I
Preliminaries

much should be allocated to children, then, is hard to say, for "there is no knowing what they cannot be given credit for," that is, there seems to be no way in which an interpretive model, "knowing," can be secure in drawing limits. What is it that cannot be attributed to children and their powers? A question to be asked, precisely because the conception of power here seems to be so mysterious, beyond the reach of understanding. We cannot *know* power. We cannot produce explanations of power that hope for anything more than being powerful, that somehow partake of the power they are not explaining but entering into. One negotiates with power for a share of the pot. One hopes, out of power, to produce accounts which succeed not in presenting but in coercing. Power is everywhere.

And nowhere. It is not easy to determine what this power is, much less why it is so often used to form the center for investigations, the metaphoric base from which we construct our world. We might consult two authorities on power, the police and Michel Foucault. First the police. Here are R.P. "Toby" Tyler and Lore E. Stone, in testimony to the United States Senate Committee investigating "Child Pornography and Pedophilia": "Children have been sexually exploited by adults since homo sapiens acquired the intelligence and reasoning capabilities to recognize that sexual activity can provide a sense of *power*, control, gratification, and recreation" (my emphasis).[11] Speaking out of rich experience in these matters, they do not hesitate to extend their observations to all homo sapiens, and to "sexual activity" generally. It does seem that the police tend to see sexual activity, like all other human ventures, in terms of power.

The same is true for Michel Foucault, though he would disdain the psychologizing, the universalizing sweep, and the linking of sexual deployments to a "sense of recreation," whatever that may be. Foucault plays in a much higher league than that in which Tyler and Stone bumble, but he plays by the same rules.

He has, in fact, laid out those rules with an unprecedented and dazzling sophistication. Most centrally concerned with the "technologies of the self," he has produced a sustained inquiry into the connections of power and knowledge: "The exercise of power perpetually creates knowledge and, conversely, knowledge constantly induces effects of power."[12] He has provided a history of the development of "a power whose highest function was perhaps no longer to kill, but to invest life through and through."[13] Power has invaded "the social body" by way of "a tightly knit grid of material coercions" enforced by "surveillance."[14] Escaping from this grid or from this way of thinking is unthinkable. Foucault has mounted a devastating critique of the illusion of "liberation," of the sad and dangerous pretense of standing "outside the reach of power."[15] Deliverance, possible only in those rare instances when the normally variable and fluid power relations become "congealed," operates even then simply to "open up new relations of power."[16]

The liberation we are most proud of in this century is of course the liberation of "sex," "sex" being nothing more than a recent "deployment of sexuality" "that we must break away from." "Sex," far from liberating us, simply encases us within its "speculative," "ideal," "internalized" realm, a realm created by a move by "power in its grip on bodies and their materiality, their forces, energies, sensations, and pleasures."[17]

Foucault insists that this power is not located anywhere:

> Power in the substantive sense, *"le" pouvoir*, doesn't exist. What I mean is this. The idea that there is either located at—or emanating from—a given point something which is a "power" seems to me to be based on a misguided analysis.... In reality power means relations, a more-or-less organised, hierarchical, coordinated cluster of relations.[18]

Power is certainly not to be identified with a sovereign who wields it or with an agency of state; "it becomes a machinery that no one owns."[19] Power "*is* 'always already there.' " One cannot be beyond it or find in it "margins" for play.[20] Power, centrally, cannot be grasped in static or abstract terms: "power is neither given, nor exchanged, nor recovered, but rather exercised ... it only exists in action."[21] Power, Foucault often says, is not what he is interested in or talking about. "I hardly ever use the word 'power,' " he claims, thereby amazing anyone who reads him. Instead of "power," he analyzes "the relationships of power": "I mean that in human relations, whatever they are—whether it be a question of communicating verbally ... or a question of a love relationship, an institutional or economic relationship—power is always present; I mean the relationship in which one wishes to direct the behavior of another."[22]

"Power is always present." The subtlety of Foucault's analysis of the techniques of surveillance and the compelling hints on how to mobilize ourselves against power are so unexpected and so radical they perhaps obscure the deep complaisance of the power-based project, the way in which it proceeds from within and flatters our normal cultural procedures, whereby power is allowed unquestioned control of discourse and of vision. Just as Foucault says, whether it is a question

Theoretical, Cultural, Personal / 33

up of gaps, the erasure of otherness brings the alien under control and murders desire. And the hit men are explainers.

Explanation is akin to erotic fulfillment and thus hostile to desire. This is doubtless one reason why pedagogues are so often figured as enemies of youth, as sterile, wizened, impotent. According to this irresistible comic formulation, we hate those youth, more particularly we hate their sexual energy and are anxious to neutralize it by forcing on them the saltpeter of explanations construed in the form of power. Explainers detest desire. They want to copulate with the other, more exactly to *have* copulated with her. We want to present to students and to others who will listen what we have already so that they have it already. We want it in the past. We want fulfillment; and fulfillment, as Joyce Carol Oates has observed, is the feeble and unerotic pleasure we derive from having it all over with.[63] Pedagogues and cultures who figure their world in reference to power are the enemies of otherness and the enemies of desire. They want no more cakes and ale; they want the banquet to have ended some time ago. They don't want appetite; they want digestion.

We were not always so drearily fogged in by power. Our grandparents, for instance, could look at the subject of Victorian sexuality and locate some luscious gaps there. Where we see the dullness of domestic explanations, they saw a tantalizing game. They called the Victorians "prudish." We call them "repressed." There is a great difference. Our explanatory agriculture covers the whole landscape, blankets everything. "Prudishness," on the other hand, is a very poor thing as explanations go, offering more of a description than an analysis, a description, further, where the stress falls on what resists or lies outside the field of explanation, on the impossibility, the alien otherness. It is, we note, an otherness which is constructed. The Victorians for our grandparents were thus as exotic, as much an object of erotic longing, as the promiscuous tribes described by anthropologists. The Victorians lived in another country, one saturated with desire and very much unlike our own suburban terrain of impotent explicableness. Our grandparents were erotic readers of the Victorians; they drew back the curtains and let the spotlight play on the sequined spangles of desire.

The Past

According to Freud, reading the hidden is duck soup: "He that has eyes to see and ears to hear may convince himself that no mortal can keep a secret."[64] No doubt Freud achieved that conviction, but we have now come to a state where at least the past can go back into hiding, knowing its secrets are pretty safe. Traditional views of the Victorians, especially the Victorians on sex, now seem smug and self-congratulatory, bolstered by a false sense of security, a sense of knowingness as regards not only the position of the Victorians but the position from which they were being sighted.[65] Now we have learned that we must look to our own positioning, reassess how we are finding and viewing facts, be prepared to hear that facts do not come to us clean and fresh: "Against the positivism which stops before phenomena, saying 'these are only *facts*,' I should say: no, it is precisely facts that do not exist, only *interpretations*."[66]

How are we, as interpreters, situated in reference to the already-interpreted past? I cannot begin to know where that past is, without knowing where I am in relation to it. My own landscape is pretty much hidden from me, and my own interpretations have already been made; but that must not stop me from trying to discover some of the ways of their making. I cannot, then, ask what the Victorians thought but rather why it appears to us that they thought as they did. More specifically, our question is, "What is it that enables or forces us to see as we do in reference to the way the Victorians formulated 'the child' and 'the body' and 'sex'?" When we add that we start by assuming that the Victorians are making sounds our ears can no longer pick up and are writing in an alphabet now lost, we will probably have no right to expect straight answers. We'll search out that which is hardest to hear and see, that which doesn't sound or look right.

The most remarkable re-seeing of the sexual past has liberated us from the burden of liberation and brought the Victorians out from under the smothering overlay of "repression." Failing to hear the Victorians talk about sex or not wanting to hear them, we had chalked all that silence (our deafness) up to (their) repression, to a hypocritical or cowardly cooperation with a cultural coding that insisted sex was not there. The Victorians were repressed, and repression, we know, "produces inhibition, fear, and aggression."[67] Such a popular, reductive view derives from Freud's classic formulations—"excitations . . . prevented by psychical obstruction from attaining their aims [and] diverted into numerous other channels till they find their way to expression as symptoms"[68]—which in turn owe some debt to Nietzsche.[69] There had been a few early protests against the notion of repression, it is true. Havelock Ellis, in his own inimitable way, piped up, "I have never repressed anything,"[70] and Alfred Kinsey lets loose some of his best sarcasm against the efforts of legislators, federal agencies, and "certain organizations" willing to spend millions to "repress" the na-

CHILD-LOVING

CHILD-LOVING

**THE EROTIC CHILD
AND VICTORIAN CULTURE**

JAMES R. KINCAID

ROUTLEDGE · NEW YORK AND LONDON

Published in 1992 by

Routledge
An imprint of Routledge, Chapman and Hall, Inc.
29 West 35th Street
New York, NY 10001

Published in Great Britain by

Routledge
11 New Fetter Lane
London EC4P 4EE

Copyright © 1992 by Routledge, Chapman and Hall, Inc.

Printed in the United States of America

All rights reserved. No part of this book may be reprinted or reproduced or utilized in any form or by any electronic, mechanical or other means, now known or hereafter invented, including photocopying and recording, or in any information storage or retrieval system, without permission in writing from the publisher.

Kincaid, James R. (James Russell)
    Child-loving : the erotic child and Victorian culture / James R. Kincaid.
      p.   cm.
    Includes bibliographical references and index.
    ISBN 0-415-90595-8 (HB)
    1. English literature—19th century—History and criticism.
2. Children in literature. 3. Erotic literature, English—History and criticism. 4. Children—Great Britain—History—19th century.
5. Great Britain—Civilization—19th century. 6. Love in literature. 7. Sex in literature.   I. Title.
PR468.C5K56   1992
820.9′352054′09034—dc20   92-20741
                                                                                   CIP

ISBN 0-415-90595-8

For Nita

Contents

Acknowledgments	ix
Part I: Preliminaries	
Chapter 1: Positionings: Theoretical, Cultural, Personal	3
Part II: Victorian Constructions of Children and Eros	
Chapter 2: The Child	61
Chapter 3: The Budding Body	104
Chapter 4: Sex and Its Uses	134
Chapter 5: Child-Love	183
Part III: Figures of the Child	
Chapter 6: The Gentle Child	217
Chapter 7: The Naughty Child	246
Chapter 8: The Wonder Child in Neverland	275
Part IV: Reading, Watching, Loving the Child	
Chapter 9: The Pedophile Reader: Texts	303
Chapter 10: The Pedophile Reader: Events	341
Chapter 11: Our Own Child-Loving	359
Index	395

Acknowledgments

As one advances in years—not that I'm old—and spends, let's face it, nearly a decade on a project, one would have to be uncommonly noxious or self-sufficient to avoid running up so many happy obligations that the listing of them becomes a dive into panic. I know I will, as you would too, leave out the very person for whom I have vowed to cut off my hand sooner than ignore. I would ask her or him to forgive me, but there's no hope for that, so the hell with it.

I cannot forget Eve Kosofsky Sedgwick, who took on thinking for me and helping me at a time when those less gallant and courageous would have folded in on themselves. There is no way I can thank her, only wave a tribute to her generous smartness. My dear friends U.C. Knoepflmacher and Linda Shires read and talked me through the whole decade, never flagging in their brilliance or patience. J. E. Rivers got me started on this project, gave me hundreds of important tips, and kept telling me when I needed to hear it that I should get to work and stop stewing. Regina Schwartz has always understood better than I what it was I was doing and has left her wonderful intelligence open for me to raid. Jeffrey Robinson is both wiser and more daring than I, but he never let on when helping me. Julian Markels and Robin Bell Markels between them poured enough shrewd care, learning, and love over the ideas in this book that there is no excuse for it not being better than it is. Robert Polhemus read much of this and spent more time than any ordinary friend ever would talking me through hard times and notions. Garrett Stewart laid his staggering wit and kindness onto large parts of this, calling my attention to many howlers, continuing to do so even when it was clear that I deeply resented his attentions. Patricia Cherin gave the first chapter a rousing and funny reading that was more sympathetic than it deserved, but I didn't mind. Sweethearted Allen Mandelbaum introduced me to Barry Moser, who then saw, drew, and spoke of possibilities that could never otherwise have entered my head. Cathy Comstock saw so much here that was really within her own wit and blissful imagination that I was able to revel in her comments and imagine myself writing terrific things. Gerhard Joseph sought out ways to make the manuscript sharp and engaging; its many failures are certainly not those of this bountiful friend. N. John Hall is not really, as he has been called, the Darwin of Depravity, but he was very useful to me as a resource on many matters, depravity among them. Keith Fitzgerald gave me the benefit of his detailed knowledge of the McMartin case and his superb analysis of it. Joseph Litvak, serving as a publisher's reader, offered me as intelligent and generous a reading as I've ever received and saved me from several hundred pages worth of blunders.

Many others contributed as much or more as those already cited, but it would be unreasonable to expect me to discuss each one at length, wouldn't it? No one ever does that. So my thanks to the following friends and scholars, each of whom deserves more than this, more than I can ever give them, so they had better look elsewhere: Lesley Brill, Chris Zacher, Timothy d'Arch Smith, Nina Auerbach, Edward Guiliano, Michael J. Preston, Dale Kramer, Patricia Yaeger, Richard D. Altick, Bruce Kawin, David Simpson, John Glavin, Peter Manning, John Stevenson, Buck McMullen, Joseph Boone, Anthony Reid, Arthur A. Adrian, Len Findlay, Margaret Higonnet, Marshall Brown, Ron Gottesman, Michael Moon, Sue Lonoff, Alan Sinfield, David DeLaura, Juliet McMaster, Gerald Graff, Sidney Goldfarb, John Jordan, Hilary Schor, Margaret Ferguson, Selwyn Goodacre, Al Hutter, Tom Mitchell, John Rechy, Adrian Richwell, Daniel Tiffany, David Frantz, Richard Ide, Larry Swingle, Jay Martin, Vincent Cheng, David Eggenschwiler, Molly Bendall, David St. John, and the staff at the Kinsey Institute at Indiana University.

Diane Germano was a wonderful copy editor, and I greedily adopted virtually all of her corrections and suggestions, thanking her for good ideas and good prose to match.

Anne Kincaid, Elizabeth Kincaid, and Matthew Kincaid did excellent library work, card shuffling, and general high-voltage research for me. They were paid for it, true, but paid so poorly that only their graciousness kept them going. They deserve something better than thanks; but it's a tough world, as I'm always telling them, and thanks count for something, I should think.

I am also am very grateful to the John Simon Guggenheim Foundation for its support both during the fellowship year and ever since; to the University of Colorado for a Faculty Fellowship and my Chair there, Lesley Brill, for his constant help and affection; and to The University of Southern California, my Chairs Peter Manning and Richard Ide and my Dean, Marshall Cohen, for arranging the time, resources, and merry environment that have buoyed me up ever since I came.

Gerald Bruns, whom I have in an excess of bounty thanked in the past but who never deserved it, had nothing whatever to do with this project, beyond some attempts (foiled) to meddle.

The book is dedicated to the one who does most to honor the truths of the human heart.

A portion of chapter 9 dealing with *Tess* appeared in an earlier form in *Sex and Death in Victorian Literature*, ed. Regina Barreca (London: Macmillan, 1990), pp. 9–31, and is reprinted here with the permission of Professor Barreca; a summary of some of the points in chapters 6 and 7 appeared as "The Manufacture and Consumption of Children" in *Victorian Review* 17 (Summer 1991): 1–17, reprinted here with the permission of the editors; a few pages from chapter 9 appeared in an essay co-authored with Buck McMullen, "Tennyson, Hallam's Corpse, Milton's Murder, and Poetic Exhibitionism" in *Nineteenth-Century Literature* 45 (1990): 176–205, used here with the consent of the editors, the Regents of the University of California, and Mr. McMullen. Some of the ideas on latency in chapter 3 and on silence in chapter 4 appeared first in "What the Victorians Knew About Sex," *Browning Institute Studies* 16 (1988): 91–99 (now *Victorian Literature and Culture*) and are used here with permission of the editors.

1

Positionings: Theoretical, Cultural, Personal

We all know that there is a difference between a healthy and normal love of children and a love which is sick and freakish. Given that most of what is involved in thinking of a child and loving it is mysterious, it's surprising that we know so much. I want here to explore how we come by that knowledge, how it is constituted, why it is so important to us, and what it costs us to maintain. You've guessed that the exploration is funded entirely by skepticism, by an idea that what passes for knowledge among us on this subject is more likely a prescribed cultural agreement cemented by fear, desire, and denial. I suspect that this knowledge is really "knowingness," a pact that authorizes us to treat our ignorance as wisdom and to make that ignorance the basis for action.[1] What if we looked at the discourse on pedophilia and its history ironically, as if we were somehow outside of it? What would happen? That we are not and cannot be outside does not entirely disable our expedition; it simply means that we will have to distrust our own maps, try to unsettle our most confident sense of where we are, include ourselves in our own satiric accounts. And we have no certain destination, no permanent truth to find; we have only various planes on which to travel.

So, what about the way we talk of child-loving? The talk is monster-talk, first of all, talk that is busy rejecting the pedophile that it is, at the same time, creating. It assembles in order to fling aside, imagines so that it might recoil in disgust. This is not to say that pedophiles are imaginary, just that our discourse creates a space for them, a space that we can bet will not go unoccupied. It is clear that we invest a great deal of cultural capital in the importance of pedophilia, though it is not so clear why we do so.

My hope is that a home-version form of deconstruction might be useful in jolting this discourse enough so as to make more vulnerable some of the assumptions it is busy engaging and disguising. I believe the first step could be to center the Other, to welcome home the monster we are so busy exiling: we make the definition of our health in this regard so entirely dependent on being non-pedophilic that we find ourselves willy-nilly entangled with that we are shooing away. We need the pedophile to fill our emptiness, provide the matter we otherwise miss, create our own form of existence. That which we deny returns by the back door and sits comfortably in the living room; at least that's where we are going to put him and see what he does. More to the point, we'll see what we do.

The Victorians are employed here to assist in exposing our discourse and its compulsions; they display their own prose primarily to help them in reading us. I am, that is, less interested in reconstructing the past than in examining what our methods of reconstruction might tell us about our own policies. Victorian discussions of the child, the body, sexuality, pedophilia are often fascinating and surprising in themselves, no doubt, but for my purposes these discussions do not exist "in themselves" but only as they provide a field on which we train our historical lenses. The past does not exist as a solid ground from which to assess the present; the past is there for us in reference to present needs. We can find some measure of liberation, I believe, by examining the directions we receive for reading the past and then disobeying them as brazenly as we can, flaunting them, turning them back on themselves. The point of doing this is less to re-read the past through some off-center, fun-house mirror than to find out a little of why we are reading as we are. To this end, I am most interested in ways in which it can appear that the Victorians (or some of them) did *not* read as we do, did not see the same things or respond in the same way, did not go to the same schools. All the Victorians in this book, then, are Other Victorians—strange, inhospitable, nearly undecipherable. The point is not to read them but to look for ways in which they resist reading, to estrange them or find those who already seem to have their teeth bared.

The argument is that what we think of as "the child" has been assembled in reference to desire, built up in erotic manufactories, and that we have been laboring ever since, for at least two centuries, both to deny that horrible and lovely product and to maintain it. Pedophilia, by this reckoning, is located at the cultural center, since it describes the response to the child we have made necessary. If the child is desirable, then to desire it can hardly be freakish. To maintain otherwise is to put into operation pretty hefty engines of denial and self-deception. And that is what we have done. By insisting so loudly on the innocence, purity, and asexuality of the child, we have created a subversive echo: experience, corruption, eroticism. More than that, by attributing to the child the central features of desirability in our culture—purity, innocence, emptiness, Otherness—we have made absolutely essential figures who would enact this desire. Such figures are certainly not us, we insist, insist so violently because we must, so violently that we come to think that what we are is what these figures are not. They come to define us: they are the substance we feed on. The pedophile is thus our most important citizen, so long as he stays behind the tree or over in the next yard: without him we would have no agreeable explanation for the attractions of the empty child. We must have the deformed monster in order to assure us that our own profiles are proportionate.

I hope it is clear, then, that the terms "pedophile" and "child," point, for me, not to things but to roles, functions necessary to our psychic and cultural life. We find people to play these parts, certainly, bodies we can thrust into the performance; but their presence testifies only to our need. My "child," then, is not defined or controlled by age limits, since it seems to me that anyone between the ages of one day and 25 years or even beyond might, in different contexts, play that role. What a "child" *is*, in other words, changes to fit different situations and different needs. A child is not, in itself, anything. Any image, body, or being we can hollow out, purify, exalt, abuse, and locate sneakily in a field of desire will do for us as a "child," I contend. The "pedophile," similarly, is a role and position, brought into being by and coordinate with the eroticizing of the child. Defining the child as an object of desire, we create the pedophile as the one who desires, as a complex image of projection and denial: the pedophile acts out the range of attitudes and behaviors made compulsory by the role we have given the child. Demonizing this figure at the same time we call loudly for his presence, asserting his marginality as we proclaim his importance, dissociating as we make alliance, we anoint as we execute the pedophile. At least that's the argument here: the outcast pedophile is somehow on the throne. Having said that, having centered pedophilia, we should be in a position to see what such a wedging into our discourse might uncover.

It shouldn't be necessary to say this, to insert this interruption, but it is: the purpose of centering pedophilia is not to celebrate it or display its virtues. I wish to do two things: to show the extent to which it is already there at our heart and, more important, to throw open to the light (or to such light as we can generate) the tricks we now have come to depend on to sustain our ideas of what is natural. It will be hard enough to hold pedophilia at the center, given our repulsion to it and our rampaging need to return to normal. I think there are good reasons for this pedophile spotlighting, not the least of which is that our present devices, meant to assure us and protect us from unwelcome ideas, do not work very well. These same agencies have, however, no way to admit defects; and so their response to doing such a lousy job of controlling matters is to do the same lousy job with more and more energy. As these things do not work we call upon them more strenuously; as our protections fail we rely upon them desperately. I will argue that the chief casualties are the very children we think we are protecting: needing the *idea* of the child so badly, we find ourselves sacrificing the bodies of children for it.

Even an initial peek at the sanctified notion of child-loving renders obvious right away some startling features of this discourse: its urgency (or shrillness), its uniformity, and its extraordinary redundancy. The talk at once appears ritualized: the same thing is said very often, in unison, in the same tone and with the same beat. That this is a chant does not suggest anything like insincerity. On the contrary, there is no subject on which we are more in earnest, less given to casual gestures or the mere observance of forms. This is a ritual that seems to be directed by and enacted through panic. Orthodox talk on the subject—and nearly all the talk we have is orthodox—inflates us with anger and disgust. We can be said to have a visceral reaction to it, if by that we mean that our bodies participate in our rhetoric, indicate unmistakably our wholehearted probity. Our hands become clammy and our mouths dry, our stomachs tighten and eyes narrow, the skin covering our forehead stretches hard and our nostrils flare.

That it should be so almost suggests that our response is "natural," a suggestion many would love to accept. But can this cultural redundancy really be the sound of nature being discovered; or is it the bark of power giving orders? That we quiver at the mention of child-love does not mean there is anything natural about our response; maybe it is just that the physiology of disgust is prescribed as a requisite accompaniment to the words. Can it be that we have found ways to bow down so sublimely to the power of an idea that all is one: words and music, body and mind? We have not so much "naturalized" a single explanation of pedophilia, I am guessing, as been naturalized *by* it.

This possibility in turn allows us to unglue a whole host of other binaries involved here: inverting their order, connecting them (denying their separateness), and then examining the assumptions on which they rested in the first place. Most apparent is the division between adult and child, a dissociation which, I will claim, has been at least for the past two hundred years heavily eroticized: the child is that species which is free of sexual feeling or response; the adult is that species which has crossed over into sexuality. The definitional base is erotic: our discourse insists on it by loudly denying its importance. Of course other binaries are involved too, those involving innocence and experience, ignorance and knowledge, incapacity and competence, empty and full, low and high, weak and powerful. All of these divisions are very wobbly, requiring massive bolstering by this discourse. Deconstructing them means, I hope, exposing their pretenses, their hilarious *un*naturalness, their comic attempts to cover their own private parts. I hope it also leads to showing what damage we are doing and to locating a way out.

If the child is not distinguished from the adult, we imagine that we are seriously threatened, threatened in such a way as to put at risk our very being, what it means to be an adult in the first place. My own focus on pedophilia here suggests that what is most at stake is our capacity to know desire: the child is not simply the Other we desire but the Other we must have in order to know longing, love, lust at all. The child is that which we are not but almost are, that which we yearn for so fiercely we almost resent it, that which we thought we saw in the mirror and almost wanted to possess yet feared we might. The child is the embodiment of desire and also its negation.

Other deconstructive centers would open up other possibilities, of course, and the study which follows is not pursued in order to find a new set of strategies or a new scheme we can put in place and then trust, hoping it would, like our present ordering devices, function on its own and leave us free to pursue other interests. I wouldn't know what it meant to think of other interests, interests divorced from these centerings, and the purpose of deconstructive play with such centers is not to provide us with new ones but with the license to travel from one to another—and, of course, to yet another. In the process, though, we can, I think, act strategically and politically, act to devise ever more flexible, subversive, even liberating modes of perceiving and acting. We can, in this case, help worm ourselves partly free, squirm out from under—and we can allow children to wriggle with us. The dream of total liberation may be itself the greatest snare: no center is ideal, unequipped with methods of protecting itself. Still, in the moving itself we will find points of insight, fields for action, moments of exhilaration.

But I notice in my own prose and my own thinking on this a reliance on metaphors of power that makes me believe that deconstructing child-love had better open up more than the techniques by which we maintain desire. It had better show us why we are drawn to metaphoric structurings like those embedded in "techniques" and "maintaining."

That is, I hope we will not simply find pockets of opposition or points of resistance to power. Such talk grants to power the very authority that should be at stake, or at play. I hope we can understand better why we think in terms of power in the first place, naturalize it, center it, idealize it, make it metaphysical, bow down to it.

Thus much of the book which follows is an intertwined meditation on desire and power, trying to acknowledge and to elude both. I am interested in what series of metaphors we commit ourselves to when we center power and to what depths these commitments run. To slant away from power or dodge it, to search for alternate, provisional centers, I have found myself immersed in strategies of whose utility (make that necessity) I have, from time to time, convinced myself but whose true attraction may well lie in their tolerance for my exhibitionism. The first is an attempt to find centerings antithetical to power, centers which creep in from below (they are not "serious") or slide in from the side (they are "peripheral"). While both could conceivably simply take over from power and start centering our ways of seeing and being in the world, I have tried to hedge them round with jokes and mumbled apologies in order to keep them from even thinking of such pretensions to authority. They are meant as instrumental only, tools or (better) game equipment. The main tools have come to me as affinity/connection and as play/inconsequence. The first provisional center (affinity) disrupts power's dependence on hierarchies, on separating and ordering by units; in the place of atoms held in place by complex lines of force, this center amalgamates, slops over, hugs together; in place of the purified logic of paranoia (who's got power over me?) it plops down the logic of community (who's there for me to join?). The second, play, subverts the insistent causality of power by a model of inconsequence, of disconnection. In play, controls are given over or, better, are never thought of, since there is no place for them. There is no power (or none that goes anywhere), no logic, no order of any kind, even grammatical. In the benign form of play, races are run so that we may hear that "Everybody has won and all must have prizes"; in its dark form trials are held where sentences precede verdicts and where we may (or may not) have our heads ordered off at any moment. In either case, it's all nonsense, all an absurdist wonderland.

But I do not pretend that I can take up a position outside of power by these means, that I can do more than write in-and-out of power. Doing so demands sneakiness, or so I tell myself, demands obliquity. I know from experience that this can be maddening to others, however delightful to me; but I see no way to employ a precise lucidity directed to causal development and to truth-unfolding, even were such lucidity available to me. I believe the directives ordering such consecutive lucidity and then applauding it issue from the same headquarters I am trying to blast or ridicule or convert or hide from. Doubtless my procedures are far more timid and conventional than I imagine, and I do not pretend to send down this writing from some planet where conventional academic discourse is unknown. But I have tried to take liberties and to indulge in some moments that violate and insult the demands of power, or at least imagine they do so. That these insults and outrages should be visited on my readers is probably not inevitable, but I tell myself that it is.

I also have taught myself to believe that there is justification for a persistent use of the first person plural to discuss the cultural positioning *we* have taken up and the responses *we* dutifully allow to be elicited from us—especially erotic responses. This practice has proved annoying to some of my friends, good friends, who have read parts of the manuscript. "This book really seems not to be about the pedophile but about *we*. Who's this *we*?" "This *we*'s not me!" Some have suggested that the *we* is insolent; some have said it is evasive: "Try putting an *I* there, if that's how you feel, but don't include me without asking. Just go ahead! Put an *I* there—see how *you* like it!"

There are two responses I've used to this, one not so good and the other better. The first (windy) is that I wouldn't like it at all, such personalizing, such confessing, as if what I felt were of any particular importance, as if I had the slightest idea what "I felt." I am afraid that an *I* would be far more artificial than any *we*. The assemblage that goes by "we" in the book before us is a cultural *position*, a place where we must be, if we are to exist at all. It is, this *we*, a field of complex desire, in reference to children, not a single, willed desire but a general cultural geography of and for desire. It is a desire that works through *us*, writes into us; it is not something we bring into being but rather the other way round. Doubtless there are many local and diverse manifestations of this desire, but I am dealing here with a form of desire figured socially and historically and not psychologically and individually. In my view, we are all part of this *we*, can't help it, unattractive as that collective may be. We can resign our membership about as easily as we can get out of our century or our culture's assumptions. For those who insist that they have found, even within our episteme, some safer place to stand over and against the child, a position that is altogether different from the one I describe, I can only suggest that they read the "we" as a form of Other. Every time the second person comes up, such a reader, estranged entirely from the dynamics being assumed, can vote to abstain. For her or him, the *we* is not a cultural spot carved out for all of us; the *we* is simply "Kincaid and those Others." Such a reading would seem to be a strongly resistant one, but resisting readers are certainly among the best, the ones most likely to bring the arguments into new lands.

Yeah, but that response has about it both a slight rhetorical flim-flam and even a kind of bullying—I see clearly where we are as a culture and you don't, ha! ha!—that makes it not so good. The second is better and simpler. I don't know whether I am right or whether others occupy the position I think I occupy. Different people in different places at different times feel wildly different things about quite specific children (and differently, of course, about different children). People have very different notions about what "a child" is and what counts as attraction. Probably most of us, but certainly I, find it hard to locate exactly what it is we do feel. The homogenizing of *we*, like the unreal category "the child," tends to make talk of desire seem both disinfected and strangely disembodied. Still, I can say this much (and suspect a great deal more): I do not find it hard myself to understand the way our culture's general standards of beauty mesh with the appearance of children or how it is that often children have won contests (beauty contests) to determine for the rest of us what should constitute desirability; I can see and feel that the enticing images of purity and almost formless innocence are fulfilled not simply in heaven, the virgin, and Ivory soap but in the child; I can understand why all television sitcoms require an androgynous and beautiful child; I do not find the appeal of Shirley Temple or Freddie Bartholomew or Brooke Shields or Ricky Schroeder a mystery; I do not think Coppertone ads are merely cute or that they appeal only to Others; I can see why we need the various monster myths of pedophilia. That much is clear. I suspect I am not alone and send out the *we* on the strength of that suspicion.

And what's the point, what political and practical aims are embedded in this book? I cannot pretend to be offering an effective liberal or idealist program (or rhetoric) here: I do not aim, that is, to suggest changes in laws or institutional structures, on one hand, or to alter "attitudes," on the other. The aims are, rather, utopian and revolutionary, both in the sense of toppling and of circling around to hit from the rear. By arguing that the outside (pedophilia) is inside and that the one being protected (the child) is being assaulted by its protections, I am trying to locate a field of difference wherein the child, its needs, its loves, and its lovers will not only appear but be entirely new.

And that's plenty for a preamble to the Introduction. What follows in this first section is meant to set up for you (set you up for) four major topics: the child, gender, power, and time. I want to consider just a little more fully the preliminaries necessary to our thinking about the concept of children, about gender constructions, about the dominant metaphor ("power") we're abusing so, and the ways in which we might go about reading the past. Sex we'll save for later.

The Child

The constructivist view is well-known: "the child" was invented in the late eighteenth century to occupy an empty psychic and social space. The consequences of that view for us are explored in a long chapter later, so here I'll be allowed to drop in only an anecdote. Here it is.

Ask those interested in the subject to name the greatest lovers in Victorian fiction, and they'll say, "Cathy and Heathcliff." They've got to. Ask them to flesh out the image, give some details, and this is what they'll do: they'll talk about these two titanic lovers on the wild moors, running, fueled by rebellious energy and a passion that recognizes no conventional bounds. I know that's what they'll do because I do it. It is curious, though, that the novel never depicts Heathcliff and Cathy on the moors. What we see most vividly through our memory of the novel that novel does not see at all.[2] Keep that in mind. We might also note the situation and ages of the lovers. There are other points worth noting, but these will do.

Here's the passage where we are decidedly not shown the lovers in action. The beleaguered Lockwood is reading Catherine's makeshift diary, in which she records the history of abuse she and Heathcliff are absorbing and the pluck with which they confront it. On the particular Sunday Catherine describes in her writing, the two children have been forced to writhe under a sermon from Joseph that "lasted three hours precisely," emerging from that, not into their usual play but into a silence enforced by Hindley and his mewling but equally sadistic wife. Cathy tries to fashion a snug retreat for the two by fastening their pinafores together and hanging the splicing over a dresser arch, but Joseph rips it down, boxes Cathy's ears, and forces on them religious tracts. Pushed beyond any limit, Cathy pitches "Th' Helmet uh Salvation" into a corner and Heathcliff follows with "T' Brooad Way to Destruction." For this they are banged about some more and "hurled" into the back kitchen, where Cathy begins writing the diary entry Lockwood is presenting to us. Her writing is, we probably assume, soon interrupted:

> " ... my companion is impatient, and proposes that we should appropriate the dairy woman's cloak, and have a scamper on the moors, under its shelter. A pleasant suggestion—and then, if the surly old man come in, he may believe his prophesy verified—we cannot be damper, or colder, in the rain than we are here."
>
> * * * * *
>
> I suppose Catherine fulfilled her project, for the next sentence took up another subject; she waxed lachrymose.
> "How little did I dream that Hindley would ever make me cry so...."[3]

Did they go onto the moors? Lockwood supposes they did, but Lockwood's suppositions are never on the mark. Even if they did, is this the image we want of these sweethearts from hell, Satan and his bride? After all, we have here two little figures huddled under a cloak to keep dry, children who are chased from hiding place to hiding place and who seem much more pathetic than titanic, more like Hansel and Gretel than Antony and Cleopatra.

But we don't really *have* the two little images under a cloak or on the moors at all. We don't have anything. We have a row of asterisks, an emptiness. And it is out of that emptiness that we have produced these blazing images of romantic tragedy. There's something else: those pinafores. Heathcliff in a pinafore? Demonic passion in a skirted twelve-year-old? (Heathcliff may be thirteen at the time, but Cathy is only twelve.)

Well: this great image of erotic passion in the modern Anglo-American imagination is put together out of childhood and emptiness. Pure energy, nature, love—pure nothingness. As we will see later, none of this should surprise us. Childhood can be made a wonderfully hollow category, able to be filled up with anyone's overflowing emotions, not least overflowing passion. Into this vacuum, then, strong desire can leap, calling itself pure and calling what it finds not pedophilia but tragic romance. Two little children stand at the center of our erotic figurings, and they do so precisely because they are so pure.

Their purity, like all purity, is figured as negation. The only time we see the children alone together in their bedroom is immediately following the death of Mr. Earnshaw. Actually, we don't see them but we do, by way of Nelly, listen at the keyhole as Peeping Toms, accepting second-best in the way of titillation. We hear the tots discussing pious matters. Nelly says, "The little souls were comforting each other with better thoughts than I could have hit on; no parson in the world ever pictured Heaven so beautifully as they did, in their innocent talk" (V). Such an emphasis on the sanctimonious here acts dramatically to empty out the actors, those indistinguishable "little souls" by way of the cleansing negations of innocence. These genderless angels appear all over Victorian culture and all over ours. They are our mutual centerfolds.

We will have more of this later in the book, much more; just one further dribble here. Take David Copperfield. As a child he sees himself as an insistently empty figure: "I have been Tom Jones (a child's Tom Jones, a harmless figure) for a week together."[4] This purity, this harmlessness is presented as complete vacancy; the absence of harmfulness amounts, in fact, to nothing at all, a blank image waiting to be formed. As emptiness, the child David can be variously eroticized by those around him: his kissing mother, his hugging nurse, his beating stepfather and schoolmaster, the adult narrator, and, arguably, the reader. Purity, it turns out, provides just the opening a sexualizing tendency requires; it is the necessary condition for the erotic operations our cultures have made central.

Gender

Gender or any other set figure of sexual opposition is of very little importance to child-loving. From our authorized, common-sense perspective, gender is obvious, gender is nature; and we are virtually forced to understand pedophilia in terms of male or female adults and male or female children. Our statistics and our attitudes are directed by these conceptions, by the assumption that these are categories that are both fixed and determinate. Adults and children are separated by puberty; men and women are separated by—well, everything. Freud conjured up a visitor from another planet who was struck by nothing so "forcibly" as "the fact of the existence of two sexes among human beings." But such differences, Freud also noted, did not seem to strike children at all, did not form the base even for their exploration of sex.[5] Those who love children, who enter into the child's world through love, we might say, have a similar capacity for ignoring what is so obvious to Martians. Child-loving demands a release or displacement of our habit of creating oppositions, slides us toward a paradigm that does not make things distinct but blurs them. That this deconstruction is never complete, that gender is still somehow present[6] should not surprise us so much as the fact that it is asked to be satisfied with a bit part.

I do not dispute historical constructions which insist on the importance of gender to the understanding of forms of sexual attraction other than pedophilia, Victorian or modern. It is in part because such arguments have been so successful that I am set loose to make what I can of this pedophile margin, this area of radical deviance. Thus, throughout this book I have been allowed to slight or even ignore gender, to suggest that these categories, which seem so necessary to us, simply are not present within this mode. I will grant that any study of child sexuality might be connected in some manner to, might throw some light upon, cultural constructions of female sexuality. Women's presumed delicacy and tenderness have occasionally been explained as the preservation of "the infantine constitution," and her "natural" closeness to children as the way in which "woman herself . . . remains almost always a child in regard to her organization."[7] One should, however, note also the strength of similar cultural myths connecting men to children, by way of sports, irresponsibility, and dependence on others for the satisfaction of basic needs: only men and children play with balls and can't cook. My point is, though, that these are not my points. Gender is a construction far less important to pedophilia than to other forms of perception: that's my point.

Of course all manner of cultural impositions take the form of marking gender difference, both for children and for adults. The very fact, however, that these mandates may be contested marks their artificiality, our sense that we are, in some measure, able to manipulate for ourselves what we choose to make "male" and "female" mean. For example, the view that women have less interest in or capacity for sex than men, a view found in this century and the last, exists side by side with the view that women have much more, or that there is no difference after all between men and women in this regard. Elizabeth Blackwell said that things were, on the whole, pretty equal all around.[8] This insistence on equality is an insistence that sexual passion is not to be measured through gender categories, which in turn suggests that those categories can mean what we take them to mean, that there is nothing necessary or natural belonging to either gender or, more importantly, to the concept of gender.

At least so say the pedophiles—almost. Pedophilia can no more fly entirely free of dominant paradigms than can any other deconstructive maneuver, which means that traces, at least, of power and of powerful binary categories can usually be found. That qualification aside, however, pedophilia is remarkable for melting down gender difference in the same way it abolishes distinctions between ages. We tend to understand all sexuality in oppositional terms, but such oppositions just do not enter much into the play of child-loving. Such ungendered seeing is not quite comprehensible in our culture, but there is reason to suppose that a century or so ago gender was of little importance in the usual sort of thinking on children, that many Victorians were comfortable in minimizing gender differences in children, in regarding them, like Krafft-Ebing, as "neuters."[9] It seems clear that we have lost the easy security which would have allowed such merging, such a relaxation of enforced divisions.

Such a merging, in any case, is extended in pedophile discourse to the entirety of one's emotional life, where the child and adult move toward a state where there is no child/adult or male/female barrier marking off distances, creating endings. This state, this world where play is unconstrained and never-ending, represents a goal which itself is always being sought for, never found. Still, as pedophile eroticism partakes of play it loses any sense of "fulfillment" (or closure), of pleasure that is fundamentally genital or copulative. Gender becomes not something to be transcended but something that is trivial, not a part of the game, even the sexual game. And thus, just as children tend toward becoming a kind of uniformly formless cuddle-bunny, so do the adults, male and female alike. It doesn't matter—almost.

Of course it matters greatly to our conventional understanding of pedophilia, which asserts usually that the entire phenomenon is a male activity and a male fantasy, directed by the way males are positioned in the power field. As beings taught that sexuality is the exercise of power against some object, males do sometimes, we are told, turn to extraordinarily illegitimate exercises of that power against manifestly powerless objects, namely children. All pedophilia, thus, is male-molestation, is a form of male-rape. I believe such a construction follows cogently enough from the initial assumptions connecting sex and power. If sex is power; if all forms of human contact can best be understood as power negotiations; if power itself is to be exempt from scrutiny, made ideal—then there is a certain logic in channeling all this to a male source. But even here there are problems. No one claims, for instance, that women are exempt from the power paradigm, just that they are disadvantaged by it. Why they would not themselves turn to exploiting weaker beings is not clear, especially when one recalls the deterministic argument that child abusers have themselves been abused as children ("the cycle of abuse") and further notes that most victims are said to be female. Our own most prized nostrums would seem to indicate that women simply must be doing most of the sexual abusing of children.

Such arguments, however, are so hurtful and so clearly designed to bring forth no fruit, that surely we can find other grounds. Of course the genderless world suggested by pedophilia is dangerous, taking away as it does our methods for spotting the villains. Here we declare not only that men and women are both involved in the play but that such distinctions are next to meaningless. What we gain by such a move, we hope, is some insight into the machinery that constructed those differences in the first place and the needs which caused us to build those machines. We lose some protections, that is true; but what good have those protections been to us, anyhow? How well are we protecting right now? And who are we protecting from what?

Power

At the very end of "History of an Infantile Neurosis," Freud allows himself what must have been some satisfying sneering at the attempts of Jung and Adler to escape some "paltry but unimpeachable facts." In particular, Freud ridicules their idea that the "phantasy of rebirth" is a cause and not a symptom. Freud summarizes their argument, not very fairly we may be sure, and smirks, "All this would be very nice, if. . . ." The satire gathers steam and bursts: "the patient, at a time only four years after his birth, may after all have been too young to be already wishing to be born again." Mocking the Jung/Adler notion with potent common sense, Freud flicks the lash for the perfect final stroke. One more word would be too many.

But Freud is too candid to rest with common sense, particularly that which would deny almost all psycho-sexual power to children. So he spoils the art altogether: "But no, I must take this last argument back; for my own observations show that we have rated the powers of children too low and that there is no knowing what they cannot be given credit for."[10] This is so discordant with the cocky tone preceding and so nearly leads Freud back into the Jung/Adler camp that he is forced to add a footnote to reclaim his lost ground: "I admit that this is the most delicate question in the whole domain of psycho-analysis. I did not require the contributions of Adler or Jung to induce me to consider the matter with a critical eye. . . ."

The question of the powers of childhood is the most delicate in the whole of psycho-analysis and, for Freud, the most important. He is willing to botch his satire so as to insist on "the powers of children." Those powers have been rated too low; they need to be reassessed and the whole field of power redistributed in our understanding. Just how of love or ideology, institutional maneuverings or sexual ones, understanding is subject to the controls of power. Questions are posed and answers formulated in terms dictated by power. Nothing is so powerful as power.

And what is it? How can Foucault get away with saying that, because he is not interested in the thing but in its doings, the nature and existence of the thing can be taken for granted? What justifies the evocation of whatever it is power can be taken to be?[23] Is he appealing to common sense, to nature, to a power lying outside of any historically or culturally determined apprehension of it? Is power a centered agency, ideal, situated beyond time and beyond the reach of questioning? Each of these appeals is nonsense to any poststructuralist, of course, and no one can accuse Foucault of not being that. But his center, this concept of power, remains strangely secure, mystic and immune, protected and idealized, metaphysical through and through.[24]

And so it is in our culture generally and in our most advanced critical model, the new historicism.[25] Even such thoroughgoing poststructuralists as George Lakoff and Mark Johnson are infected. Their *Metaphors We Live By* proceeds to show how "our ordinary conceptual system, in terms of which we both think and act, is fundamentally metaphorical in nature"[26]; "in all aspects of life . . . we define our reality in terms of metaphors and then proceed to act on the basis of the metaphors" (p. 158). Whether the reality we live by bears any relation to anything but the metaphor is an open question, truth being merely "a function of our conceptual system" (p. 179): "metaphors are basically devices for understanding and have little to do with objective reality, if there is such a thing" (p. 184). If. Very shrewd in showing how a culture's values cohere in its metaphoric apparatus and how even subcultural groups preserve and perpetuate central metaphors (Trappist monks see virtue as up), Lakoff and Johnson nonetheless see power not as metaphoric but as natural or, more properly, metaphysical: "Whether in national politics or in everyday interaction, people in power get to impose their metaphors"; "new metaphors, like conventional metaphors, can have the power to define reality" (p. 157). Power seems to be granted some kind of being outside of metaphor, which, in the terms employed here, means outside conceptual systems, culture, history.

Power, thus, even in Foucault is made strangely coherent. Robbed of a definite source and a set location, power nonetheless (or therefore) is able to work for him as a hegemony, making his analyses severely inclusive. Even more so are those of Freud, whose adoption of the power model similarly left no room for anything else, no "margins," as Foucault said. Despite the guile and reflexive irony often found in

Freud's actual procedures, when he came to reflect on method, he generally saw power as tidying up loose ends: "It is always a strict law of dream-interpretation that an explanation must be found for every detail."[27] Similarly, "I am ready to assert that *every* neurosis in an adult is built upon a neurosis which has occurred in his childhood" (emphasis mine).[28] Sometimes he sounds almost jocular on this point, having a laugh on (or with) the totalitarian appetites of power: "Other complications, too, may arise, but they can easily be fitted into the general scheme."[29] It is not Freud's compliance with our culture's centering and mystifying of power that is remarkable, but his self-conscious awareness. He was, as a matter of fact, his own best deconstructionist: "thoughts in the unconscious lie very comfortably side by side, and even contraries get on together without disputes—a state of things which persists often enough even in the conscious."[30]

But power has too seldom been at risk from deconstruction or any other form of inquiry. Its security is nowhere so evident as in writings on sexuality, where the subject becomes more than just another subject, becomes, in fact, the center of being and the key to all knowledge, precisely because it is empowered. Sexuality, that is, becomes identified with power and thus takes on some of its monolithic characteristics. As usual, it is Freud who speaks most plainly and eloquently on the subject: ". . . I can only repeat over and over again—for I never find it otherwise—that sexuality is the key to the problem of the psychoneuroses and of neuroses in general. No one who disdains the key will ever be able to unlock the door."[31] And no one who loses the key to the understanding of neuroses is likely ever to know anything about modern life.

For some Victorians, as for us, the way to find that key was to name things aright, to tag things properly. "Discard euphemism," says William Acton, and "call it by its true name."[32] The true name in this case was "prostitute," but it might have been any name attached to sexuality, the utterance of which presumably gives the speaker power and also fixes the sexual quality within a name. Thus, for those working with power and with the power of naming, sexuality becomes connected with being, and naming that type of sexuality provides access to primary essence. One becomes, within the paradigm of power sexuality, what one does with ones's genitals.[33] As Foucault puts it, "The sodomite had been a temporary aberration; the homosexual was now a species."[34] The allure of this species thinking is undeniable. Moll notes that homosexual adults, convinced that that's what they *are*, tend to report that they have had purely homosexual experiences because the heterosexual ones have become unreal.[35] Sexual essentializing brought on by power thinking is enforced by the same means. Havelock Ellis observed that the category of the "frigid" woman was an invention of the nineteenth century, an invention whose status as the natural and the real was rigorously policed.[36]

But this nineteenth century which saw the beginnings of sexual essentializing, identifying the person with the sexuality (or the sexual behavior), also saw vigorous protests against it. The same William Acton who wanted us calling a whore a whore also carefully distinguished the activity from the person, terming "a vulgar error" the idea "That once a harlot, always a harlot." The woman, the being, was not, for Acton, the same as the prostitute.[37] Even more tellingly, Josephine Butler, in her moving attempts to show that prostitutes are simply "altogether human beings like ourselves," not only attacked the cruel "wholesale labelling" of these women but went further to question even the sacred polarities of good and evil: speaking of the poor, she said, "the boundary line between the virtuous and vicious is so gradually and imperceptibly shaded off, that there is no one point at which it would be possible to affix a distinct name, or infallibly assign a class."[38]

It is just that sort of quick acuity, that ability to see what price we pay for the joy of affixing distinct names and assigning classes, which is so strikingly absent from thinkers caught within the traps of power. Victorian protests against sexual species-thinking are fairly common,[39] but Alfred Kinsey's echoes of these protests in this century seemed strange unto perversity. Kinsey patiently asked us to consider regarding human sexual experience and longing in terms of varieties and dynamic change rather than fixed determinate categories.[40] But his very brilliance and clarity were so at odds with our time that he is now buried under silence. The prescribed line on Kinsey today is that his statistics were wrong, his sampling techniques naive, that he has been totally discredited. Alas.

So we are left with the power of names, sexual essences, and what Foucault has called a " 'reverse' discourse": what looks like an oppositional discourse, a minority or persecuted group speaking out for itself, but in fact is simply a tactical element operating within the same field of force, "in the same vocabulary, using the same categories" by which it was once attacked or disqualified. Thus, "homosexuality begins to speak in its own behalf," but it does so by accepting the specifications and deployments of power.[41] Specifically, the equation of homosexuality and being is ironically seized upon as a key to "liberation." One comes out of the closet and into the cell.

It is interesting that Foucault's model of dominant and reverse discourses is set up to discourage multi-leveled thinking and to advance the cause of a unitary notion of power. It is not, for him, a question of a dominant force and an oppositional force that springs up in reaction to it, but of one dominant which formulates a complex pattern of accords, some of which are made to look like contradictions. Everything proceeds by the same methods and within the same general assumptions, thus fostering the dominant mode that orchestrates reactions. Under the guise of protest, this reverse discourse is worse than quiescent, since it is drawn into the service of the very master it hates.

As Foucault suggests, our Western cultures have located themselves or been located in reference to a unitary though remarkably insinuating deployment of power that tends toward polarizing the world in order to provide the illusion of free thought and free choice. We are confronted with metaphors of opposition that constitute our only means of perceiving things. Monolithic forms of power divide the world into impossibly stark binaries and present them to us as the real: up/down, in/out, day/night, man/woman, adult/child, normal/abnormal.

I hope it is clear that the list of oppositions presented above is arranged in order of decreasing "naturalness"; that is, we are less likely to perceive the opposition as wholly "real" or "innate" as we proceed down the line. It is not entirely for nothing that a small guerrilla force of poststructuralists has been at work on the fundamental mechanisms of power. Perhaps the most important sneak attacks have been directed at the idea of the normal and its equation with the natural. The notion that the "norm," established by a coalition of custom and counting and enforced by power, can function both as a regulative center in culture and as the primary tool for social understanding is especially strong in sexual matters. As Foucault points out, the agencies of power in the nineteenth century worked to reinforce the concept of regular, normal (adult heterosexual) sex by being increasingly silent about it, armoring it with the strength of an unspoken assumption. What was spoken about incessantly, he argues, were matters which had previously scarcely been noticed, among them, children's sexuality, madness, criminal sex, homosexuality or inversion, reveries, and obsessions.[42] The abnormal, in other words, was spoken of in order to increase its separation from the home of normality and to make that home all the more alluring and substantial. Havelock Ellis, in this regard almost wholly typical, explained his procedures by way of this dualism:

> The original inspiration of my own work, and the guiding motive throughout, was the study of normal sexuality. I have always been

careful to show that even the abnormal phenomena throw light on the normal impulse, since they have their origin either in an exaggeration or a diminution of that impulse; while, reversely, we are better able to understand the abnormal when we realise how closely it is related to the normal.[43]

Ellis's otherwise neat conformity to the dualisms of power is dangerously compromised by his final subversive sentence, his bland marking of how close, after all, are the relations of the abnormal and the normal, the pervert and the family man.

Such a suggestion clears the way for the unrelenting mockery of the normal-abnormal equipment carried on most notably by Alfred Kinsey. Kinsey was outraged by the dreary predictability and cruelty of thinking which confused analytical categories with loose ethical ones and thus was doomed to remain within the boundaries of the most obtuse commonsense. It was not, for Kinsey, the way of science to accept "philosophic, religious, and cultural" legends; that so many had done so, had proceeded eagerly with the normal/abnormal (right/wrong) distinction would, he predicted, "provide the basis for one of the severest criticisms which subsequent generations can make of the scientific quality of nineteenth century and early twentieth century scientists."[44] Particularly incensed by the folly, still common today, of studying "abnormal" sexuality in clinics, hospitals, and prisons—"The incidence of tuberculosis in a tuberculosis sanitarium is no measure of the incidence of tuberculosis in the population as a whole"— Kinsey brought to bear on the idea of the abnormal both brilliant sarcasm and the results of massive statistical research. His goal was simple, to show that "whatever the moral interpretation . . . there is no scientific reason for considering particular types of sexual activity as intrinsically, in their biological origins, normal or abnormal."[45]

It seems clear, however, that Kinsey has had no permanent success, perhaps no real influence at all. There are periodic relaxations of these enforced dualisms, as in the 1960s (maybe), but we seem to return always to the security of binaries, no matter how vicious they may be. When asked, we will probably agree with Rupert Croft-Cooke's scornful dismissals of norms and normality: "When we are young we think there is a norm in human behaviour, particularly in sexual behaviour."[46] But we tend to retreat under pressure, to insist on these distinctions. Just as Foucault says, the discussion of power which takes place within its boundaries is forced to act as a promoter of company policy.

It is not that "power," and particularly the raw pursuit of personal power is always celebrated, of course. Nietzsche spoke plainly on the brutalizing effects of power, on its connections to "stupidity," and Orwell's *1984* is a sustained attack not just on political power but on those who make power an end in itself. Even more useful are Gregory Bateson's penetrating comments on how it is not *power* but "the *idea of power*" that corrupts:

> But the *myth* of power is, of course, a very powerful myth and probably most people in this world more or less believe in it. It is a myth which, if everybody believes in it, becomes to that extent self-validating. But it is still epistemological lunacy and leads inevitably to various sorts of disaster.[47]

Inured as we are to disasters, we may need manifest lunacies to provide a wedge into the myth of power. In the field of sexuality, power-thinking sometimes exposes its own rapacious urgency, here, uncharacteristically, in Nietzsche: "The reabsorption of semen by the blood is the strongest nourishment and, perhaps more than any other factor, it prompts the stimulus of power."[48]

Turning briefly to the subject that will later absorb us, we can see in common concerns about pedophilia some of the difficulties within power explanations. Accustomed to thinking of sexual relations in terms of power, we turn to pedophilia as an easy case, a clear instance of distorting the power equilibrium that must, if all is to be fair and square, obtain. It is because big and older people are more powerful than small and younger people that sexual contact between them is wrong.

But are things in fact so simple? Accepting for a moment the inevitability of the power-terms in understanding this issue, we find, even so, a murky picture. Anyone involved with the issue of pedophilia, even the police, admits that violence or physical force are almost never used by pedophiles. As for subtler forms of power, Theo Sandfort's study of the children involved in pedophile relationships concludes that coercion was not a factor. Since Sandfort is Dutch and published his findings in Amsterdam—and since his conclusions do not square with the demands of our cultural beliefs—we are unlikely to attend to him. Still, all who have had any dealings whatever with children recognize that they are not entirely powerless and are often equipped with a considerable arsenal. The sentimental image of complete weakness will not stand up against direct experience. When that experience is sexualized, the child may be further equipped with the power attached to the emotional vulnerability of the older partner and to the much blunter threat of exposure or blackmail. Byron was victimized by the former and Wilde by the latter; and many others have preceded and followed. Perhaps power hates pedophilia so because it actually threatens to grant power to the child, placing the adult in a weakened, sometimes dependent position.[49] Power would never admit this, of course, and says just the opposite; but that is its usual way.

It's not of course that we should turn the tables, declare children the offenders, and warn adults about the dangers lurking around every corner. The question is not the redistribution of power but its adequacy in the first place, its limitations as a tool for understanding and for living. When we come up against a situation like the one dramatized with pedophilia, where the evident power relations are shaken by a further look, where power simply provides inroads into hopeless contradictions, what can we do? Where can we look for help? To power, of course, since it's the only thing in our bag. Haul out the lighter fluid to fight the fire.

I suggest that power can deal with issues that evade its grasp or that threaten to expose its deficiencies only by saying no, telling stories of denial. In terms of pedophilia, one can locate these tales everywhere, in the gothic construction of the pedophile, for instance: the lurking stranger with the candy, the mentally retarded village hang-about, the homicidal wanderer. That people who in fact do engage in sexual relationships with children virtually never fit these images does not seem to matter. It appears to be a cultural necessity, a requirement of power-discourse, to declare over and over again that these matters are marginal, controllable by power, and thus safely distanced from us, from me: whatever is going on in the heads of pedophiles, my head is clear of it. Power seems to promise me at least that protection.

But my warrant for such a claim can be contested. Uncomfortable questions may be posed pretty easily. Why do we talk about this subject so much? Why do we want to look at the faces of missing children on milk-cartons, willing to assume that they have been abducted for sexual purposes even when we know that most are runaways or involved in custody battles only? Why does the subject of children sexually-at-risk provide such an inexhaustible lode for television and film writers to mine? Why do we entertain or even perhaps believe wild stories about a multi-billion dollar kiddie porn industry in this country? Why do we gorge ourselves with statistics that would seem to indicate that no child has much of a chance to reach age 12 without being entrapped by at least one pervert? Why all this chatter? Why the hypnotic interest? And what is it we are in need of hearing? Exactly the same thing, said or represented over and over again. Faultless feelers of the public pulse like *The Reader's Digest* know this and run substantially the same article, with a different title, about every second month. Almost all television programs, sit-coms included, repeat the same dealings with the subject. *Ms.* and *Hustler*, NOW and the Rev. Jerry Falwell, Jesse Jackson and Jesse Helms echo one another. What explains this passion for repetition—other than passion itself? Isn't it just possible that our culture is wildly busy estranging pedophilia in order to guarantee its otherness and drench it with desire? In saying so loudly that pedophilia is monstrous, even impossible, aren't we building up a chorus that sings of how the sexual attractiveness of children is indubitable and pedophilia is inevitable? What could be more normal than this monstrousness?

Has power brought us to this? Do our procedures of denial circle back to affirm resoundingly? If so, how do we understand this peculiar and contradictory maneuvering of power? The most direct answer would seem to be that we are, as Kinsey pointed out, often determined to deny what was well known in the past: the remarkable sexual capacities of the very young.[50] The Victorians, we will find, could be much more open than we in acknowledging this fact or possibility (or myth), though they often seem just as uncomfortable with it: in order to "avoid a tendency toward lust," writes H.S. Pomeroy, "chocolate as a beverage . . . should never be given to children."[51] We seem to have given up on chocolate and have turned to a silence diet. For us, the issue is never raised. It is not good form. Perhaps our posture on this point is a result of being stationed in a post-Freudian, partly anti-Freudian world, suspicious of Freud's flood of enthusiasm for the untold "powers" of children generally and the special sexual powers even of infants. One of the consequences of Freud's abandonment of the seduction theory was his embrace of the hypothesis of full and intense infantile sexuality.[52]

But Freud's zeal cannot by itself explain our almost manic resistance, our fierce denial. For these, there are at least two quite plausible explanations advanced from within the power paradigm: first, that recognizing children as sexual beings means recognizing one's own children that way, which in turn may force us far too close to incestuous ponderings[53]; second, that pedophiles respond to the politeness and helpfulness of children, attitudes, ironically, that we strive to promote.[54] In both these explanations, pedophilia emerges as a basic and subtly embedded threat to the power of parents, to the institution of the family, and to implicit hierarchies within the culture. It threatens to become an instrument of exposure. I mean to suggest also that there are within power, conceived of as a way of seeing and figuring the world, limitations that can be masked or censored only by a circular employment of power itself. The power metaphor sustains and protects itself, when necessary, by turning to power—as a bludgeon.

However, power cannot speak to those whose faculties it has not already formed. Without power-forged eyes and ears, we will find its songs and scenes discordant. There may be none around who have not been worked over by that particular smithy, but even so, some, like Edward Pechter, have recognized in the power invoked by the New Historicists simply a new "essence," not a step beyond humanism but an exchange of a cynical essentialism (power) for a flattering one (humanism). With deceptive simplicity, Pechter says that he is simply "reluctant to accept the will to power as the defining human essence," as if it were a matter of temperament or taste.[55] It is not that simple, true enough, but Pechter's graceful strategy points to the arbitrary nature of the power center and even its fragility—and that's all good.

For power is so often moved to action, and it so often acts to hurt. Indeed, it knows only how to hurt. This is especially true of our mental procedures within power and their consequences. With pedophilia, where power agencies are most obviously operative, it is useful to look at what we actually seem to know about the adults and the children involved in this practice, as opposed to what we commonly say. Even those most absolutely hostile to it, firm in their views, and smug in their conclusions will, when pressed, tell a story quite at odds with the prescribed cultural fable. The following is from the report to a 1984 Senate Investigating Committee holding hearings on "Child Pornography and Pedophilia," a report from "The Sexually Exploited Child Unit of the Los Angeles Police Department." The children, they say, "are lacking a loving, attentive home environment." The pedophiles "offer friendship, interest and a concerned attitude that many parents are unable or unwilling to provide."[56] Children, they would say, are seduced and molested by way of being loved; but they cannot disguise that their narrative is all about love and concern and the failure of the family. How does power deal with all this? How do we deal with it?

We tend to turn the whole theater of pedophilia into a melodrama of monsters and innocents, and we do so for many reasons, all of them bad. Doing so assures us that there are no complex issues and none that threaten. It allows us to overlook both contradictions and cruelties in our logic, in our family structure, and in our social system at large. It allows us unlimited and gratuitous *talk* on the subject. There is a parallel case in the Victorian discussion of prostitution, a discussion which will emerge again more fully later. For now, I want simply to note that the "issue" of prostitution seems to have been successfully turned by well-meaning reformers of the time into a narrative of male lust and unwilling female victims. By ignoring the possibility, raised directly by most who spoke with prostitutes and believed them, that many prostitutes "chose" their line of work, that is to say, were forced into it not solely by male seducers but by economic need and fierce cultural demands, the reformers managed to promote starkly conservative ends, securing the very structure that was making prostitution inevitable. At the very least, they diverted attention away from one set of problems to a personalized power-drama that, however troubling, could be played out without altering the rules of the game.

Just so with pedophilia, where the morality play dictated by power tries to divert the suspicion, simple and shattering, that directing all this unspeakable activity we want both to deny and to heighten is the terrible absence of love. Too many of us do not give children attention, sympathy, affection; therefore they go to those who will. Little Pip, denied love by his sister, goes to his stepfather Joe, who gives him plenty of that and plenty of gravy. Had it been plenty of sex instead, perhaps at least there would have been some facing of the problem and some attempt, however furtive and shamefaced, to solve it.

But what about the damage? What about Pip or the exploited, molested, and abused child? And those questions, those protests, it must fairly be said, do arise immediately and with urgency from the position of power. We must say that power's most pressing claim on our allegiance, or the one that is always pressed on us in any case, is its ability to spot the victims and mobilize power to protect them. Being sensitive to power, we gain the increasingly sophisticated ability to spot its abuses. Imbalances become sharply visible, and we add our weight, the weight of the law, and the heft of public opinion to equalize things. The strength of power in this field, then, lies in its readiness and ability to insert proper protections.

But what price do we pay for those machines of protection, what risks are we taking in so moving to avoid risks? I think that, in the area of human sexual relations (as in all others), we run the danger of sexualizing force itself. That is, as we become more and more aware of power imbalances in sexual relations, it finally becomes simply obtuse not to see any sexual encounter as coercive, subtly coercive perhaps but definitely so. Paradoxically, as we extend the great benefit of the power paradigm, its ability to enable the operations of decency and mutual protection, we mix the categories so badly that sex becomes violence and all human encounters are rapes. I do not wish to be understood as ridiculing the important advantages we have derived from power analyses in this area, the way we have come to understand more fully and compassionately what "consent" might mean and often does not mean. I merely point out what I take to be apparent: all forms of human contact involve uneven power equations and thus, potentially, the need for the machinery of protection, protection from the very agencies of power that caused the problem in the first place.

What empowers the protective agencies? Isn't there a danger of the very protections becoming coercive? Isn't it possible that the need to protect can run amok, as has perhaps happened with the fight against pornography, where the worthy and sensitive have joined hands with the coarse and indecent. More importantly, isn't it possible that denying to those under 18 (or whatever age) the ability to consent risks denying them the competence to exercise a whole host of other rights? Most important of all, how do we control the damaging effects of connecting so closely sexuality and power, thus brutalizing the human body and laying on us an inescapable mixing of love with force?

I do not think there's a way to control the damage done by power, but its authority might still be subverted or ignored. Power might be not so much replaced as tripped up, made the victim of a whoopee cushion. Deconstructed, in a word, de-centered by way of alternate centers: in this case, affinity and illogic.

To get there, let's look at a particularly annoying attribute of power, its unfailing way of taking itself so seriously. It is so solemn about everything, even sex. Here, for example, is the imposing Havelock Ellis talking about inverts, a now-extinct class: "The frequent inability of male inverts to whistle was first pointed out by Ulrichs, and Hirschfeld has found it in 23 per cent. Many of my cases confess to this inability, while some of the women inverts can whistle admirably." There follow some comments on related deficiencies in areas like smoking, dart-throwing, and spitting; some case-histories; and a judicious qualification to put the brakes on those prone to run wild on the whistling point: "It is scarcely necessary to add that the inability to whistle by no means necessarily implies inversion. Shelley, for instance, was unable to whistle. . . ."[57]

Actually, this humorless tone is less a reflection of Ellis than of the mode in which he is working. His tone, like his "thought remains the captive of the linguistic mode in which it seeks to grasp the outline of objects inhabiting its field of perception," according to Hayden White.[58] That "mode," in this case, is, as I have indicated, the melodramatic or the serio-tragic, the approved genre for writers on sexual abnormality. (Kinsey is the only scientific writer on sex I know to tend toward the comic-satiric.) White has, of course, outlined in his famous book the various modes or emplotments by which history is written and the world understood. If writing on sex has tended to be trapped in the tragic and the tragic-romantic (or melodramatic), we might do something to free not simply the tone but the whole discourse by switching the center to something like sentimental comedy or even vaudeville. We might find in this process an alternative to the totalitarian protections of power. We might find in this deconstruction of power not freedom but a new set of possibilities.

On the way to decentering it, we must encounter at least one more charge, battle-bulge, from power, the accusation that we are deluding ourselves by imagining a point of absolute liberation, free from power altogether. Foucault, according to Jana Sawicki's brilliant analysis, while quite aware that his own argument is itself involved in power relations, still feels that it can be liberatory: "This is not liberation as transcendence of power or as global transformation, but rather as freeing ourselves from the assumption that prevailing ways of understanding ourselves and others, and of theorizing the conditions for liberation, are necessary, self-evident, and without the effects of power."[59] We are, one is tempted to say, freed from the preposterous notion that we can be free. But that would be cynical and evasive. It is true that one cannot first construct a center, in this case power, and then free one's discourse from it by claiming to be outside all centers, though perhaps Foucault's discourse can be implicated in power and still have some capacity to emancipate. But why need we continue to spin round this prime mover of power? If power defines and controls any response to it, why then, why respond to it? Why give it credit for being so powerful? Why acknowledge its existence? Why, especially, allow it to exist beyond the reach of inquiry, of skeptical examination, of play? Why posit it as the metaphysical center of a stable structure of meaning and perception?

That last is, of course, a set-up, the question from the shill in the crowd paid to feed the person on stage, though our headliner, Jacques Derrida, hardly needs a shill: "the concept of a centered structure is in fact the concept of a play based on a fundamental ground, a play constituted on the basis of a fundamental immobility and a reassuring certitude, which is itself beyond the reach of play."[60] Power constitutes, for many of us and not just Foucault and Stephen Greenblatt, exactly that center beyond the reach of play. As such, it can claim a great deal of explanatory or at least rhetorical significance. Power explanations are powerfully persuasive, precisely because they are so flattering, anxiety-relieving. They reinforce the center, assure us that there is no rupture and that nothing is lost. Of course these power explanations seem to be dealing with rupture and loss all the time, and to be dealing with them in a particularly unflinching way. Power explanations flaunt the courage with which they are advanced. But they function as strokings, upsetting no one, even with their fiercest quarrels. One more analysis of the currents of power circulating through the state, through discourse, and through the body gives us the good news that Power's in Its Heaven, All's Right With the World.

But Power's no better than God in this regard, though they have a great deal in common. Both act as unifying agencies that come at us in our lives, through our eyes and into our bodies, as totalitarian. Thus the need to breach, to decenter, to deconstruct. I have been trying throughout, at least here and there, to indicate the artificiality of power's protected status, the dangers involved in its functioning smoothly. I do not intend a challenge, a guerrilla movement against power. As we know, that would simply trap me within the power I was foolishly proposing to fight. I mean simply to set up camps in other counties, if I can, not a rival's though, since the communities I have in mind would have little sense of what it would mean to go to war or collect tariffs or control the population or keep things orderly. These are not better than the Power county, nor do they escape totalitarian dangers. All they can lay claim to is differing. But in the present circumstances, that's a great deal.

Which brings us to desire; and eventually to the kind of writing and analysis we might desire. We wisely turn to Roland Barthes, who knew all there was to know on these subjects: "Is not the most erotic portion of a body *where the garment gapes* . . . : the intermittence of skin flashing between two articles of clothing (trousers and sweater), between two edges . . . ; it is this flash itself which seduces, or rather: the staging of an appearance as a disappearance."[61] Barthes is ambiguous, if we want, providing us with some gaps of his own: is it the thing staged, the flash of flesh, or the staging which seduces? One thing is certain, he says, "Desire is no respecter of objects," that is, the object or meaning being shifted or displaced, flashed, matters not at all; "the only thing that counts . . . is *the transference itself.*"[62]

It is the process, not the thing, the way the game is directed and not the outcome, much less the "point" of the game, that matters. With desire, one can take up and leave off, but never begin or end it. For one thing, the games are infinitely repeatable and thus never over. "Do it again!" squeals the loved child who has just been thrown again and again to the ceiling. But no repetition is an exact repeat. This game is forever new, forever encouraging us to create, to invent and stretch rules, to extend into infinity the variations. Desire thus perpetuates itself by concocting a universe of empty spaces into which we can bounce. By holding open to alteration or to subversion or to ticklish adjustments every boundary, every order, every sweater and trouser of officialdom, we can stage a kaleidoscopic panorama of desire. A refusal to take things seriously, then, is a refusal to close with things, to copulate with them, to shut them off. Such desire lives on the flash, the change, the distance; and not on the grunt and sweat and rub of contact; it does not fulfill itself, does not violate or rape. Desire places the banana peel and then hides around the corner. And as you fly through the air, it will watch to see if your clothes, arranged and under orders to conceal, do not break ranks and reveal, in a glimmering second, the forbidden and funny and desirable bit of skin.

There are other names for this sort of theater of course and other names for the operations of desire. Power tends to be hostile to deconstructing desire, to place under arrest the desire which scurries across the border only to execute annoying pranks. For power, desire must come in with tanks, intent on occupation. Power cannot imagine a desire that is not intent on fulfilling itself, on ending itself in a grand and destructive act of orgiastic violence, extinguishing itself and annihilating the Other it thought it wanted.

If the murder-suicide image is too melodramatic, how about this? Power's explanatory systems commonly act to erase distance, to bring what we thought was alien and strange, that is desirable, under control, to familiarize it and thus make it domestic and undesirable. I think it is clear that our procedures for understanding our subject, let's call it Victorian sexuality, have substituted power and control for otherness and desire. Any upstart system hoping to gain our interest ought at least to restore Victorian otherness and offer the prospect of renewed desire.

Otherness is always situated at a distance so great it becomes a dim blur and then disappears. The other is that which we place outside our perceptual field, which we will not allow our metaphorical lens to cover. It's not just that we cannot explain it; we cannot quite *see* it; it does not lie within our conceptual field. We seem to take pleasure in constructing the other not simply as an absence but as a seductive inexplicableness. It cannot be, therefore it is not—as far as explanations go. On the other hand, this impossibility, this that which is not, becomes the core of erotic energy. We need very badly this otherness, this elusive image that evades our mechanisms of explanation, this lack that will fuel desire. So we stage the gaps and eroticize them. Now, though eroticism is a happy condition, most people find, we seem reluctant to experience it at the cost of all control, so we also try to fill in the very gaps we have dug. The first activity fuels desire; the plugging tion's sexual habits, efforts which have managed only to increase nocturnal emissions and premarital petting.[71] But these voices were lost in the dominant cultural drone about repression.

Michel Foucault's critique of repression is familiar,[72] but worth waving to as we go by. He managed to startle us into recognizing the constructedness of the idea, first simply by referring to it as an idea, "the repressive hypothesis." Never denying that sex was or can be prohibited, he argued that "it is a ruse to make prohibition into the basic and constitutive element" in understanding modern sexuality.[73] Such a ruse masks the extent of power's dominion, and presents to us the pleasant suggestion that we can resist power by resisting its prohibitions. However, "power would be a fragile thing if its only function were to repress."[74] "In actual fact," Foucault says, "what was involved . . . was the very production of sexuality": "the stimulation of bodies, the intensification of pleasures, the incitement to discourse, the formation of special knowledges, the strengthening of controls and resistances."[75] Of particular importance was this "multiplication of discourse," the way we have been drawn to telling everything about sex, valorizing sexual discourse, and paying agents to listen to our sexual secrets.[76]

This talk, he says, suggests compulsion, not freedom, a cooperation with the agencies of power and not an effective marshalling of resistance to them. Our proud sexual liberation thus confirms our continuity with the Victorians, not a break from them. When we look again, we note ruefully that the Victorians are wont to claim the same sort of liberation: every nineteenth-century sex manual washes in self-laudation, gloating over its enlightenment and the ignorance of its competitors. We read such things and see that the tale of sexual liberation can be figured easily as an ongoing cultural necessity, a lie we tell ourselves about our own emancipation. Foucault's deconstructive new historicist move thus translates power from a tool we thought we could employ to an institution employing, even creating us. Our talk is not empowering us but empowering power; our sexuality serves neither us nor liberation from repression, even had there been a repression to be liberated from.

With repression at hand we were able to read silence. If all else failed, silence could be felt as a form of denial, signaling at some deep level actual assent: Freud's discussion of Dora is the most famous employment of this interpretive technique.[77] Without repression, we still want to speak of silences, still suspect that we cannot write history without interpreting the unsaid, without some means for rejecting the face value of things, locating that which, hiding behind silence, was shameful or private and therefore sexual. We were tempted to assume that "even the refusal to talk about it [sex] . . . marks it as *the* secret and puts it at the heart of discourse."[78]

There is no reason to center sexuality in this way, to assume that it is *the* secret just because someone doesn't talk about it. Plenty of things are not talked about without necessarily qualifying as *the* secret, *the* metaphoric center of a field of discourse. Right now, for instance, I am not talking about my weight problems, deeply interesting, but, not even to me, *the* secret. But this centering of sex, even or especially when it does not seem to be present, has been occupying us for so long that its tie to silence can hardly be waived aside.

Silence is connected to sexuality for the Victorians by a strong negative tie: silence excludes the possibility. That's what we think they thought—or used to think they thought, before Foucault. We can still actually hear them saying something like that now and then. William Acton occasionally suggests that if we can find ways not to let in the words or thoughts, then the actions will also be blocked: since it is, he argues, impracticable and genetically undesirable for a male to marry immediately at the onset of puberty ("Stallions are not put too early to the stud"), "let him eschew sexual thoughts and obscene conversation, and give himself to healthy exercise and vigorous study."[79] As late as 1921, we find Lord Desart, Director of Public Prosecutions, and Lord Birkenhead, the Lord Chancellor, suggesting that maybe if the word lesbian isn't uttered, it won't exist: it'll not cross anybody's mind to do it or be it.[80]

But it is actually more common to find Victorian discourse asserting some form of the opposite, some hint of a connection between silence and action. Mary Wood-Allen explained that her series of sex manuals were designed to promote innocence, an innocence which, she claimed, was dependent on knowledge and not silence. Silence simply would render youth, female youth particularly, liable to corruption.[81] Mrs. Child, similarly, argued that failing to talk frankly to daughters would excite their natural curiosity on the subject to unnatural heights.[82] Some iconoclastic Victorian analysts drew a general connection between silence and indecent behavior: "in proportion as manners become corrupt, language becomes more guarded,—modesty, when banished from the heart, taking refuge on the lips."[83] Finally, we have recently been taught to entertain the possibility that the unspeakable may be connected to the do-able: "Just as the incest taboo makes it possible in our century for near relatives to live together without censure or suspicion, so by treating homosexuality as something unthinkable, earlier ages in effect facilitated the expression of sentiment between members of the same sex."[84] Clearly, silence can operate not as an opposite of what is said and done but in complex cooperation with them.

It is just as possible that silence indicates indifference, ease, or an unwillingness to be drawn into arenas defined by others. It is in the nature of cranks to hog almost all of the discourse, when no one cares to issue rebuttals. Those who loudly claim that Elvis lives or that millions are worshipping Satan go largely unanswered; will future historians suppose that we were consumed with such things and thought alike on them? Similarly, the silent may have been seeing differently from the vocal (and from us). Perhaps many Victorians felt that the truth was not only disconnected from language but also from the self, even if there were such things as truths and selves:

> Nay, we learn to know that it is so impossible to see ourselves altogether truthfully (our own breath obscuring the mirror in which we attempt to gaze), and still more impossible to convey to another mind by spoken words what we truly are. . . .[85]

And finally, on the principle that the more we talk the less we are likely to be understood, silence may be figured as the desire to communicate fully.

That covers a pretty wide range of possibilities, but there is one further and that is that silence and action are not connected at all, even by oppositional or ironic ties. We have to allow for the possibility that silence conceals nothing, to envision the chance that when the magician opens the box, nothing will be there. Perhaps the Victorian code of action was one thing and that of speech was another: "Certain things were not to be talked about; that was really all that was asked."[86] This is not hypocrisy; it is unrelatedness. Of course that unrelatedness comes from us as much as do the connections; it is not more accurate for us to see things in the past as sundered, floating free—but it may be more fun.

That Victorian culture was no monolith and that Victorian people were highly variable seems perfectly obvious. And many would agree that "it is not true, as we earlier thought, that there was a single, unchallenged prudish position among Victorians."[87] Even so, it is not uncommon to find scholars talking about the period or the people as if they were one thing, using newer terms like "episteme" not all that differently from older homogenizations like "spirit of the age" or "representative." In order to speak at all, I suppose, we must generalize; but it is as well to do so about diversity or disorder.

And it is a very disorderly group we find in nineteenth-century England, varying from region to region, from decade to decade, by gender and by religion, by schooling and trade, and, most obviously, by class. An awareness of class permeates even the most resolutely disinterested scientific texts. William Acton, our old friend, here pauses in his consideration of how female delicacy operates to hinder medical care by dropping a few hints to young bumpkins entering into the trade:

> To prevent unnecessary exposure, the patient should be dressed and wear drawers, or a towel or napkin should be folded around each thigh before proceeding to the examination. Inattention to these little circumstances will soon betray that the operator is not in the habit of conducting an examination among the upper classes.[88]

Whereas, presumably, proper attention to these little circumstances will enable any stable-boy to bamboozle the rich and famous. Not all books dealing with sexuality are silver-fork novels in disguise, of course, though one does notice how much writing the middle class did for the class below it. Among other things, they wrote telling that class how to take care of its children along the lines of received middle-class practices, often, no doubt, sending hurtful signals, pieces of advice quite irrelevant to a situation so different. Now and then, the thought of this difference breaks through; here it suddenly strikes the author (of *Little Children*) that, in contrast to her own easy life, the burdens under which poor mothers groan are almost unimaginable; and we can watch in this passage as her compassion reaches out and then withdraws, leaving behind nothing better than God:

> We richer mothers, when we are tired, or sick, or want to be alone, have others to whom we can trust the care of our children. You have to bear with yours always. Yes, it is very hard. So hard that to yourselves alone it would be impossible. But then you are not alone. God knows how much harder it is for you than for us, and He will give you so much the more help, if you will but ask Him.[89]

Our own attempts to reach this Victorian past must somehow avoid detouring round these enormous class differences. Child mortality rates (from 1837 to 1843), for instance, "doubled and tripled as the social level of fathers dropped."[90] Almost all writers assumed that what was said about modesty, delicacy, and innocence, even the innocence of small children, did not apply to the poor: Acton prints a powerful letter from Henry Mayhew arguing that the indecent living conditions which must be endured by the impoverished cause the minds of females to be "wholly divested of that sense of delicacy and shame which, so long as they are preserved, are the chief safeguards of her chastity."[91]

Nor is this class situation by any means as simple as the usual three-part articulation would suggest. R.S. Neale has shown how much more intricate the social layering and the social movements really were, arguing that even the middle class, which is usually (by literary critics, at any rate) identified wholesale with "Victorian," included a very wide range of social strata. Further, there were always in this culture what Neale calls "important minorities and deviations."[92]

Deviations from what? We have just argued that there is no what to deviate from, no certain way to spot the center and thus no way to mark a stray. Strong voices which are, so far as we can tell, saying what we thought Victorians on the whole did not say, we will therefore call not "deviant" but "various." These are especially valuable sounds, not because they are bizarre—who knows about that?—but because they tell us something about our desire to make them marginal.

What are texts evidence *of* exactly? Does the existence of a document, even in many editions, mean a lot? What does it mean? How many books are bought for show, for amusement, for arousal, for any number of reasons other than because they accord with our own views? In fact, some, not wanting to be bored, buy very few books that confirm their views. If that were entirely so (which of course it is not), large sales figures would indicate marginality. In any case, even if we knew how to recover texts and how to read them with certainty when they were recovered, which we don't, we would not know for whom these texts spoke.

And of those whom tradition has fixed as most resistant to our own views, and thus most conveniently discarded as "eccentrics": we have no way of knowing how many Victorians felt themselves vibrate in tune to these singers. We assume that few did, but it may be worth bearing some discomfort in order to examine a few who are undoubtedly subversive, but perhaps much more subversive of our received values than of their contemporaries'.

A. Charles Knowlton

Charles Knowlton's *Fruits of Philosophy* seems clearly to be an outlaw book, or at least we can say that if we like. It was published by Charles and Annie Bradlaugh and prosecuted, later republished as a test of the law. But does the fact that the law is after it justify us in marginalizing it? First of all, the law is always several generations behind the feeling of the public; second, perhaps the forbidden is expressing a very deep and general wish of the populace. But Knowlton's book, concerned with birth control, does not really seem to travel very far down the dark roads of desire. Though still protected by the British Library's comic procedures for preventing the misuse of awakening books—signing forms declaring the purity of one's intent, reading the book only in plain view of the librarians—*The Fruits of Philosophy* will disappoint most of those willing to invade the "cabinet" of erotica in the North Library. Still, it contains some daring arguments on behalf of contraception, some startling positions embedded in the clear and reasonable prose. For instance, using a shrewd if odd coalition of Darwin and the decent life, Knowlton confronts the objection that sheathing the penis is "against nature" by rudely retorting that it's a very good thing that it is: "Well, what of it? In this restricted sense of the word, it is also against nature to cut our nails, our hair, or to shave the beard. What is civilized life but one continual warfare against nature?"[93]

Even more daring is his use of Bentham: "Owing to his *ignorance*, a man may not be able to gratify a desire without causing misery (wherefore it would be wrong for him to do it), but with knowledge of means to prevent this misery, he may so gratify it that more pleasure than pain will be the result of the act, in which case the act to say the least is justifiable" (p. 3). Note the merry "to say the least." This "act," we may not have noticed, which causes an overplus of pleasure over pain and which is brought about by a defeat of *ignorance* and which proceeds with due regard for the prevention of misery, is nothing less than coitus, pure and simple, with nothing said about marriage either.

B. John Davenport

John Davenport is the author of such works as (short-titles) *Aphrodisiacs and Anti-Aphrodisiacs: Three Essays on the Powers of Reproduction* (1869) and *Curiositates Eroticae Physiologiae; or, Tabooed Subjects Freely Treated in Six Essays* (1875). These titles perhaps do not tell all, but they tell much. Inside are wonders more directly rattling than those in Knowlton. Right off in the Preface to *Curiositates*, for instance, Davenport lets fly with his irritation at what he calls (apparently with terrible sarcasm) *"linguistic purists,"* those who want to mutilate "the brave old English word *cock*" and turn it into *"co,"* as in turnco.[94] He has much, very much, to say on this matter.

He then sprinkles his text with statements that would seem to be outrageous—but who really knows? On the subject of women and sexual passion, say, we have what we think of as an official line on the subject from William Acton, a line made much mock of by Steven Marcus: women generally have little or nothing in the way of sexual feelings.[95] Now comes Davenport, saying as if there were no two opinions on the matter, that "the amorous desires of women are not under such control as those of our sex." He becomes rhapsodic on the issue: "women are far better adepts in the *ars amandi* and its mysteries than men; . . . they have a much keener relish for the tender bliss to which they deliver themselves up with a zest and an *abandon* unknown to men; in short . . . at the feast of Love, women are *gourmandes par excellence*" (pp. 17, 22). Apart from Davenport's silly prose—and how do we know it sounded silly?—is there any reason beyond our own needs in the matter to throw away his opinion and save Acton's?

Similarly, his fierce opposition to celibacy may have had some voters behind it. He argues that celibacy is clearly "in opposition to the laws of nature" (nature serving flexibly as friend or foe, depending on the argument), condemning the practitioners to a "state of nullity." So far so good, we might assume, considering that such an argument probably drew on some still-fierce anti-Catholic feeling and that Davenport is, or so he says, a staunch friend to chastity. He goes on, however, to say that celibacy is debilitating because it "throw[s] back upon the animal economy, a superabundance of vigour," clearly a bad thing in his view (p. 38). All this about the "animal economy" and "vigour" refers to semen and the effects of retaining or "reabsorbing" it, often said to be nourishing or invigorating. One starts to wonder if Davenport doesn't have some secret mission.

Is his hatred of celibacy a mask for something else, something he is promoting? Is he, like Knowlton, flirting with free love? Promiscuity? Masturbation? He does mention that "the over excitement of the organs, abating their tone and vitality, unfit them for the discharge of their office," which sounds to us orthodox enough, if we need to invent an orthodoxy. Davenport seems to be using a recognizable economic model: these organs only have so many miles in them. A few pages later, however, he is referring to another model altogether, one that seems directly contradictory: "Another cause of impotency is the allowing the parts of generation to remain too long in inaction. Those parts of the body which are most exercised are always found to be better grown, stronger, and more fitted for the discharge of their natural

42 / *Positionings*

functions provided the exercise be neither too violent nor too frequent."[96] This model of exercise, equally familiar to the Victorians, suggests a wholly different sort of economy than the fixed, stable economy of scarcity advanced earlier. Now we have an economy of plenitude and surplus; in fact, it is not even a question of surplus but of economic magic: the more you spend the more you have (within reasonable limits, maybe, but there isn't much fretting about limits).

My pun on "spend" by the way is no more outrageous than Davenport's on "discharging" duties and functions. But why does he pun at all, and why does he risk absurdity by applying the notion of building biceps or of developing the lungs through healthy outdoor exercise to other muscles and organs altogether (and to exercise probably not conducted outdoors)? Is his anti-Catholicism sincere, or the defense of chastity, or his patriotic fervor in defending that good old English word "cock"? Is Knowlton serious in invoking Darwin or Bentham? To what extent are men like Davenport and Knowlton speaking from within an episteme and to what extent are they being ironic and playful with the very forms of that controlling structure? My money is on deconstruction.

C. *George Drysdale*

Drysdale and his *The Elements of Social Science* (not a descriptive title) are generally taken more seriously by historians,[97] but his position does not differ much from Davenport's. If anything, he is blunter (or less confused). It would be possible to quote just enough from Drysdale to make him fit in with what we take to be the conventional: he speaks of a *"germinal capacity"* in human beings that sounds very much like a fixed sperm pool and he does pretty well in advancing frightening ideas on the horrors of masturbation, an act which reduces that pool alarmingly. Masturbation is so debilitating, such a "fatal drain," that there are "few rocks on which the health of more individuals is wrecked."[98]

But, like Davenport, Drysdale has metaphors more insidious than draining pools and reasons more involved for insulting masturbation. While masturbation, he says, pulls the plug on the pool, sexual intercourse, like a fresh rain, fills it again, replenishes seminal strength. Even worse than masturbation is the dehydrating sun of celibacy, which Drysdale for some reason (perhaps an impish one), calls "chastity": "Chastity, or complete sexual abstinence, so far from being a virtue, is invariably a great natural sin" (p. 162). And why does chastity fit into this interesting if rather preposterous category of "natural sin"? Because it violates wantonly the sovereign law of physiology: "One physiological law of supreme importance and universal application in our constitution is, that every member must, in order to be vigorous and healthy, have a due amount of exercise, and that of the normal kind" (p. 78). Again, the exercise model confronts the simple economic one, this time dividing over the two expenditures of sperm in masturbation and in intercourse, each of which, for some reason, obeys a radically different economy. Why this is so, whether the attack on masturbation is tongue in cheek, whether there are secret understandings with the audience, who that audience is and how they are responding: all these things are mysteries, mysteries that cannot, however, be solved by trying to cage Drysdale and ship him to the margin.

D. Richard Burton

Burton's translation of *The Arabian Nights* is remarkable, but no more so than his "terminal Essay," especially "Section D: Pederasty."[99] It seems devised as a slap-in-the-face introduction to cross-cultural analysis, an indictment of Podsnappery: "We are overapt to apply our nineteenth century prejudices and prepossessions to the morality of the ancient Greeks who would have specimen'd such squeamishness with Attic salt" (p. 164). That's a mild example of his assault on "an age saturated with cant and hypocrisy," nursing an "impure" obsession with the sins of others and too stupid to see the vileness of its own "holiness" or to set about, as it should in consistency, "to purge the Old Testament of its allusions to human ordure and the pudenda; to carnal copulation and impudent whoredom, to adultery and fornication, to onanism, sodomy and bestiality" (p. 192).

This is an angry and insulting book, often overtly so. Burton's notes alone constitute a gallery of outrage. A single one (p. 171) contains speculation that the first try at creation recorded in *Genesis* aimed at a hermaphrodite, that Adam carnally copulated with all the animals, and that God fouled things up by failing to make man "self-reproductive" like vegetables. Later notes are spiced by reflections like "The more I study religions the more I am convinced that man never worshipped anything but himself" (p. 163). But are these insults or, just as likely, sophisticated jokes? Are Burton's solemn references to sodomy as "unnatural," as "the Vice," to be taken at face value (and what *is* face value?)? What about his theory on the "Sotadic Zone," a climactic and geographic region, having no connection to race or even culture, where pederasty is "popular and endemic" (p. 159)? "Within the Sotadic Zone there is a blending of the masculine and feminine temperaments" (p. 160), possibly related, he says, to a "pitiful" condition, having to do with "the nerves of the rectum and the genitalia, in all cases closely connected, [but] abnormally so" here in the Sotadic (NL43–NL30). To be fair, Burton does not unequivocally support the mix-up-of-nerves theory, the offspring of Prof. Mantegazza; he simply presents it to us for our consideration. What are we to make of this material? Is it a hoax? Is Burton himself a pederast or something? Does he only pretend to find the practice abhorrent? If he finds it abhorrent, why give us all these pages on it? How do we take the tone? Is he punning when he says such things as "Balls of sodomites were held. . . ." (p. 190)? To whom is this material addressed? How do we read it?

Very carefully, of course, though it's not clear that will help us much. Burton's rhetoric looks slippery even under quite traditional analytic lenses. Note how deftly he mixes together learning, observation, and rumor; sarcasm, eroticism, scatological leering, and scholarly piety. He can also do wonderful things with a breezy, informal style: "puberty, they say, is induced earlier [in cities] than in the country sites . . . causing modesty to decay and pederasty to flourish" (p. 187). Just how much of this statement are "they" responsible for? Is it "they," for instance, who give us the connection between the decay of modesty and the flowering of pederasty? Again: "Under Louis Philippe, the conquest of Algiers had evil consequences, according to the Marquis de Boissy" (p. 190). Just how much of the account that follows of French troops and Arab boys is due to the Marquis, and is it he who calls the matter "evil"?

There is no pinning down these fugitive texts. Maybe they belong dead-center—the tail pinned right on the donkey's *clazomenae*. Burton, the source (p. 166) for that impressive learned term (though maybe he stole it from somewhere else or made it up or is offering it as a joke), would have liked playing that game. Like the other voices offered up in this section, Burton's is not to be trapped within an ethos or a conventional episteme. He—and all the others—are too *Cinaedus* for that.

It is true that to our ears these texts sound remarkably contentious and pointed. In fact, however, nearly all Victorian discourse seems to present itself to our recording apparatus as manically positioned and individualized. What we—and Oscar Wilde—regard as Victorian earnestness is our reading of this strangeness, the feeling we have that every writer feels compelled to stake out a highly idiosyncratic claim on every issue under the sun. It is extraordinary to us, for instance, that as we see it, each individual Victorian forced himself to go through a theological boot camp, wrestling in detail with such things as apostolic succession, the doctrine of the Trinity, and the Monophysite heresy. For those of us living in an age when the most vigorous religious movement, fundamentalism, does not bother itself with theology at all, such things as one Victorian party having to prepare a second Victorian party for the news that a third Victorian party was having doubts about the Holy Trinity seem unthinkable.[100] Again, we can read such things only as funny or mad. We imagine that the Victorians were compulsive, since that is the only tool given us for understanding. But isn't it possible that they were so willing to go after everything, to state every possible position on every issue with such vigor and apparent conviction, not because their lives depended on it, but because very little or nothing (in our sense) depended on it? Isn't it possible that this ability to enter into every fray, for the rankest amateur to produce confident analyses of science, religion, sociology, ethics, proceeded not from compulsion but from ease, not from the insane feeling that their utterances would move mountains but from the pleasure in the utterance as an utterance, something very different from a monstrous bulldozer?

The question, in any case, is how knowledge or the pursuit of it gets formulated by the Victorians—and how we go about trying to locate such formulations. One starting point might be found in all the Victorian boosters clubs formed behind inquiry itself, the confidence expressed in looking long and hard, asking inconvenient questions. The very boldness of the process itself is heady and satisfying, never mind the outcome. Perhaps there is something transgressive in all this questioning, something erotic in opening all the doors and inviting the curious to nose about at will and to leave no question unasked. Certainly there is something wonderfully ingenuous in this enthusiasm for inquiry, the self-indulgent refusal to submit to or acknowledge any constraints: "*This* is an age . . . for inquiring into the *how* and *why* and *wherefore* of everything."[101] The boundless sweep of *everything* suggests childlike anarchy, which is perhaps one reason the child became so central in this period: the child was the inquirer, the theorist, the scientist, the reformer, the unacknowledged (or not so unacknowledged) legislator.

Not surprisingly, this inquiry appears to us as empirical, conceived of largely as focused and specific, concerned with little things that would somehow grow into big things, define a field, define a method, define what we would now call a theory. There were of course many exceptions (and there may be more exceptions than I want to acknowledge), but there was often a tendency to distrust theory: "As a rule . . . theoretical controversy is unfruitful,"[102] said Freud, the greatest of those who believed his method and "system" evolved straight from the material being observed: "I can only assure the reader that I approached the study of the phenomena revealed by observation of the psychoneuroses without being pledged to any particular psychological system, and that I then proceeded to adjust my views until they seemed adapted for giving an account of the collection of facts which had been observed."[103] Freud leaves out of this story where his views came from in the first place, how he adjusted them, and what standards he used to decide when they had been sufficiently adapted for giving an account. He also doesn't tell us what he counted as "phenomena," how he looked at it, or where he derived his notion of what an "account" might be. He would have said all this came from the phenomena themselves. The early empiricists all seem to talk that way: extensive enough inquiry into the phenomena will provide the theory whereby the inquiry may be conducted in the first place. The only problem they tend to acknowledge is that in some fields there aren't yet enough good observations: "in the field of sex we content ourselves with the smallest and vaguest minimum of information, often ostentatiously secondhand, usually unreliable."[104]

Even when the facts are there in plain view, people often stupidly/stubbornly can't/won't see them—or that's what the inquirers like to say. William Acton roared, "It is useless to shut our eyes to a fact,"[105] and he thought his society was doing just that; Freud said the fact that certain sexual perversions were "very widely diffused among the whole population" is acknowledged by everybody except medical writers, who "take care to forget it at the very moment when they take up their pens to write about it"[106]; and Kinsey lamented often our general "unwillingness to face the facts."[107] What this grumbling usually suggests is that others do not arrange the facts in the same order, do not see quite the same facts, do not, in other words, live within the same theory or the same metaphor. When this happens, empiricists, who imagine there are only one set of facts and one way to see them, generally hurl insults at the others: Freud says all resistance to his system comes from simple "narcissism of men, their self-love."[108]

Meanwhile, this tyranny of facts quickly becomes a tyranny of systems. But what a grim way to put it! As I suggested earlier, this power explanation of the turn to facts is not the only one: facts also release words, release play, and have a slipshod, irresponsible way of avoiding rigid and consistent theorization. There are, in other words, happy sides to this story. As systems come into play, even psychoanalytic systems, they come bolstered by facts which they are, in turn, prepared to explain fully. Psychoanalysis is a system of explanation rigorously and firmly built on facts; or perhaps it is built on nothing at all and is an ingenious game with infinite applications. Either way, it is now showing itself as a *system* and not a collection of inquiries into facts. As a system it makes different claims—or allows more freedom to the players. One thing is certain: with the authority of the system (under cover of the system), one can do things the unlicensed empiricist would never get away with. Indeed, one *must* often do things that are offensive, simply because the system moves in that direction. William Acton, we have seen, indicates how the system makes it lamentably necessary to examine naked ladies, even naked ladies of quality; equally repugnant to him is the way his subject forces him to talk about blennorrhagia of the anus (and anal sex): "Had I the option of passing over the subject of this chapter in silence, I would gladly do so. Nothing but the fact that it is a definite part of the subject which I am describing. . . ."[109] The "subject" leads one on willy-nilly; if into unpleasant places, well, what is one to do? Most writers, of course, offer more than this apologetic helplessness; they say that the revolting is good for us. Ellis, for instance, acknowledges that many do not want to hear what he has to tell them but that silence on such a topic is "disastrous" and, worse, "unwholesome."[110] Subjects come at us as castor oil.

And we like to think that the Victorians were subject- or system-crazy. After all, this was the period of such things as the electromagnetic system, the patented use of that "great agent of organic life," *electricity*: in belts, lung invigorators, liver and digestive organ stimulators certain to cure, among many, many other things, spinal afflictions, heart complaints, tumors, consumption, cold feet, deafness, gout, paralysis, indigestion, and "complaints suffered while in a railway accident."[111]

But the great Victorian systems, we imagine, were moral and ethical: "It cannot surely be questioned but that we want a System of Morals better than any of those which are currently around us," wrote Frances Cobbe in 1855, in a Preface to a book offering just that article.[112] The most popular system going, in our view, was a slap-happy sort of optimism, combined with a grinding devotion to duty that makes our eyes glaze over: "Duty alone is true; there is no true action but in its accomplishment."[113] That's coming it pretty strong, but it would strike most of us as representative Victorianism, especially when we hear that it's from Samuel Smiles, reckoned to be a major voice of the greatest of Victorian systems, the Compromise. But one wonders if these neat systems, apart from the electro-magnetic ones ("magnetic currents sustain energy"), aren't mostly modern constructs.[114] Smiles, for instance, does not seem to me nearly so univocal or chipper as I had been led to believe: "The wise person gradually learns not to expect too much from life. Nor will the wise man expect too much from those about him."[115]

This sort of stoicism is not what we recognize as Victorianism, though we are deeply familiar with a new growth in their landscape that accompanied the emphasis on subject and system like the aphid the rose, namely the expert. These experts were generally steely-eyed, terrifying in their insistence on the importance of their expertise. Here's Smiles again, from a different book and in a different mood: writing on physical education, he announces that the laws of growth, the ones he is articulating in his book (by the way), are "invariable," and that, further, "to be guided by these certain laws . . . is the duty of all, and especially parents." Why? Because otherwise your child will die! Infant mortality is high and the cause is singular: "it *is* a want of knowledge."[116] A failure to consult this expert, then, amounts to criminal negligence. Most experts are not so directly horrifying, but they do make clear that there is no such thing as natural or intuitive knowledge or skill in anything, least of all in being a parent:

> Many people have an idea that it comes intuitively to women to take care of children, and that every woman is naturally endowed with the knowledge of how to take care of a baby, which knowledge will develop of itself, without any help, as soon as occasion arises. That this is fallacious requires only a little thoughtful consideration to make itself manifest to any reflective mind. There are schools of cookery. . . .[117]

Even the switch from considering certain activities (masturbation, for instance) as vices to thinking of them as diseases,[118] acted greatly to heighten the importance of the expert on diseases, the physician.

In order to gain power, however, or, from our point of view, in order to gain an audience, Victorian experts were often required to sacrifice some of their austerity and descend unto the multitude. They had to talk to the customers, the fans. A.F.M. Willich introduced the new century (the nineteenth) to this democratic specialist type, by way of a particularly massive tome, *Lectures on Diet and Regimen: Being a Systematic Inquiry into the Most Rational Means of Preserving Health and Prolonging Life: Together with Physiological and Chemical Explanations, Calculated Chiefly for the Use of Families, in Order to Banish The Prevailing Abuses & Prejudices in Medicine.* It's no small thing to bring these physiological and chemical explanations within the reach of every family. Willich agrees: "We apparently live in an age, when every branch of human knowledge is reduced to a popular system; when the most important sciences lay aside the garb of pedantry and mysticism; when, in short, the sources of information are open to every rank, and to both sexes."[119]

This *accessible expert*, the explaining genius, is a legacy we have lost from the nineteenth century; it survived for a time in medicine shows and street-corner prophets but now appears only in the degraded form of Christian evangelists. It makes you long for the electro-magnetic man with his rowdy flim-flam and his digestive-organ stimulators. I'm sure they worked.

Actually, it is most likely that this proliferation of experts-at-your-elbow acted not so much to consolidate knowledge and give a boost to human certainty but to open up to many more people a baffling but delightful world of pure difference. Still, it was that brand of difference that insisted on counting and on being counted, that asked for choices and selections or, at the very least, strict attention. Things were consequential, ideas and words were influential, nothing was wasted. Whatever system of accounting was used within these various systems, each must account for absolutely everything. Systems must be complete and unified or they are nothing worth. Child-rearing systems, for instance, must include every influence on the child. And everything *was* an influence on the child: "It cannot be too strongly urged that, unless the plan of education adopted with children does them a positive physical good in all its details, it does them a positive physical harm—it cannot be neutral."[120] The "plan," thus, supplants earlier conceptions of "nature" and takes over full and absolute responsibility for good or for evil. Neutrality is unthinkable since there is no motive force outside of the plan; the plan does not provide assistance to other agencies of growth but *is* the agency of growth.

The plan is centered, made quickly into an essence. And this is one aspect of Victorian thinking, particularly sexual thinking, to which our attention is always directed by modern scholars: its faith in essences. Categories of perversion, for instance, and people to fit them in both came into being in the nineteenth century.[121] Actually, what we tend to see most often in the discourse are alternatives to or protests against what we might call species-thinking or essentialism. George Ives argued that we should conceive of all human possibilities from "ultra-masculine to the infra-feminine" as shifting and as existing not as types but as "spread out like a spectrum."[122] William Lecky's extraordinary *History of European Morals* is not a relativist work, but it does make clear that there are in different periods and cultures different emphases on different virtues and shifting "moral types."[123] Charles Bell Taylor said that even the essence of chastity is not very clear: "I must remind you that to distinguish between chaste and unchaste women ... is a most delicate task for a special jury and a learned judge."[124] And William Acton, as we noted previously, attacked the essentialism laden in the conception of the "prostitute."[125] It must be admitted, however, that these voices might well arise simply because the essentializing is so widespread and habitual. Entrenched visions and mental procedures never speak for themselves until they are no longer entrenched. They are protected by silence.

Or so they imagine. There is a way in which the passion for recording, for getting things right, for cataloguing and classifying, for essentializing tended to provide its own deconstructive fun. The mania for scientific or pseudo-scientific cataloguing, for instance, forming a part of the popular natural history craze, soon got happily out of hand.[126] Popular books with titles like *Romance Under the Microscope* or *A Naturalist's Walks in Country Lanes* often paid a kind of rudimentary attention to classification systems but really displayed disruptive profusion, suggesting that the thousands of different ferns or bugs they listed pointed to the inexhaustible variety that you could find right out in your own garden or in the nearby woods. Nature, these books suggest, is not to be caught and contained by essentialist categories or any other device. Whatever you've got, there is always more of it, slightly different too.

Further, right in the middle of Victorian essentializing one finds an equally central formula or structure that is not so much contradictory as potentially deconstructive: change. As the Lecky example above suggests, the idea of change crept over the period like a glacier, or maybe something faster than that. Foregrounded paradigms of change seem to be observable in almost all discourse,[127] perhaps because that's what we like to see. It does seem that, just as neutrality is ruled out as an effect, so is the concept of a steady-state condition lost: things must either advance or decline; they cannot stand still. Ideas of progress are common but so are ideas of degeneration: Macaulay is countered by Carlyle, Krafft-Ebing by Acton.[128] We will see in the next chapter how these paradigms were fitted to the child, which became both the image of "an instrument for change" in social and political conditions[129] and a melancholy fix on a golden time that we all slip away from.

Notes

1. The landmark ironic exploration of modern "knowingness" and its terrors is Eve Kosofsky Sedgwick's *Epistemology of the Closet* (Berkeley: Univ. of California Press, 1990).

2. For a rich discussion of emptinesses in the novel and particularly its lovers see John Stevenson's excellent "'Heathcliff is *Me*!': *Wuthering Heights* and the Question of Likeness," *Nineteenth-Century Literature* 43 (1988): 60–81. It is possible that Hollywood, which has not shrunk from showing us the moors, and Cathy and Heathcliff on them, is partly responsible for this. However, I have run the test on students who have never seen the television and movie versions and have found the same results.

3. Emily Brontë, *Wuthering Heights* (Boston: Houghton Mifflin, 1956), ch. iii.

4. Charles Dickens, *David Copperfield* (Oxford: Oxford Illustrated Dickens, 1948) ch. iv.

5. Sigmund Freud, "On the Sexual Theories of Children," The Standard Edition of the Complete Psychological Works of Sigmund Freud, trans. and ed. James Strachey, with Anna Freud (London: Hogarth Press and the Institute of Psycho-Analysis, 1953), IX, 210. Subsequent references to Freud will be from the *Standard Edition*.

6. I grant that many famous child-lovers had their gender preferences, Carroll favoring girls just as clearly as Barrie sought to live with boys. I do not, however, think we can understand even such preferences in power terms. Carroll, I suggest, did not hate boys but certainly had an aversion to what he called their "appendage," an aversion he said was aesthetic. Even if we scoff at such an explanation, I think it is plausible that he regarded the penis simply as too unmistakably gendered and "adult," too closely associated with the power sexuality he disdained. For Barrie, boys were simply both temperamentally more akin to his more athletic interests and, bluntly, much more easily available. Judging from his photographs, however, Barrie's boys, always shot from the rear, are as genderless as Carroll's girls, just as removed from the dying finality of heterosexual copulation.

7. The first is from Michael Ryan, *The Philosophy of Marriage in Its Social, Moral, and Physical Relations*, 3rd ed. (London: H. Balliere, 1839), p. 143; the second from Alexander Walker, *Woman: Physiologically Considered as to Mind, Morals, Marriage, Matrimonial Slavery, Infidelity and Divorce* (Birmingham: Edward Baker, 1898), pp. 39–40.

8. Dr. Elizabeth Blackwell, *Counsel to Parents on the Moral Education of Their Children* (London: Hirst Smyth and Son, 1878), p. 37 and *The Human Element in Sex*, 2nd ed. (London: J. and A. Churchill, 1884), p. 49.

9. See Deborah Gorham, *The Victorian Girl and the Feminine Ideal* (Bloomington: Indiana Univ. Press, 1982), pp. 68–83; Richard von Krafft-Ebing, *Psychopathia Sexualis*:

A Medico-Forensic Study, trans. Franklin S. Klaf (New York: Bell Publishing, 1965), p. 186.

10. Sigmund Freud, "From the History of an Infantile Neurosis," XVII, 103.

11. R.P. Toby Tyler and Lore E. Stone, "Child Pornography: Perpetuating the Sexual Victimization of Children" testimony to "Child Pornography and Pedophilia" hearings, Sen. William V. Roth, Jr., chair, United States Senate Subcommittee on Investigations of the Committee on Governmental Affairs, 98th Cong., 2nd sess. Washington: GPO, 1985, p. 93. Characteristic of the level sustained throughout is the following note: "Gender, whether stated as masculine or feminine, should be read as masculine or feminine" (p. 93).

12. Michel Foucault, "Prison Talk," in Colin Gordon, ed., *Power/Knowledge: Selected Interviews and Other Writings by Michel Foucault, 1972–77*, trans. Colin Gordon et al. (New York: Pantheon, 1980), p. 52.

13. Michel Foucault, *The History of Sexuality, Volume I: An Introduction*, trans. Robert Hurley (New York: Pantheon, 1978), p. 139; see pp. 135–59.

14. Michel Foucault, "Two Lectures" in Gordon, ed., *Power/Knowledge*, p. 104.

15. Foucault, *History of Sexuality*, p. 6. Foucault does, of course, allow for "resistances" to or within power, but I am concerned here with his granting to power centrality and totality.

16. Michel Foucault, "The Ethic of Care for the Self as a Practice of Freedom: An Interview with Michel Foucault on January 20, 1984," conducted by Raul Fornet-Betancourt et al.; trans. J. D. Gauthier, S.J., in James Bernauer and David Rasmussen, eds., *The Final Foucault* (Cambridge, MA: MIT Press, 1988), pp. 3–4.

For a very useful analysis of Foucault on power, see Sheldon S. Wolin, "On the Theory and Practice of Power," in Jonathan Arac, ed., *After Foucault: Humanistic Knowledge, Postmodern Challenges* (New Brunswick: Rutgers Univ. Press, 1988), pp. 179–201.

17. Foucault, *History of Sexuality*, pp. 155–57.

18. Michel Foucault, "The Confession of the Flesh," in Gordon, ed. *Power/Knowledge*, p. 198. See also Maurice Blanchot, "Michel Foucault as I Imagine Him," trans. Jeffrey Mehlman, in *Foucault/Blanchot* (New York: Zone Books, 1987), pp. 95–98.

19. Michel Foucault, "The Eye of Power," in Gordon, ed., *Power/Knowledge*, p. 156.

20. Michel Foucault, "Power and Strategies," in Gordon, ed., *Power/Knowledge*, pp. 141–42.

21. Foucault, "Two Lectures," in Gordon, ed., *Power/Knowledge*, p. 89.

22. Foucault, "Ethic of Care," in Bernauer and Rasmusssen, eds., *The Final Foucault*, p. 11.

23. See Blanchot, "Michel Foucault": ". . . nor is he interested in the concept of power in general, but rather in relations of power, their formation, specificity, and activation" (p. 90).

24. For similar and more detailed critical analyses of Foucault's employment of "power" see Jeffrey Weeks, *Sex, Politics and Society: The Regulation of Sexuality since 1800* (London: Longman, 1981), pp. 6–11 and John Kucich, *Repression in Victorian Fiction: Charlotte Bronte, George Eliot, and Charles Dickens* (Berkeley: Univ. of California Press, 1987), pp. 14–15.

25. See, for the best examples, the work of Stephen Greenblatt or the recent collection

he edited, *Representing the English Renaissance* (Berkeley: Univ. of California Press, 1988).

26. George Lakoff and Mark Johnson, *Metaphors We Live By* (Chicago: Univ. of Chicago Press, 1980), p. 3. Further references will be cited in the text.

27. Freud, "History of an Infantile Neurosis," p. 42.

28. Freud, "History of an Infantile Neurosis," p. 99.

29. Sigmund Freud, "Fragments of an Analysis of a Case of Hysteria," VII, 55.

30. Freud, "A Case of Hysteria," VII, 61. Freud's comment is echoed in Gerald Bruns's observation that "norms of rationality are social: they are rooted in ways of life rather than in processes of knowledge"; see *Inventions: Writing, Textuality, and Understanding in Literary History* (New Haven: Yale Univ. Press, 1982), p. xii.

31. Freud, "A Case of Hysteria," p. 115.

32. William Acton, *Prostitution: Considered in Its Moral, Social, and Sanitary Aspects in London and Other Large Cities and Garrison Towns, with Proposals for the Control and Prevention of Its Attendant Evils* (London: Frank Cass, 1972; reprint of 1870, 2nd ed.), p. 207.

33. See Arnold I. Davidson, "Sex and the Emergence of Sexuality," *Critical Inquiry* 14 (1987): 16–48. Davidson argues that the tie between sexuality and essence comes into being in the nineteenth century; then, "to know a person's sexuality is to know that person" (47).

34. Foucault, *History of Sexuality*, p. 43.

35. Albert Moll, *The Sexual Life of the Child*, trans. Dr. Eden Paul (New York: Macmillan, 1913), p. 5.

36. Havelock Ellis, *Studies in the Psychology of Sex*, 4 vols. (New York: Random House, 1936), I, ii, 193–203. Unless otherwise noted, all further references to *Studies in the Psychology of Sex* will be to the 1936 edition.

37. Acton, *Prostitution*, p. 27. Acton's position was that prostitution was amenable neither to "absolute repression" nor to licensing. He advocated a middle ground he called "RECOGNITION" (his caps), a term, state of mind, and argument that will not seem so innocent or reasonable now as he hoped they would then.

38. Josephine Butler, "Paper on the Moral Reclaimability of Prostitutes, read by Mrs. Butler at a Conference of Delegates from Associations and Committees Formed in Various Towns for Promoting the Repeal of the Contagious Diseases Acts, Held at Freemason's Tavern, 5th and 6th May, 1870" (n.p.: n.p., n.d.), pp. 3–6.

39. Along with Acton, Havelock Ellis called such classifications as "homosexual," "bisexual," and "heterosexual": "superficial," "scarcely scientific," and "of no great practical use." See *Psychology of Sex*, 3rd ed. (Philadelphia: F.A. Davis, 1913), II, 88.

40. See, for example, his (with Wardell B. Pomeroy and Clyde E. Martin) *Sexual Behavior in the Human Male* (Philadelphia: W.B. Saunders, 1948), pp. 636–39. Many recent studies reject sexual essentialism, notably the excellent works by Jeffrey Weeks.

41. Foucault, *History of Sexuality*, p. 101.

42. Foucault, *History of Sexuality*, p. 39.

43. Ellis, "Foreword" (1936) to *Psychology of Sex*, I, xxi.

44. Kinsey, *Sexual Behavior in the Human Male*, p. 7.

54 / *Positionings*

45. Kinsey, *Sexual Behavior in the Human Male*, pp. 201–3.

46. Rupert Croft-Cooke, *Feasting with Panthers: A New Consideration of Some Late Victorian Writers* (New York: Holt, Rinehart and Winston, 1967), p. 11.

47. Gregory Bateson, *Steps to an Ecology of Mind* (New York: Ballantine, 1972), p. 486.

48. Friedrich Nietzsche, *Notes* (1880–81), X, 414, in *The Portable Nietzsche*, ed. and trans. Walter Kaufmann (New York: Penguin, 1976), p. 75. Subsequent references to Nietzsche will quote from this source.

49. Theo Sandfort's study, *The Sexual Aspects of Pedophile Relations: The Experience of Twenty-five Boys* (Amsterdam: Pan/Spartacus, 1982) is notable for considering the children involved; on pederasty and power, see pp. 81–82, 86. The most extended treatment of the power available to the child in such relations is in Tom O'Carroll's *Paedophilia: The Radical Case* (Boston: Alyson Publications, 1982), pp. 166–82. For other thoughtful considerations of this issue, see Eve Kosofsky Sedgwick, *Between Men: English Literature and Male Homosocial Desire* (New York: Columbia Univ. Press, 1985), pp. 5–6; Vern L. Bullough, *Sexual Variance in Society and History* (New York: John Wiley, 1976), pp. 590–91; and (on Byron) Louis Crompton, *Byron and Greek Love: Homophobia in 19th-Century England* (Berkeley: Univ. of California Press, 1985), p. 238.

50. Albert C. Kinsey et al., *Sexual Behavior in the Human Female* (Philadelphia: W.B. Saunders, 1953), pp. 13–14. See also O'Carroll, *Paedophilia*, who presses the issue of why our culture is so eager to deny or suppress the fact of child sexuality.

51. H.S. Pomeroy, "Introduction" to Rev J.F. Flint, *The Temptation of Joseph*, 5th ed.(Boston: Arena Publishing, 1896), p. 22.

52. See Jeffrey Weeks, *Sexuality and Its Discontents: Meanings, Myths, and Modern Sexualities* (London: Routledge and Kegan Paul, 1985), p. 133.

53. See Larry L. Constantine and Floyd M. Martinson, eds., *Children and Sex: New Findings, New Perspectives* (Boston: Little, Brown, 1981).

54. See Mary Ann Largen, "Foreword" to Ann Wolbert Burgess et al., *Sexual Assault of Children and Adolescents* (Lexington, MA and Toronto: D. C. Heath, 1978), p. ix. Largen says the fact that pedophiles test victims for these qualities is appalling: "The prevention dilemma this poses for parents is enormous. How, in fact, do we teach our children to protect themselves without giving up all the social values we may wish to instill in them?" One notices that all the concern, even pity, is focused not on the children but on "we" parents, apparently the real victims in all of this.

55. Edward Pechter, "The New Historicism and Its Discontents: Politicizing Renaissance Drama," *PMLA* 102 (1987): 292–303.

56. U.S. Senate, "Child Pornography," p. 132.

57. Ellis, *Psychology of Sex*, II, 291.

58. Hayden White, *Metahistory: The Historical Imagination in Nineteenth-Century Europe* (Baltimore: The Johns Hopkins Univ. Press, 1973), p. xi.

59. Jana Sawicki, "Feminism and the Power of Foucauldian Discourse," in Arac, ed., *After Foucault*, p. 167.

60. Jacques Derrida, *Writing and Difference*, trans. Alan Bass (Chicago: Univ. of Chicago Press, 1978), p. 279.

61. Roland Barthes, *The Pleasure of the Text*, trans. Richard Miller (London: Jonathan Cape, 1976), pp. 9–10. See also 14–15, 51–53, 58 and Roland Barthes, *Sade/Fourier/Loyola*, trans. Richard Miller (Berkeley: Univ. of California Press, 1976), pp. 7–8. The finest use of these Barthesian insights I know is in Cathy Comstock's brilliant *Disruption and Delight in the Nineteenth-Century Novel* (Ann Arbor: UMI Research Press, 1988).

62. Roland Barthes, *Roland Barthes*, trans. Richard Howard (New York: Hill and Wang, 1977), p. 123.

63. In comments during a Forum on "Androgyny: Fact and Fiction" at the Modern Language Association Annual Convention on December 27, 1973 in Chicago, Illinois.

64. Freud, "A Case of Hysteria," VII, 77. Later in the same essay, Freud makes a similar point: "It is easy to learn how to interpret dreams . . . for the patient himself will always provide the text" (p. 116).

65. Steven Marcus, *The Other Victorians: A Study of Sexuality and Pornography in Mid-Nineteenth-Century England* (New York: Basic Books, 1966), p. 1. Marcus is given to recurrent sarcasms about "the point of intellectual development to which thinking about sex had attained" in Victorian England (p. 112). Others, far less responsible than Marcus in discussing the Victorians, feel free to report gossip as fact, the outlandish as the commonplace: see, for example, Samuel X. Radbill, "Children in a World of Violence: A History of Child Abuse," in C. Henry Kempe and Ray E. Helfer, eds., *The Battered Child*, 3rd ed. (Chicago: Univ. of Chicago Press, 1980). Radbill's idea of history is to tell us about nurses stroking children's genitals "to stimulate their own lust" and about the "skilled baby killers" hired to nurse illegitimate children, killing, he says, 80% of them (pp. 9, 13).

Even the best are at their weakest when they read the past as positivists: "But it was in the middle class that youthful sex was most firmly policed," says Weeks (*Sex, Politics*, p. 40), never stopping to ask how it is we would ever know something like that or, more importantly, why we are so ready to believe such an assertion and what our readiness might reveal.

66. Nietzsche, *Notes* (1888), *The Portable Nietzsche*, p. 458. Compare Foucault's hectored insistence that he is *not* saying "that there is nothing there and that everything comes out of somebody's head" ("Ethic of Care," in Rasmussen and Bernauer, eds., *The Final Foucault*, p. 17).

67. *Show Me! A Picture Book of Sex for Children and Parents*, photography, captions, designs by Will McBride; explanatory text by Dr. Helga Fleischhauer-Hardt; English language adaptation by Hilary Davies (New York; St. Martin's, 1975), p. 145

68. Sigmund Freud, "Three Essays on Sexuality," VII, 237–38.

69. See Hayden White, *Metahistory*, pp. 365–67.

70. Quoted in John Stewart Collis, *Havelock Ellis: Artist of Life* (New York: William Sloane, 1959), p. 16.

71. Kinsey, *Human Male*, pp. 415–16.

72. For an especially well-informed and intelligent analysis of Victorian sex studies generally and their turn away from theories of repression, see Carol Z. Stearns and Peter N. Stearns, "Victorian Sexuality: Can Historians Do It Better?," *Journal of Social History* 18 (1985): 625–34.

A vigorous defense of repression is mounted by Crompton, who also proposes that "the 'discursive explosion' Michel Foucault purports to have discovered in eighteenth- and nineteenth-century French sexology did not cross the channel" (*Byron and Greek*

Love, p. 4). A striking employment of the term as suggesting inwardness, a refusal to speak; and a brilliantly original analysis of the "productive role these refusals could play in the development of Victorian emotional life" (p. 3) is offered by Kucich, *Repression*; see esp. pp. 1–33.

73. Foucault, *History of Sexuality*, p. 12.

74. Michel Foucault, "Body/Power" in Gordon, ed., *Power/Knowledge*, p. 59.

75. Foucault, *History of Sexuality*, pp. 105–6.

76. Foucault, *History of Sexuality*, pp. 30, 23, 7.

77. Freud, "A Case of Hysteria," VII, especially 59–60.

78. Weeks, *Sex, Politics*, p. 19.

79. Acton, *Prostitution*, pp. 163–64.

80. See Weeks, *Sex, Politics*, p. 105.

81. Mrs. Mary Wood-Allen, M.D., *What a Young Girl Ought to Know* "Purity and Truth Series" (Philadelphia and London: Vir Publishing, 1897), p. 20.

82. Mrs. Lydia Maria Child, *The Mother's Book* (Glasgow: Richard Griffin; London: Thomas Tegg, 1832).

83. John Davenport, *Aphrodisiacs and Anti-Aphrodisiacs: Three Essays on the Powers of Reproduction, With Some Account of the Judicial 'Congress' as Practised in France During the Seventeenth Century* (London: privately printed, 1869), pp. v–vi.

84. Crompton, *Byron and Greek Love*, p. 73.

85. Frances Power Cobbe, *Auricular Confession in the Church of England* (London: H. Brace, 1872), p. 21.

86. Richard Lewinsohn, *A History of Sexual Customs*, trans. Alexander Mayce (New York: Bell, 1958), p. 290.

87. John Maynard, "The Worlds of Victorian Sexuality: Work in Progress," in Don Richard Cox, ed., *Sexuality and Victorian Literature* (Knoxville: Univ. of Tennessee Press, 1984), pp. 259–60.

88. William Acton, *A Practical Treatise on Diseases of the Urinary and Generative Organs (in Both Sexes)*, 3rd ed. (London: John Churchill, 1860), pp. 217–18.

89. Anon., *Little Children: A Few Words to Mothers. By a District Visitor* (London: Society for Promoting Christian Knowledge, [1872]), p. 6.

90. Thomas Edward Jordan, *Victorian Childhood: Themes and Variations* (Albany: State Univ. of New York Press, 1987), p. 84.

91. Acton, *Prostitution*, pp. 181–83.

92. R.S. Neale, *Class and Ideology in the Nineteenth Century* (London: Routledge and Kegan Paul, 1972), pp. 121, 141–42. See also Gorham, *The Victorian Girl*, pp. 15–16, 31.

93. Charles Knowlton, *Fruits of Philosophy: An Essay on the Population Question* (London: Freethought Publishing Co., n.d. [1877]), p. 6. This book is in some reprints subtitled "The Private Companion of Adult People," but I believe the caution to be a twentieth-century addition. Subsequent references are cited in the text.

94. John Davenport, *Curiositates* (London: privately printed, 1875), pp. vi–vii. Subsequent references will be cited in the text.

95. Marcus reads Acton as saying this: *The Other Victorians*, pp. 29–33.

96. Davenport, *Aphrodisiacs*, pp. 29, 34.

97. See, for example, Peter T. Cominos, "Late-Victorian Sexual Respectability and the Social System," *International Review of Social History* 8 (1963): 44–45.

98. George Drysdale, *The Elements of Social Science; or Physical, Sexual and Natural Religion: An Exposition of the True Cause and Only Cure of the Three Primary Social Evils: Poverty, Prostitution and Celibacy*, 35th ed. (London: G. Standring, 1905 [first pub., 1854]), pp. 55, 87. Subsequent references will be cited in the text.

99. Reprinted in Brian Reade, ed., *Sexual Heretics: Male Homosexuality in English Literature from 1850 to 1900* (London: Routledge and Kegan Paul, 1970), pp. 158–93. Further references will be cited in the text by page number.

100. As G.M. Young wittily suggests: *Victorian England: Portrait of an Age* (New York: Oxford Univ. Press, 1964), p. 14.

101. Robert Holt, *"How has it come about that there is a Church in Every Parish in England? and How are the Parson's Paid?": A Speech Delivered at a Meeting of the Inhabitants in Hillesden and Others, on Wednesday, Jan. 16, 1884* (London: Rivingtons, 1885), pp. 3–4.

102. Freud, "History of an Infantile Neurosis," XVII, 48.

103. Freud, "A Case of Hysteria," VII, 112–13.

104. Ellis, "Preface to First Edition," *Psychology of Sex*, p. xxxiv.

105. Acton, *Prostitution*, p. 177.

106. Freud, "A Case of Hysteria," p. 51.

107. Kinsey, *Human Male*, p. 21.

108. Sigmund Freud, "A Difficulty in Psycho-Analysis," XVII, 139–44.

109. Acton, *A Practical Treatise*, p. 241.

110. Ellis, "1897 Preface," p. xxviii.

111. Richard C. Shettle, *Curative Magnetism: The 'Magneticon'* (London: n.p., 1882), p. 3.

112. [Frances Power Cobbe], *An Essay on Intuitive Morals, Being an Attempt to Popularise Ethical Science*, 2 vols. (London: Longman, Brown, Green, and Longmans, 1855, 1857), p. v.

113. Samuel Smiles, *Character* (London: John Murray, 1871), p. 371.

114. Cominos, "Late-Victorian Sexual Respectability," 228–31, provides a good example of intelligent system-building. See Ellis's sophisticated objection to such procedures (*Psychology of Sex*, II, 90).

115. Smiles, *Character*, p. 370.

116. Samuel Smiles, *Physical Education; Or, The Nurture and Management of Children, Founded on the Study of Their Nature and Constitution* (Edinburgh: Oliver and Boyd, 1838), pp. 7, 10.

117. "A Mother," *A Few Suggestions to Mothers on the Management of Their Children* (London: J. and A. Churchill, 1884), p. x.

118. See John Rutledge Martin, "Sexuality and Science: Victorian and Post-Victorian Ideas on Sexuality," a Ph.D. dissertation (Ann Arbor: UMI, 1978), pp. 168–212.

119. A.F.M. Willich, *Lectures on Diet and Regimen*, 2nd ed. (London: T. N. Longman and O. Rees, 1799), p. 25.

120. Dr. Elizabeth Blackwell, *The Religion of Health*, 3rd ed. (London: Moral Reform Union, n.d. [1889]), p. 19.

121. See Davidson, "Sex and the Emergence," pp. 40–47.

122. George Cecil Ives, *The Classification of Crimes* ([London]: privately printed for private circulation, 1904), pp. 54–58.

123. William Edward Hartpole Lecky, *History of European Morals from Augustus to Charlemagne*, 2 vols. (London: Longmans, Green, 1869), p. 154.

124. Charles Bell Taylor, *The Contagious Diseases Act, Showing Its Cruelty, Injustice, Demoralising Tendency, & Inexpediency in a Sanitary Point of View; a paper read before The Medical Society of London, January 17, 1870* (n.p.: n.p., n.d.), p. 8.

125. Acton, *Prostitution*, p. 270. Kinsey's protests against essentialism were eloquent and relentless: "It would encourage clearer thinking on these matters if persons were not characterized as heterosexual or homosexual, but as individuals who have had certain amounts of heterosexual experience and certain amounts of homosexual experience. Instead of using these terms as substantives which stand for persons, or even as adjectives to describe persons, they may better be used to describe the nature of the overt sexual relations, or of the stimuli to which an individual erotically responds" (*Human Male*, p. 617). For a magisterial critique of sexual essentialism, see Weeks, *Sex, Politics*, pp. 2–4.

126. See Lynn Merrill, *The Romance of Natural History* (Oxford: Clarendon, 1988).

127. Peter Gay, *The Bourgeois Experience: Victoria to Freud, Volume 1: Education of the Senses* (New York: Oxford Univ. Press, 1984), pp. 52–54, discusses paradigms of change, and Weeks, *Sex, Politics*, pp. 153–55, shows how important was Freud's reconstitution of sexuality as something constructed in the process of development.

128. On ideas of progress, see Hayden White, *Metahistory*, pp. 47–8; on ideas of degeneration, see Martin, "Sexuality and Science," p. 233. For the second pairing, compare Krafft-Ebing, *Psychopathia Sexualis*, p. 3 (morals have advanced) and Acton, *Prostitution*, p. 299 (morals are declining).

129. See J.S. Bratton, *The Impact of Victorian Children's Fiction* (London: Croom Helm, 1981), pp. 13, 42.

II

Victorian Constructions of Children and Eros

2

The Child

> Let us live for our Children!
> *Friedrich Froebel*[1]

> If mankind had been able to learn from a direct observation of children, these three essays could have remained unwritten.
> *Sigmund Freud*[2]

As the last decade of the nineteenth century opened, H. Clay Trumbull, editor of the *Sunday-School Times* and published expert on the care of children, was able to announce that "the child" had become not only a legitimate object of notice but a major hit: "For a century or more the progress of interest in and attention to the children has been steady and rapid. And now the best talent of the world is laid under contribution for the little ones."[3] It had not always been so. These little ones, variously designated, had been around in one form or another. It's just that they hadn't exactly been seen, not, anyhow, as we see them. As Freud says, direct observation has its limitations.

That, at least, is the contention of an interesting group of modern historical constructionists, led by Philippe Ariès. Looking back through twentieth-century lenses, Ariès can see little before the seventeenth century that is recognizable as a child: "it seems . . . that there was no place for childhood in the medieval world."[4] Studying medical records, portraiture, literature, costume, language, the history of education, and various other social documents, Ariès concludes that what we think of as the child was not there, that "the child" became a conceptual and thus biological and social category much later, flowering in the nineteenth century. Lawrence Stone's study of the historical development of family formation lends further support to this conception of the child as a historical and linguistic phenomenon, as do Richard Lewinsohn's comments on the absence of children from the pictorial representations of the Aurignacian Age, Peter Coveney's observation on the unimportance of the child in literature until the last decades of the eighteenth century, and Deborah Gorham's tracing of the rapid development of toys and books for children during that same period.[5]

There have been some heated objections to this thesis, based mostly on a reluctance to attribute to earlier ages a callousness toward their offspring and a skepticism toward a version of history which can be made to look so flattering, a steady advance toward our kindness and sensitivity.[6] But it is safe to say that Ariès and his followers have driven a sharp wedge between the child and nature, shown us the contingent, determined nature of this phenomenon, the child.

It is Ariès's procedures and not the accuracy of the new blueprint that concern us here. Whatever one thinks of these historical recuperations, Ariès's analyses of the present are brilliant. If we take him to be saying that there simply *is* no child in the past, we trudge down dusty and familiar roads to dreary positivist debates. If, on the other hand, we hear him more directly or simply, his arguments become productive: looking as closely as he can, he can spot nothing in the past that he would, personally speaking, call a child. He is like a puzzled bird-watcher, declaring that, while there may perhaps be warblers on the Waterloo Bog, he cannot spot any. It's not the absence of the warblers that should interest us but the procedures of the bird-watcher and the quality of the binoculars. Ariès is doing the rarest kind of history, a history of the present, aiming at de-naturing "the child," exposing our own constructing apparatus, freeing us, at least a little, from the tyranny of our eccentric seeing. He points out, in other words, radical difference, a difference so great that it seems to take the form of the difference between something and nothing, between a modern child that is there and a medieval child that is not. The effect of such a project is not to substantiate our modern perception but to show that the child is the perceptual frame we have available to us for fitting in just about anything we choose—or nothing. What the child *is* matters less than what we *think* it is and just why we think that way.

The Victorian child, for instance, takes on considerable remoteness once again, the exotic term "Victorian" now being coupled with the unanchored "child." The distance threatens to become so great, in fact, that we notice a perhaps understandable tendency to deny it, to make us into Victorians and our children into theirs. "The child," says Ariès, was marked off as separate and distinct, distinguished from and understood as somehow in opposition to "the adult," this move becoming apparent by the late eighteenth century.[7] For Ariès, however, this shift from a blurred and mixed world to one so demarcated was quite gradual. Not so, his followers, who seize control of the past by erasing distance, turning Ariès's gradualism into Noah's flood: "The point in cultural history when childhood and adulthood become separate and opposing worlds is clearly the late eighteenth century"; or

"Whatever its origins, the separateness of childhood was axiomatic in Victorian ideology."[8] In this version of history, at some point things are transformed into a single "ideology" that turns out, unsurprisingly, to be identical to our own.

If we think of Victorian culture and Victorian constructions of children as shifting, various, and mysterious, we have some hope of catching a glimpse of where our own unwarranted certainties come from. All we have to do is allow difference—easy enough to do if we listen to voices that sound different. Perhaps the Victorians did not so uniformly separate the child and adult, for instance. Gathorne-Hardy points out that special clothes designated or thought of as children's clothes were not made until the 1920s.[9] Peter Coveney argues that the influential Romantic conception of the child did not support any such separation between adult and child, certainly not a separation between two species.[10] However much of childhood radiance is lost by the adult and however difficult the connections may be to recover, Wordsworth and Coleridge are not talking about two species staring at each other across the chasm of puberty but about a form of imaginative and spiritual continuity. Unfamiliar costume and standard literary tradition thus suggest historical difference, a tie between adult and child we no longer see very well. Finally, we hear difference in some Victorian voices that seem to be protesting against the very species thinking that, perhaps, is invading them but has not yet made many inroads. The protests come from two directions, first against the homogenizing effect such thinking has on the children themselves. According to such individualist notions, children are not a species but a rag-tag bunch without essence or even defining characteristics: "A child is liable to be looked upon as if he were simply one child among many children generally; but every child stands all by himself in the world as an individual."[11] The second protest admits (for the sake of argument) the generic class of "children" but denies they are to be seen as different from adults: "many are too apt to treat children as if they are another order of creation, different to [sic] themselves."[12] All this, I submit, is more than enough to laugh off the field those who, while admitting the constructedness of the child, would somehow privilege our own constructions. By making the Victorians, the Victorian child, and the Victorian understanding of the way the child was formulated so very strange we reinstate as our center difference or otherness itself.

There are many ways to figure this otherness, though there is no way to control it, even if we wanted to do so. Psychoanalysis itself throws up its hands: Freud says that whereas with adults it is now possible "to divide mental processes into conscious and unconscious" and to "give a clearly-worded description of both," "with children this distinction leaves us almost completely in the lurch. It is often embarrassing to decide what one would choose to call conscious and what unconscious."[13] We might thus deliberately search out in the past grating voices that disrupt the harmony of our expectations, Rousseau, for example, whom we usually take to be the source for the sentimental exaltation of children: "What the child should know is that it is weak and that you, adult, are strong; and from this difference it follows that it is under your authority. That is what the child should know, that is what it ought to learn, that is what it must feel."[14] This sounds more like a camp commandant than Rousseau; even the syntax thuds with the bullying mash of power, and the "it child; you adult" formula descends to comic levels of Tarzaniana. But here we find the sort of unexpected otherness we were looking for, an indication that this concept, "the child," was as strange then as it is now—but not in the same way.

This difference in the past might suggest something about the quality of difference we force on the child in the present, a difference which can resemble very closely the otherness with which we formulate women and minorities. Like these, children are "denied direct access to legal and social institutions; not permitted to decide their own fates; expected to defer to the preferences and judgments of the upper class (adults); and denied specific privileges reserved for the upper class, such as self-determined bedtimes, use of social drugs, and the right of free association." We live under the assumption that children are especially privileged and that our entire culture is "child-centered," but the "romantic mythology" encrusting childhood is very much like that used for racial and gender power-moves: "children, 'coloreds,' and women are all depicted as naturally carefree, fortunate to be unsuited to the burdens of autonomy and decision-making, and better off protected by those in control."[15]

The links here might be especially suggestive as regards gender, the cultural ties between women and children. What really is the gender of Oliver Twist, say, or of the children who have recreated that part on the screen? What is the gender of the comic-strip character Buster Brown, with his long lashes and long locks and skirt-like affair, not very different, one might assume, from the pinafore worn by Heathcliff? What is the gender of Little Nell—or any of the Brady Bunch? Victorian advice manuals tend heavily to discourage too much gender discrimination in the rearing of children, suggesting that they be treated pretty much the same.[16] Krafft-Ebing said bluntly that they *were* the same: "The child [before puberty] is of the neuter gender." He proceeds to argue, even more remarkably, that the most strenuous attempts to develop in this child a gendered consciousness, by way of education, employment, dress, and the like, are "devoid of psychical significance": the child remains possessed by "sexual neutrality."[17] Our own view of the matter tends, significantly, to be more edgy: we look back and see not neutrality but some kind of cross-dressing. Small boys dressed "like girls" until the end of World War I, says Ariès; and Jean Hagstrum speaks of the Romantic legacy of the *feminized* child.[18] Engrossed with enforcing gender distinctions, we risk reducing to simple perversity the difference of the past.

Reading perversity, we avoid difference; and the same might be said for what we construe as enlightened notions (ours) of personal freedom. We may be surprised to see the number of Victorians, even official Victorians writing official manuals, who went about encouraging children to be independent and parents and teachers to allow them to be so. Early Victorian public schools deliberately gave boys a great deal of freedom and eschewed such controls as spying (though later such freedom all but vanished)[19]; the fiction of Sarah Smith ("Hesba Stretton") in the 60s suggested openly that children should not "regard their parents as infallible, or even [feel] that it is their duty to obey them, if they are in the wrong."[20] Child-rearing books seldom advocated breaking the will, since it acts "to destroy the child's privilege of free choice,"[21] a privilege we never supposed Victorian children had, much less a "right to privacy," "to justice," "to his childhood," and a right to avoid the miseries of excessive cleanliness.[22] All of this seems refreshing, as if the past had caught up with us, was echoing our progressive concern for the child's independence. But why haven't we wanted to hear this before? Also, does a celebration of the child's freedom really manifest a concern for health or a concern for distancing, a fear that the demands for obedience are working too well, drawing the child into a predictable, monotonous, and unerotic closeness? The encouragement of individualism, even of naughtiness, then, can be read as a way to maintain the gap, to formulate the category of "child" so as to make it safely other.

Molds for Casting Childhood

The child was a difference, but it was a difference formed by a culture and inscribed within categories of the perceivable. All this means is that the other-child must have been formulated within recognizable bounds of otherness, most clearly (for us) otherness thought of as fluid, changeable. In fact, the child seems often to have been identified directly with motion. Mary Wood-Allen defined an infant as "that little helpless bundle of capabilities,"[23] the dynamism in the last word nicely playing off the cuddly stasis of "bundle." Usually, the emphasis on change was even more direct: "We must not think of a child's mind as of a vessel, which it is for us to fill, but as a wonderfully organized instrument, which it is for us to develop and to set in motion."[24] Even religious writers spoke of children making "an everlasting approach to goodness and to God."[25] This torpid but steady pace recalls the emphasis Thomas Arnold placed on the patient encouragement of a "gradual change" from childhood to adulthood, a change taking several years.[26]

So, a developmental model appears to be at work, an idea of change growing out of a "nucleus" in the child: "There is no doubt, that whatever the Boy is, so the Man will be."[27] The particular sort of development is often explained in terms of the stages of evolution, where bodily changes recapitulated in abridged form the growth of life itself in its various stages:

> We find, throughout nature, that every creature possesses its peculiar type, towards which it must tend, if it is to accomplish the purpose of its creation. There is a capacity belonging to the original germ, which, if necessary conditions are presented, will lead it through the various stages of growth and development to the complete attainment of this type. This type or pattern, is the true aim of the individual.[28]

But, as always happens or as always should happen when we are going along so well in constructing a unitary view, disruptive figures appear. In the process of convincing ourselves that a paradigmatic notion of change and development (or at any rate motion) obtained for the Victorians, we run into something like this: "We are not required to give the *whole* attention directly and exclusively to securing a change of heart. Improve, by all your ingenuity, the natural temper and disposition [of children]."[29] The part about improvement we can deal with, improvement suggesting the glacial crawl Thomas Arnold seems happy with. But securing changes of heart sounds like something different—like murdering one thing and setting up another in its place.

And indeed we find a model contradictory to the gradualist one running happily along side it as in the quote above, where one can presumably recruit Darwin and Noah for the same team, somehow coordinate "improvement" with instantaneous changes of heart. The child, that is, could do just as well for an image of transformation, of change figured not in evolutionary but in catastrophic terms. Evangelical models might see the child as depraved and very much in need of complete overhaul; or the child could itself figure as the instrument of sudden redemption, as in *Silas Marner* or much of Dickens: Little Nell, though she doesn't much help those around her in the novel, is often felt to be an agency offered up for massive social transformation.

But this equation of the child with "change," even contradictory models of change, is too simple, failing to account for the way the child can be and is slotted into a psychology and an erotics of loss. Though loss is itself a function of change, its particular dealings with the child tend to freeze any movement, to create a kind of affective tableau, one in which the child always *is* (and always is fixed) but always is beyond reach. Change is thus arrested, made an object for contemplation, for tender regret, for sexual arousal. Such a mechanism is often attributed to Wordsworth and to a readiness we all have to wallow in nostalgic melancholy of a more or less gratuitous kind[30]; it is said to come to the fore in the Victorian age (and our own) as "a natural form of escapism,"[31] a retreat from the cold world of getting and spending, imperialist plunderings, and, according to Lewis Carroll, bathing machines. As the popular Victorian song put it, "Backward, turn backward, O time, in your flight,/ Make me a child again just for tonight."[32]

Even that song, with its curious situating of the child and our desire in the womb-dream, death-bed nighttime, seems to be issuing from more than a "natural" (whatever that may mean) escapism. The fervent hope to catch the child and hold it, even at a distance, suggests, I think, a well of desire deeper and more unsettled than anything either purely natural or simply escapist. The following, for instance, is from A.R. Hope, writing what he claimed was the first book really about boys. If so, and it may be, it sets up a classic framework for looking at boys, fixing them at a distance, and then longing for them. In this passage, Hope, a schoolmaster now retired, remembers, with an aching fondness that is almost unbearable, how he watched the boys in their rough and tumble play: "And looking on such scenes from a quiet corner, I used to long for a fairy to touch me with her wand, that I, too, might become small and lithe and smooth-faced and light-hearted, and might roll and tumble, and hurt and get hurt, and shout out for very carelessness and fulness of life."[33]

There is much one might say about this embarrassingly open admission of voyeurism. Here I wish only to point to its voyeurism and its power to embarrass. First, is it not remarkable that Hope, once he gets going on this celebration of boyhood and his desperate wish to join with it, does not, though he easily could, remove himself to a time when he in fact *was* lithe and smooth-faced and tumbling and hurting and being hurt to his heart's content? Instead, he creates a scene where he indulges only in longing, in watching from afar, looking out "from a quiet corner," as if what he wanted to recall was not the activity, the motion, but his very distance from it. Second, we might wonder just why this scene is so embarrassing to us, whether A.R. Hope is not simply a happy pioneer in a now-thronged field, blazing about too openly for current comfort. We might ask ourselves why we photograph our own children with such intense and confused emotions, and why manufacturers of film sell us their product by promoting, to the virtual exclusion of all other lures, the claim that their product will enable us to impound the child, hold it forever. How is it we find ourselves, like Hope, "looking on such scenes from a quiet corner"?

Official Definitions of the Child

Even the schools, we are told,[34] did little to mark out childhood prior to the late eighteenth century. Very small children and older adolescents (as we would now think of them) were mixed together indiscriminately and were regarded as a uniform group. But not for long. By the nineteenth century, schools began separating their charges into "forms" or "classes," thus suggesting a new interest in these people and a determination to understand and control them analytically, by separation.

According to the law generally applicable throughout the country and throughout the century, a person under seven years of age was presumed incapable of committing a felony; between seven and fourteen, the presumption still held but could be contested and rebutted; a male under fourteen was thought to be incapable of committing rape. The only deviation from the 7–14 demarcations of which I am aware occurs in reference to the number of strokes of the birch allowed in whipping convicted criminals, where the dividing line is 12 (no more than six strokes; from 12–14, twelve strokes were permitted).[35] When the law finally turned its attention, or part of it, away from beating little people itself and towards protecting them from the beatings of others, it held, even well after the turn of the century, to the same arbitrary numbers, much to the disgruntlement of child-advocates: "If they have passed this magic age of fourteen years, they are legally children no longer, and the law takes its eyes off them and lets them wander at will."[36]

Legislation's relative consistency, however groundless, is nowhere echoed in the work of the experts writing extensively on these very children. Unsatisfied with the law's crude rule of seven (and multiples), those more attentive produce before our eyes a much more engaging range of categories. William Acton began in his popular *The Functions and Disorders of the Reproductive Organs in Youth, in Adult Age, and in Advanced Life*, with the clean simplicity of a three-part stages of man. By the third edition, however, only five years later, he had to change his scheme and his book's title, inserting *in Childhood* before *in Youth*. It wasn't that Acton had discovered with further study that children also had functioning and disorderly reproductive organs; he had discovered a new entry in the stages of man, a new category he called the child.[37] Others were even more exacting, adding an "Infancy" in front of Childhood, so as to make it Infancy-Childhood-Youth or, possibly much the same thing, Infancy-Childhood-Boyhood & Girlhood.[38] Just as we were fearing, experts were not slow to complicate the complications, introducing, among other things, overlapping categories, as in Moll, where infancy extends through the first year; childhood, including that same period, advances to the end of the fourteenth year; boyhood and girlhood, as I make it out, cutting into that and running from age seven to twenty-one, a span that further takes in but is not limited to "youth," ages fifteen to twenty-one.[39] Got it?

All of this indicates a "natural" phenomenon (the child and its near neighbors) in the process of being artificially constructed and then quickly rushed into action. The process is perhaps even clearer, though essentially quite the same, in reference to adolescence, which virtually all writers, not just Ariès,[40] recognize as a social institution and not a natural state, an institution that has, once manufactured, given us more trouble than Hyde gave to Jekyll. Among other things, as a "stage" designed to encourage and thus contain a medley of rebellious, unproductively selfish, nominally revolutionary, and uncontrollably erotic feelings, adolescence has become both amorphous and inconveniently lengthy. "The child" is under somewhat better control.

If that is true, it may be because we have, slowly but certainly, agreed on a collective illusion that the child is a biological category, not, like adolescence, some mishmash of pubescent eruption, a stage in school, and one's marital situation (one automatically ceases to be an adolescent upon marriage). The child, we have come to feel, is defined biologically, even better, sexually (or non-sexually).

As we will see in the next two chapters, there is nothing less certain than the body and its figurings, unless it is sex and the way we understand it. That we should feel some assurance in a fiction, "the child," secured through these means is perhaps remarkable, but it seems to be so. Though earlier conceptions of childhood had to do with social situation, specifically with dependence,[41] by the Victorian period, the new dividing line seems to have achieved general currency under the name of puberty: "The commencement of menstruation is the borderline between childhood and womanhood."[42] The borderline for males was also marked, if a little less clearly, by liquidity: the tendency to nocturnal emissions, accompanied by some secondary signs. We will deal with all this more fully later, but it is important here to note that the dividing lines, like the child itself, was, first of all, constructed, and second, often constructed sexually. Childhood ended with the onset of puberty, of sexuality. Such logic required that the child be thought of as that which is non-sexual, a conception which seems always to have required some elaborate mental slithering and some brash pseudo-science. The most lasting of the labels used to stick non-sexuality onto the child has been "latency," a fiction variously understood as sublimation, negation, repression, dormancy, or absence, but aggressively naturalized all the same: it is, says Freud, "organically determined and fixed by heredity."[43]

Despite such public assurances, officials have betrayed a great deal of uncertainty on these literal definitions of children, an uncertainty that seems not to decrease with time. The most obvious sign of trouble is the proliferation of categories and numbers to mark them with. Is a child something from 7–14 or something from 0–21? And what's a youth, an infant, a boy or girl, an adolescent? Mr. Podsnap may have been quite sure in his own mind precisely what constituted "the young person," but few others seem to have been. One way to chart this confusion is through the debates on age of consent legislation proposed and enacted. This boundary was established in law as a signal that a female could after that age give consent to having sexual intercourse. Such a determination is perhaps broader, but it surely centers on what is taken to be "a child" and it defines that child in two ways that are, as Ariès points out,[44] relatively new: age and sexuality. In 1861 the age of consent was raised from 10 to 12, in 1875 to 13, and in 1885 to 16. That marks quite a range both in concern for and in conception of what constitutes a child. There are important complications embedded in the "consent" controversy I will return to later, but it is not too early to point out here how this tactic for defining childhood establishes even more firmly at the center of the child a kind of purity, an absence and an incapacity, an inability to do. All are fundamental in our thinking about this figure.

The Nature of the Child

Unencumbered by any necessary traits, this emptiness called a child can be construed in about any way we like. One of the first ways to present itself figures the child's nature as the fallen nature we adults have left behind with the old Adam. Here, for instance, is a little lesson on politeness meant for children, an exemplum that becomes so caught up in the evil of its audience that it lets go of its own avowed purpose:

> Remember then, my dear children, the little history of this day: and, if you would wish to please God, strive to be really polite. But remember, too, that you have naughty hearts, which are full of envy, pride, and selfishness, and that you cannot be really polite, till a new heart is given you.[45]

So there's no point in trying to please God, the author, or parents, since all the politeness one can muster would not really be politeness at all. But, like most writers of this stamp, the author is clear enough about the bad qualities in the child's heart, a clarity notorious in the novels of Mrs. Sherwood: "... he knew no naughty words and naughty tricks; notwithstanding which, like all little children, who have not yet received new hearts, he was full of evil inclinations.... Every child born of the family of Adam is utterly corrupt from his birth."[46]

Thomas Arnold's similarly low opinion of children (or boys) derives from a different source. While Arnold can speak of children in reference to the fall and regeneration, he seems much more interested in civilization than salvation: "... my object will be, if possible, to form Christian men, for Christian boys I can scarcely hope to make; I mean that, from the natural imperfect state of boyhood, they are not susceptible of Christian principles in their full development upon their practice, and I suspect that a low standard of morals in many respects must be tolerated amongst them, as it was on a larger scale in what I consider the boyhood of the human race."[47] He does worry about the boys' souls, but more about what he calls their "moral childishness," a quality he can civilize out of them. The salient characteristics of boyhood he enumerates as "teachableness, ignorance, selfishness, and living only for the present."[48] Luckily, that first trait lays the child open to the teacher, who will erase the other three or know the reason why.

Arnold's model is not so much the innately depraved being as the savage, a parallel picked up later by Herbert Spencer: "Do not expect from a child any great amount of moral goodness. During early years every civilized man passes through that phase of character exhibited by the barbarous race from which he is descended."[49] Savages are there, of course, to be turned into something else entirely, perhaps not British gentlemen but something not savages. As such, they are attacked resolutely. Resolutely but not fiercely, since they have about them a something almost like innocence—an artlessness, a spontaneity. One can hardly decide whether to win them to Christ or teach them a few tricks and domesticate them. They are, after all, so cute. And so it is perhaps that the child can be tolerated, not because it will change but because there's something winning about it as it is. Deborah Gorham shows that often daughters were taught to be pets for their fathers[50]; one suspects there were many boys playing those roles as well. Whether the little person, "the child," was much better off being cute than being depraved is open to question; but there seems little doubt that they were and are thus regarded: cute and innocent.

There are three essential things to note about this innocent child: first, it was concocted and not discovered; second, the quality of innocence was not only "protected" but inculcated and enforced; third, we vastly overstate the dominance of this view of the child in the Victorian period, expressing and exposing a need of our own. The first point is most obvious. Few would question that the innocent child was manufactured by Rousseau, with refinements by Wordsworth and a thousand lesser writers, interior decorators, and producers of greeting cards. Prior to the eighteenth century, says Ariès, nobody worried about soiling childish innocence because "nobody thought that this innocence really existed."[51] Now, however, the notion that the child was innocent, valuable, and weak became common.

For several reasons, this sort of child might need or merit protection, though much of this protection seems to take the form of preventative medicine, hindrances based on a rather insulting estimate of the child's immense capacity for blundering into error or sin. Here, for instance, is the Rev. S.S. Seward, addressing The National Purity Congress on this subject: "It should be understood at the outset that the child's mind is perfectly pure at the beginning. It is a tablet prepared for the tool of the engraver, but as yet virgin." I confess that I do not follow the part about the engraver, but we may assume the Rev. Seward's audience could do so. In any event, this "perfectly pure" mind of the child is open to many threats (from "the engraver"?), threats the Rev. Seward has a plan for warding off. His strategy is to guard the child, around the clock, and be certain that nothing whatever enters in: "I am fully convinced that if the children of the rising generation should be fully protected in the way I have indicated against the wrong habits and 'evil communications' to which all are exposed, they would grow up perfectly innocent and free from all impure thoughts and desires."[52] Keeping every pen away from the virgin tablet, Rev. Seward could as much as issue guarantees of perfect innocence, a mind forever free from thoughts and desires, impure ones anyhow.

These well-meaning (maybe) protectors often adopt the line that the innocence needing protection is so feeble and is beset by foes so numerous and wily that any measures are justified, including putting innocence into protective custody or solitary confinement. Innocence is always seen as being defiled, slipping away, not what it used to be. The child's innocence, then, becomes a vulnerability. Here is an expert on purity and consequently on degradation, the notorious Anthony Comstock, representing the New York Society for the Suppression of Vice and speaking at the same Purity Congress as the Rev. Seward but going him one better:

> These brutal assaults upon the native innocence of youth and children is [sic] laying burdens upon the rising generation which will be grievous to their future welfare and heavy to be borne.... The degrading of our youth is a crying evil to day. It is a seed sowing from which brothels, dives, prisons, penitentiaries, asylums and early graves are fast being recruited.[53]

Perhaps Mr. Comstock's fury drives his last sentence a little off the pavement, but we get his drift. One wonders why, facing this sort of thing, children would not be quick to denounce innocence altogether and take their chances with depravity? Indeed, many children tried (and try) hard to escape the burden of innocence. But it is not easy. Innocence is not, as we said, detected but granted, not nurtured but enforced; it comes at the child as a denial of a whole host of capacities, an emptying out. Left to themselves, Ellis says, children are "wholly devoid of modesty."[54] Of course children never *are* left to themselves and of course modesty is not quite the same thing as innocence. But it is close, and the observation is significant and potentially disruptive. Whatever the child may naturally be (if anything), Ellis makes it pretty clear that innocence is a faculty needed not at all by the child but very badly by the adult who put it there in the first place. Giving this innocence to a child, then, may satisfy our needs but possibly not the child's.

But this innocent child may be a very-late-Victorian or, more likely, modern imposition. The image does not seem to me all that common in the nineteenth century, propaganda about "the cult of the child" notwithstanding.[55] One must, at least, somehow account for widespread contradictory images, the noxious or savage child mentioned earlier and the "child of feeling." This last possibility, though also associated with Rousseau and the "cult of sensibility,"[56] unleashes dangers not usually associated with mere "innocence." If the child of nature is figured not as an emptiness but one more in touch with primal sympathies, we have a creation more complex and threatening. No longer a blank tablet waiting for or being shielded from the engraver, this child is actively benevolent, compassionate, loving. "Innocence" for us may still suggest this artless tenderness; but largely we have tried over the last century to remove from innocence any substance whatsoever, to figure its purity as nullity. The active, loving child is too demanding, too difficult to control, too hard to love. We prefer those we love, it seems, to have less obtrusive matter; we would rather not have them exuding feeling, since that might intrude on ours. So the innocent child becomes increasingly vacant, drained of any capacity to feel.

But for the Victorians, as near as we can tell, innocence was a more intricate matter and innocent children not so common as now. Some Victorians scoffed at the idea: "the popular idea that children are 'innocent,' while it is true with respect to evil *knowledge*, is totally false with respect to evil *impulses*; as half an hour's observation in the nursery will prove to anyone."[57] Some who granted children some kind of innocence didn't think it was worth much: "the simple credence of the child, though so often lauded and coveted, is useless, or at least hazardous, for the man."[58] And far more important than these rather theoretical expressions of resistance to the power of the innocent child are some looming images from the Victorian period that we are hard-pressed not to read as the signals of general cultural barbarism, of a cold disregard or contempt for the child.

One of the most baffling of the many mysteries of Victorian culture is this split between little Oliver Twist in the novel and little Oliver Twist in life. One is fawned over, protected, lusted after; the other is beaten, starved, imprisoned, transported. It's not that Dickens is unaware of this split; in fact, he exploits it. And it's not a simple dichotomy between literature and life, between the child one imagines and the child one kicks aside at the crossing or burns alive in one's chimney. Both images obtained and both children lived (though the first had a good chance of outliving the second). It's just that we are very likely to maunder on about the Wordsworthian child and forget the thundering counter-chorus of carelessness, contempt, and abuse.

For that reason, we'll take a quick tour through this chamber of horrors. Thomas E. Jordan's *Victorian Childhood* provides a full, statistically bolstered view of how children were misused while alive and how quickly they died. Alfred Fennings, in 1856, announced that "nearly half the children born in this country, die before they are five years old"; Arthur W. Edis, in 1879, put the figure at one in three, not a wonderful improvement, particularly among the working classes, where, Edis says, fully half the children die before five.[59] What appears to us to be a kind of wholesale slaughter needs to be seen over against an extraordinary expansion of the number of children born; during the century, says Gathorne-Hardy, the total population grew "by *over eleven per cent every single year.*" Further, "in 1830 the *average* family had six or seven children."[60] If these figures are even close to correct, they indicate, or seem to, something like that "torrent of babies" Tennyson said he dreamed of.[61] Certainly there are, in sum, more than enough new babies to make up for those who are dying; probably, if we inquired closely, we would discover that for each baby buried about one and a half new ones came to take its place. But, maybe not everyone really wanted replacement babies, having become attached to the original.

But were they so attached? How did they regard these individual babies, so likely to die and so much a surplus commodity as to be nearly a nuisance? They were everywhere, under foot, coming and going in such numbers as to rival fruit flies. As critics of Ariès have pointed out with some vigor, however, high rates of child mortality do not necessarily indicate parental or societal indifference to the child; and it would be just as foolhardy to argue this from the basis of a teeming or even excess child population. But how do we read the massive exportation of surplus children to all parts of the empire, Canada for instance?: "Between 1868 and 1925 eighty thousand British boys and girls were sent to Canada to work under indentures as agricultural labourers and domestic servants. All were unaccompanied by parents, although only one-third of them were orphans. Most were not yet fourteen."[62] And so it was across the empire, and there is something unsettling, at the very least, in the image of these droves of little children being shipped off forever to strangers. How precious or how innocent could they be?

Most of these young children, of course, left because of economic necessity, the same force that drove many into the labor force at home. We have heard so much about child-labor during the period, even about how its cruelties have been exaggerated by left-wing histories,[63] that we are likely to be bored by the subject or take it for granted. It may be well to remind ourselves of what we think it may have been

76 / *The Child*

like to clean the gears and belts of great monsters of machines while they were still running, to be harnessed to a cart and forced to crawl up a mine shaft hauling it, to be a sweep, a climbing boy. These little boys, the littler the better, even unto deformity, crawled up chimney after chimney, squeezing into impossibly small places, swallowing soot and grinding it into every part of their body, suffering from "knap knee" and twisted ankle joints, open sores, various lung diseases, burns, cancer of the lip, and the special "chimney sweeper's disease," cancer of the scrotum, cured, if at all, only by cutting away the diseased part and often the testicles as well. Boys became lodged in tight places. If that happened, other boys might be sent up with pins to drive into their feet or a fire might be lit. Some boys were roasted alive: "On inspecting the body, various burns appeared; the fleshy part of the legs, and a great part of the feet, more particularly, were injured; . . . the elbows and the knees seemed burnt to the bone."[64] Weigh that charred corpse against Lewis Carroll's "child of the pure unclouded brow."

It is not that the Victorians were unaware of these atrocities or that they failed to point to them with indignation. William Acton said it was impossible to walk the streets of any large city "without feeling that the neglect of children is a reproach to us," a reproach in the form of lurking child criminals and prostitutes. Acton also sought for causes and for remedies, investigating, for instance, the very high rate of illegitimate births (about 8% by his figures) and the terrible fates awaiting these bastards on the streets or in baby farms, at least some of which, Acton implies, were little more than licensed slaughter houses.[65] Others, like Mary Carpenter, worked tirelessly in studying and helping the juvenile criminals.

But the primary focus of attention seems clearly to have been the prostitute, a figure and a locus of controversy we will examine later. Here, however, we might note that the age of these prostitutes was not often an issue, not an issue in the way we would make it an issue, at least. Many of these are, after all, child prostitutes, or what we would think of as child prostitutes. It may well shock us that in reading through the many words written on this issue, so few seem even to notice what for us is the major point. We are told that prostitutes as young as 8 or 9 were not uncommon[66]; just how many prostitutes we would think of as children is uncertain, figures on those under 15 or 16 ranging from .27% to over 12%.[67] At the outside, there seem to have been fewer than a thousand child prostitutes known to police; but the problem was very real. The question is what the problem was. Henry Robinson tells the lengthy stories of two girls of 13 lured into prostitution but seems completely unaware that he ought to be, we would think, foregrounding their age. He is much more interested in arguing that, given that they grew up "familiar with the language, the manners, and the *morale* of the brothel," "it is next to impossible" to imagine them not adopting the same line of work, and as quickly as possible.[68] Some Victorians seem concerned that children may have their moral sense blunted by contact with prostitutes,[69] but there is not a great deal of evidence, until very late in reformers like Stead, that the *child*-as-prostitute is much of an issue. Acton's voice is never representative of anything in particular, but here he usefully brings to the surface what others are ignoring—and then proceeds to ignore it. First, the issue: "The extreme youth of the junior portion of the 'streetwalkers' is a remarkable feature of London prostitution." But he then employs that "remarkable feature" only to debunk the myth that these girls have been victims of panders and debauched gentry: "their seduction—if seduction it can be called—has been effected, with their own consent, by boys no older than themselves, and is all but a natural consequence of promiscuous herding, that mainspring of corruption among our lower orders."[70] One can call Acton callous, but perhaps he is simply avoiding a gendered analysis for an economic and social one no less humane. It may be for this reason that he appears, like most others in this controversy, male and female, unwilling to center "the child," perhaps unconscious that the problem could be profitably put that way—and maybe it cannot.

In any event, the point here is the strangeness, the distance of the past revealed by these quite unsentimental imagings of the child. This was a century which was as legislatively active in liberal causes as any at any time, but it was comparatively neglectful of the young in its reforms.[71] Opposition to any association offering to protect children was fierce throughout the period, blocking any such organization until 1884, though the Society for Prevention of Cruelty to Animals had existed since 1824 (granted the prefix "Royal" in 1840). None of this obliterates the notion of the sentimentally fixed, "innocent" child—but it casts doubt on it.

So much doubt that we can, if we like, go further, first by noting the strong connection at least since the seventeenth century[72] of innocence with weakness and ignorance. The child is endowed with blessed or natural innocence, its most valuable, perhaps its only, attribute, its only possession. But it is not clear that the child thereby owns much, innocence being a negative quality, more or less, defined as the absence of things like strength, knowledge, corruption. Of the many *OED* listings under "innocence," only two seem substantive: a half-wit and a child. The rest of the listings are negations or lacks: "free from evil," "lacking knowledge." Innocence is a beginning state, uninscribed, a blank. If the child is innocent, actually innocence itself, what is a child?

One could say that innocence is more than a blank, that it takes on substance by feeding off its polar opposite, which we might call depravity, a word with plenty of substance. The *OED* suggests clearly that innocence has been traditionally opposed from its beginnings to the broader term "evil," the "innocent" simply being free from "evil." Such a definition is fair, but it does not register as well as "depravity" the passivity we associate with innocence—"evil" calls up the more active opposition of "good" for us—or the tendency over the last two centuries to narrow "innocence" to a sexual meaning. In any case, it takes little maneuvering to make depravity (corruption, evil) the superior term in this opposition; innocence is the absence of it. (Try thinking of depravity as the absence of innocence; it can be done, but only by straining.) But are the terms really separate? If innocence depends for its existence on depravity, how can it be said to be free of the depraved? Isn't it possible that depravity is not around on the other side of the world from innocence but at its core? When we search about for the most disgusting word for the most disgusting activity, do we not often light on "regressive"? What do we mean when we say that pornography, for instance, describes and caters to "regressive and infantile fixations"?[73] As we regress, push backward to the child, into the heart of innocence, we seem to find the foulest depravity. One might say that this trick was played on us by Freud. I suggest that Freud had nothing to do with it, that it was the work of innocence itself, a word created as a state of being that was pure nothingness, secretly nourished by its opposite. Abhorred vacuums get filled up, and depravity will do as well as anything else.

The child was there waiting for Freud as for all of us, defenseless and alluring, with no substance, no threatening history, no independent insistences. As a category created but not occupied, the child could be a repository of cultural needs or fears not adequately disposed of elsewhere. For Freud, for pedophiles, for parents and pedagogues, for all of us, the child could carry meaning, a meaning that might, moreover, easily be deleted. The child was impermanent, untrustworthy, protean, here-today-gone-tomorrow. Whatever meaning we placed there wouldn't last too long. The child could be erased, was in fact in the process of being erased even as we packed the meaning in. If the child had a wicked heart from birth, that heart could be ripped out and a new one planted there in no time. If the child was ignorant, that wouldn't last long; if disobedient, there was always the whipping cure; if angelic, death would take him or, more likely, her; if loved or loving, that too would pass. Any meaning would stick, but no meaning would stick for long. The child, coming unglued itself, could not hold the glue of labels.

The point of pursuing at such length this particular figure is that its emptiness lays particular claim to our attention. The vacant child has been able to rivet the attention of our culture for some time. How many people do, one way or another, follow Froebel's urging, and live always for their children, even if those children don't want it, even if those children don't exist in material form? What could J.M. Barrie possibly mean by saying that "nothing that happens after we are twelve matters very much"?[74] Was he completely aberrant, maybe joking? What of our own focus on the child, especially the victimized child?

None of this proves that the child is a fixed cultural center. I do not mean to argue any such thing, only that the vacuity of the child makes it available for centerings we do not want to announce openly. It's not that the child can hold only guilty secrets; we also pack into this knapsack special treats we love but feel are not so good for us. The child carries for us things we somehow cannot carry for ourselves, sometimes anxieties we want to be divorced from and sometimes pleasures so great we would not, without the child, know how to contain them. People, we know, sometimes beat children because the child can be filled up with whatever must be beaten. It's the same with love.

Figures of the Child

A. *The Happy Child at Play*

Play is one thing children are allowed to do, though we tend to be fonder of the concept than of the thing itself, more likely to warm to child's play in a novel or painting than actually to enjoy its repetitive monotony in life. Even if we don't actually like play, though, we think that we do, and we attribute to the child the ability *really* to play, to know what play is all about, and to be happy doing nothing but play. Play for them is gratuitous, of course, and inconsequential. Adults work and children play, so we pass child labor laws to keep the demarcation steady, to keep children rollicking around in a state of freedom. To allow them to avoid work, we force them not to work. We must have them playing. Alfred Kinsey's observations suggested to him that children had little tolerance for free or inventive play: "children are, on the whole, conformists."[75] They love routine, steadiness, security even unto tedium. We may have noticed something like this ourselves. But in the face of that, we insist that the child will play, wants to play. Playing children are free, we believe, without a hint of the many cares that will come. They are blissfully happy.

An unhappy child was and is unnatural, an indictment of somebody: parent, institution, nation. Hugo, Dickens, Dostoevsky, the Brontës, Gaskell, Stowe, Hardy all channeled fierce indignation through the weeping child. Oliver Twist's unhappiness is enough to penetrate even the parochial breast, lumping the throat of Mr. Bumble the beadle (ch. iv). Even the tough-minded Trollope, often given to parodying Romantic sniveling over children, has a favorite character argue that "the principal duty which a parent owed to a child was to make him happy."[76] The child was not to be unhappy; or not, as a severe child-rearing manual put it, to be *seen* as unhappy: "childhood should not be regarded as a time of probation, but of complete happiness."[77] We must, whatever may befall, *regard* children as happy; if we so regard them, that's what they will be.

Even the Sunday School Union recognized the importance of keeping up this image of the happy child, moving deliberately after mid-century toward something they called "recreative instruction." We have a glimpse of what that may have been: in 1861 the Union purchased from a ragged school worker a panorama called "The Overland Route to India," a pedagogical tool they said found great popularity (whether with the students or teachers is not made clear). This popularity, indicating the successful union of happiness and tutelage, caused the Union to react in ways since become habitual to church and school alike: they formed a committee, more exactly "an exhibition subcommittee" who, as the years went by, added new panoramas, lantern and slide shows, and, in a burst of hilarity, "Oriental costumes."[78]

B. The Holy Child at Rest

But we will guess that the Sunday School had on its mind something other than fun. The child was also the baptized soul; the duty of those who attended on children was to preserve this purity, not by promoting happiness but by pointing the way to salvation, a very different matter.[79] The child as holy (or potentially so), as sanctified (if perilously) is an image as important as that of the depraved child, though, given our own preferences, we hear much more about the latter. A kind of reverence for the child and a concern for its purity contributed to the manic insistence on obedience we meet everywhere we look. "Obedience, it must be remembered, was instilled less as a convenience to parents than as a prerequisite to faith," says M. Nancy Cutt.[80] Well, it suits Cutt's purposes to arrange the balance this way, but of course there is no knowing exactly why obedience was instilled, much less measuring the motives. As we will see later, obedience was a virtue handy for many models of child-rearing. Still, it is certainly true that many people did speak of the religious child in terms of obedience, a point presented with a impressive rotundity in Frances Cobbe's *Intuitive Morals*:

> It is not the concern of the moralist, but of the psychologist to investigate the fundamental principle of the Religious Sentiment in the human soul. That sentiment may be, in its germ (as Schleiermacher has affirmed), a mere "sense of dependence." More accurately defined (as by Schenkel), it may be "a sense of dependence ethically induced." In its perfect form it would seem to be best described as *"the sense of absolute dependence united with the sense of absolute moral allegiance,"* the Being on whom we depend being recognised as possessing the Right to claim, as well as the Power to enforce, our absolute obedience.[81]

The pure child is thus the absolutely obedient child, the child of God (and a joy to its parents). It would also be a child whose sense of absolute dependence (however induced), united with a sense of absolute moral allegiance, would render independent (or any) action on its part difficult. The absolutism here amounts to a demand that the child have no reservations, no withholding some secret part of itself that is the Right of the Being (not the child) to claim. The child actually cedes its being to another—or so another hopes. This dispossessed child, little Miles of *The Turn of the Screw* perhaps, giving itself over to purity or to the parent, has nothing left and nothing left to do but to die.

The child seems often formulated so as to be subject to absolute claims, claims that may take its life. Miles's shocking death seems a playing out of the rights of those over him, a ghastly game between the Governess and Quint, between obsessions that destroy the field in the contest. Many children die for love, particularly in pedophile fables like "The Priest and the Acolyte" that helped draw Wilde down. Rather than yield to the demands of this brazen world, the priest and the child remain pure to their love and to one another into death. The child yields the absolute Right over himself to a Being called Love, just as Little Nell yields her self absolutely to Righteousness. With characters like Smike or Paul Dombey, the Being who claims such absolute Rights may be said to be some principle of Pathos. The popularity of these images of dying children is often attributed to nostalgia run amok, to outrageous sentimentality, to escapism so extreme as to suggest the entire culture's death-wish, its feeling that life would be better rejected, negated[82]; to a psychotic desire to possess, consume the child.[83]

It is also possible that the actual fact of children's death was swimming into view along with the child itself. As the child becomes known and valued, its actual loss is noted—a loss that can come either through growth or death. When we lose to growth this desirable child and the love we feel for it, the ache is keen enough; but such loss is also banal, a grinding-down rather than a lightning bolt. Child corpses, a cynic would say, are far more satisfying aesthetically and erotically than a child grown out of childhood and into a gangly, bepimpled adolescent. At any rate, we do see the fact of children's death being noted, generally with alarm; we read of mortality rates, analyses of causes, plans for alleviation. We also see this dying child attached to class issues, an emergence of a discourse quite at odds with the romantic or erotic one. The lower-class child does not fade away like Little Nell; it is wasted by typhus, ripped apart with cancer of the scrotum. Against the soft haziness of a middle-class sentimental romance is thrown this lower-class naturalism.

C. The Worrisome Child

And of course the genres and the diseases and the classes and the actual children can hardly be kept so conveniently distinct. Even the most protected middle-class child will come into contact with servants, at the very least; and there is, finally, the collective nation to think about and to think about with anxiety. Along with a growing self-consciousness about the expansive possibilities of national identity comes a tendency to center that potential for expansion in the child: "the nation comes from the nursery," says an exuberant Samuel Smiles.[84] *All* nurseries are involved in this process, even the most humble or, more likely, squalid. Thus not just Dickens but a host of workers among the poor can argue that the treatment and condition of the least of these is indeed an index of the national character and the national heart. Veterans of the battle to save children from the conditions of the slums thus commonly state that "the care of her children may well be a nation's chief concern,"[85] without feeling any compulsion to specify who these children are.

This is not to suggest that perceived class differences did not color or direct some thinking on children: lower-class children were thought of as even more "dangerous" than their parents. Still, the species "child" often had, I believe, great monolithic power, so much so that even large differences, like class, could sometimes be explained as environmental effects on children, the fundamental "child" in these cases being the same across class lines. That the child could now and then achieve such status as an idealized or universal category is part and parcel of its movement into the area of inquiry. Hardly had the child come on the scene than it was made the object of study, flattened out and held steady so that the "laws" governing the child and its world could be discovered:

> I am firmly convinced that all the phenomena of the child-world, those which delight us as well as those which grieve us, depend upon fixed laws as definite as those of the cosmos, the planetary systems, and the operations of nature; and it is therefore possible to discover them and examine them.[86]

Thus the child enters into discourse as an article for inquiry and concern, as a visible image of expansion and degeneration, of happiness and play, misery and exploitation, of the future and the past, of faith and death, of the existence of class lines and their dissolution.

D. The Child at Home

This multiform, shifting image takes on its greatest social importance in reference to the historical development of the family, an institution, some feel, that grew up around this new creature. It is, they say, the child which shapes the contours of the home and the family, hence of modern social formation. As a more analogy-prone Victorian writer put it, "The nest of the feathered kind is for the nestlings, the home of human-kind is for the children."[87] Ariès has been foremost in tracing how the child gradually came to define what the home and family were and how they would function. Thus the family, like the child, is not an institution that can be traced to some primal "need" but to specific and fairly recent historical developments. It is, then, the family which defines the shape of the modern world (rather than, say, individualism) and the "child" which has made possible this modern family:

> The family ceased to be an institution for the transmission of a name and an estate—it assumed a moral and spiritual function, it molded

bodies and souls. The care expended on children inspired new feelings, a new emotional attitude, to which the iconography of the seventeenth century gave brilliant and insistent expression: the modern concept of the family.[88]

Ariès speculates on the importance to this new-molded family of physical resemblance, the ability of parents to see themselves (or imagine that they do) in the features of their children, quoting Erasmus's important words on the subject: "One cannot admire too greatly the astonishing pains taken by Nature in this respect; she depicts two persons in a single face and a single body; the husband recognizes the portrait of his wife in his children, and the wife that of her husband."[89] The whole unit is fastened together by way of the projection of parental fantasies onto the child, who functions also to reflect back to the looker whatever is desired. The bond in fact becomes so close and necessary in the nineteenth century that it wasn't until the passing of the Custody of Children Act (1891) and the Prevention of Cruelty to Children Act (1894) that it was possible, under any circumstances, to remove a child from the custody of both its parents, simply because the very notion was "so foreign" to the spirit of English law and English thinking.[90]

But the adherence of the family in and through this child can also be reckoned as brittle, apt to crack. In fact, many, most notably Freud, accepting the centrality of the family to social structuring, proposed a model not of bonding but of uneasy, even hostile relations, of chafing under authority and the opposition between generations, on which "the whole progress of society rests."[91] Foucault, reshaping slightly Freud's family romance, discusses how the body "became the issue of a conflict between parents and children, the child and the instances of control."[92] But it was Oscar Wilde who told this story most succinctly: "Children begin by loving their parents; as they grow older they judge them; sometimes they forgive them."[93]

According to this model, the family unit, unnatural and historically accidental to begin with, is riddled by unending warfare between this artifice, the child, and the parent, this modern "parent" being as much a concoction as the "child." In Victorian times, we might assume, the concept of the parent was as yet a little shaky and needed a great deal of bolstering in the form of buck-up discourse meant to provide some backbone for this newly put-together, barely dry model. The parent is assured, for instance, that the child is, after all, the parent's: "The whole of life that he had ever known, had its center and all its vital springs in you."[94] "It is important to remember," says another author addressing those in no danger of forgetting, "that as the home is so is the boy."[95] This sort of flummery is meant to inflate morale, to reassure parents that, at bottom, they do indeed exist. They need to be told that they are the sole and absolute source of the child, because there is always the possibility that it's really the other way round.

The whole business of forming or defining the child through the parent, then, is an anxious way also of forming and empowering the parent. "The parent" is not an easy role to play or to learn, for that matter. One has to master a set of rules, a set of method-acting procedures: "I will strive to govern myself. Self-control and perfect self-possession are essential to a proper exercise of authority." In this theater, one runs the risk of being controlled by the audience, by the rabble in the pits, who need lots of instruction before they can recognize you for what you are: "I will train them to believe that I know what is best."[96] That belief is by no means implicit; the parent has to *create* or beat into shape his own being in relation to the child. In order to make sure you as parent are the one holding the reins, a little tactical trickery may be necessary: disguising oneself in enemy uniform, for instance, and sneaking into their camp: "And here was the great and powerful charm I held over my children. In the play hours I became one of them, so that their play did not often become a romp."[97] Became one of them?

Such devices suggest that the situation is felt to be desperate, and so do the shrill battle cries that sound more and more as if they were trying to halt a retreat. Finding ourselves in a field controlled by power, we are glad to come upon even false assurances that we have some of it: "I think we err very much, and very generally, in not expecting enough from children."[98] Such statements proceed as if our authority were a matter of course. Usually we require something more direct: "God has placed in your hands an influence over your children which is almost boundless. We underrate this power."[99] This may be a little like telling a woozy fighter who has just taken a nine-count to go in there and git 'im, but perhaps adults deserve such hokem for having conceived of the whole situation in terms of power to begin with.

One thing is certain: if we think of our relation to children in reference to power, there is nothing to keep them from thinking in the same manner. More to the point, we will certainly imagine that they are thinking that way, since we can imagine no other way of thinking. We will, thus, inevitably produce statements like this one: "There is a stage in which almost all children form their concepts of relationships in terms of power and control."[100] Once we allow that, we will discover, just as inevitably, that the parents are losers, adopting the complaints of losers: they have been misused, neglected, cheated:

The protection and the benefits flow all *the other way* [from the parent to the child]. We might have expected that *filial* affection would be strong, being based upon gratitude and a sense of dependence, and that if indifference should be manifested at all, it would be the parent's indifference towards the child. But no. The coldness is always on the part of those who *receive* the favours.[101]

It is perhaps for this reason, to save face or to find a way to displace the conflict, that this presumably solidifying Victorian middle-class family was so anxious to fragment itself, to introduce into its midst servants, nannies, and governesses. Servants, says Peter Laslett, were the largest single occupational group in England up to the early 1900s,[102] and we know that public schools not only grew in popularity throughout the century but that children tended to leave home for them at an increasingly earlier age.[103]

Gathorne-Hardy says that parents on a broad scale "simply abandoned all loving and disciplining and company of their little children, almost from birth" to the nurse or nanny.[104] Generally seeing the children less than an hour per day, these fairly well-to-do middle-class parents ceded virtually all authority to that nanny.[105] Then, at least within that class, the male child was sent speedily off to boarding schools which, even at their best, offered raging epidemic diseases, widely publicized "immorality," and plentiful battering. Honey suggests that parents were willing to expose their children to such things not simply from a desire for status or in tribute to a code of manliness that demanded "toughening," but also in recognition of a basic "transfer of function" between family and school, a general reorganization of society around the school. Honey's analysis sets the school not as an analogous family but as "a powerful rival institution capable of generating alternative values,"[106] flourishing because the middle-class Victorian family, swarming with children who often died early and were seldom seen by the parents anyhow, was not held together by any cohesive affection: "It is a mistake to assume that propaganda, however powerful, can make parents love their children or even desire prolonged contact with them."[107] Though contradictory readings of the situation are available—Ariès argues that the school substituted for apprenticeship and thus strengthened the position of the child as the center of the developing family[108]—this stark counter to sentimental images of the child is sobering.

There are, predictably, nineteenth-century voices raised against parental avoidance of children. William Cobbett urged parents, men included, to involve themselves fully with their children and spend ample time with them, doing away with surrogates and rivals; he disapproved strongly of public schools for boys or girls, of wet-nurses, nannies, and other hired substitutes: "many are but too prone to think that when they have handed their children over to well-paid and able servants they have *done their duty by them*, than which there can hardly be a more mischievous error."[109] And the author of *The Children's Wrong* puts the matter even more strenuously: "What we do mean to say is this, that both by nature and by revelation children are committed to the care of *parents*, and that he who without an absolute necessity gives up his charge to other hands is guilty not only of a grievous wrong to them, but of treason against his God."[110] But such voices and their urgency may as likely suggest that it's a middle-class wilderness they are crying in. In any case, we too easily assume that our version of the Wordsworthian child was the one current then. The child figure is surely more threatening and amorphous than such soft certainty would allow.

Managing the Child

T. L. Nichols' popular mid-century medical-marriage manual, with the wonderful title *Esoteric Anthropology*, talked about the whole range of what one did with children as the "Management" of them.[111] This term seems to have become the standard by which parents measured their activities and their position relative to the child—or at least the standard by which they were *told* to measure themselves. Management, a term which the *OED* says has enclosed from the very beginning broad traces not only of "control" but of "manipulation," also has a secondary meaning applicable here in full: "The working or cultivating (of land); hence *dial.* the process of manuring." Any sort of iron-fisted "management" was also a form of cultivation, enrichment for the child's own good, even if the child did see the loading on of manure in a different light. Management might include a hearty dose of aversion therapy, for instance: "While parents teach their children to do right, they should *make it as difficult as possible* for them to do wrong."[112] Generally, however, the secret was to insist on a strict and unvarying routine in order to train the young "in proper habits of order."[113]

Children, we are told, greatly benefit from such orderly management, even when it is necessary (it always is) for the managers to extend themselves into every detail of the child's life. Children don't mind that; they actually have some kind of instinct for being managed and feel lost when unmanaged, positively "demanding"[114] from their parents the infliction of the best available business and agricultural techniques.

But what we hear over and over from the experts is that this demand is not being met, very far from it. It is the parents, more especially the mother who is the one in the managerial chain bearing direct responsibility: "She is the one who [sic] nature has appointed to rear the child . . . and woe betide her and it if she fail in her solemn duty."[115] That, from one of the innumerable *Guides to the Management of Children*, makes it clear why so many woes are now betiding these defective mothers who have brought into being just what Samuel Smiles said they would, the child's and society's worst nightmare, "the bad home": "it will become a dwelling of misery—a place to fly from, rather than fly to; and the children whose misfortune it is to be brought up there, will be morally dwarfed and deformed—the cause of misery to themselves as well as to others,"[116] including, we may be sure, the guilty mother. And those guilty mothers and nearly-as-guilty fathers were everywhere, ignoring directives and turning out a miserable product: "the present race of children and young people are not hopeful for the future of our nation."[117] Irregular, disorderly parents cannot turn out regular and orderly children; it's as simple as that.

The situation is so chaotic that it spawns a form of black humor, borne of despair: Mrs. Bray, author of *Physiology for Common Schools*, cites the case, not all that unrepresentative (would that it were!), of a mother of a sick child who thought the child "ought to be well, since she had given him all the physic that was left in the bottles at his grandfather's death."[118] One can hear in Mrs. Bray's tones the tragic-saintly, I'd-be-cynical-were-I-not-so-good ring of the missionary unable to keep clothes on the savages. One cannot, of course, blame the child: "We do not hesitate to blame parental misconduct for a great deal of the domestic disorder commonly ascribed to the perversity of children."[119] It is the managers who have to be managed.

During the nineteenth century, the child seems to have become so mysterious that what one did with them, how they were to be administered, became itself a mystery. What once was thought to be instinctive (if it was thought about at all), came to constitute a special field of knowledge[120]: "The training of children—physical, moral, and intellectual—is dreadfully defective. And in great measure it is so, because parents are devoid of that knowledge by which this training can alone be rightly guided."[121] This new thing, the child, is terribly important, the full weight of both the importance and the terror landing squarely on the new form of the parent. No one, says the child-guidance books, could be less suited for bearing the weight. Those books are up to the job, but not the parents. Willich ushers in the century by suggesting, with a moderation that later would seem pussy-footing, that parents perhaps were not doing all they could and that he had a little to offer in the way of some good-sense measures: "There is little room to doubt, that by a more rational mode of nurture, during the first years of infancy, many subsequent diseases might either be wholly prevented, or at least greatly mitigated."[122] The tone changes as the century moves along and the child-managing experts gain confidence. The first thing one encounters in these later books, almost always, is hair-raising self-promotion. Arthur Edis claims he is doing no more than quoting Lord Shaftesbury in saying that "one hundred thousand children die annually in Great Britain from preventable causes," preventable, Edis implies pretty clearly (not claiming in so many words Lord Shaftesbury's endorsement), by the book right in front of you.[123] Alfred Fennings, not one for implications, says straight out that the management principles clearly outlined in his *Every Mother's Book*, rigorously applied, could save the lives of 4 out of 5 of the very many ("nearly half of the children born") who are now dying in the first five years of life.[124]

Trying to manage on one's own is, then, not simply misguided; it is murderous. These books petrify and then insult so directly that one wonders why they were so popular. After all, they were relentless in reminding their startled readers that "the responsibilities devolving upon parents, if they would have their children grow up clean and pure [or grow up at all], are indeed almost numberless."[125] To compensate for such heart-benumbing words and to balance the self-promoting bullying, these books offered power to parents, something parents were glad to be told that they had: "Mothers, I say to you, your influence for good or evil on your children is *immense*,"[126] said the Rev. Alfred Bligh Hill, incumbent of St. Paul's Tiverton, on the 29th of May 1856 in an address to mothers of schoolchildren attending a "tea feast." One can guess that the Rev. Hill (perhaps just "Alfred") was a popular man indeed. He was joined by many others in offering a trade, or even a kind of bribe: buy my book and I'll save your child's life and, not incidentally, give you a power boost that's absolutely tremendous. I'll show you how "parents may make of their children almost what they will."[127]

And out of all this power brokering, this negotiating between parents and experts, out of all this intricate manipulating, this haggling over who is to be in control of the controlling, this careful cultivating of the land, we are left with a child even more empty than before.

The Child of Wax, The Ceramic Child, The Child Botanical

Over and over, this child-rearing discourse transfers the being of the child to the parent (or to the discourse itself), reaching for a variety of metaphors to suggest openly that the "child" is nothing more than what it is construed to be, nothing in itself at all. Soft wax is a common figure for expressing our ability to stamp onto the child what we will: "Children's minds are like wax, readily receiving any impression."[128] Just as popular was a ceramic-products metaphor, with its proverbial and authoritative-sounding image of the potter and his clay: "Like clay in the hands of the potter, they are waiting only to be molded," presenting to us the opportunity to make something beautiful: "They may be moulded like potter's clay to graceful and harmonious shapes or the reverse."[129] Gliding past the rude notion of "the reverse," we are sure to find this altogether fitting: the child can be molded to be something lovely to look at, which is, even better, a something, quite wonderfully, *us*. The child is more than our little clay pot; he is a mirror. Though he uses an uncouth metaphor to explain this self-replication, Samuel Smiles does make the process clear: "Whatever children see, they unconsciously imitate; and they insensibly become like to those who are about them—like insects which take the colour of the leaves they feed on. . . . The characters of the parents are thus constantly repeated in their children."[130] And very graceful and harmonious those characters are too!

The most common of these models for evacuating "the child" and exalting "the parent" is clearly that of "the nursery." We see the term everywhere: "Home is the grand nursery for virtues"; or, more extensively, "We would rather consider the nursery as a garden into which trees and flowers of various kinds have been transplanted in their wild state, to be developed into all the beauty of which their nature, and the highest perfection of cultivation make them susceptible."[131] We notice in this last analogy, otherwise so pleasing, a buried but noxious suggestion that the child/plant has a "nature," an inner being we can only help perfect. Such a suggestion is, happily, quite uncommon in this widespread connection of children with plants, a connection so pervasive that the same word, nursery, can be used for the place where both are brought up and managed.[132] Generally, that nursery and its "little tender flowers"[133] "have no will of their own," are entirely dependent on the gardener-parent, on "the wisdom with which the frail and delicate plant is reared and nurtured."[134] "There is," we are told, "a pliability in the young mind, as in the young twig; which renders it apt to take any shape into which circumstances may press it. It is of great consequence, therefore, not to let it shoot awry; nay, to train, and gently bind it, in the best attainable direction."[135] The plant will grow into most anything the parent wants, or will be *apt* to do so. Even better, in Trumbull's later (1891) *Hints on Child-Training*, any limitations on the gardener's inclinations imposed by the plant's aptitudes are explicitly removed: "Children can be trained in almost any direction—despite their natures."[136]

The Watchers, The Influencers, The Habit-Formers

The nursery analogy has an advantage over the wax or ceramic models in that plants, unlike pots or seals, keep growing and keep changing, thus necessitating or excusing a inspection both more intensive and prolonged. When one considers the frailty of the young plant and, even more significant, the quality of the scrutiny that can be brought to bear upon it, says Pye Henry Chavasse, "it would appear that too much attention cannot be paid to the subject."[137] Chavasse's "attention to the subject" may be an excuse for the book he is trying to promote; but others provide the natural extension of the gardener image to the parent, emphasizing that in order to produce good plants one has to keep a sharp eye on them: "The watchfulness over the young child, by day and night, is the first sacred duty, to be universally inculcated."[138] This might seem to be, even for voyeuristic parents, overdoing; but one cannot be too careful. The watchfulness of course is not extended simply to curtail opportunities for masturbation or sex play; it strives to control the flow of "influences" coming into the child's life and forming its contours.

These influences are widely thought to determine the outer form of the mind as it "condenses into shape" and to impregnate it with features which are "taken up into the very tissue" of its making, "evermore to hold a place in it."[139] Such influences reach deep into the individual and into the national fiber: such things as "the heaviness of the Dutch and the vivacity of the French" likely come from different ways of influencing children, the Dutch keeping them "in a state of repose" and the French "perpetually tossing them about."[140] Makes a lot of sense when you think about it. And all influences, as I noted earlier, are seen as active influences: "unless the plan of education adopted with children does them a *positive physical good* in all its details, it does them a *positive physical harm*—it cannot be neutral."[141] It may then be inevitable that these books so often open with pointed sermons on *influence*:

It is not easy to estimate the influence even of what may seem an inconsiderable effort, when directed to such an object as education. It has been said, that a stone thrown into the sea agitates more or less every drop in the vast expanse of waters. So it may be with the influence we exert on the minds and hearts of the young. . . .[142]

This is a teacher talking, so allowances must be made; but Mrs. Child is quoting the teacher in her *Mother's Book* so that parents may do their part, not perhaps agitating every drop of water in the oceans, as does the teacher, but doing something considerable. The parent has the power to control the diet of impressions that will feed the subject throughout life: "their early impressions generally continue to old age," toned down and modified a little by later experiences, perhaps, "but the *shadow* is there."[143] The last metaphor is a strong one, hinting that the shadow of the parent reaches from beyond the grave, a specter that evokes Freud, who indeed carries on this Victorian chorus on influences: "We have . . . good reason to believe that there is no period for which the capacity for receiving and reproducing impressions is greater than during the years of childhood."[144]

We did not have to wait for Freud to invent the impressionable child, or to extend the receptivity into infancy. The time at which they may receive influences is, writers commonly urge, much earlier than we might suspect, even from birth, though not all of these come from parents: before a child can "take notice," "I believe they are receiving impressions indeed, not from this world, but from the holy angels."[145] A reliance on angelic agencies to keep up the influence is uncommon, most writers being willing to settle for mother: "Strange to say, the influence of the mother upon the child begins even during months of pregnancy."[146] Actually, given this line of thinking, there's nothing the least bit strange about it.

This emphasis on influence and the power of the parent to exercise it helps explain an aspect of the "innocent child" that may be confusing to us. The innocent child is empty, all the more susceptible to influence. It is not a compliment to the child, then, to insist that deceit, for instance, is nothing more than "an *acquired* vice," that "children are not naturally deceitful."[147] Not naturally deceitful does not suggest that they are naturally truthful, just that they are not naturally anything.

But this not-anything is quick to *acquire* various things, like a magpie; and it acquires nothing more readily than habits. Usually habits, unlike character traits, seem to be bad things, a burden the adult must carry from childhood.[148] Habits also seem to come along later and thus be, perhaps alarmingly, outside the control of the parents. One often meets with talk about habits in such things as Advice-to-Public-School-Boy manuals: "Remember that you are now forming your character, that you are acquiring habits; which, whether good or bad, will not be easily changed hereafter."[149] Nothing about acquiring habits in the womb or from the angels here. Often this discourse even gives the child some choice or at least responsibility in the acquisition of habits: "It is an old saying that 'habit is second nature;' consequently you will see the necessity of being very particular what habits you contract."[150] "Habit" seems to enter this discourse, then, on the other side from "impressions." Habit holds all the negative possibilities, not in the sense of bad habits but in the sense that the child might have control of them, that the child might, in other words, have some substance, a possibility that would be undesirable in every sense and that "habit" is assigned to contain and make manageable, just like the child.

On Idleness and Obedience

Lewis Carroll may have felt at ease parodying Isaac Watts's "Against Idleness and Mischief,"[151] but that poem's fierce sentencing of children to hard labor was a feature of much writing on the subject—not just of bees and how they doth, but of children. Less memorably than Watts, *Children and What to Do With Them* argues that "regular employment, and a total banishment of idleness, are *requisite* in the life of a properly brought up child."[152] Requisite or not, the constant harping on the theme might tempt one to suspect that idleness had not been stamped out. Further, it is just possible that these books are not so much calling for a halt as they are calling attention. Do we really want anything like "a total banishment of idleness" in children or do we simply want excuses to talk about this idle child? Are we, in fact, creating and then dwelling on an image of the inert child, the child of stasis, uncontaminated by the threat of change, growth, independence of any sort? An idle child can be watched, after all, or even photographed, framed, made permanent. Idleness is the best thing in the world for us, next to emptiness—in fact is nothing more than the outward and visible sign of an inward and spiritual nothingness.

And as for obedience: we've saved it for last (apart from a brief earlier fling under religion) because it looks like the dominant, the key to child management. When writers of manuals of the sort we have been examining come to the issue of obedience, you can sense them getting a firmer grip on the pen, reaching for a dictionary of military terms, snorting a little. I don't know how to give a sense of this passion

94 / *The Child*

for redundancy—and it is both redundant and passionate—without having recourse to a list:

> —The state of boyhood begins under a law. It is a great mistake to address always the reason of a child, when you ought to require his obedience.
>
> —Instant and unquestioning obedience is a duty which every child owes to its parents, and which is the bounden duty of every parent to enforce.
>
> —A child's first duty . . . is Obedience; that is, doing what he is told to do, cheerfully and readily.
>
> —Teach them to *obey* you: that one great lesson of all life, *"to submit."*
>
> —I will remember that the *will* must be subdued and habits of obedience formed very early; believing that if I have complete control of the child before five years of age, I shall have little trouble afterward.
>
> —[to children]: By obedience and affection you may make your parents happy, and be happy yourselves.[153]

And one more, this one a long one, in order to give us a clearer look at the logic, if that's the word, controlling this mania:

> I would also remark, that parents cannot take a single step to advantage in endeavouring to train up their children to piety, without first obtaining their *unlimited, unqualified, entire submission* to their authority. The *very first* lesson to be taught the child is to *submit*, to *obey*. There are various methods of obtaining this ascendancy. In some cases it is to be done by kindness, in others by severity; but in some way or other it *must be done*. Your children must be habituated to do what you command, and to refrain from what you forbid; not because they can see the reason for it, but because you *command* or *forbid*: submission, not to your *reason*, but to your *authority* [is vital]. . . . Be it remembered, insubordination is the essence of irreligion. I repeat it—insubordination is the essence of irreligion.[154]

This passage seems to enact its instructions, seeking to move us into enforcing obedience above all, not because we see the *reason* for it but because it is commanded. Reasons are waved aside so that the way may be cleared for the main attraction. One doesn't command obedience for any particular reason, not even to make things easier on oneself. (Indeed, the regimen suggested to require obedience would take so much effort a sensible person would happily settle down with moderate-to-heavy disobedience.) One hammers at disobedience because, as with idleness, it is so thrilling to talk about its opposite, though for reasons that appear at first to be contradictory.

The idle child is fixed, available, manipulable. So, we might say, is the obedient child, who becomes in the models presented above not a choice but an echo, a dullish sort of replication of ourselves. But the obedient child sacrifices otherness in the way the idle child does not. Consider Dickens's Fat Boy, who hangs about Dingley Dell and makes people's flesh creep. He is Idleness incarnate (along with some other interesting vices like Gluttony), but his hollowness is the mysterious hollowness of fascinating caverns. The obedient child, however, has nothing behind the mirror, which might suggest why the image of the disobedient child is so hypnotically alluring. Insisting on obedience is a way of pulling before us, kicking and screaming, the child who is said to be like us, exactly like us, with a broken will or no will and no desires that are not our own. But we know very well that the issue of the struggle of wills is not the only game in town, that there is also the issue of the play of desire. And there the struggles, the kicks and screams, the evidence of independence come to the fore. The child can serve as a mirror, certainly, happily reflecting back to us a pleasing image of ourselves. But children robbed of otherness are finally repulsive. If children were not bad, it would be impossible to love them.

Notes

1. Friedrich Wilhelm August Froebel, *Letters on the Kindergarten*, trans. and ed. Emilie Michaelis and H. Keatley Moore (London: Swan Sonnenschein, 1891), p. 169.

2. Sigmund Freud, "Three Essays on the Theory of Sexuality," VII, 133.

3. H. Clay Trumbull, *Hints on Child-Training* (London: Hodder and Stoughton, 1891), p. 52.

4. Philippe Ariès, *Centuries of Childhood: A Social History of Family Life*, trans. Robert Baldick (New York: Knopf, 1962), p. 33.

5. Lawrence Stone, *The Family, Sex, and Marriage in England, 1500–1800* (New York: Harper and Row, 1977); Lewinsohn, *History of Sexual Customs*, p. 9; Peter Coveney, *The Image of Childhood; The Individual and Society: A Study of the Theme in English Literature*, rev. ed. (Baltimore: Penguin, 1967), p. 29; Gorham, *The Victorian Girl*, p. 18.

See also the effective employment of this thesis by Robert Etienne, "Ancient Medical Conscience and the Life of Children," *Journal of Psychohistory* 4 (1976): 131–61, who claims that the indifference to what we think of as the child was so marked in classical Greece that infanticide was an everyday event and infant deaths so commonplace and

96 / The Child

insignificant that they were often scarcely recorded, even for imperial families; by Stevi Jackson, *Childhood and Sexuality* (Oxford: Basil Blackwell, 1982), who says that in Tudor England children of seven years of age were considered adults, legally responsible for their actions and liable to be (and sometimes actually) hanged (p. 34); and by Jonathan Gathorne-Hardy, *The Rise and Fall of the British Nanny* (London: Hodder and Stoughton, 1972), pp. 42–43, who supports Ariès's citation of the high rate of infant and child death in earlier centuries as making unlikely a great emotional investment in children.

6. Keith Thomas's criticism of Stone ("The Changing Family," *TLS*, 21 October 1977, 1226–27) is an example. The case of traditional historians against Ariès is stated fairly by Linda Pollock, *A Lasting Relationship: Parents and Children Over Three Centuries* (Hanover, NH and London: Univ. Press of New England, 1987), pp. 11–13. A defense of Ariès against the psychohistory of DeMause is in Valerie P. Suransky, *The Erosion of Childhood* (Chicago: Univ. of Chicago Press, 1982), pp. 5–6.

7. Ariès, *Centuries of Childhood*, p. 38 and passim.

8. The first is from Mark Spilka, "On the Enrichment of the Poor Monkeys by Myth and Dream; or, How Dickens Rousseauisticized and Pre-Freudianized the Victorian View of Childhood," in Cox, ed., *Sexuality and Victorian Literature*, p. 162; the second is from Weeks, *Sex, Politics*, p. 48. For echoes, see Bratton, *Impact of Victorian Children's Fiction*, p. 11; Jackson, *Children and Sexuality*, pp. 22–27; and J.H. vand den Berg, *The Changing Nature of Man: Introduction to a Historical Psychology* (New York: Dell, 1961), p. 71.

9. Gathorne-Hardy, *Rise and Fall of the British Nanny*, p. 175.

10. Coveney, *The Image of Childhood*, pp. 68–90.

11. Trumbull, *Hints on Child-Training*, p. 69.

12. "A Mother," *A Few Suggestions to Mothers*, p. 17.

13. Freud, "History of an Infantile Neurosis," pp. 104–5.

14. Quoted in vand den Berg, *Changing Nature*, p. 23.

15. Constantine and Martinson, eds., *Children and Sex*, p. 6.

16. Gorham, *The Victorian Girl*, p. 80.

17. Krafft-Ebing, *Psychopathia Sexualis*, p. 186.

18. Ariès, *Centuries of Childhood*, p. 58; Jean H. Hagstrum, *Sex and Sensibility: Ideal and Erotic Love from Milton to Mozart* (Chicago: Univ. of Chicago Press, 1980), p. 266.

19. See T.W. Bamford, "Thomas Arnold and the Victorian Idea of a Public School," in Brian Simon and Ian Bradley, eds., *The Victorian Public School: Studies in the Development of an Educational Institution* (Dublin: Gill and Macmillan, 1975), pp. 64–67.

20. Bratton, *Impact of Victorian Children's Fiction*, p. 87.

21. Trumbull, *Hints on Child-Training*, p. 36.

22. Kate Douglas Wiggin, *Children's Rights: A Book of Nursery Logic* (Boston: Houghton Mifflin, 1892), pp. 10–19.

23. Mrs. Mary Wood-Allen, M.D., "Moral Education of the Young," in Aaron M. Powell, ed., *The National Purity Congress: Its Papers, Addresses, Portraits: An Illustrated Record of the Papers and Addresses of the First National Purity Congress, Held*

Under the Auspices of the American Purity Alliance, in the Park Avenue Friends' Meeting House, Baltimore, October 14, 15 and 16, 1895 (New York: The American Purity Alliance, 1896; rpt. New York: Arno Press, 1976), p. 224.

24. Anon., "Children's Literature," *The Quarterly Review* 13 (26 January 1860) in Lance Salway, ed., *A Peculiar Gift: Nineteenth-Century Writings on Books for Children* (Harmondsworth, England: n.p., 1976), p. 317.

25. Cobbe, *Intuitive Morals*, I, 100.

26. Thomas Arnold, "Sermon 1" and "Sermon 2," in *Christian Life: Its Course, Its Hindrances, and Its Helps: Sermons, Preached Mostly in the Chapel of Rugby School* (London: B. Fellowes, 1841), pp. 9, 12, 15.

27. The "nucleus" quote is from Smiles, *Character*, p. 33; the rest is from Anon., '*The Boy Makes the Man': By a Sunday Scholar: A Prise Essay* (Leeds: J. Heaton and Son, 1862), pp. 6–7.

28. Blackwell, *Counsel to Parents*, p. 3. See also Froebel, *Kindergarten*, pp. vii–viii, 10; and Willich, *Lectures on Diet and Regimen*, p. 89.

29. Rev. Jacob Abbott, *Parental Duties in the Promotion of Early Piety* (London: Thomas Ward, 1834), p. 37.

30. See Coveney, *The Image of Childhood*, p. 80.

31. Eric Trudgill, *Madonnas and Magdalenes: The Origins and Development of Victorian Sexual Attitudes* (New York: Holmes and Meier, 1976), pp. 90–91.

32. Elizabeth Akers Allen's "Rock Me to Sleep" (1869), Stanza 1.

33. A.R. Hope, *A Book About Boys* (Boston: Roberts Brothers, 1869), p. 21.

34. Most enthusiastically by Ariès, *Centuries of Childhood*, p. 164.

35. These details are lifted from W. Clarke Hall, *The Law Relating to Children: A Short Treatise on the Personal Status of Children, and the Statutes that Have Been Enacted for Their Protection* (London: Stevens and Sons, 1894), pp. 21–27.

36. Edward Jones Urwick, "Introduction" to John Howard Whitehouse, Geoffrey Gordon, and N. Malcomson, *Report of an Inquiry into Working Boys' Homes in London* (London: Arnold Fairbanks, 1908), p. 3.

37. The full title of Acton's work is *The Functions and Disorders of the Reproductive Organs [in Childhood,] in Youth, in Adult Age, and in Advanced Life, Considered in Their Physiological, Social, and Psychological Relations* (London: John Chandler). The first edition was published in 1857, the third in 1862. Some of the other changes in these editions (through the sixth in 1875) and the character of Acton's work generally are examined in Chapter 7.

38. On the first division, see Pye Henry Chavasse, *The Young Wife's and Mother's Book: Advice to Mothers on the Management of Their Offspring during the Periods of Infancy, Childhood, and Youth; Advice to Young Wives on the Management of Themselves During the Periods of Pregnancy and Lactation*, 2nd ed. (London: Longman, Brown, Green, and Longmans, 1842). On the second, see Anon., *The Mother's Medical Adviser; on the Diseases and Management of Children, With Recipes* (London: Cradock, 1843), p. 1; and also, somewhat confusingly, the versatile Chavasse in another book, *Advice to a Mother on the Management of Her Children and on the Treatment on the Moment of Some of Their More Pressing Illnesses and Accidents*, 13th ed. (London: J. and A. Churchill, 1878).

39. Moll, *The Sexual Life of the Child*, pp. 1–2. To help clarify things, Moll adds that these categories are rough-and-ready, individual variations being quite large.

40. See Ariès, *Centuries of Childhood*, pp. 25, 29–30, 329; and also his "Thoughts on the History of Homosexuality," in Philippe Ariès and Andre Bejin, eds., *Western Sexuality: Practice and Precept in Past and Present Times*, trans. Anthony Forster (Oxford: Basil Blackwell, 1985), pp. 67–68; Gorham, *The Victorian Girl*, pp. 369–70; and Jackson, *Childhood and Sexuality*, p. 105.

41. See Ariès, *Centuries of Childhood*, p. 25.

42. Lionel Weatherly, M.D., *The Young Wife's Own Book: A Manual of Personal and Family Hygiene; Containing Everything that the Young Wife and Mother Ought to Know Concerning Her Own Health and That of Her Children at the Most Important Periods of Life* (London: Griffith and Farran, 1882), p. 28.

43. Freud, "Three Essays," VII, 177.

44. Ariès, *Centuries of Childhood*, pp. 15–18.

45. [Lucy L. Cameron], *The Polite Little Children*, 6th ed. (London: Wellington Sallop, 1822), pp. 31–32.

46. Mrs. Mary M. Sherwood, *The History of Henry Milner*, Part I, Chapter IV; quoted in M. Nancy Cutt, *Mrs. Sherwood and Her Books for Children* (London: Oxford Univ. Press, 1974), p. 70.

47. Thomas Arnold, Letter to Rev. John Tucker, 2 March 1828; quoted in J.J. Findlay, *Arnold of Rugby: His School Life and Contributions to Education* (Cambridge: Cambridge Univ. Press, 1897), p. 30.

48. Arnold, "Sermon 2," *Christian Life*, p. 14.

49. Herbert Spencer, *Education: Intellectual, Moral, and Physical* (London: G. Manwaring, 1861), p. 135. See also Cobbe, *Auricular Confession*, p. 5, and *Intuitive Morals*, I, 112.

50. Gorham, *The Victorian Girl*, pp. 38–41.

51. Ariès, *Centuries of Childhood*, p. 106.

52. The Rev. S.S. Seward, "Purity—How Preserved Among the Young," in Powell, ed., *National Purity Congress Papers*, pp. 208–9.

53. Anthony Comstock, "Demoralizing Literature," in Powell, ed., *National Purity Congress Papers*, p. 421.

54. Ellis, *Studies in the Psychology of Sex*, I, 36–37.

55. See J. P. Ward, " 'Came from yon fountain': Wordsworth's Influence on Victorian Educators," *Victorian Studies* 29 (1986): 405–36. Ward suggests that the influence of the Wordsworthian view of the child on Victorian educationists has been overestimated.

56. For a discussion of the Child and Feeling in literature, see Coveney, *The Image of Childhood*, pp. 40–42.

57. Spencer, *Education*, p. 136.

58. Cobbe, *Intuitive Morals*, pp. x–xi.

59. Alfred Fennings, *Every Mother's Best Book; Or, The Child's Best Doctor* (London: n.p., n.d. [1856]), p. ii; Arthur W. Edis, "Introduction" to Anon., *Children: Their Health, Training, and Education, with Valuable Health Notes for Young and Old* (London: G.W. Baron, n.d. [1879]), pp. 2–6.

60. Gathorne-Hardy, *British Nanny*, p. 65.

61. Quoted in Hallam, Lord Tennyson, *Alfred, Lord Tennyson: A Memoir*, 2 vols. (New York: Macmillan, 1898), I, 314.

62. Joy Parr, *Labouring Children: British Immigrant Apprentices to Canada, 1869–1924* (London: Croom Helm; Montreal: McGill-Queens Univ. Press, 1980), p. 11. For emigration to other parts of the empire, see Gillian Wagner, *Children of the Empire* (London: Weidenfeld and Nicolson, 1982).

63. See, for example, Clark Nardinelli, "Child Labor and the Factory Acts," *Journal of Economic History* 40 (1980): 739–55. To be fair, Nardinelli is addressing only the importance of child labor to the success of the industrial revolution, an importance, he says, which has been exaggerated.

64. This report and the general information concerning sweeps is drawn from Peter G. Clamp, "Climbing Boys, Childhood, and Society in Nineteenth-Century England," *Journal of Psychohistory* 12 (1985): 193–210.

65. Acton, *Prostitution*, pp. 289, 280–86.

66. See William Logan, *The Great Social Evil: Its Causes, Extent, Results, and Remedies* (London: Hodder and Stoughton, 1871).

67. For various figures, see Clement Dukes, M.D., *The Preservation of Health, as It Is Affected by Personal habits Such as Cleanliness, Temperance, &c.* "The Essay on Social Statistics for the Howard Medal of the Statistical Society of London for 1884" (London: privately printed by Messrs. Rivington, 1884), pp. 168–69; G. Richelot, *De La Prostitution en Angleterre et en Écosse* (Paris: J.B. Bailliere et fils, 1857); and A. Vintras, *On the Repressive Measures Adopted in Paris, Compared with the Uncontrolled Prostitution of London and New York* (London: Robert Hardwicke, 1867), pp. 34–35.

68. [Henry Robinson], *The Whole Truth and Nothing But the Truth About the Social Evil: Being Deeper Glimpses of the Business of Prostitution in Edinburgh, &c.* (Edinburgh: Henry Robinson, 1866), p. 9.

69. See Logan, *The Great Social Evil*, p. 18.

70. Acton, *Prostitution*, pp. 185–86, 295–96.

71. See Jordan, *Victorian Childhood*, pp. xiii-xiv.

72. Ariès, *Centuries of Childhood*, p. 122.

73. Edward J. Bristow, *Vice and Vigilance: Purity Movements in Britain since 1700* (London: Gill and Macmillan, Rowan and Littlefield, 1977), p. 32.

74. Quoted in Andrew Birkin, *J. M. Barrie & The Lost Boys* (London: Constable, 1979), p. 8. This line is used again in the 1987 Rob Reiner film, "Stand By Me," based on a Stephen King story.

75. Kinsey, *Human Male*, p. 445.

76. Anthony Trollope, *Doctor Thorne* (Boston: Riverside, 1959; first pub. 1858), ch. 3, p. 37.

77. *Children: Their Health*, p. 115.

78. William H. Groser, *A Hundred Year's Work for the Children; Being a Sketch of the History and Operations of the Sunday School Union from Its Formation in 1803 to Its Centenary in 1903* (London: The Sunday School Union, n.d.), p. 67. Groser also discusses an interesting-sounding "Children's Holiday Homes" program for "poor or

ailing scholars," a program that by the time of the writing (1903?) involved 19,000 children (pp. 163–64).

79. See, for one of many examples, Anon., *Hints on Early Education. By a Mother*, 2nd ed. (London: Joseph Masters, 1852), p. 5.

80. M. Nancy Cutt, *Mrs. Sherwood*, p. 48.

81. Cobbe, *Intuitive Morals*, II, 2.

82. Coveney, *The Image of Childhood*, pp. 192–93, 340–41.

83. Morris Fraser, *The Death of Narcissus* (London: Secker and Warburg, 1976), pp. 55–56.

84. Samuel Smiles, *Self-Help; with Illustrations of Character and Conduct* (London: John Murray, 1859), p. 294.

85. William Mitchell, *Rescue the Children or, Twelve Years' Dealing with Neglected Girls and Boys* (London: William Isbister [1886]), p. ix.

86. Froebel, *The Kindergarten*, p. 91.

87. Anon., *The Children's Wrong: A Book for Christian Parents* (London: Jackson, Walford, and Hodder, [1864]), p. 10.

88. Ariès, *Centuries of Childhood*, pp. 412–13; see also pp. 10, 353, 364, 375, 398, 405–7. See also Peter Laslett, ed. *Household and Family in Past Time* (Cambridge, Cambridge Univ. Press, 1972), p. 13.

89. Ariès, *Centuries of Childhood*, p. 364.

90. Hall, *The Law Relating to Children*, p. 11.

91. Sigmund Freud, "Family Romances," IX, 237.

92. Foucault, "Body/Power," in Gordon, ed., *Power/Knowledge*, p. 57.

93. Oscar Wilde, *The Picture of Dorian Gray*, ch. 5; in *The Annotated Oscar Wilde*, ed. H. Montgomery Hyde (New York: Clarkson N. Potter, 1982).

94. *The Children's Wrong*, p. 24.

95. Anon., *Boys and Their Ways: A Book for Boys and About Boys; By One Who Knows Them* (London: John Hogg, 1880), p. 9.

96. Anon., *Resolutions Respecting the Treatment of My Children* Tract #1594 (London: Society for Promoting Christian Knowledge, n.d. [1860?]), p. 3.

97. Mrs. Eliza Warren, *How I Managed My Children from Infancy to Marriage* (London: Houlston and Wright, 1839), p. 34.

98. Anon., *Hints on Early Education*, p. 5.

99. Rev. Jacob Abbott, *Parental Duties in the Promotion of Early Piety* (London: Thomas Ward, 1834), p. 58.

100. Jack Novick and Kerry Kelly Novick, "Beating Fantasies in Children," *International Journal of Psychoanalysis* 52 (1972): 238.

101. Abbott, *Parental Duties*, p. 5.

102. Peter Laslett, *The World We Have Lost* (London: Methuen, 1965), p. 35.

103. J.R.DeS. Honey, *Tom Brown's Universe: The Development of the Victorian Public School* (London: Millington, 1977), p. 126.

104. Gathorne-Hardy, *British Nanny*, p. 19.

105. Gathorne-Hardy, *British Nanny*, pp. 61, 74–77.

106. Honey, *Tom Brown's Universe*, p. 205.

107. Honey, *Tom Brown's Universe*, p. 206; see also pp. 19–20, 203–21.

108. Ariès, *Centuries of Childhood*, p. 369.

109. William Cobbett, *Advice to Young Men and (incidentally) to Young Women, in the Middle and Higher Ranks of Life, in a Series of Letters Addressed to a Youth, a Bachelor, a Lover, a Husband, a Father, a Citizen or a Subject* (London: Griffin, Bohn, 1862), pp. 237–42.

110. Anon., *The Children's Wrong*, p. 17.

111. T.L. Nichols, *Esoteric Anthropology* (New York: Arno and The New York Times; 1972 rpt. of 1853 London ed.), pp. 210–22.

112. Mrs. J.H. Kellogg, "Purity and Parental Responsibility," in Powell, ed., *National Purity Congress Papers*, p. 219.

113. See Gorham, *The Victorian Girl*, pp. 67–68, and the anonymous negative exemplum, *The Disorderly Family; or, The Village of R****: A Tale for Young Persons. By a Father* (London: Bell and Dalby, 1860). For a protest against this reliance on structure and regimentation, see Suransky, *Erosion of Childhood*, pp. 64–65.

114. Clement Dukes, M.D., *An Address in School of Hygiene on Medical Guidance in the Selection of Schools for Certain Children; Delivered at the Sanitary Institute of Great Britain, Before the Medical Profession, on July 16, 1889* (London: Cassell, 1889), p. 9.

115. Dr. Henry Arthur Albutt, *Every Mother's Handbook: A Guide to the Management of Her Children* (London: Simpkin, Marshall, Hamilton, Kent and Co., 1897), n.p. [Preface].

116. Smiles, *Character*, pp. 41–42.

117. Anon., "Defects in the Moral Training of Girls; by a Mother," in Rev. Orby Shipley, ed., *The Church and the World: Essays on Questions of the Day* (London: Longmans, Green, Reader, and Dyer, 1868), p. 80.

118. Mrs. Caroline Bray, *Physiology for Common Schools in Twenty-Seven Easy Lessons* (London: Longman, Green, Longman, and Roberts, 1860), p. 67.

119. Spencer, *Education*, p. 109

120. See Gorham, *The Victorian Girl*, pp. 65–66.

121. Spencer, *Education*, p. 31.

122. Willich, *Lectures on Diet and Regimen*, p. 78.

123. Edis, "Introduction," *Children: Their Health*, p. 2.

124. Fennings, *Every Mother's Best Book*, p. ii.

125. Kellogg, "Purity and Parental," in Powell, ed., *National Purity Congress Papers*, p. 222.

126. Rev. Alfred Bligh Hill, *Address to Mothers, Delivered at a Tea Feast Given to the Mothers of the Children Attending the Various Schools of the Town [of Tiverton], on the 29th of May 1856* (London: Wertheim and Macintosh), p. 15.

127. Mrs. Emma F. Angell Drake, *What a Young Wife Ought to Know* "Self and Sex Series" (London: Vir Publishing, 1901), p. 142.

102 / The Child

128. Anon., *Children, Their Health*, p. 111.

129. Mitchell, *Rescue the Children*, p. 16; and Rhoda E. White, *From Infancy to Womanhood: A Book of Instruction for Young Mothers* (London: Sampson Low, Marston, Searle, and Rivington, 1882), p. 101.

130. Smiles, *Self-Help*, pp. 293–94.

131. The first citation is from Isaac Taylor, *Advice to the Teens; or Practical Help towards the Formation of One's Own Character*, 2nd ed. (London: n.p., 1818), p. 65; the second from Mrs. [Matilda Marian] Pullan, *Children and How to Manage Them* (London: Darton and Co., 1856), p. 3.

132. Gathorne-Hardy, *British Nanny*, p. 45, says English is the only language for which this is true.

133. Mrs. Warren, *How I Managed My Children*, p. 37.

134. E.C., *Our Children, How to Rear and Train Them: A Manual for Parents, in the Physical, Educational, Religious, and Moral Training of Their Children* (London: Cassell, Petter, and Galpin, [1874]), p. 9.

135. Taylor, *Advice to the Teens*, p. 89.

136. Trumbull, *Hints on Child-Training*, p. 17.

137. Chavasse, *Young Wife's and Mother's Book*, p. vii.

138. Blackwell, *Counsel to Parents*, p. 65.

139. Anon., *Do-The-Girls Hall, or Coventual Life Unveiled; Addressed More Particularly to Parents of Young Girls; "By a Parent"* (London: N. Wilson, [1875]), p. 8.

140. Mrs. Child, *The Mother's Book*, p. 1.

141. Dr. Elizabeth Blackwell, "The Religion of Health," quoted in Anon., *Children: Their Health*, p. 129.

142. Mrs. Child is here quoting with great approval "Mr Francis' Discourse on Error in Education" in her *The Mother's Book*, p. ix.

143. The first part is from Michael Ryan, *The Philosophy of Marriage*, p. 47; the second from Anon., *Children and What to Do With Them: A Plain, Simple, Common-Sense Guide to Mothers Respecting the Health, Ailments, Diet, Clothing, Exercise, Education, Employments, Amusements, and General Management of Their Boys and Girls* (London: Ward, Lock, and Co., [1850]), p. 93.

144. Freud, "Three Essays," VII, 175.

145. Quoted in Anon., *Hints on Early Education*, p. 4.

146. Mrs. Warren, *How I Managed My Children*, p. 7.

147. Anon., *Children and What to Do with Them*, p. 94.

148. See, for instance, Anon., *Boys and Their Ways*, passim.

149. Rev. Frederick Poynder, *A Few Words of Advice to a Public School Boy*, 4th ed. (London: Rivington, 1860), p. 13.

150. Anon., *A Father's Advice to a Son* (Manchester: John Heywood, [1872]), p. 4.

151. Watts's poem was published in his *Divine Songs for Children* (1715) and had considerable currency during most of the nineteenth century too. The poem and Carroll's (or Alice's) parody of it are in *Alice's Adventures in Wonderland*, "The Pennyroyal Alice" (Berkeley: Univ. of California Press, 1982), p. 48.

152. Anon., *Children and What to Do with Them*, p. 106.

153. The sources are, in order, Thomas Arnold, *Christian Life*, Sermon X, p. 105; Mrs. Pullan, *Children and How to Manage Them*, p. 15; Mrs. Charles Bray, *Elements of Morality in Easy Lessons, For Home and School Teaching* (London: Longmans, Green, and Co., 1882), p. 23; Ellice Hopkins, *On the Early Training of Girls and Boys: An Appeal to Working Women* (London: Hatchards, 1882), p. 34; Anon., *Resolutions*, p. 3; Rev. Jacob Abbott, *The Child at Home; or, The Principles of Filial Duty* (London: James Blackwood, [1860]), p. 10.

154. Abbott, *Parental Duties*, pp. 10–11.

3

The Budding Body

Body Power

The modern "body" is an invention at least as startling as the modern "child." There was a time, says A. F. M. Willich (1799), and that time seems only yesterday, when most people, on a rough-and-ready, day-to-day basis, really were not aware that they had a body: "Formerly, people were not accustomed to think of the physical state of their body, until it began to be afflicted with pain or debility."[1] It was not the custom to regard such things, the things not being there to regard; at least not there in the same way that they now, most indubitably, are. Willich makes it clear that, whatever former customs may have been, the upcoming century will see innovative fashions, different things to think on. One of the fads that stuck was the body.

It stuck so well that it has become, along with the child, a part of what we take "nature" to be. Weeks points out how even Foucault resorts to a "latent essentialism" in "his use of 'the body' as a final court of appeal." "It is difficult," Weeks concludes, "to see why the 'body' should have a 'reality' denied other social phenomena."[2] If we consider the body to be an assemblage of various cultural needs and anxieties, we do more to honor its great dexterity, its ability to answer to many calls. We also better suggest something of its unpredictability.

There is no blinking the fact that it has an unruly way of being less obedient than we would like, of taking on an unwelcome autonomy. This modern body sometimes goes off on its own, detaching itself from our counsel and control. It gives us the sense of having much more power over us than we have over it, though it will submit sometimes to being studied, even, when it is young and without much choice in the matter, to steady scrutiny: "The body of the child, under surveillance, surrounded in his cradle, his bed, or his room by an entire watch-crew of parents, nurses, servants, educators, and doctors . . . has constituted, particularly since the eighteenth century, another 'local center' of power-knowledge."[3] We have gained so little either of power or knowledge, however, that one wonders whether this "surveillance" isn't much more like attendance at an exhibitionist's concert. What can we do but watch the body, any body, and do homage to it? If we try to duck out or if we nod off during the show, it exacts terrible penalties.

We cover the body to protect its rights to privacy. It is the body which blushes; we don't. We give it what it wants. We wash it free from sin and sexual stain. We legislate on its behalf, trying to placate it. The flood of public health measures enacted during the nineteenth century, especially in England, is commonly attributed to the horrors brought on by the industrial revolution, its swelling cities and so forth.[4] It is just as likely that these bills were forced on us by the "body," by way of its new physician-priests. For what had we ever received that we might call benefits from the body? Gregory Bateson points out how medical science has even lost consciousness of "the body as a systemically cybernetically organized self-corrective system" and thus has no wisdom at all to offer, simply "a bag of tricks," some of them flashy, but amounting to nothing more than random entertainments for the body.[5] For all its feistiness, this new body is nothing if not delicate, forever demanding attention and seldom making it clear just what kind of fixing it needs. It is all very well for Willich to announce triumphantly that "every individual of any penetration now claims the privilege of being his own physician" (p. 26); such things sound generous and help to sell the training manual he had written. But the truth is that it is about as much a privilege to be one's own physician, as it is to carry out one's garbage. There's no alternative. We have arranged things so that, according to Mrs. Bray's *Physiology*, "our bodies will not keep healthy of themselves."[6] Mrs. Bray is enunciating the sad truth everyone recognizes, the truth that gives the lie to Willich's drivel about privileges. There is, as even Willich later admits, not a lot to cheer about over this new bogeyman of a body, which has made "health" something of a chimera, a golden image vanishing over the horizon: "I do not mean to insinuate, that a perfect and permanent state of health is compatible with the delicate organization and complex functions of the human body" (p. 97). Willich begins to see that health itself is inscribed in that which it seeks to exclude: "I am well aware that [the body's] most healthy condition closely borders on disease" (p. 97). Considerable fuel is thus added to evangelical distrust of the body, to formulating the body as enemy.

Body-Laws

Even the laws which the body was presumed to follow, though usually hidden and more or less indecipherable, were nonetheless inexorable, commonly operating to penalize: "Nature is a strict accountant; and if you demand of her in one direction more than she is prepared to lay out, she balances the account by making a deduction elsewhere."[7] No friendly loans, just frosty cash-and-carry. Many of these fierce laws governed sexual behavior and the lack of it too. Edward Carpenter invented (discovered?) the law connecting the avoidance of sexual expression to growth itself, that is, the bodily-law which punished impurity by refusing to permit any more development whatsoever:

> To prolong the period of continence [purity] in a boy's life is to prolong the period of *growth*. This is a simple physiological law, and a very obvious one; and whatever other things may be said in favour of purity, it remains perhaps the most weighty. To introduce sensual and sexual habits ... at any early age, is to arrest growth, both physical and mental."[8]

Sex is the subject of our next chapter, but we can slide enough of it in here to note how even that bully could be brought to its knees by the body. Whether the laws Carpenter notes are indeed "simple" and "obvious" matters a good deal less than that they are *laws*, and that they issue from the body. A physiological law is not so much a law controlling the body as a law the body uses to control us. The body is not a subject in this community; it is the police, the secret police, an authority so cryptic that it writes its laws and then buries them, destroying all the maps. The trick, as Browning's Caliban says, is to find the laws—or die. In the dominion of the body, as in Setebos's, it can only be a matter of engaging frantically in the hunt, never so much as knowing whether we are getting warm.

It may seem odd that what seem to us the obvious places to look for body-laws did not always seem so obvious to our great-grandparents. While they were wildly (or merrily) off chasing wild geese in the thickets of electro-magnetism or the economics of semen expenditure, we have adjusted our lenses to points about the developing body that we suppose really do matter: gender differences, for instance. Freud's interplanetary visitor, we recall, was struck with nothing "more forcibly than the fact of the existence of two sexes among human beings," a fact which did not, however, present itself to children as a fact at all.[9] Nor did it, perhaps, to the Victorians, at least as regards children.

Before the time of puberty or "adolescence," they did not take much official notice of gender. We are probably not surprised to come upon Victorian worries about the mixing of boys and girls in "dangerous" situations: "Do not let girls and boys sleep together, or share the same bedroom"; "Try and be careful not to tub the girls before the boys."[10] What will surprise us is the rarity of such expressions, or even of such distinctions between the sexes. Advice manuals, when they did note the difference, most often actually urged parents to minimize rather than emphasize it; and it wasn't, as I have noted, until this century that gender differences in infancy and early childhood were at all marked in dress.[11] We can assume that Victorians *saw* gender differences; but it does seem that they were far less eager than we to make them linchpins of an entire conceptual system. They noted such things as the comparative changes in the size of the larynx at puberty—in proportion of 5 to 7 for girls, 5 to 10 for boys[12]—but never in order to build a way of viewing on the basis of that difference. Their tendency was to find ways of using even what seem to us obvious points of difference, like the penis, as lines of connection. When we find a Victorian calling the clitoris "a miniature, imperfect penis,"[13] we are not wrong to read it as sexist; but are less literate in their vocabulary of affinities, their very different construction of the body.

To what extent, for instance, could actions performed by or on the body be reversed, to what extent, if any, was healing possible? Were the body and its functions to be understood in reference to models of change (or redemption) or models of fixity (or retribution)? These complex issues of perception were battled over or played with most openly (or most obviously to us) in reference to the Victorian positioning of prostitution. This prolonged and complex battle has been ably put into modern terms by historians[14]; I wish only to look at what it was the Victorians may have seen in the first place. What is it one finds when one sets out to look for a prostitute? How does one go about looking? According to some guides, one looks for a thing, a distinct thing altogether. A prostitute for them is not like anything but a prostitute, not, for instance, like other women. Prostitutes may once have *been* women, but they have "descended," as it is usually put, to another order of being or species.[15] That species can, of course, be studied; and it forms itself into "distinct grades or classes"[16] that may ape human society. But those who have stepped down into this order have entered a new world. They have embodied themselves differently. Once there, it is "absurd" to suppose they can be somehow rescued or "amalgamated" with the rest of humanity[17]; "escape themselves they cannot."[18] This last is an especially revealing way of putting it: a prostitute can as easily escape being a prostitute as a frog can escape being a frog. It is only in fairy tales that frogs become princes or prostitutes respectable women.

But many Victorians, we know, not only believed in such fairy tales but worked to enact them. Gladstone's reclamation projects and Dickens's work at Urania House are best known; but such attempts to counter an essentialist model of the prostitute seem to have been fairly common. Behind much of this work was the liberal force of William Acton's *Prostitution* (1857), a hard-nosed argument on behalf of the reclaimable body. Rejecting out of hand the notion that prostitutes are commonly "recruited" or that they are "seduced" into the profession,[19] Acton refuses to tell his story as a moral fable. He understands that there is a way in which the prostitute has chosen her position and that, in a capitalist democracy, she has every right to do so: "we cannot but admit that a woman if so disposed may make a profit of her own person, and that the State has no right to prevent her" (p. x). But for Acton the issue cannot be understood in these narrow personalist terms. Prostitution he regards as a system, supported in part by a sexual desire that operates on an economy of balance: the more prostitutes there are available, the more desire there is. But it seems to Acton impractical and inhumane to attack the problem by attempting to interfere with this network of desire. The deeper motive force empowering the system he sees as economic: prostitutes do not in actuality choose their position but are "driven" to it "by cruel biting poverty" (p. 180). He proposes no broad solution to this problem, beyond that implied in the increased compassion or charity his Dickensian outrage might evoke. Rather, he suggests that measures be taken on behalf of the prostitute "to ameliorate her condition, so as to enable her to pass through this stage of her existence with as little permanent injury to herself and as little mischief to society as possible" (p. xi). For Acton, it is clear that "once a whore, always a whore" is absurd; for him, the body is healable, not just in theory but in plain fact: "the great mass of prostitutes in this country are in course of time absorbed into the so-called respectable classes" (p. xi).

The body, thus partially freed from essentialist moorings, was perhaps no better understood and no less threatening; but the dangers were not those of deterministic shacklings but of open uncertainty. This Actonian body could be changed, transformed, not simply reclaimed. We have trouble understanding this model, since the transforming of bodies has now solidified into various industries: fat farms, aerobics, plastic surgery, and a host of other grim manufactories. It is conceivable, though, that bodies, like any other construction, could be located within play. Bodies could be like ideas in Wilde: tossed in the air, transfigured, pulled out of hats.

Body-Centers

The question is how one could understand this new body. One answer was to propose a structure whose coherence is guaranteed by the authority of a center of some kind, a center which directs all other activities in the body and, most important, commands and secures our understanding. There were many candidates nominated for this position in the nineteenth century, it appears, each of whom advances a surprisingly all-inclusive program. The various centers, in other words, are quite distinct one from another. There are some trifling overlaps—nerve force may include magnetic energy; the blood may be energized with sperm—but mostly this election offers clear choices.

A. Nerve-Force Centers

The idea that the body was ruled by some kind of engine or dynamo came quite readily to an age fascinated by the machine and by such things as the "forces" in nature. "Energy of will—self-originating force—is the soul of every great character," said Samuel Smiles.[20] Great characters aside, these sort of macho nouns often butt their way into discourse on the body as "nerve force," "vital energy," "vital powers." Bodily growth, says one expert, "involves an expenditure of nerve-force—in other words, a drain upon the store accumulated in the masses of cells and networks of fibres of the central nervous organs." This nerve force actually forms new flesh and tissue: "it is this nerve-force sent down to the limb from the brain and spinal chord which presides over this molding."[21] The mention of brain and spinal chord suggests a complex nervous *system*, but the fuel both driving that system *and* produced by it is this amazing nerve force. Not just body molding is assigned to this power, but health as well. More exactly, ill health or death are caused by a lack of it. Infants die of what amounts to " 'old age,' i.e., of natural decline, a few weeks, months, or years after birth" because of *"a deficient original endowment of vital energy,"*[22] vital energy, we take it, being a mass-market version of nerve force.

The fact that this energy is often figured as a reservoir or a fixed supply makes it a useful model to employ against precocity of any kind and, we will not be surprised to see (in the next chapter more fully), against masturbation. Henry Clarke Wright quotes the following, quite orthodox letter from a masturbator: "The vice has gained upon me for several years, and has worn out my vital powers of body and soul. The essence of life has left me."[23] Lest the pathos of such a letter move us to self-righteous and gratuitous anger, let me insist that this model could also produce results we might call enlightened. Jacob Abbott, for instance, one of the most prolific writers of advice-for-parents manuals, used the model in his *Gentle Measures in the Management and Training of the Young* to present strong arguments against corporal punishment. Beating a child, he says, probably does indeed reinforce one's authority (and that is important), but it also can "shock the whole nervous system" and cause "excessive cerebral action," leading in turn to "derangements or actual disorganizations," which of course no one wants. He prefers gentle measures that "do not react in a violent and irritating manner, in any way, upon the extremely delicate, and almost embryonic condition of the central and nervous organizations, in which the gradual development of the mental and moral faculties are so intimately involved."[24] One can find good in every body-model.

Notice the slight readjustment in the model used by Abbott, where the simple notion of force or energy is replaced by a "central and nervous" organization. This pattern allowed for more complex thinking and also for the beginnings of a synergistic model. The nervous system was here often conceived of as a shifting, highly tuned, infinitely sensitive register of various stages of human development, altering to direct the growth of the body and adjusting itself, its "internal structure," as it went along.[25] Such is the interdependence of the components of this organization that "every part of the nervous system makes its influence felt by all the rest."[26] Doubtless this concept of a system which tingles throughout its many branches at the slightest jar to any fiber owes a great deal to the more primitive concept of force and to the demonstrations of popular physics, the action on a row of dominoes, for instance.

B. Chemical Centers

Some who found themselves attracted to the idea of vital power were not satisfied to build a factory, the nervous system, charged with producing such energy. Nothing would make them happy short of analyzing the secrets of that energy, the constitution of life itself, or at least the "life force." Since none of the writers pursuing this chemical heart of things seems to have been a chemist or at least to have been willing to be very specific about the sort of chemistry being studied, I will allow one example to serve: "In order that we may be able to grow and act, our bodies have in them a power, or 'force' called *chemical affinity* (affinity means *liking*, or one thing *preferring* another).... A very tiny chemical change, such as a very little more or less of any of its ingredients, may cause a complete change in the thing itself; and an enormous power lies in the *slightest chemical change*."[27] There you have it. We must not lose confidence in this centering just because the author speaks of elements and compounds as "ingredients" and their action together as "things"; this is probably an expert kindly adjusting downward a technical vocabulary for us. In any case, as far as the body is concerned, in chemistry we have all we know on earth and all we need to know: "The power of the body arises simply from the chemical changes that take place within it."[28]

C. Blood-Centers

"The blood is the life!" said Stoker's Count Dracula, who knew whereof he spoke. But that's not very interesting, apparently. It's not that the Count is perverse; it's that he's too conventional in announcing what is common knowledge and thus not worth printing. Blood is a center, but a dull one, providing wide-ranging but yawn-enforcing explanations: "in the organic world the blood or other nutrient fluids in animals, or the sap in vegetable life, is the material agency by which the conversion of potential into kinetic energy is maintained."[29] The business about maintaining the kinetic energy seems respectable, even if it's not clear that much kinetic energy is needed in "vegetable life." Generally, though, blood flows quietly.

D. Electro-Magnetic Centers

But not magnetism, or electricity, or any combination of the two. One enthusiast, Dr. Richard Shettle, Senior Physician at the Royal Berkshire Hospital and President of the Reading Pathological Society, not only found in magnetism a healing power (made available to all in his *Curative Magnetism*) but claimed for his subject the very life essence. "I have," he says on the cover of a published address, "been making some investigations on the blood, with the view of showing the precise nature of the force by which all the processes of animal life are kept up. When arterial blood circulates in the capillaries, there it has the properties of giving out or imparting to the texture a force which is none other than Electric and Magnetic." None other than that! Carried along by the blood, or perhaps somehow causing the blood to flow, these "currents of energy" have a very simple source: "every form of matter is permeated by the magnetic force of the earth." What this Electric and Magnetic ("for I believe the two forces cannot be separated," says Shettle) power does more specifically is to maintain the growth of tissue and monitor the balance between nutrition and waste.[30] It imparts all this "to the texture."

E. Brain-Centers

I am not sure why, but I find very few statements which seem to center the brain within the body. Perhaps, as with blood, the possibility is too insipid to invite comment. More likely, I think, the "mind" is still thought of as something other than the body, very possibly linked with or analogous to the body but not really an integral part of it. Writers who do situate controlling powers in the brain tend to be writers on sexuality, especially those striving to free the study of sexuality from biological determinism. Dr. Elizabeth Blackwell insisted in all her many writings that "a fundamental error as to the nature of human sex too often exists, from failure to recognise that it is even more a mental passion than a physical passion."[31] Krafft-Ebing located even radical sexual deviations in the mind: "as in all pathological perversions of the sexual life, the cause must be sought in the brain,"[32] a point echoed enthusiastically by Freud, who said that it was "precisely with the most repulsive perversions that the mental factor must be regarded as playing its largest part."[33] Somewhat ironically, it was these very writers on sex, so badgered and censored, who moved the study of the subject away from the genitals and into the head. Perhaps that is why their culture and our own have found them so threatening.

F. Sperm-Centers

We find more comfortable those we can ridicule, for instance those who did nothing more than connect the manifestly obvious role of semen in the creation of life with its maintenance. Even the most moderate of writers on the body considered this liquid "a highly vitalised fluid,"[34] "the most subtle and spiritous part of the human frame [which] serves to support the nerves"[35]—and some were willing to go further. For Davenport, it was "the very quintessence of life,"[36] a meager tribute compared with Samuel Butler's cheer-leading: "All our limbs and sensual organs, in fact our whole body and life, are but an accretion round and a fostering of the spermatozoa. They are the real 'He.' . . . They are the central fact in our existence, the point toward which all effort is directed."[37] One could hardly be more emphatic in asserting a core for a conceptual system.

It was a system that, whether widespread or not, certainly attracts our attention, especially when it is used to understand masturbation. Again anticipating the next chapter, I will glance at the subject here to suggest how visible such causal thinking may have been or at least how readily we are able to see it. The loss of semen, by way of masturbating, nocturnal emissions, and seepage, was sometimes thought to be more disastrous than massive bleeding. We read often that the draining of semen is equivalent to pouring out twenty or even forty times that much blood.[38] Such depletions could lead to a terrible disease, spermatorrhoea, or something even worse. Henry Verley's *The Curse of Manhood* employed a striking analogy from nature to drive home the peril: we do, he admits, take sap from maple trees; "but now, sirs, remember the cost to the maple-tree. It declines and dies."[39] And, just as the careless discarding of semen could lead to ill, so could the retention of it lead to bliss, or to vigor anyhow. According to Mary Wood-Allen, there seems to be no limit to the force one can gain by remaining continent, a fact a young boy especially needs to be taught: "he needs to know that Tennyson expressed scientific truth as well as poetry, when he wrote,

> 'My strength is as the strength of ten,
> Because my heart is pure.' "[40]

This is certainly an interesting gloss on the source of Galahad's strength and of his purity too.

In case we are wondering how Wood-Allen could call all this "scientific," we might turn to the accounts of the research of one Dr. Brown-Sequard. Not content with theories alone, Dr. Brown-Sequard made experiments upon himself to check out the claims for the virtues of seminal retention. Injecting himself with "an infusion freshly made from the sexual glands of a rabbit" (we need not ask why a rabbit was his animal of choice), he "found a notable increase in strength," not simply of "muscular strength" either "but of general vigor and vitality." Given that Dr. Brown-Sequard was eighty years of age, such results are no small potatoes. Waving aside as the issue of "careless methods" the many related experiments that had produced "negative results," Dr. Brown-Sequard could point to his unmistakably "increased intellectual vigor" and to the fact that problems with which he had been "greatly troubled," namely, "inactivity of the bowels," had disappeared with the rabbit-gland injection and that now "both mechanical and medicinal means for aiding the bowels were entirely unnecessary."[41] Just what Tennyson had in mind.

Before leaving the wilds of masturbation, it is worth considering a statement of Davenport's that may be simply devilish but that may speak earnestly to this sperm-center: "the best medical authorities are of the opinion that the retention of the seminal fluid is liable to very serious ends."[42] The retention model does indeed conflict with several popular Victorian ideas, most notably that connected to exercise. Retention also activates the censure against hoarding, the fierce cultural detestation of the miser, of anal collecting, of dust-piles and Silas Marner and Fagin, the last suggesting a "racial" fear as well. And celibacy, especially for males, was too closely connected to Roman Catholicism to be untainted. The spermatic center, in other words, insofar as there was such a center, was bubbling with conflict, busying itself in undermining its major supports.

G. Sex-Centers

Clearly related to other model-building, but somewhat more abstract is the apparent tendency here and there not simply to center the body in sex but to identify the two. Acton is not the only writer to understand humans in terms of "their threefold organization of body, mind, and spirit" or to see the dominance of the first over the other two as the triumph of lust.[43] Deslandes attributes to sex the power to touch balefully all other parts of the body: "The influence of the genital organs is so great, and extends so perfectly to all parts of the organism, that the slightest morbid disposition of the latter is favored by its action."[44] The sentence does not wind up where one thinks it will, but it seems to be arguing for a terrifying causality, one which proceeds directly from the centering of the "genital organs" to their misuses and to a long list of miseries, including tumors, consumption, apoplexy, blindness, St Vitus' Dance, diseases of the spinal marrow, and brain ailments.

On which cheering chord we leave this survey of the "centered" body, noting only that the sight of so many candidates in an unseemly scramble for the top job has a way of calling attention away from the candidates and to the job itself. It might even make one wonder whether we really need a person in that slot, whether, when you come right down to it, the slot itself is all that essential. Maybe the body can do very well undirected.

The Body That Runs Itself

There is nothing natural about the notion that the body should have some controlling agency. Even if we think of the body as "functioning" in the way a state functions, there is no reason to conceive of that state as autocratic. Cooperative or socialist models are available to us, and anarchy is an inviting possibility. In fact, we can often locate in this Victorian discourse a good many contradictory patterns, not so much competing with one another as bouncing along side by side in an incoherent game. The body can be the field for such play, presenting itself to us in the hierarchical, ordered forms we have just outlined; in more haphazard shapes, where boundaries can be transgressed or erased; or as self-enclosed units that invite us to play *with* and not *on*, as a toy rather than a field. The body-as-toy concept isn't common, I expect, outside of certain forms of pornography we construe as reprehensible. But the self-sufficient body has been around for some time, certainly since the last century, when it was common to talk about it as a machine or organism that worked (or should work) with self-regulating precision, with timely cooperation among its members.

Thus we find frequent reference to the "harmonious" body, each part, as in a madrigal, coming in on tune and on schedule: "And not only should all his powers be developed, but they should be developed harmoniously, and at the proper time."[45] Such a conception of the body is quickly attributed to nature, such harmonies as the writer finds pleasing being called "natural": "The stages of evolution, in its different organs, take place in regular succession;—no power, no capacity, outstrips another.... Every period of its progress to maturity comes on in a *natural* and gradual manner."[46] This image of nature's mellifluous unity often controls the idea of what the home and family should be:

> Home neglects no faculty whatever. It works upon all. It keeps each in its proper place. It supplies what they all require. There is nothing congenial from which it bids any of them keep aloof. It balances one

by another. It promotes the harmonious cooperation of the whole; and it thus produces a perfectly developed child.[47]

Though with a style less hammering, Thomas Arnold conceived of the ideal Church similarly: "The true church of Christ would offer to every faculty of our nature its proper exercise, and would entirely meet all our wants."[48] All that is wanted by and for the body is patience, understanding, and some occasional balancing—not much. It works very well by itself. It requires only that one not get inside and bumble with the delicate workings and that one not make demands on it that are unreasonable.

But it seems that we *will* meddle, and make unreasonable demands, forgetting what Spencer said about the fair but strict accounting which the body keeps: "if you demand of her in one direction more than she is prepared to lay out, she balances the account by making a deduction elsewhere."[49] And we can be sure the deductions will show up just where we can least afford them. These dilemmas are what we most often hear about: "A love of appetite established in one direction will be hard to restrain in others."[50] This song that is the body is forever being thrown into discord, a point I will postpone examining for a moment so as to consider how the unity of this harmonious body was also a shifting, *developing* unity.

As applied to the child, this model of development helped mold at least one thick strand of popular thinking. Froebel conceived of his kindergarten as reproducing natural development: "Therefore, in actual fact, the bodily development of each one of us is in some measure an enormously compressed abridgement, a quick recapitulation of the creation of the higher vertebrate animals in its various stages. Is it not true, then, that the purely physical development of man from the simple to the complex, from the lower to the higher, is 'an exhaustive representation of true education'?"[51] All this seems very well, though it is worth noting also that this evolutionary concept of development did not seem to deny the child's body access to sexuality. It is not clear that any developmental model would do so, without some pretty heavy tinkering.

The tinkering we have done shows through most clearly in reference to our manipulations of the body's relationships to exercise. Exercise would seem to be akin to "practice" and thus a perfect accompaniment to a harmonious and happy body. To a certain extent it is: we teach children to use the body in order to help it get stronger, keep it "in shape," allow it to develop "naturally." The natural economy of the body, by this reasoning, depends on nourishing the supply by keeping up the demand. But there are certain parts of the body we do not want developing naturally, that are therefore declared exceptions to the exercise rule. We have been known to go even further, to maintain that exercise directed elsewhere, to the legs and the lungs, say, will actually help block any temptation to work out on other parts: "In order to postpone the advent of uncontrollable sexual desire in the young, there should be an absence of exciting thoughts and temptations throughout early life; and in their place a systematic use of mental and physical exercise."[52] Since the exercise which was enforced seems usually not to have been mental, all this had the effect of substituting the locker room for the bedroom, a logic and practice we retain.

Exercise did not always serve a fear of the body's uncontrolled desires, of course. Mandatory physical activity fed directly into the cult of body worshipping, which was (and is) not seldom erotic, to drooling after athletes, and also to a pattern of moderation and temperance quite at odds with the manic, all-or-nothing models of sexuality we have been discussing. Many felt that exercise, like almost everything in life, should be taken "with great moderation," that excess of anything might be damaging to the body.[53] Even "playing the flute, blowing the bugle, or any other wind instrument," said Chavasse, could be "decidedly injurious to the health" of a child, since "the lungs and the windpipe are brought into unnatural action by them."[54] The longest section of Dukes's *Preservation of Health* is entitled "Temperance," a term he applies to moderate exercise of the organs (he does not say which ones), exercise that will apparently limber things up without draining, shocking, or exhausting.[55]

So, the harmonious model of body development that counters the solo or autocratic one is modified, riddled with contradictions, perforated by inviting gaps for play. This form of the body, finally, is no more coherent than any other, and we say that even before we introduce the "mind," which may be separate from the body, part of it, or linked by ingenious analogy.

Minding the Body

"The union between the physical, moral, and intellectual elements of our nature cannot be dissolved during our lifetime," announced Elizabeth Blackwell.[56] Many writers on the body might not think to tie the "moral" so explicitly into this union, but otherwise this view seems orthodox. It finds its way into fiction: in *Persuasion*, Captain Harville says, "I believe in a true analogy between our bodily frames and our mental; and that as our bodies are the strongest, so are our feelings."[57] His argument is directed, however playfully, toward proving the superiority of men; but he does see an untroubled cooperation between mind and body. So do a few other writers, among them the author (anonymous) of *Youth and True Manhood in the Highest and Best Sense*, a surprisingly upbeat tract, given its dire talk about "the Snares and Pitfalls of Youth and Manhood": "all that tends to strengthen and develop the muscular portion of their body also helps the development of their mental qualities."[58] So long as the argument soars along at this level, no one gets hurt.

The difficulties begin when we get to specifics or when we remember that all this strengthening and developing is not unproblematic, that we don't really desire development across the board. The unpredictable Drysdale hits at the heart of the problem. "The mind and the body," he says, "are inseparably linked together, so that the health and happiness of the one involves that of the other."[59] So far, so good. In the very next sentence, however, he turns away from health and happiness: "every imperfect moral [i.e., mental] state, at once reacts on the body." And that is just the start of our distress. We jump right into the problem of excessive development: "In consequence of this intimate connection between the mind and body, we cannot doubt that mental labour calls into action some organ, and that if continued for a great length of time, it will fatigue, and may injure this organ."[60] Depending to some extent on what the organ is, such a linkage can be troublesome. It is all very well, then, to urge that someone facing a potentially injurious bodily urge "keep the mind well occupied,"[61] but what if the occupation of the mind is the problem in the first place?

What if the development of the mind, which sounded fine when it was linked with the development of biceps, has so little sense that it proceeds to link up with just those organs we were eager to keep quiescent? What if there is even a tie between intelligence and the temptation to vice? "Intellectual boys," says the author of *What a Young Boy Ought to Know* (whether he wants to or not), "because of a more highly wrought nervous organization and because of keener sensibilities, are much more liable to become addicted to this vice [guess which one] than boys of a lower grade of intellect and with less sensitive bodies."[62] This locates the central predicament; but there are others, equally familiar in our own culture. One is the fear that the mind-body union will leave the young person unprotected against the powers of inflaming ideas, that mental productions of the imagination, fed through print, will find their way to the body. "Young people in America," frets Julia Ward Howe, "read so much and so miscellaneously that they will be apt to come often in contact with the misleading sort of romance which I have in mind."[63] This suggests yet another fearful consequence of the mind-body model, one which invests its worries not just in the imaginative faculty but, more directly, in the eye: "This mysterious [sexual] instinct develops earlier in proportion as the eye and the imagination are soonest furnished the materials upon which it thrives, and long before the age of puberty it is strong and well-nigh ungovernable in those who have been allowed these unfortunate occasions."[64] The notion that the mind and body are joined by some directly proportional ratios of growth, then, not only does not guard against perils but may be the source of them.

Things are not much better, though they are certainly different, in models which abandon the metaphor of harmony and cooperation between mind and body for one of warfare or inverse proportions. Here, whatever acts to the good of one agency weakens the other. "It is folly," says Albutt, "to cultivate the brain at the expense of the body."[65] Samuel Smiles's agreement is so deep it looks almost like plagiarism but is probably just reiteration of a cultural commonplace: "The brain is cultivated at the expense of the members, and the physical is usually found in an inverse ratio to the intellectual appetite."[66] These "inverse ratios" suggest that mental and physical development or activity should occur in some kind of balanced distribution or, more likely, alternately, first one and then the other. It is clear, in any case, that this model does not make it easy to do two things at once, not if one is cerebral and the other corporeal: "if the brain sets to work hard just as the stomach is digesting, the blood rushes fast into the brain and leaves the stomach with too little blood. This stops the digestion, and makes all go wrong with the stomach and the parts connected with it."[67] It is no laughing matter to have all go wrong with the stomach and connected parts; but it is perhaps no worse than the case cited by Davenport of the celebrated mathematician whose interest in his work made all go wrong sexually:

> The interval of time which occurred between the commencement of his labour of love [with his attractive wife] and the end was always sufficiently long to allow his mind, which had for a moment been abstracted by his pleasure, to be brought back to the constant objects of his meditation—that is, to geometrical problems and algebraic formulae. At the very moment even of orgasm, the intellectual powers resumed their empire and all genital sensation vanished.[68]

Once mind and body are linked, then, such hazards are born as to make it nearly a matter of indifference whether the linkage is harmonious or hostile, in direct or inverse ratios. Especially with the developing child, we must be wary not only lest the mind or body perish from too little food but luxuriate dangerously from too much. What is sure to strike us most forcibly in advice manuals and home medical guides is the emphasis on the latter.

The Precocious Brat

The Young Wife's Own Book put it most calmly: the mother "must remember that early development of body or mind is a thing not to be desired."[69] Thomas Arnold, in his more robust way, called this thing, "a thing to be deprecated," and Rhoda White in her *Book of Instructions for Young Mothers* did not hesitate to name the thing "a dangerous thing."[70] Even Spencer, writing to promote education, agreed on "the dangers of over-education during youth."[71] It is common to attribute much of this fearful chorus against precocity to Rousseau and the passage in the *Confessions* where he speaks of his reading as a "dangerous method" for inciting "passions peculiar at my age" before he had the power to control or even to understand them.[72] Doubtless such an attribution is cogent, but another way of figuring the culture and its apparent interest in precocity is to see the matter as embedded in the body-models available to them. These models, by the way, made all forms of precocity dangerous, not just sexual quickness, though it does seem that some writers emphasized the sexual. At least that's what *we* tend to see in this discourse.

In any case, warnings against any kind of precocity seem to have been widespread and to have received the backing of some strident rhetoric. The gentlest line was that what we saw in the child was reversed in the adult: "it is the dull child that usually becomes a bright man; the bright child too often becomes a fool."[73] There were worse things than foolishness ahead for children allowed to be precocious: "inflammation, and either convulsions, or water on the brain, or insanity"[74] were on the horizon, a forecast on which there was considerable agreement: "water in the head, diseases of the brain, and frequently idiotcy [sic]."[75]

Explanations for this often cited "the radical difference between the youthful and adult nature," claiming that the child's brain, like every other part, became more easily tired and, when tired, could be strained by continued use. "The over-taxed brain," Dr. Blackwell continues sarcastically, "cannot be righted by boating and cricketing."[76] For many, it could not be righted at all. Chavasse tells the sad story of Henry Kirke White, precocious of course, who died at 21 from overwork of the brain, as did Lucretia Maria Davidson at a similarly early age. "If," he says, "an over-worked precocious brain does not cause the death of the owner, it, in too many cases, injures the brain irreparably."[77] Death is to be preferred.

Those who find nothing more in precocity than the dangers of overwork, however, seem myopic to those who connect it to disease, either as symptom or cause. Here are some experts: "Children who are prodigies in learning, music, and other pursuits, are generally destroyed by premature disease in the brain"; "premature and luxuriant growth of mind will seldom, if ever, be found to spring from a vigorous root; it is, indeed, a species of disease"; "some children . . . are stimulated and urged into all sorts of unnatural mental exertion, until the poor little brain which, from its very activity, requires all possible strengthening, becomes diseased, the body is enfeebled, and the precocious child becomes the stultified and stupid adult, if indeed life is spared to it."[78] It is true that this disease is seldom given very specific features. Some attribute what is *"the tomb of their talents and of their health"* to a misappropriation of energies: *"the most noble part of the vital force is withdrawn from perfecting the organization, and is consumed by the act of thought."*[79] That provides some explanatory force, I suppose, but not much. When we get more detailed expositions, they tend to look to us not at all like science but like a series of assertions, disguised only slightly by some high-sounding hokum about "the fibers of the nerves" or "the internal fibers of the brain." The following example is very long, but I quote it in full, since I think its very length and tedium are part of the machinery of authority being cranked up here to hornswoggle the reader:

> The act of attention, or work of the mind, is accompanied by a discharge of force from the masses of cells in which it accumulates, quite analogous to that involved in the movement of the limbs. Only, this force, instead of passing externally along the nerves to muscles, is discharged along the internal fibres of the brain. This internal expenditure of force causes really more fatigue than does the external expenditure; in other words, mental activity is relatively more fatiguing than muscular action. It is so even in the adult; but still more in the child, from the fact we have so many times insisted upon, namely, that the fibres of the nerves are well developed, and able, therefore, to transmit impressions with facility; but the internal fibres of the

brain are imperfectly developed, and the work of transmission of impressions along them is, therefore, more burdensome.[80]

This is the rhetoric of absolute certainty: a series of facts, related in confident declarations—A "is" B—leading, "therefore," to a conclusion that no one would question. I do not mean to suggest that we do any better or any different. It is just that here, as elsewhere, such rhetorical bullying reveals more openly than usual that something other than the demands of science and truth are at work, that we need to have all this said in this way because we need to believe it and to have it confirmed. We require reasons for fearing and reviling the precocious child, reasons perhaps having to do with jealousy and neurotic demands and deep longing; but we can scarcely even pretend that they spring from the requirements of "truth," whatever that may be.

But if we need this kind of talk, the child likely does not; nor is it the only kind of talk around. There are voices from the past that counter any monotone we may try to record. Mrs. Child's *Mother's Book* told its readers that they were doing "an immense deal of good" by exercising the brains of infants and children, thus "giving their minds active habits." These little ones, she says, should be told that "the more knowledge you gain, the more useful you can be." She concludes, "if the mental faculties are kept vigorous by constant use, they will excel in anything to which their strength is applied."[81] No mention of exhaustion, of drawing vital force away from other organs, of water in the head or "idiotcy"; just a placid, if grim, recommendation for prodding children into "constant use" of their brains. Even some of the books on or for schoolboys suggest that the worries about precocity have been exaggerated and that a little more work wouldn't hurt: "Dull boys, so far as my experience goes, are generally made by all play and no work."[82] Even Thomas Arnold, no special friend to the precocious, felt that the duty of the teacher was "to hasten growth."[83] And many who deplored precocity nonetheless saw it as often inevitable: "Its mind has opened prematurely and unwholesomely, no doubt; but the action of it cannot be ignored. The modern mother's business must be to train, as best she can, a growth which it is impossible to check."[84] When things have come to be regarded as "sad but true," they are on their way to being celebrated, just around the corner from modern programs for the "talented and gifted" child, the child everyone wants to have and an alarming number do. But things are not so simple: Victorian views, even when sanded down to fit nicely into a subsection of a chapter, are anything but uniform and uncontradictory; and we still live with a marked dislike for the very precocity that is celebrated, a strong even if sneaking aversion to the self-assured, knowing child, the brat.

When we look squarely at the issue of sexual precocity for the Victorians, we are unlikely to notice a lot of difference from our own views, much less a primitive base from which we have progressed. Elizabeth Blackwell, often the most sensible-sounding of Victorian medical writers, argues that in the orderly processes of bodily development, sexual development has a natural place, a place that should not be artificially advanced: "if the faculty which is bestowed as the last work of development, that which requires the longest time, and the most careful preparation for its advent—the sexual power—be brought forward prematurely, a permanent injury is done to the individual which can never be completely repaired."[85] The only fault many of us would find with Blackwell's arguments, arbitrary though they may be, is that she bothers to argue at all on a point which we would like to regard as beyond contestation. The Victorians tend to make us uncomfortable by talking so much on the subject of child sexual precocity, and especially when they ladle into their talk embarrassing bits of folklore we imagine we have outgrown. T.L. Nichols is not, like Blackwell, a soothing and reasonable voice from the past; and he is nowhere more annoying than when he throws the full force of his ignorance into agreeing with us:

> It would be well if children had no sensation and no idea of sex. Unfortunately, the exciting and diseasing habits of civilization tend to produce an unhealthy precocity in the young of both sexes. Children either fall into habits of solitary vice—from hereditary predisposition or a stimulating diet,—or they are taught libidinous and destructive practices by ignorant or unprincipled servants, or companions or schoolfellows who have been in some way corrupted.[86]

We would love to think too that it would be well if there were no child sexuality, and it would be comforting to blame what we cannot but admit exists on the diseasing effects of our culture or on somebody else who was unprincipled or in some way corrupted, never mind how. But we don't want Nichols, who seems to believe masturbation is induced by eating pepper, on our side. He threatens not so much to lose the game for us as to expose the rules by which we are playing.

One of the regulations clumsily bared by Nichols is a class rule, the notion, which we will give more time to later, that children of the urban lower class, children of the street, are so commonly precocious that it is foolish to speak of their innocence: "it is part of a street-bred child's precocity that he acquires a too early acquaintance with matters which, as a child, he ought not to know about."[87] There is suggested here too a notion that probably would not bear scrutiny: that simply knowing about sex will make the child not only eager but able to do it. No doubt such views are often held, but we usually hear them spoken openly only by writers of child-pornography—"Mona's puberty of course followed very rapidly on these excitements"[88]—and Sigmund Freud—"A neurotic wife who is unsatisfied by her husband is, as a mother, over-tender and over-anxious towards her child, on to whom she transfers her need for love; and she awakens it to sexual precocity."[89] We may find quaint the biological models used here, but there are at least two others, crucial to thinking about the body and about the child, that we moderns have drawn out from the Victorian past and cozied up to happily: puberty and latency.

Puberty and the Body Transformed

The creation of puberty seems to have solved a good many problems. It provided a means for preserving childhood innocence, more important childhood difference and childhood emptiness. It showed how the child could be considered a separate species without violating utterly the metaphor of "development": one simply posited that puberty marked the moment of metamorphosis, where the child was recast as an adult.

Puberty was often figured as suddenness, as "revolution," an abrupt re-formation of the body: "A complete revolution is effected in the human economy at the age of puberty; the bones harden, the constitution becomes strong and vigorous . . . and many diseases . . . disappear. The brain becomes developed, the intellectual functions are augmented."[90] At this point, "genital organs suddenly and astonishingly develop" and "sexual desires are awakened."[91] This great awakening is not ordinarily described so graphically, with genital organs blossoming overnight; but perhaps that lies beneath more poetic descriptions:

> As [they] approach the height of maturity, they pass through the mysterious land of the "Teens," at the gateway of which is conferred upon them the gift of creative power. This gift is accompanied with the wonderful unfolding of powers, physical, mental and moral. The body develops into greater beauty and perfection; new avenues of thought are opened. . . .[92]

The door closes forever on childhood.

It is almost a pity to complicate this neat picture by saying that what we take to be modern notions of puberty as a gradual and progressive development were common in the last century as well. Mrs. Child spoke of puberty as occupying "the period from twelve to sixteen years of age," and Krafft-Ebing saw puberty not as a jack-and-the-beanstalk growth but as the slow development of hitherto "vague and undefined" "impulses of youth" into "conscious realization of sexual power."[93]

Gradual or sudden, though, puberty carried with it serious consequences, most of them grave. The pressures exerted by these astonishing new organs is so great, in fact, that, whether we like it or not, "it is well known that rigid continence is seldom observed about the age of puberty."[94] Not everyone will admit anything of the sort, but the fact that a conservative writer could so throw in the towel suggests that this form of "puberty," so handy in some ways, could also be a monster. By acting as a dam, holding back utterly the sexual powers, puberty also had to take on the responsibility for releasing all that pent-up pressure. Puberty-as-flood became an awesome catastrophe, the invasion of sexual need and interest: "But it is particularly before and during puberty that these [sexual] organs deserve the most serious attention, for then they possess the most power."[95] If sexuality is strongest at puberty, declining thereafter, what does that suggest about nature's plan for reproduction? Such a rhythm does not accord particularly well with the idea that the body develops according to the needs of our culture and in everybody's best interests. We do not, after all, want people reproducing at 11 or 12 years of age.

And there are, of course, many other problems with puberty as a construction used both to explain and to control sexuality, problems pointed out by Kinsey, who argued that in many cases there was a steady progress from child sex play to adult sexuality, and by Freud, who said puberty simply gave "infantile sexual life its final, normal shape."[96] Freud called the idea that puberty suddenly let loose a torrent of sexuality hitherto unknown "a gross error."[97] The model served so very well, however, to preserve what we needed in this necessary construction of the "child" that it still maintains almost unchallenged authority. Freud's efforts to modify our understanding of the body so as to make puberty less catastrophic, less absolutely determinate seem to have failed. Kinsey's even calmer voice has been displaced, made marginal by a chorus of ridicule succeeded by a conspiracy of silence. But it was Kinsey's proposal of an unbroken line from child to adult that really would have threatened the catastrophic puberty model and perhaps given us a way to think of the child that didn't put it on the far side of a barricade. Freud, after all, proposed nothing so radical, settling instead for the culturally conservative model of latency.

The Latent Body

Freud did not invent the idea of the body hibernating during a period of sexual latency. He lazily picked it up and tacked it onto a scheme where it made very little sense, far less sense than it had previously. If children are somehow figured so as to be missing completely sexual feelings or instincts, it doesn't require any special concept of latency to explain what is going on with their bodies sexually. Nothing is going on. Still, a few Victorian writers did use the term, probably to help explain how street children could do as they did. Blackwell said sexual feelings in the child "are entirely latent," a point emphasized also by Krafft-Ebing, who suggests that latency is synonymous with "sexual neutrality," in the sense of genderless or, more exactly, sexless.[98] Mary Wood-Allen gave voice to the parallel term nearest to hand: before puberty, she said, "your reproductive organs have been asleep."[99]

Such notions are repeated today in the breezy writings of orthodox Freudians everywhere: "With the passing of the Oedipus complex, the period of latency is ushered in."[100] After such an enthusiastic sexualizing of infancy, Freud's slide back into this way of thinking and this terminology must seem surprising—or it would if we did not need what he has to say so badly. Latency, after all, does not so much render the connection between sex and the child unthinkable as make it necessary to think about it. The latent body is being controlled by sexual energies, working beneath the surface perhaps but directing the progress of the creature. After infancy, Freud says, the activity of sexual forces continues, but "their energy is diverted, wholly or in great part, from their sexual use and directed to other ends."[101] Latency is an erotic term, an erotic projection onto the body of the child that renders that child fully an object of sexual forces, forces that operate deeply in and through the child and manifest themselves in any and all directions: thus, while no activities are *really* sexual, there are no activities which are really *not* sexual either. Of course these sexual forces are not in any sense exercised *by* the child. Latency is not, Freud insists, a matter of cultural training or education; children are not *taught* latency. It is what they *are*, "organically determined and fixed by heredity."[102] Just so, we have constructed this organic determination and are prepared to fight for it.

And there *is* an enemy, certainly, a large number of voices raised in protest against the very idea of latency. Kinsey was probably the first to assault the idea head-on, saying that, Freud and his followers to the contrary, pre-adolescents knew a thing or two and put those things into pretty general practice and, further, that such sexual inactivity as did exist in children was certainly not "organically determined and fixed by heredity," but simply "imposed by the culture upon the sociosexual activities of the maturing child."[103] Some have followed Kinsey, particularly those engaged in empirical studies; Constantine and Martinson's recent *Children and Sex* turns over an entire section to writers eager to bombard it, and there are others arguing with a mixture of anger and bemused resignation that latency simply does not exist.[104]

But none of that matters a pin: we must have the idea and the word. "Latency" evacuates the child and also invests it with precisely the agency being kicked out. It is a revolving door, causing to enter on one side what is leaving by the other. Actually they are the same side, what leaves is what enters and at just the same place; the exiting and the entering are the same; the bouncer is the hostess. "Latency" is not so much double-edged as happily deconstructed.

The word "latency" grows from the notion of lateness—some agency sneaking into the room (or into the body) after the meeting has been going on for some time. That doesn't fit the Freudian model directly; for him, sexuality is not made to enter where it was not but to leave where it was. But things are not so simple: latency, the forcible eviction of sexuality from the child's body, calls so much attention to itself, we might say, that the child is inevitably sexualized. Dragged screaming from the room, sexuality leaves behind more than traces; it marks the body indelibly as "open," invites to it attention that can hardly be other than sexual.

And we have just begun with "latency," which may originate with this image of lateness but which carries within it also the possibility that the latent agent has been present all along but has managed to remain unnoticed, slouching in the back row of the meeting snoozing or silent. This fits Freud's model a little better, though still not very well, since it is not clear what puts sexuality to sleep (since it was fully awake during infancy) or why it can't wake up after a short nap.

More subversive still is the meaning embedded in "latency" that, while what is present may not be active now, it is fully alert, concealing itself and biding its time. This possibility of disguise opens the door for the fully subversive suggestion, developed especially in the medical meaning of latency, that the agency is not only present but active and centrally active. It simply disguises its activities, artfully making them appear as something else, just as a latent disease, masking itself as an absence, puts forward the symptoms of another disease that actually isn't there. Such sneakiness certainly bears no resemblance to the comforting idea of sublimation. There sexual energies were diverted to other ends; here they only pretend to be. Here there are no other ends: the body is fully sexualized.

Sexual latency, thus, figures the body in terms of an absence that is also a presence, a benign non-activity that is also on a rabid terrorist campaign. The body of the child, protected by these means from internal and external agencies of sexuality, at least before the age of puberty, finds itself exposed by the same means. The curtains that were meant to veil become props for a theatrical staging, fall away during the strip tease. The reading of the child's body in our culture is invaded by a code, provided by sex. To say such a thing doesn't suggest that the body is any different from the mind, soul, or spirit; or that the child is any different in this regard from the rest of us. We are all in the same boat on this particular voyage; we all have the same difficulties locating any charts, maps or pilot. We have been told, though, that they are all below deck, far below deck.

Notes

1. Willich, *Lectures on Diet and Regimen*, p. 26. Subsequent references will be cited in the text.

2. Weeks, *Sex, Politics*, p. 10

3. Foucault, *History of Sexuality*, p. 98.

4. See, for example, Jeanne L. Brand, *Doctors and the State: The British Medical Profession and Government Action in Public Health, 1870–1912* (Baltimore: The Johns Hopkins Univ. Press, 1965).

5. Bateson, *Steps to an Ecology*, p. 433.

6. Mrs. Bray, *Elements of Morality in Easy Lessons*, p. 1.

7. Spencer, *Education*, p. 179.

8. Edward Carpenter, *The Intermediate Sex: A Study of Some Transitional Types of Men and Women*, 2nd ed. (London: Swan Sonnenschein, 1909), p. 93.

9. Freud, "On The Sexual Theories of Children," IX, 211–12.

10. Ellice Hopkins, *On The Early Training*, pp. 20, 23. See also William H. Walling, *Sexology* (Philadelphia: Puritan Publishing, 1902). Walling is adamant about the necessity for "the early isolation of the sexes" (p. 27). He is, however, writing very late, as an American, and for a publishing company that seems tied to a particular point of view. I have not studied closely this issue of distinguishing children by gender, but it is my impression that it becomes an issue primarily on this side of the Atlantic and in this century.

11. See Gorham, *The Victorian Girl*, pp. 68–83.

12. Ellis, *Studies in the Psychology of Sex*, IV, 124–5.

13. Nichols, *Esoteric Anthropology*, p. 42

14. See especially Paul McHugh, *Prostitution and Victorian Social Reform* (New York: St. Martin's Press, 1980) and Judith R. Walkowitz, *Prostitution and Victorian Society: Women, Class, and the State* (Cambridge, Cambridge Univ. Press, 1980).

15. See James Beard Talbot, *The Miseries of Prostitution*, 3rd ed. (London: J. Madden, 1844), p. 43.

16. See Ralph Wardlaw, *Lectures on Female Prostitution: Its Nature, Extent, Effects, Guilt, Causes, and Remedy* (Glasgow: J. Maclehose, 1842), pp. 15–16; and William Tait, *Magdalenism: An Inquiry into the Extent, Causes, and Consequences of Prostitution in Edinburgh*, 2nd ed. (Edinburgh: P. Rickard, 1842), p. 45.

17. William Logan, *The Great Social Evil*, p. 104.

18. W.R. Greg, *The Great Sin of Great Cities*, rpt. from *Westminster & Foreign Quarterly Review*, July 1850 (London: John Chapman, 1853), p. 8.

19. Their first sexual experiences are, he says, with boys their own age, fully consensual, and simply the "all but natural consequences of promiscuous herding" springing from the horrid conditions in which they are raised. I am quoting from the second edition (1870), pp. 295–96. Further references will be given in the text by page number.

20. Smiles, *Character*, p. 15.

21. Mary Putnam-Jacobi, "The Nervous Diseases of Infancy and Childhood," in Frederick A. Castle, ed., *Wood's Household Practice of Medicine, Hygiene and Surgery: A Practical Treatise for the Use of Families, Travellers, Seamen, Miners, and Others* (London: Sampson, Low, Marston, Searle, and Rivington, 1881), I, 542.

22. Henry Hartshorne, "Disease: Its Nature, Causes, and Manifestations," in Castle, ed., *Wood's Household Practice*, I, 287. Bullough traces the idea that "all diseases could be reduced to one basic causal model, either the diminution or increase of nervous energy" to the late eighteenth-century Edinburgh scientist John Brown; see *Sexual Variance*, p. 542

23. Henry Clark Wright, *Marriage and Parentage; or, The Reproductive Element in Man as a Means to His Elevation and Happiness*, 2nd ed. (Boston: B. March, 1855), p. 79.

24. Jacob Abbott, *Gentle Measures in the Management and Training of the Young; or, The Principles on which a Firm Parental Authority May Be Established and Maintained, Without Violence or Anger, and the Right Development of the Moral and Mental Capabilities Be Promoted by Methods in Harmony with the Structure and Characteristics of the Juvenile Mind* (New York: Harper and Brothers, 1872), pp. 17, 18, 25.

25. Putnam-Jacobi, "Nervous Diseases," in Castle, ed., *Wood's Household Practice*, I, 536.

26. Mrs. Hilton Dothie, *Health in the Home* (Greenock: Orr, Pollock, and Co., 1886), p. 21.

27. Dothie, *Health in the Home*, p. 15.

28. Dothie, *Health in the Home*, p. 16.

29. R.C. Shettle, *Address Delivered at the Annual Meeting of the Reading Pathological Society on September 11th, 1889* (Reading: J.J. Beecroft, 1889), p. 6. See also Ben

Barker-Benfield, "The Spermatic Economy: A Nineteenth-Century View of Sexuality," *Feminist Studies* 1 (1972): 49. Barker-Benfield relates the ancient belief in blood as life to the masturbation taboo.

30. Shettle, *Address*, pp. 1, 11, 14, 12.

31. Blackwell, *The Human Element in Sex*, p. 15.

32. Krafft-Ebing, *Psychopathia Sexualis*, p. 222.

33. Freud, "Three Essays," VII, 161.

34. Blackwell, *The Human Element in Sex*, p. 23.

35. Wllich, *Lectures on Diet and Regimen*, p. 539.

36. Davenport, *Curiositates*, p. 44.

37. Samuel Butler, *The Notebooks of Samuel Butler*, ed. Henry Festing Jones (London: A.C. Fifield, 1912), p. 17.

38. The source may be Tissot, but the figures are widely repeated. See, for example, Davenport, *Curiositates*, p. 138 and Willich, *Lectures on Diet and Regimen*, p. 539. Davenport, who cites Buffon for the terrifying 40-factor, clearly has his own subversive reasons for hustling aboard this particular bandwagon.

39. Henry Verley, *The Curse of Manhood, Containing Invaluable Information for Young Men and All Those Who Are Married, A Lecture to Men in Exeter Hall, London* (London: n.p., 1887), p. 7. See Bullough, *Sexual Variance*, pp. 78–79, for speculation on the origins of this fear of semen loss in the Judaic tradition.

40. Mary Wood-Allen, "Moral Education of the Young," in Powell, ed., *National Purity Congress Papers*, p. 234.

41. J.H. Kellogg, "Chastity and Health," in Powell, ed., *National Purity Congress Papers*, pp. 259–60.

42. Davenport, *Curiositates*, p. 67

43. See Acton, *Prostitution*, pp. 162–63.

44. L. Deslandes, *Manhood: The Causes of Its Premature Decline, with Directions for Its Restoration: Addressed to Those Suffering from the Destructive Effects of Excessive Indulgence, Solitary Habits, Etc., Etc., Etc.*, trans. "with many additions" by "an American physician" (Boston: Otis, Broaders and Co., 1843), p. 70.

45. Amariah Brigham, *Remarks on the Influence of Mental Cultivation and Mental Excitement upon Health*, notes by Robert Macnish, 6th ed. (London: A.K. Newman, 1844), p. viii.

46. Willich, *Lectures on Diet and Regimen*, p. 89.

47. Anon., *The Children's Wrong*, p. 15.

48. Arnold, *Christian Life*, p. lvi.

49. Spencer, *Education*, p. 179.

50. Mrs. J. H. Kellogg, "Purity and Parental Responsibility," in Powell, ed., *National Purity Congress Papers*, p. 221.

51. Froebel, *The Kindergarten*, p. 7.

52. Dukes, *Preservation of Health*, p. 145. See also Wood-Allen "Moral Education of the Young," in Powell, ed., *National Purity Congress Papers*, p. 235, and, on the

existence of this logic in the public schools, Honey, *Tom Brown's Universe*, pp. 104–17.

53. Anon., *Letters from a Father to His Son* (London: S. Straker [1869]), p. 35.

54. Chavasse, *Advice to a Mother*, p. 272.

55. Dukes, *Preservation of Health*, pp. 93–191.

56. Blackwell, *The Human Element in Sex*, p. 12.

57. Jane Austen, *Persuasion*, in R.W. Chapman, ed., *The Novels of Jane Austen*, 3rd. ed., Vol. 5 (Oxford: Oxford Univ. Press, 1933), IV, ch. xi, p. 233.

58. Anon., *Youth and True Manhood in the Highest and Best Sense: Specially Written by a Physician and Surgeon; Being an Exposure of Unscrupulous Persons, Their Modes of Procedure and Extortion; a Safeguard against the Snares and Pitfalls of Youth and Manhood; Diseases and Ailments Incident to Youth and Manhood, with Practical Treatment, General Advice, Hints, and Warnings* (London: The "Family Doctor" Publishing Co., [1895]), p. 9.

59. Drysdale, *Elements of Social Science*, p. 37.

60. Brigham, *Mental Cultivation and Mental Excitement*, p. 18.

61. Rev. George Everard, *Your Innings: A Book for Schoolboys* (London: James Nisbet, 1883), p. 63.

62. Sylvanus Stall, *What a Young Boy Ought to Know*, "Self and Sex Series" (Philadelphia: Vir Publishing, 1897), pp. 98–99.

63. Julia Ward Howe, "Moral Equality Between the Sexes," in Powell, ed., *National Purity Congress Papers*, p. 67.

64. Walling, *Sexology*, p. 15.

65. Albutt, *Every Mother's Handbook*, p. 166.

66. Smiles, *Self-Help*, p. 241.

67. Mrs. Bray, *Physiology for Common Schools*, p. 108.

68. Davenport, *Aphrodisiacs*, p. 28.

69. Weatherly, *The Young Wife's Own Book*, p. 156.

70. Arnold, *Christian Life*, p. 23; White, *From Infancy to Womanhood*, p. 102.

71. Spencer, *Education*, p. 179.

72. Jean Jacques Rousseau, *Confessions*, revised and completed by A.S.B. Glover, 2 vols. (London: Nonesuch Press, 1938), I, 9.

73. Fennings, *Every Mother's Best Book*, p. 10.

74. Chavasse, *Advice to a Mother*, p. 289

75. Anon., *The Mother's Medical Adviser*, p. 20.

76. Blackwell, "The Religion of Health," quoted in Anon., *Children: Their Health*, p. 129.

77. Chavasse, *A Young Wife and Mother's Book*, pp. 119–22.

78. In order, Michael Ryan, *The Philosophy of Marriage*, p. 315; Anon., *The Mother's Thorough Resource-Book, Comprising Self Discipline of the Expectant Mother; General Management During Infancy and Childhood: Also Children's Complaints; Children's*

132 / *The Budding Body*

Cookery, Etc. (London: Ward and Lock, 1894), p. 197; Mrs. Pullan, *Children and How to Manage Them*, p. 25.

79. Anon., *Children: Their Health*, p. 125.

80. Mary Putnam-Jacobi, "The Nervous Diseases of Infancy and Childhood," in Castle, ed., *Wood's Household Practice*, p. 541.

81. Mrs. Child, *The Mother's Book*, pp. 10, 17, 141.

82. Anon., *Boys and Their Ways*, p. 8.

83. Bishop of Hereford, "Introduction" to Findlay, *Arnold of Rugby*, p. xx.

84. Anon., "Defects in the Moral Training," in Shipley, ed., *The Church and the World*, p. 83.

85. Blackwell, *Counsel to Parents*, p. 8.

86. Nichols, *Esoteric Anthropology*, p. 116.

87. Edward Jones Urwick, in Edward Jones Urwick, ed., *Studies of Boy Life in Our Cities; Written by Various Authors for the Toynbee Trust* (London: J.M. Dent, 1904), p. 307. See also Krafft-Ebing's observation "that girls who live in cities develop about a year earlier than girls living in the country, and that the larger the town the earlier, other things being equal, the development takes place" (*Psychopathia Sexualis*, p. 16).

88. Anon., *When a Child Loves and When She Hates: A Tale of Birch and Bed, by a Gentleman* ([London]: privately printed, [1890]), p. 36.

89. Sigmund Freud, "'Civilized' Sexual Morality," IX, 202; see also, Freud, "A Case of Hysteria," VII, 56.

90. Ryan, *The Philosophy of Marriage*, p. 143.

91. Ryan, *The Philosophy of Marriage*, p. 67; Drysdale, *Elements of Social Science*, p. 65.

92. Wood-Allen, "Moral Education of the Young," in Powell, ed., *National Purity Congress Papers*, pp. 231–32.

93. Mrs. Child, *The Mother's Book*, p. 129; Krafft-Ebing, *Psychopathia Sexualis*, p. 22.

94. Ryan, *The Philosophy of Marriage*, p. 64.

95. Deslandes, *Manhood*, p. 19.

96. Kinsey, *Human Male*, p. 182; Freud, "Three Essays," VII, 207.

97. Sigmund Freud, "Sexual Enlightenment," IX, 133.

98. Blackwell, *The Human Element in Sex*, p. 36; Krafft-Ebing, *Psychopathia Sexualis*, p. 186

99. Wood-Allen, "Moral Education of the Young," in Powell, ed., *National Purity Congress Papers*, p. 184.

100. Daniel Offer and William Simon, "Stages of Sexual Development," in B.J. Sadock et al., *The Sexual Experience* (Baltimore: Williams and Wilkins, 1976), p. 134

101. Freud, "Three Essays," p. 178.

102. Freud, "Three Essays," p. 177.

103. Kinsey, *Human Female*, p. 116.

104. Constantine and Martinson, eds., *Children and Sex*, Section III, pp. 73–107. See

also J.W. Mohr, "Age Structures in Pedophilia" in Mark Cook and Kevin Howells, ed., *Adult Sexual Interest in Children* (London: Academic Press, 1981), who calls the latent period "on the dimension of actual behavior . . . not latent at all" (p. 45); Ronald and Juliet Goldman, *Children's Sexual Thinking* (London: Routledge and Kegan Paul, 1987), who attack the latency myth not simply because there is no evidence to support it but because it retards the movement for vital sexual education for children; and Tom O'Carroll, *Paedophilia*, pp. 35–44.

4

Sex and Its Uses

> Sex is boring
> —*Michel Foucault*[1]

It is time we stopped imagining that the subject of sex tied the tongues of all Victorians, made them blush and stammer and stare at their shoes. It just as often brought a happy glint to the eye and inspired a poetry embarrassing perhaps only to us. Mary Wood-Allen, for instance, finds her reflections on human power drawing her irresistibly to sex. While the earth itself is, she says, "a great Wonder Ball which has been put into the hands of man" and on which he is busy "building cities, making railroads and ships," this industrial might is comparatively nothing: "the most wonderful power of which he has control is over this principle of life, by means of which he changes the waste places into gardens and makes the desert to bloom as a rose."[2] It is true that talk of horticultural sex and Wonder Balls may be more enthusiastic than specific, but it clearly constructs "this principle of life" as primary.

Just as enthusiastic is Krafft-Ebing's way of placing sex at the bottom of it all: "Sexual feeling is really the root of all ethics, and no doubt of aestheticism and religion"[3]—and no doubt of just about anything else that comes to mind. Krafft-Ebing does have a particular axe to grind, as do most of the writers we will be quoting, writers who, while searching for the truth, may also be pumping up the volume of their subject in order to hawk their wares or justify their own fascinations. There surely is a danger in citing writers on sex to demonstrate that writing on sex is important. There is an even greater danger in accepting their totalitarian claim that sex is the dominant from which all else—ethics, aesthetics, religion, and field sports—springs. What we can do instead is try to glimpse a little of the way in which sex and sexuality were staged. Those who made themselves happy with sex in the leading role often (though certainly not always) tended to write narratives of fierce causality, with sex as the main causal agent.[4] Since narratives of the causal exclude improbabilities or miracles (romance and comedy) and swing toward the tragic or ironic, they tend to be dismal. These are the tales in which masturbation leads inexorably to acne and death, impure thoughts to insanity. We regard such stories as hilarious and find comfort in imagining that they were the only stories told in the unliberated days of our greatgrandparents.

We are less pleased to hear our own fables being told by the Victorians, so we do not listen. We imagine that because we have exchanged one form of causality for another we have escaped from bondage; but at issue is the imprisoning authority of causality itself, of assigning to sex a determining power. Here we are perhaps not seeing so well, are unlikely even to notice the stage machinery grinding away to hoist *sex* over to join *power*. Sex is not simply given top billing; it is allowed to order about the other actors. We tend to accept that assignment of power as natural, but there is nothing natural about it. The question need not be whether sex is the central authority; we might ask if we want to grant "authority" in the first place. But it is just this question power metaphors render inaudible.

The association of sex with power is by no means universal, much less "natural" for the Victorians and tends therefore to be asserted, when it is asserted at all, pugnaciously, as if there were a stiff opposition. Charles Knowlton uses the browbeating rhetoric of Mrs. Proudie to intimidate us into sanctioning the marriage of sex and power: "surely no instinct commands a greater proportion of our thoughts, or has a greater influence upon our happiness for better or for worse."[5] Elizabeth Blackwell joined in, hammering out the message that sex, "this strongest part of our nature,"[6] was securely in command, one with power.

Sex, for writers working within this paradigm, is the cause of everything, literally everything: "sexual purity purifies all, whilst sexual corruption corrupts all." So said one O.S. Fowler in 1869, adding as a clarifying example the observation that "by nature, and as long as they remained virgins, they were as spotless as other virgins, but it was sexual impurity alone which changed them from angels into demons."[7] And this is not the only realm which sex controls: nursing mothers, for instance, are advised to moderate their desires, keeping sexual relations "in considerable check," since "sexual emotions of frequent occurrence deteriorate the milk."[8]

Given this enthusiastic welding of sex and power, it may surprise us to come upon the eagerness with which Victorians sometimes also talk of the joys of sex. One example: the 1882 *The Secrets of Life*, by Dr. Lucas, conceded that "no passion is more intricate or more powerful in its working" than "the sexual instinct" and conceded too that it could force us to drink "the bitterest waters of human misery." But Dr. Lucas's heart is not awash in bitter waters: "At every stage in life's journey from the cradle to the tomb it is the never failing spring from which flows the sweetest streams of earthly bliss." This sweetness is not only delightful but essential: duty itself would have been an insufficient motive for undertaking the work of reproducing ourselves; therefore wise nature threw in passion to keep us going.[9] We may be tempted to regard Dr. Lucas as a quack, but the orthodox Freud made his definition of hysteria, the major sexual disorder, hinge in part on an inability to find pleasure in sex: "I should without question consider a person hysterical in whom an occasion for sexual excitement elicited feelings that were preponderantly or exclusively unpleasurable."[10]

Perhaps that is enough to create the suspicion that any reconstruction of Victorian sexual thinking had better be ready for surprises. We can locate sex as the center, if we like; we can watch as power is grafted onto sex and can, following Foucault, imagine that what we are viewing is the invention of modern sexuality (sex-discourse). Sex and sexuality enter the world as legitimate subjects, we can say, and present themselves immediately as texts. Ellis is a pioneer in arranging things so that sexuality becomes a matter of images and groupings of "erotic symbolism," arranged in fields much as they are in poetry, where we see "the part becoming a symbol that stands for the whole."[11] The way the Victorians wrote that text is an intriguing subject for study, Freud's "Dora," for instance, offering as its main plot a drama of "knowing."

But, before enlisting in this sex-as-text campaign,[12] we might tune in on two cautions: first, one can textualize without empowering; second, such textualizing is, to begin with, only what we design from our looking. If we say sex was made text, we ought at least to deal with other possibilities, with the sex that was not text at all but whatever else it was. And that raises the question we probably should have begun with.

What Was Sex?

If sex was invented in the nineteenth century, not everyone seems to have gotten the word. Though we will confront more directly the issue of silence later in this chapter, it is well to observe here that many texts that should have, by our model, textualized sex simply don't do it. Writings on the developing child and even on the boy away at school sometimes act as if their only concerns were diet and dress and how to make the right friends. Without recognizable sexual sounds, we have a tough time locating our subject, much less grappling with it.

For one thing, we don't know if what we have on our hands, if we have anything on our hands, is a matter that the Victorians regarded as biological or psychological or, somehow, both. It matters a great deal, clearly, whether we find sex in the head or somewhere else. Krafft-Ebing, for instance, was able to support the wobbly concept of "latency" by distinguishing between physical and "psychical" sexuality: "abnormally early excitation of the genitals may occur, either spontaneously or as a result of external influence, and find satisfaction in masturbation; yet, notwithstanding this, the *psychical* relation to persons of the opposite sex is still absolutely wanting, and the sexual acts during this period exhibit more or less a reflex spinal character."[13] But Krafft-Ebing's distinctions (spine-head) are not widespread; so we are left in the dark as to the essence or location of this sexuality.

How it was to be gauged or judged is no less baffling. John Rutledge Martin argues persuasively that throughout most of the nineteenth century the standard for understanding and regulating sexuality was "nature," a "static, mechanistic, and Newtonian" model (of the "natural") that began to yield only in the last decade of the century to the "dynamic, developmental, and Darwinian" standard of the "normal."[14] Many would put the transition earlier or would adjust the terminology—Davidson marks the change as from anatomy to psychology[15]—but the general features of this mapping of the past are widely accepted as accurate. What Blackstone understood as a "crime against nature"[16] at some point became thought of more and more as a deviation from or perversion of the normal. The *OED* says that the modern sense of normal is common only since about 1840 and that the equation of "normal" with "usual" or "average" occurred later still, not until the 1890s.

All this sounds like an advance, this replacing of the "static" with the "dynamic," the arbitrarily "anatomical" with the descriptively social and psychological. But of course our constructions of the normal are no more disinterested or objective than our constructions of the natural. Any number of sexual surveys have revealed enormous gaps between our practices and our pretenses without disturbing in the slightest our insistences on what constitutes normality. Kinsey, for instance, found that nearly two-thirds (60%) of his respondents said they had engaged in homosexual activity in their pre-adolescent years, the mean age being 9.21 years.[17] But it is doubtful if many so engaged would have called the practice "normal" then—(or now?).

Normality seems to be a standard constructed much more out of anxiety and wish-fulfillment than out of a regard for behavior. "One of the obvious social injustices" growing out of this standard, wrote Freud, is that it "should demand from everyone the same conduct of sexual life."[18] The clash between a democratic view which honors diversity and a single standard of sexual activity is obvious but apparently not generally troublesome. Kinsey reported that, ideology aside, the range of actual conduct made the adoption of one mode of sexual understanding palpably absurd.[19] Our tolerance for absurdity is, however, clearly capacious enough to allow us to maintain unscathed our standard of the normal. For this, Freud must bear some responsibility, despite his occasional protests. While recognizing that what he called perversions were embedded in "what passes as the normal constitution,"[20] he could nonetheless, in the same essay, go on to discuss both the perverse and the normal as if they were clear descriptive categories rather than absurd impositions:

> In the majority of instances the pathological character in a perversion is found to lie not in the *content* of the new sexual aim but in its relation to the normal. If a perversion, instead of appearing merely *alongside* the normal sexual aim and object . . . ousts them completely and takes their place in *all* circumstances . . . then we shall usually be justified in regarding it as a pathological symptom.[21]

When the pioneers are bolstering such categories, there is little hope that the followers will break from them. Sure enough, the Freudian establishment has been resolutely quiescent and normative, dedicated to what has politely been called the "equilibrium model."[22] Only in rebels like Nietzsche and Foucault is there a concerted effort to "undermine the fetish of *normality* which is used to justify the mistreatment of those failing to conform to the current norm."[23] In general, then, we must be wary of congratulating ourselves on finding a model that is really more flexible or even serviceable than the Victorian "nature." There are even times when some of us might cast our lot with "natural" sexual behavior. As Kinsey points out, "in some instances sexual behavior which is outside the socially accepted pattern [i.e., abnormal] is the more natural behavior because it is less affected by social restraints."[24]

It is, then, difficult to see that the substitution of "norm" for "nature" has constituted an advance. Both are regulatory fictions, "norm" perhaps being the more dangerous since it wears such an innocent descriptive mask. It depends on who is regulating, I suppose, and where they are operating from.

Sex and Talk

Foucault says that we could not have been more absolutely wrong about the Victorians: "Rather than a massive censorship, beginning with the verbal proprieties imposed by the Age of Reason, what was involved was a regulated and polymorphous incitement to discourse."[25] Sex was not something to be hushed up but something new to be discussed: "sex became something to say," indeed, something that insisted on being said: "sex . . . had to be put into words."[26] Modern sexuality exists in and through discourse, a situation we have not created by means of "sexual liberation" from the Victorians but have inherited directly, even meekly, from them. Such a goading of discourse Foucault ties to a Western tradition that links sex, through the confessional, to truth and knowledge, eventually to a *scientia sexualis*, as opposed to the *ars erotica* of the East.[27] The public discourse that controls sexuality is connected to vague but ubiquitous agencies of power that serve nothing but their own ends.

His subversive paradigm is sharply inserted into our own discourse on sexuality and has quickly become very nearly an orthodoxy. It is much more common to take Foucault for granted these days than to challenge his model, much more agreeable to talk about Victorian discourse than Victorian repression, about texts than silences. We will return to repression and silence later, but it is only fair to note that Foucault's popularity owes something to the skill with which he has satirized the modernist version of sexual history, the myth of liberation. He has provided us with an escape from the smug discourse which equated sex talk with progress and with social good; for instance: "Psychiatrists began [about the middle of the nineteenth century] to publish case histories, and, though some of these had a negative effect by stereotyping homosexuality as an illness, they at least broke the taboo of silence."[28] We are now enabled to figure matters so that this stereotyping appears complicit: there was no taboo of silence to break, first of all; and second, the translation of sex into discourse did not transfer power from the system to individual agents. Sex and sexual experience were so deeply *interpreted* for us that it became possible to ask whether sexual assault was really more damaging than being told what it meant: was it worse to be violated or to have that violation tattooed into us by some Kafkaesque piece of babbling social machinery?

The enthusiasm with which Foucault advances his thesis and with which it has been received should not obscure for us, however, important points at which this spread of sexual discourse or the union of sex with talk has been resisted, locations in Victorian culture and in our own where sex talk is not only not encouraged but actively opposed. Where sex talk does not exist, of course, we have the most active resistance of all, but that which is hardest to trace, blunt silence. But we can easily enough locate a point short of that, what we used to call militant prudery, stern warnings against sex talk, a line of discourse on sex arguing that there should be no line of discourse on sex. C. Plummer, Victorian editor of the works of the Venerable Bede, suggested that the naming of some sex acts might somehow make them tangible and dangerous:

> Penitential literature is in truth a deplorable feature of the medieval church. Evil deeds, the imagination of which may perhaps have dimly floated through our minds in our darkest moments, are here tabulated and reduced to a system. It is hard to see how anyone could busy himself with such literature and not be the worse for it.[29]

Worry about these dimly floating evil deeds creeps into cautions about the talk felt to be common among boys at school, talk that would be much better if it were "entirely avoided."[30] Such anxieties apparently spilled over into curricular matters, into fears that the "unnatural vice," as J.A. Symonds sarcastically calls it, was brought into being by the required reading in Greek and Latin authors. Symonds rejects the notion but still feels called upon to sneer at it: "I should doubt much whether ever any one at school was first put upon the track of it ['spooning' or homosexual love] by his classical studies."[31]

Younger children were often felt to be even more at risk from corrupting words. In his "Purity—How Preserved Among the Young," the Rev. S.S. Seward told parents "to guard the child . . . against impure suggestions" and "evil communications,"[32] warnings repeated so often, especially in reference to girls, that it is easy to wax caustic on how frightfully suggestible they must have been. But we are still far from easy on extending sexual discourse to children, a point insufficiently noted by Foucault. Stevi Jackson suggests that we have simply found "new ways of rationalizing the need to keep them in ignorance."[33]

At the very least, we have tiptoed round the subject. The Victorian Rev. Seward, perhaps not a fair example but an interesting one, acknowledges, though with some pain, that sexual curiosity will arise and will, somehow or other, be satisfied. If the child is "left to learn what he must learn sooner or later from the tainted lips of playmates and companions, accompanied with many impure suggestions and vain imaginings, the result cannot but be disastrous." Therefore, the mother must, in a series of "sacred confidences," talk to the child, knowing that "the Lord and the angels will co-operate with us if we will cooperate with them" in these matters. Specifically: "The simple story of the egg and the chick . . . will solve the whole mystery of their origin beyond all childish questions." This story will leave "not the slightest taint of impurity," so long as the child is made to understand that he must never speak of these things with others.[34] Children receiving this barnyard talk from mother, God, and the angels might perhaps seek out "others" for a different sort of conversation.

Many Victorians knew this very well and were willing to support a way of talking to children much bolder than the line advanced by Seward. Even the same National Purity Congress at which Seward spoke featured others, equally anxious for virtue on a broad scale, who saw the issue differently. The Rev. J.B. Welty argued that the purity movement could only work by explicit "instruction" in these matters and that such instruction was at present woefully "inadequate." Another speaker, Elbridge T. Gerry, said the enemy to be wrestled and thrown took the form not simply of ignorance but of a kind of half-knowledge of things sexual: "side by side with ignorance, which proverbially is the parent of vice, comes what is still worse—*partial knowledge.*"[35]

Even with children, then, one sometimes is told that throwing open the windows will let in air. Whether that's really what was wanted for children was such a ticklish matter, however, that few writers rested with the ventilation argument. Ordinarily we hear, as we did from the Rev. Seward, that we had better pass along to the child these secrets of adulthood, not because the child has some right to them but because withholding them (which is what we really would like to do) will result in even greater peril for the child, and greater inconvenience for us. A sly or just possibly sincere form of this argument was sometimes used as a justification for making pornography available to all ages: it will give children the true facts on sexuality, making unnecessary the straining of their imaginations, a straining which leads to the agonies of "precocious sexual desire": thus, reading pornography will maintain their innocence.[36] A more common form of this same argument is that straight talk will preserve not only innocence but health. When parents encourage ignorance, it was often said, they defeat their own ends, "since it leads the active mind of the child to seek for information in bad quarters, often to its own injury." What's more, parental mysteriousness "magnifies" the importance of sex and may cause the child to grow up "morbidly over-sensitive about the whole subject." Worse, "for fear of leading a boy into bad habits, his parents will not instruct him how to pull back his foreskin and wash away the accumulation of white rancid material," which causes irritation and itching and thus "leads directly to masturbation, and produces the very vice which the fond parent stupidly supposed he was helping the child to avoid."[37] Talk was essential for children but not easy to manage. Those presumably in the best position to provide it too often did not do it or did it "stupidly." This vital talk was obviously a monster of a chore, partly (and inevitably) because of the uncertain relationship of the child to sex, and partly because many felt that the matter was far too important to be left to parents or teachers or even pastors.

Sex Talk and the Expert

What Foucault is responding to is what he takes to be a flood of books on the subject during the nineteenth century; but the existence of many such books does not necessarily indicate a great deal of talk. Possibly the responsibility for talking about the subject was assigned to experts, thereby relieving the general public of the chore. For us, the barrage of cookbooks and home doctoring books serve many who don't care about food or the body; books which offer "readings" of literary texts are very handy for those who don't care enough to devise their own. But since we have nothing much more than the books to go on, we will never know. It is just that the number of books published on a subject (and even sales) may run in direct, inverse, or no particular relation to public interest and public chatter.

Still, the volume of Victorian books on sexuality is considerable, as is the way in which experts moved in to multiply the available manuals. Though few of these books addressed themselves exclusively to child sexuality and though some actually waived the subject, the child still figured as one of the pillars of this discourse. Most of these works, even those concerned entirely with what went on or should go on between adults, claimed as justification the necessity for the proper education/protection of children. The expert took on the familiar role of pedagogue, running an adult-education course so that the latest in sexual information could be transmitted to (or withheld from) the child.

Perhaps the growth of this species of sex-pedants can be attributed in part to the growth among the middle class in the popularity (and feasibility) of the concept of "privacy" during the period, a concept that not only shielded the family from outside but shielded members of the family one from another.[38] Children thus had less opportunity to learn from direct observation or from chance acquaintances, placing the burden increasingly onto parental talk. The parents, in turn, looked to shift the burden to other shoulders or, at least, to find some helpers.

They had not far to look for those happy to take on the whole job and more. The experts not only pushed their subject but tended to berate the ones who were listening to them for not listening to them sooner: "Our early neglect [of the sexual education] of youth, is one of the greatest causes of social immorality," thundered Elizabeth Blackwell[39]—to those who had purchased her in hopes of compensating for early neglect. Even worse, these experts seemed to recognize no limits to their authority. They claimed for "the sacred ministry of the physician," a calling which, "while obliging him to see everything, also permits him to say everything."[40] From such a perch, they allowed themselves to revile bitterly those who offered even mild resistance to their preaching. Freud, entering late in the game but playing by the rules, provides the best example:

> What can be the purpose of withholding from children . . . enlightenment of this kind about the sexual life of human beings? Is it from a fear of arousing their interest in these matters prematurely, before it awakens in them spontaneously? Is it from a hope that a concealment of this kind may retard the sexual instinct altogether until such time as it can find its way into the only channels open to it in our middle-class social order? Is it supposed that children would show no interest or understanding for the facts and riddles of sexual life if they were not prompted to do so by outside influences? Is it thought possible that the knowledge which is withheld from them will not reach them in other ways? Or is it genuinely and seriously intended that later on they should regard everything to do with sex as something degraded and detestable from which their parents and teachers wished to keep them away as long as possible?[41]

Freud almost overdoes the satire by adding that he finds all these motives for concealment "equally absurd" and that it is "difficult to honour them with a serious refutation."

It seems to him, as it did to his forebears, that the necessity for talk, at least *his* talk, was plain but did not go without saying. If we wished to have control over children, he said, we had better listen to him, give him control. With enough talk, what was present in the child's unconscious can be brought into the form of conscious ideas and there "treated" or regulated:

> There is no necessity for feeling any compunction at discussing the facts of normal or abnormal sexual life with them [children]. With

144 / *Sex and Its Uses*

the exercise of a little caution all that is done is to translate into conscious ideas what was already known in the unconscious; and, after all, the whole effectiveness of the treatment is based upon our knowledge that the affect attached to an unconscious idea operates more strongly and, since it cannot be inhibited, more injuriously than the affect attached to a conscious one.[42]

Freud is nowhere more modern than in such talk about power; but not all of his forebears seem to have been so relentlessly in pursuit of control. Both Richard von Krafft-Ebing and Havelock Ellis seem playful by comparison, exploring their subject with all the wild excitement and lack of selectivity of any amateur let loose at a shell beach or among the flowers.

A. *Krafft-Ebing*

Perhaps the most engaging assessment of Krafft-Ebing's work was offered by the man who was also, in some sense, his rival, Havelock Ellis:

> Krafft-Ebing's methods were open to some objection. His mind was not of a severely critical order. He poured out the new and ever-enlarged editions of his book [from 1877 onward] with extraordinary rapidity, sometimes remodelling them. He introduced new subdivisions from time to time into his classification of sexual perversions, and, although this rather fine-spun classification has doubtless contributed to give precision to the subject, it was at no time generally accepted. Krafft-Ebing's great service lay in the clinical enthusiasm with which he approached the study of sexual perversions.[43]

"Enthusiasm" is the right word. He was always willing to add another case study or two, new ideas, new types of psychopathologies. Much like the fern-rock-shell classifiers Lynn L. Merrill discusses in *The Romance of Victorian Natural History*,[44] Krafft-Ebing tended to suggest with his ever-expanding categories not mastery of a subject but a sense of pure bliss in its inexhaustible fertility, its capacity to produce abnormalities that would defeat any neat classifications. This is not to say that either Krafft-Ebing or Victorian scientists were silly; they seem simply to have operated under more expansive paradigms. Krafft-Ebing also added to his enthusiasm a firm conviction that his subject was central to human concerns, so that it defined not simply their mating and herding rituals but their highest and most sublime leaps as well. Love, he insisted, was always and only possible in "the presence of sexual desire [and] can only exist between persons of different sex capable of sexual intercourse." Platonic love was an inane "platitude, a misnomer"; if sexual difference and the capability and desire for coitus were not there, all we could hope for was friendship.[45] Assured of the significance of his work, Krafft-Ebing proceeded with much of the recklessness and courage of the pioneer he knew he was.

Not everyone has admired his unruly way of clearing the wilderness. One historian of the subject has concluded that Krafft-Ebing, repulsed by his subject, "viewed human sexual behavior as a collection of loathsome diseases." As a consequence, his famous book "probably did more to elicit a disgust with sex than any other single volume."[46] It is true that Krafft-Ebing framed his subject in such a way as to require him to explore many by-ways. It is also true that occasionally these abnormalities seem repellent to the author. He can speak of those who are "tainted, as a rule hereditarily" (p. 295) with a shudder that still quivers in his pages, and he takes pains to indicate his disgust with masturbation: "It despoils the unfolding bud of perfume and beauty, and leaves behind only the coarse, animal desire for sexual satisfaction" (p. 189). Masturbation not only leaves us coarse, ugly, and smelly, but leads as well to bestiality, homosexuality, and finally, by some degenerate logic not clear to me, to indifference. As long as Krafft-Ebing sticks to masturbation, he confirms the diagnosis that he was driven to write by some kind of abhorrence for the subject.

But he isn't always writing on masturbation, in fact, seldom bothers with the subject. Generally he is off chasing other possibilities which, even if they are "diseases," seem to strike the author as quite fascinating, not at all "loathsome." The very fact that he is so eager not to reify but to alter and expand his listings suggests genuine liberality, I think. It is not just the various abnormalities which keep growing from edition to edition but the conditions which give rise to them. Here, for instance, are the causes of incest: hereditary tainting, drinking, weak-mindedness, "defective separation of the sexes among the lower classes," epilepsy, and paranoia (p. 409). As he thinks of new possibilities, he is happy to include them; and their constant growth suggests not disdain but something like generosity.

Krafft-Ebing can sometimes also cover with quite conventional language some unorthodox insistences. Those who practice sex with children under the age of fourteen, for instance, he regards with horror: "The finer feelings of man revolt at the thought of counting these monsters among the psychically normal members of human society" (p. 370). The language seems to invite easy agreement, flattering us with the attribution of finer feelings and separating us off from these monsters. But there is something odd about the sentence when we look closely, something about its peculiar destination. All this moral huffing and puffing leads to nothing more than saying that pedophilia is not the activity of the psychically normal, which isn't to say that practitioners should be driven from our midst or burned alive. It is to say that they should be looked after: "the proper place for such persons is a sanitarium established for that purpose, not prison" (p. 374). Further, he never supposes that sexuality is the exclusive property of adults: "manifestations of sexual instinct may occur in very young children" (p. 36).

Krafft-Ebing's refusal to succumb to a model of power also allowed him to move, sometimes great distances, in his thinking. Most impressive to us, surely, is the shift, however incomplete, in his view of homosexuality, from degeneracy to illness to unusual development. A statement like the following was regarded as contentious when a form of it appeared in Kinsey, but it is there in Krafft-Ebing, part of his elaborate play in and with his subject: "Thus it happens that the individual, according to the predominance of favourable or unfavourable influences, experiences now heterosexual, now homosexual, feeling" (p. 232).

B. Ellis

Havelock Ellis felt it necessary to correct a serious imbalance in the work of Krafft-Ebing. In his 1936 "Foreword," Ellis says that the label "pathological," often stuck to his own work by the ignorant and the cowardly, actually does belong on Krafft-Ebing's book, "in which," Ellis charges, "the whole field of normal sexuality was dismissed in half a dozen feeble and scrappy pages." In contrast, he says, he has been all along a student of the normal: "the original inspiration of my own work, and the guiding motive throughout, was the study of normal sexuality." It is just this emphasis that strikes us as shocking, given his view of what constitutes the normal: "I have always been careful to show that even the abnormal phenomena throw light on the normal impulse, since they have their origin either in an exaggeration or diminution of that impulse; while, reversely, we are able to understand the abnormal when we realise how closely it is related to the normal."[47] And all this is advanced in Ellis's characteristic courteous, matter-of-fact tone as if it were itself the most normal thing imaginable. Ellis's genealogical skill, his ability to show how deeply "related" were the normal and abnormal, is exactly the point on which he seemed "pathological" to many of his contemporaries and seems so to many of us.

Actually, Ellis is echoing Krafft-Ebing's claim to have unveiled the mysteries surrounding human attraction, love, sexual selection. Krafft-Ebing, as we noted, tended bluntly to equate the three; Ellis is subtler, craftier—but it is not clear that his conclusions are any different. He develops his argument indirectly, around an attack on what he takes to be Darwin's confused importing of an aesthetic principle, "beauty," into his explanation of sexual selection. Beauty, Ellis contends, has little to do with love, unless "beauty" is inflated to include the vast "complexus of stimuli which most adequately arouses love" (IV, v). And how are we to understand this complexus of stimuli that really does bring love into being? Ellis's answer is buried in the middle of a difficult paragraph and is placed in a sequence of syntactical patterns that appear very nearly tautological. Still, his point can, I think, be found. "Love springs up as a response to a number of stimuli to tumescence, the object that most adequately arouses tumescence being that which evokes love" (IV, v). The test for love springing up is thus Krafft-Ebing's, perhaps dressed up for company a little but still deeply imbued with the capacity to offend. Whether Ellis's intricate but unpretentious style and jokey buried metaphors strike us as playful or not likely depends more on how we're situated than on Ellis's comic timing and delivery.

Ellis, we remember, called attention to Krafft-Ebing's "methods," said they were "open to objection" (II, 69). As if his own were really all that different. Both writers pursue lines of argument where, though the content is boisterous enough in itself, the method is dramatically foregrounded. Ellis in particular draws our attention to the conduct of the inquiry, the way in which evidence is sorted through and then piled up, mostly piled up. Neither Krafft-Ebing nor Ellis seems to care much for the sorting; they are unselective, sociable to a fault, inviting into their books virtually anything that might illuminate something else and a good many things that are unlikely to illuminate anything but insist on entering anyhow.

But Ellis does also take care at least to start his inquiries with a sharply defined focus (modesty, for instance). Ellis's technique is to begin by defining the term, presumably in order to restrict the field, make his subject and reader snap to attention. Not surprisingly, definition often works actually to introduce multiple possibilities, contradictory lines of inquiry, humorous muddyings of the water. Even when it does not, when the definition is restrictive enough to hold things in place, what follows introduces the merry cumulative hurly-burly of

148 / *Sex and Its Uses*

accumulation: examples drawn from numerous medical authorities and other forms of literature covering a vast range, a host of case studies and hearsay reports, and brief, moderate-sounding conclusions.[48]

Ellis is master of a prose sufficiently flat and a syntax sufficiently complex and lumbering to be reassuring, suggestive of a disinterested, cautiously qualified argument trudging along. After all the clinical reports and citation of opinions, the references to tribal rites and the behavior of animals and insects, modesty, he concludes, can be analyzed into diverse "factors," five of them, and submitted to some fair-minded conjectures as to its place in an advanced society. Now Ellis is about to say that, apart from serving as a kind of seductive warm-up in the mating game, modesty, even in its form as a gesture of sexual refusal, is really "only imperative among savages and animals." Further, "the socio-economic factor of modesty, based on the conception of women as property, belongs to a stage of human development wholly alien to an advanced civilization." All that can be claimed for modesty is that it provides a "delicate" "grace of life" (I, 82), whatever that may be. This is clearly subversive material, set up masterfully:

> We have seen that the factors of modesty are many, and that most of them are based on emotions which make little urgent appeal save to races in a savage or barbarous condition. (I, 82)

We hardly need Stanley Fish—though it would be nice to have him—to lead us through this dingbat of a sentence. The opening clause is fatuous enough to have come from Mr. Pecksniff, another blowhard who loves the sheer gratuitousness of the first-person plural, when it means nothing and includes no one. "We have seen that the factors of modesty are many." And we see too what a trite view that is. When Ellis proceeds apace—"and that most of them," it hardly matters which ones, since no one cares—we are eager only for the end of this sentence. "And that most of them are based [who bases them?] on emotions which make little. . . ." We done yet? By the time we hit the sharp words at the end, we are so serenely bored we may not quite register either their audacity or their unorthodox playfulness. Modesty should appeal only to barbarians?

It is not that Ellis has nothing in his act but method, nothing but a series of sentences that act like exploding cigars. He can also jolt us by reversing the technique above and parading some rattling specifics, as in his distinction between normal and perverse sexual employments: using orifices other than vaginal ones to induce tumescence is perfectly "normal," but their use to procure detumescence is "perverse" (IV, 20).

Ellis can be, now and then and when we least expect it, thoroughly conventional. But he tends to be conventional in pieces, not in wholes, to mix in with what may be orthodox views others which seem bizarre. He does not, for instance, deviate as much from conservative opinions on masturbation as we would expect him to. On some points, to be sure, he defies convention: "Acne very frequently occurs without masturbation, and masturbation is very frequently practiced without producing acne."[49] But he is willing to entertain seriously the possibility that masturbation is connected, if loosely, to inversion: "That masturbation, especially at an early age, may sometimes enfeeble the sexual activities, and aid the manifestations of inversion, I certainly believe. But beyond this there is little in the history of my male cases to indicate masturbation as a cause of inversion" (II, 276). With women, masturbation can be "a favoring condition for the development of inversion" (II, 277). Such daffiness may expose, at least for some readers, the weaknesses of such causal and empirical reasoning; but generally Ellis is not very interesting on the masturbation issue.

Inversion is another matter. Ellis thought that there was such a thing—"sexual instinct turned by inborn constitutional abnormality toward persons of the same sex" (II, 1)—but saw it as just one form of "homosexuality," which he defines as "all sexual attractions between persons of the same sex, even when seemingly due to the accidental absence of the natural objects of sexual attraction, a phenomenon of wide occurrence among all human races and among most of the higher animals" (II, 1). Despite Ellis's apparently conventional employment of "normal" and "natural" standards, he seems to be saying, blandly, that homosexuality is the usual thing. This same odd conglomeration of opinion and observation, some of it bolstering received views and some not, marks the entire discussion.

Ellis seems ready to consider any possibility, whether or not it is plausible or coherent. Homosexuality, he allows, may be a matter of geography, so much more common in the South than the North that one can observe a division even between Northern and Southern Italy. On the other hand, it may not, in Italy, be geography, but "blood" or, again, an inheritance of purely social customs from ancient Greece, or perhaps it is just that Italians are generally more "open" about their sexual practices. And, come to think of it, "there is some reason for believing that homosexuality is especially prominent in Germany and among Germans." All of this, along with some remarks on Greek pederasty and infanticide, sweeps before us in the space of three pages

(II, 58–60). As he goes along, then, Ellis throws up at us the possibility that "in the opinion of some" homosexuality has become more widespread or maybe just more conspicuous, perhaps because of the Oscar Wilde trials, though that would be "paradoxical," or perhaps because of urbanization, "one may say" (II, 63).

If one is Havelock Ellis, one may say anything at all. "Paris, Florence, Nice, Naples, Cairo, and other places, are said to swarm with homosexual Englishmen" (II, 63): since it is said, never mind by whom, Ellis is willing to say it also. He suggests that, just possibly, inverted women "present a favourable soil for the seeds of passional crime," which would account for the fact(?) that they are, unlike normal women, more criminal than their male counterparts. As for the number of homosexual women, Ellis says that it equals that of men, with this difference: "in its more pronounced forms it may be less frequently met with in women; in its less pronounced forms, almost certainly, it is more frequently found" (II, 195). He knows this because a friend of his told him what a friend of his had told him: "A Catholic confessor, a friend tells me, informed him that for one man who acknowledges homosexual practices there are three women" (II, 195).

Such evidence is plenty good enough for Ellis, who seems to support any observation he has collected without regard to consistency. It would, for instance, be wrong to think of his work as being persistently homophobic, though he often gives voice to disabling myths. He just as often entertains against-the-grain explanations, and he advances comments that seem deliberately to buck the tide: "it has not, I think, been noted" how frequently "elevated forms of homosexual feeling" are present in "moral leaders and persons with strong ethical instincts," and, "without possibility of doubt," among religious leaders (II, 27–28).

In other areas, Ellis's arguments do tend to be more consistently rebellious or playful. This is clearest in his long meditation on the connections between love and pain: he breezily defends Sade as a person whose sexual theater featured "pain only, and not cruelty." The sadist generally, he said, arranges matters so that the pain being inflicted "should be felt as love." Pain is just part of the game, the ground rules mutually agreed upon. Thus, "we have . . . to recognize that sadism by no means involves any love of inflicting pain outside the sphere of sexual emotion, and is even compatible with a high degree of general tender-heartedness" (II, 165–66). Sadistic tendencies seem about to spill over into sentimental virtues.

This is true even or especially when the sadists are children and when the subject is flagellation. This subject looms so large that I will linger over it for an entire chapter (7) later. But I'll note now that Ellis regards the definite "sexual associations" and sexual pleasures children receive from watching or imagining other children being whipped as "well within the normal range of emotional life" (II, 141). Ellis is, finally, too unpredictable to be tied securely to a paradigm of power. We may say if we like that the Victorians transformed sex into discourse and then turned that discourse over to experts. But we need not figure those experts as stern pedagogues or moralists; they as often seem playful, maybe clownish.

Sex and Silence

And what do we do with that which didn't make it into discourse, all the sexual practices which were private or sneaky or taken for granted; all the attitudes and beliefs that were a matter of course or a matter of shame, whatever the experts might be saying? Doubtless something about sexuality was spoken in the nineteenth century, but was there a direct connection between what was spoken and what was done or felt? Of course not; and that means we must try to hear the silences and to read what is altogether blank. We must allow not simply for a discrepancy between what was prescribed by experts and what was done but for a range of activity and opinion that was nowhere discussed because nowhere challenged or even noticed.

Sometimes these silences speak loudly, if not very clearly, to us, as in the curious neglect of young prostitutes noted earlier. Such silence can be explained in many ways: perhaps the girls were not regarded as innocent *or* perhaps their innocence was so obvious as to make reference to it unnecessary. Perhaps the issue of age was felt to be less important than other issues, a potential distraction, rhetorically ineffective; perhaps it was felt to be a blackmail-bomb, far more powerful when planted but left undetonated. Perhaps age distinctions so obvious to us were not so pointed then; perhaps they were not present.

Similarly, anyone now reading through Victorian advice-to-parents (or to youths) manuals is likely to be as struck by the occasional absence of certain opinions or subjects as by their presence. Manuals written in the first two or three decades of the century, Cobbett's *Advice to a Youth* for instance, very often say not a word about sex and children. Whether they thought there wasn't any or knew there was and didn't care or simply didn't locate the issue as a problem demanding treatment isn't at all clear. It probably *is* clear that I like the last explanation best and have tried to phrase it in more persuasive terms; but it cannot make very strong claims. The fact that these manuals are early might allow us to concoct a chronological argument whereby what was not a problem early on (for whatever reason) clearly became a problem (for whatever reason) later. But there are a good many instances of silence later on that seem just as baffling. Both *Children and What to Do With Them* (1881) and *Children: Their Health, Training, and Education* (1879) enter into tedious detail about dressing, bathing, bedding; but neither makes any mention of sex, not even of masturbation. Such manuals so often do discuss these matters that we can hardly attribute their omission here to prudishness. Perhaps these writers simply didn't notice the issue, didn't regard it is bothersome?

That a culture, particularly the Victorian culture, could be more or less aware of sex without paying it a lot of attention seems to us impossible. But that is just one of the attractions presented by the idea. Another is that we could then understand better why some writers were so zealous about combatting silence. Acton's argument on prostitution, for instance, can be seen as an attempt to raise the subject into speech, without exactly making prostitution "natural." He repeatedly sought that middle path between licensing and ignoring, "recognition." Recognition would allow for a certain restrained discourse, a via media between the dangerous silence now prevailing and the ugly prattle so common among those licensing French.

Silence was as dangerous as France, possibly, because silence might signal acceptance. At the opposite pole from the repression argument lies the possibility that many Victorians did not discuss sex because they felt no anxiety about it. Even Foucault, rejecting outright the repression hypothesis, can imagine no substitute other than equally frantic discourse. It is possible that other ages did not share our terrors, were sometimes silent not because they were unliberated but because they had never been invaded in the first place. We get some hint of the possibility of this quiet nonchalance in the fervor with which writers who do consider sex often position their subject: they are, they like to say, speaking out the alarming truth in the face of apathy that has laid hold of the land. Now this general insouciance as regards, say, masturbation may be a quite unreal invention of these very writers, a way of making what they have to say appear all the more novel and commercially attractive. But it may also reflect a genuine feeling that most people find "physiological reasons against continence" and regard even masturbation as "inevitable, and therefore wisest to let it alone."[50] In any case, this projection of indifference gives voice to an opposition, provides a form to silence, suggests strongly that we cannot read these silences easily, if at all.

At least we might abandon the once-popular caricaturing of the Victorians, reading silence as ignorance and hypocrisy.[51] It hardly seems useful now to view the nineteenth century as a period when facts just weren't faced: "socially and biologically, sex was denied."[52] The silences we certainly do notice seem to be more productively recorded as difference, sometimes great and threatening difference. It would be a shame to respond to that gaping strangeness with self-protective sneers: "This momentary bewilderment on our part [at the difference in Victorian sexual thinking] can be dispelled if we remember that the Victorians tended to argue along lines that accepted racism, sexism, and class inequality as part of the natural order."[53]

I do not mean to suggest that all recent work has stayed within these boundaries[54] or that one cannot locate in Victorian discourse (as in our own) what appear to be attempts to impose silence, to throttle sex and talk about it once and for all. We might assume that, since sex is horrifying to some of us, it may have been to some Victorians.[55] Lord Lyttleton said that despite eighteen centuries of Christianity, "the lust of the flesh" still constituted the greatest social pollutant and the "worst enemy" of young men.[56] That's pretty mild compared to what emerges from the religious Right today. More in their league was the American Rev. Flint, who wrote so as to help the young deal with the "newly-awakened" creature within and see that it is not "transformed into a devouring monster." Like the Reagans on drugs, the Rev. Flint sees the answer to the problem he locates ("sensual needs") in slogans, bromides of denial: "Ignorance and moral weakness say, yes! and invariably the result is disastrous to body and mind and soul. Wisdom and self-control say, no! and vigor and happiness are the sure reward."[57] Developing the capacity to say no does have its backers, but surely they are not so many nor so enthusiastic as to justify us in saying, as Marcus does of William Acton, that everything in his book and "all it represents" is controlled by fear, "fear of sex in general and particular."[58] Victorian silences, like Victorian speeches, do not seem to tremble. The wonder is that we ever wanted to feel them that way.

The Wisdom of Our Ancestors

But apparently we did need to hear the story of how foolish and timorous the Victorians were, how liberated are we. Such a fable features William Acton, resurrected as lead singer in Steven Marcus's brilliant and highly successful costume drama, *The Other Victorians*. Marcus's success can be attributed to his having provided with such intelligence and wit exactly what we wanted, an account of the Victorians that would allow us to regard our own sexual history as no history at all, as the emergence of wisdom from out of the blackness. Marcus's historical model comes from *Genesis* or from fairy tales; sexual enlightenment appears ex nihilo. William Acton, called "Dr.," by Marcus, certainly not out of courtesy, is made Overseer of the Old Order in this myth, the man who can consolidate the sequence of error, born of fear, that is, for Marcus, the nineteenth century.

Marcus's legend has the quality of melodrama not simply in its broad comic plotting but in its powerful allegorizing. He says, for instance, that the anonymous author of *My Secret Life* was "raised in a typical Victorian household,"[59] the household standing for everything that is "Victorian," also a monolith. Acton enters into this field as the author of writings that "represent the official views of sexuality held by Victorian society—or, put in another way, the views held by the official culture" (p. xiv). According to the first formulation there are a block of official views on "sexuality," a uniform body of opinion, we can trace to "Victorian society"; Marcus's other way of putting it merely allows for a satiric split between an "official" culture and its dark or hypocritical underside.

John Maynard presents a fair summary of recent reassessments of Marcus's narrative and the challenges to his procedures. F. Barry Smith, in particular, has skewered the method Marcus employs: the arbitrary elevation of a single figure into an ideal type and the subsequent attempt to use the exegesis of that figure as historical evidence. Smith adds, wearily, that such techniques are "common in literary circles," despite the best efforts of historians like himself.[60] But all of this leaves uncertain the position of Acton. Certainly he is hard now to ignore, not simply because of Marcus's attention but because so many other historians and critics have landed on him. How important he was in his time is another matter, the number of titles and editions being notoriously poor markers of public interest. It is difficult to accept Weeks's confident conclusion—"Acton was certainly a minority spokesman"[61]—but it is clear that he was challenged in his own time and that he did not speak for any "official culture," since there was none. M. Jeanne Peterson, who seems terribly angry with Acton, charges him with being a writer of "medical pornography," a "near-quack," a conclusion there is absolutely no reason to accept. She does point helpfully to the career of Dr. James Paget, a physician whom she thinks is more "representative" than Acton and certainly more "moderate."[62] But "moderate" is just the term applied to Acton by two thoughtful historians, Peter Cominos and John Rutledge Martin.[63]

My own inclination is to side with Cominos and Martin, shoving Acton a little to the right on some politico-medical spectrum. I think he tends to be more cautious than many on some issues, masturbation and female sexuality among them. But his positions matter less to us than the complexity and flexibility of his thinking, illustrative not, certainly, of any views held by the "official culture"; but of the fact that Victorian discourse on sexuality, even that of what may have been a physician of only "average" penetration, is far more challenging and difficult to assess than we have often been led to believe.

Like almost everything out of the past, he can be made to appear ridiculous. As Acton moves from edition to edition (six in all) of his *The Functions and Disorders of the Reproductive Organs in Childhood, Youth, Adult Age, and Advanced Life; Considered in Their Physiological, Social, and Moral Relations*,[64] he not only marks deliberately any changes in his opinion but also indicates with scrupulous care the nature of any opposition to his ideas. It is mostly when this opposition becomes heated that Acton can seem to us excessive. In the first two editions, for instance, he has argued, really quite nonchalantly, from a simple economic model: the organs (or semen) can be "used up," "exhausted." Gradually he is forced to modify the concept of fixed supply considerably, but he is not willing to yield any ground on the question of continence, not willing to allow that a failure to use the sexual organs early on might cause them later to atrophy. By the sixth edition, Acton has pretty much been driven to distraction by enemies to his position, forced finally to resort to the rhetoric of shrill insistence: "there exists no *greater error!*" (6th ed., p. 37). To show what an error it is, he turns, perhaps unwisely, to what he regards as evidence, albeit evidence in the form of a story told to him by a friend who had it straight from this other friend, who knew about this horse:

> That continence is not followed by impotence is shown most forcibly in animals. Mr. Varnell, late a professor at the Veterinary College, told me of an entire horse [sic], kept by a friend of his for hunting. This animal early in life was not allowed to mount mares, yet was quiet in their presence and hunted regularly. When twenty years old he was put to the stud and became a sure foal-getter. (6th ed., p. 38)

For myself, the undisguised innocence with which such evidence is presented seems quite compelling; I am willing to be persuaded that if a horse can do it, I can. I can see, though, that Acton's procedures might strike others as insufficiently rigorous.

Probably more bothersome to many today are his views on masturbation, views which may have caused real pain and which, reversing his usual tendency, become more obdurate as time goes on. In the first edition (1857), Acton gives one of those breathlessly cascading, infinitely extendable listings of the horrors awaiting those who cannot keep their hands off themselves, such a list as is reproduced in the next paragraph. What is remarkable here, though, is not the list, pretty much the standard item, but Acton's acknowledgment not only that many others feel differently on the subject but also that these others may be right:

> . . . my opinion probably stands alone. Only lately, I was advancing it to an able physiologist, who told me he believed that one-half the boy population masturbated themselves more or less, and that the consequences were very slight. He saw much of conscience-stricken young men, who consulted him; but, in his opinion, they exaggerated their sufferings, and writers on the subject had magnified the ill effects of self-abuse. Whether this gentleman's statements or mine be the more correct I must let others decide. (1st ed., p. 58)

So shines an honest man in a weary world. Unhappily, this golden moment fades as time and editions go by and Acton falls victim to his own conviction. By the 6th edition, the views of "this gentleman" are being printed only to be mocked. The lovely last sentence has vanished, and Acton now sneers: "This gentleman and those professional men who agree in this view have probably only met with slight cases, for there can be no doubt that there are others, whose wretched condition, mental and bodily, can hardly be exaggerated" (6th ed., p. 61). Acton is now convinced not only that the inevitable tie between masturbation and insanity is "beyond doubt" (6th ed., p. 62) but that advances in science have allowed us to track all manner of terrible things back to that practice, things so horrifying we don't even know what they are: "many eminent surgeons now admit that various unrecognisable ailments are caused by these practices" (6th ed., p. 60).

There are also plenty of quite visible consequences, Acton says, and we may as well haul out one of his lists. Later in this chapter, we'll come on masturbation again, but watching the parade now will save us time later:

> The frame is stunted and weak, the muscles undeveloped, the eye is sunken and heavy, the complexion is sallow, pasty, or covered with spots of acne, the hands are damp and cold, and the skin moist. The boy shuns the society of others, creeps about alone, joins with repugnance in the amusements of his schoolfellows. He cannot look

anyone in the face, and becomes careless in dress and uncleanly in person. His intellect becomes sluggish and enfeebled, and if his evil habits are persisted in, he may end in becoming a drivelling idiot or a peevish valetudinarian. Such boys are to be seen in all the stages of degeneration, but what we have observed is but the result toward which *they all* are tending. (6th ed., pp. 15–16)

In this, Acton can seem to us funny, contemptible, or both.

But, having exposed what will seem to us the worst of him, we can pursue Acton's shifting, complex, often witty play with sexuality. Despite the horrific line on masturbation, he ordinarily is relaxed on sexual matters, anxious to soothe and to reassure where he can, to guard against the excesses of hypochondria and the damaging effects of sexual myths. He takes pains, on the whole, not to alarm or to cause unhappiness. When he isn't talking about masturbation, he sounds much more like Dr. Spock than Dr. Jekyll: he is no monomaniac, but a physician who, by his lights, is eager to help others and to exercise what becomes an almost excruciating sense of decency.

He is anxious, for instance, to guard against the destruction of "the happiness of the purest family circle" by the mistaken belief that "blennorrhagia" of the female is caused by incontinence[65]; and he vigorously protests against the horrid fantasy that venereal disease can be cured by sexual intercourse with a virgin.[66] In discussing the harm done by that fable, though, Acton also displays a seasoned pessimism that is nearly cynical: "Whatever its origin, this vile idea will still, I fear, do much mischief before being eradicated, so deeply is it rooted in all parts of the world." This tone is characteristic and indicates, doubtless, a certain coldness in his views on some subjects; but also suggests a mature aversion to enthusiasm, a recognition that sexual practice and belief are so closely connected to fable that only minor social adjustments are possible. It is this wariness that makes him so circumspect about legal matters, about the difficulties of proving child rape, for instance. We may be appalled that he is so cautious, full of so many warnings about the signs of self-abuse and the like that the physician will need to look for. I believe, however, that he is simply attempting to protect the physician and the child from the futility (or worse) of being defeated in court. He is blunt enough about the sort of evidence which is needed: the presence of semen. Anything less, he says, is likely to fail, and failure is devastating to the child.[67]

Even more impressive are his attempts to ease the minds of those who are troubled, those who suffer from all manner of sexual worries, real and (mostly) imagined. Recognizing that more than a few (all) men worry about the size of their penis, for instance, Acton addressed the issue directly and kindly: "The size of the penis varies greatly, and it has been a great source of consolation to many patients to be told that its efficiency bears no relation whatever to its size. A small penis, indeed, is often a more efficient organ than a large and massive one" (6th ed., p. 75). This cheers up the small-penised at the expense of those with large and massive ones, but the latter, one feels, can take care of themselves.

Acton was sensitive to the widespread fear of sexual disorders, the unhappiness and physical damage that could spring from phobias. Phobias related to syphilis greatly occupied him; and he wrote with feeling of the mental illness he called "syphilophobia," a malady that sometimes caused people to copy symptoms from quack medical texts and even to adopt those symptoms. Acton's insight into this psychosomatic phenomenon and his compassion for its sufferers seem to me remarkable. He stresses firmly that syphilis is not an inescapable scourge on prostitution or vice but a treatable disease. The idea that God would resort to something as grim and unfair as syphilis as a form of punishment moves Acton to anger: "if syphilis be a retribution, it would appear to be inflicted on the children with far greater severity than on the parents."[68]

He is willing to bend toward pity even when the subject touches on semen, not generally his point of greatest tolerance. Unlike many others, Acton does not finally recommend the simple retention of semen but rather its "healthy secretion," by way of "the natural action of the testicles" (6th ed., pp. 10–11). Now, by "healthy" and "natural" he does mean "continent," to be sure; but he does try not to frighten, relaxing on the issue of nocturnal emissions. By the sixth edition, in fact, he has expanded to two full pages his reassurances, letting his readers know that such emissions were commonplace and, what's more, indicative of no impurity (pp. 13–15). The dangers of masturbation can, he acknowledges, be exaggerated, causing considerable damage. By the fifth edition, Acton is concerned lest excessive worries and guilt make life "a hell upon earth" for decent people of both sexes (p. 110). "Conscience," he sees, "tells many that their previous lives have not been faultless, and . . . pseudo-medical books exaggerate the consequences of indiscretion, and predict the most awful consequences, describing trains of symptoms enough to frighten the most courageous" (6th ed., p. 172). He adds in the last two editions an Appendix, "Exposure of the Quack System," designed to guard his readers from these excesses.

Finally, we should stress once again Acton's openness and his willingness, perhaps eagerness, to change. There is nothing very consistent about the direction of such changes; what is remarkable is that he worries these shifts so publicly, makes such a display of them. We become accustomed in the later editions to a phrase like, "Admitting, then, as I now do" or, even more elaborately, "In former editions of this work I was not prepared to entirely acquiesce in these opinions of the reabsorption of semen, but I am now disposed to think . . ." (6th ed., p. 128). He comes to think there is something in the reabsorption of semen, but he also comes to think that the loss of semen can hardly be equated, as had been widely thought, with the loss of forty ounces of blood: "Of course," he adds in the 5th and 6th editions, "these alarming statements are not such as modern science can at all endorse" (p. 96). In the last edition, he "admits" that celibacy itself, while necessary, "is attended with many drawbacks and temptations, much sexual and mental suffering" (p. 198).

Most significant for our purposes is Acton's gradual and more subtle changes as regards children. Often regarded as hilariously inconsistent on the sexuality of the child, as arguing that the child was both entirely free from sexual capacities and chock full of them, Acton actually makes the *potential* sexuality of the child clear from the start, noting the common presence in male infants of erections and even of orgasm prior to developing the ability to ejaculate. He doesn't think child sexuality is healthy, but he never says that it cannot exist. As the editions move along, Acton keeps fiddling with modifications to his image of the child.

In the first two editions, childhood is not given a section of its own. "Extreme youth" is mentioned, but only briefly: "Extreme youth should be attended by complete repose of the generative functions, unbroken by anything like intense feeling for their employment" (p. 6). This is fairly slippery prose, of course, with its equivocal *should be* and murky *anything like*. By the third edition we have the following:

> I believe that healthy children's curiosity is hardly ever excited on sexual subjects except in cases where such questions are purposely suggested, or where bad example has demoralized them. (p. 2)

In the fourth edition this is shortened to:

> I believe that such [healthy] children's curiosity is seldom excited on these subjects except where they have been purposely suggested. (p. 2)

In the fifth edition only the ending phrase is changed:

> ... except as the result of suggestion by persons older than themselves. (p. 2)

The sixth edition retains this but adds the following curiosity:

> At any rate in healthy subjects and especially in children brought up in the pure air and amid the simple amusements of the country, perfect freedom from, and indeed total ignorance of any sexual attraction is the rule. (p. 2)

Acton's honesty keeps him from ever saying what he seems to want to say: that children are asexual. Perhaps they *ought* to be or *might* be under certain circumstances, but *ought* and *might* are very often not *is*, and Acton knows it and says it.

All in all, I see no warrant for condescending to this intelligent and candid physician. His instincts were on some matters what we would call conservative; and he wanted some things to be as he thought they *should* be. But he tried very hard not to let his wishes determine what he saw, and he almost certainly fooled himself less than do those who have located in him nothing more than an occasion for mocking the wisdom of our ancestors.

Masturbation and Other Attractions

Our reading of the sexual past has tended to rely on certain themes, so apparent to us that we assume they must certainly be *there* and not merely phenomena appearing in response to the dictates of our own perceptual categories. We find ourselves drawn to particular features of sexual discourse during the period, largely because they tickle some concern of ours. I do not propose to begin noticing other things, since that would be very nearly impossible; but it is important to attend to the fact that this form of history is inevitably a boomerang.

A. Female Sexuality

One of the things we definitely construe from the Victorian past is a tendency to depend on conventional gender categories and on heterosexual reproductive activity as normative; and a tendency at least as strong to resist such dependencies. Gender determinants often become visible only when they are called into question, when, for example, writers reject certain qualities commonly attributed to "women" (sometimes attributing them to men) or when categories of significance are defined in terms other than gender: age, class, geography. I think we are more likely to naturalize this gendered way of thinking than were the Victorians, and thus to read their thinking as more strictly gendered than it may have been. The Victorians themselves often seem to have employed "male" and "female" as counters in a loose and free-flowing game, pleasurable but of little consequence.

When they thought to speak of the difference between male and female, that is, they often seem to adopt the tone of people gossiping. The rhetoric is unbuttoned, the method anecdotal. Hyperbole is excused, and no one is held to very strict account. One is free, for instance, to speak of puberty not simply as a time of sexual but of ethical metamorphosis: "A great change takes place in the girl at the time that puberty commences. She changes both in outward aspect and in moral feelings."[69] One gets the feeling that a writer could, if the idea floated into view, claim with impunity that the female blood suddenly began to circulate in the reverse direction at this time. It's not that the issue is not taken seriously; it's just that different rules apply, more like the loose rules of a game.

There doesn't seem to us to be much that is playful in the discourse on female masturbation, but perhaps the writers enjoyed themselves inventing symptoms and consequences; certainly there were no firm checks on imaginative fertility in these areas. Female masturbation seems usually to have been regarded as just as damaging and as prevalent as in boys.[70] There were some catastrophes either reserved especially for or at least handed out in greater quantity to females: the destruction of the "taste for healthy matrimonial intercourse,"[71] sterility (due to the wasting of the limited number of eggs—between 15 and 20—assigned to each woman),[72] unpleasantly overheated sexual needs and the inability to form friendships,[73] death and the loss of beauty.[74] Just as titillating as extending the list of disasters was detailing the traces by which one could locate unmistakably these practitioners of what they supposed was a secret vice. "It leaves," says Mary Wood-Allen, "its mark upon the face so that those who are wise may know what the girl is doing."[75] What these marks are exactly isn't very clear, but luckily the author continues, suggesting that those who don't know whether they have spotted marks or not can double-check by observing the little girl's eating habits, a signaling device beyond even the most devious child's ability to disguise: "She will manifest an unnatural appetite, sometimes desiring mustard, pepper, vinegar, and spices, cloves, clay, salt, chalk, charcoal, etc., which appetites certainly are not natural for little girls."[76] It was left for the twentieth century to disrupt all this float-and-glide with statistical studies, the first I know of on gender distinctions in masturbation issuing from Kinsey. He found that 93% of males and 62% of females masturbated, that women tended to do it more as they grew older and men less, that it wasn't clear whether female mammals other than humans masturbated to orgasm (though some males certainly did), that twice as many girls as boys were able to teach themselves how to masturbate, boys feeling the need much more heavily for instruction. Kinsey found out other things too: with females, the more education one received, the more one masturbated, though one's chances of reaching orgasm by this means were not affected by educational level. Urban women, however, were not only more likely to do it but, once doing it, more likely to reach orgasm than those in rural locations; women were less likely than men to accompany masturbation with fantasy (or so they said), but both groups reported that masturbation was to them a "source of pleasure."[77]

So much for modern play. Victorian free-form openness on the question of gender certainly had its grim side, one must hasten to add, a way of formulating female sexuality as foul and threatening. Krafft-Ebing reports a French case history from 1882, what he calls "a disgusting story," to be sure, though one suspects the sources for his disgust are not the same as ours:

> ... the disgusting story of two sisters afflicted with premature and perverse sexual desire. The elder, R., masturbated at the age of seven, practiced lewdness with boys, stole whenever she could, seduced her four-year-old sister into masturbation, and at the age of ten was given up to the practice of the most revolting vices. Even a white hot iron applied to the clitoris had no effect in overcoming the practice, and she masturbated with the cassock of a priest while he was exhorting her to reformation.[78]

The last detail, worthy of Genet, would make us cheer, were it not so very sad. But there is that white hot iron, the instrument of torture Krafft-Ebing seems to emphasize only to highlight the depravity of the poor little girl. One is almost tempted to say that Krafft-Ebing's callousness is more repulsive than the torture; and though this would be gratuitous, it would serve to recall us to the very somber features of the past and the limits of any purely textual activity. In any case, the operation Krafft-Ebing is referring to seems to be a form of clitoridectomy, the removal of a piece of skin, sometimes called the "hood," above the clitoris, apparently to alter sexual behavior, most clearly masturbation. It is important to note, though, that, according to Barker-Benfield, the man who re-introduced this operation in England, Dr. Isaac Brown Baker, "was expelled from the London Obstetrical Society almost immediately after the published results of his clitoridectomies in 1866, and the operation was not performed in England thereafter."[79] It seems to have had some currency, however, in America.

The more general questions on female sexuality, how strong it was and what forms it took, at least evoked no mutilating surgical procedures. In fact, Victorian writers tended to delight in arguing for a level of female sexual desire, capacity, or both far beyond that of men. T.L. Nichols said of little girls that "her passions are as strong, and her power of gratification even greater" than that of boys; in maturity, correspondingly, "some women seem to have the capacity for greater and more frequent enjoyment than men."[80] Krafft-Ebing spoke with assurance if not total clarity in announcing that "sexual consciousness is stronger in woman than man."[81] It is certainly possible that, in an area where anything goes, people choose to say what will get attention, what will go against the grain of popular belief. All the same, the common idea that the Victorians denied female sexuality has no basis at all beyond our desire to flatter ourselves.[82] Woman was doubtless made "Other" during the period, but not without resistance from many quarters, some of which seem to have made conscious efforts to combat or explode gender stereotypes; for instance, this from Havelock Ellis: "Masochism is commonly regarded as a peculiarly feminine sexual perversion, in women, indeed, as normal in some degree, and in man as a sort of inversion of the normal masculine emotional attitude, but this view of the matter is not altogether justified, for definite and pronounced masochism seems to be much rarer in women than sadism," though, as he goes on to show, masochism is quite a common feature of the makeup of a man.[83]

Depending on how one looks at it, then, the Victorians were either freer or less responsible as regards gender distinctions. It is possible that they saw something other than the distinctions we see; if they did, it would be out of our range anyhow.

B. Masturbation

This feature has been heavily anticipated. I am, however, sitting here with such a large number of notecards on the subject that it would be a pity not to use them. Besides, the subject of Victorian masturbation is irresistible; and that, perhaps, is the most interesting point: our willingness to hear once again the same story. We are apparently prepared to believe that with the dawn of the nineteenth century "the age of masturbation insanity was upon the Western world,"[84] seldom considering why such condescension comes so easily to us. We may even regard as typical Dr. Lucas's *Secrets of Life*, where he unveils with fanfare "the king of dissipations," "the solitary vice of self pollution," which "spreads desolation throughout the land"[85]; or the following from *The Magnet*, recommending Deslandes's *Manhood*:

> The vice of which it treats is supposed by competent judges to be generally prevalent and growing; it is spreading through the community decrepit bodies and decayed minds, and peopling insane hospitals and the grave. Some of the highest medical authorities pronounce it the great scourge of civilization.[86]

We may use such things to establish our own enlightenment. Whatever our faults, we know about masturbation. Along with Kinsey, we ridicule the notion of wasting semen, asking why the same principle doesn't apply to spitting.[87] For much of our culture, masturbation is "essentially neutral"; certainly "we have never seen a case where masturbation in and of itself [whatever that might mean] had any deleterious consequences, physical or emotional"; in fact, we will go so far as to say that as "a source of pleasure," it "deserves to be regarded as a potential asset in life."[88] We say we take it for granted, perhaps even regard it as a condition of health: "the nonexistence of masturbation during adolescence is usually a sign of serious illness."[89] This seems close to a naive mirror image of Victorian thinking on the subject, a point also noted by John Rutledge Martin, who wryly comments that "the logic and observation employed in modern writings on masturbation seem to be about the same order as that of a century or so ago."[90]

Actually, sober histories of the masturbation controversy, although tracing the source of the furor to S.A.D. Tissot's famous 1758 monograph (or even earlier), tend to see the real power of the social purity movement and its sweep both to center and wipe out masturbation as relatively short-lived and also late: in the 1880s and 1890s in England.[91] What might be called an epidemic of preoccupation among medical men and some of the clergy seems also to have been a latter-day phenomenon, though it lasted longer, from the 1870s until perhaps the Great War.[92] Furthermore, it appears that the decline in the tendency to blame masturbation for all sorts of disorders came not from enlightenment or from research disproving the relationship between the practice and the diseases, but from a decline in the diseases themselves, brought on by general medical advances having nothing to do with masturbation.[93]

None of this fine historical work has stood in the way of the comedy still to be found in Victorian masturbation panic. Though I promised to give no more lists of the likely or certain results of the solitary vice, I will anyhow: beyond acne, sweaty palms, and sunken eyes, there are: loss of memory, tremors, "a besotted stupid look," "morbid appetite," repugnance to marriage, broken teeth, spinal curvature, loss of flesh, constipation, diarrhea, and, the old favorite, insanity. Ellis gives a much longer inventory, cites a physician willing to accept "considerably over one hundred" effects of masturbation, and suggests that this carnival of enumeration has perhaps gone on long enough.[94] Before it stopped, it claimed its victims, some of whom wrote letters to doctors, detailing what masturbation had done to them:

> I cannot walk two hundred steps without resting, so extreme is my weakness. I have continual pains in my body, particularly the shoulders, and suffer greatly from those in the chest. My appetite is good, but this is rather a misfortune, as I have dreadful pains in my stomach after eating. If I read a page or two my eyes fill with tears, and create great suffering; and I am constantly sighing involuntarily.[95]

Equally pitiable are the cures advised for masturbation. Even if clitoridectomies were rare in England, one wonders how many children were driven to exhaustion by conscientious parents who, following what they thought was the best advice, tried frantic exercise to drain "nervous energy" and thus render "erotic desires less prominent."[96] One wonders what cost was exacted from children, and parents too, by the insistence that mothers especially needed to be "Argus-eyed." Since "the art with which they elude vigilance is often inconceivable," parents needed not simply to watch but to watch with wily "art," watch in a way that was, in fact, spying, even on the sleeping child, surprising it in the night with unannounced checks. This same authority gives permission to tie hands, day and night, or to employ "a straight waistcoat."[97] Now this same authority is also a nearly manic enthusiast on the subject, perhaps a crackpot; but we know that such appliances as armored belts, toothed penile rings, and electric genital alarms existed.[98]

Such a focus on humor and horror may cause us to ignore the more

166 / *Sex and Its Uses*

prosaic questions about masturbation that should, all the same, present themselves: To what extent was masturbation actually a concern and to what extent was it condemned and by whom? To the extent that it was made a subject for study and for some degree of anxiety, how did it achieve that status?

The presence of masturbation worries could hardly have escaped any writer on children, at least after mid-century, and, one suspects, few middle-class parents. This is not to say that everyone was equally infected or infected at all by such concerns, just that they were in the air, or at least in books. By the turn of the century, the assertions in William Walling's *Sexology* (1902) to the effect that masturbation was "the most frequent, as well as the most fatal of all vices," practiced commonly even by infants,[99] were run-of-the-mill. Over forty years earlier, O.S. Fowler had announced that there were "very few boys" who did *not* do it and that "the great majority of girls are more or less addicted to it."[100] Those who did discuss masturbation—and not everyone, as we will see, did so—seem to have regarded it not so much as a symptom but as a cause. Elizabeth Blackwell, for instance, is pretty vague on why one might want to masturbate in the first place—perhaps because of "transmitted sensuality," she says or from a "nervous sensation, yielded to because it 'feels nice.' "[101] Compare this casual simplicity to the elaborate and extensive analysis given to the results of masturbation and we get some hint, perhaps, of why masturbation loomed so large: not because it was a consequence of man's evil nature but because other things were the consequence of it, other maladies which could not otherwise be explained. These were physicians more than moralists, and their interest was in disease, not sin. Masturbation was thought by some to be the cause of many medical problems and thus the location for medical solutions: "in innumerable cases it [masturbation] induces precocity of physical sensation, and prepares the way for every variety of sexual evil."[102] Notice that masturbation is not the result of but induces "physical sensation"; it is the cause of "every variety" of sexual evil, for which, in part, we can read "disease."

Not every physician chose to depend on this etiology, however, nor did every moralist follow this causality. Many manuals say not a word about masturbation, not even a veiled word, so far as I can tell. Pye Henry Chavasse's *Advice to a Mother on the Management of Her Children* does not, even in the 13th edition (1878), mention the subject, and Chavasse seems to me a liberal, highly opinionated writer who is delighted to have the responsibility to speak unwelcome truths as he sees them. The Rev. Frederick Poynder's *A Few Words of Advice to a Public Schoolboy* (4th ed., 1860), though promising and delivering "plain words" (p. 5), has no words at all on masturbation, though plenty of them on the innumerable dangers that lie in wait at school. These are examples of the silence one meets with, I would say, at least half the time. How we read that silence depends on what we need to hear. I suggest that one way to interpret it is the simplest: masturbation was not mentioned by many because many did not think it worth mentioning. It was not mentioned, that is, because it was felt to be insignificant, not because it was terrifying, unspeakably indecent, or too obvious.

In truth, as we look back at this Victorian discourse, we find difference all over the place, not simply a flattering difference between us and them but confusing differences within their culture. "Much contradiction of thought exists on this subject," says the scrupulously honest Elizabeth Blackwell, who goes on to cite two views as equally unhelpful and "extreme": one is the doctor (unnamed) who claims masturbation is utterly harmless; the other is Tissot and his followers, with their "pictures of mental and physical ruin," pictures that Blackwell labels "frightful."[103] Her position is one common to Victorian thinking, even medical thinking, a carefully situated *moderation*.[104] This does not mean that she approved moderate amounts of masturbation (though some clearly did); but that she accepted its presence, and tried to understand and deal calmly with the issue.

These contradictory voices that Blackwell cites do not always resolve themselves so cleanly in compromise: some seem to raise the issue precisely because they fear there may *be* no issue, or at least that few of their readers think there is: "It is an indubitable fact that the vice [masturbation] is one which meets with too little discouragement on all hands; and is therefore practised with too little shame."[105] We can even locate some outspoken promoters of masturbation as the holy "mode by which God in Nature provides that he shall have no unhealth through chastity," a mode, we are told, far preferable to seduction or employing prostitutes.[106]

Even among those who noticed masturbation and then condemned it, the reasons for that condemnation varied significantly. Some found the loss of semen weakening, citing Tissot (seldom by name) and his dreary 1–40 calculus; one early writer said the enfeebling process proceeded "by geometrical progression,"[107] which sounds even more frightening. In addition to being a "drain," several writers said it was also a "shock" to a system, usually the "nervous system," ill prepared to withstand it. These conservative writers often expanded the idea of masturbation to include other forms of "unnatural" sex, "from the use of contraceptions to homosexuality," says Bullough.[108]

168 / *Sex and Its Uses*

But not all reasons were this simple or predictable (if indeed the ones cited above were either simple or predictable). The habit of thinking about masturbation as a *cause* of sexual activity, as a way of inducing "uncontrollable lust," say, made it possible to link the act to a variety of social problems and condemn it on those grounds, as, for instance, *"the root of the evil of prostitution."*[109] Some protests against masturbation drew attention to what we would now think of as the general problem of child abuse, here the "vile plan" adopted by some nurses of quieting "peevish" children by "tickling the genital organs."[110]

In addition to these social analyses, a good many critics of masturbation located the problems in psychological terms, worrying not only about the mental habits induced thereby but about the effects of horror stories: the all-too-common problem of the man who, experiencing some slight problem, "magnifies the possibilities of his misfortune by recalling all the terrors painted for him years before by some overkind adviser, and he becomes a hopeless victim to melancholy and hypochondria, not on account of his masturbation so much as from the terrible results of nervous apprehension."[111] Similarly, psychological and social analyses sometimes lead to warnings against masturbation on the grounds that it was secretive, "the supreme narcissistic act."[112]

There are other angles on masturbation as well, one of the most startling, at least in its candor, being Freud's early attack on the practice as, first, offering an image of a sexual object so idealized that reality would always be disappointing and, second, teaching practitioners "to achieve important aims without taking trouble and by easy paths instead of through an energetic exertion of force."[113] Masturbation, in other words, is both too nice and too easy, objections that present what used to be called the Protestant ethic with an unusually high pitch of naivete. And finally, there is the most harrowing of all ways to understand the masturbation controversy: in the absence of anything better in the way of an explanation, it gave the medical profession something to say to the bereaved parents of dead children—dead, as Dickens said, and dying thus around us every day. Worries about masturbation functioned as excuses for cruelty, as self-protection for quacks, as inducements to hypochondria and suicide, as attempts to help and to comfort, as the basis for social improvement. Sometimes those worries did not exist at all.

Schoolboy Immorality

J.R.deS. Honey's *Tom Brown's Universe: The Development of the Victorian Public School* has provided such a detailed account of the controversy over the sexual (if that's what it was) behavior of Victorian schoolchildren that we need do little more than summarize his arguments. Generally, he shows how terms like "vice, immorality, wickedness, corruption, evil and sin" "changed their connotation" as the century advanced, acquiring sexual meaning only after about 1860.[114] Before that time, with Thomas Arnold, for instance, "evil" might refer to idleness, a want of manliness, lying, or a series of "communal rather than private" much less sexual vices.[115] Arnold's silence on sexual matters seems unlikely to have been caused by either ignorance or reticence. Perhaps he regarded the matter as relatively insignificant or better left unnoticed.

By the time of *The Children's Wrong* (1864), one begins finding much more ominous references to "breeding grounds of immorality," "the deepest degradation," the inability of respectable men and women "to look back upon their schooldays without a blush."[116] Such coded talk seems, within another decade or so, more closely tied, first to masturbation and then to homosexuality. Unmistakable references to the latter are common by the 1895 *Youth and True Manhood*, where "practices impossible to describe in greater detail without disgusting the reader" are described in great enough detail so that we know what is happening.[117] In fact, perhaps the leading figure among masturbation worriers, Edward Lyttelton, had, by the 1890s, to do battle with a fierce competitor: the "immorality" caused by "bad friendships," by "affection" which becomes "debased, and leads to the worst results."[118] And promoters of elevated forms of schoolboy affection, like Edward Carpenter, had to admit to very careful distinctions.[119]

One must remember, though, that none of this tumult had much apparent effect on the popularity of Victorian public schools or even with their tie to an ideal of manliness. Children were still packed off to boarding school in droves, as parents could afford it, in part, says Honey, to protect them from the temptations offered by servants.[120] There were even some analysts, like Ellis, who were able to use the publicity about schoolboy vice to argue that adolescent or childhood homosexual relations were generally "spurious" and "normal."[121] As with every other feature of the Victorian landscape, then, this one is by no means uniformly smooth and easy to traverse.

Pornography

"Pornography" is a very inexact and dangerous term; but it may convey to most of us more sharply than "erotica" the sort of material I have in mind. It is probably present in Victorian discourse; beyond that, nothing is very certain about its status or extent, about how we can locate it and understand it.

We tend to think, partly as a result of Marcus's *The Other Victorians*, that Victorian culture unloosed a flood of pornography, that it flowed heavily throughout the period and across the land. Such an image fits well with orthodox notions of sexual history, of Victorian repression and modern liberation, of Victorian duplicity. But an orthodox historian is going to be disappointed in the extent of the evidence: instead of the deluge of pornographic volumes expected, one finds hardly more than a trickle. This is, admittedly, a fugitive genre; aside from a few collectors, many have been anxious to rid themselves of any they have inherited, and thus the material tends to disappear. But that, in itself, does not give us reason to assume that massive amounts of it existed last century. Pisanus Fraxi's [Henry Spencer Ashbee's] *Bibliography of Prohibited Books* consists of three fat volumes, each running to over 500 pages and each packed with nothing but pure porn. However, that source, which is, to my knowledge, not only the richest but about the only one we have, really is much less abundant than it appears. Once one subtracts the various indices and appendices, the works written in earlier centuries, reprints and slight variations on one title, translations of the same work, and the often bulky annotations, the number of titles is certainly not large, with fewer than half of those actually in the British Library's collection. I think the sensible conclusion is that a small amount of specifically erotic literature was available at least on a limited scale at least late in the century. There may have been more, earlier, with wider distribution; but no reason exists for thinking so beyond our supposing it must have been true. That we do so tells us something about our own relationship to the Victorian past.

What most people know about Victorian pornography they know by way of Marcus, which is certainly a mixed blessing. Marcus has been justly praised for attacking the material in the first place and for his abilities to draw together the discourses of erotic and high-canonical literature. On the other hand, there are many points in his procedures that I would not want to let slide by without questioning. For one thing, he seems to be upset by the very idea of pornography, to reach for the most strident prose he can grasp whenever he approaches the topic: pornography is "a genre whose only secret sometimes seems to be its ability to persuade the reader that psychosis is merely a heightened form of normality," and he implies that the conditions for an interest in the subject are "defective powers of concentration."[122] More serious are his dubious historical arguments concerning pornography, especially the speculation that it gains force precisely as the condition it describes, in this case powerful phallic sexuality, ceases to be a real social presence (p. 212). He also is a very solemn reader of the genre, seeing in it nothing but neurotic earnestness. However tricky and self-reflexive legitimate novels are, he says, porn is busy trying "precisely to subdue or extinguish" any consciousness we may have of the fictionality of the narrative (p. 46), an astounding conclusion to reach regarding these chatty, winking-at-you works. And he takes the openness of erotic fiction, its move toward endless development and its resistance to closure, as a weakness, indeed a sickness: "the author does not permit the counter-idea of genuine gratification, and of an end to pleasure, to develop" (p. 195). Somehow, for Marcus, "genuine" gratification seems tied to its cessation. Similarly, he argues that the open energies of this material make it formless, non-literary: "If it has no ending in the sense of completion or gratification, then it can have no form; and it is this confinement to the kind of form that art or literature must by nature take which is noxious to the idea of pornography" (pp. 195–96). Any argument that refers form to "nature" ought to have us checking the silver, especially when "nature" turns out to be so stolid.

For these works can be read from other, playful lines of sight, even in the most self-consciously dreary of them, *My Secret Life*, where "Walter" calls attention to the fact that his numerous sexual exploits sound a good deal alike, a redundancy he says is "inevitable, for human copulation, vary the incidents leading up to it as you may, is, and must be, at all times, much the same affair."[123] It depends on how one looks at it, surely; and Walter's view of his own adventures may not be that of every reader. There is something in the sheer length of the work that supports its almost ridiculous thirst for experience, its playful allegiance, as Marcus admits, to experience "as an end in itself and not merely a means to something else" (p. 189).

We will have many occasions to return to this genre in upcoming sections. I would like to close out this one by looking briefly at the justifications which pornographic works almost inevitably feature, formal explanations or apologies, sometimes instructions on how to read or how to categorize (and thus make acceptable) the book in question. Since there is no reason not to accept these offerings as jokes, I am happy to do so: *My Secret Life* hails itself as a "contribution to psychology"; *Lustful Adventures* as a triumph of literary realism, an advance in "truth and justice"; *Mysteries of Venus* as a sex manual for young brides; *The Confessions of Nemesis Hunt* "as either a warning or a guide" (take your pick); and *Suburban Souls* as, of all things, a moral exemplum on how "to be intensely wicked on an honourable, chivalrous basis."[124] To these, Ashbee adds, in the "Introduction" to his *Bibliography of Prohibited Books*: advancing the "science of Bibliography" (p. ix), filling in gaps in our present knowledge (p. xviii), providing information on "manners and customs" invaluable to future generations (pp. xx–xxi), protecting what is rare for its own sake (p. xxvi), and presenting volatile material in a safe form (pp. xxvii–xxviii). He admits that his work is not the sort of thing everyone will welcome; and, in one of his finest asides he "anticipates" the storm that is to come: "I cannot help, nor do I for one moment expect that my work will pass uncensured. Many will justly proclaim it incomplete."[125]

The Sexualizing of the Child

We now look at the sexuality of the child right next to us through such a haze of opinion, myth, and denial that it is difficult to know what it is we are seeing. How much harder it is to look back at something else, the Victorian child, and ask how it became so laden with sexuality, why the culture invested so heavily its sexual capital in this child. If that's what happened. Even assuming that the Victorians had some glimmering of what was occurring, which isn't likely, and even assuming we could reconstruct other parts of the past, which we can't, the causes of this joining of the child and sex would still elude us: we have so many heavy screens thrown up between us and the object of our study. We have accumulated a great deal of unhelpful learning in the meantime; we have had to deal with Freud and then, almost as bad, Foucault; we care no less intensely than did the Victorians for this child, and we have no clearer path to follow to the secret that will reveal to us what this child is and what all this intensity means.

We now hear that the idea of the pure or innocent child, at least if those words mean "asexual" or "non-sexual," is medically and scientifically unsound. Wardell Pomeroy, following Kinsey, proudly gave us the latest word in 1968: "Today we know that both male and female babies as young as four to six months have orgasms."[126] It's not clear that we found that such good news, but we had those four to six months of purity to treasure. Before long, however, we were told that there was literally no life before sex: "It is now known . . . that fetuses sometimes suck their thumbs, fingers, and toes, and that male babies are capable from birth of penile erections, and female babies of vaginal lubrication."[127] This sort of knowledge is likely to rattle around in our heads, like loose change, never lodging anywhere. Much the same might be said for our awareness of the fact that our attitude toward childhood sexuality is not shared by all peoples:

> The traditional cultures of the West generally take the attitude that children are not naturally sexual creatures, should not *be* sexual creatures, and should at all costs be kept away from sexual knowledge and ideas lest they somehow *become* sexual creatures before their appointed hour arrives. Yet the members of relatively few cultures studied by anthropologists would have anything but derision for such notions. Indeed, the overwhelming majority of preindustrial cultures consider sex to be an inevitable and harmless aspect of childhood.[128]

We know that; but, again, we keep our knowledge from interfering inconveniently with our more settled ideas.

And we also have Freud to see through, Freud with his vinegary sarcasms about parental idiocy: "He does not credit [his children] with having any sexuality and therefore takes no trouble to observe any such thing, while, on the other hand, he suppresses any manifestation of such an activity which might claim his attention."[129] Freud also pushes his way into our mental parties with his bumptious tales about children seducing adults: "He therefore began to play with his penis in his Nanya's presence, and this, like so many other instances in which children do not conceal their masturbation, must be regarded as an attempt at seduction."[130] It is not, however, through anecdotes that Freud interposes what would be, if we attended to it, the most disruptive of his claims: that infant sexuality not only exists but, in its unrestrained dedication to sexual pleasure and its disregard for the demands of civilization (much less the demands of reproduction), establishes a pattern that will make us unhappy the rest of our lives. Freud's insistence on infantile sexuality, that is, constitutes much more than an irritant. It is the foundation of a theory of mind and culture we would rather forget. Thus, at least in part, the rejoicing over recent charges that Freud's abandonment of the seduction theory (and his adoption of the paradigm of infant sexuality) were accompanied by inhumane sexism and general caddishness. We would love to return to the opinion apparently dominating conservative Victorians, the one Freud held uneasily up to 1897: that children were asexual but could be made sexual by outside stimulation. Such a view, ridiculed by most moderns when it appears in its Victorian dress, has still a vigorous, if absurd, life in our culture. As Matthew Arnold's Parliamentary buffoon says, a thing's being an anomaly does not constitute grounds for objecting to it.[131]

174 / *Sex and Its Uses*

Compared to Freud, more recent historians have made hardly a ripple. The one exception is Foucault, though his influence is as yet confined. While not dealing extensively with the child, what he has had to say about its investment with sexuality is vital. Foucault figures that prior to the end of the eighteenth century child sexuality was a matter of "indifference,"[132] but that with the nineteenth century the child was sexualized. This had the "spectacular" result of problematizing not the child's sexuality but the adult's: by way of a "secret causality" between childhood and adulthood (e.g., the long-term effects of masturbation), sex became characterized not by an adult presence but by "the interplay of presence and absence, of the visible and the hidden."[133] Child sexuality becomes the measure of the adult's. And it is, he says, a child sexuality that we affirm by denying. We might suppose that the purpose of most Victorian and modern talk on the subject was, precisely as Foucault says, "to prevent children from having a sexuality." "But," he continues, the "*effect*" of this endless, anxious talk "was to din it into parents' heads that their children's sex constituted a fundamental problem ... and to din it into children's heads that their relationship with their own body and their own sex was to be a fundamental problem as far as *they* were concerned; and this had the consequence of sexually exciting the bodies of children."[134]

But exactly how were children sexualized? To say that they were invested with sexual capacity surely does not say all. What position were they given in our culture's allotments of desire? How was their difference placed in reference to the erotic? Were there consequences of our unrelenting denials of child sexuality, other than the simple boomeranging Foucault notes?

A. *The Non-Sexual Child of Desire*

Say we believe all the propaganda, fully and unreservedly believe it. Even our unconscious has no doubts on the matter, no tricks up its sleeve. The child of Rousseauist theory,[135] completely free from sexual passion, is our child. We regard the following as obvious: "It should be understood at the outset that the child's mind is perfectly pure in the beginning." Blotches, such as unfortunately do threaten, come from the outside; properly screened and protected, the child could "grow up as free from taint in this world as we may imagine those do who have been transplanted in infancy to the other world."[136] Should accidents occur, like premature puberty, we can still preserve purity and defeat the tainting powers:

Under these circumstances, the patient should reside in the country and lead a quiet life; she should have regular, moderate out-of-door exercise; she should have a cold bath of short duration—say two to three minutes—every second day, followed by a brisk friction of the skin; she should avoid anything calculated to arouse the passions, such as going into gay company, reading exciting works of fiction, etc.[137]

Those who take their stand with purity find some unexpected support from Havelock Ellis. Ellis wanted to qualify Freud's theory of infantile sexual operations by calling them "really presexual feelings"; he was even willing to argue that things like tickling, though certainly connected to sexuality when practiced on adults, are entirely free of that association for children.[138]

Even if we take this position ourselves, just where are we? I have suggested earlier that this hollowing out of children by way of purifying them of any stains (or any substance) also makes them radically different, other. In this empty state, they present themselves as candidates for being filled with, among other things, desire. The asexual child is not, as we will see, any the less erotic but rather more.

B. The Sexual Child of Desire

Besides, this belief in purity was tough to sustain. Even true believers faltered: "For the first few days, at any rate, of an infant's life, it is not needful to attend to its morals."[139] Those clouds of glory dissipate rapidly.

The dangers are everywhere. In the nursery, most parents know, infants will likely display a "proneness to touch and 'play with' their sexual organs." But most parents seem not to recognize that such things are dangerously polluting, not "play"; most parents actually ignore or encourage such things and, what's worse, turn children over to nurses who actively participate in this "tickling."[140] So many books warn against nurses and servants that one wonders (a) why any were kept, (b) how they could reasonably have been made responsible for child sexuality, and (c) how it is no one blew the whistle on such obvious scapegoating. Operating here is a very handy class biology, a notion that the lower orders not only are performing under much lower moral standards but a different bodily organization as well, one which does not extend the benefits of purity even to children: "instances innumerable, I am grieved to state, have come under our notice where the grossest licentiousness has been found to exist [in the working class] even among children of tender years."[141] Observers often found themselves grieved to state such things, things that must surely have infected to some extent the sanitized notion of children from other classes.

In fact, one has to wonder whether such disinfected notions really were so widespread after all, whether even the propaganda to that effect does not sometimes reveal the strain of keeping up the pretense. It is arguable that no one needed Freud or Moll or Krafft-Ebing's case studies of eight-year-olds on sexual rampages. Even in conservative writers like Ellise Hopkins or Clement Dukes, we see what can certainly be construed as admissions of child sexuality. Hopkins seems quite direct: "I fear that there is a great deal more filthy, indecent play, amongst our girls and boys, then we have any idea of."[142] Dukes uses a different tactic, first going on for nearly thirty pages (144–71) about "the importance of total abstinence from sexual excitement in the young" and then admitting at the end that such abstinence is, after all, an "uncommon virtue."[143]

There are, finally, a few indications that, for all the worries expressed about child sex play, other things worried the Victorians more. It is curious to us, for instance, that discussions of homosexuality, even by specialists like Carpenter or Symonds, almost always failed to distinguish adult homosexuality from pederasty. Richard Burton's spectacular "Terminal Essay" similarly is never clear on whether what is being discussed involves men, boys, or some mixture. Didn't it matter? Was the anxiety over childhood innocence secondary to concerns about homosexuality? To what extent were children actually made innocent? To what extent were they protected from one kind of sexuality in order to be turned over to another? To what extent were they made available for adult desire, opened up to an eroticism much more complex and demanding than the masturbation they were being guarded from?

Notes

1. Michel Foucault, "Genealogy of Ethics," in Herbert L. Dreyfus and Paul Rabinow, *Michel Foucault: Beyond Structuralism and Hermeneutics* (Chicago: Univ. of Chicago Press, 1982), p. 229.

2. Wood-Allen, *What a Young Girl Ought to Know*, pp. 58–59.

3. Krafft-Ebing, *Psychopathia Sexualis*, p. 1.

4. See Foucault, *History of Sexuality*, pp. 65–66.

5. Knowlton, *Fruits of Philosophy*, p. 41.

6. Blackwell, *The Human Element in Sex*, p. 17.

7. O.S. Fowler, *Offspring and Their Hereditary Endowment: or, Paternity, Maternity, and Infancy; Including Sexuality; Its Laws, Facts, Impairments, Restoration, and Perfection, as Taught by Phrenology and Physiology, Together with Warnings and Advice to Youth* (Boston: O.S. Fowler, 1869), pp. 42, 40.

8. Albutt, *Every Mother's Handbook*, p. 23.

9. Dr. Lucas (pseud.), *The Secrets of Life: Issued by the Private Dispensary* (n.p.: privately printed, 1882), pp. 9, v, 10.

10. Freud, "A Case of Hysteria," VII, 28.

11. Ellis, *Psychology of Sex*, I, 188.

12. Arnold Davidson, in "Sex and the Emergence," presents a brilliant example of this turn, enlisted on behalf of a precisely restricted narrative: "sexuality itself is a product of the psychiatric style of reasoning" (p. 23).

13. Krafft-Ebing, *Psychopathia Sexualis*, p. 187.

14. Martin, "Sexuality and Science,", pp. iii-v; see also pp. 88–123.

15. Davidson, "Sex and the Emergence."

16. See Bullough, *Sexual Variation*, p. 565.

17. Kinsey, *Human Male*, p. 168.

18. Freud, "Three Essays," IX, 192.

19. Kinsey, *Human Male*, p. 197.

20. Freud, "Three Essays," VII, 171.

21. Freud, "Three Essays," VII, 161.

22. See Suransky, *Erosion of Childhood*, p. 183.

23. Hayden White, "The Archaeology of Sex," *TLS* (May 6, 1977), p. 565. See also Murray S. Davis, *SMUT: Erotic Reality/Obscene Ideology* (Chicago: Univ. of Chicago Press, 1983). Davis's book searches not for the causes of deviance but for the forces that come together to constitute normality; he assumes that sexual behavior will be diverse, not normal (uniform).

24. Kinsey, *Human Male*, p. 59.

25. Foucault, *History of Sexuality*, p. 34.

26. Foucault, *History of Sexuality*, p. 32.

27. Foucault, *History of Sexuality*, pp. 57–73.

28. Crompton, *Byron and Greek Love*, p. 368.

29. Quoted in Bullough, *Sexual Variance*, p. 357.

30. Anon., *The Children's Wrong*, p. 48.

31. J.A. Symonds, *The Memoirs of John Addington Symonds: The Secret Homosexual Life of a Leading Nineteenth-Century Man of Letters*, ed. Phyllis Grosskurth (Chicago: Univ. of Chicago Press, 1984), p. 295.

32. Rev. Seward, "Purity—How Preserved Among the Young," in Powell, ed., *National Purity Congress Papers*, pp. 203, 209.

33. Jackson, *Childhood and Sexuality*, p. 48.

178 / *Sex and Its Uses*

34. In Powell, ed., *National Purity Congress Papers*, pp. 205, 206.

35. Rev. J.B. Welty, "The Need of White Cross Work," p. 246; Elbridge T. Gerry "Child Saving and Prostitution," p. 336. In Powell, ed., *National Purity Congress Papers*.

36. James Holmes, *Memoirs of Private Flagellation* (Paris: Librairie des Bibliophiles, 1889), pp. 5–6.

37. Edward L. Keyes, "The Male Genito-Urinary Organs," in Castle, ed., *Wood's Household Practice*, p. 497.

38. See Bullough, *Sexual Variance*, p. 540.

39. Blackwell, *Counsel to Parents*, p. 50.

40. Krafft-Ebing, *Psychopathia Sexualis*, p. xiv.

41. Freud, "On the Sexual Enlightenment of Children," IX, 132.

42. Freud, "A Case of Hysteria," VII, 49.

43. Ellis, *Psychology of Sex*, II, 69.

44. Lynn L. Merrill, *The Romance of Victorian Natural History* (New York: Oxford Univ, Press, 1989).

45. Krafft-Ebing, *Psychopathia Sexualis*, p. 8. All further references in this section to this work will be cited in the text.

46. Edward Brecher, "History of Human Sexual Research and Study," in Sadock et al., *The Sexual Experience*, p. 71.

47. Ellis, *Psychology of Sex*, I, xxi. All further references in this section to this four-volume work will be cited in the text.

48. For a similar description of this method see Vincent Brome, *Havelock Ellis, Philosopher of Sex: A Biography* (London: Routledge and Kegan Paul, 1979), p. 121. Brome calls Ellis's tendency, at least in the early part of his study, to take "his data too easily at its face value" a "flaw" (p. 21), which, from many points of view, it may be.

49. Ellis, *Psychology of Sex*, IV, 10.

50. Dukes, *Preservation of Health*, pp. 165, 155. Dukes does not, needless to say, side with these voices.

51. See Marcus, *The Other Victorians*, p. 163. Marcus cites Gladstone as proof: "Gladstone, for example, was totally unable to understand any joke that contained a sexual reference." A historian so convinced of the truth of his constructions as to see nothing problematic in this assertion and no other possibilities in the evidence is working positivism with a vengeance.

52. John Farley, *Gametes & Spores: Ideas about Sexual Reproduction, 1750–1914* (Baltimore: The Johns Hopkins Univ. Press, 1982), p. 111.

53. George Frederick Drinka, *The Birth of Neurosis: Myth, Malady, and the Victorians* (New York: Simon and Schuster, 1984), p. 171.

54. For a fine survey of some of the best recent work, see the Stearns's review essay, "Victorian Sexuality," *Journal of Social History*, 625–34.

55. Trudgill, *Madonnas and Magdalenes* (pp. 49–55) develops the line that the Victorians regarded sex with terror.

56. Edward Lyttleton, *The Causes and Prevention of Immorality in Schools* (London: Social Purity Alliance, [1887]), pp. v, ix.

57. Rev. Flint, *Temptation of Joseph*, pp. 7–8, 9. This last peroration takes a form very similar to that employed by Mr. Micawber in his famous advice to David: "Annual income twenty pounds, annual expenditure nineteen nineteen six, result happiness. Annual income twenty pounds, annual expenditure twenty ought and six, result misery" (*David Copperfield* [London: Oxford Univ. Press, 1948], ch.xii).

58. Marcus, *The Other Victorians*, p. 28.

59. Marcus, *The Other Victorians*, p. 111. Further references in this section will be cited in the text.

60. Maynard, "the Worlds of Victorian Sexuality," in Cox, ed., *Sexuality and Victorian Literature*, p. 259; F. Barry Smith, "Sexuality in Britain, 1800–1900: Some Suggested Revisions," in Martha Vicinus, ed., *A Widening Sphere: Changing Roles of Victorian Women* (Bloomington, Indiana: Indiana Univ. Press, 1977), pp. 184–88.

61. Weeks, *Sex, Politics*, p. 39.

62. M. Jeanne Peterson, "Dr. Acton's Enemy: Medicine, Sex, and Society in Victorian England," *Victorian Studies* 29 (1986): 588, 569–90.

63. Cominos, "Late-Victorian Sexual Respectability," p. 24; Martin, "Sexuality and Science," pp. 54–55.

64. William Acton, *The Functions and Disorders of the Reproductive Organs in Childhood, Youth, Adult Age, and Advanced Life; Considered in Their Phsiological, Social, and Moral Relations*, 6th ed. (London: J. and A. Churchill, 1875). The first edition (also published by Churchill, then John Churchill) was in 1857 and bore a slightly different title, leaving out "Childhood" and using "Psychological" instead of "Moral." The 2nd edition was in 1858, the 3rd in 1862, the 4th in 1865, and the 5th in 1871.

65. Acton, *A Practical Treatise*, p. 184.

66. Acton, *A Practical Treatise*, p. 60.

67. Acton, *A Practical Treatise*, pp. 200–7.

68. Acton, *A Practical Treatise*, pp. 523–27.

69. Dr. Henry Arthur Albutt, *The Wife's Handbook: How a Woman Should Order Herself During Pregnancy, in the Lying-in Room, and after Delivery; with Hints on the Management of the Baby, and on Other Matters of Importance Necessary to Be Known by Married Women*, 2nd ed. (London: W.J. Ramsey, 1886), p. 50.

70. See Gorham, *The Victorian Girl*, pp. 89–90.

71. Albutt, *Wife's Handbook*, p. 53.

72. Davenport, *Aphrodisiacs*, p. 23.

73. Deslandes, *Manhood*, p. 7.

74. Jean Dubois, *The Secret Habits of the Female Sex: Letters Addressed to a Mother on the Evils of Solitude and Its Seductive Temptations to Young Girls, the Premature Victims of a Pernicious Passion* (New York: "Sold by All Booksellers Generally," 1848), p. 356.

75. Wood-Allen, *What a Young Girl Ought to Know*, p. 106.

76. Wood-Allen, *What A Young Girl Ought to Know*, p. 107.

77. Kinsey, *Human Female*, pp. 173–75.

78. Krafft-Ebing, *Psychopathia Sexualis*, p. 37.

180 / *Sex and Its Uses*

79. Barker-Benfield, "The Spermatic Economy," p. 59.

80. Nichols, *Esoteric Anthropology*, p. 83.

81. Krafft-Ebing, *Psychopathia Sexualis*, p. 9.

82. See John Rutledge Martin, "Sexuality and Science," for the most authoritative argument on this subject (pp. 50–64). He says that the Victorians may have "reduced" female sexuality but never denied it. Only Acton, he points out, said anything of the sort; and he was really not so much denying female sexuality as arguing that it existed in moderate forms (see *Prostitution*, p. 178). Acton was mainly concerned, Martin says, with combating the spermatorrhea quacks, a context in which women play little or no part.

83. Ellis, *Psychology of Sex*, I, 111.

84. Bullough, *Sexual Variance*, p. 499.

85. Dr. Lucas, *Secrets of Life*, pp. 25, 35.

86. Printed on the front wrapper of *Manhood*.

87. Kinsey, *Human Male*, p. 297.

88. Paul H. Gebhard et al., *Sex Offenders: An Analysis of Types* (New York: Harper and Row and Paul B. Hoeber, 1965), p. 488.

89. Annie Reich, "The Discussion of 1912 on Masturbation and Our Present-Day Views," *Psychoanalytic Study of the Child* 6 (1951): 88. Reich is here speaking specifically of boys.

90. Martin, "Sexuality and Science," p. 84.

91. See Bristow, *Vice and Vigilance*, pp. 127–29. See also Martin, "Sexuality and Science," pp. 2–38; Bullough, *Sexual Variance*, pp. 496–99; and Robert H. MacDonald, "Frightful Consequences of Onanism: Notes on the History of a Delusion," *Journal of the History of Ideas* 28 (1967): 423–31.

92. F. Barry Smith, "Sexuality in Britain," p. 197.

93. For an admirably intelligent and sympathetic account of the masturbation controversy and of medical practice during the time, see Arthur N. Gilbert, "Doctor, Patient, and Onanist Diseases in the Nineteenth Century," *Journal of the History of Medicine and Allied Sciences* 30 (1975): 217–34.

94. Ellis, *Psychology of Sex*, I, 249–50.

95. In Dubois, *The Secret Habits*, p. 49.

96. Dukes, *Preservation of Health*, p. 166.

97. Deslandes, *Manhood*, pp. 167, 233–34.

98. See Alex Comfort, *The Anxiety Makers: Some Curious Preoccupations of the Medical Profession* (London: Nelson, 1967), pp. 104–5. His chapter 3, "The Rise and Fall of Self-Abuse," pp. 69–113, is the best in this mode I have come across.

99. Walling, *Sexology*, p. 41.

100. Fowler, *Offspring* (1869), p. 60.

101. Blackwell, *The Human Element in Sex*, p. 34.

102. Blackwell, *The Human Element in Sex*, p. 32.

103. Blackwell, *The Human Element in Sex*, pp. 32–33.

104. Martin, "Sexuality and Science," for a persuasive analysis of how moderation worked in other areas of Victorian sexual thinking generally: the condemnation of both excess and celibacy, for instance (p. 29).

105. Dukes, *Preservation of Health*, p. 149.

106. Francis W. Newman, *The Cure of the Great Social Evil, with Special Reference to Recent Laws Delusively Called Contagious Diseases' Acts* (London: Trubner and Co.; Bristol: Arrowsmith, 1869), p. 23.

107. Henry Thomas Kitchner, *Letters on Marriage: On the Causes of Matrimonial Infidelity, and on the Reciprocal Relations of the Sexes*, 2 vols. (London: printed for C. Chapple, 1812), I, 25–26.

108. Bullough, *Sexual Variance*, p. 546.

109. Dukes, *Preservation of Health*, p. 161.

110. Acton, *A Practical Treatise*, p. 9.

111. Keyes, "The Male Genito-Urinary Organs," in Castle, ed., *Wood's Household Practice*, p. 524.

112. Gilbert, "Doctor, Patient," 224.

113. Freud, " 'Civilized' Sexual Morality," IX, 199.

114. Honey, *Tom Brown's Universe*, p. 194. On this general issue, see pp. 178–96.

115. See Arnold, *Christian Life*, p. 37, for example; and Honey, *Tom Brown's Universe*, pp. 25–26.

116. Anon., *The Children's Wrong*, pp. 46–48.

117. Anon., *Youth and True Manhood*, p. 14.

118. Lyttelton, *Causes and Prevention of Immorality*, p. 7.

119. Carpenter, *The Intermediate Sex*, pp. 92–94. For more on this subject, see Honey, *Tom Brown's Universe*, pp. 167–96; and John Chandos, *Boys Together: English Public Schools, 1800–1864* (New Haven: Yale Univ. Press, 1984), pp. 284–319. On lesbian schoolgirl love, see Martha Vicinus, "Distance and Desire: English Boarding-School Friendships," *Signs* 9 (1984): 600–22.

120. Honey, *Tom Brown's Universe*, p. 207.

121. Ellis, *Psychology of Sex*, I, 216.

122. Marcus, *The Other Victorians*, pp. 73, 80. Further references in this section will be cited in the text.

123. Anon., *My Secret Life*, 11 vols. (Amsterdam: privately printed, [1967]; rpt. of original c.1885 ed.), I, 9.

124. Anon., "Introduction," *My Secret Life*, p. 6; Anon., *Lustful Adventures* (n.p.: n.p., 1900), pp. 6–7; Anon., *The Mysteries of Venus, A Nuptial Interlude; A Preceptor for Ladies and Gentlemen on Their Wedding Eve* (London: Mary Wilson, 1882), p. 4; Anon., *The Confessions of Nemesis Hunt* (London: privately printed, [1902?]), p. 2; Anon., *Suburban Souls: The Erotic Psychology of a Man and a Maid* (Paris: privately distributed, 1901), p. 4.

125. Pisanus Fraxi [Henry Spencer Ashbee], "Introduction," *Bibliography of Prohibited Books*, 3 vols. (New York: Jack Brussel, 1962), I, lxv.

126. Wardell B. Pomeroy, *Boys and Sex* (New York: Dell, 1968), p. 17.

127. Floyd M. Martinson, "Eroticism in Infancy and Childhood," in Constantine and Martinson, eds., *Children and Sex*, p. 23.

128. Richard L. Currier, "Juvenile Sexuality in Global Perspective," in Constantine and Martinson, eds., *Children and Sex*, p. 12.

129. Freud, "On the Sexual Theories of Children," IX, 209.

130. Freud, "History of an Infantile Neurosis," XVII, 24.

131. "A member of the House of Commons said to me the other day: 'That a thing is an anomaly, I consider to be no objection to it whatever.' I venture to think he was wrong...." "The Function of Criticism at the Present Time" (1864) in *Matthew Arnold*, ed. Miriam Allott and Robert H. Super, "The Oxford Authors" (Oxford: Oxford Univ. Press, 1986), p. 323.

132. Foucault, *History of Sexuality*, p. 37.

133. Foucault, *History of Sexuality*, pp. 99, 153.

134. Michel Foucault, "Truth and Power," in Gordon, ed., *Power/Knowledge*, p. 120.

135. Hagstrum, *Sex and Sensibility*, p. 222.

136. Rev. Seward, "Purity," in Powell, ed., *National Purity Congress Papers*, pp. 208, 212.

137. A. Reeves Jackson, "Diseases Peculiar to Women," in Castle, ed., *Wood's Household Practice*, p. 542.

138. Ellis, *Psychology of Sex*, II, 306–7; IV, 16. Bristow, *Vice and Vigilance*, says Ellis "shared the pre-Freudian notion that sex was dormant in children" (p. 135), a somewhat misleading way of putting it, since Freud believed sex was dormant/latent in *children* (as opposed to infants), and since Ellis's view of childhood sexuality is, in truth, somewhat more open and ambiguous than I have made out.

139. E.C., *Our Children, How to Rear and Train Them*, p. 15.

140. Richard J. Ebbard et al., *How to Restore Life-Giving Energy to Sufferers from Sexual Neurasthenia and Kindred Nerve and Brain Disorders (Neurosis, Hysteria, etc.)* (London: Modern Medical Publishing Co., 1903), p. 37.

141. Mitchell, *Rescue the Children*, p. 114.

142. Hopkins, *On the The Early Training*, p. 44.

143. Dukes, *Preservation of Health*, p. 171.

5

Child-Love

> The man who kills does no more than shorten a human life, but a man who corrupts a young lad or girl destroys one—and that is worse.
> —Mr. Justice Stable[1]

It strikes our contemporary Mr. Justice Stable that it is better to murder an infant in its cradle than to nurse to fruition a desire that would corrupt a young lad or girl. We all know, approximately, what Mr. Justice Stable means when he talks about the "young," and we also think we know what he means by "corrupting" them. We recognize, further, that his position on the matter is a platitude in our culture. It is shared by all, the political Left and Right, men and women, the liberated and the prude. Even the imprisoned are one with the respectable on this issue: the fairly commonplace murdering of those doing time for sexual involvement with children seems a natural consequence of Justice Stable's views, a performance of a drama scripted by our own normality. But how did such a drama arise? Who built the theater? What's the play about? What's the attraction?

To begin: Victorian talk on children, on the body, and on sex did not dissociate but combined the three, did not make the figure of the erotic child's body unthinkable. Discourse that directly sexualized the child, as I have argued, was no more effective than that which purified it in terms of successfully divesting the child of desirability. That this should be so comes, as Foucault says, from the presence of all the talk about sex and the child, all the evident anxiety. Making the child's sexuality a central problem, we have married them, even when we deny that they are on speaking terms. In addition, we have loaded all this discourse with such desperate energy that it has taken on a dualistic fierceness: the child is either free of any whiff of sexuality or is, somehow, saturated with it. The idea that children might be invested with a low-level, junior-grade sexuality—something between nothing whatever and full-fledged carnality—is seldom advanced and less often welcomed. This all-or-nothing rhetoric reflects a process of imaging the problem that makes the eroticizing of the child inevitable.

Our culture deals with this inevitability by issuing orders to deny it.

It is imperative that we declare to be obvious what our way of doing business and seeing our world makes impossible. The child has been made desirable, and we must blame someone, namely the pedophile, as much a necessary cultural construction as a real-life criminal. My aim in this chapter is to find perspectives on the development of this dominant line on child-loving, to construct some counter-narratives on how the child came to be loved and by whom, and to pause over why some stories are more popular than others.

The explicit relationship of pedophilia to our present culture will not find its way to the center until chapter 10, but a brief reminder of where we sit at present will perhaps help us settle in more clearly in reference to the past. As a starter, here is a familiar statement. The game is to guess the author: "Criminal statistics prove the sad fact that sexual crimes are progressively increasing in our modern civilization. This is particularly the case with immoral acts with children under the age of fourteen."[2] Not a contemporary of ours (as you were thinking, right?) but the Victorian Krafft-Ebing.

Generally, our great-grandparents didn't bother much with such narratives. It has been left to us to puzzle helplessly over what we have done, to search for a scheme to contain the sexual attractiveness we have implanted in the child. We have not outgrown Krafft-Ebing's story of moral decay, but it hardly seems sufficient. It is better, though, than the blank confessions of bafflement that now and then break through: "Given such strong social and legal sanctions against such behavior, why would any adult turn to a child in search of sexual gratification rather than other, more acceptable, outlets? Such behavior seems unreasonable."[3] Attempting to rule unthinkable the way in which the child has been linked to sexuality in our culture, such denials make it mandatory to think about the sexualized child. And we think in terms of a traditional fable which has served us faithfully, if not well:

> Many adults are concerned these days about older men who hang around schools and corner candy stores, hoping to lure some boy or girl into sexual behavior with them. Parents and police departments are rightfully concerned with these people, because they are sexual exploiters and bullies. . . . Sometimes, as the newspapers remind us so often, they can be a great deal worse. They can even be kidnappers and murderers.[4]

One thing in this account is accurate: the newspapers do remind us of this story. Other than that, as Theo Sandfordt comments, this image of the stranger luring children off the streets and into sex "does not correspond to the paedophile as seen by these young people [those having sex with adults], and it probably doesn't offer much insight into the phenomenon in other cases either."[5] Those most closely involved with the concrete details of the problem commonly lament that the popularity of the myth so overrides actual evidence that "many cases are missed": for example, the assumption that "a violent, forcible attack" is involved on the child is contradicted by the "large body of evidence showing that child sexual abuse often involves nonviolent, nonforcible contact."[6] Kenneth Plummer has gone so far as to compile a point-by-point refutation of the common line: in place of a dirty old man we have an average age of 35 (Kinsey); only as few as 12% are strangers; in the overwhelming majority of cases, the attentions are not forced on the child; very seldom is sexual intercourse attempted or intended; far from traumatizing the child, these experiences are usually felt to be pleasurable.[7] Very few of us would accept Plummer's arguments, certainly not the last one, even as we note how young those beauty-contest-winners tend to be.

One has the feeling that all the counter-evidence and ridicule in the world would not shake the ability of this tale of the molestation of innocence by strangers to get itself told. Why it is told so often and with such passion is by no means clear, though it is the central question. Our own insights into our cultural myth-making here are classically weak. They get no better than the chilling ironic form of suggesting that we inadvertently subject our finest and most alert (or at least most passive and obedient) children to a kind of training course for pedophile relations: "many of the same qualities that make a child a 'good' child also make him or her an 'easy' victim."[8] But surely we can dive deeper.

Deep-diving is a metaphor not only annoyingly self-congratulatory but probably inaccurate. The most stunning answers to our questions have been taken from the surface, plucked up by the placid empiricism of Alfred Kinsey and related with the same sly bluntness with which he spoke of sex with calves.[9] For the most part, Kinsey gives the impression of neutral reporting—that very small children and many infants may experience orgasm, for instance, even without the emission of semen.[10] But now and then the mask drops and we see the social critic and reformer: "it is probable that half or more of the boys in an uninhibited society could reach climax by the time they were three or four years of age, and that nearly all of them could experience such a climax three to five years before the onset of adolescence."[11] Clearly Kinsey has a great deal of sympathy for this "uninhibited society" and an equal amount of scorn for the one around him. He is here talking about boys, but he can be just as deadpan outrageous when it comes to girls. Noting how beneficial youthful orgasms are, he allows that many females "appear to get along without such an outlet" but still maintains that "the chances that a female can adjust sexually after marriage seem to be materially improved if she has experienced orgasm at an earlier age."[12]

When Kinsey turns to pedophilia, he often achieves his bone-rattling effects through the same imperturbable prose: "Older persons are the teachers of younger people in all matters, including the sexual."[13] I'm sure there is a name for this satiric technique, where a scorpion's tail is attached to the most commonplace crawling thing of a statement. Sometimes Kinsey can do similar things simply by scattering flat, low-toned words into a context we want to regard as highly charged. Note in the following the unexpected zing of the folksy tone and of relaxed terms like "somewhat older," "more experienced," "a good many," "effective," and especially "help":

> Manual manipulation is more likely to become so specific [leading to arousal and orgasm] if the relation is had with a somewhat older boy, or with an adult. Without help from more experienced persons, many pre-adolescents take a good many years to discover masturbatory techniques that are sexually effective.[14]

Kinsey is fully aware that we regard it as better to chop off a child's head than to give a little "help" in masturbation. But he has no sympathy with such views, sees no reason why "more experienced persons" should not lend a hand. What harm could it do the child, he asks, apart from the harm *we* inflict through our attitudes? "It is difficult," he says, "to understand why a child, except for its cultural conditioning, should be disturbed at having its genitalia touched, or disturbed at seeing the genitalia of other persons, or disturbed at even more specific sexual contacts."[15] That such disturbances do take place he acknowledges, and he acknowledges that they can be terrible in their power. But he blames them on us, on "the public hysteria" which lands harmless adults in prison and makes it very hard for the child to grow up to enjoy sex or much of anything else.[16]

Kinsey readily concedes that in cases where physical damage has been done to the child, where force has been used, criminal acts have clearly taken place. But it upsets common views to imply that there is a distinction, that power can be used to understand only some of these instances. From within power, all sexual encounters between adults and children involve a self-evident power imbalance and are thus deeply coercive: the adult is larger; has invested in her or him psychological and cultural authority; is more experienced at manipulating the child, who has been conditioned to be obedient.[17] Through power, the narrative can only be told in one way, as a story of rape, it being "patently ridiculous" to suppose that the child can ever be the instigator in such relations.[18] Furthermore, the damage to the child is inevitable and inevitably severe. The very fact that so few children mention these events to parents or authorities is itself proof of the damage, of the power of the molesting adult. Such power narratives sound wholly persuasive; but if they were, the argument could be put to rest. Somehow, child sexuality and child eroticism elude the control of power. To this point, we have dealt with that annoyance by applying yet more power, on the principle that if something does not fit, pound on it.

What Is It?

Admiring children, responding to children as erotic forms, investing one's primary emotions in children, desiring children, engaging in sex with children, helping children, molesting children, worshipping children, devoting one's life to children, living for children, living through children: all these forms (and more) are available to us under the general rubric of "child-love." Some are sanctified; others are censured. How they are to be distinguished one from another is never, in practice, very clear, though there is pressure to pretend that nothing could be clearer. Loving children does not mean doing so in *that* way, which is the way of "pedophiles" (lovers of children) or "pederasts" (lovers of boys). We use those terms as if they marked off an area of the population and an area of modern experience entirely distinct from the rest of us. We conduct clinical studies on them, the medical establishment having been called in to confirm what the law has asserted: that pedophilia exists and can be cut out of the herd. What can be arrested can be studied, and science thus completes the circle and confirms what it was necessary to have settled: that pedophilia is a condition. We called out the police to confirm that it exists. Having established that, we are free to detest it, pity it or, if we are crazy, honor it.

To help encourage acknowledging it, we conduct studies of pedophilia mostly in jails or hospitals, the two institutions most clearly set up to reassure us that there are those who are different. Even so, the results of these inquiries can be unsettling. They often do not indicate marked deviations in this population. In one important study, most of the subjects were not old; most did not abuse drugs or alcohol; there were "no significant differences in intelligence between child offenders and the general population"; and none were homosexuals.[19] Some groups studied have indicated an "abundance of marital coitus and [a] high degree of happiness in marriage."[20] Parker Rossman cites unpublished studies which show that more pederasts are arrested from among the clergy than any other vocational group, perhaps, Rossman says, because they "tend to be more naive and innocent."[21] These are not the sorts of things we want to hear, nor do we want these studies telling us of "accidental" or "situational" pedophilia. Pedophilia must be premeditated and congenital, though it is probably permissible to say also that it is widespread, so long as you keep to certain rules. That is, it is legitimate to say that one out of every three children is molested; or seven out of every ten. It is also fine to assert that molested children grow up to be molesting adults. But one cannot say that one out of every three or seven out of every ten adults are molesters (though that would seem to follow). Such studies are being conducted, perhaps, to keep such things from being said. All such studies confirm the segregation of child-lovers; and so long as the findings are not gruesome it doesn't much matter what they are. No one wants to see the clergy tarnished, but it is a price we will pay for the benefits conferred.

One of the benefits is the bolstering it gives to reassuring categories of perversion, categories that protect us from looking too hard. Such thinking is needed with figures like Swinburne, whose relationship with Adah Menken is seen as conveniently bizarre and whose reference to her as "a mistress" is simply disbelieved.[22] After all, if Swinburne is allowed any sort of conventional heterosexuality, even as an interlude, our categorizing habits might be in trouble. The categories and the protective habits of mind that bring them into being are what matter.

In reference to pedophilia, these categories are, it is true, multiplied in clinical analyses: girl-lovers, boy-lovers, those attracted to the prepubescent, the adolescent, the young adult. It is customary also to assert that these are all members of the same "psychodynamic constellation."[23] But it seems to me that even what we admit to in the way of child-loving complications outruns this "variation-on-a-theme" model. It is not just a matter of distinguishing the ages of the children in question but their appearances and relative physical maturity. The gender of the child may matter, but so may the gender of the adult. It may seem important to determine whether the child and the adult or both are heterosexual or homosexual, assuming those terms are in any way fixed. Further, there seem to be important differences between fantasy and actual behavior, between aggressive sexual advances and sex play, between coitus and fondling, between rape and consensual connections, between premeditated and situational sex, between long-term affairs and single encounters. All of this befouls the waters, since the multiplication of difference inevitably causes a confusion of categories that in turn calls into question the distinction between the perverted and the normal love for children. "Perfectly normal men and women often participate in children's play and activities, hence distinguishing between the normal and abnormal is a bit difficult."[24] "No it isn't!," we want to respond. But we are forced to admit that these studies, on one hand so reassuring, have a way of clouding the categories they are set up to clarify, opening the way for a form of sexual thinking that abandons fixed categories in favor of a scale of dynamic and relativistic measure of a shifting range of possibilities. Such models, proposed as early as Edward Carpenter and aggressively promoted by Kinsey, never seem to make many inroads in our culture. I am unable to see why this should be so, and am not satisfied that it can be adequately explained in terms of fear, but the fact remains that there are some categories whose fixity we are unwilling to regard as negotiable.

The Gender Issue

Though gender issues and gender-thinking are these days both fluid and complex, they tend to harden into simple form in the case of child sexuality. I think it is possible that we assert the importance of gender all the more confidently because of our lack of confidence in our ability to figure and place it. We are confused about the nature or location of gender in both the child-lover and in the child being loved, and so reach certainty.

It is true that, for whatever reason, some child-lovers seem consistent in their gender preferences; but many, like the Victorians and like Freud, see little difference between the sexes in children: "it is not until puberty that the sharp distinction is established between the masculine and feminine characters,"[25] an amalgamation perhaps especially marked during a period that discouraged (in advice manuals anyhow) very much gender discrimination with children.[26] What's more, pedophiles, some experts tell us, have sexual preferences which are "blurred" as regards gender.[27]

Still, our culture does not allow the gender of the child to be a matter of indifference in such situations. We attach to the gendered child an evaluation that is as insistent as it is muddled. First of all, as Francis Newman pointed out last century, "manifestly, the fact is, that people desire chastity in their daughters *greatly*, and in their sons *very feebly*: that is the true key to the whole."[28] Newman seems indeed to be onto something, though it is doubtful that he has the only key. Certainly we do place a higher value still on female chastity and delicacy and react with a different quality of anger to the violation of a female child: purity is attached to children and to females. On the other hand, it appears that there is a different level of fury that comes into play, as it did against Oscar Wilde, when a people feels that its young manhood is being threatened.

When one considers the gender of the adult (the pedophile), our attempts to gain clarity seem no more successful. For some time, we seemed able to maintain pretty successfully the story that gender simply was not an issue, that all pedophiles were male. Women, says Gebhard in his study of sex offenders, fail to excite public concern, and justifiably so: "The average female has a much weaker 'sex drive' than the average male; consequently she is less likely to behave in a sexually illegal manner."[29] This exposes the uncomfortable logic at work in decriminalizing the female, the price that apparently must be paid. But for some time it was exacted, partly because women had so much contact with children that it was necessary to insulate the two parties sexually. The result may have been less happy. Freud said women were sexually magnetized by children (as they were not by men): "In typical cases women fail to exhibit any sexual overvaluation towards men; but they scarcely ever fail to do so towards their own children."[30] Ellis, further, had dutifully recorded instances of assaults on children by women as evidence that his age tended to undervalue the range and power of "the sexual impulse" in women.[31] But it wasn't, I think, until quite recently that the possibility has been raised that women's virtual immunity from suspicion (and prosecution) in this regard had been unwarranted. John Crewdson suggests that at least as many women as men are active pedophiles, posing the uncomfortable dilemma raised by any belief in the cycle-of-abuse theory: abused children grow up to abuse children, and the majority of those abused are female. He suggests that young boys molested by women are too ashamed to report it and are laughed at when they do; lesbian relations with children simply go unnoticed.[32] Whatever the persuasive force of these arguments, they do act to confuse further what already is in a terrible jumble, even as regards gender.

Homosexuality and Child-Love

There is of course a pervasive modern tendency to declare that, whatever else may remain unclear about this child-love, it is our main perversion. What interested the Victorians in the way of perversion, at least in the last three decades of the century, seems primarily to have been not the size (or age) of the people involved, but the gender. The "invert" or, increasingly, the "homosexual" held public and medical attention.

The Victorians, though often including pedophilia or pederasty within homosexuality, did not use the former as a club to beat the latter. Instead, they focused on the nature of the same-sex attraction (or, really, male-male attraction, the discourse on lesbianism remaining almost entirely the sole possession of pornography). When they happened to speak about the attraction to children, they tended to mark its *difference* from homosexual behavior. Even Havelock Ellis, who found child-love of so little consequence that he seldom noted it, did agree with Moll's view of pederasty as "that form of inversion which comes closest to normal sexuality," the child attracting the male adult because of its resemblance to a woman.[33] Krafft-Ebing went further: "Practically speaking, acts of immorality committed on boys by men sexually inverted are of the greatest rarity."[34]

These off-hand dissociations of pederasty from homosexuality became the basis for some modern opinion. Victorian notions that pederasts are associating boys with something feminine (in the normal heterosexual way) find some recent echoes,[35] and the most respected empirical studies reluctantly admit that adult offenders against boys are "almost uniformly heterosexual and not homosexual," that perhaps not just offenders but pederasts in general are heterosexual, that there is even a possibility that what we think of as "homosexual pedophilia" may be not only unrelated to but mutually exclusive with what we think of as "homosexuality."[36] This is not to say that the ignorant, the unscrupulous, and the brutal have discontinued making the association between these two bogeys, homosexuality and pedophilia. It is just that no respectable explanation of the second "perversion" can depend on the first for support.

Respectable Explanations

Before launching into the multitude of entirely proper explanations of child-love (including my own), I might consider briefly why we have so many, why they take the strenuous form that they do, why each is so self-contained and coherent. Why are we so eager to scurry to find causes for variance? What function is served by the enunciation of causality, its embodiment in official forms, its elaboration? And by what means do we determine which explanations will suit our needs

192 / *Child-Love*

and which will not, which ones are sound and which defective? Here are a couple of explanations offered up for testing:

> The loneliness engendered by the early loss of his [John Addington Symonds's] mother, and the emotional rejection by his father whom he strenuously feared and revered, helped to fixate him at the homosexual level from which he was never able to rise.[37]

> It is not uncommon for a man with paedophilic tendencies to marry and become a father, but it is often the case that these tendencies declare themselves more overtly in the offspring.[38]

The first seems crudely homophobic, the second to announce its silly causality too openly. Are these statements any different in kind, though, from those now accorded respect? And why are such explanatory statements licensed, encouraged?

Psychological Explanations

The most popular form of explaining isolates the phenomenon of child-love within the mind of the adult participant. Such personalizing of pedophilia makes complex, peculiar, and distinct the causes which give rise to it and the impulses which drive it. The influential Brandt Steele allows that other modes of explanation may possibly contribute a little to our understanding, but that social explanations, for instance, cannot possibly give us "a deeper, more subtle psychological understanding of these individuals."[39] The depth of such explanations is itself reassuring, providing distance and encasement; the claim for subtlety is a red herring. As I mentioned before, collecting data to support this deep subtlety from prisons and mental institutions is curious. Just as curious is the rarity of protests. It is as if we were to accept without question conclusions on marriage drawn from a study of those who had assaulted their partners or been driven mad by them.[40]

Even in psychological studies, however, there are often incidental deviations from the main cultural narrative, though such discordant matter is usually ignored. We do not especially want to hear that the average pedophile is married, perhaps more happily than most, and has sexual intercourse within that marriage a little more often than the average. It is incoherent to report that this pedophile is rather prudish, conventional, possibly more "controlled than the average male,"[41] showing only an average-at-best response to sexual stimuli. Most of all, we regard as never having been said the following news: "Few sexual offenders against children are demonstrably psychotic in any obvious way."[42] Such a profile does not suit the character in the story. Much worse, the story itself is sometimes upset by those who say we have gone to the wrong shop (psychology) for our plot: "the psychology of pedophilia remains pretty much an enigma."[43]

We might scorn Krafft-Ebing's guess that "erotic paedophilia" was caused by "a morbid disposition,"[44] but our own notion that pedophilia is a "condition," a "disease" was the view held also by Krafft-Ebing—"the proper place for such persons is a sanitarium established for that purpose, not prison"[45]—and before him by Justinian.[46] Further, we should recall how a similar "informed" connection between homosexuality and disease was used to such cruel ends, how any conception of "disease" is sure to lead to ideas of contagion. With this in mind, we can understand the words of the pedophile "Norman" studied by Bell and Hall: "I would prefer to have been called bad rather than sick."[47]

But the connection with disease is very strong—"there is no known cure for the pedophile"[48]—and a minor industry sets about finding such a "cure," often by way of the barbarism called "direct behavioral intervention."[49] Almost invariably, however, the pedophile is mulishly resistant to well-intentioned therapy, stubbornly refusing to change. Pedophiles almost never refer themselves for treatment or, when placed there by force, fully cooperate with it. Apparently accepting our culture's deep beliefs, pedophiles may simply be rejecting the superficial blather about disease, regarding their activity as a consequence of their "nature," seeing their feelings as essential. It is also very likely that the almost complete failure of any devices for helping indicates that the pedophile likes things the way they are and regards the cure not as something worse than the disease, but as something intruded into what they are. They are not eager to have their life taken away, even if they are promised another and better one.

In any case, what seems to be at stake is not a cure anyhow, but the explanatory mechanisms we invest in, and our need to keep the explaining machinery going. Such machines can objectify and distance that which has come uncomfortably close. A popular explaining formula draws upon the disturbed-childhood fund, an almost invulnerable source since no one can ever remember enough from infancy or early childhood to refute it. "The common denominator," says Steele, in the life of child molesters is the absence of adequate parental models during childhood, "the lack of appropriate sexual education, and, most important for all [child abusers], lack of empathic, sensitive care during the early impressionable, developmental years."[50] It is true that some people often included in studies or surveys of sexual maladjustments, Swinburne for instance, would appear to have had plenty of "empathic, sensitive care" during those "impressionable, developmental years"; but who can say for sure? Besides, maybe he had too much empathy and sensitivity, which would lead to the same results as too little, especially when the mother is involved. Many authorities agree that too strong an attachment to the mother can lead to a form of mutual admiration which can lead to narcissism[51]—and then to pedophilia, as one tries to recapture the boy that knew so fully the mother's love. So, a tilt in either direction as regards the closeness of mother and infant will, we are told, lead to pedophilia, evidence for this to be found not only in case histories but in the presence of the Great Mother or anima archetype in the writing of adult pedophiles.[52]

One can also see pedophilia as caused by one form or another of fantasy or at least the dependence on fantasy. This argument is seldom to be distinguished from the first, since a reliance on fantasy is usually said to be rooted in some disturbance in early life. Still, one can study the nature of pedophile fantasy, the unusual amount of intense imaginative activity, the remarkable fact that most pedophiles are poets and all are photographers. The presence of this imaginative life was, to John Addington Symonds, a horrible burden, a sign that he could not repress his desire at all, only "stifle" its outward expression and "wallow" in the "pernicious sins of the imagination."[53] Symonds was aware that his tastes were not sublimated by such an inner life but fed by the narratives constructed there.

The question then, to try another explanation, is why the pedophile would turn to weaving such stories. Because, we are often told, the pedophile is fixated or, more likely, regressive to such an extent that he or she is no more than a child, a case of arrested development or of pathological retreat from an overpowering adult world: "Chronologically Norman is an adult; psychologically, he is a child, an infant, possibly even a fetus."[54] Such a diagnosis is close to being a judgment. The "fixated pedophile" is said to be a victim of "maladaptive" adjustment, but he is not a victim we need have much sympathy for: "he appears to be a marginal or inadequate individual who is somewhat overwhelmed by the ordinary demands of life."[55] Such inadequates are sometimes diagnosed as spoiled brats "unable to defer the gratification of their impulses."[56]

It is possible that such expressions of pique are touched by a sense we have, supported by pedophile writings, that pedophilia poses as fastidious, claims for itself a superior refinement. Disdaining the ordinary close connection of the sexual and the animal (hair, sweat, smell), the pedophile implicitly accuses us of being swinish in our tastes and practices. The child is imaged in pedophilia as clean, fresh, unmarked: a reproach, however absurd, to conventional behavior. The pedophile somehow manages this half-subversive positioning, puts forward this nagging and preposterous claim that it is *we* who are defiled.

Such offenses perhaps add fuel to the most gratifying explanation of the problem, that there is no problem after all, that we are right, and that our way of regarding and doing sex couldn't be more satisfactory. Pedophiles would very much like to be like us if they could, but they can't. Therefore, they try to be as much like us as they can and use substitutes: unable to attract or be attractive to adult men or women, they settle for children. Since these children are "displacements from the original object, and [since] displacement can only be partially satisfying,"[57] they are doomed to be unsatisfied, unlike us.

You will notice that the tone changes now and becomes, while no less animated, free from any irony. I realize I shouldn't address you directly, but it's important that you understand that what has preceded were the ideas of others, explanations of pedophilia arranged by me into groupings but not otherwise what I could call my own. Because I did not want to stand behind them and because I also wanted to keep you from back there too if I could, I attempted mild satire. But what follows here very shortly are my explanations, which should not be understood as being presented satirically. It is true that they are, pretty much, in the form of "explanations" and that I have just been arguing that such explaining may be a kind of denial, a way of asserting a control we cannot really muster. True, but aside from that, I think what follows are pretty good as explanations go. I do not claim that these are right, that they really explain, only that they function very impressively as explanations.

This child, the image formulated in response to desire is really a complex and dynamic function. The child is not a fixed counter, even in photographs, and acts not only as a distant allurement but as a moving conveyor belt, propelling the adult dreamer into the child's world, a world that immediately becomes the sole property of the dreamer. In this sense, the child is constructed as a mirror that is also a window, reflecting back to the adult viewer a child, a true child. The child, then, is at the same time alien and familiar, that which is different and that which can pass for the self. We as adults look and, lo, we see

196 / *Child-Love*

the true child, a form of our own self, or at least a self we can recognize. The child performs as a complex narcissistic image[58] offering entry into a vision of play.

Pedophiliac figurations situate the child at a distance impossibly remote and in a focus impossibly blurred; but such an image really allows the adult to leap into this blur, somehow without canceling the desire—and, what is more crucial, without capturing or canceling the child who was originally there. The original child keeps its distance, that is, offering the adult the way to maneuver into a new position but, in doing so, moves to a new position itself, maintains its Otherness. The child thus is split into the true child, the one who was there in the first place and whose spot is now occupied by the adult, and the false child, the one who has moved away.

This psychic theater, so popular in Victorian and modern cultures, thus allows the adult to be more the child than the child is. While the true child is consistently sentimentalized, the false child, who is doing no more than playing its part, is forced into a drama of betrayal, is compelled to remain Other and act out the familiar role of the false child. The false child is resistant, does not understand, does not come close, and is therefore commonly resented. But of course it is this distance from the true child, the adult, that allows for the maintenance of desire. Using Lewis Carroll as a familiar example, one might say that Alice plays brilliantly her false-child role, never is a true child, never responds to Carroll himself when he enters as the true child, as the Dodo, gnat, or White Knight. We do, thus, get a strong sense of a true child in these books, one who is central to the nonsense, who not only does not want to grow up but has no way of imagining such a thing. But that true child is not Alice. Alice aggressively resists that role—but it is played to the hilt by Carroll—or perhaps projected by Carroll. The Alice figure, then, is shadowed by this true child, but is distant enough from it to occupy the position of a faintly hostile, defensive Other, both longed-for and feared. The pedophile, in short, plays the part of the child in order to play with the desire for the child-who-ought-to-be.

Such terms as molestation are meaningless to an operation like this one, not only dictated by desire but guaranteed to preserve that desire by preserving distance. A pedophile operating within a paradigm of play is not seeking fulfillment, wants not even to construct a seduction drama but to stand on the threshold of such a drama. It is an erotics of temptation and flirtation, a chase after a signified one will never catch because, in the catching, the world would collapse and desire would end. The paradigmatic operations of play thus most clearly mark themselves off from those of power: power leads to a collapsing of distance and of desire; it can eroticize only itself and thus tends toward completion and even toward violence, toward rape and toward a world divided between the satiated and the brutalized. Play, feasting on its own inventiveness, does not lead to anything but its own perpetuation; it does not know conclusions. Play eroticizes the whole world—and keeps it that way.

Historical Explanations

Explanations of pedophilia that appeal to history have been far less popular than psychological ones. Partly, I suppose, it is less sparkling to have sexual practices described as if they were nothing more than shifting patterns of trade or the rise of the middle class. But it does seem to be significant that the full range of explanatory models employed to such wonderful effect with difficult contemporary issues like gender are denied to pedophilia. While other areas, even of sexuality, are subject to a full range of disciplinary discourses, pedophilia seems to be locked into psychological vaults. There may possibly be complex reasons for this segregation, but the one that presents itself to me is that psychological discourse alone gives us the totalizing shields we need from the implications of this subject: the individualizing hypotheses and the vocabulary of aberration. Psychological talk names the subject handily, explains it in such a way as to keep it away, and derides it.

This is not to say that we are totally without a history or some materials for a history of this subject, just that what we have often looks outlandish. J.Z. Eglinton's *Greek Love*, one of the fullest accounts, is so full of personal judgments and specialized arguments that it is hard, despite its capaciousness, to credit its reliability. It sails, however, far above such things as Drew and Drake's *Boys for Sale*, which advertises itself as a "sociological study" and contains a considerable number of historical assertions, but which could do more to resist being used as a guidebook for the pederastic tourist. Some of the histories that do exist have claimed that pedophilia increases along with the prosperity and general success of a nation; it seems to thrive "wherever people have leisure and wealth to enjoy themselves."[59] Those sorts of findings are, we might assume, so unwelcome to a culture possessed of much leisure and wealth and badly wanting more, that encouragement for further research would be wanting.

There are many studies of Greek and, to a lesser degree, Roman pederasty; and we have snatches of knowledge from the centuries after. Bullough cites a seventh-century Irish penitential which lists penances, curiously "light ones," for the explicit practices of "the sinful playing of boys," a subject which has some bearing on the subject.[60] It is not generally until the European Renaissance, however, that things pick up slightly. We know that the tradition of modern pederastic erotica can be traced back at least to *Alcibiade Fanciullo a Scuola*, attributed to an early seventeenth-century Venetian, Ferrante Pallavicino and published (posthumously) in 1652.[61] In Renaissance England, the presence of boys on the stage has stirred some interest,[62] but to a large extent what we know about the history of pedophilia begins with the nineteenth century.

That is not the same thing as saying that pedophilia itself begins with the nineteenth century. However, it can be argued that the special historical construction of "the child" during this period and slightly before made it available to desire in a way not previously possible, made it available by, among other things, making it different, a strange and alien species that was once, and in some way is still, continuous with the adult. This highlighted, special, and different child was also made radiant, by way of the Romantic exaltation of the child, an exaltation furthered by the revival of fundamentalist Christianity in Victorian England. The contributions of Christianity to pedophilia are hard to measure but probably heavy,[63] considering what force was placed by that religion on purity, how closely purity was associated with children (and, of course, women), and how vital, if partly submerged, was the connection between this purity and the sexually prohibited, desirable, sanctioned, and necessary: violating purity was perhaps the major crime; but the enjoyment of purity was also the reward held out to the faithful, both in marriage and in heaven. Purity was, in any case, defined by and thus riddled through with sexual desire in Victorian England. The alliance of purity and sexuality rules its religion, its poetry, its commerce; it reached its zenith in the home, and in the center of the domestic sphere, the child.

All of which is high-sounding but dubious. So negative a game as purity could never attract so many players, and even sexuality's imperialist claims deserve to be questioned. *I* want to claim that the way in which we have constructed the child, the way in which it has been constructed historically, makes its desirability inevitable. But I do not say that the erotic appeal of the child is the center of the culture or a key with which to unlock its secret. That we have so incessantly disclaimed responsibility for eroticizing the child makes the subject particularly seductive, but it does not guarantee any sort of centering.

But who knows? Anyhow, attending to details, we ought to ask what we do know of Victorian pedophilia. The three chapters following will take up this theme as regards discourse that is mostly literary. We should also acknowledge the spectacular public issues of prostitution and "white-slavery," however little the Victorians focused those problems on child victims, and nod toward the low-level public scandals caused by schoolmasters suspected of pederasty or even sacked because of it, William Johnson (Cory) and Oscar Browning, both at Eton, for instance.[64] We know of the existence of cults worshipping little girls and of groups of child-loving (mostly boy-loving) poets, organizing themselves with various degrees of unanimity and strength from the 1860s through the 1930s under rubrics like "The Calamites" (after Whitman's "Calamus" poems) or "The Uranians" and including such figures as Symonds, Edward Carpenter, John Francis Bloxam, John Gambril Francis Nicholson, Frederick Rolfe ("Baron Corvo"), and a great many others.[65] We know that Greek pederasty was studied, doubtless distorted (or adapted), and to some extent promoted, and we know that this took place within a context, the public schools, where the very practices discussed were also practiced. Whether such practices were growing steadily throughout the century we have no way of knowing, but the expanding discourse on the subject suggests that the conversion of the practice into a "problem" proceeded rapidly toward the end of the century.

We can, also in passing, note some forms of Victorian pedophilia that seem especially marked, perhaps specific to the period. The particular attractions of the sick or dying child seem to have figured importantly for the culture generally, and certainly for pedophiles. The surviving pedophile poetry and what we know of public activity suggests that, next to dying and the even-more-popular flogging, bathing may have provided the most important subject: "Breasting the wavelets, and diving there,/ White boys, ruddy, and tanned and bare."[66] Francis William Bouidillon's "The Legend of the Water Lilies" (1878)[67] is one of several poems of this sort that combine naked bathing with death: when one of the group swims out too far, the others, all of them, try to save their comrade and drown in the attempt. Some water lilies (the ones referred to in the title of the poem) grow there to mark the grave and preserve the erotic image of the bonanza of naked, dying bodies. This memorializing raises another common feature of pedophilia, the action taken against transience on behalf of the desire to possess and hold the child in time. The incessant nineteenth-century (and modern) child-photographing seems to be a form of this erotic urge, and the photographing can, in turn, be related to the close connections between pedophilia and voyeurism, all of which I will save for later chapters. Finally, we can locate in Victorian pedophilic discourse what look like various displaced or substitute fetishes or practices: spanking, most notably, but also enema cults and underwear cults. In *When a Child Loves*, for instance, the chief adult figure, General Hill, was "one of those persons for whom the little lady's underclothing had a great and especial fascination."[68]

This last example leads me, not very artfully, to an acknowledgment of the existence of some erotic or pornographic material directly involving children. As I mentioned earlier, I believe we have greatly exaggerated the quantity of this material, probably because we get pleasure in imagining it to have been there, much as we now relish the idea of some "billion-dollar kiddie porn industry." There was at least a little Victorian child erotica. The bulk of what survives focuses on flagellation (see ch. 7); there is not a great deal of "straight" material—depictions of seduction, sex play, intercourse between adults and children—that I know of. There is, however, a lot of windy propaganda about the importance of sex starting very young:

> At the age of twelve I had practiced every form of sexual desire that my vigorous imagination could conceive. I had "had" several beautiful boys of my own sge [sic] with whom I indulged in sll [sic] sorts of sexual acts. I had also played with and "had" several young girls from the age of six to twenty, which, together with my carnal knowledge of all of father's farm. . . .[69]

Even this, however, seldom takes narrative form. What we generally find, in place of detailed depictions of adult-child sex, is one form or another of general discussion, extended arguments on the subject. Here are two examples, the first being somewhat rudimentary, the second more advanced. The first:

> Is it any wonder that men of refinement and feeling, seek above all things the mutual indulgence of sensuel [sic] passion between themselves and pretty child-girls? Surely not. Fors [sic] is not the naked form of a healthy well grown girl of twelwe [sic] or thirteen years . . . a picture for any man's desire?[70]

This "surely not" is so weak as arguments go that one wonders why the "is it any wonder" was introduced in the first place. I guess the appeal to "any man's desire" is an appeal to the desire of those already in the fold, that this is preaching strictly to the converted. The second example at least makes a pass at something other than argument-from-experience:

> Again, what is the reason that a man vigorous of build, and capable of gratifying a fully developed woman, prefers a mere child of fourteen? I answer, because that very disparity affords him delight, gratifies the imagination, and constitutes that exact adaptability of circumstances of which I speak. In effect it is, of course, the imagination which is at work. The law of contrast is constant, in this as in all else.[71]

I thought for some time that this was parodic, a put-on which employed all the pompous puffery of explanation—the question-and-answer format and the elaborate overkill of "very"s and "of course"s and "all"s—and said, on purpose, absolutely nothing at all. I find, however, that this universal and constant "law of contrast," is recognized (only in a footnote, but recognized all the same) by Havelock Ellis: " 'Men,' remarks Q, 'tend to fall in love with boys or youths, boys or youths with grown men, feminine natures with virile natures and *vice versa*, and different races with each other.' "[72] Does this mean that this contrast-principle was in fact not only around but accorded respect, made into a "law"? Doubtless more inane regulations have been formulated through similar means; perhaps they all are. In any case, it is remarkable that even these works which deal directly with child sexuality expend so much energy justifying sexual attraction to children and so little depicting it. And since the justifications are meager-unto-mockery, one is almost tempted to regard this kind of pornography, apparently rare in any case, as a minor form of misfiring satire only and to conclude that most forms of kiddie porn are modern inventions.

Such a conclusion would perhaps be warranted but would not lead anywhere very interesting. More intriguing, I think, is the possibility that the Victorians, busy sexualizing the child, still did not invest in the process the degree of anxiety common in this century. It is possible that they did not regard the erotic child as a problem in the way we suppose they must have. What is a commanding problem for us did not always seem a problem at all to those making it so. Even Freud did not bother enough with the issue of sexual attraction to children to make it into a separate category or discuss its etiology and treatment. He usually suggested, in an offhand way, that children become sex objects only with those among the cowardly and the impotent who haven't the occasion for sex with adults. The "uncanny frequency," he says, with which "school teachers and child attendants" turn up as sexual abusers of children can be attributed to the fact that they "have the best opportunity for it," just as, one supposes, those who live near water tend often to go swimming. The nonchalance of this has offended even devout Freudians, who like to point out that the sex doesn't follow the vocation but vice versa, that such people don't have sex with children because they are around them but seek out ways to be around them so as to have sex with them.[73] But that is modern orthodoxy, quite at odds, it appears, with the Victorians who sexualized and made desirable this child, all the while not much noticing the process or, perhaps, noticing but not caring, or caring but not turning the issue into the particular sort of problem that would demand discursive treatment.

Social Explanations

Not all cultures think alike on the issue of pedophilia: why does that fact register so faintly? The scandals of ancient Greece, Rome, or the Ottoman Empire are known but are absorbed comfortably into the remote past. Rumors of child prostitutes in modern-day Naples or reports of shocking attitudes toward the issue in Scandinavian countries strike closer to home. While much of this talk is alarmist or downright false, there are, certainly, many cultures which would (and do) find ridiculous a denial of childhood sexuality. Though as I write this much of the Scandinavian liberalism on sexuality has disappeared or been modified severely, we still have around imports from the recent past, like the textbook *Show Me!*, which offered the most unlikely counsel: "when playing with the child, the mother caresses and names not only the face, stomach, and back, but also the genitals. Embraces and caresses are fun and pleasurable for both children and adults."[74] Even more alien to our notions was the news, however inaccurate, that "the National Bar Association of Holland, to which all attorneys must belong, has called for the abolition of all sex laws involving children except intercourse with a girl under twelve, on the ground that police inquiries and court trials do more harm to children than does the illegal sexual activity."[75] I hasten to say that this "news" from Holland is now quite dated (1976) and may reflect nothing at all of the present attitudes. However, most Americans would scarcely be surprised to read that all of Scandinavia had set out not just to legalize but encourage kids in their pursuit of sexual merriment. The significant point is not the inaccuracy of this view but the querulousness we feel about our own rigidly held attitudes, held all the more rigidly because we fear that on this issue others may think differently, more confidently, or better.

Just as unwelcome is the argument that there are class differences on this point, that different economic and social levels hold to different positions and tolerate different practices in reference to the sexual being of children. Even many Victorians, generally less universalizing in their dogma, were clearly uneasy at subscribing openly to a causal connection between class and sex for children. But then the lower orders did appear to believe differently and even to *do* differently in this area somehow, giving rise to the notion that there is another genre of childhood present among the lower classes, other ways for puberty to function, other applications of words like "purity" or "innocence": we live with this still.

In pedophile writing we note the persistence of Prince and Pauper myths, a structure Michael Moon has brilliantly traced through the Horatio Alger narratives of American capitalism.[76] In this fable, the well-to-do (or at least better-to-do) adult loves and helps the poor child to rise. Often, as with Carpenter, this social perspective is made into an ideology, a series of democratic vistas opened up by way of pedophilia. The extent to which this passion for lower-class children is more than myth I do not know. My guess is that we have undergone a change in this regard and that Victorian Horatio Alger legends have been replaced by modern pedophile images of the middle-class child: Buster Brown, Lords of the Flies, E.T.'s family. However that may be, the propaganda in the nineteenth century and early into this one stressed heavily the attractions of this poor child. Timothy d'Arch Smith feels that such stories reflected clear practices and preferences and equally clear reasons for them. The relationships were, because of different moral standards believed to exist among the poor, easier to enter into, less risky, and (especially) easier to break off for the adult; the social inequality mirrored a psychological and physical inequality and thus was inevitable; the adult's insecurity and fear of failure would have made him seek out a social inferior as a safer possibility. But d'Arch Smith also feels that the democratic urge was genuine, a legitimate and "laudable drive to rear the boy from his menial environment into a better life wherein he could share the heritage of art, literature, the sciences, and eventually take his place as an equal."[77] It is possible that the pedophile's marginal position alerts him not only to self-interest but to the pains suffered by all the outcast. This is not a necessary consequence of pedophilia, of course, any more than virtue is of poverty. Still, the passion for helping the child is so strong in pedophile relations that even the police acknowledge it.

The police, in fact, are often shrewder and more sophisticated analysts of this phenomenon than are social scientists or even the general public. They also tend to be cynical, blunt, and melodramatic; but they are fully aware that a good many parts of the popular explanation of pedophilia, often those most fervently held, are weak or even wholly fallacious. Here is one policeman, testifying to Congress:

> Approximately 85 percent of all child molestations are committed by somebody the child knows, either a parent, family friend or a person entrusted with the custody of the child. Yet frequently we tell our children to be aware of the total stranger, not to get into the stranger's car, and not to take candy from a stranger.[78]

Why is it that we repeat this so often, and why do we not have deep explanations of the particular sort of family romance that animates the tight sexual circle of child and parent, family friend, or "custodian"? Where are the extensive studies of pedophilia as a form of incest? It is true that "incestuous pedophilia" is admitted as a type, but why not investigate the possibility that the substantive term, the motivating activity is incest, not pedophilia? I suggest that the answers to these questions would be similar to those we would find to questions about why the testimony above, though so familiar in form, makes so few inroads into popular belief. The narrative that is told, that is current, demands the abducting stranger. The love story is certainly not to be played out at home—or we don't want to acknowledge that it inevitably is played out at home. Thus the fable that thousands of children each day are victims of playground kidnappers continues. We have few stories about the kind of exploitation that does go on.

Explanations from the Other Side

Most explanations of pedophilia, along with most of the narratives that embolden those explanations, seem to come from those who are anxious above all to have us believe that they have nothing to do with the subject, know nothing first-hand about it. These story-tellers are telling tales of immunity. The very fact that they are squealing indicates, of course, that they have something to tell. The state would never provide protection unless they had some inside word to reveal. But the state and those blowing the whistle are locked into a secret agreement on this, an agreement secured by the fact that the state and those singing are one and the same, with the same vital interests in maintaining the guise that public explanations/myths of pedophilia are disinterested and elevated.

If that sounds too conspiratorial, perhaps it is equally to our purpose to listen to the voices of the pedophiles themselves and, as near as one can make them out, the children. What the pedophiles say is, most often, that it's love: "any sexual *acts* which may, and generally do, accompany, follow or precede this mental joy are adjuncts—prologue or epilogue to the essential monograph of the mind . . . which I call love."[79] Sex is perhaps less often an adjunct than a mere hope or acknowledged hopelessness, an impossibility that nonetheless helps drive the relationship between the adult and child. The 1985 movie *Dreamchild* (directed by Gavin Miller) thus construes the relationship between Lewis Carroll and Alice Liddell, granting to Carroll a dignity and stiff courage that, whether present in the real Charles L. Dodgson or not, clearly marks the long but telling letter from T.H. White:

> I have fallen in love with Zed. On Brave Beach with Killie I waved and waved to the aircraft till it was out of sight—my wild geese all gone and me a lonely old Charlie on the sands who had waddled down to the water's edge but couldn't fly. It would be unthinkable to make Zed unhappy with the weight of this impractical, unsuitable love. It would be against his human dignity. Besides, I love him for being happy and innocent, so it would be destroying what I loved. He could not stand the weight of the world against such feelings—not that they are bad in themselves. It is the public opinion that makes them so. In any case, on every score of his happiness, not my safety, the whole situation is an impossible one. All I can do is behave like a gentleman. It has been my hideous fate to be born with an infinite capacity for love and joy with no hope of using them.
>
> I do not believe that some sort of sexual relationship with Zed would do him harm—he would probably think and call them t'rific. I do not believe I could hurt him spiritually or mentally. I do not believe that perverts are made so by seduction. I do not think that sex is evil, except when it is cruel or degrading, as in rape, sodomy, etc., or that I am evil or that he could be. But the practical facts of life are an impenetrable barrier—the laws of God, the laws of Man. His age, his parents, his self-esteem, his self-reliance, the process of his development in a social system hostile to the heart, the brightness of his being which has made this what a home should be for three whole weeks of utter holiday, the fact that the old exist for the benefit of the young, not vice versa, the factual impossibilities set up by law and custom, the unthinkableness of turning him into a lonely or

sad or eclipsed or furtive person—every possible detail of what is expedient, not what is moral, offers the fox to my bosom, and I must let it gnaw.[80]

But, if we are admitting the full chorus of pedophile voices, we must not pretend that they all sound as tragically rich as White's. A more characteristic tone is comic self-mockery, a light self-consciousness manifested in overtly pedophile stories and autobiographies. Here, for instance, is Michael Davidson, telling of a friendly, bluff, breezy, "man-to-man" Dr. Fraser, who used to take him on rounds with him and, one memorable day, asked the child Davidson if he "played with himself":

> This overwhelming question . . . made me squirm with embarrassment; not because of the subject, which I guessed at, but because I was ashamed of not knowing exactly what he was talking about: somehow I felt that at my age, about twelve, I should have understood what he meant and should already have been performing this secret act, whatever it was, that he seemed to expect me to perform. Mortified to the point of sweating, I whispered No; and he, thank heaven, left it at that.[81]

Also common is an outrageous punning style whose flaunting, sometimes coarse gesturing might also be seen as self-protective. The title of Nicholson's *Love in Earnest* is a pun, as d'Arch Smith has pointed out to me, and a terrible pun too, though no more silly or flagrant than the dedication of Drew and Drake's study of boy prostitution, *Boys for Sale*, "To those boys who have contributed great quantities of their time and energy so that this book could be written," or the characteristic style of Dukahz's *The Asbestos Diary*: "The Mann Act is not the Boy Act" (p. 138); "Carry me Back to Old Virginity" (p. 153); "Never send a man to do a boy's job" (p. 139). When this style is toned down for fiction, it often still pokes fun at the subject and, especially, at the adult pedophile, who is typically portrayed as victimized by the wiser, more experienced, less scrupulous child.

This sort of reversal of what are taken to be obvious power inequalities is a standard comic formula, of course. But where we might find it great fun with henpecked husbands, with the Wife of Bath or Jiggs and Maggie, we are unlikely to be amused here, where the child is cast in the role of the seducer. We are disposed to find such reversals less laughable than nauseating. We take them seriously, see them as arguments, immoral arguments, deserving not giggles but prosecution.

There is, though, a danger of labeling any attention to such children which suspends even temporarily the requisite framework of seducers and victims and its foregone conclusions as "blaming the victim."[82] But why need any response or any understanding be confined to generating "blame"? That our reactions should be so prescribed and so violent is unfortunate, making it at least an open question where the damage to the child is coming from. Groth, for instance, reports this scene following an assault (by a friend of the family) on a six-year-old boy:

> At the hospital, the victim, John, was quiet and alert, answering questions briefly. He showed interest in the hospital equipment and was cooperative during the physical examination, which was primarily visual. His parents, in contrast, were crying, chain-smoking, and talking obsessively about the event and their fears of the aftereffects on their young son.[83]

The damage that can be done by such parents and by the police, judges, courtroom personnel, doctors, psychologists, social workers behind them is not to be underestimated. It is not here a case of "blaming the victim," but of recognizing the dangers which are unleashed when a simplistic melodramatic formula is applied to life. John's parents have simply been responsive to an explanatory model that leaves them with nothing to do but express their terrors about the damage done to their young son and thereby assure that the damage will take hold.

The severely suppressed child-love story that runs counter to the official narrative is no less self-interested, but it is illuminating. There are those who tell it this way: that child-love is marked by a maternal solicitude, a high degree of good-natured tolerance, a selflessness, an altruism, or a genuine caring that makes it as fine as any other form of human love—or even much finer. Richard Burton held that while affection among adults, at least adults of different genders, always involves sexual feeling in some form, affection for children, especially boys, need not, the implication being that the latter was more refined and valuable.[84] One doubtless wants to stop considerably short of such idealizing, but it is remarkable that even those researchers holding conventional views tend to point out that it's very rare that the adult is activated by anything like aggression toward the child victim.[85] Fewer than 1% of convicted offenders use drugs or drink on children, kidnap or harm them physically.[86] If we stop to ask what, in fact, pedophiles *do*, we discover that their activities are confined pretty much to cuddling, kissing, touching, looking, and exhibiting; Gebhard, dealing again with a sampling made up entirely of the imprisoned and reporting

208 / *Child-Love*

the highest incidence I have seen, says that 6% of his adults attempted sexual intercourse.[87]

Such softening touches to the pedophile portrait are customarily, when noted at all, read as malevolent. The adult becomes a rapist and a seducer, playing insidiously on the child's need for love and affection, enticing him or her by "counteraggressive" behavior and acts of seeming kindness into "a situation in which he or she [the child] feels indebted or obligated."[88] That's one way to look at it, but it's not the only one. O'Carroll mentions clinical studies that report, with some surprise, that "children are *likeable* to pedophiles in ways that are not purely physical," that "their sincere fondness for the objects of their sexual desire sometimes leads them to quite striking acts of charity in efforts to further the child's happiness or future prospects."[89]

Pedophiles do care about the child; so much seems obvious. It also seems obvious that the caring is entwined with sexual desire in such complex ways as to make either a cynical or an idealist argument insufficient. That is, it seems to me equally simple-minded to argue that the pedophile's apparent love and concern are no more than deliberate tools of seduction or to claim that the love is exalted, existing only to serve the child. The latter is a common boast in some forms of pederastic propaganda, usually formulated to feature a civic-spirited adult male willing to help the adolescent on the way to grown-up, heterosexual life, guiding him by means of "greek love" through this otherwise rough period of adjustment. Such claims are perhaps not so ludicrous as the contention in Drew and Drake's *Boys for Sale* that anal penetration will lead to "the gaining of a new self-understanding,"[90] but the idealism involved will hardly pass unsuspected. It might even deserve comparison with the unembarrassed, full-toned poetic connections made by the Rev. Edwin Emmanuel Bradford between boy-love, patriotism, and Christianity:

> Is Boy-Love Greek? Far off across the seas
>   The warm desire of Southern men may be:
> But passion freshened by a Northern breeze
>   Gains in male vigour and in purity.
> Our yearning tenderness for boys like these
> Has more in it of Christ than Socrates.[91]

What, in fact, do people like the Rev. Bradford, assuming he acted somehow on his "yearning tenderness," do to or for children? How do children view the matter? It is surely a matter of note that we so seldom ask that question, that we know so little about how children experience these relationships. In the few cases where researchers have listened to the children, the results, however incomplete, have usually been unsettling. Perhaps that is why such studies are rarely conducted and never listened to. Theo Sandfort's painstaking research on twenty-five boys involved in such affairs with adults concluded from the data that "the sexual contacts had no negative influence upon the general sense of well-being of these boys," such negative feelings as existed (having to do mostly with fears of being caught) "played hardly any role at all."[92] Similarly, Fritz Bernard's "Pedophilia: The Consequences for the Child" offers the following "provisional conclusions": the experience can be positive for the child; there is no evidence of traumatic influence; there seems to be no direct influence on later sexual orientation; the only negative effects are produced by the attitudes of society generally.[93] To be sure, neither study pretends to be comprehensive and both come from The Netherlands.

But they do raise a question we seldom ask: why is it that the pedophilia we say is thriving thrives? Insisting on a single story perhaps blocks what could be more complex and useful responses and keeps us from helping the very children we are anxious to protect. Could it be that the child responds to the pedophile's love because there isn't otherwise much love around? Do we have a nation full of "protected" but unloved children? It is possible too that the very low valuation of children that leads to the sorts of protective custody arrangements we prescribe for every home leads also to a loss of freedom, a sense of rebellion.

Who owns the child? The wonderful Kate Douglas Wiggin raised this question in her *Children's Rights* (1892) and answered it with a ringing affirmation of the right of the child to his or her own being: the child, she said, "has the right to his childhood" (p. 10), an absolute right that must not be trespassed even by our demands for obedience. Wiggin is a radical, perhaps, but she is maintaining a view of childhood which we all, when we relax a little, can see and even enjoy seeing: the image of the unfettered child, Blake's happy child, filling the glade or the world with laughter. It is the child we glimpse briefly when Kim walks with the lama, when Maggie Tulliver runs in the fields, when Oliver Twist plays merrily with Fagin and the thieves, when Alice throws herself down the rabbit-hole, Huck swims naked and then lazies about smoking with Jim, when Joe Gargery looks at Pip with secret understanding and ladles yet more gravy onto his plate. But of course these are moments caught in passing, when the child is on the lam.

And the child is, in every case, running from power. "It is difficult," says Stevi Jackson, "to imagine any sexual contact between a child and

210 / Child-Love

an adult" which would not be "coercive," "given adults' power over children." But she goes on: "The problem is not sex itself, but its association with power."[94] If we then proceed to dissolve the association of sex with power we may have made the problem itself seem both unnatural and soluble. Noting all this does not, of course, naturalize pedophilia, much less justify it. But it does suggest that our resistance to child-love helps ensure the perpetuation of the activity. Child-love, in this figuring, is an attempt to fly free from power, to fly by the nets created by our way of catching meaning. Damaging and furtive, child-love is an "escape" not just allowed but demanded by our paradigms, our ways of seeing. But to suggest that child-love cannot be controlled by power, that it represents some effective pocket of resistance may seem naive. We could just as well say that the form of child-love our culture constructs and brings into being lies within power, power which turns all loving of the child finally into molestation, allows no other way of figuring it. In that sense, child-love is not an escape at all but an act of obedience, prescribed by the very agencies of power that mandate our horror of it.

Notes

1. The item is quoted from "a newspaper" in Michael Davidson, *The World, The Flesh, and Myself* (London: Arthur Barker, 1962), p. 171. I cannot say for certain that Mr. Justice Stable said this or that there is or ever was a Mr. Justice Stable, but such voices are all around us, and they all sound the same.

2. Krafft-Ebing, *Psychopathia Sexualis*, p. 333.

3. A. Nicholas Groth, "Patterns of Sexual Assault Against Children and Adolescents," in Burgess et al., *Sexual Assault of Children*, p. 3.

4. Wardell B. Pomeroy, *Boys and Sex*, p. 26.

5. Sandfort, *Sexual Aspect of Paedophile Relations*, p. 38.

6. Suzanne M. Sgroi, "Introduction: A National Needs Assessment for Protecting Child Victims of Sexual Assault," in Ann Wolpert Burgess et al., *Sexual Assault of Children*, p. xv.

7. Kenneth Plummer, "Pedophilia: Constructing a Sociological Baseline," in Cook and Howells, eds., *Adult Sexual Interest*, pp. 223–28.

8. Ann Wolbert Burgess and Lynda Lytle Holmstrom, "Accessory-to-Sex: Pressure, Sex, and Secrecy," in Burgess, et al., *Sexual Assault of Children*, p. 89.

9. Davis, *SMUT*, says, "Almost alone among Naturalist social scientists, he did not disparage even child molesters" (p. 205).

10. Kinsey, *Human Male*, p. 158.

11. Kinsey, *Human Male*, p. 178.

12. Kinsey, *Human Female*, p. 14.

13. Kinsey, *Human Male*, p. 167.

14. Kinsey, *Human Male*, p. 170.

15. Kinsey, *Human Female*, p. 121.

16. Kinsey, *Human Male*, p. 238; Kinsey, *Human Female*, p. 121.

17. See, for example, Gebhard et al., *Sex Offenders*, pp. 54–55; C. Henry Kempe, "Incest and Other Forms of Sexual Abuse," in Kempe and Helfer, eds., *The Battered Child*, p. 198; Constantine, "The Effects," in Constantine and Martinson, eds., *Children and Sex*, pp. 232–36.

18. Brandt Steele, "Psychodynamic Factors in Child Abuse," in Kempe and Helfer, eds., *The Battered Child*, p. 75.

19. Burgess et al., *Sexual Assault of Children*, pp. 4–5.

20. Gebhard et al., *Sex Offenders*, p. 65.

21. Parker Rossman, *Sexual Experience Between Men and Boys: Exploring the Pederast Underground* (New York: Association Press, 1976), pp. 173–74.

22. See Croft-Cooke, *Feasting with Panthers*, pp. 84–85.

23. Steele, "Psychodynamic Factors," in Kempe and Helfer, eds., *The Battered Child*, p. 73.

24. Bristow, *Vice and Vigilance*, p. 17.

25. Freud, "Three Essays," VII, 219.

26. See Gorham, *The Victorian Girl*, pp. 68–83.

27. Fraser, *Death of Narcissus*, p. 43.

28. Newman, *The Cure of the Great Social Evil*, p. 28.

29. Gebhard et al., *Sex Offenders*, pp. 9–10.

30. Freud, "Three Essays," VII, 151.

31. Ellis, *Psychology of Sex*, I, 224–27.

32. John Crewdson, *By Silence Betrayed: Sexual Abuse of Children in America* (Boston: Little, Brown, 1988), pp. 69–73.

33. Ellis, *Psychology of Sex*, II, 286–87.

34. Krafft-Ebing, *Psychopathia Sexualis*, p. 372.

35. Dr. Andrew Bradbury, in his "Foreword" to Dennis Drew and Jonathan Drake's *Boys for Sale: A Sociological Study of Boy Prostitution* (New York: Brown Book Co., 1969), says, "In every case . . . the man who seeks young boys for sexual relations is seeking something *feminine*" (p. 11).

36. See, in order, C. Henry Kempe, "Incest and Other Forms of Sexual Abuse," in Kempe and Helfer, eds., *The Battered Child*, p. 204; Rossman, *Sexual Experience*, p. 14; and Aloysius Nicholas Groth and H. Jean Birnbaum, "Adult Sexual Orientation and Attraction to Underage Persons," *Archives of Sexual Behavior* 7 (1978): 175.

37. Louis J. Bragman, "John Addington Symonds: A Study in Aesthetic Homosexuality," in Dr. Hendrick M. Ruitenbeek, ed., *Homosexuality and Creative Genius* (New York: Astor-Honor, 1967), p. 110.

38. Fraser, *Death of Narcissus*, p. 221.

212 / Child-Love

39. Steele, "Psychodynamic Factors," in Kempe and Helfer, eds., *The Battered Child*, p. 51.

40. Objections to these procedures are not common, but they are heard now and then. Among the most strenuous and clear-sighted are in Kinsey, *Human Female*, pp. 18–19, 116–22. See also Moll, *The Sexual Life of the Child*, p. xii; Rossman, *Sexual Experience*, pp. 40, 43; Sandfort, *Sexual Aspects of Paedophile Relations*, p. 3; and especially Kevin Howells, "Adult Sexual Interest in Children: Considerations Relevant to Theories of Aetiology," in Cook and Howells, eds., *Adult Sexual Interest*, p. 86.

41. Alan P. Bell and Calvin S. Hall, *The Personality of a Child Molester: An Analysis of Dreams* (Chicago: Aldine, Atherton, 1971), p. 89. See also Gebhard et al., *Sexual Offenders*, pp. 69, 282–84.

42. A. Nicholas Groth, "Guidelines for the Assessment and Management of the Offender," in Burgess et al., *Sexual Assault of Children*, p. 30.

43. A. Nicholas Groth, "Patterns of Sexual Assault against Children and Adolescents," in Burgess et al., *Sexual Assault of Children*, p. 6.

44. Krafft-Ebing, *Psychopathia Sexualis*, p. 371.

45. Krafft-Ebing, *Psychopathia Sexualis*, p. 374.

46. According to J.Z. Eglinton (pseud.), *Greek Love* (London: Neville Spearman, 1971), p. 363.

47. Bell and Hall, *Personality of a Child Molester*, p. 16.

48. William Dworin, Detective, Los Angeles PD, Sexually Exploited Child Unit, "Child Pornography and Pedophilia" hearings, United States Senate Subcommittee on Investigations, of the Committee on Governmental Affairs, 98th Cong., 2nd sess, p. 122.

49. A possible "cure" for pedophilia discussed by D.R. Laws and A.V. Pawlowski, "An Automated Fading Procedure to Alter Sexual Responsiveness in Pedophiles," *Journal of Homosexuality* 1 (1974): 149. See also Fraser, *Death of Narcissus*, pp. 230–36.

50. Steele, in Kempe and Helfer, eds., *The Battered Child*, p. 74. See also Gebhard et al., *Sex Offenders*, p. 322.

51. William Kraemer, "A Paradise Lost," in William Kraemer, ed., *The Forbidden Love: The Normal and Abnormal Love of Children* (London: Sheldon Press, 1976), pp. 2–3. The fullest and most elaborate psychoanalytic investigation of pedophilia, Morris Fraser's *The Death of Narcissus*, is a considerable work, representing as good an attempt at containing the subject by these devices as has been made. It should be pointed out, though, that this model, though neatly accounting for some cases, fails to explain why other figures, Dickens and Trollope say, both with childhoods that can be made to fit the mold, do not, so far as we can tell, turn out to be pedophiles. Even with agreed-upon pedophiles, the results are inconsistent: the argument fits J.M. Barrie, perhaps, but how about Lewis Carroll?

52. Fraser, *Death of Narcissus*, p. 19.

53. Symonds, *Memoirs*, pp. 128, 127.

54. Bell and Hall, *Personality of a Child Molester*, p. 19. See also Gebhard et al., *Sex Offenders*, p. 63; A. Nicholas Groth, "Patterns of Sexual Assault," in Burgess et al., *Sexual Assault of Children*, pp. 22–23 ("In essence, he is a psychological child in the physical disguise of an adult"); Casimir Dukahz (pseud.), *The Asbestos Diary* (New York: Oliver Layton, 1966), p. 13; Davidson, *The World, The Flesh, and Myself*, p. 1.

55. Groth, "Patterns of Sexual Assault," in Burgess et al., *Sexual Assault of Children*, p. 7.

56. Gebhard et al., *Sex Offenders*, p. 81.

57. Bell and Hall, *Personality of a Child Molester*, p. 123.

58. As suggested before, it is common enough to evoke this myth and this "complex" in discussing pedophilia. Crewdson, for example, speaks of "the grossly narcissistic nature of most child molesters" (*By Silence Betrayed*, p. 63). In psychoanalysis, the term "narcissism" refers to "the condition in which the ego retains the libido" rather than having it pass to an object (Freud, "A Difficulty," XVII, 139). It is not often noted that Freud emphasized that the transfer from ego to object was never complete, that "a certain quantity of libido is always retained in the ego" (p. 139). Hagstrum, *Sex and Sensibility*, has a fascinating discussion of narcissism and Milton's Eve (pp. 44–46).

59. Rossman, *Sexual Experience*, p. 102.

60. Bullough, *Sexual Variance*, p. 360.

61. See Wayland Young, *Eros Denied: Sex in Society* (n.p.: n.p., 1964), p. 80. Pallavicino, according to Young, was born in 1616.

62. See, for example, Jackson I. Cope, "Marlowe's *Dido* and the Titillating Children," *English Literary Renaissance* 4 (1974): 315–25. Cope argues that Marlowe uses boys in love scenes for complex comic and satiric effects, playing in sophisticated ways on the audience's recognition of the actors' sexual immaturity. A more recent and broad-ranging study is Stephen Orgel's "Nobody's Perfect: Or Why Did the English Stage Take Boys for Women?," *South Atlantic Quarterly* 88 (1989): 7–29.

63. Ellis, by way of a very interesting "Russian correspondent," connects Christianity with the erotic attraction to little girls; see *Psychology of Sex*, I, 43–44.

64. Croft-Cooke discusses these cases and others; see *Feasting with Panthers*, pp. 103–18.

65. See Eglinton, *Greek Love*, pp. 227–28, 378–79; and especially, Timothy d'Arch Smith, *Love in Earnest: Some Notes on the Lives and Writings of English "Uranian" Poets from 1889 to 1930* (London: Routledge and Kegan Paul, 1970). D'Arch Smith's work sets a standard in scholarship, sensitive reading, and calm lucidity that has not been approached by any other work in the field.

66. Frederick William Rolfe (Baron Corvo), "Ballade of Boys Bathing" (ll. 12–13), reprinted from *The Art Review* 1 (April 1890) in Brian Reade, ed., *Sexual Heretics*, p. 227.

67. See Reade, ed., *Sexual Heretics*, pp. 146–53.

68. Anon, *When a Child Loves*, p. 8.

69. Anon., *Lustful Adventures*, p. 1.

70. [Phyllis Norroy, pseud.], *Private Letters from Phyllis to Marie, or The Art of Child Love, or The Adventures and Experiences of a Little Girl* (London and Paris: privately printed, 1898), p. 12.

71. Anon., *The Autobiography of a Flea* (London: privately printed for the Erotica Biblion Society, 1901), p. 8.

72. Ellis, *Psychology of Sex*, II, 286.

73. See Fraser, *Death of Narcissus*, p. 119; Freud's views are quoted in Fraser.

74. Fleischhauer-Hardt, *Show Me!*, p. 149.

75. Rossman, *Sexual Experience*, p. 5.

76. Michael Moon, " 'The Gentle Boy from the Dangerous Classes': Pederasty, Domesticity, and Capitalism in Horatio Alger," *Representations*, 19 (1987): 87–110.

77. d'Arch Smith, *Love in Earnest*, p. 192.

78. William Dworin, U.S. Senate, "Child Pornography," p. 45.

79. Davidson, *The World, The Flesh, and Myself*, p. 47.

80. Quoted in Sylvia Townsend Warner, *T.H. White: A Biography* (London: Jonathan Cape/Chatto and Windus, 1967), pp. 277–82; quoted also in Tom O'Carroll, *Paedophilia*, p. 17.

81. Davidson, *The World, The Flesh, and Myself*, p. 5.

82. See, for example, Jeffrey Moussaieff Masson, *A Dark Science: Women, Sexuality, and Psychiatry in the Nineteenth Century* (New York: Farrar, Strauss, and Giroux, 1986), pp. 10–11; and Groth, "Patterns of Sexual Assault," in Burgess et al., *Sexual Assault of Children*, p. 3.

83. A. Nicholas Groth, Ann Wolpert Burgess, and Lynda Lytle Holmstrom, "Crisis Issues for an Adolescent-Aged Offender and His Victim," in Burgess et al., *Sexual Assault of Children*, p. 46.

84. In Reade, ed., *Sexual Heretics*, p. 159.

85. Suzanne M. Sgroi, "Child Sexual Assault: Some Guidelines for Intervention and Assessment," in Burgess et al., *Sexual Assault of Children*, p. 131.

86. Rossman, *Sexual Experience*, p. 29.

87. Gebhard et al., *Sex Offenders*, p. 71.

88. Groth, "Patterns of Sexual Assault," in Burgess et al., *Sexual Assault of Children*, p. 11.

89. O'Carroll, *Paedophilia*, p. 59.

90. Drew and Drake, *Boys for Sale*, p. 103.

91. Quoted in d'Arch Smith, *Love in Earnest*, p. 3. The poem was published in *The New Chivalry and Other Poems* (1918).

92. Sandfort, *Sexual Aspects of Paedophile Realtions*, p. 80.

93. Mark Cook and Glenn Wilson, eds., *Love and Attraction* (Oxford: Pergammon Press, 1979), p. 501.

94. Jackson, *Childhood and Sexuality*, p. 63.

III

Figures of the Child

6

The Gentle Child

The loved child is very often the gentle child:

> He was all beautiful: as fair
> As summer in the silent trees,
> As bright as sunshine on the leas,
> As gentle as the evening air.[1]

Like the evening air, gentleness is all softness, yielding, calm, touched a little, perhaps, by twilight's shadowed dimness, slight obscurity, faint sadness. The quality of gentleness must be felt, not rudely spoken, as Byron knew so well in addressing the choir boy, John Edlestone:

> And thou my friend, whose gentle love
> Yet thrills my bosom's chords,
> How much thy friendship was above
> Description's power of words![2]

Byron appeals to the experience of "gentle love," an experience which must be shared to be known, which words would only sully, and which the uninitiated (those unacquainted with Edlestone perhaps) cannot hope to know. Gentle love seems to be connected to the friendship which unites adult and child, but clearly far surpasses that commonplace tie.

Gentleness is that which the adult finds in the child or hopes to find in the child or attributes to the child or crams into the child by force. More than just a question of gentle birth and blood, gentleness is a matter of doing tenderly. The common synecdoche for such thrilling behavior is the hand, the gentle hand, which knows how to be properly receptive to the adult, how to accept, store up, and, in a subtler way, reciprocate the precious gifts being given:

> Alice! a childish story take,
>   And, with a gentle hand,
> Lay it where Childhood's dreams are twined
>   In Memory's mystic band. . . .[3]

Alice's gentle hand will (or had better, if "take" is felt as an imperative) puff and pillow the story into the downy cloud of "memory," a place where the adult and child are twined together, a band of two, mystically playing forever.

The gentleness discovered, wished for, or implanted in the child is a prescription for responsiveness, for fully sympathetic reading. The gentle child is that most hallowed of author's fantasies, the "gentle reader"—alert to every delicate nuance, unafraid of syntactical and grammatical traps ahead, delightfully willing to be surprised. This gentle reader is, if juvenile, still super; and just the sort of child Lewis Carroll saw in his best dreams:

> Some perhaps may blame me for thus mixing together things grave and gay; others may smile and think it odd that any one should speak of solemn things at all, except in Church and on a Sunday: but I think—nay, I am sure—that some children will read this gently and lovingly, and in the spirit in which I have written it.[4]

Carroll's care in sorting out for membership in his special club those who read "gently and lovingly" is also a caution against reading like those "some" or "others" who are prone to blame him or find him odd, those others who are the unloving and ungentle and consequently undeserving of gentleness or love in return. More than a caution, this passage gives a recipe for reading; and, more than that, it issues a command, a "gentling" forcibly applied, an expression of a determination "to gentle" the reader, in the fiercer more impatient senses of that verb: "to render gentle, to soften, to tame, to break in." The gentle child is not always simply found hanging around, then; sometimes it is the product of heavy industry. Sometimes, the gentling must come in the way of tenderizing in the old-fashioned way that used to be common with ungentle meat: pounding on it.

If the child is an artificial product to begin with, it might as well be fitted up to one's liking. Gentleness can be made to order. It can be found or it can be constructed, the two procedures really amounting to the same thing.

The Ideal Child

The intensity of the idealism marking the gentle child's attraction is often put in curiously argumentative form, a form which seems to reach toward absolutes, especially the absolute of "purity." As with Ivory soap (99.44% pure!), this purity is figured as an absence that can be filled by the poet or ordinary adult, and filled often with a desire so exalted and scoured as hardly to require justification, but which commonly gets a good deal anyhow, by being contrasted with the muck surrounding it, as is the Rev. E.E. Bradford's fresh-from-the-bath-boy named Alan:

> And thus I see him, naked, clean and warm,
> Framed by the uncurtained casement close behind,
> Placed in a picture lowering with storm,
> Mid myriad snow-flakes whirling in the wind.
> His radiant face, illumined by the fire,
> Gleams out against a dark and troubled sea:
> The shore, here dark with snow, there foul with mire,
> Lies all around his form yet leaves it free:
> So is it with his heart, 'mid shame and sin
> Unstained it glows with love's pure light within![5]

The glowing purity of unstained love is, I gather, analogous to the illuminating fire which allows the Rev. Bradford to inspect Alan's nakedness. I am not sure which side of which casement the speaker of the poem is on, whether he is peeping in or looking out. In any case, the foul and miry shore, like the shame and sin which Alan's heart is surrounded by,[6] acts to frame his purity and set it off for special attention and admiration.

The bases for such exaltation were various, but some were laid out quite clearly by Symonds in his *A Problem in Modern Ethics*, where the "pure and sweet," "spiritual," "democratic," "passionate," and "intense" ideal of "adhesiveness" is traced to Whitman and, behind him, to "the early Dorians, those martial founders of Greek love," "a form of paiderastia upon which the Greeks prided themselves, [and] which had for its heroic ideal the friendship of Achilles and Patroclus."[7] Even beyond any service in providing rationalizations for practices and feelings difficult to maintain, these exalting procedures purified not only the loved one but the love—and hence the lover:

> His love is pure as thy own life is pure,
> And passionate as thy dreams are passionate,
> And there is none thou canst so much allure,
> And none thou couldst so little satiate.[8]

220 / *The Gentle Child*

Notice how Raffalovich's poem connects the purities of life and love to such unlikely accompaniments as passion and a roaring capacity for sex-without-satiation. The logic is not entirely clear, but it is presumably welcome. And it is clearer in later poems like "A. Newman's" [Henry Moore Pim's] "Perfectly Contented," where the self-consciously Narcissistic figure presented exposes how the lover can possess the purity of the beloved:

> Since your sweet lips were made for mine,
> Your heart around my heart to twine,
>   Your eyes to look in mine and see
>   Reflected there your purity,
> All other loves you must outshine.

Having made such lips and heart "mine," the speaker has also taken over (or somehow provided) the purity, a purity which is set off by the slime about them:

> For coarser joys let others pine;
> To you alone I will confine
> My heart. My perfect melody
> You are.[9]

Ownership of heart and song conferred on the adult this transcendent moral authority, an escape by way of the child from adult corruption. It was common to see the child as pristine, offering a purifying draught to take in and make part of one's own system.

Children were and still are subject to the most widespread and bizarre extremist siftings. *Boys and Their Ways*, written it says "by one who knows them," deftly sorted out its subject into two areas, "the good boys and the bad," and went on to mark out the critical moment when each child "has to make up his mind to which section he will belong."[10] The good child, our present concern, is more than just so-so good; it is angelic, holding out the promise of a happiness that is complete and divine. These gentle, saintly children, fulfilling the hopes of orthodox Anglicanism for "embodied perfection," carried their beholders (or a few of them anyhow) into the realm of "credible angelic presences."[11] Actually even more alluring than these already finished angels were those who still needed to be shaped by the pedophile potter: "though at first view the lurid lights of the savage element alone appear, there is a rich background formed of the finer shades of the angel element, waiting for the skilled hand to bring forward and develop." "Therein," says the author, "lies the charm of it."[12] Certainly that is true: this charming child, hiding the angel element, offers inviting material for the hand that is not only skilled but positively itching to get to work.

The World of Childhood

The images of reciprocity in pedophile verse depend, perhaps paradoxically but absolutely, on constituting childhood as an entirely separate, even remote sphere. The gentle child lives in a beautiful and tender world, but one that is far away, self-sufficient, and sealed-off. It takes a special invitation to enter. The child lives in a world that is not only made but made-up, in the sense outlined by Oscar Wilde when he said that true art must never substitute an imitative for a creative medium.[13] That is, the child and his world must never be approached with vulgar mimetic or realist expectations but with imaginative ones; correspondingly, the area of childhood must never be drawn into the rude world of use, necessity, or concern:

> The only beautiful things, as somebody once said, are the things that do not concern us. As long as a thing is useful or necessary to us . . . it is outside the proper sphere of art. To art's subject-matter we should be more or less indifferent. We should, at any rate, have no preferences, no prejudices, no partisan feelings of any kind. It is precisely because Hecuba is nothing to us that her sorrows are such an admirable motive for a tragedy.[14]

The child's world is the world of pure art, which means it is unnecessary, useless, and "nothing to us." Because it is everything to us. It is a world beyond the reach of common notions of what counts and how to count it, of causality and logic, of naming the facts, of truth-telling. Those who, like Jeffrey Masson, regard the statement that children are liars not as a truth but as a slander are living in a cozy suburban geography quite distant from the untamed lands the child-lovers seek in childhood.[15]

This difference, though perhaps not the sublime artistic indifference to the subject, is illustrated by Theodore Wraitslaw's sonnet "To a Sicilian Boy" (1893), which, after some admittedly concrete (mimetic?) celebrations of the boy's "exquisite breasts and arms adorable," along with a "heavenly throat" and some amazing "blossoms of [the] mouth," moves to show how this image is a magic carpet for carrying

222 / *The Gentle Child*

the adult into the undoubtedly erotic but, more crucially, distant land of the child. Sexual rapture is but a vehicle wherein the trip to oblivion can be made:

> I love thee, sweet! Kiss me again, again!
> Thy kisses soothe me, as tired earth the rain;
> Between thine arms I find my only bliss;
> Ah let me in thy bosom still enjoy
> Oblivion of the past, divinest boy,
> And the dull ennui of a woman's kiss![16]

The last line, with its snide misogyny, reaches out from the child's world, now safely gained, with an arrogant gesture of contempt, sticking out its tongue to mark the separation that has been achieved. Such a poetic union of pedophile and child is often strutted, sometimes by way of direct expressions of scorn for parents, for the conventional world and the conventional controls on children (and, not incidentally, on the pedophile). Alone at last, the pedophile and child (or the pedophile on behalf of the both of them) cannot resist a triumphant jeer. In *Peter Pan*, Barrie has the boys get in a mock tussle about mothers, "not that they are really worrying about their mothers, who are now as important to them as a piece of string."[17] More homicidal, Michael says in the last act: "Let me see father. (Disappointed.) He is not as big as the pirate I killed" (Act V, p. 152).[18]

There is, of course, some quavering bravado associated with such gestures, some sense that it would not be necessary to declare childhood such a safe enclave if one were certain that it were—or certain one had reached it. Child-love is a perilous undertaking and would be so even if the police were not so alert and so often alerted. It is terribly risky to strike off backwards into waters that may perhaps never have been navigable in search of islands that may never have existed. Wilde spoke of the allure of feasting with panthers, of the titillation of risk, and Raffalovich boasted, "All things I love are dangerous."[19] But not all are so bold, and the idealizing conceptions of what the child was and where he lived seem to be spawned partly by fear.

Idealized Sex

Such fear may flow most freely when the subject turns directly to sex. Freud suggested that it was necessary to exalt something about sex in order to do it, such mechanisms being observable in history, though operating differently at different times: "The ancients glorified the [sexual] instinct and were prepared on its account to honour even an inferior object; while we despise the instinctual activity itself, and find excuses for it only in the merits of the object."[20] Since the "inferior object" referred to by Freud seems to stand for "child" or "animal," the child lover, according to this account, must be prepared either to find ways to counter the despising of the activity or to promote enthusiastically "the merits of the object"—or both.

As we have seen, it is both which are called on. In its most extreme form, the child is made angelic and transformative, the act of love a mystical experience. Just as often, the burden on such discourse is to boost the act, not the object. References to the superiority of the erotic experience, often argued at the expense of adult heterosexuality— "the dull ennui of a woman's kiss"—are uncommon, apparently less effective than arguments that picture the adult transforming the child (not vice versa). Such arguments, as we have seen, are made either along class lines (democratic "lifting" of the poor child) or psychological ones ("Greek-love" benefits to the boy's adjustment).

The good child we have before us now, however, is so alluring that justifications seem superfluous. I do not mean that pedophile discourse is insincere or untrue, just that it has difficulty substituting ethical argument for the pull of strong desire. This good child is, after all, so invitingly vacant that the goodness is utter blankness. Such blankness can suggest that the child's goodness, like that of Oliver Twist, is ordained, impervious to any wicked influence. Such a figuring may ironically open the good child up to sexual desire as no amount of imputed knowingness could. This blank child could be so loved, so made love to, that the goodness might rub off; if not, one can move forward with a clear conscience, the child being so very incorruptible. Doubtless this is one reason the Oliver image is so popular and why the child can be subject to such flagrant and unrestrained sadistic sexual mishandling.

Similarly, the good child's innocence is figured as shamelessness: like Adam and Eve in the garden, naked and proud of it. With children, their goodness thus would make them all the more ready to satisfy desires, at least voyeuristic desires. "Small children," Freud notes, "are essentially without shame, and at some periods of their earliest years show an unmistakable satisfaction in exposing their bodies, with especial emphasis on the sexual parts."[21] Modesty, then, is associated with corruption, with the fall. The good child will maintain this innocence, this delightful "satisfaction" in exposing itself.

Not surprisingly, this association of goodness with happy nakedness is employed in a good deal of what we think of as art and/or entertainment: paintings, decorative illustrations, films, and literature—Huck Finn's nude evenings with Jim and Brooke Shields sunbathing in *The Blue Lagoon* (1980) being prominent examples. In explicitly erotic fictions, the readiness of children to strip and strut is more pronounced. A couple of examples from *The Pearl* will suffice. In "Memoranda from Mr. P——" two adult males manage to seduce a fifteen-year-old boy by allowing his pleasure in displaying himself full sway. They take him swimming, share the same bathing machine, and let his nature take its course. All that is needed in the way of encouragement is to notice him and be good-natured about it: "How we joked him about his little doodle." They then move to mutual exhibition, to comparisons of various sorts, and then, building on the boy's Edenic shamelessness, to what they have been after from the start.[22] In "Young Beginners," four children ranging from nine to fourteen exercise their unblushing immodesty. It all starts with the delights of showing all-round:

> "Let us have a good look. Why need you mind? You may see mine if you like. Let's all look at one another, and see which has the nicest."
> "Oh, do!" cried John and Janey, "it will be great fun."

We are not surprised that John and Janey react in the same terms as the Bobbsey Twins—"Oh, do!"—since they are alike good children. These particular children see no reason to be ashamed of anything or to restrain their natural enthusiasm for play. When Gussy (a male) suggests to Nelly that they imitate the little animals they have seen on the farm, John and Janey respond again like the sweet innocents from the Sunday School stories:

> "Do let him," cried John and Janey. "It will be such fun."[23]

The fun to be had here is not, after one or two numbers, judged to be sufficiently enticing to *The Pearl*'s readers, so these young actors are soon dropped from the story and the focus shifts to the older children and, actually, to the adults whose goings-on they spy out. My guess is that there is not as yet that much interest in child erotica, a form that develops along with the cultural strength of the erotic child and does not reach full flower until this century.

Such erotica of this sort as there is (or that survives) more commonly employs a counter-image of the modest child, equally idealized but showing goodness by contradictory means: quickness to feel shame rather than immunity to it. This material seems always at least mildly sadistic, offering some sort of pleasure in the humiliating of the radiantly perfect child. The presence of sexual aggression directed at goodness or at cultural definitions of goodness really places this subject in the next chapter, but we might note here how frequent are the expressions of annoyance at good children like Sid Sawyer and the inducements to excitement at their pain. In the Victorian material, the sadism is less pure, mixed as it is with the common ingredients of seduction erotics: the child's modesty provides not simply (or even mainly) a provocation for torture but a barrier to be overcome, a device for plot complication, suspense, and arousal. In an early scene in *When a Child Loves*, the good child Mona is molested by a General Hill in the lavatory of a railroad car. The details of this scene are drawn out relentlessly and painfully, the child not so much resisting as expressing in certain terms her misery, particularly her shame at being looked at: "Oh, no, no, you shan't look! You mustn't look! I won't let you see me! You shan't lift my frock up any higher! Please, please don't look any more. I am so dreadfully ashamed!" This good child is not the shameless innocent of Freudian and Christian legend: she feels no "satisfaction" in exhibiting herself, nearly dies with mortification: "Crying and sick with shame, Mona felt her frock and petticoats lifted up to her waist and the man's eyes fixed on every secret part of her body. He felt her and studied her without cessation or mercy for nearly ten minutes, and only ceased at last because her agitation began to frighten him."[24]

I cannot see that expressions of indignation serve much purpose in this discussion, but one may perhaps usefully inquire whether such forlorn material as I have just quoted can ever have aroused anyone? I can only say that this sample is typical for the most part, that it is unusual only in emphasizing as it does the child's terror and physical shock and the adult's fear. But the narrative, in fact this same chapter, goes on to show how Mona, initiated more gently by a slightly older girlfriend, comes to relish the whole business and to lose any shame she originally felt. Her goodness seems to have been employed simply to increase the challenge and the excitement. So, just like the contradictory conception of goodness discussed earlier, Mona's is available for erotic consumption.

The Vanishing Child

Pedophile relations exist for a time, a very short time, and then they are not there. They do not develop into any other form, nor do they decay. Now and then some kind of mild friendship develops between the adult and growing adolescent, but that is different, bearing no relation at all to the intensely romantic prior union. That union just goes away. The adult turns his back for an instant and wheels around to find the room empty: "suddenly," Michael Davidson says, "overnight like an overblown flower, it is dead"[25] The child does not grow or even grow up; it becomes extinct. In part, these metaphors express the fact that the child becomes unattractive to the adult, becomes just another ordinary adult and no longer anything magical—disfigured by body hair and erupting skin and ungainly height. Gone forever is what Eglinton, with supreme corniness, calls the child's "bloom": that "brief period in a boy's or girl's adolescence during which the skin acquires a peculiar silky texture and color heightens,"[26] a period so brief that it is lost almost before we know it, before we even saw it and responded to its promise.

Thus the prosaic fact that children do not stay children takes on enormous psychological and poetic force in the imaginings of childlove. There are, in an upbeat vein, a few rousing carpe diem poems addressed to shilly-shallying children; but predictably much more common are the laments, here stated in typical style by "A. Newman," in "Aged Fifteen" (a fateful age):

> The passing bell for your dead years
> Is tolling . . .
> ....
> I know, alas! the sad day nears
> When my boy's love no longer cheers
> My life.[27]

Though more complex, Byron's Thyrza lyrics, attributed by Crompton to his memories of Edlestone, address this sense of precious evanescence:

> The flower in ripen'd bloom unmatch'd
> Must fall the earliest prey,
> Though by no hand untimely snatch'd,
> The leaves must drop away:
> And yet it were a greater grief
> To watch it withering, leaf by leaf,
> Than see it pluck'd to-day. . . .[28]

The fact of transience and the foreknowledge of it, however, often lend to child-love a rather joyless urgency, a sense that romance is a holding action or, more commonly, a form of denial. If one can make the experience intense enough, perhaps it will make it stay, contain both time and the child. Maybe by looking hard enough, long enough I will occupy the territory myself.

Such, we are told, is the aim of voyeurism, to secure the viewer against pain to the ego that would come from being looked at, by being made an object. By turning the world into a permanent object, I become permanent subject, no longer threatened and now completely (if neurotically) in control. With pedophilia, the crucial feature of this fantasy is its promise of constancy, the way it offers up to us the child in a frame, held by our gaze and preserved from time and from running off.

Pedophilia seems almost always to be on intimate terms with such possessive looking. The pedophile does not so much want to look in order to imprison the actual child but to imprison the sight. Just as the pedophile does not really want to own the child but the *idea* of the child, so the vision seems to provide permanent access to that idea. But the envisioning is also an end in itself, an erotic world on its own. "Thinking," says W. David Allen, in a wonderful insight into the phenomenon, "is more interesting than knowing, but less interesting than looking."[29] Thus the popularity of pornography, the evocation of pictures and not bodies. "A. Newman's" poem, "Bare Knees," beginning "On Norman's knees I fix my eyes,"[30] seems almost a parody of this compulsive voyeurism, but it is everywhere in erotic literature. Prior to Mona's seduction in *When a Child Loves*, she is made the object of the lustful looking of many characters—and readers:

> [Mona] wore very short frocks, her thin white drawers fitted tight to her round limbs, and as she climbed railing [sic] or flew to and fro in a swing, all the pretty curves and inlets of a little maiden's body were shown freely and heedlessly to these eager eyes. There was more than one man among Mona's acquaintance who found it one of the considerable pleasures of his life to take the child out for walks, where, with her short skirt and babyish unconsciousness, she would have to climb half-a-dozen fences.[31]

The impulse of these acquaintances, in life or in literature, seems to be to mount a gallery of images. It is not by accident, therefore, that so much pedophile activity, among the Victorians and among us, has been connected to the camera. Photographing children before they slip away, before that "bloom" can no longer be caught, is a need felt by Lewis Carroll, by J.M. Barrie, and, judging by the television and magazine

228 / *The Gentle Child*

advertisements of film companies like Kodak and Polaroid, by nearly everyone today.

Nostalgia

Photography also feeds an emotion not far from voyeuristic possessiveness, the sad feeling of nostalgia. The vanishing child is typically succeeded by the lost child, panic by a sensation of warm self-pity and luxurious melancholy. Nostalgia is a great set-up for story-telling, largely because the feelings have no existence outside of stories that bring to the past a life so intense it becomes the only life. Susan Stewart gets it exactly right: "By the narrative process of nostalgic reconstruction the present is denied and the past takes on an authenticity of being, an authenticity which, ironically, it can achieve only through narrative."[32] I would add only that what we call "the present" is no less dependent on narrative: this past is not different in kind but just in location from the stories we are bound to tell.

Stewart goes on to argue that "nostalgia is sadness without an object,"[33] by which I take her to mean that the object is so blurred and softened by sentiment that it becomes part of the general coloring of the scene. Nostalgia is not like looking for a lost shoelace but like trying to recapture the "feel" of autumn, a glimpse of hair, a smile, the curve of a cheek. Nostalgia can make us weep more surely than any immediate calamity or even a blow to the nose. It is one of the penalties and rewards of trying for an impossible permanence, of loving and losing.

But there is more to the child-lover's nostalgia than a reaction to lost love. The romance was, after all, not ended but initiated by loss, by the attraction for a past one has lost long before the child came along. "You can't go back," says Dukahz, "but you can borrow an illusion so powerfully valid it at times overwhelms reality."[34] Better, it becomes reality, this drive back into loss, this immersion in nostalgia for one's own child-being. Pedophilia is so deeply colored by a desire to return, to be the child, that it does not take the loss of that loved child to induce nostalgia. The pedophile lives in and through nostalgia all the time; it is the romantic heart of the relationship.

Pedophile poets love to write of the pain caused by the traumatizing growth of the child: "And till I find those eyes of blue/ And golden curls, I walk in pain."[35] The discourse feeds the feeling, even creates it or makes it possible. One of the poems from *Love in Earnest* is so unusually candid about how soft and lovely the recollections are and how readily they are made the substance of life that it deserves quoting in full:

> I live in the light of fancies fled,
>   Of days and dreams gone by;
> My heart is linked to passions dead
>   By an eternal tie;
>   Fond memories live, and triumphs high
> Despite oblivion fell,
>   All Time and Change and Death defy,
> And nothing breaks the spell.
>
> My soul, through sullen clouds o'erhead,
>   The love-light can descry
> Where, by sweet recollections fed,
>   My spirit loves to lie;
>   The happiness can never die
> Of days remembered well,
>   Old Love breathes soft as Summer sigh,
> And nothing breaks the spell.
>   ENVOY
> Dear, since the last good-bye was said,
>   The dead Past where I dwell
> Has ever been Love's daily bread,
>   And nothing breaks the spell.[36]

This supply of Love-food must be maintained if the happiness that "can never die" is to be kept from dying. The spell which nothing can break is attached to his lodgings there in the dead Past, as he says; but that Past must be carefully arranged and ordered. It must be imagined in exactly the right terms, must be "remembered well." Remembering *well* does not mean remembering "accurately" or even with great attention to details. Remembering well means remembering erotically, remembering so as to feed the present. For these purposes, inaccuracy and some fogging may serve very well. The important thing is to put together a theater of memory that will stage dramas so vital that they will not only convince us that the past is there before us but that this "past" is in fact the present. Memory will hold the child, allow its sexuality to be re-presented over and over, allow us to play on the stage we have built the drama we have written.

Through these erotic plays of memory we also reach back to an uncanny union with childhood, a sense that we are, in the very process of remembering, acting as children. The child is construed as the great rememberer, though it is the child being remembered. This is neither logical nor easy to follow, I know; but the process can be sorted out: memory is constructed from observation; the powers of observation are never so strong as when we are young; though most adults lose such powers, they can cast back into childhood and perhaps regain contact with them; thus, we can remember childhood only by asking the child to do the remembering for us. We must seduce the child into playing this musty old game, remember our childhood through the child, who can only be asked out of and will only consent because of love.

To see this, we can look to the greatest Victorian memory work, *David Copperfield*, where David (as adult narrator) says much of what I have been saying, only better:

> This may be my fancy, though I think the memory of most of us can go farther back into such times [infancy] than many of us suppose; just as I believe the power of observation in numbers of very young children to be quite wonderful for its closeness and accuracy. Indeed, I think that most grown men who are remarkable in this respect, may with greater propriety be said not to have lost the faculty, than to have acquired it.[37]

This adult narrator says he is not just prosing: "I build these conclusions in part upon my own experience of myself." Set in memory, the novel is also built on "my own experience of myself," an experience so drenched in longing that the child, thoroughly loved by the adult, is willing to return that love and be remembered through it, be the one who remembers, offering himself up to us as a never-changing, well-remembering mirror.

That the offer carries with it no counter-demands makes it all the more moving, convincing the adult that the union he is forming with the child-of-memory, this "experience of myself" is a democratic, free union, a vision of the world as it ought to be. Pedophilia which engages itself with the good child is also likely to invoke an idealized form of anarchy. Notice how much of what Hayden White says about the typical emplotments of ideological anarchy fit with those of pedophilia. White is speaking of a view of total human history, but it fits almost exactly our personalized view of the good child's decline into adulthood and an attempt to turn that prelapsarian past into a here-and-now:

> Anarchists are inclined to idealize a *remote past* of natural human innocence from which men have fallen into the corrupt "social" state

in which they currently find themselves. They, in turn, project this utopia onto what is effectively a non-temporal plane, viewing it as a possibility of human achievement *at any time*, if men will only seize control of their own essential humanity, either by an act of will or by an act of consciousness which destroys the socially provided belief in the legitimacy of the current social establishment.[38]

Anarchy, the political celebration of play and of nostalgic pedophilia, seeks to blow up the wholly illegitimate world of the adult, and build in its place the free kingdom of the good child.

Since this linkage of pedophilia with ideological anarchy may seem unconvincing on the face of it, perhaps we should look at what common sense would tell us are the least likely candidates for anarchic sentiments: nostalgic ex-schoolboys and silly schoolmasters. The first seem to set the past in an ornate frame so as to stare at it, not use it as a bludgeon against the existing social order; the second spend their lives, it would appear, as the most severe policemen of the current social order, stamping out not just rebellion but rudeness. Taking the old-boy reminiscences first, we might ask what it is they want to preserve. It is not always easy to discover this, the author of *Boys and Their Ways*, for instance, going on, in a way wholly typical of this discourse, with an enthusiasm so great that it overwhelms any specifics. Schooldays, he says, without a speckle of originality, are "the happiest period of a man's career," largely because of the intimacies formed and operating then: "Such friendships we shall never know again!" One would probably want to know just why such friendships are a thing of the past, but all we get is some disappointing prating: "In after life we are incapable of so much disinterestedness, so much self-control, so ready and willing an obedience."[39] These qualities, however valuable in an accountant or member of organized crime, seem hardly likely to have lit the fire that burns through this discourse. Other writers are more direct. Symonds for instance, who recalls the joys of Harrow school not in terms of high-flying virtues but of a great deal of pinch and cuddle, leading to dizzying love: "Twice only in my life did I kiss him on the lips. The first time I did so I almost fainted from the intense rapture of the contact."[40] Symonds is speaking here of Willie Dyer, a boy three years younger than he who transformed the world in such a way that we can better understand the anarchist dream:

> My love enisled me in an enchanted garden, round which the breakers of the world of fact fretted without disturbing the delightfulness of dreaming. I no longer cared for work. I ceased to be ambitious. It

was enough to live. My love seemed to me more real than aught in life beside.[41]

While such prose may no longer find favor, the condition it describes may. It is a condition far removed from the virtues of disinterestedness, self-control, and obedience. What may surprise us is the extent to which schoolmasters celebrated that dangerous anarchy, the ability of schoolboys and especially schoolboys in love to create an ideal order so superior to the existing social realm as to be threatening to it. We may remember the schoolmaster A.R. Hope from back in Chapter 2, peeping out at his playing boys with ever so much yearning: "I used to long for a fairy to touch me with her wand, that I, too, might become small and lithe and smooth-faced and light-hearted, and might roll and tumble, and hurt and get hurt, and shout out for very carelessness and fulness of life." The full life, for this schoolmaster, is certainly not the ordered, adult life but the howling world of (male) childhood: "jumping, wrestling, chasing each other round tables, scrambling, rolling on the floor, and otherwise behaving in a way calculated to terrify prudent mothers and sisters, the whole performance being accompanied by a mingled din of shouting, laughing, whistling, chattering, and pure howling for howling's sake, which I confess was music to my ears."[42]

Some of these schoolmasters carried their alternative views and practices so resolutely into the public eye that they caused small scandals. Oscar Browning's dismissal as an assistant master at Eton made the *Times*, the *Daily News*, and the House of Commons. Dr. Horner is said to have remarked on his dismissal of Browning, "I have not charged him with *immorality* in the ordinary sense of the word,"[43] making it quite clear that he was charging him with *immorality* in some extraordinary sense. Croft-Cooke reports, persuasively but rather too confidently, that "no one had any doubt" what the real reason for the dismissal was: "he was sacked because he was a homosexual."[44] Browning did go on to take up with young sailors and blacksmiths and stable lads in the style of democratic "adhesiveness," and it does seem likely to me that he was much involved sexually with boys at Eton. Still, I do not think that his threat to the Eton way and ours can be adequately explained as simply that of the pedophile.

Browning later came to be known as the king of the snobs, but during his Eton days he seems to have represented fully the sentimental anarchism associated with the idealizing of children. Browning may not have, like Hope, found the howling boy music to his ears; but his love for the child took the form of creating a counter-world, a deeply subversive world that put the last first. Although he drew up lists of formal reforms he had in mind for Eton almost as soon as he stepped in the door as an assistant master, those Browning actually carried out ran much deeper. In his house, different values reigned—an indifference to sports, for instance, and an almost equal indifference to instituted hours, assignments, and due-dates. Browning, who himself often set the example of cutting Chapel, seems to have regarded religion as a matter on which the well-bred hardly bothered to have views, and he managed thereby to agitate the more orthodox among his charges. He appreciated fine food and wine and saw to it that his boys did too. Like Spark's Miss Jean Brodie after him and many another too, he thought his charges were far better occupied conversing with him than doing their ordinary reading, and he made himself available for long talks of this powerful sort. Against the expressed wishes of the headmaster, he promoted an interest in poetry other than classical (modern English poetry). He arranged theatricals and the visits of musicians and daring writers and artists, Pater among them.[45]

He created, in short, what we might now call an alternate paradigm, a vision of the world quite like Oscar Wilde's. In fact, his close attention to the decorations of his rooms and delight in their beauty bring to mind irresistibly the Wildean worship of atmosphere. One wonders how Browning felt about cucumber sandwiches and, really, how he felt about boys. His anarchic and free-wheeling rebelliousness, however, was clearly shared, was made available, even to Browning himself, only with and through his young friends and lovers.

Less obviously political, though also influential on the young was Browning's teacher and, in more ways than one, predecessor at Eton, William Johnson. More traditionally aristocratic in his views, certainly, than Browning and a little more conventional in such things as room decor, Johnson, from a different angle entirely, offered a threat to the established order so menacing as to bring down upon him too the dismissal and disgrace that later came to his pupil. In Johnson's case, there were no attempts to subvert the classical curriculum or to encourage any laxity in the traditional forms of learning. Johnson was not a sophisticated man and did not seek to lead his pupils to broader vistas. He simply loved Eton and the boys, some of them especially, and wanted that world to be there forever. He took boys on holidays, on boating parties, to his home in Devonshire. Just as often, he visited in their homes. He wanted to extend Eton into the whole world, but it was of course his own special warm and unified Eton, caught in the "Eton Boating Song," which he wrote. Testimonials to him in later memoirs show how deeply he was loved by his charges, and some of

234 / *The Gentle Child*

his extraordinary verse shows how deeply he could love in return. His dismissal is shrouded in mystery, though it is assumed by one and all that he went too far in one of his sentimental-sexual affairs with a boy. Perhaps that is so, or perhaps, though again in a way different from Browning, he was regarded as an alien, one who might colonize the boys into another way of life, a life truly adhesive. From the vantage-point of the adult, this world of the Eton Boating Song and games and long talks and adolescent confessions and boyish love was fixated and regressive. But to Johnson, who was a simple and dignified man, not given to elaborate discourse, what he had found at Eton and offered to the boys was "freedom":

> And when I may no longer live,
> They'll say, who know the truth,
> He gave whate'er he had to give
> To freedom and to youth.[46]

Freedom was doubtless as threatening as the moving, sentimental visions of permanence he created, permanence in the school, in childhood, or in death—sometimes all three in one:

> They told me, Heraclitus, they told me you were dead,
> They brought me bitter news to hear and bitter tears to shed.
> I wept, as I remembered, how often you and I
> Had tired the sun with talking and sent him down the sky.
>
> And now that thou art lying, my dear old Carian guest,
> A handful of grey ashes, long long ago at rest,
> Still are thy pleasant voices, thy nightingales awake;
> For Death, he taketh all away, but them he cannot take.[47]

Out of death and darkness come the sounds that feed the memory and awaken it to a pleasure so vital that it is all but a recompense. Death manages to shape things, allowing us to see clearly and in a pleasant hazy-dark light. And what we see, we see with pleasure. It is almost as if the last line, with its mildly confusing paradox, presented itself to us as this: *Because* Death taketh all away, he creates a delight that cannot die. Death removes all complexity, purifies, puts what we love at such a distance that it becomes sadly pleasurable and irresistibly erotic.

The Dead Child

The good child is patient, quiet, submissive; the best child is eternally so: that overstates the case—only slightly. "The Priest and the Acolyte," the story with which Wilde was bespattered so unfairly in his trial, ends with the orgasmic apotheosis of the priest and his loving choir-boy in death. They hold onto one another forever; and the reader can hold onto the image. Cathy and Heathcliff exist in our imaginations as corpses as much as scampering children, and Count Dracula with his "child-brain," promising the purest union of death and eros, has never had difficulty gaining entry to our hearts or bedrooms.[48] Oscar Wilde, who understood holding actions better than anyone in the century, still had a distaste for cadavers, substituting perfectly in his lovely half-parodic epigram: "Those whom the gods love grow young." And stay young, of course, which is a little like staying dead. The fantasy of death as a dissolver of barriers, as a doorway into union between adult and child is not an undignified one; it is the myth of romantic tragedy. It is a belief in a good ending for the good child, a world of heavens but no hells.[49]

But actually, as we mentioned earlier, the equation of pedophilia with necrophilia is mischievous. Few pedophiles actually want death in that form, though perhaps something on the road to death would do, something *dying*. It's hard to deny a strain of pedophilia that longs for the expiring child, but it is a morbid strain that is much more active in what might, hopelessly, be called mainstream culture than in practicing pedophiles. For pure drooling eroticism over this figure, one needs to turn to Victorian popular songs or popular literature (or to our own right-to-life narratives). Here is an important example:

> Speak gently to the little child!
>   Its love be sure to gain;
> Teach it in accents soft and mild—
>   It may not long remain.[50]

This poem still is familiar because Lewis Carroll parodied it in *Alice's Adventures in Wonderland*. Carroll had too much regard for children to find them very interesting when they were in decline. His Duchess, a comparatively attractive figure, has no worries that the child will soon be leaving:

> Speak roughly to your little boy,
>   And beat him when he sneezes:
> He only does it to annoy,
>   Because he knows it teases.[51]

In the Duchess's comic view, there is no danger and no death. There is not even any fear (or the boy would not be so anxious to tease—or sneeze either). Her sadism, if that's what it is, seems perverse only if we forget (which we will) that it counters the more monstrous, culturally central perversity that equates goodness with a degenerative, finally fatal, and luscious disease.

A. Little Paul

Paul Dombey's quest to find out about the wild waves is as tempestuous and as much a landmark in his culture as Burt Lancaster and Deborah Kerr writhing in the tidal wash in the 1953 *From Here to Eternity* was in our own. The obsessive focus of the first quarter of *Dombey and Son* is the quite lovely gliding of this archetypally "gentle boy"[52] toward the old fashion that consummates the old fashion of the boy, "the old, old fashion—Death!" (ch. xvi). Dickens' punning on the old-fashioned tag at such a point makes us uneasy, but less uneasy than Paul's dying words, "Mama is like you, Floy. . . . But tell them that the print upon the stairs at school is not divine enough." Perhaps that hint inspired Holman Hunt and Millais to do popular Jesus pictures with a higher divinity quotient. This sort of thing embarrasses us, and we dwell on such "sentimentality" if we do not like Dickens or feel the need to say we don't. But actually Paul's death comes and goes in a five-page chapter, and there are only a half-dozen sentences of the exalted prose we love to cringe over. There is something here beside the last choke-and-sputter. Peter Coveney noted that "Paul Dombey's *dying*, not *why* he died, becomes the focus of interest."[53] Really, it is his dying and not his *death* that consumes us, the titillating movement toward, the strip-tease prior to the naked climax that occupies us.

This gentle boy on his way to death is laid before us from the very first as a tidily arranged bundle of morbid childish eroticism, "tucked up warm in a little basket bedstead" in the first paragraph of the story and seldom allowed out of beds or baskets thereafter. He is a pure child, and "a pretty little fellow too," with "something wan and wistful in his face" (ch. viii). He is a pedophile pin-up, obscurely alone and "put upon" as Mrs. Wickham is always saying. He is a frail baby and is doing even less well when we come on him again in the interesting stage of boyhood, wasting and pining after his dismissed nurse, temperamentally melancholy, and "naturally delicate" (ch. viii). Paul enters onto childhood as most people enter onto their nineties. He is, after all, so attractive in repose: "What a pretty fellow he is when he's asleep!" (ch. viii). Just right for freezing. Exactly like Peter Pan, Paul cooperates with the pedophile fantasy to the point of announcing his disinclination ever to be anything but a child:

> "Shall we make a man of him?" repeated the Doctor.
> "I had rather be a child," replied Paul.
> "Indeed!" said the Doctor. "Why?"
> The child sat on the table looking at him, with a curious expression of suppressed emotion in his face, and beating one hand proudly on his knee as if he had rising tears beneath it, and crushed them. (ch. xi)

Peter Pan is more cheery about all this, but the image of eternal allure is the same. Peter Pan is equally "curious," enigmatic, unexplaining—equally, we would say, Other, an object of desire. Neither figure is quite accessible to this sort of contact; neither will yield his secrets or his love to schoolmasters who set them in the middle of tables and start the grilling.

But both are capable of pumping up enormous gushers of desire in onlookers, especially those who understand, even nourish and pet the otherness. Paul exercises on people, even old Mrs. Pipchin, an "odd kind of attraction" (ch. viii), an attraction to his very oddity and difference. Paul, in turn, is attracted to those older than he, to adults like Mrs. Pipchin and Glubb, dismissing a "lad" as drawer of his carriage in favor of the boy's grandfather (ch. viii). Paul's alien old-fashionedness, in fact, is once even directly attributed to and identified with the Victorian buzz-term for dangerous child-sexuality, "precocious" (ch. viii). This precocity suggests that his childhood, though just what we want, is shadowed by an odd knowingness. He has a way of looking at you "with an expression, half of melancholy, half of slyness" (ch. viii), a "sly and quaint yet touching look" (ch. xi). He's a sly one, but touching all the same. The slyness suggests that his "old-fashioned" quality reaches backward into the past of the adults who surround him and long for him. They share a secret kinship, even oneness with this distant, strange creature. At the same time, his slyness reaches forward, touching these adults in a way equally secret, in the center of their sexual learning and desires. The child knows and shyly, slyly advances anyhow.

The question must be whether this knowing child can coexist somehow with the pure child we had been given so many opportunities to construct, whether the gentle child can be sexualized. There is nothing blocking such a happy contradiction, nothing keeping us from responding to purity and also jumping into that emptiness with attributions of

238 / *The Gentle Child*

our own, slipping in a little sexual knowledge and sexual desire. For Paul Dombey seems to be a morsel offered up to readers, a child in need of adult lovers. After all, his mother is dead and his father, in idiotic defiance of all natural instincts, is impatient for him to grow up. Readers know better and are given an open invitation to swallow this little toasted crumpet if they like. But there are better pleasures than those of swallowing, and we find them through watching a contest between those who want the child to grow up and those who do not. On one side we have Mr. Dombey and his perverse desire[54] and the linear plot and its perverse desire. If they had their way, Paul would get over whatever it is and mature. But child-loving readers, who regard maturing as rotting, are opposing all this and have on their/our side the desires of the sly knowing child, along with the attractions of Death. We win.

B. *Little Nell*

But Paul's is only a one-act play. For the full thing, a world-famous seventy chapters of dying, we turn to Little Paul's predecessor, Little Nell. But, unlike Paul's death and to the surprise of those who have only heard of this event and are expecting something lavish and wallowing, Little Nell's end occurs when we and the narrator are not around. We only hear about it, and not very much about it at that. By the time we get there, "She was dead. Dear, gentle, patient, noble Nell was dead."[55] She was dead and two continents let loose with what they had been holding back for so very long, tears mostly. The extent of this public mourning has doubtless been exaggerated, but it makes a good story, which is all one ought to ask of history.

In any case, in addition to being allowed full-scale dying, Nell also has that wonderful knowing innocence Dickens later copied with Paul, the impossible joining of purity and awareness. Nell, who opens the novel at 13, a nicely ambiguous age, is eroticized as fully as Paul and by much the same means. She is the absolute Other, the adult-child or child-adult who has no echoing surroundings, who is alien everywhere. She has no place in London and when she heads for the hills with her moronic grandfather she is alone in the country and even more alone when they venture among people: "more alone than she had ever been before; alone in spirit, alone in her devotion to him who was wasting away upon his burning bed; alone in her unfeigned sorrow" (ch. xi). Like Paul, Nell is precocious, more the adult than her own grandfather, as he admits with irritating readiness (ch. i). As every reader (or at least every critic) has noted, her ability to attract sexual interest is focused in Quilp, who makes rude comments about her bed and her body, a regular "bud," he says, "with such blue veins and such a transparent skin"; altogether "such a chubby, rosy, cosy, little Nell!" (ch. ix). Just as Paul is "sly," both empty and full, so is Nell both ethereal and palely angelic but also chubby and rosy, other-worldly and of the bedroom. Even her brother adds to the almost unseemly rush to invest the child with the capacity to attract desire: "The girl has strong affections, and brought up as she has been, may, at her age, be easily influenced and persuaded" (ch. vii). This is almost too much.

But Nell is more than just the blooming child out of pornography, caught by death just as that bloom is at its height and preserved like freeze-dried corn. Her erotic appeal is much more closely tied to death even than Paul's, largely because she and her sexual interest are defined throughout by sharp contrasts with everything living. Dickens says he thought of the novel in terms of contrast and the first chapter baldly gives us the plan of the book: "to imagine her in her future life, holding her solitary way among a crowd of wild grotesque companions." All those wild and alive, then, are figured not just as "grotesque," but as antithetical to the centered child. We are thus drawn away from all life, which is drained of interest and potency by the magnet of childish death. One might test this thesis by checking one's response to the curiously dominant Kit Nubbles group, ask why they are one and all tedious and faintly repugnant, and conclude that they are simply too healthy, too unknowing, too far removed from sexual death.

Or, consider how it is we are able not only to stomach but to cheer such things as the narrator's observations on what "a bright and happy" fate awaits "those who die young" (ch. xxvi) or the bachelor's concluding comments to his brother (the grandfather) on how at death they will become children again, thus cementing the naturalness of the tie between death and the child. How can such statements be made to seem natural? Consider Nell's bird. Discovered at one point by the sentimental Kit, he shows it to Quilp, who is less sentimental:

> "Here's a bird! What's to be done with this?"
> "Wring its neck," rejoined Quilp.
> "Oh no, don't do that," said Kit. (ch. xiii)

Who are you rooting for? Look again at the thundering paragraph that so stirred the hearts of later satirists:

> She was dead. Dear, gentle, patient, noble Nell was dead. Her little bird—a poor slight thing, the pressure of a finger would have

crushed—was stirring nimbly in its cage; and the strong heart of its child-mistress was mute and motionless for ever. (ch. lxxi)

This deflection of our attention from the corpse onto the bird seems tasteless, blundering. But it is this contrast that makes Nell's dying and her death so blissful, such a model of perfect eros. That hopping bird, draining off any resentment or guilt, allows us to melt in simplicity of tears or perfect desire, to swoon right into the bed or coffin without the slightest compunction. Even at the funeral, the contrast is there and the unlocated anger too, this time directed at the old people who were more dead than Nell, who come to represent everything repulsive, everything above ground: "What was the death [the coffin] would shut in, to that which still could creep and crawl above it!" (ch. lxxi). Up here are the creepers and crawlers; down below is youth and beauty. We would dive six feet under with Nell for aesthetic reasons, even if we were not already driven there by desire.

The Pastor and His Flock

There are many who might serve to conclude this chapter on the good, gentle child. Ernest Dowson's attraction to children and his affecting poems would do, as would Symonds and his candid *Memoirs* and poems. Both might be made to represent the constructing and loving of this figure. The Rev. Francis Kilvert (1840–79), however, provides an instance of one whose range of feelings were far less distant than Dowson's and less aware or honest than Symonds's. His *Diaries* are, however, full, anecdotal, and deeply soaked in his own sexual and pastoral experiences. Kilvert seems to have been blessed with the sort of selective innocence that allowed for pretty complete self-indulgence, though it is entirely possible that he *did* nothing that his parishioners or the children found untoward.

His interests were varied. He even records in later volumes of his diary a considerable capacity to be aroused erotically by child-whipping.[56] And now and then he seems interested in little boys. He records an instance of a mother, "evidently very proud" of her son, inviting Kilvert in to see him naked; announcing "I'm not ashamed to show him," she then takes off his clothes "so as to show his bottom and thighs naked from the waist downward" (III, 242). Earlier, he and a friend "adjourned to my bedroom and had a great romp with the boys who mounted on our backs" (I, 24). On the whole, however, the boys of the parish did not interest Kilvert or set him ablaze in the way the small girls did.

He describes them with a lascivious freedom that could only have been available to him through a conception of the child as completely good. He provides elaborate descriptions of little girls whose looks capture him, descriptions that carefully frame the subject in a seductive pose: children's faces are often "shaded" (I, 94), screened yet slyly open to his view: "beautiful large soft dark eyes" look out "from beneath their long dark silky lashes" (I, 83; see also I, 47). Action is arrested, dazzling smiles revealing little white teeth and a momentary full glimpse of a face "as she tossed her dark curls back" (I, 155). Several times in these descriptions we can observe what seems to be a quick reversal: suddenly recalling his vocation, the language, somewhat absurdly, changes from the erotic to the soapy-pious. A beggar child with luxuriant hair "tossed and tangled wild," peeps out at him from behind a door with "beautiful wild eyes": "It was irresistible. Christ seemed to be looking at me through the beautiful wistful imploring eyes" (I, 31). The following passage illustrates more clearly than a brief excerpt can do both Kilvert's obsession with the "pure" and his slipping and sliding between the call of the wild and the call of God:

> How is the indescribable beauty of that most lovely face to be described—the dark soft curls parting back from the pure white transparent brow, the exquisite little mouth and pearly tiny teeth, the pure straight delicate features, the long dark fringes and white eyelids that droop over and curtain her eyes . . . and seem to rest upon the soft clear cheek, and when the eyes are raised, that clear unfathomable blue depth of wide wonder and enquiry and unsullied and unsuspecting innocence. Oh, child, child, if you did but know your own power. Oh, Gipsy, if you only grow up as good as you are fair. Oh, that you might grow up good. May all God's angels guard you, sweet. The Lord bless thee and keep thee. The Lord make his face to shine upon thee and be gracious unto thee. The Lord lift up his countenance upon thee peace [sic], both now and *evermore*. Amen (I, 168–69)

Sometimes the metaphors become even more overt: in a reverie his gipsy girl wakes to the invading sun, which "has stolen into her bedroom and crept along the wall from chair to chair till he has reached the bed and has kissed the fair hand and arm that lies upon the coverlet and the white bosom that heaves half uncovered after the restlessness of the sultry night, and has kissed her mouth whose scarlet lips, just parted in a smile and pouting like rosebuds to be kissed, show the pearly gleam of her white teeth, and has kissed the sweet face the blue veined lashed eyelids and the white brow and the soft bright tangled hair" (I, 173–74). Language as thinly veiled as the girl continues moving from body part to part in a kind of erotic tap-dance.

Often there are no veils at all. He describes walking ten miles just "to kiss that child's sweet face" (I, 123). Merry children at play always delight him, especially when their clothes become loosened, turned up, or, best of all, ripped open or off, "showing vast spaces of white, skin as well as linen" (I, 103). Better even than children on swings are children bathing:

> Being tub night, Polly with great celerity and satisfaction stripped herself naked to her drawers before me and was very anxious to take off her drawers too for my benefit, but her grandmother would not allow her. As it happened the drawers in question were so inadequately constituted that it made uncommonly little difference whether they were off or on, and there was a most interesting view from the rear. (I, 325)

How much awareness Kilvert allowed himself of the nature of interests like these we cannot know, just as we cannot be sure what exactly his consciousness of such matters really could amount to. He does not generally reflect on these points; we could not hear him very well had he done so. What is clear is that he did not regard these children lightly: "She was perfectly bewitching and I fell immediately deeply in love with her" (I, 132). There is no reason not to take him at his word. His love often amounted to outright worship, and he consecrated bits of ground or clothing or even machinery because a loved child had touched them. He saw these children, then, as icons or as framed images of irresistible beauty, much the same thing in his case: "I wish I could get a likeness of the child. If her picture were in the Academy it would be thronged, unapproachable" (I, 381).

Finally, as with all lovers of the good children, Kilvert dreamed of taking possession of the emptiness, somehow transporting himself into it. On being asked to be Godfather to a little girl he had long had his eyes on and long adored, Kilvert was overjoyed: "Now I shall have a real right in the child" (I, 304). Of course, the sort of rights he had a mind to claim were never recognized. It is likely he would never have exercised them anyhow. But the good child's final inaccessibility, even, if the truth were known, in the grave, confronts somehow or other all the idealizing child-lovers. The gentle child may peep shyly out from under long lashes or slyly cuddle up to us or laugh and invite us into the tomb. That's as far as it goes; that's where goodness gets you. But it was the child-lover's destination all along, so this goodening of the child was no mistake.

Notes

1. John Addington Symonds, "Lad's Love, ll. 1–4, in [Edward Mark Slocum], ed., *Men and Boys* (New York, 1924; rpt. New York and London: Coltsfoot Press, 1978), p. 43.

2. Lord Byron, "The Adieu," in Slocum, ed., *Men and Boys*, p. 41.

3. Lewis Carroll, "All in the Golden Afternoon," prefatory to *Alice's Adventures in Wonderland*, "Pennyroyal Alice," p. 34.

4. Lewis Carroll, "An Easter Greeting to Every Child Who Loves *Alice*," in The Pennyroyal Edition of *Through the Looking-Glass, and What Alice Found There*, "The Pennyroyal Alice" (Berkeley: Univ. of California Press, 1983), p. 147.

5. Rev. E.E. Bradford, "Alan," in Slocum, ed., *Men and Boys*, p. 49.

6. I think the reader is perfectly free to regard this "sin and shame" as Alan's body (apart from his heart), as his activities, or more broadly as the activities of other people, not Alan at all.

7. John Addington Symonds, *A Problem in Modern Ethics* ([London: privately printed by Davos, 1891]), pp. 185–93; also in Symonds, *A Problem in Greek Ethics* ([Bristol: privately printed by Ballantyne and Hanson, 1883]), p. 19.

8. Marc-Andre Raffalovich, "Rose Leaves When the Rose Is Dead," ll. 5–8, in Reade, *Sexual Heretics*, p. 197.

9. "A. Newman," "Perfectly Contented," *Rondeaux of Boyhood* (London: privately printed, 1923), p. 35.

10. Anon., *Boys and Their Ways*, pp. xiii–xiv.

11. Fraser, *Death of Narcissus*, p. 215.

12. "Introduction" to Urwick, ed., *Studies of Boy Life in Our Cities*, pp. xii–xiv.

13. Oscar Wilde, "The Decay of Lying," *Intentions* (Portland, Maine: Thomas B. Mosher, 1944), p. 22.

14. Wilde, "The Decay of Lying," *Intentions*, p. 17.

15. Masson, *A Dark Science*, pp. 14–16.

16. In Reade, ed., *Sexual Heretics*, p. 306.

17. J.M. Barrie, *Peter Pan, or The Boy Who Would Not Grow Up*, "The Uniform Edition of the Plays of J. M. Barrie," (New York: Charles Scribners' Sons, 1928), Act II, p. 52. Subsequent references to this play will be cited in the text.

18. Interestingly, Barrie suggests that the demarcation between parents and children is so great that even parents, otherwise dim and sluggish, recognize it. What's more, they are perhaps as happy to be rid of the children as the children are to be shut of them. At least Mr. Darling may be: "George," says his wife, "you are sure you are not enjoying it?" (Act V, p. 149).

19. Raffalovich, "Lovelace" (1886), in Reade, *Sexual Heretics*, p. 199.

244 / The Gentle Child

20. Freud, "Three Essays," VII, 149; this occurs in a footnote Freud added in 1910.

21. Freud, "Three Essays," VII, 192.

22. Anon., "Memoranda from Mr. P——" *The Pearl: A Journal of Facetive and Voluptuous Reading*, No. 17 (Nov. 1880); (rpt. New York: Ballantine, 1973), pp. 598–601. It is fair to add that this voluminous journal shows very little interest in children and contains not much that even we would think of as "kiddie porn."

23. Anon., "Young Beginners," *The Pearl*, No. 4 (Oct. 1879); in Ballantine rpt., pp. 123–29.

24. Anon., *When a Child Loves*, pp. 24, 25.

25. Davidson, *The World, The Flesh, and Myself*, p. 111.

26. Eglinton, *Greek Love*, p. 479.

27. "A. Newman," "Aged Fifteen," *Rondeaux of Boyhood*, p. 61.

28. See Crompton, *Byron and Greek Love*, pp. 186–87.

29. W. David Allen, *The Fear of Looking, or Scoptophilic-Exhibitionistic Conflicts* (Charlottesville: Univ. Press of Virginia, 1974), p. 7.

30. "A. Newman," "Bare Knees," *Rondeaux of Boyhood*, p. 22.

31. Anon., *When a Child Loves*, p. 6.

32. Susan Stewart, *On Longing: Narratives of the Miniature, the Gigantic, the Souvenir, the Collection* (Baltimore: The Johns Hopkins Univ. Press, 1984), p. 23.

33. Stewart, *On Longing*, p. 23.

34. Dukahz, *Asbestos Diary*, p. 13.

35. Symonds, "A Dream," in Slocum, ed., *Men and Boys*, p. 43.

36. Anon., " 'Of the Land We Love'—To C.C.B.—a Ballade," in d'Arch Smith, *Love in Earnest*, pp. 75–76.

37. Dickens, *David Copperfield*, ch. II, p. 13.

38. White, *Metahistory*, p. 25.

39. Anon., *Boys and Their Ways*, pp. 45, 126.

40. Symonds, *Memoirs*, p. 105.

41. Symonds, *Memoirs*, pp. 105–6.

42. Hope, *A Book About Boys*, p. 21.

43. See Chandos, *Boys Together*, p. 287.

44. Croft-Cooke, *Feasting with Panthers*, p. 114.

45. See Croft-Cooke, *Feasting with Panthers*, pp. 111–18. Croft-Cooke supplies most of the details cited here, though his assessment of Browning—"an aggressive and conceited man" (p. 111)—is, I think, quite unnecessarily harsh. Croft-Cooke seems to have a distaste for almost all the figures he writes about, a distaste he expresses with a facetiousness of which he never tires. Still, I am grateful for the material I have used here and in the discussion of William Johnson (Cory), pp. 103–11.

46. William Johnson, "Academus," reprinted in Croft-Cooke, *Feasting with Panthers*, p. 111.

47. William Johnson, "Heraclitus," reprinted in Reade, ed., *Sexual Heretics*, p. 68.

48. According to Bram Stoker's version of the legend, Dracula can enter no room into which he is not invited.

49. Fraser, *Death of Narcissus*, points out how many Victorian pedophiles angrily rejected the doctrine of eternal punishment—or any punishment at all: Carroll, MacDonald, Farrar.

50. This popular children's poem, published in 1848, was probably written by David Bates, though originally attributed to G.W. Langford. See The "Pennyroyal" *Alice's Adventures in Wonderland*, p. 77.

51. Carroll, The "Pennyroyal" *Alice's Adventures in Wonderland*, p. 77.

52. Charles Dickens, *Dealings with the Firm of Dombey and Son; Wholesale, Retail and for Exportation* (London: Oxford Univ. Press, 1950); originally 1846–1848, ch. xvi, p. 223. Subsequent references to this novel will be cited in the text by chapter.

53. Coveney, *The Image of Childhood*, p. 161.

54. From this point of view, Mr. Dombey is punished not for his treatment of Florence but for his unnatural rejection of the pedophile energies that drive parenthood.

55. Charles Dickens, *The Old Curiosity Shop* (London: Oxford Univ. Press, 1951), originally, 1840–41, ch. lxxi, p. 539. Subsequent references to this novel will be cited in the text by chapter.

56. Rev. Francis Kilvert, *Kilvert's Diary: Selections from the Diary of the Rev. Francis Kilvert*, ed. William Plomer, 3 vols. (London: Jonathan Cape, 1938–40). The diaries cover the period from 1 January 1870 to 13 March 1879. Subsequent references will be cited in the text by volume and page number.

7

The Naughty Child

> Well, I'm sorry for Algy, but still
> it's a spree;
> And his floggings are always so
> jolly to see.[1]

The good child is always the obtuse child. The good child attends dutifully to the cultural orders it hears, the ones telling it what it is and what it should do. But it is such a simpleton that it reads all on the surface, takes the sanitized slogans for the real thing. The good child is like the football player who believes winning isn't everything, the attorney who believes honesty is the best policy, the consumer who believes insurance companies care. The good child practices an hour a day, tries not to lie, believes that parents and teachers have its best interests at heart. And for all this it is pretty much despised.

Luckily, not all children are good children. We do not allow it. Since the child is a construction in the first place, there is no reason we would settle for such tedium. Instead, our culture constructs the way the pedophile constructs: the child, made mirror-like in order to transport us into the land of true childhood, is then displaced and made to play the part of the false child, the naughty child. This child does not, like the good child, listen to the chirpings of the official aviary but attends to a more subtle semiotics of desire that require the child to evade the demands that are placed on it, the ones defining it as a good child. This resisting child thus keeps its distance from the professed standard, remains Other, does not so much rebel as respond more acutely to what is wanted. What is wanted is not goodness, and definitely not rebellious independence; that would be worse than goodness. The wise child conforms to another measure, that of the naughty child. The wise child finds its body called upon to represent a good many forms of complex distancing and mirroring, but it's an acting job that, though demanding, can actually be mastered with ease. That's because, as Eve Kosofsky Sedgwick wryly points out, the child has so much help, so many lessons given gratis.[2]

The major lesson this naughty child must learn is "how to stay away from goodness." It could be argued that the deviances of attractive naughtiness are rigidly prescribed, that we want neither genuine nor central challenges coming from children we are setting out to adore, that naughtiness is goodness with a wink. But I think it would be minimizing the Otherness we need from the naughty child to regard it as no more than a slight rumpling of the approved model. I think the naughtiness comes at us from an angle more acute. The contract governing the behavior of the naughty child is perhaps specific and rigid in its terms; but we have pretended so long not to know of this contract that the behavior of the child always seems surprising. Good children are so strenuously advertised for that we almost suppose we would hire them, losing sight of the critical requirement that only those who do not at all fit the bill need apply.

Resenting the Child

Our culture has for some time forced its best and brightest into naughtiness. More exactly, it has draped a costume of naughtiness over the child and directed it to play that role, offering rewards for doing so: the child is loved, the child is spanked. That's what the child wants and needs, we are told. It is our duty to play our part as adults, to muster the assigned feeling toward the naughty child, a feeling corresponding to the activity demanded of us, one which will hurt us much more than the child. We love and therefore we spank—or flog, beat, whip. Our culture provides us with courses in the Method so that we can, on demand, call into play the designated emotion: neither outrage nor amusement (both representing the adult's failure to read his part) but a stern, resolute disapproval, moderated by a half-weary, almost good-natured acknowledgment that the child is, after all, a child: a kind of glare with a grin behind it, a loving walloping. We'll call it "resentment."

We call it resentment because the child will not fully participate in the game, will not holler down our rain barrel. The child is naughty because it gets out of the way and stays out of the way. Of course, this *is* the game: the child must vacate the position of true child, become Other, so that the child-spot is left open for the adult. The child becomes naughty so that we may be the good child. Once sent around the corner, the naughty child can be longed for and resented. It can be whacked for daring to leave. Were it somehow not to leave, of course, the game would end. The game is "let's resent": an invitation to play at a violent attack on naughtiness. The drama is fierce—anger, tears,

248 / *The Naughty Child*

howls—but nothing holds, even the pain; it is all a fabrication for the sake of the game, for the sake of eros. Pocketed within this game is another: "let's love": where love is confirmed by having approval smacked, stamped on it. The game is one game, not paradoxical and not ironic: we distance the child because we so need it close, yell at it because we approve, give pain as love.

Thus we follow a set of cultural exercises on how to resent children. Wordsworth was important in providing a discourse that could be so easily held up satirically against the actual, no-clouds-of-glory-behind-them beings that so annoyed later writers. But even before Wordsworth, the child was resented; one supposes resenting it accompanied inventing it—resenting it and thus pining for it. The childlike quality most firmly implanted by tradition and most justifying resentment was ingratitude, an ingratitude Samuel Butler (the elder) shrewdly ascribed to Nature herself, that is to the very architectural plans on which the child was built: "Nature hath order'd it so, that Parents have a great Inclination to the Love of their Children, because they cannot subsist without it: But takes no course that children should Love their Parents, because they have no such neede of it."[3] Butler's ambiguous "they" may suggest that parents subsist on the love of children, an unrequited love, of course.

In any case, by the nineteenth century child-resenting could be made into a cult. A few of the streams feeding into this swelling lake of feeling are unmistakably bitter. Some represented children as morally deficient, "usually more inclined to be selfish than adults,"[4] and the passivity demanded of them, like the static femininity expected of girls, was often subject to scorn. Mostly, however, the resentment was advanced facetiously, with the sort of roaring hyperbole with which we disguise our most questionable feelings. An example of this half-muffled explosion is *The Artificial Mother* (1894), a story, dedicated "to the oppressed husbands and fathers of the land," of a robot who tends to the nine children or "mother-devourers" of a much-beleaguered and jealous father. This robot does just fine with the "wretches," who have "no souls that needed nurturing" anyhow and who are now no longer bothering the narrator. When, at the end, the whole thing turns out to have been a dream, the narrator is deeply disappointed, as are his readers; but it is the dream-cover which has allowed all this annoyance to spill out in the first place.[5] Such annoyance infuses canonical literature in the period through such images as the babies of Eleanor Bold and Celia Chetham (in *Barchester Towers* and *Middlemarch*), babies who are nothing but blobs of flesh, "living toys" that mindless people bounce around and then adore. The sarcastic counter to baby-worship is the use of children as stage props by Becky Sharp and Madeline Neroni. In Dickens, the resentment is expressed more directly, as child after child is beaten on stage, sometimes piteously but often in fun, the most merry target being Alexander Mac-Stinger in *Dombey*, whose only part in the story is to be periodically spanked and to sit on the curb cooling his besparkled bottom.

Victorian Child-Correcting

Spanking is the usual way in which love and resentment have been exercised, thereby keeping desire at a healthy level—especially in England and America, where flagellation, lacking the religious sanction given it throughout most of Europe, has been available for secular deployment across a broad front.[6] Possibly the practice became especially prominent in England because the French made some moves in the nineteenth century to outlaw it.

The Victorians, like us, hardly needed the spur of foreign competition to incite the activity. What they needed, apparently, was a discourse of explanation and justification, a discourse they adapted quite skillfully from what they found lying around. The handiest talk was the pious and the simplest use of that was the claim that one whipped because God said to: "That God has ordained corporal punishment no man can doubt." That's very assured rhetoric, a little too assured, since it occurs to the author at once that not all men believe in God. Nothing ruffled, he switches from one absolute to another: "even the atheist allows that Nature has ordained it."[7] Suspicious readers will be checking the footnote and discovering that the source for this is a volume compiled by one who is an "amateur flagellant," and maybe not a scholar. But I had no intention of disguising as sound the work of eccentrics. To prove it, I will provide evidence that divinity and spanking were indissolubly linked, that the author of *Experiences of Flagellation* (cited above) speaks from within the same episteme as Bishop Wilberforce and the Queen. Take the emphasis in Evangelical tracts on beating children to save their souls[8] or the slightly more gentle stories of Mrs. Sherwood. Here is the climax of *The Little Woodman*:

> William lived very happily with his grandmother, because she brought him up in the fear of God; and while he was little she punished him when he was naughty.
> She often used to say, "I loved your father so foolishly that I never corrected him, so God corrected me. But I will love you, my little

grandson, with a wiser love, and will not fail to punish you when you are naughty."

When William grew up he thanked his grandmother for having preserved him from doing wrong. And thus their days were spent happily in diligent labour; while their evenings were closed with reading God's book and praying together; till, at length, the pious old woman died.[9]

God sees to it that she whips him and that William is thankful for it, once he grows up and the whippings (one assumes) stop.

Similarly, Penny History No. 10 of "Houston's Juvenile Tracts for the Amusement and Improvement of Young Persons" is entitled (improvingly and amusingly), "The Rod." Here the speaker, Mrs. Rowland, gathers about her some children for a fireside chat, occasioned by her observation that, unlike William in the story above, most children were perversely resistant to being slashed with rods. "Every child," she goes so far as to say, "looks upon the rod as a very unnecessary thing." Far from being unnecessary, the rod is, she says, God's major tool for fashioning the world just the way he likes it. People like Isaiah and Solomon are quoted as being much in favor of the rod, but the major testimony comes from God himself, "in his gracious promises to David": a pledge to send "the rod" and "stripes" to David and his people. The special graciousness of this might not be especially plain to the witless children, but Mrs. Rowland reveals how it is all done "to make his people better." Just like God, then, adults wish to make children better, but it isn't easy: "O how much punishment it sometimes takes to wean us from our sins!" But God, and Mrs. Rowland too, will not give up: "If one affliction will not do, God is pleased to send another."[10]

Those who do not want God playing a part in all this often evoke a more general concept of correction: that it is being done for the child's own good, good that will be available for use in this life, as the habits or ideas absorbed in the beating will make one rich, happy, or something equally satisfactory. The parent is doing, if not God's work, then, at least moral work—as in a *good* spanking—and also hygienic work—as in a *sound* or *healthy* spanking. Often it is felt to be imperative, a duty performed to save, if not souls, then lives. Better pain now than pain or death later. It is educational, instilling, as Ellice Hopkins says, "wholesome terror":

One really careful mother I know was told by her little girl in all innocence of heart that a strange gentleman had given her some money, and been very kind to her, and asked her to go a walk with him. She at once took the child aside and gave her a sound whipping for taking the money. You may think it harsh, as the child knew no better. I believe it was the very best thing she could do.

The child might have forgotten a simple injunction, but "the whipping would fill her with a wholesome terror of strange men in the future, and of some unknown peril connected with them which made mother so angry."[11] The possibility of the child feeling an unwholesome terror of mother because of a quite well-known peril is never entertained; probably that never happens.

As well as acting as a preventative, whippings could function as cures. Some took the short route through the forest of difficulties surrounding childhood masturbation, for instance, and advised that the whole problem would disappear with "a good thrashing."[12] Even "spoiling," the condition spankings were designed, above all things, to protect against, they could somehow also repair, a drama of reformation recorded, in part, in *Sandford and Merton*. Thomas Arnold suggested that judicious correction could help us in the main business of life, the "return to that better and holy nature, which, in truth, although not in fact, is the proper nature of man."[13] But Arnold was no Wordsworthian, and he equated that "better and holy" and "proper" state of man with the state of adulthood. Childhood was, at best, a condition of "essential inferiority," one which must be positively labeled as such in order to assure the movement out into adulthood. Whipping, "as fitly answering to and marking the naturally inferior state of boyhood,"[14] became a tiresome but necessary duty.

A. Home-Spanking

Home-beating of children is now as private a matter as sex, which means that we have little to go on in judging the range of this domestic practice in our own culture. What breaks through to our attention are extremes like the murdering and crippling of children, incidents that we take to be atypical. The Victorians were nearly as secretive about their disciplinings. There is something about it in novels, in a few case histories in Krafft-Ebing and Ellis, and in some pornography—none of which counts for a lot as evidence. Memoirs and autobiographies from the period often talk about floggings at school but are usually reticent on home activities.[15] Most of the discourse we have comes from the advice manuals, but we all know how tenuous is the connection between good advice and good behavior (or any advice and any behavior). Besides, the advice on this point was decidedly mixed, tilting toward opposition. We do have sporadic bits of ugliness popping up from the newspapers. *A Few Suggestions to Mothers* quotes an ad from *The Times*, Christmas Day issue, 1888:

> *Unruly Girl—Wanted*, a high-class *SCHOOL*, where the rod is used. Address R. B., May's Advertising Offices, 162, Piccadilly.[16]

Now and then ads were run offering to chastise children, trying to hire people to do so, seeking buyers for special birch-rods. And occasional bursts of correspondence appear on the subject in respectable places like *Notes & Queries* and, most notoriously, *The Englishwoman's Domestic Magazine*.[17] The latter published from 1867–70 a series of letters on the whipping of children (mainly girls), not only on whether it was advisable but, more commonly, on the various (and minute) details connected with the operation. Many of the letters took a high moral line in fixing our attention on some particular feature of this practice: "I do not think any of your correspondents have drawn attention to the fact that girls while under punishment at schools are often left exposed an unnecessary length of time in order to gratify the vile propensities of brutal onlookers, both male and female."[18] The correspondent does not specify the length of time that would be reasonable and that would frustrate all vile propensities.

How many people regarded whippings as necessary or, in any case, carried them out? Under what circumstances and in what manner? How did they feel about it? And the children: how did they feel? We know that "spanking" as a form of chastisement distinguished from "whipping" and usually offering a milder alternative (hands, hairbrushes, or slippers instead of whips and rods) came into common use as a "legitimate discipline" in the great decade of Reform, the 1830s.[19] That, at least, seems to be the case in America, where things British were often imitated. It seems to me most reasonable to follow recent historians who have sought to moderate somewhat the melodramatic Dickensian narrative of Victorian childhood as a series of buffetings.[20] There is at least as much of what we think of as evidence pointing in the direction of relative gentleness as toward the existence of a culture of licensed child-abusers. That we should ever have wanted to believe the latter story is of greatest interest to me. We devised that story and then repeated it as often as the correspondents to *The Englishwoman's Domestic Magazine* repeated their descriptions; and for the same reason: because we needed to hear the story. If the brutal Victorian home did not exist, we needed to invent it.

B. School-Spankings

Here there is no need to invent, we suppose. We have the firmly-established or at least often-repeated stories of such savages as Nicholas Udall, part-time playwright and full-time flogger at Eton, Dr. Busby of Westminster, and especially Dr. Keate of Eton, whose reputation seems based largely on his having flogged 80 boys one day and, on another, having lit into a number of innocent candidates for confirmation, mistaking them for the daily lineup of miscreants. It is estimated that he averaged about ten boys a day, not including in the calculations Sunday, when he rested.[21] These floggers, we can assume (if we like), are weak versions of what came later, in terms of severity and sadistic terror. Thomas Arnold, for one, says that flogging in the early days of the century may have been frequent but, partly for that very reason, too much like a joke and not nearly painful or horrifying enough: "the fault of the old system of flogging at Winchester was not its cruelty, but its inefficiency; the punishment was so frequent and so slight as to inspire very little either of terror or of shame."[22]

We know a great deal about what these floggings, or the worst of them, were like. Usually ceremonial, they involved the reading out of names or the singling out of one name for invitations to the master's room at some later time. Often two older boys were assigned to lead the culprit at the appointed hour to the room, where more pronouncements were made, before forcing the boy to lower or remove his trousers, lift up his shirt, kneel before and bend over a block, often draped in black. He was then held down by two older boys and the swishing carried out. The rod used, one source on the spot says, was about 14 ounces in weight and 64 inches long.[23] Another witness reports that the beatings were prolonged until "the wretched boy's bottom was a mass of blood."[24] Still other autobiographical records suggest that less uncouth measures may have been nearly as painful:

> He [Mr. Dunbar, a master at Wixenford] was a master of spanking, though he used to say that it hurt him nearly as much as it did us. I remember that it was at about the 15th blow that it really began to hurt and from thence the pain increased in geometrical progression. At about the 28th blow one began to howl. The largest number of smacks I ever received was I think 42.[25]

There seems to be no end to such stories. At least it is not easy to overestimate our interest in them or our willingness to expand a few old-boy stories into a general pattern.

After all, there is counter-evidence: bare-bottom birching was replaced by the use of the cane on fully clothed bodies by mid-century,[26] a move that probably reduced the terror and shame Arnold sought. An 1877 report on Christ's Hospital, the school of Coleridge, Lamb, and Hunt, says that "for some years past the average annual number of floggings has been only eight in a school of eight hundred."[27] While this figure is reported as if it were unusual, it is so wildly at variance from what we supposed that it should give us some pause. And the 1864 Government Report from the Taunton Commission presented evidence that showed "that corporal punishment was exceptional everywhere," that "the most common form of penalty was the writing of lines."[28] This assaults the spectacular images we have evoked, evoked despite the plenitude of humane protests from Victorian writers on children: a boy who is flogged "looks upon his school as his prison, and his master as his prison-keeper."[29]

C. Spanking-Bans

I have found few child-rearing manuals which are enthusiastic about the benefits likely to derive from whipping children, many more which are fiercely against it, and a large majority which are very cautious on the subject. The most common line is that "personal chastisement" ought to occur only "in extreme cases,"[30] and that it should be discontinued after the child is four or five.[31] Many, like Mrs. Child, worried that whipping, quite apart from any humiliation or pain to the child, actually made the parents' job harder: "mere fear of suffering," she said, only makes the child "*conceal* what is evil."[32]

The various societies growing up to protect children, numbering in the hundreds by the early part of this century, and the legislation, beginning to roll in England by the 1860s, aimed in the same direction: to save children from assault, neglect, and other forms of ill-treatment. Always, however, these movements have had to gulp down somehow what is generally perceived, in England and America anyhow, as the right to whip children. There was even a period late in the nineteenth century when liberal reformers sought to protect child-offenders from the damaging effects of imprisonment by substituting court-ordered whippings: in 1893, 2858 children were sentenced to be whipped in England, plus a few more at assizes and courts of quarter sessions.[33]

Even when questions have been raised about sticks and rods wielded by judges, schoolmasters, or nurses, the rights of parents have generally been secured. The 1894 "Prevention of Cruelty to, and Protection of Children Act" explicitly held out to parents and teachers the right "to administer punishment to such child."[34]

Whether children are actually hit or not, the idea, the narrative seems vital. The stories are kept alive, the stories of Keate of Eton, of Swinburne, of Pip, of Tom Brown, of Tom Sawyer, of the kids in the next block, the next room.

Spanking-Sex

Our culture does not want to mislay the tie between spanking and desire, just as it does not want to acknowledge it. Past generations were often more candid about the arousals of child-beating. The general connections between flogging and sexual excitement had been mentioned in the *Satyricon*, by Festus, and by Lucian,[35] the more particular association with children recognized in England at least as early as 1541, when Nicholas Udall, mentioned earlier as a legendary flogger, "was charged with unnatural crime and confessed his guilt before the Privy Council."[36] The anonymous 1669 *Children's Petition* accuses schoolmasters of exercising "lechery" in their disciplinary operations and of running houses of "Prostitution, in this vile way of castigation in use, wherein our secret parts, which are by nature shameful and not to be uncovered, must be the Anvil exposed [sic?] to the immodest eyes, and filthy blows of the smiter." "As soon as the flesh is bare," the author says, the "appetite" of the master is aroused and becomes "an unquenchable fire."[37]

However uncommon such protests may have been then, by Victorian times, it is the rule for the experts to speak plainly on the issue. Acton says that whipping leads to bed-wetting and other emissions,[38] and Krafft-Ebing argues more directly that often "the first excitation of the sexual instinct is caused by a spanking," that masturbation follows, and that it would, therefore, "be better if parents, teachers, and nurses were to avoid it entirely."[39] According to Davenport, "flagellation exercised upon the buttocks and the adjacent parts, has a powerful effect upon the organs of generation" because of "the many intimate and sympathetic relations existing between the nervous branches of the extremity of the spinal marrow."[40] Other, more accessible reasons also lay near to hand. Freud said "it has become well known to all educationalists that the painful stimulation of the skin of the buttocks

256 / *The Naughty Child*

is one of the erotogenic roots of the *passive* instinct of cruelty (masochism)."[41] It seems doubtful that quite all educationalists knew anything of the kind; but to the extent that they did, as Freud points out, they knew it from the spectacular and widely discussed childhood of Rousseau.

In the *Confessions* he records how he reacted to being spanked by his governess Mlle. Lambercier:

> I felt in my pain, and even in my shame, a mixture of sensuality which left more desire than fear to experience it again from the same hand. It is certain that, as there was, without a doubt, a forward instinct of sex in it, the same chastisement from her brother would not have appeared in the least pleasing.

What is remarkable is not so much Rousseau's frank connection of this punishment to sexual excitement as his dire insistence that the experience set for good not only his sexual tastes but his sexual being: "Who would believe it, that this childish chastisement received at eight years old [he was actually ten] from the hand of a girl of thirty, should decide my taste, my desires, my passions, for the rest of my days?" "The method taken with youth," he says, "would be changed, if the distant effects were better seen,"[42] rather an understatement, if one accepts his causality. It is not that Rousseau had much direct effect on the practice of parents or even fully aware educationalists, simply that he articulated a tie between spanking and sex that was widely felt and energetically denied.

The denial took the form of concocting a perversion, of asserting loudly that those who saw or felt the tie were little better than criminals. The most spectacular example of this form of Victorian and modern thinking is the popular (or scholarly—they are no different) conception of Swinburne. His trips to the flogging parlor at St John's Wood, his fascination with the Marquis de Sade, his many letters about Eton and the details of flogging and flogging blocks all are well known. Even more useful to us are his poems:

> The supple Twigs, the swelling Buds I view,
> That once too well my burning Buttocks knew.

Or

> You don't mean—you, who know how the birch makes one's skin burn—
> That this cousin of yours, Redgie—what's his name?—
>   Swinburne,
> Gets whipped more severely than this?[43]

If one ignores the light and parodic elements here and the Byronic rhyme of skin-burn/swin-burne, Swinburne can be made to provide just what is needed: a moderately respectable but indisputably freakish container for the attraction, a container that gives us the requisite lie. Swinburne is mad, at least a monomaniac. He represents what everyone else is not. Thus his writings on the subject are said to be little short of gibberish, never playful or amusing, the reverse of arousing. Certainly the varieties of pain Swinburne found irresistible are miles away from any land where sex lives—for normal people, that is. By saying this sort of thing loudly and with assurance, we may continue to enjoy Swinburne and Swinburne's own enjoyments in one form or another with impunity.

The connections between erotic feelings or activity and pain are not often explored in relation to child-spanking, though there are a few important exceptions.[44] The hush is convenient and allows the practice of corporal punishment to flourish and to defend its imposing legal fortress. Only two strong voices break the silence, those of Havelock Ellis and Freud. These would be considerable sounds, were there any chorus with them; but there is none. As a result, despite their prestige, Ellis and, to a lesser extent, even Freud are records that are never played.

A. Ellis on Pain and Love

Of the many unexpected things a modern reader finds in *Studies in the Psychology of Sex*, the most startling must be the extended section Ellis entitled "Love and Pain." Even the title is nose-thumbing, with its aggressive substitution of "love" for "sex," the word we would expect in a discussion of S/M. Ellis here sounds very much like Kinsey and gives one a renewed respect for the principles, however corrupted, of scientific disinterestedness. Neither Ellis nor Kinsey fly free from their historical and cultural moorings, of course; but both are stoutly resistant to certain features of those paradigms, write directly *against* such prescriptions. Both refuse to regard conventional expressions of repugnance and the repetition of fixed views as sufficient. In fact, neither even is willing to acknowledge such reactions, proceeding for the most part with the calm, speculative openness that has misled some into regarding them as naive.

Ellis sees as impediments simple-minded views which equate pain with the exceptional, the undesirable, and the perverse; and mild-mannered as he is, he has no time for those who block the road.

He rolls straight forward, right over the objectors, with a massive examination that begins by assuming and then by demonstrating that pain is inextricably entwined throughout human societies of all types and "stages," with animals too and with insects, in their (and our) techniques of arousing one another, courting, mating, expressing preference, and love.[45] The use of that term *love* frees his analysis from the question-begging identifications of sexual pain with cruelty, arguably, of course, only to tilt him over into a sentimental position wherein pain looks like fun. But Ellis is a writer as fully aware of the cultural context he is addressing as one can be: he knows that his audience will gladly provide the entirely predictable counter-weights to his provocative refusal to see why love should *not* be linked to pain, why pain should *not* be dissociated from cruelty.

Pain and even the noblest expressions of erotic (and divine) love seem to him often interestingly allied, and he says so. More remarkably, he places such things before us as if he were serving up just one more peanut-butter sandwich. He sees nothing especially surprising in what he is saying, just as he sees nothing extraordinary, much less unnatural or perverse, in the alliance of pain and eros.[46] He even investigates dispassionately what is to us the most unspeakable (though certainly a very do-able) erotic activity, child-beating. "There is," he tells us, "nothing necessarily cruel, repulsive, or monstrous in the idea or the reality of whipping" (III, 129). So far, Ellis might sound like those legislators who are equally anxious to protect both children and the right of parents to hammer them. But Ellis is talking about whipping and sexual arousal, specifically the sexual arousal of the child. The sentence quoted above continues: "and it is perfectly easy and natural for an interest in the subject to arise in an innocent and even normal child, and thus to furnish a germ around which, temporarily at all events, sexual ideas may crystallize" (III, 129). Spank a child, then, and you provide the innocent, natural, easy stimulus and focus for the development of sexual ideas and emotions. It is a temporary focus, maybe—I am unable to decide what Ellis may mean by "temporarily at all events"—but it is an unequivocally erotic focus, and, Ellis says, "normal." The effectiveness of child-whipping in arousing the sexuality of children is thus argued with what one might call satiric relish, what with the deadpan roll-call of conventional epithets all displaced from their customary station. What may look to us like equally sarcastic rhetoric accompanies his extension of this scene of titillating theater from the one being spanked to the spanker, from child to adult: "the general sexual association of whipping in the minds of children, and frequently of their elders, is by no means rare and scarcely abnormal"

(III, 137). It's a delicate, stiletto-like thrust, as if Jane Austen had taken to writing on the subject.

Ellis's bland prose often contrasts strikingly with the subject in this way. Whipping, he says, not only provides pleasurable sexual kindlings but has a "general tonic influence" which "naturally extend[s]" from the buttocks directly effected "to the sexual system" as a whole (III, 137). Pain is especially productive because it is "the most powerful of all methods for arousing emotion" (III, 172), including the emotions of moderate (stimulating) fear and anger. Such anger is divorced from cruelty or desires to dominate, and thus seems part of a ritualistic, playful heightening of feeling. Ellis's awareness of the theatrical nature of whipping scenes pushes him further to connect the sexual activity with children, even very young children: "it is natural that an interest in whipping should be developed very early in childhood," and that such associations should enter into their games and activities as "a much relished element" (III, 140).

Ellis's views are so distant from those generally accepted that they cry for special explanation. Possibly he had a particularly bleak view of children, but there is little evidence that Ellis finds children monstrous. He is not especially interested in them, but on the whole seems to like and respect them. I think we must accept Ellis at his insistent word: he regards child sexuality and what we think of as sadism and masochism as normal and natural. The pain that is essential to the erotic whipping of children is given, and felt, as love. It is love that directs the entire operation, not the desire to give pain, which is only a means. The child and the adult are joined in an erotic play that features the most up-to-date, shake-you-in-your-seat stage effects of thunder and tempest. But these are only accompaniments to a plot that is gliding along well-known paths, paths that will lead to what is desired, which is not damage but more desire. That naughty child is so cunning and natural, so much like the adult, that no one would want to hurt it. This spanking story reaches outward, though somewhat heavy-handedly, to take in everything with that "high degree of general tender-heartedness" (III, 166) that characterizes Ellis's staging of the way pain and love come together in the child.

B. *Freud's Comfort: A Child Is Being Beaten By Someone Else*

There are some valuable things squirreled away in Freud's famous " 'A Child Is Being Beaten.' " He notes, though only in passing, that the "phantasy" is remarkably common in analysis and speculates that it "very probably" is frequently found in those not obliged to undergo treatment.[47] He interestingly textualizes the subject, treating it as a pleasurable story or movie run in the head rather than an event. That is, though he acknowledges that such texts are often sparked by actual spankings and are certainly populated by identifiable figures from life, his primary interest is in the teller's relation to his text, in sophisticated narratology and not blunt biographical criticism. He draws attention to the fact that the phantasy invariably protects the very child being beaten, never seriously harming it (XVII, 180); and he raises for further investigation the importance of the issue of gender in the construction and content of these narratives. All of these points, however skimpily developed, must count as provocative contributions to the study.

Generally, however, Freud shields us from the subject by telling us what we want to hear, assuring us that the topic is, however fascinating, entirely unthreatening. He takes the most resolutely right-wing Victorian opinions on the body and sexuality and discreetly reclothes them in modern analytical rigor. Freud traces the roots of the sexual beating story to the Victorian bugaboo, precocity, a "component" of the sexual system which "has made itself prematurely independent" (XVII, 181), and which "was able for constitutional reasons to develop prematurely" (XVII, 189). Faced with this familiar specter, the reader can relax. This whole business is, as Freud's essay soothingly repeats about eighty times, only a "perversion," thus of merely clinical interest—very great interest, of course, but not personal. Freud introduces a reassuring empiricism that handily examines case studies and sorts them out into neat classes or configurations of the beating scene: direct sadism in the story of a rival being beaten, masochism in being beaten oneself, a secret masochism under a sadistic form in being a spectator at the beating of others. Freud's analysis is a superb form of denial: tough, strictly objective, yet modulated through distaste. Freud finds the whole thing as creepy as he knows we do, and thus allows us the same protections he needs himself, the guarantees that we are none of us implicated. Just so, he provides us with the assurances of absolute certainty. There is no doubt whatever about the distance we have put between us and this perversion; our tongue is oiled with confidence: "All of the many unspecified children who are being beaten by the teacher are, after all, nothing more than substitutes for the child itself" (XVII, 191). "After all, nothing more than": is this finally reassuring or does it give the game away, expose the carnival of question-begging and arbitrary assertiveness going on here? The psyche is a strange place to go looking for reassurances; one might find there unpleasant connections between oneself and the monsters one was trying to disown. Freud, trying to confine everything to the tent where they keep the freaks, has taken us all around back for a sneaky, dirty peek under the canvas. Perhaps he has let out the monsters among us.

Modern Spanking

It is curious that forms of understanding in thrall to power should coexist peacefully with a refusal to connect the spanking of children to power. Whatever needs are satisfied by that activity are apparently so vital that we need a glitch in our logic, an area of enforced stupidity in order to protect ourselves. Admirably alert to seeing the sexual direction of most human activity and to locating the agencies of force compelling us in those directions, our culture nonetheless claims that undressing a child and beating it on an erogenous area is benign. We may even allow schoolteachers to do it when parents are not around, perhaps as a form of compensation supplementing what will not be provided in cash. I do not mean to be arguing that spanking must be connected to power; one can imagine playfulness entering in. But we see here in our culture an obvious form of the sexualizing of power and the most cowardly form of denial. As Shaw is supposed to have said, if we enjoy beating our children so much we cannot stop doing it, fine; but we should not pretend it is for their own good. If we are going to center power as a mode of behavior and understanding, we should at least not allow power-driven behavior an exemption from power's way of understanding.

The Victorians tended to encounter fewer absurdities here, since most of their discourse was more aware and honest than our own. They saw spanking as a sexual activity, risky for children, and probably best avoided; some were repulsed by the brutality of the operation, the undisguised application of force to human affairs. Contrary to popular opinion (contrary to what would be very nice to believe), the Victorians do not seem to talk very much about this subject. Such an assertion is impossible to establish, but few of the advice manuals I looked at devoted much attention to spanking or seemed especially interested in it when they did; there is not a lot of flagellation erotica (surviving anyhow) dealing with children; apart from stories of public schools, it plays little part in novels and poems.

But it is there now and then in the past, and we can find it, the zeal of the hunt probably being much more significant than the availability of the game. What we find should offer us the same insights into what we have done by mixing sex and power as is offered, presumably, by S/M theorists and practitioners today.[48] At one extreme we find Victorian enthusiasts for power, those who should embarrass us by their naive fervor, their boorish notion that since sex, power, and whipping children are sanctioned, one might as well say so. Having inadequately digested the rules for decorous behavior, they recognize no limits. Sometimes the flagellation erotica becomes too bloody and redundant, leading in one case to the depiction of the murder-by-whipping (and rape and cannibalizing) of an eight-year-old girl.[49] Also, some of those few advice manuals which are enlisted on the side of child-beating are unsubtle in their use of power metaphors:

> In judicious correction, courage and perseverance are alike requisite. The child should never be allowed in this contention to gain a victory. Crying is the defensive weapon of the child, and if this resistance is successful, by the yielding of the nurse or mother, she will often find difficulty in regaining her lost dominion.[50]

Such analyses seem driven by anxiety: the "defensive weapon" of the child may not be so defensive, may somehow be used to attack. "Children command us by their tears," says Stendhal.[51]

That's the problem with explanations that want to use power to hold things steady. It's much like trying to move a large mattress alone: the object keeps sliding and walloping, mocking our attempts to establish control and threatening finally to knock us over and smother us. Even in this area where the power relations seem so clear—one person is bigger, wiser, older, wholly entitled—it does not take much cunning to see that the configurations may easily be reversed, transferring control to the child.

The most evident demonstration of the ability of the weaker party to seize power is provided by the life of Leopold von Sacher-Masoch, who was single-minded in his pursuit of power-to-the-beaten and equally successful in gaining it—he managed not only to have himself whipped by those who did not want to whip him but forced his wife into unfaithfulness, even placing newspaper ads to hasten on the adultery.[52] Masochists provide the clearest instance of a contractual power arrangement which is dictated entirely by the submissive party, who builds the set and writes the script, the whipper being "merely an employee, a slave of the self-styled victim."[53] Children, not necessarily masochists of course, can still seize power by their very aggressive naughtiness, taking over the law by regulating its most dire penalties. Freud claimed that children "trying to provoke punishment" were seeking masochistic pleasure and a relief from psychic guilt.[54] Perhaps they are also trying to attract attention or love, but they are certainly attracting and seizing power. As Foucault points out, the law must locate ways to foil the transfer of power that takes place when the violator can control the law by "arbitrary actions," attracting the law to himself at will—his will.[55] Foucault makes explicit what is plain in the idiom of correction, which commonly transfers power to the child: are you forcing me to spank you again? You have brought this on yourself!

It is power that makes power not just powerful but desirable and the exercise of it erotic. The easy accessibility of the child to the most palpable form of power seems to render erotic beating inevitable. The child learns to participate, even to invite it; and we manage to deny what we are doing, even fail to see that we are violating the best excuse we have for power: that it protects the victims. Thus too, beatings are conducted with hypocritical righteous fervor. We have no ground whatever for doing such a thing, so we need to assure ourselves that our ground could not be more solid: we are not doing this for our pleasure but for the good of the child. Shaw was right: if we would admit the sexual grounding of the activity, we might then see no need to injure, sometimes murder the child. We might even stop it, were we able to find a paradigm other than power. Even if it continued in some form under different auspices, it would no longer be sound or healthy, hurting us more than the child, calling forth our most ingenious hypocrisies. If one spanked playfully, for instance, it might be harder to sustain. I do not know where to view such play right now, but we get glimpses of it sometimes in the punning dialogue of spanking foreplay:

> You *will* do that?
> I had to. I'm sorry.
> Well, I'm sorry too. Because now I have to spank you.
> Please don't.
> I wouldn't if you didn't ask for it.

Especially the open *will* is useful here, suggesting that the child is both insisting on being naughty but also answering to a command, an imperative. But what follows on such comic confrontations is seldom happy. The closest it gets to fun is, I will say, in pornography—but that is seldom very funny.

Stories of Child Spanking

By "pornography" I refer to any arousing work which seems to carry the charge of the forbidden, usually marked by the means of production and distribution: privately printed, circulated selectively, not only deviating from but challenging the official views of what one does with the body and how one regards such doings. This is not a formal definition, but then definitions depending on formal features are hopeless, here as elsewhere. Especially here, where what was commonplace to the Victorians may be so shocking to us no publisher would touch it—and, now and then, vice versa. Pornography, a power-analyst would say, is the form you are told *will* excite you and *will* make you feel guilty while doing so. It is not forbidden, but prescribed, an area of eroticism made necessary by being made desirable. Agencies of power assure that certain images and representations will remain erotic by forbidding them, thus subsidizing their production and guaranteeing a steady market.

I prefer to think of erotica as less constrained than this, and power as less shrewd. Doubtless it is true that there are not six people now alive who will openly admit to being sexually aroused by spanking children—among the several billion who actually are—but that fact can just as well indicate that power is failing as that it is doing its job. In any case, I would like to use as exemplary the story of the child being lustfully beaten.

The first thing most people notice about child-spanking porn is that it is not realistic (naively mimetic). Marcus says that this literature is marked by its redundancy, "the elaboration of a single fantasy," and its "radical incoherence," its "absence of focus." Such features seem to Marcus both artistic faults and symptoms, "twisted" and "grotesque," of "the pathos of perversity," "an imprisonment for life."[56] While Marcus is too shrewd a literary critic not to notice the "sophisticated" variety of forms employed with this narrative, he brushes all those "surface" features aside in his search for the single perversion he is uncovering beneath. One could as easily compare these narratives with modernist fictions that are similarly self-reflexive and playful, similarly at ease about foregrounding and making obvious the very codings being employed. Marcus sees the allusiveness, range, and openness of these forms as evidence of a desperate and impoverished (twisted, childish, pathetic) need to repeat one anecdote forever, without the benefit of plot or coherence. But why is coherence such a virtue, and why need we see this baring of the device as a defect?

The most obvious point of entry into Marcus's formulation is by way of the absence of much actual flagellation in these flagellation fictions. There is much talk, not only in the way of erotic foreplay—misdeeds, accusations, denials, sentencings—but in general reflections on the subject,[57] attempts not so much to "justify" it as to expose the language of justification to ridicule and substitute, as Barthes says Sade did, "a new 'language,' no longer spoken but acted; a 'language' of crime [or deviance], or new code of love."[58] This code of love is established in defiance of the "real," specifically in defiance of power. It takes us to the very center of power, physical domination and cruelty, and shows us, by playing so wantonly with these images, that power is, if not hallucinatory, a bad bargain we can dissolve at any time. Flagellation fantasies do not spring from out the prison, as Marcus would have it; they illuminate the prison of power, and they smuggle in explosives to all the prisoners.

At least that's a way of reading, according to which these stories are not punitive but parodic. There are seldom bullies or villains in these decidedly comic plots. Spankings are rewards, not come-uppances; the child being spanked directs the plot that leads toward the spanking. The child either learns very quickly to desire the whippings or somehow feels that way right from the start.[59] The joy is said to come from the pain and from exhibiting oneself: "I found delight in the pain that birching produced, and lustful joy in turning and writhing my body under the rod, lewdly presenting every part in its full nakedness to eyes of [the child's tutor]."[60] But usually the pain "is but the condition under which the pleasure is permitted; it is not the end pleasure itself."[61] These pleasures are placed subsequent to and consequent on the pain, which is said to be a mere nothing in comparison: "it leaves such a delightful glow which more than repays for the momentary inconvenience."[62]

This *glowing* always, in one way or another, comes into being in these radiant tales, both as a warming reward to the child and also to the adult, who flushes-glows with excitement as she or he looks on at the blushing-glowing being produced. These tales are scarlet-dyed, red-saucy. They move from "bum to blushing bum," to one or another "red quivering nether part" with a "red rod,"[63] suffusing everything in a sunset glow of erotic blushing, modesty coyly issuing an invitation from the center of immodest exposure, titillating in the midst of violation. The child is caught at the moment of greatest "bloom," flushed at that moment of perfection. The spanking is a way of appreciating its rare charm: "Like most childish beauty, Mona's was less the beauty of feature than of colour."[64] And this color comes to be something not simply to admire but to bring into being. The adult becomes the child through the ruby glow encompassing all.

What looks like a portrayal of dominance and separation, marking the inferior and distant state of the child, becomes a fable of joining. In a typical scene, the adult soothes the sobbing child after the whipping, wiping her brow and kissing her hands, only to be told that "The whipping wasn't there!"[65] What follows on this is obvious, but it is important to insist that very often these spankings do lead to other activities, that people of all genders and ages are usually effected by the experience, either end of it, in such a liquefying way that they all swim together in the radiance. In the following example, a woman is birching a young girl of thirteen: "A melting sensation came over me, and I felt all wet between my thighs, my head swam, and I dropped the rod. . . ."[66] Dropping the rod, she does not leave the room. This mutuality is said to extend to psychological effects like embarrassment: "pain, shame and humiliation exciting to the highest point the nervous system of *the givers and takers* in either sex" [67] (emphasis mine). Power's individualizing and hierarchizing is washed into a merging crimson sea.

Results

A few specific questions remain, among them why the child's buttocks should be so alluring. We know that they are and that people like the Rev. Kilvert spend much of their lives trying for glimpses of them, setting little girls into swings, for instance, in such a way as to bunch up the clothes and expose the bottom "in excellent whipping condition."[68] Kilvert wants not just to see but to smack. He offers his services readily to parents who want daughters spanked and he speculates, not very fruitfully, on whether "bottoms [were] so formed that they might be whipped."[69] Putting aside for a moment the vicious consequences of this, we might notice how asinine such ideas are, how comic. There is, after all, something funny in buttocks, twin mounds of protruding pads that quiver and blubber out of our control. We cover them not because they are indecent but because they are silly; we worry not about giving offense but cause for giggles. Why is mooning uproarious? Why are there so many comic stories about floggings, like Thomas Hood's outrageous "The Death of the Domini": "I have heard of a road to learning, and he did justice to it; we certainly never went a stage in education without being well horsed."[70] Similarly, Victorian school stories customarily assumed that "the height of humor was for a boy to impregnate his trousers with snuff or pepper before a beating."[71] The answer to our question, then, is that the child's bottom is desirable because it is funny, because it releases us for a moment from power and into a completely nonsensical world of pointless hilarity.

Other answers to the question are available, I know, answers that will seem just a little more sophisticated.

But the sharing in a joke on power and its particular sophistications is the point here. The naughty child is created in order to have fun and be funny. In the fun is a form not just of play, but of love. That the child may seek love in this form or that it may substitute for the scene of incest is a commonplace of orthodox psychiatry, but I have in mind something simpler. Here are two accounts from the public schools of the 1850s and 1860s, from Sewell at Radley, each expressive of the engulfing love said to be a part of such experiences:

> Both of them . . . when they got up from their knees came to me and burst into tears and put their arms around my neck and kissed me—as a child would its father. They knew I had a great affection for them and that what I did was for them.

> Then I flung away the cane. . . . I think when I made that boy get up from his knees, and he put his arms round my neck was the most exquisite moment of enjoyment I ever had.[72]

This doesn't seem particularly funny, I will admit, but perhaps it is comic in the grim way Northrop Frye would have Dante or the New Testament or Tennyson's *In Memoriam* to be. It is a kind of resurrection: up from the knees and into new life.

"It's as good as a play!," as Dickens's fun-lovers are always saying. These flagellation narratives are elaborately, self-consciously *staged*, made spectacle. As Smirnoff says, even in direct masochistic activity, the "essential phenomenon may well be not in the suffering but in the position of the masochist"[73]: getting everyone to their marks, saying the lines, doing the dance, involving the spectators in the action. This is people's theater, no more ritualized than any theater and with the raucous willingness, characteristic of comedy, to include the meanest spectator. As we watch, we participate; and vice versa. The gestures of spanking are made blatant, "theatrical" so as not to be mistaken for the real and cruel. Much as in the wrestling matches Barthes analyzed, suffering is no part of the event or the experience; we enjoy "the perfection of an iconography." The single spank is like "the forearm smash," where "catastrophe is brought to the point of maximum obviousness, so much so that ultimately the gesture appears as no more than symbol."[74]

It is more than symbol to the abused child. It is about time we said that, drew attention to the fact that, under power, no activity is allowed to be playful and that spanking, perhaps the chief official thing done for and to the child in our culture, can only take the form of brutal and damaging assault. It can be no other. Its eroticism is undeniable and will therefore be denied; it is an erotics of the sneaky and the perverse—and of violence. I am claiming only that the narratives of playful, consuming, theatricalized child-spankings deconstruct our earnest forms of rape and battery carried out on children in the name of "correcting." Refiguring the terms of the drama, repositioning the actors, relocating the entire theater, we can see differently what we are about: murdering children in order to protect them, denying the mutuality of the narratives for the destructive separations, the distinctions necessary to the clarities of power.

The most fundamental of these are distinctions of gender, precisely the area where the narratives we are discussing take most pains to elide difference. The resistance to power in these stories takes the form of a resistance to fixity: locating the child as both us and Other, sliding in and out of focus. In the game of resentment we discussed earlier, the child is chastised for refusing to play the game but keeps the game going by that very refusal. The bottom thus is not fixed nor, as we shall see, really vulnerable to injury. It just keeps appearing and disappearing, never there to be possessed but never lost. The bottom is genderless and allows us to escape gender: "children are of no sex,"[75] says the porn; and neither, when entering this world, are the adults.

With a flourish, this genre switches the apparent sexes of the spankers and the recipients so wantonly we don't know how to apply our usual distinctions. Both men and women, sometimes children, do the spanking; and the receivers are a mixture—sometimes boys, sometimes girls, sometimes one in the disguise of the other. Such fluidity can be upsetting. Marcus noted it and then denied it with an argument that is about as good as the power metaphor can manage. Marcus admits that "the sexual identity of the figure being beaten is remarkably labile" and sees that we might be tempted to conclude that the actual gender does not matter, that "the ambiguity of sexual identity seems in fact to be part of the pleasure that this fantasy yields."[76] Yet such a conclusion "one cannot hold for long," at least if, like Marcus, one recalls the demands of the explanatory metaphor controlling things. He straightens things out, therefore, by claiming that, appearances notwithstanding, "the figure being beaten is originally, finally, and always a boy."[77] That he is originally and finally a boy means, I suppose, if it means anything, that his gender is not transformed by the spanking; but we recognize the cadences of "originally, finally, and always" for what they are: thumping reassurances that the power metaphor can assert power, that it can beat down any obstacle and do some spanking itself. For Marcus, the lack of interest in genitals displayed in this fantasy indicates a form of regression, a "perversion" that reminds him of homosexuality, an unhappy state "qualitatively different from other perversions" in its shifting of the erotic zone from where it belongs onto the buttocks.[78] Hence, "this fantasy is a homosexual one: a little boy is being beaten—that is, loved—by another man," beaten instead of being loved more sensibly because the transformation of boy into girl is "both a defense against and a disavowal of the fantasy it is simultaneously expressing."[79]

Marcus locates signifieds, halts the presto-chango, freezes the action all in ways dictated not so much by his Freudianism as by the way power says we must construct explanations and protect ourselves (or it) from other metaphors. Here we are asked to overlook the manifest gender fluidity, the ease with which costume or sexual organs are put on and off. We are asked to assume that, contrary to all reports and all experience, spanking and pedophile fantasies (and presumably activity) are confined not just to men, a palpable absurdity, but to gay men, an ugly and hurtful allegation. Here is power at its most obviously coercive, policing with attack dogs the boundaries between genders.

Why should the playful collapse of controlling structures and especially dualistic structures not extend to gender? If the line between backwards and forwards, up and down, now and then, important and unimportant, growling and purring can be so merrily deconstructed, why not that between male and female? The magic wand waved over pedophile discourse releases signifiers from conventional stockades and releases the magician from the laws of age. Becoming the child, the author yields the right of adult control, even over the false and naughty child, but also lays claim to a state of being beyond time and beyond any artificial distinctions between child and grown-up. Similarly, the barriers of gender vanish in smoke. They do not exist.

Consider, for instance, our own century's pedophile pin-ups, the child you love to spank. Buster Brown, say, a figure we will return to at the close of this book, is both stereotypically boyish *and* girlish: active, mischievous, and sneakily defiant, on the one hand; but, on the other, sporting long blond hair and a blank and featureless face that our culture always finds "sweet" and "cute" in females. His clothes are unisex fashions that he made briefly the rage: a puffy playsuit with a skirted pinafore that has to be hiked up and thrown back over his shoulders for every spanking. Notice how this image of androgyny is repeated later in Perry Winkle, in Shirley Temple, in Mark Lester, in Patty McCormack, in Jeff East, in Tatum O'Neal, in Ricky Schroeder, in River Phoenix, in Kristy McNichol. The figures in this pedophile play have no particular gender, gleefully switch back and forth in an erotic, non-climactic, never-ending farce.

These narratives offer to decenter power so completely that we stand for a moment in another field, within a different metaphor. We notice how such stories defy logic, consequence, what Marcus thought of as "coherence." The situations are repetitive precisely because there is no reason they should not be. The child is never damaged by the spankings, nor is it deterred one whit from repeating the same or similar offenses over and over again. It never strikes the adult that the spankings are having no effect on the misbehavior they are designed to control or halt, since the spankings are designed to do no such thing, but rather to ensure their perpetuation. This illogic preserves desire by preserving the playfulness of the situation and the comic resiliency not only of the child but of the adult too. The child's willingness to be forever naughty helps pull the adult into a world which has no effective lessons, no consequences, no endings, no fulfillments, no growings up. The child and the adult are thus joined not in a melodrama full of enemies but in a comic spectacle like a sunrise: spreading, fusing, luminous.

Notes

1. Algernon Charles Swinburne, "Algernon's Flogging," *The Whippingham Papers*; quoted in *Lesbia Brandon*, ed. Randolph Hughes (London: Falcon Press, 1952), p. 503.

2. Eve Kosofsky Sedgwick, "A Poem Is Being Written," *Representations* 17 (1987): 126. Sedgwick's essay is so much the finest thing written on the subject of the place of erotic child-beating and the erotic child generally in our culture that it seems very much like the only thing written.

3. Samuel Butler, *Prose Observations*, ed. Hugh De Quehen (Oxford: Clarendon, 1979), p. 95.

4. Anon., *Children: Their Health*, p. 111.

5. [G.H. Putnam], *The Artificial Mother: A Marital Fantasy* (New York and London: Knickerbocker Press, 1894), pp. 1, 13, 27.

6. This is the explanation given by the absolutely unreliable Dr. Iwan Bloch, *Sex Life in England* (New York: Panurge Press, 1901), p. 191. Marcus, *The Other Victorians*, p. 78, points out that the erratic character of this book is not entirely Bloch's fault, that what we have now is a mishmash translation by Richard Deniston of Bloch's 1901 book (published in German).

7. Anon., *Experiences of Flagellation: A Series of Remarkable Instances of Whipping Inflicted on Both Sexes with Curious Anecdotes of Ladies Fond of Administering Birch Discipline; Compiled by an Amateur Flagellant* (London: privately printed, 1885), p. 2.

8. Also see Gathorne-Hardy, *The British Nanny*, pp. 48–57.

9. Reprinted in Cutt, *Mrs. Sherwood*, pp. 86–87.

10. Reprinted in Victor E. Neuberg, *The Penny Histories: A Study of Chapbooks for Young Readers Over Two Centuries*, Vol II of *The Juvenile Library*, gen. ed., Brian W. Alderson (London: Oxford Univ. Press, 1968), pp. 195–206.

11. Hopkins, *On the Early Training*, p. 52.

12. August Adrian Strasser, "Masturbation in Childhood," *Medical Record*, June 17, 1905, p. 931.

13. Arnold, Sermon 1, *Christian Life*, p. 2.

14. Thomas Arnold, "On the Discipline of Public Schools," *The Miscellaneous Works* (London: B. Fellows, 1845), p. 365. Arnold's essay was originally published in *The Quarterly Journal of Education* (1835), signed "A Wykchamist."

15. The fullest evidence and best analysis is in Elizabeth Pleck, *Domestic Tyranny: The Making of American Social Policy Against Family Violence from Colonial Times to the Present* (New York: Oxford Univ. Press, 1987).

16. "A Mother," *A Few Suggestions to Mothers*, p. 49.

17. See Ian Gibson, *The English Vice: Beating, Sex and Shame in Victorian England and After* (London: Duckworth, 1978), pp. 54–64 (on ads) and pp. 198–229 (on correspondence). Gibson discusses and gives examples of the correspondence in five periodicals, usually spanning a period of several years.

18. Reprinted in Anon., ed., *Indecent Whippings* ([London]: privately printed, [1880?]), p. 12. The letter is from "G.W.L."

19. See Pleck, *Domestic Tyranny*, p. 414.

20. See Linda Pollock, *A Lasting Relationship*, pp. 165–67 and *passim*; and Margaret May, "Violence in the Family: An Historical Perspective," in S.P. Martin, ed., *Violence and the Family* (Chichester and New York: John Wiley, 1978), pp. 151–54.

21. These stories are repeated in many places, often with minor variations. See Anon., *Boys and Their Ways*, pp. 52–54; and Chandos, *Boys Together*, p. 221. Chandos's chapter "The Unspared Rod," pp. 221–46, offers a host of examples, all of pretty much the same thing.

22. Arnold, "On the Discipline," p. 365.

23. William Harnbett Blanch, *The Blue-Coat Boys; or, School Life in Christ's Hospital; with a Short History of the Foundation* (London: E.W. Allen, 1877), p. xv. Blanch is here comparing the smaller rod used at Christ's Hospital to the standard item.

24. Roger Fry, quoted in Honey, *Tom Brown's Universe*, p. 198.

25. The young Curzon, quoted in Honey, *Tom Brown's Universe*, pp. 198–99.

26. George Ripley Scott, *The History of Corporal Punishment: A Survey of Flagellation in Its Historical, Anthropological, and Sociological Aspects* (London: Torchstream, 1949), p. 104.

27. Blanch, *Blue-Coat Boys*, p. xv.

28. J.H. Adamson, *English Education: 1789–1902* (Cambridge: Cambridge Univ. Press, 1964), p. 253.

29. Chavasse, *The Young Wife and Mother's Book*, p. 111.

272 / *The Naughty Child*

30. Anon., *Children and What to Do With Them*, p. 95.

31. Anon., *Hints on Early Education*, pp. 22–24.

32. Mrs. Child, *The Mother's Book*, p. 36.

33. W. Douglas Morrison, *Juvenile Offenders* (New York: D. Appleton, 1898), p. 213.

34. Joseph Bridges Matthews, *The Law Relating to Children and Young Persons* (London: Sweet and Maxwell, 1895), p. 30.

35. Scott, *History of Corporal Punishment*, pp. 197–99.

36. Ellis, *Psychology of Sex*, II, 42.

37. Anon., *The Children's Petition: or, a Modest Remonstrance of that Intolerable Grievance Our Youth Lies Under, in the Accustomed Severities of the School-Discipline of This Nation; Humbly Presented to the Confederation of the Parliament* (London: Richard Chiswell, 1669), pp. 49, 7, 11, 15.

38. *A Practical Treatise*, p. 181.

39. Krafft-Ebing, *Psychopathia Sexualis*, p. 22.

40. Davenport, *Aphrodisiacs*, p. 113.

41. Freud, "Three Essays," p. 193.

42. Rousseau, *Confessions*, p. 16.

43. The first is from the "Prologue" to *The Flogging-Block*, the second from "Charlie's Flogging" in the same work. Both are quoted in *Lesbia Brandon*, ed. Hughes, pp. 531, 513.

44. The most significant exceptions, Ellis and Freud, are dealt with presently. Essays examining sadism and masochism are fairly common, sometimes extending usefully into literary discourse. A good example is Richard McGhee's " 'Swinburne Planteth, Hardy Watereth': Victorian Views of Pain and Pleasure in Human Sexuality," in Cox, ed., *Sexuality and Victorian Literature*, pp. 83–107. Even Kinsey did nothing with the subject of child-spanking and, beyond reporting some limited data on biting and nibbling (Paul Gebhard and Alan B. Johnson, *The Kinsey Data: Marginal Tabiulations of the 1938–1963 Interviews Conducted by the Institute for Sex Research* [Philadlphia: W.B. Saunders, 1979], p. 265, for instance), ignored the more general issues of sexuality and pain.

45. In the second edition, "Love and Pain" is in the third volume, though in other editions it is moved around from volume to volume, most commonly coming to rest in volume I. The examination of courtship and combat rituals, the connection between them, and the tie of both to pain in animals, insects, primitive peoples, and modern society is in III, 66–103 (second edition). Subsequent references in this chapter will be cited in the text.

46. Well, this is going a little far, I will admit, in making Ellis sound like Masters and Johnson or Kinsey. Ellis does hold to the notion that normal sexuality is to be equated with heterosexual intercourse. Anything which becomes so attractive as to act as a *substitute* for such intercourse he does find abnormal; but he is certainly free and easy about anything at all which will stimulate one into preparing for or desiring intercourse. In other words, he would find whipping as a means of achieving orgasm (for either party) abnormal, but perfectly normal as a means of foreplay or preparation for orgasmic intercourse.

47. Sigmund Freud, " 'A Child Is Being Beaten': A Contribution to the Study of the

Origin of Sexual Perversions," XVII, 179. Subsequent references in this chapter will be cited in the text.

48. See Weeks, *Sexuality and Its Discontents*, pp. 236–41, for an examination of the argument that S/M offers a privileged insight into sexual power and the infusion of sexuality by power, and that it comes close to being a kind of parody of ideological control (of "fascism") rather than an homage to it.

49. Anon., *Confessions of a Royal Rake, Being the Autobiography of Charles Godfrey Fleetwood, 7th Earl of Essex, the amazing revelation of his dissolute life and monstrous perversions* (Atlanta: Pendulum Books, 1968), pp. 22–29. I am not at all sure that this work is "Victorian," of course, since it seems to be common practice for many twentieth-century novels to be post-dated for some reason, presumably because more readers find Victorian sex enticing than are aroused by their own.

50. Anon., *The Mother's Best Book or Nursery Companion; by a Committee of Experienced Ladies* (London: Kent & Co., [1859]), p. 15.

51. Stendhal [Marie-Henri Beyle], *On Love*, trans. H.B.Y. under direction of C.K. Scott Moncrieff (New York: Da Capo Press, 1983), p. 286.

52. Ellis has a good account, I, 114–19. The term "masochism" was apparently first used by Krafft-Ebing.

53. Victor N. Smirnoff, "The Masochistic Contract," *International Journal of Psychoanalysis* 50 (1969): 667.

54. Freud, "History of an Infantile Neurosis," XVII, 28.

55. Michel Foucault, *Foucault/Blanchot*, p. 35.

56. Marcus, *The Other Victorians*, pp. 252, 263, 127.

57. The "authoress" of *Lady Gay Spanker's Tales of Fun and Flagellation, Etc.*, for instance, offers a long disquisition on the defects of "realism," which, though "a fad of the present day," is "brutal, bordering on the obscene" because it is inconsistent, arbitrarily cutting off the most interesting scenes and switching to prudishness just when it ought to go on. The present work, we are told, will be true to its genre and provide "actual realism," "which the authoress trusts her friends will agree with her . . . is beautiful anjoyable [sic]" ([London?]: privately printed, 1896, pp. 5–6).

58. Barthes, *Sade/Fourier/Loyola*, p. 27.

59. This is virtually always true, even in cases where the beatings seem to be quite terrible. A good example is Lord Kidrodstock, *Stays and Gloves: Figure-Training and Deportment by Means of the Discipline of Tight Corsets, Narrow High-Heeled Boots, Clinging Kid Gloves, Combinations, Etc., Etc.* (London: Carrington, 1909), where the 10-year-old boy-narrator is subjected to what certainly seems like real pain and lots of it but learns to desire these severe, even bloody whippings.

60. Anon., *Lady Gay Spanker's Tales*, pp. 24–5.

61. Esther Menaker, "Masochism: A Defense Reaction of the Ego," *Psychoanalytic Quarterly* 63 (1953): 205–20.

62. [Algernon Charles Swinburne et al.], "A Visit to Mrs. Birch," *The Whippingham Papers; a collection of contributions in prose and verse, chiefly by the author of the 'Romance of Chastisement'* (London: privately printed, 1888), p. 18.

63. [Swinburne], "Arthur's Flogging," *Whippingham Papers*, p. 5.

64. Anon., *When a Child Loves*, p. 5.

65. Anon., *When a Child Loves*, p. 50.

66. Anon., *Lady Gay Spanker's Tales*, p. 17.

67. Anon., *Venus School-Mistress, or Birchen Sports* ([London]: privately printed, [1898]), p. 125.

68. Kilvert, *Diaries*, 12 August 1875, p. 218.

69. Kilvert, *Diaries*, 17 December 1878, p. 439.

70. Thomas Hood, *The Comic Annual* (London: Charles Tilt, 1834), pp. 79–80.

71. E.S. Turner, *Boys Will Be Boys: The Story of Sweeney Todd, Deadwood Dick, Sexton Blake, Billy Bunter, Dick Barton, et al.* (London: Michael Joseph, 1975), p. 73.

72. Quoted in Honey, *Tom Brown's Universe*, p. 192.

73. Smirnoff, "The Masochistic Contract," p. 665.

74. Roland Barthes, *Mythologies*, trans. Annette Lavers (New York: Hill and Wang, 1957), p. 20.

75. Anon., *Experiences of Flagellation* (London: privately printed, [1885]), p. 8.

76. Marcus, *The Other Victorians*, p. 259.

77. Marcus, *The Other Victorians*, p. 260.

78. Marcus, *The Other Victorians*, p. 262.

79. Marcus, *The Other Victorians*, p. 260.

8

The Wonder Child in Neverland

One of his arms droops over the edge of the bed, a leg is arched, and the mouth is not so tightly closed that we cannot see the little pearls.[1]

First, [Alice's sister] dreamed about little Alice herself: once again the tiny hands were clasped upon her knee, and the bright eager eyes were looking up into hers—she could hear the very tones of her voice, and see that queer little toss of her head to keep back the wandering hair that *would* always get into her eyes.[2]

The two most persistent and stimulating images of the erotic child we possess are inherited from the Victorians, and neither fits the gentle-naughty schematic we have set up. We will (surprise!) still cling to that scheme, admitting that Peter Pan and Alice are not presented to us to be spanked or to be nuzzled. They will neither bend over nor cuddle, refuse to be either naughty or nice. Yet no children have ever been more desirable.

They keep us up on our toes, sprinting after them and never getting close, seldom catching more than a glimpse. Those who imagine that the child offered and offers nostalgic "escapism," soft regression, "ease and repose from the troubles of the day," something "safe and simple"[3] seem to have looked past the formulations of erotic Otherness in these complex images. Try to find "ease and repose" with them and they'll pull the chair out from under you, give you nitroglycerine hotfoots. They are not offering anything; they are taking. Peter and Alice demand to be loved on their terms entirely, and they are not easy terms. Such love must be complete, unquestioning, and entirely its own reward. No love is given in return. Both are supremely indifferent to the adult's feelings and desires. They have their own needs, to which one can, now and then, minister. That is the most they will allow. One can hope to sneak a peek—at Alice resting fretfully on the bank and provocatively tossing the hair from her eyes; at Peter asleep and exposing his arched knee and his pearls. But, even at these rare moments, no one can violate the "Do Not Disturb" signs worn by these scenes.

No figures are more insistently Other, more adept at resisting satisfaction, blocking fulfillment, keeping the chase and desire alive. They do this not by vanishing but by moving in and out of the next room, tantalizing us, coming almost within reach, almost within focus, and then scooting off. They do not, then, set up a static binary with the adult; they engage in a shifting dynamic, seeming to allow both seeing and being seen, a move from subject to object and back, but no chance to hold the child or the desire. One may admire the sleeping Peter or even try to trap his shadow; but he will wake and steal back his own shape. Alice eludes even her own photographs, smiling slyly out of them with an enticing knowledge of her own reserve, declining our invitation to be captured in the frame. This child is like Looking-Glass jam, which is available only on the "*other* day" today isn't.[4] Alice, we remember, doesn't want the jam anyhow. But we do, want somehow to make today one with that other day, the day when we were the child, had the jam.

But this child will not hold still to be properly tidied up and admired. It is tempting (I am tempted) to start making charts comparing and contrasting the Alice books with *Peter Pan*, thus fixing things and having done with the play and the longing. There's nothing like a chart to kill desire; the illusion of understanding promoted thereby is very strong. I might say, for instance, that both works, counting the Alice books as one thing, run with the following counters: the child and the adult, the world of play and the world of power. Peter, the child, is lodged in the world of play and the adult is stuck in the world of power; Alice, the apparent child (actually the adult) is firmly in the world of power and the apparent adult (actually the child) is in the world of play. The adult, accordingly, tries to wiggle into various forms and habitations, including that of the playful child. The child, however, is too much for the adult, always one step ahead and out of reach in the other world and shape. As I move to the sandbox and swings, the child moves to the board room and the pulpit; as I put on a pinafore, the child reaches for a girdle, a top hat, a cigar. I shift along with the child, but the child is quicker. Wonderland creatures can certainly be bossy and sententious when they choose, at which point, however, the grown-up Alice becomes sweet and childlike; when they are playful, she becomes Mr. M'Choakumchild. Peter Pan's adults often try regressing, Mr. Darling all the way down the Darwinian ladder and Hook back through memory to his days at Eton; but neither can get any closer to the erotic dream-child. Otherness cannot be made into a formula with these characters; it is not a question of lining up a few oppositions and watching them exhaust themselves. This play is too rubbery for that, too adept at keeping itself from ever being played out. These are dramas of perpetuation, plays of the elusive maneuverability of the child. That we are unable to close the distance seems melancholy to a few. But the true child-lovers know the pleasures of these failures, the pleasures which would not come except from failure. You can be invited back to play this game only if you lose it; you can win your way to a sight of the child and a hope for an audience, only by releasing that hope and the child with it. The stories taking place in Neverland and in the Wonderland behind the looking-glass are never going to let themselves down to give the adult what he wants. But if we were not foiled every time, we would have no hope of succeeding and no reason to return. These may be very melancholy comedies we pay so eagerly to see, but they've always drawn capacity crowds.

Growing Up

As we are sliding down toward the child, the child is roaring past us in the opposite direction, growing up. Nothing contributes more clearly to the child's fluid status than this sense of being in motion—and in the wrong direction. Whether seeking to please or to vex, the child imitates (mocks) the adult, and through its representations seems to be preparing for a life as our flattering mirror—or replacement. "As if its whole vocation were endless imitation," the child sets about playing adult, perhaps in order to learn the tricks of the trade—or perhaps in order to propitiate and ward off the demons. There is really no need to interpret such activity as work, as eager apprenticeship, when it might just as well be seen as ludic displacement or simply as romping with the materials closest at hand: give children two stones, an old hat, and some string, and they will make up a game; and so they do with adult lives that present themselves to them. But we generally read their play in the most depressing way and often impose the view of childhood that most alarms us: that it is nothing more than schooling for adulthood. Freud's view of the matter is instructive:

> A child's play is determined by wishes: in point of fact by a single wish—one that helps in his upbringing—the wish to be big and grown up. He is always playing at being "grown up," and in his games he imitates what he knows about the lives of his elders.[5]

As one skids through Freud's sentences, one sees him artfully slimming down the problem, first reducing all play to wishing and then trimming the multiform "wishes" to a manageable "wish" to grow up. Freud exposes the way in which we take the variety of children's play, open to any interpretation, and construct a single restrictive story: the child plays at one thing and for one reason; and that is how you must see it. Why should we see it that way? Freud says it will "help in the child's upbringing." Telling the story in this way allows us to use the child's own activities to gain what we want, namely, for the child not to be a child, merely an adult-in-training. But of course that is not at all what we want. The child functions as a mirror for us, certainly, but it is a complex mirror yielding oblique, distanced views of desirable otherness. If the child should grow up, it would become not a trick mirror but a cheap dime-store reflector, providing nothing in the way of obliquity and nothing for desire. Freud, we remember, was a storyteller especially fond of irony.

Both Carroll and Barrie use our awareness of this terrible story as an ominous backdrop against which to develop their much more alluring plots. Alice and Peter are asked to decide about growing up, to mold their lives and the plots of their stories around this decision. These are crisis stories, like those crisis-of-vocation or of-faith plots so loved by the Victorians. The question raised for both figures is, "Will you agree to grow up?" Alice seems to find the prospect so untroubling she recognizes no dilemma at all, while Peter sees adulthood as a trap and is willing to give up everything in order not to fall into it.

Yet the tensions in each story are the same: an urgent need for the child, the elusive child-forever, is played off against all the sensible, Freudian-ironic, and undesirable powers that would erase distance, make the child manageable, catchable, and thus just another grown-up-soon-to-be. Everywhere around Peter, children are betraying his vision, moving up even when they sense what a mistake they are making. "All children," Barrie wrote in opening his Peter Pan novel, *Peter and Wendy*, "except one, grow up."[6] And they grow up with the speed of darkness, even the Davies boys, for whom Barrie made such a special world and to whom these Neverland stories were first told: "They had a long summer day, and I turned round twice and now they are off to school" ("A Dedication" to *Peter Pan*, p. xxix). Alice rushes by just as rapidly, hardly noticing the landscape and the lovers she is leaving behind. There are a few hints, usually contained in jokes or puns, that she might very well have left off growing altogether at seven—"with proper assistance" (*Looking-Glass*, p. 64). This is usually seen as a grim suggestion that Alice could have arranged for her own execution, but it also might be taken, more literally and dearly, as offering a whole world of help to Alice in remaining a child. Alice's language sometimes teases us with the same kind of wishing: "At least," she says from within the mashed quarters of the Rabbit's house, "there's no room to grow up any more *here*" (*Wonderland*, p. 59). As long as she is in these magic worlds, perhaps she can be *held*, kept as a child, cozied close to the child-lover:

> Without, the frost, the blinding snow,
>   The storm-wind's moody madness—
> Within, the firelight's ruddy glow,
>   And childhood's nest of gladness.
> The magic words shall hold thee fast:
>   Thou shalt not heed the raving blast.

The child blindly chooses the blindness, rejects the warmth of the nest for the raving madness outside. The magic of the words can no more "hold fast" the child than can Peter's play hold onto the lost boys who are for a time his friends but then fall, let themselves down to growing up, become truly lost.

Peter Pan

Barrie's play is usually received as a bittersweet piece of nostalgia, a self-protective lament for the remoteness of the child that creates that very distance. We could not love Peter half so much were he not able to fly and escape us. Knowing very well what he is and what he needs to protect, Peter announces three times in the play that he wants, in the name of "fun," to be always a "little boy" and that he is willing to put up quite a fight to remain so. Peter Pan is that most leathery and alluring of Others, the absolutely self-possessed, with no interest in imitating the grown-up, with no need of anyone outside himself. We cannot resist the child who is so determined to resist us.

Peter Pan is so compelling that it is embarrassing, especially when there seems to be so little reason for responding to one so unresponsive. That is just the point, but we may feel the need all the same to apologize. One way to do so is to abuse Peter—"an affectionless psychopath!"[7]— or, since it seems a fairer match, his author. Barrie can so easily be seen as a case of arrested development, frozen by early trauma and rivetted either by his own childhood or by his mother's.[8] There is no doubt that the image of his mother as a girl meant much to him, at least in the way of material he could plunder for stories. But we do not generally allow that Barrie might have had the freedom to be opportunistic. We trap him in much the way his words trap Peter Pan. We declare the Barrie cult of the first two decades of this century an unhealthy dip into sentimentality, a mania for regressive satisfactions we no longer need. Barrie, we hear, hardly even liked childhood, so much did he bathe it in regret and a desire not to be. *Peter Pan*, the work most expressive of the "author's sickness," does not tell the story of the boy who wished not to grow up "but, carrying the sentiment to its deadly conclusion, of the boy who wishes so plainly that he had never been born."[9] The work, says the same analyst, develops an undeniable "power," but a power that is, somehow, "debilitating."

A verdict of "debilitating power" is protecting something, perhaps an unwillingness to accord to this odd narrative and its boy-hero the cultural centrality they hold. Biographical criticism offers a form of armor, reminds us of Barrie's freakishness, the way his notebooks record a repulsive sexual terror, for instance: "Greatest horror—dream I am married—wake up shrieking."[10] His relationship with the Davies family, especially the five boys, is generally thought to have consumed all the time and energy (sexual energy) he had to offer. But it was energy enough, we are told, to eat up that family. Peter Davies later stated that Barrie was such a strong character "in his own strange way" that he could charm people into playing parts into which he cast them, that "when he was strongly attracted by people, he wanted at once to own them and to be dominated by them," managing at least the first pretty well.[11] But that ownership was, as Davies also says, balanced by a generosity, even a modesty that put the relationship into a "peculiar equilibrium." We can read the language of otherness here—"strange," "peculiar"—as indicating Davies's uneasiness and buried anger or simply his way of fumbling toward the extraordinary. Another of the boys, Nico, said "I haven't the skill to answer" questions about the nature and quality of Barrie's love, feeling that his own mind was too "ordinary" to encompass Barrie's and express what it held. Nico thought Barrie was "in love" with his two oldest brothers (and with his mother) and that "things obviously went through his mind." But he added that he "never heard one word or saw one glimmer of anything approaching homosexuality or paedophilia."[12] It is possible that these strained explanations, Nico's and our own, express a need to locate Barrie (not his play, however) at some distance, to make him bizarre. Thus, little attention is paid to evidence of his strong interest in adult women, his considerable professional and social success, the fact that a great deal of his writing and almost all of his plays are without interest in or for children, and the highly unneurotic ease with which he could joke about himself, even about those who were real-life Peter Pans: Thomas Hardy at one point did not want to leave childhood, marking him, Barrie thought, as possessed by a pathetic-funny "complex," even though "one hardly thought of Hardy as a Peter Pan."[13] And what do we make of Barrie's enthusiasm for D. H. Lawrence, a "vivid," "passionate," "big," "lovable," writer whose "coarsenesses" "are a very small affair"?[14] We make nothing of this, since it does not fit.

But we continue to chase after the erotic boy-phantom he devised for our fancy, the image that remains so commanding precisely because it insists on its half-alien quality. It is odd that the charge of sentimentality is brought against a figure who is antithetical to syrup, who is so unsoft and unfurry as to bite all those who try their hand at petting. "No one must ever touch me" (p. 29), he declares right off. His is the skin you love to touch but dare not, an inviolate spotlessness. "No one is going to catch me, lady!" (p. 157), he accurately forecasts. Because the child is himself so uncoercive, he gives the sense of wanting nothing more than for nature to take its course, so long as he is not ambushed, forced into doing something so unnatural as growing up. He is made into an argument for health, all the rest being depravity and illness. At the same time, this health is never made available to us. We are not nostalgically beckoned by Peter Pan but reminded sternly and without tears that such a child cannot be, at least cannot be ours.

The child scorns the comfort of sentiment. Peter Pan is one of the "gay and innocent and heartless" (*Peter and Wendy*, p. 186) who always is "thinking chiefly of himself" (*Peter and Wendy*, p. 188), so much so that he easily forgets Hook, the lost boys, Wendy, and even Tinker Bell, whom we had wanted so much to find sweetsie. Peter and the other children so long as they are under his spell have absolutely "no compunction for what they have done" (*Peter Pan*, p. 151), no regard for what others may be feeling, no real consciousness of another. This is not the Wordsworthian child, but it is not the child of the spanking stories either. Peter does not seem to arouse resentment, the feeling that we can exercise ourselves familiarly on one part of the child while keeping other parts Other and desirable still. Barrie could play with such titillations, as in his late play *The Boy David*, where the exasperated mother, driven beyond limits, begins the foreplay by talking about what will happen when father gets home. The child, entering readily into the erotica, keeps the conversation going for some time with cute lines and Swinburnian begging: "David (imploringly). 'Not Father's belt.' "[15] But in *Peter Pan* the refusal of the child to notice the adult, even to annoy by being naughty heightens the attraction: "the most heartless things in the world, which is what children are, but so attractive" (*Peter and Wendy*, p. 119). The question is how to get his attention.

Peter's toughness is vitally connected to his innocence, an innocence nowhere more relentlessly tied to ignorance. Peter knows so very little, is maintained by his not knowing. Wendy's canny sexual advances have no chance with an imperious boy who is quite sure that "kisses" are acorn buttons. Barrie identified the Peter Pan quality in A.A. Milne and wrote urging him to keep to his wonderful not-knowing:

> The gaiety and irresponsibility of your work . . . are rarer gifts that you wot of now. When you know you won't be so gay. So don't know as long as you can.[16]

Ignorance really is bliss here, a state that is blessed because it does not *know*, does not partake of the limitations of what passes for *knowing* among the grown-ups. With grown-ups, being is dispersed along various dribbles of knowledge. With the child, all is compact within the certainty of the not-knowing, refusing to know. The identity is whole, focused, absolutely assured: "There never was a cockier boy" (*Peter and Wendy*, p. 27). He holds his body cocked and ready, struts, asserts his being unself-consciously, happily exposed.

Peter is unabashed, as near naked as the stage will allow; Barrie's stage direction says, "In so far as he is dressed at all it is in autumn leaves and cobwebs" (*Peter Pan*, p. 27). "I'm sweet, oh, I am sweet!", he sings while flying, not so much registering his effect on us as his erotic delight in himself. It is a delight the audience is allowed to share—from a distance. It is best when he can be seen napping, leg arched and hand thrown over the edge of the bed like a serpentining Cleopatra in drag. But not really in drag, being so genderless. One of the things he does not *know* is gender, or maybe it is one of the things we are allowed for a moment not to know. Peter is resolutely boyish and is customarily played by females; it could as well be reversed. His position is not so much androgynous as beyond gender, his erotic fascination being focused especially in his pearly teeth. His most provocative acts come when he sends energy into these teeth: "Peter gnashes his pretty teeth with joy" (*Peter Pan*, p. 89). Twice in the play we are reminded that these are his "first teeth " (pp. 11, 88), his "baby teeth," teeth that exist to expose the very bone but that comes prior to gendered sex: "Here was a lovely boy, clad in skeleton leaves and the juices that ooze out of trees; but the most entrancing thing about him was that he had all his first teeth" (*Peter and Wendy*, p. 11). Even more than the lovely form and the oozing juices, these first teeth move and beguile, as Eden does. These first teeth will never be supplanted, made to give way to grown-up replacements.

But these teeth are not often on view; they are not displayed as fixed artifacts. So much, I hope, has been made clear. What is not so clear is the nature and direction of Peter's dynamism. It is directed only, as he says over and over, toward having fun, toward inconsequential play. So obvious it may escape us, this playing forms most of the action and most of the appeal of the drama. It is not simply that Neverland is set up and equipped with all the apparatus necessary for fantasy play; it is that Peter manages to conduct the adventures so that they are repeatable and yet infinitely variable. His life is centered in play and thus naturally works to perpetuate that play, to keep things going. If it looks as if he might possibly win, he simply changes sides (*Peter Pan*, p. 89), a wonderful technique that even his opponents learn to adopt (*Peter and Wendy*, p. 83). Peter's position on all matters is dictated by this form of being: play does not serve other ends but acts as the center to explain and allow all else. Even death will be no more than "an awfully big adventure" (*Peter Pan*, p. 93), one more way to play.[17]

The enormously successful children's pantomime written as an awfully big treat for adults is more than a landscape for Peter Pan to fly through. It does not make a spectacle of desire but provides a gymnasium for the exercise of it, reminding us even in such things as sit-com jokes about women and cheque-books (*Peter Pan*, p. 51) that the child does not form the real audience here; the child is the main attraction. The play, dedicated to the five Davies boys, made up of stories told to them, and written, possibly, as "a last desperate throw to retain the five of you for a little longer" ("Dedication," p. viii), creates a carefully laid out and demarcated field for pedophile frolic. It is play that is neither so fanciful nor idealized as to be cleansed from the ugliest racial and class fantasies. The pirates are bumptiously lower class and the redskins present a coalition of red, black (they are the Piccaninny tribe), and yellow, their speech being a version of stage-hall (and later movie) Chinee: "Me his velly nice friend," says Tiger Lily (*Peter Pan*, p. 103).

This play about the child for the adult designates very carefully the sort of adult it has in mind: white, middle class, British (preferably), erotically unengaged. We must accept the role assigned or we have no business in this play, or even observing it. We cannot, for instance, accept the part of the parent. Probably most children's literature that pretends to understand the child does something to release it from being tethered to parents. In many, parents never appear at all, are presumed to be irrelevant. Here, however, we get a strong dose of parents, in the flesh at the beginning and end, and by implication throughout. The senior Darlings are immediately diminished by the stock comic roles they are quite content to play—the bumbling, blustering father and the cooing mother. They have been deactivated, robbed of any threatening potential before the play begins. Even so, even in this cartoon state, they are attacked, subject to the violent therapeutic beatings a child will mete out to a doll. Mr. Darling's part and that of Hook were originally played by the same actor,[18] thus linking the major enemies (if Hook is really an enemy); and there is, we saw in Chapter Six, one remarkably hostile joke allowed to Michael, where he compares (unfavorably) his father to the pirate he managed to murder (*Peter Pan*, p. 152). Generally, however, parents are put in their place by being forgotten. Once away from home, once they have turned the first corner, the children have no reason to account for these parents, to tend to their orders, to acknowledge their authority or their being. They kill them by insouciance and thus regain their liberty. Mr. Darling, uncharacteristically "doting" on his children, crows, "There is not their equal on earth, and they are ours, ours!" (*Peter Pan*, p. 14).[19] Peter Pan provides them the chance to be not *his-his!* but their own. Refusing to grow up means refusing to cede the rights to yourself to mere predecessors.

The aggression against the parent and the adult generally is fairly strong in this fable, suggesting that one way to turn the whole world into Neverland would be to evacuate the parts now inhabited by killing off the occupants. Perhaps it would take little effort *not* to grow up if there were nothing to grow up *to*. This murderous impulse is not given major play; but it does find expression now and then. Peter's anger is only really aroused by elders and their intrusions:

> [He was] full of wrath against grown-ups, who, as usual, were spoiling everything. . . . There is a saying in Neverland that, every time you breathe, a grown-up dies, and Peter was killing them off vindictively as fast as possible. (*Peter and Wendy*, pp. 120–21)

But the one adult he does, more or less, manage to kill does not seem to be an enemy at all but a bellowing, funny parody, a player who, like Peter, does not *know*, a child who has agreed to play Daddy and is having a fine old time of it: "A holocaust of children, there is something grand in the idea!" (*Peter Pan*, p. 144). This is the little kid as bogeyman. Or perhaps it is the one adult who is allowed in, the one who is much closer to Peter even than the lost boys, the adult as lover. Peter has set it up as a rule that no one is to close with Hook but himself, and he especially glories in stalking the Pirate and being stalked by him, as if they were connected, tied together in this game. The hook becomes for Peter both a symbol of the power of adulthood and of the ease with which he controls that power. Peter has put the hook there, after all, the hook that can duel but not spank. For the garden-variety father, dully tyrannical, he has substituted an enormously appealing monster.

And that monster, for his part, is not so much murderous as obsessed. He is obsessed with Peter, cannot leave off looking for and at him: "There is something in PETER that at all times goads this extraordinary man to frenzy; it is the boy's cockiness, which disturbs HOOK like an insect" (*Peter Pan*, p. 116). The sentence here seems almost to enact the feeling by which Hook is possessed, the itching desire he feels for the boy: the "something" undefined in the first clause is suspended, held open, until its release into "cockiness," the self-possessed figure of energy about to explode that has attracted so many readers and watchers. Hook is the privileged lover who knows how to get close by never touching (despite his great advantage in reach). With "a touch of the feminine" (*Peter Pan*, p. 86), Hook is the complete person: the complete pedophile and the perfect child. He plays either the game of resentment and danger or the game of sentiment and nostalgia (by way of his quivering public school memories). Hook is the entry adults have into the itch that is Peter; he shows us how to scratch enough to keep it alive.

The adults who would kill it off, the actual enemies, wear skirts instead of hooks, come in the form of women who threaten to disrupt the pederastic unity being forged. Even Mr. Darling "might have passed for a boy again if he had been able to take his baldness off" (*Peter and Wendy*, p. 170). But Mrs. Darling is another matter, as are mothers in general and especially that youthful incarnation of smothering motherdom, Wendy. Various commentators have suggested that Wendy appears as an idealized form of Barrie's mother, a possibility which fits well with other theses, no doubt, but not with mine; for the mother I construct from the play is both oafish and deadly, a cross between Edith Bunker and Medusa. Wendy comes into the play as an intruder, a disturber of the peace and play, sets up a school, and is last seen on a broomstick, where she should have been all along.

In his "Dedication," Barrie had joked with the Davies boys, with whom he had often shared Neverland times, about an intruder (possibly their nurse or mother) into their mutual games, a female they had considered inviting but never did because of the risk. Wendy becomes that "disturbing element," one who "bored her way in at last whether we wanted her or not"; "she would not stay away" (p. xxvii). Perhaps not so accidentally, she is shot; and for a time we are allowed to suppose that she is a goner. Peter's response—"Wendy is dead!"—is not "so much pained as puzzled" (*Peter Pan*, p. 64): Wendy's corpse is simply a bother. When she revives and begins mothering them, she takes on a part that the boys would just as soon no one played: "They knew in what they called their hearts that one can get on quite well without a mother and that it is only mothers who think you can't" (*Peter and Wendy*, p. 120). Peter concurs, with a somewhat stronger expression of dislike: "Not only had he no mother, but he had not the slightest desire to have one. He thought them very overrated persons" (*Peter and Wendy*, p. 25). At the end of the novel version, future mothers and daughters succeed one another with depressing redundancy, the old ones sliding into the grave and out of memory: "Mrs. Darling was now dead and forgotten" (p. 185).

In the meanwhile, though, Wendy enters to skew the play's erotics by getting between Peter and his admirers: Hook, Barrie, and us. (She gets some interfering help too from Tinker Bell, whose death is also waved before us.) Wendy really wants Peter to herself; not content to watch him with Hook and us, she wants to touch, kiss, possess. We enter into a contest with her, not to see who can *get* Peter but to see whether our desire can outlast or outface her wish to cancel that desire. We want to keep him free, and squirm not with embarrassment but with fear when the mushy stuff starts. In the novel, Peter even allows himself to be kissed, which is enough of a setback to make us declare this later work unauthentic. It is not that Wendy brings in the specter of heterosexuality; it's that she is "one of the kind that likes to grow up" (*Peter and Wendy*, p. 184) that makes her so dangerous. She introduces the ideas of contact and consummation, the bland acceptance of the grown-up that is murderous. Somehow she already knows all the unfairness, loves it, and is anxious to get on with dealing out her share. Peter is youth and joy, and she is age and death; Peter is the little bird broken out of the egg, and Wendy is the mother who would still sit on him until he is suffocated. Wendy shows us that real monsters have warm bosoms. She drains off from us any desire to fix, and releases the energies of play.

But the skillful channeling of resentment and danger into the feminine and maternal does not really do what we expect; it does not clear the way for pure, untroubled joy. Neverland does indeed offer a world where random adventures follow one another in a riotous carousing, an immersion in carnivalesque "fun." It would seem to be a realm of romance, untroubled by memory, anticipation, or any other causal tie.

No "logic of events" or any other kind of logic is going to hamper the demands we might, on the spur of the moment, feel like making. Thus the novel celebrates through self-reflexive jokes the freedom both writer and reader may feel from traditional constraints: we get to flip a coin to decide on adventures, and we do not have to depend on the laws of physics to determine whether the Darling parents will reach the bedroom in time to prevent the flight of their kids:

> Will they reach the nursery in time? If so, how delightful for them, and we shall all breathe a sigh of relief, but there will be no story. On the other hand, if they are not in time, I solemnly promise that it will all come right in the end.

Like Trollope, Barrie turns it all into a romp, makes play not a glitch in the real but the measure of it. For Barrie, for Peter, and for us, "make believe and true [are] exactly the same thing" (*Peter and Wendy*, p. 71)—or should be. *Peter Pan* is, however, about our inability to have make-believe and the true stick together: it dramatizes an artistic failure, the failure to make the vision of play persuasive. Even while the lost boys are with Peter, they hold to the pernicious distinction between the true and the make-believe. They are unable to forget all the unfairnesses that are thrust on them by adults. Not being able to forget, they come to know, to grow up and start inflicting unfairnesses of their own (*Peter and Wendy*, p. 98). The boys leave Peter, changing from the wondrous and lost to dismally found and "ordinary" (*Peter and Wendy*, p. 182).

The play cannot resist the force of the unfair, of knowing, cannot establish its own rhetoric in the face of these powers. Even Tinker Bell is slaughtered. Despite the applause, we do not believe in fairies or cannot sustain the image that, for a moment, we glimpsed disappearing round the corner. Peter offers his secret to all these children and to us, but remains alone. Saddest of all, the one who did actually catch on, who knew how to make unfairness not into education but into frolic, who would never leave willingly, is removed by the great enemy of all lovers and all children. Hook is swallowed by that force of time, lodged in a crocodile, which busies itself turning out grown-ups and wounding pedophiles like Hook. Barrie records a failure in the lost boys, in Wendy, even in the fairies to measure up to Peter's standards, to understand what he is saying. Peter undergoes one desertion after another, countless acts of ignorant betrayal. And those loyal to him are gulped down by the growing up that blots out the pedophile love. The crocodiles of this world, not all of them female, win.

On the other hand, they never get to Peter, never have the slightest chance against that image of desire which can live in a play and through play, unthreatened even by crocodiles.

Alice[20]

The crocodiles in Wonderland are different, are, in fact, our friends. But, sadly, they don't stand a chance, which is a pity. They are overcome by the busy little bee. Alice, with her all-too-common perceptual apparatus unhinged by the fall down the rabbit hole and into another mode of being, tries to regain touch with what she takes herself to be and what she can expect from things around her. She figures, like the unfailingly shrewd little girl she is, that she can hardly go wrong if she recalls a set of maxims, poetically expressed, that speak from the heart of her adult culture. She knows that if she can just get hold of a particular poem, the one telling her what she is, the one telling her what adults say she is, all will be dandy. She will know what the world is and how she fits into it, if she can just process through her brain and mouth this official set of definitions and instructions on how to grow up. Alice, just like Wendy, wants so badly to grow up, she more or less is grown-up now, probably was born grown-up. As a consequence, she is a great menace to the child. But, to return to our story, Alice is distressingly disoriented and turns for the stability of conventional moorings to "Against Idleness and Mischief."

In that poem, the bees work snugly if manically within time to "improve each shining hour" with skillful "labours hard" that extend through "all the day." This insect model, once constructed, is then mashed down over the child:

> In works of labour, or of skill,
>   I would be busy too;
> For Satan finds some mischief still,
>   For idle hands to do. (*Wonderland*, p. 48)

So we pass our "first years" in imitation of the bees, hoping thereby to elude Satan and stock up enough virtue so as to be able to give "some good account at last." According to this, childhood is defined not merely by adulthood but by death, by "last" things. All things are consequential, matters for accounting; and prudential and linear rules should therefore be in place from the first minute of life. The child is made at once into the aged, aged man, grown-up and glad that not a second was wasted, not a flicker of idleness or mischief—of play or childhood.

That Alice would want to regain her place in such a world tells us a great deal about her. So does the wonderful crocodile ode which comes unbidden from her lips. In this version, all good things come to him who does nothing at all, come to him for no reason whatever. The crocodile sits in the ooze of the Nile, swishing water on his tail and grinning. Nothing more. The sweet little fishies just swim right into his "gently smiling" jaws. This model is all idleness and mischief, all imprudence and miscalculation—and no sentiment. The crocodile and he who writes of him have as much time for such slush as did Peter Pan. Wonderland and its crocodiles are pure Neverlands, thoroughly oblivious to the rules of power, entirely at home with play.

But Alice is not at home with play. She is at home with the bees—with logic, accounts, work, death, and sentimentality: the rewards that come to those willing to grow up. The Otherness represented by Alice is even more elusive than Peter's, more subtle and indistinct, more a photograph we can set in the past and tell stories about, more a memory her sister can dream when Alice runs off, more a child who never was. If we were not allowed to enter Neverland, except through the Hook who is consumed by time, never allowed to approach the child who made and ruled that land, here we are welcomed into the magic world, enter easily—but we find no child at home. We find only Alice, the false child, resisting the play, telling us coldly at every turn in the game that we are being silly, that we must wake up, grow up.

Alice remains so distant and desirable because she vacates the position of the true child, leaves it for us, and becomes the false child, the child who betrays by growing up. Of course if things were this static the work would be very uninteresting, or at least unerotic. Alice often seems as if she *might* move into the play, go in for a little idleness and mischief. She is, after all, propelled toward *adventures* by an eager and winning "curiosity" even more capacious than Peter's, whose own adventures are comparatively controlled. Alice is also just as resistant to being fawned over or touched and is just as self-possessed under most circumstances, nearly as "cocky." Her push forward, toward the future, is in part a perky resistance to the cult of femininity we are told the Victorians honored, the vision of a static woman with no thought of a direction or needs of her own.[21] Alice knows what she wants and pushes toward it with a boldness often found admirable.

But what is it she wants, and why does she want what she wants? Who has told her she wants it? The little bees and Isaac Watts and her culture? Here comes Lewis Carroll offering something else quite at odds with all that, quite in another country. Alice exercises power, resists the lure; but what does she gain? She gains power, the power to resist play. But she had the power in the first place, and it seems to be a sort of power that carries with it a good many rules, the first one being that power is never to be questioned. Alice seems trapped, given only the power to resist, to decline invitations but never accept them.

It is this same power which sets her off, separates her from the world we have moved into and thus makes her both exasperating and desirable. Nina Auerbach has brilliantly exposed for us how Carroll's granting of power to the child, the child being photographed, was not an imposition but a form of understanding what was the child's, a power nakedly erotic, passionate, and seditious.[22] Alice's resistances—to Wonderland, Carroll, play, and us—then, are expressions of her sexuality and her appeal. This eroticism is by no means imposed, simply allowed, photographed in a setting that will make it available to us.

That setting, Wonderland, is fuller than Neverland, fuller of risk, absurdity, freedom from sense. There is danger everywhere but no consequence. Bees do not accumulate accounts here, and a royal order of execution has nothing to do with death. They "never executes nobody, you know," or at least that's what the Gryphon says (p. 107), and it ought to know. No effect ever follows on a cause, one of the ways in which the game is maintained. We can understand Wonderland in negative ways, as a world where such things as death and time are psychically "economized," if we like. The narrative is initiated by a rabbit terrified of being "too late," an ominously open and resonant phrase we can scare ourselves with, and such things as time and death are recurrent subjects for conversation. But the conversation seems mere horsing around, these topics carrying no more weight than any others, than haddock's eyes or tea. Tea is in fact more important, since tea fixes the time and not vice versa. It is always tea-time, the time having been murdered by the Hatter, whose head was ordered off by the Queen, in consequence of which it was not taken off. In Wonderland, play is not purchased at the cost of hiding from terrors like time and mortality; time and mortality are made subject to play, give up their power in order to join in the fun.

Everything in Wonderland either generates a game or has to go sit and sulk. Since no attention at all is paid to the sulkers, they soon see the error of their ways and offer themselves up to the game. The Mock Turtle dallies with deep sadness, the Queen with death, the Duchess with sentimentality and with morals. This last, her quick ability to locate the moral that everything has within it, is of great interest to us, since it seems so close to textual interpretation, and may offer the secret of how to make interpreting fun. For the Duchess, the comment "The game seems to be going on rather better now" can be taken to mean "Oh, 'tis love, 'tis love, that makes the world go round." Or, she says, it can mean that the world goes round by everybody minding his business (much the same thing), in turn meaning "Take care of the sense, and the sounds will take care of themselves." The Duchess, poststructurally adept, seizes on secret puns, hidden disconnections, takes them in her beak, and drops them into craters, just like Jacques Derrida. It is a proud interpretive activity and a frisky one. Even the concluding Wonderland trial offers a hilarious romp with logic, linguistic certainty, and the control we imagine we have over events and consequences.

But the most unembarrassed view of what play can do comes in the simplest of the frolicsome activities, the Caucus Race. Here Dodgson is drawn in himself, taking on the form of the Dodo, just for the fun of it. The Dodo reads out the non-rules, not to constrain but to shoo away any constraints. Instead of giving rules, he gives out invitations, not a representation of experience but the thing itself: "the best way to explain it is to do it" (p. 53). The course is marked out "in sort of a circle"—" 'the exact shape doesn't matter,' it said"—and all who were nearby and wanted to join in (which was everybody) "began running when they liked, and left off when they liked." Though it is not clear that the race has anything like an ending, it is felt only fitting that there should be a prize; so the Dodo, after some thought, declares, "*Everybody* has won, and *all* must have prizes" (p. 54). Such play opens us up to wild delights.

Delights which Alice would prefer, thank you just the same, to forego. She responds to the invitations offered to her with polite refusals, though she keeps going, keeps being tempted, keeps making us think that just possibly she will slide over into sloth and devilment. Despite her curiosity, however, she is generally a well-ordered adult, prudent and respectful of conventions, even when she fails to recognize the basis for or implications of these conventions. She wants above all to stay in command of her world, Wonderland included, and reaches time and again for just those devices which had seemed so natural when she had been taught them—the ordering of predatory hierarchies, for instance. She tends to understand and value levels of being in terms of who eats what or whom, a grisly view whose genteel disguises are quietly removed in Wonderland. "Do cats eat bats?," she wonders as she falls, and sometimes " 'Do bats eat cats?' for, you see, as she couldn't answer either question, it didn't much matter which way she put it" (p. 40). Any warm-blooded noun might be inserted, we suppose—bat, cat, rat, gnat, slug, or Alice—so long as the key, *eat*, remained constant. She seems unable to avoid connecting the eaters with their dinners, chatting up mice and birds about cats and turning the delightful lobster quadrille into a feast, where the merry dancers are threatened by her own practices—"I've often seen them at dinn--" (p. 112).

As with "Idleness and Mischief," she often turns for security to prim prudential poems of the sort adults thrust at children (then and now). Trying to recover a sense of who she *is*, Alice runs for answers to the worst part of her culture. It is very sad and irksome, what with all the Wonderland creatures singing to her and waving brightly colored (if not very tasteful) banners telling her not to worry about the sort of identity that grown-ups give you. But Alice keeps after these poems, poems with titles like "'Tis the voice of the sluggard" (p. 114) or "The Old Man's Comforts and How He Gained Them" (p. 67). This last, better known as "You are old, Father William," stands as a direct rebuke if not to Alice then certainly to the cautious, CPA assumptions she is wanting to make. The poem Alice is trying to remember features an old man braying about how he spent all his youth preparing for his nineties and now what an abundant payoff he has had. He never once forgot, he says, that "youth could not last;/I thought of the future, whatever I did,/That I never might grieve for the past" (p. 67). As a result of hoarding his youth in this way, he is now "cheerful," collecting divine interest and entertaining callers with reflections on his favorite topic: "You are cheerful, and love to converse upon death,/Now tell me the reason, I pray." Not even Alice can hold such a vision in Wonderland; its prudential economy has no meaning there. As a result, all Alice can get from the situation is a rollicking poem about a somersaulting, upside-down, eel-balancing, ointment-selling, punning old man who has no notion that yesterday has any connection to tomorrow, that one might or might not save, or that there is any God or Death one might be "cheerful" about. He even becomes tired with his questioner, bored with anyone who really would think to ask for advice, when he could ask for marmalade.

But Alice remains in the position of the poem's questioner, so firmly resistant to entering into the world of the child that she sometimes appears stupid. Take the episode with the Duchess's baby. The Duchess seems to treat the baby like an old football that can take a lot of dirt and pounding. Alice is appalled in just the prescribed ways, regarding babies as "*precious*" little bundles. Now it is a rule in pedophile writing that babies are entirely without interest to sane people and that expressions of interest are so much flummery. Alice, however, can hardly help herself, since she is so committed to aping grown-up responses. The Duchess is dousing the baby in pepper, bouncing it about, and singing a great parody of yet one more poem of prudential economy, this one, "Speak gently!," softly reminding us that little ones are likely as not to die, and that it therefore behooves us to make things as much like a perpetual funeral as we can: "Speak gently to the little child!/Its love be sure to gain;/Teach it in accents soft and mild—/It may not long remain" (p. 77). The Duchess's version blasts through that simpering like an express train: "Speak roughly to your little boy,/ And beat him when he sneezes:/He only does it to annoy,/Because he knows it teases" (p. 77). Alice learns nothing from this, and rescues the baby—or takes it on the fly—carrying "the poor little thing" (p. 78) away, only to discover that it is or has turned into "neither more nor less than a pig" (p. 79), which should tell her something about babies and about sentimental ordering systems, but doesn't.

Nor does she learn the most important lessons of all, that things do not conclude in Wonderland, that they cannot be understood in terms of goals or ends, and that new modes of seeing might be not only useful but happy substitutions. Time and again, she wants to tie things up and send them off, write a report and file it. The Mock Turtle's old-boy (or -girl or -it) memories (or anticipations or lies) of a quite remarkable school it attended (or is attending or will be attending or never did attend) include an idea whose time had certainly come: lessons should lessen, else there is no reason for their name—ten hours one day, nine the next, and so on. Alice feels, first, stung by this praise of a school she did not frequent; but then she tries to understand the lessening system. What, she wonders, happened on the eleventh day, a vacation? That's it! " 'And how did you manage on the twelfth?' Alice went on eagerly" (p. 110). Earlier, at the great tea-party, formed as a ring of eternity, Alice tries to find in the circle a stopping point, tries to reinsert linear time into a world where it's always tea-time; she wants it all to be over: as the party moves round and round, Alice cannot keep from asking "what happens when you come to the beginning again?" (p. 88). Where Wonderland has most to offer, Alice calls up her strongest resistance.

All the same, we never lose hope of somehow educating this child into childhood. She does not, for one thing, always have her back up, hissing. We are led into this work by the promise that the child can be cuddled. The prefatory poem, "All in the golden afternoon," is a basking verse, one that laps and strokes and suggests a recapture in memory so perfect that the past will flood the present, erasing that distinction and, with it, the one between the adult and child. Early on, as Alice goes down the rabbit hole, there is a nestling intimacy implied between the narrator and the child who allows such attentions: "She generally gave herself very good advice (though she very seldom followed it)" (p. 44), humor whose very feebleness signals a private understanding. Again, at the very end, the child is there, or seems to be, for snuggling. She is still "little Alice," and through her sister provides the final enticing image (quoted at the head of this chapter). But notice how it is no longer suggested that Alice participates in this, even hears the jokes. They are still private jokes, but they are now so confidential as to be solitary. Through our surrogate, Alice's sister, we can only moon over memories or paint a picture of the future that tries to soften the pain of the child's desertion. Alice has run off from the scene; the sister, the adult, is left alone to make the best of things; though the best doesn't amount to much:

> Lastly, she pictured to herself how this same little sister of hers would, in the after-time, be herself a grown woman; and how she would keep, through all her riper years, the simple and loving heart of her childhood; and how she would gather about her other little children, and make *their* eyes bright and eager with many a strange tale, perhaps even with the dream of Wonderland of long ago; and how she would feel with all their simple sorrows, and find a pleasure in all their simple joys, remembering her own child-life, and the happy summer days. (p. 130)

The adult tries to hold something, to keep the child from becoming so resoundingly ordinary and familiar. The adult wants not to bring the child close but to keep it at a distance, hold it at arm's length. Otherwise, we cannot move in a field of desire at all. We can always pretend, with Alice's sister, that somehow Alice will be different, that adulthood will not destroy her Otherness, that she will keep, in memory and in her heart, something simpler. But deep inside, even while spinning this story, we acknowledge that the magic did not take, that Alice has no simplicity to maintain or regain, that she will not even, in a vulgar and pathetic idea we could not keep ourselves from adding, use the story to bring other children to us, others with bright and eager eyes. She could never tell the story. She didn't get it.

And the reflex of all the fawning and pretend-hoping over Alice is bitter exasperation, a full current of resentment such as never made its way to Peter Pan. There are any number of creatures who, with our cheering support, let loose at Alice a barrage of contempt. The best of these players in this spiteful game is the Pigeon. Alice's mushroom experiments have elongated and rubberized her neck until she is, the narrator says, "like a serpent," a hint picked up by our Pigeon-friend, who beats Alice over the face with her wings—vigorously, we hope—and shrieks at her: "Ugh, Serpent!" Alice tries to defend herself by claiming she is a little girl, which is just the opening we and the Pigeon are looking for. The Pigeon tests her: "I suppose you'll be telling me next that you never tasted an egg!" Alice slides right into the trap—"little girls eat eggs quite as much as serpents do, you know"—which the Pigeon slams shut with a triumphant howl: "why, then they're a kind of serpent: that's all I can say." This is such a clincher that it makes even Alice "quite silent for a minute or two" (p. 71), giving the Pigeon time to get in one or two more whacks for us.

But what good does it do? What good even is done by those jokes which pointedly contemplate the murder, suicide, or disappearing of Alice: going out altogether like a candle, say? Alice isn't even naughty for long, isn't anything for long. By the end of the book, the adult is reduced to a weary, lonely wistfulness, trying to retain the failed magic of the story.

Looking-Glass Losses

The second story almost gives up before it begins, gives up on any real recapturing effort, and sees what may be harvested from the consolations of melancholy. It is a book written not only for but by Alice's sister. But even Alice's sister is not quite resigned to going out like a candle, and, despite everything, the players behind the glass keep holding out to Alice timid entreaties, shy, red-faced, and foot-shuffling expressions of half-hope that she will yet join the fun. The erotics in Looking-Glass, in other words, are similar to those in Wonderland, depending on a fluid, shifting Other, sliding in and out of focus, offering glimpses and then taking them away, rescuing the adult from despair and then abandoning him. We are in a shaded world now, no longer in golden afternoons; but every now and then we think that—maybe, though probably not, but possibly—the clouds are parting.

The opening poem, "Child of the pure unclouded brow," provides a short form of the play of desire encouraged in the work as a whole, a desire rooted in glum loneliness and self-pity, bitterness and puzzlement, broken, though, by tantalizing suggestions that what is gone may not be gone, that what never was might be regained. The poem begins by saluting the child and then at once slipping into the lip-quivering acknowledgment that "thou and I are half a life asunder"

(p. xxiii). This distance is so extreme it nearly smothers desire: "I have not seen thy sunny face,/Nor heard thy silver laughter./No thought of me shall find a place/In thy young life's hereafter—." These are lines uttered with a sleeve brushing across eyes which are darting daggers through the tears. They look like exit lines: if what we've said were really so, if that is what we really thought, things would have to stop right here. But in looking-glass land, so much older and tireder than Wonderland, these sorts of things are always being said and then withdrawn; the child is recurrently being disowned and then given just one more chance. In this prefatory poem, we are rushed right past the sad finale into appeals to the child to keep the action going, to learn how to remember. All that is asked is that the child listen to the story, but the asking is very much in the form of threats: listen or die! Of course, we threaten in metaphors: "unwelcome beds," "melancholy maidens," and the raging, killing cold outside. "Within," on the other hand, is "the firelight's ruddy glow,/And childhood's nest of gladness." Don't leave the nest and you will not die after all! It is not too late, maybe, even now, to return. The story is written to point out the return route or, even better, to ask you to stay, since maybe you really haven't gone after all. "The magic words will hold thee fast:/ Thou shalt not heed the raving blast." That is almost believable at times; it almost seems that the magic might work its spell, name and fix the child. That it does not hold the child is obvious, is the whole point: *Through the Looking-Glass* builds its longing out of the paltry materials of what might have been.

Alice comes on the scene and at once demonstrates that she is not to be snuggled by doing some extraordinarily excessive snuggling herself: "Do you hear the snow against the windowpanes, Kitty? How nice and soft it sounds! Just as if some one was kissing the window all over outside. I wonder if the snow *loves* the trees and fields..." (p. 5). This is an Alice that has given up altogether the fragile quality of her namesake in Wonderland. Now she is confident, secure in her goals, blindly caught by the future and by growing-up. Gone for good is the open curiosity of the earlier figure, bouncing from adventure to adventure. Now she is seldom even surprised and glides serenely along, reading her mad movement from square to square as progress. In place of the early wild and alien inquisitiveness, Alice now seems to offer that most unerotic of charms, maternal kindness. It is Wendy in Wonderland.

Partly to screen ourselves from the real terror, that the child is no longer there, we enter into play with dark things. We hope somehow that we can wish into being what is hopeless, learn along with the

White Queen how to live with "impossible things," making as many as six of them come to visit before breakfast (p. 54). But we acknowledge that these things must be born out of frightening forms. Humpty Dumpty romps with rootless language, a system of connecting with one another that has no connections. There may be no ties with one's past, no remembering even the horror—unless one makes a memo of it (p. 12). Here, as in the shop run by the Sheep, the shelf we want to pick from always becomes empty; the beautiful rushes we think we have gathered melt away like snow. The Other is more than elusive here; it is always on the edge of disappearing. Perhaps grimmest of all are the pleas made through the Gnat, soft and persistent attempts to woo Alice to come join us and be a child again. The Gnat wants contact, wants jokes; but Alice knows none and finds the Gnat's offerings so poor that their communion, so much desired by the Gnat, finally dwindles to conversation about death. But we keep hoping that play somehow will be revived in the next county or in the next square. For instance, after calmly eradicating the Gnat, Alice is given another invitation, delivered by a beautiful Fawn. In the Wood of No Names where the Fawn leads her, they come together, even touch. But names in the form of order and power return to get them; and the vision is shattered—only to spring back before us again just round the next bend.

Perhaps this hope keeps a death-bed eroticism alive, but barely. There is a spark of arousing resentment against the child, it is true. The titillating notion of punishment is brought up in the frame, in the image of Alice having her punishments "saved up" and exploded on her at the end of a year (p. 5). Later the White Queen quizzes Alice at some length about her experience with being punished, observing that fine as it was that Alice had received these well-deserved chastisements, it would have been very heaven had she been punished as well for all the things she hadn't done: "better still; better and better and better. Her voice went higher with each 'better' " (p. 53), and understandably, given the pitch of imaginative excitement she is reaching. There are also a few of the rude surrogates of the sort that functioned in Wonderland, most notably here the Tweedles and the flowers. Generally, however, the threats issued against Alice are oddly abstract and disembodied—being nothing more than a fragment of the Red King's dream—as if we now had trouble believing in a body, in a real fleshly child anywhere.

The child seems to appear here only in a series of goodbyes, last encounters between a forlorn adult and a barely polite, distracted child or child-that-was. The Gnat and the fawn are succeeded by the climactic farewell with the White Knight, a scene so packed with love and self-pity it is hard to see how Alice could fail to respond. But fail she does, not crying at anything like the rate the Knight had forecast and hardly concealing her impatience as he rides off, so she can trip quickly over the last brook and be a Queen, mate a King, and confirm her betrayal.

There had once been yet another farewell, with an old wasp, where Alice had acted with more Wendy-like kindness, where the grumpy old (about-to-die, actually) Wasp is stirred to acknowledge her kindness—"Good-bye, and thank-ye"—, and where Alice gets a little warm glow from her charity: she was "quite pleased that she had gone back and given a few moments to make the poor old creature comfortable" (p. 139). This chapter on the wasp was never published, and all child-lovers know why. Alice thoughtlessly tripping over the brook, turning her back on the dear old White Knight is terrible—but it has its erotic possibilities. The scene can be replayed and made to come out differently; or, if all else fails, forced to yield the pleasures of indignation. But Alice as familiar, kindly, mothering Wendy: that is crushing. The Otherness of betrayal can be dealt with, but not the prosaic dullness of the sick-nurse. We can, after all, find a way to play with loss, with the elusive and maddening Alice and Peter Pan. We never really wanted them caged.

Notes

1. Barrie, *Peter Pan, or The Boy Who Would Not Grow Up*, Act IV, p. 119. Subsequent references to this play will be cited in the text.

2. Carroll, *Alice's Adventures in Wonderland*, p. 130. Subsequent references will be in the text.

3. Trudgill, *Madonnas and Magdalenes*, pp. 90–91.

4. Carroll, *Through the Looking-Glass*, p. 52. Subsequent references will be cited in the text.

5. Sigmund Freud, "Creative Writers," IX, 146.

6. Probably most readily available in the Signet paperback, misleadingly re-titled *Peter Pan* (New York: New American Library, 1987), p. 1. Subsequent references will be cited in the text under the proper title, *Peter and Wendy*.

7. Fraser, *Death of Narcissus*, p. 76.

8. See Fraser, *Death of Narcissus*, p. 78 and Birkin, *J.M. Barrie & The Lost Boys*, pp. 4–5.

9. Coveney, *The Image of Childhood*, p. 251. The preceding attack on Barrie was also drawn from Coveney, pp. 249–59.

10. Quoted in Birkin, *J.M. Barrie & The Lost Boys*, p. 12.

11. Quoted in Birkin, *J.M. Barrie & The Lost Boys*, p. 155.

12. Quoted in Birkin, *J.M. Barrie & The Lost Boys*, p. 130.

13. Letter to Lady Cynthia Asquith, 24 June 1928; in Viola Meynell, ed., *Letters of J.M. Barrie* (New York: Charles Scribner's Sons, 1947), p. 214.

14. Letter to Lady Cynthia Asquith, 18 January 1924; in Meynell, ed., *Letters of J.M. Barrie*, p. 200.

15. J.M. Barrie, *The Boy David* (New York: Charles Scribner's Sons, 1938), Act I, p. 20. This three-act play opened December 14, 1936.

16. Letter to Milne, 13 October 1910; in Meynell, ed., *Letters of J.M. Barrie*, p. 118.

17. This dramatic line, the curtain line for Act III, has been felt by many as ominous, pretentious, or sick. If one makes "death" the controlling word in the line, I suppose it will seem pretty awful. To me, it is incomprehensible that way. I suggest that we can also put the emphasis on "adventure."

18. Letter to R. Golding Bright (theatrical agent), 29 September [1920]; in Meynell, ed., *Letters of J.M. Barrie*, p. 62.

19. Interestingly, there are indications that the father, at least, has pretty mixed feelings about owning these children and welcomes their release on his own account. His wife, sensing this, sharply asks late in the play, "George, you are sure you are not enjoying it?" (p. 149), "it" being loose enough to include the notion that there have been worse things in Mr. Darling's life than the disappearance of the kids.

20. The discussion of Carroll and the Alice books here is soaked with the wonderful ideas and maybe even phrases of many fine critics and scholars. It is also doused in material I have previously published, repeated here unconsciously. I am especially indebted to the work of Nina Auerbach. Kathleen Blake, Lisa Ede, Donald Gray, Edward Guiliano, U.C. Knoepflmacher, Barry Moser, and Donald Rackin. Rackin especially registers, with remarkably delicate precision, both the aggression and the love flooding the Alices.

21. See Gorham, *The Victorian Girl*, p. 53.

22. Nina Auerbach, *Romantic Imprisonment: Women and Other Glorified Outcasts* (New York: Columbia Univ. Press, 1986), p. 168.

IV

Reading, Watching, Loving the Child

9

The Pedophile Reader: Texts

Look, ma—no hands!

Of course one could talk about exhibitionistic child-texts instead of voyeuristic pedophile-readers; one could say that erotic reading was a perfect match, satisfying the child-text with a watcher just as it gives the reader something evocative to watch. But such reciprocity is a Utopian vision (or excuse) constructed by a formalist/voyeur: it treats the child-text as an object to be described any way we like, imputes quite convenient intentions to it, inscribes a balanced give-and-take in perversions. It is time the agency doing this projecting received some attention.

What does it mean to read with longing, to try to maintain the currents of desire through our seeing? The child has a way not only of always skipping out of reach, which is fine, but of vanishing, which isn't. When that happens, we turn, without a hitch, to one form or another of cinema-in-the-head. J.M. Barrie, left without his boys, still had his memories and his photographs. Even Lewis Carroll, who was uncommonly gifted in procuring replacement children, lived erotically by way of his camera. But the mind's eye is just as handy, perhaps even more active and exciting than these more direct visual aids. Seeing as textual/sexual and reading as seeing: these are whirling connections we have had spun before us many times recently. For those who have trouble keeping those matters straight (me), I will go through an explanation of voyeurism in the next section, optional and not recommended for the fun-loving. Then, I will give some examples of reading the child-in-books with longing, reading as a voyeur in terms prescribed by our particular culture. Because it is our culture, we will not introduce much that is playful into our reader's erotic reading. This will be pornographic power-reading: Larry Flynt, Hulk Hogan, and Wolfgang Iser rolled into one.

Reading as Peeping[1]

In his 1915 "Instincts and Their Vicissitudes," Freud examines repression through one of its most puzzling effects, "the *reversal* of an instinct into its opposite,"[2] particularly the dynamics of sadism/masochism and scoptophilia (voyeurism)/exhibitionism. In both cases, the fundamental instinct originates within the subject: in sadism, as the impulse to master another through violence; in voyeurism, to gain mastery through vision. Both maneuvers seek to control by objectifying, turning the "other" into literal "object."

In the activity of what might be called ordinary seeing, shifts between subject and object occur continually, for seeing involves not just a single position, but a complex movement in which the subject, as part of the process of seeing, possesses the object by relinquishing visual mastery, by *becoming*, in a sense, momentarily the object. In "normal" seeing, this activity, in order to register in our understanding, necessitates an ongoing repression of the position we were in a moment before and an elevation of the substituted position we are in now. That is, it is as though the conscious mind will only tolerate or accept one position or the other, so that at any moment, because one of the positions is being repressed, there is consciousness only of looking *or* of being looked at.

There are, however, extremes, deviations from "normal" seeing, which Freud labels the "perversions" of voyeurism and exhibitionism. These extremes resist the ongoing, alternating repression necessitated by "giving up" the object of vision, and refuse to acknowledge the metaphoric system of shifts by which consciousness of one position or the other is repressed. Voyeurism is, thus, a rigid insistence on maintaining the first position—visual mastery of an object—and a refusal to be seen as an object, thus negating the temporary loss of self (or subject) demanded by the system of substitution which occurs in normal seeing. In exhibitionism, the subject settles into the lost object position with the illusion of permanence, thus erasing the threat of object loss. If *I* am the object, once and for all, there is no danger of it getting up and walking off.

Both of these extreme responses to the lost object position, voyeurism and exhibitionism, have clear and unhappy behavioral consequences. Voyeurism concentrates not only on the position of seeing, but on avoiding the opposite position. Requisite to voyeurism is not just seeing, but doing so from a position of concealment, because concomitant with the insistence on seeing is the insistence on *never being seen*, which arises from the fear that the look of another will overturn the carefully manipulated and protected power equation, threatening to make the voyeur the object of the new viewer's mastering vision. The exhibitionist, by occupying the vacant object position, is always to be looked at and insists on not looking, to show, but never to see. The exhibitionist is as blind as the voyeur is invisible. To see or be shown *something* would squeeze the exhibitionist out of the object position he has moved into precisely because he feared there was no permanent object for him.

Like most of Freud's explanations, this one is elegant, tragically engaging, and satisfying. For all that, it has an explanatory exhibitionism about it, a stability characteristic of the usurpation of the object position he discusses. Implicit in the exhibitionistic display. Freud's included, is a prescribed role and set of response for the audience: admiration and unquestioning acquiescence.

But Lacan and his followers ask the most irreverent questions and consequently destabilize the Freudian structure. To Lacan, consciousness itself is part of an ongoing process of marking and repressing differences. Consciousness, then, is the manifest level of discourse of repression and substitution, and can no longer claim the privileged status which is accorded it by Freudian ego psychology. Robert Con Davis explains this reorganization imposed by Lacan on Freud's theory of seeing: "Lacan has shown that seeing's true aim cannot be visual in any immediate sense: seeing is but a function in a largely unconscious discourse that can be glimpsed in what Lacan calls (extending Freud's discussion), the 'Gaze'—the functioning of the whole system of shifts. . . . The Gaze . . . encompasses the voyeuristic wish not to be seen, and the exhibitionistic wish not to be shown, and the relationship of these 'perversions' (as Freud calls them) points up rather directly the positionality of visual experience *as a text.*"[3] Thus, to Lacan, any conscious text (written or otherwise) is merely a part of a textual system of reciprocity and substitution—discourse—between conscious production and unconscious desire.

What Lacan has done, then, is not only to decenter and de-privilege the surface or manifest text but to call to our attention the existence of an unconscious text, which is also decentered and marked by difference, and which must be simultaneously inscribed within the conscious text. For Lacan, the words of the surface text are simply the conscious extrusion of signifiers which stand in for, metaphorically, signifiers from another chain. Though this manifest text presents the illusion of solidity and centrality, the discourse "is always centered elsewhere in an 'Other' desire. If we look closely at the manifest text, we see something else, a hollowness that inhabits the text—a mere inscription—through and through."[4]

I hasten to add that this Lacanian explanation, subtle and shifting as it is, still is dictated by power. The play must come, if it comes at all, in the deconstructive reading, in a looking that doesn't become hysterical if looked at, that is not interested in possessing—only in tickling into reciprocal activity. Such playful reading may be uncommon in a culture so imprisoned by power, but certain texts may induce an itch that we like to answer with play. These texts we set up in such a way that they can seduce us into trying to seduce them. They spurn us, but not without hinting that we may come again tomorrow. And that was all we actually wanted, all we ever hoped for from goading texts like *David Copperfield*, the arch, winking *Catcher in the Rye*, or the titillating tragedy of *Tess of the d'Urbervilles*.

Desiring David Copperfield

How do we formulate the child David so as to lust after him, not really to snare him in some sadistic/voyeuristic pen but to establish and maintain his alluring Otherness? Little David is so pure, so insistently empty, that we might have trouble not occupying him, taking him over. But even this wide-eyed innocent keeps his distance when it counts, backs off when we get close. He is, as our friend and surrogate Mr. Murdstone notes, very sharp, unpleasantly acute; he looks about him, he observes. He looks back at us, exactly what readers hiding in the bushes do not want. Still, the allures are considerable.

David's early childhood is all fluffiness, an immense feather bed. The hard pews of the church yield to warm drowsiness; soft smells, oozing fruit, lazy butterflies, and crocodiles that turn into vegetables tuck us into this world. There is some motion, but it is the motion of the dance or the welcoming hug. This is the land of cuddles, one where the connections between mother, child, and nurse are so fibrous and tactile that there are hardly clear demarcations among the bodies. With David's father only an Oedipal memory, a comic Lazarus-ghost, the feminine flow and connectiveness is pretty much undisturbed. For the voyeur-reader, it is like having front-row seats at Eden.

Even better, this is a transportable Eden, an Eden-within that goes where David goes and draws others into its purified climate. When he travels to Yarmouth in the third chapter, we glide right along and find nothing changed. Indeed, we discover even more children there, all orphans (of various sizes) with "drowndead"[5] parents happily out of the way. There's no one there to offer comfort but us, no one else to look after or at the merry innocents frolicking on the beach.

The chapter opens with a comic/magical transformation of Yarmouth into Paradise, as David recasts the bleak and flat, "spongy and soppy" landscape into "the finest place in the universe," where there is no limit to what might happen, no limit to our desire in this "Aladdin's palace, roc's eggs and all." Dan Peggotty's unreal ark is made the center of all pedophile reality, the only thing alive and bobbing after the flood in a world otherwise silenced, uncensorious. Who is to question our reading and watching in a place which knows no consequences of any sort, where an angry and punishing God, holding us sternly to account, is reduced to a joke or a gorgeous and untroubling decoration, framed and under our control: "Abraham in red going to sacrifice Isaac in blue, and Daniel in yellow cast into a den of green lions." It's not God ordering up sacrifices here in Yarmouth; it's us ordering up delightful visions. It's a chapter made for looking, David's bedroom being fitted up with a charming window and "a little looking-glass, just the right height for me" (and for us).

The introduction of Little Em'ly into this picture presents us not with a rival or a dispersion but a glorious multiplication. She and David form an affective tableau of innocent flirtation, eroticism on the surface, desire that never leaves off and never is satisfied. Em'ly is always offering her cheek and not letting David kiss her, running off and coming back. He becomes no less the object of our looking when he becomes lover, since his loving simply empties out Em'ly without filling him in: he makes her innocent by confirming his own purity: "I am sure I loved that baby quite as truly, quite as tenderly, with greater purity and more disinterestedness, than can enter into the best love of a later time of life." We know just what he means, and we love him for putting it so well and for being pure enough to think as we think.

David's pedophile reflections confirm and enable our own, guaranteeing their authority and permanence by framing them outside of time: "we had no future," David says; "we made no more provision for growing older than we did for growing younger." So long as we are able to hold our distance, keep on the other side of that enticing window, there's no reason we should ever have to stop looking. We aren't in the Edenic picture, but we never have to move from behind the camera.

It is a sign of our fallen state that we push for something more: resenting not being the star of the play, we try to barge right into the action, and thus bring the world to grief. We don't usually accept responsibility for the disaster, blaming it on Murdstone; but he and his sister parody and represent our own power-world, bring into a field of polymorphous perversity a grim, unplayful sexuality. Cast out from the full eroticism of the garden, then, of full union with the child and with the female, one must settle for what power can give. And what power can offer is just what it always does with children: the constricted game of resentment.

According to the rules of this game, we need to mark off David clearly from his mother and nurse, drive him into our corral. We need to isolate him so we can feel sorry for him and so he will need our protection. And David is as cut off from others as one can be, as Other as they get. Not only do we kill off his mother and banish old Peggotty and, through the Murdstones, put him in our own special form of quarantine; we separate him from all friendly and happy people. Mr. Omer and his family of jolly funeral furnishers giggle and flirt and sing as they work at Mrs. Copperfield's coffin, making David feel more "strange" than ever in his life, "afraid" of these "creatures" he had "been cast away among," creatures "with whom I had no community of nature" (ch. ix). No one has ever been more alone and in need of love.

That's what is finally wanted, obviously; but we have been having fun right along. We don't read patiently, waiting for the isolated child to come into being so we can find our opening; it is the very process of isolating him that is exciting, sadly enough. We mistreat the child with one hand in order to perform a rescue with the other, but we may never get around to rescuing, so enticing is the torture. Once fallen into power, we have little choice but to play at hurting or to hurt while playing. Thus we beat at David, most openly by way of the fiend Creakle, who jokes before he slashes and who finds a "delight" in whipping the boys "which was like the satisfaction of a craving appetite," an appetite that became especially ravenous at the sight of a "chubby" body like David's before him: "He then showed me the cane, and asked me what I thought of *that*, for a tooth? Was it a sharp tooth, hey? Was it a double tooth, hey? Did it have a deep prong, hey? Did it bite, hey? Did it bite?" (ch. vii). David writhes and cries quite according to form, all of these scenes at school borrowing visual and erotic strength, we can be sure, from the more detailed earlier scene with Murdstone, where David entreats and whines and begs like the boys in Swinburne—"Mr. Murdstone! Sir! Don't! Pray don't beat me! I have tried to learn, sir!"—and where the twinings and twistings, strokes of the cane, and in this case David's ill-advised aggressive biting are described lavishly (ch. iv).

We never manage to control the boy utterly—that would spoil the fun—but we are able to keep close enough to him for thirteen chapters so as to put our hands on him when we want him, which is fairly regularly. But then he somehow manages to escape from this lascivious reading: he runs away from danger, runs to Dover and his Aunt Betsey, grows up. The child vanishes from us, probably accounting for the fact that we find the rest of the book a sad falling-off. The curtain has been drawn, and the voyeur-reader is left nearly without an occupation. There are some possibilities there with the child-*like* David and his child-bride, Dora; but these are weak substitutes that themselves disappear shortly. The last four-fifths of the book, the adult part, offers nothing to peep at, nothing to read.

Holding on to Holden

The Catcher in the Rye (1951) has collapsed into the world of Snoopy, E.T., and Bill Cosby: fatuous, sentimental, childish. The book is unguarded, unashamed, show-offy, prancing. It is bratty. It is so sure of itself, so confident of its own charm and knowingness, that it doesn't care what we think. And we despise that. More exactly, we are embarrassed for the novel, embarrassed by it, embarrassed to think how we once were so drawn to it. *The Catcher in the Rye* has the capacity to move us as do memories of certain mortifying times past: not so much times when we were childish or bratty ourselves, but times when we sneakily longed for all the child held out to us. This book makes us squirm because it has not gone away. It simpers and frolics in skirts now far too short, like the forty-year-old Infant Phenomenon it is, a grotesque but still active reminder of our desires.

The long crescendo of desire for *The Catcher in the Rye* corresponds almost exactly with the decades when formalist criticism reigned alone. Thus, the novel has been endlessly *formed*, shaped, fondled, undressed and reclothed in costumes alluring but never final. It has been around for every celebration but has resisted being caught and made into a monument. Hundreds of essays, casebooks, teaching aids have been entered into the public consciousness (that part which attends to such things) on the ground that they had finally got it right, had trapped the wild and elusive Holden and his friends too. But of course they had no hope of catching anything, wouldn't have set out on the hunt if they thought they could shoot the prey, if they thought there was anything to shoot. For behind all the activity is the enticement of nothing, the knowledge that the book inscribes the emptiness we cannot resist, the nothing that was and is the mainspring of desire, the fuel for writing, for driving us to yet one more half-shameful midnight excursion to that old tease.

The Catcher in the Rye seems to us, though no longer so young and fresh as it once was, still pretty cute.[6] There's no escaping that word or that attraction. We have constructed the book as a cute-kid book, about and for cute kids; and thus, however cunningly devised, it is a bit of an embarrassment for academic critics, who are certainly not themselves cute. Any direct interest in the cute is suspect, looks like an erotic skewing; but we sidle toward it all the same. It draws us with its sharpness, pungency, pointedness; it is, to continue with the OED I've been ravaging, pretty, attractive, *taking*. And what does it *take*, when it seems ready to give so much? Well, cute is an aphetic form of acute (sharp, shrewd); and the shortened form runs parallel to cunning (possessing magical knowledge, sly, artful). The book has a craftiness, a form of *konyng* (knowing) and is never innocent. It offers, but it does not hand over; it beckons, but it does not embrace. It takes, it knows. Worst of all, it knows what we are after and, ever so cutely, mocks our desire.

What we pretend to be after is possession. We roar in pursuit of the cunning, the knowing, the cute; we want Holden, the speaker and the unknowing knower, the secret and the emptiness; we want his youth, his promise, his better suitcases. Well, we want really to want them, to chase but not to catch. A romp with this novel is a heightening of pedophilic non-fulfillment, pornography only, mere voyeuristic delight. It offers no Holden in the flesh but Holden in the mind's eye. And it is the nature of this eye (I) that causes the difficulty, hence the emptiness and tantalizing lack, and hence the need to return again and again to this novel. Erotic desire drives reading, in this case a desire to construct and then delight in the sight of an exhibitionistic figure, however vaporous, a figure we try playfully to make into an object. Our zeal to possess or perhaps just control this figure may seem to be considerable, but it rises to such heights only because we know that the figure is beyond control. We imagine that we are searching for optical consummation, a satiating feast for the eyes; but we have no intention of devouring anything or even of locating something that could be devoured. All we want, first and last, is appetite.

We read as playful mock-voyeurs, entering happily into a losing game of hide-and-seek. In this game, we never can be sure who is "it," Holden having a way of switching sides, of turning the seekers into the sought. Here we are, taking on the role of the voyeur, seeking in *The Catcher in the Rye* for the Freudian bliss of the peeper who has locked his object into his sights. But what we focus in on is not, finally, a languid exhibitionist but a productive energy, a voyeur like ourselves, a possessor and a looker, looking naughtily right back at us. This mischievous, alluring, empty child is, of course, constructed as a part of our looking, projected into the happy field of vision wherein we play the game—but that only adds to the fun.

We write as we read, then, in a wonderful, futile meet with this cute text and this cute Holden, trying our hand at objectifying in order to escape being an object, trying to use the text for erotic satisfaction so that we may not be so used—but actually not caring much either way. Only by being foiled do we keep the game and our desire going. Our knowing about the text, finally, cannot match its knowing about us, its knowing even that our serene normality, like Holden's, is shot through with the perverse: "I was probably the only normal bastard in the whole place—and that isn't saying much."[7] We might, if we wanted to, be able to rescue for ourselves some shaky notion of relative normality, even if that isn't saying much, were it not for the fact that we say so much. But our saying implicates us in a desire, however playful, for possession that is made the more complicit by our very failure to possess. We write criticism to show what master hunters we are and end up offering self-portraits of "critic left holding the bag." We want to deny our own pedophiliac voyeurism and thereby confirm it.

In what follows, I will lay out our game as if it were in stages. In the first, we play at capturing Holden, looking at him fixedly and thus fixing him. In the second stage, we discover—alas/hooray—that he has wriggled free and spot him staring impudently at *us*. He then runs slowly away: he never gets quite out of sight, just as he is never found sitting still either, for photographs or for hugs. Actually, these two "stages," separated here for clarity, merge and flash before us, alternating and playing leap-frog. Similarly, and also for clarity, the reader's complex playfulness and mock-serious (though not mock-erotic) activity will be treated with more solemnity than it ever lowers itself to in the actual conduct of the game.

A. Holden as Exhibitionist/Object

Objects of pedophilic desire must initially be vacant if they are to be occupied; that is the first rule. Whether pure or superficially naughty, the child will be in need of help, wanting a comforting parent to take possession. Critics-as-parents of *The Catcher in the Rye* have reached agreement on one significant point: Holden is searching for a "self."[8] He has lost the "self" of childhood and badly needs another. He needs the very self we are ready to give him. The reader is, we are happy to suppose, invited to write Holden, more exactly to paint him according to our fancy and then regale our eyes. Holden is the sort of child we call an "adolescent," a modern invention and a conveniently empty erotic category. As a recent entry in the stages of man, adolescence marks a vacancy, but one highly eroticized. The adolescent has no center apart from a "confused" and "transitional" sexual energy, an energy available precisely because of this emptiness, this powerfully sexualized Otherness.

Holden, then, is partially evacuated by the way his type is conventionally read in our culture. Further, the text seems to allow us even more completely to exhaust the figure of any distracting substance. The opening paragraph first threatens to put on display Holden's early childhood and "all that David Copperfield kind of crap" and then shoos it away, effectively erasing any burdensome past. He later performs a similar maneuver on his future: " 'Oh, I feel some concern for my future, all right. Sure. Sure, I do.' I thought about it for a minute. 'But not too much, I guess. Not too much, I guess' " (ch. 2). Thus he exists only as a now-thing and that now-thing is an erotically loaded no-thing, one who twice in the novel (ch. 1, 25) imagines he may disappear altogether.

I do not want to claim that Holden *is* a sexualized dream-child, only that our hollowing-out allows for that formulation. He can be made to be remarkably unspecified and thus malleable. Even his age and appearance are, so to speak, up for grabs. He is 16, he tells us, at the time of the story, but that number is not to be taken as determinate: "I act quite young for my age sometimes. . . . Sometimes I act like I'm about thirteen. . . . And yet I still act sometimes like I was only about twelve. . . . Sometimes I act a lot older than I am" (ch. 2). Choose whatever you like. Just as invitingly open is his appearance. He is now 6'2" but grew, he says, six inches last year, which allows for anything in a range beginning with a cuddly 5'8". He has grey hair, he says, or at least millions of grey hairs, perhaps all on one side, which may seem a little freakish or, worse, a little mature; but we're just as free to see it as a joke on maturity, especially since it fails to fool any of the many bartenders in the novel. This odd hair, like his size and age, blurs in our view to such an extent that we can color it as we like—also style it: "I wear a crew cut quite frequently" (ch. 1). But "quite frequently" is not always, so our own favorite fashion would do just as well. His features are pretty much a blank. We know that he is thought attractive by many, particularly men and boys but also Sunny, who, like us, finds him "cute" (ch. 13), whatever child-like configuration we may match up with that term.

Holden's language also gives us an opening for draining him and making him even younger. All of his reachings for sophistication quite charmingly exceed his grasp, suggesting a child clomping around in adult shoes: "In New York, boy, money really talks—I'm not kidding" (ch. 10). Most revealing is his management of profane and vulgar language, his ostentatious display of an ambiguous, middle-range profanity: lots of hells, Gods, goddams, a few sonuvabitches. He loves the word *crap*, a half-way house between *do-do* and *shit*. Copulation is "giving the time to." All these expressions, in other words, indicate some awareness and interest; best of all, no experience. His odd prudishness—he has no names for genitals, for instance—is readily readable as an erotic accessibility combined with vacuous innocence. The one departure from this intermediate, vacant language is *ass*. (We might expect *tail* or *butt*.) Holden is quite alert to other people's asses; goes out with the preposterous Sally Hayes only, one gathers, because he wants to see "how cute her little ass looked" (ch. 17); and constantly calls attention to his own ass. The worst thing he can think to say to Sally is that she gives him "a royal pain in the ass" (ch. 17). He has lots of pains in his ass, which must be quite delicate.

He is, in many ways, delicate: slight, lonely, sensitive, refined. He not only has dainty tastes in literature—Ring Lardner, yes; Somerset Maugham, no—but chases after the elegant and the touching everywhere: D.B.'s "The Secret Goldfish," for instance, or the dear obsession with the ducks in Central Park. He's a regular Hallmark card. Aloof not only from sweaty, grunty sports like football—"practically the whole school except me was there" (ch. 1)—he is also distant from his parents and even from the fencing team, which "ostracizes" him. He has been kicked out of school, is neither here nor there. All of this amounts to a perfect erotic figuring of a troubled, withdrawn boy of touchy sensibilities, badly in need of comfort, just the very item with which we are especially well stocked.

He is also willfully blind or, as he puts it, "yellow," precisely because he cannot look: "what scares me most in a fist fight is the guy's face. I can't stand looking at the other guy's face, is my trouble" (ch. 13): a trouble to him but a joy for us to find an exhibitionist who will not, must not, see "the other guy's face." Scared of seeing, the yellow child asks only to be seen in some unprotected way, as in a photograph, offered free as a souvenir to the voyeur-reader.

He can give things away so easily because he is rich, a crude point to raise in an academic book but unavoidable. Holden wears the smell of wealth. He has his hands on plenty of money and, what's more vital, is soiled by it, slightly but enough. He is a youthful decadent, a Yankee Oscar Wilde at puberty. For all Holden's detestation of phonies and his teeming sympathy for the nuns and others with inferior suitcases, he lets us know, often and smugly, that he is so well-heeled he can be ostentatiously indifferent to money. Pencey is "an expensive place," we learn at once; but Holden is even more "expensive," able to be contemptuous of the school and its lousy horse-jumping ads, perhaps because he is so much a part of that world. He is arrogantly boastful about the prissy non-sport of golf (ch. 11) and speaks with airy nonchalance of the "Fourth of July dance at the club" (ch. 18), as if everyone belonged to a club, albeit not the best club. He has a good spoiled-brat laugh at himself for being "a goddam spendthrift at heart. What I don't spend, I lose. Half the time I sort of forget to pick up my change at restaurants and night clubs and all" (ch. 15). His parents make big bucks, he tells us, and he adds to their hefty donations money from an "old as hell" grandmother who "doesn't have all her marbles" but is "quite lavish with her dough" (ch. 7). Poor granny doesn't buy much love from this pampered social critic, who mounts his satire on a platform nicely financed by others, never pausing to consider the source for his profligate, "madman" weekend or his luxurious breakdown. But desiring readers are not going to be balked by such things as this either, noting in his easy assumptions of wealth an important freedom, not from material need so much as from middle-class morals. The ends of the scale, poverty and wealth, goat-herders and princes each fit comfortably with pedophile eros, but not quite so easily the upright sons of shop-keepers.

But a readerly construction of Holden along sexual lines, especially along perverse sexual lines, will naturally move eventually to nothing less than direct textual sex-stuff—overt sexual doings, sexual talk, sexual symbols. There is certainly plenty in the book one might construe in this way, doubtless the reason that true moronic perverts have had good success in censoring it. But how coherent is this sexual discourse, and where does it lead? As for conventional matters, we note that Holden is befuddled but eagerly interested: "I am quite sexy" (ch. 8). He certainly is most comfortable around girls who present no particular sexual opportunity or threat: old Selma Thurmer, for instance, who "wasn't exactly the type that drove you mad with desire" (ch. 1) but who is very much the type liked by Holden despite that or, we may suspect, because of that. The nuns are a more blatant example, and in the same ballpark are Ernest Morrow's mother, who "had quite a lot of sex appeal, too, if you really want to know" (ch. 8), and the Wicker Bar's kindly hat-check woman, whom Holden tries to date and who reminds him pointedly (and he repeats it to us pointedly) that "she was old enough to be my mother and all" (ch. 20).

And we might run a very dusty course with that "and all": Holden wants to sleep with his mother, you see. From the short glimpse we have of his mother, it's not clear why; but then, according to the rules governing this game, mothers are certain to spark sexual interest/ disgust in their sons. Just so, Holden is afraid of girls his own age, at least as regards sexuality: his root problem is, by this line, his "inability to relate sexually to females."[9] The root problem with this formulation is that it is so right. The evidence can be extended forever in an orgy of case-making: Holden can be aroused only by girls from whom he can protect himself by a screen of contempt: Sally Hayes (the phony ass-pain) and the cretin ("pretty ugly" but "sort of cute") Bernice Crabs (or is it Krebs) at the Lavender Room. With Jane Gallagher, whom he likes, he plays checkers and holds hands. He grows nauseous at the idea of Stradlater's imagined violation of her,[10] and denies urgently any notion that he has sexual designs on her himself: "I really got to know her quite intimately. I don't mean it was anything *physical* or anything—it wasn't—but we saw each other all the time. You don't always have to get too sexy to get to know a girl" (ch. 11). Always? How about *never*? As he screams to Luce, "I can never get really sexy— I mean *really* sexy—with a girl I don't like a lot" (ch. 19). Or, we might say, with one he does like a lot. It is easy to see why Ernest Jones found the Freudian reading of the book (which is all he had to give it) so tedious.[11] Holden is having the banal problems that beset every adolescent male: sex is manifestly crucial but is associated with the dirty; mother is not dirty, of course; but we mustn't think of *that* association—as if we could think of anything else; and so on.

Just as drearily expectable are his mild homosexual gestures and not-so-mild homophobia. "He is," in a resoundingly obvious way, "attracted to—and attracts homosexuals."[12] Holden is fully aware of the last half of this formulation and perhaps of the first. He is fascinated by Luce and the bar full of "flits" (Luce, he thinks, being one of them); he suggests that Ernest Morrow's ass-snapping with a towel is a form of sadistic homosexuality; Mr. Antolini clearly arouses in him a tendency to project his own desires—or part of them—onto others. Even more revealing, if we make them so, are his sentimental reveries, particularly of the time "I and Robert Tichener and Paul Campbell were chucking a football around in front of the academic building," *chucking* carrying the suggestive traces of tickling under the chin and of "yielding" or "giving in." It grows darker and darker, but "we didn't want to stop what we were doing." He loves that sort of memory, he says, for the orgasm of nostalgic bliss it provides: "If I get a chance to remember that kind of stuff, I can get a good-by when I need one" (ch. 1).

In this dive back into memory, it is the dive itself rather than the content of the vision that attracts an erotic construction. It's not so much that a titillating rendering of the scene is available as the fact that the scene is set so firmly in memory and is staged so acquiescently. Perhaps surprisingly, sexual desire in this case is not fueled by direct references to sex. Holden is Oedipally troubled, misreads or overreads sexual signals, and so forth; but all in such a way as to leave him pretty much what we have been taught to regard as "normal." But that word, like "purity," asserts nothing: normal is the absence of the abnormal, nothing at all in itself. The most extended sexual episode in the novel, with Sunny and Maurice, assaults and thus confirms Holden's innocence and, more importantly, propels him backwards into childhood memories: to Allie and Bobby Fallon. The regressive turn helps fix him, empty him out, as does his rendering of the humiliating encounter with Maurice into fantasy: "Old Maurice had plugged me" (ch. 14).

Noisily overt sexual matters, then, signal little to the patterns of desire being traced, but some quiet episodes early in the novel present the possibility of a richly erotic scenario: Holden as boy-object, blind and exhibitionistic, performing for us (or our surrogate) erotically. Take the unlikely occasion of his visit to old Spencer in the second chapter. No event would seem to be designed more clearly to repress sexual interest. That's the point. The scene doesn't reek with sex; it reeks with Vicks Nose Drops, nor is Spencer described in anything like the way one would want to imagine oneself in such situations: he is decrepit, wearing pajamas and a ratty old bathrobe, draped in an Indian blanket, his bumpy disgusting chest and white hairless legs gaping through the folds. He is pretty dim-witted, a "nice old guy that didn't know his ass from his elbow." He picks his nose. This is not the distinguished, smoking-jacket fatherly, greying-at-the-temples-handsomely appearance we wanted for our surrogate. Still, the very repulsiveness of Spencer can work wonderfully as a screen to allow complete erotic expression with only minor (but crucial) displacements. Spencer, first of all, situates Holden where he wants him—on a bed. He then insists over and over on Holden's youth, pasting the term "boy" on him a maddeningly redundant fourteen times in the space of a short chapter. (Holden uses it six times himself, as if accepting the script.) So there they are, the old man and the boy alone, the boy on the bed (that word popping up seven times), where his ass—used three times (along with "crap" and "turd")—is hurting. The pedophile translation of this pain could suggest sodomy or perhaps spanking: he "looked like he'd just beaten hell out of me in ping-pong or something." The ostensible subject of their talk is *flunking* the boy, a flunking which is first re-enacted (Holden must read the exam aloud), then extended (textualized, made into pornography), and then excused:

> "Do you blame me for flunking you, boy?" he said.
> "No, sir! I certainly don't," I said. . . .
> ....
> "Tell the truth, boy."
> . . . I told him how I would've done exactly the same thing if I'd been in his place. . . .

All in all, we can fiddle this into the kind of fantasy we pretend we are looking for: a sexual encounter, carried out, memorialized, and justified.

The book, then, can be positioned as a rehearsal of voyeuristic desire, but one wonders how long it can be held that way. We can put inconvenient signals out of the way for a time, turn our back on them, but soon we get turned inside out. Voyeurism, the creation of a pure subject, defines itself in reference to exhibitionism, pure object, and is thereby dependent on and contaminated by its opposite. It wants only to be subject, only to look; but it soon finds itself being looked at. The initially compliant exhibitionist has become the threatening one who sees,[13] and we are left powerless. Try as we will to hold onto our position, this slippery transition will take place. The reader is being read, the writer written, the critic criticized.

B. Holden as Voyeur/Subject

This unwelcome turn probably starts hitting us as we try to deal with Ackley and Stradlater. Ackley, introduced first, seems a more extreme version of Spencer: he is intimately associated with fingernails, pimples, snot, toe-jam, and mossy teeth. Quite revolting (and thus a perfect cover). Sharing a bathroom with Holden, Ackley has untold advantages. He also seems a more obvious voyeur than Spencer, nervously disdainful of Holden lest he be found out but taking every opportunity to satisfy himself: "He always picked up your personal stuff and looked at it"; "He'd even pick up your jock strap or something" (ch. 3). Holden initially plays (or parodies) for Ackley/reader the desired role of object by pulling his hunting hat down over his eyes: "That way I couldn't see a goddam thing." But this compliant blindness soon becomes sadistic: he twists around on his mossy neighbor, makes Ackley into an object, upsetting any artful, displaced entry the voyeur-reader may have attempted by way of Ackley: "I know it annoyed hell out of old Ackley. He always brought out the old sadist in me. I was pretty sadistic with him quite often" (ch. 3).

Stradlater is another matter. Handsome, assuming a natural superiority to Holden, very physical with him—he greets him with "two playful as hell slaps on both cheeks" (ch. 3)—Stradlater drives out the unwelcome Ackley and puts Holden once again on display. Before long, Holden is back in character, doing a movie tap-dance, so Stradlater/reader can watch him: "All I need's an audience. I'm an exhibitionist" (ch. 4). Perfect! Finally we've got it. But we don't, of course. First, the exhibitionist turns nasty: "I didn't answer him right away. Suspense is good for some bastards like Stradlater" (ch. 4). Holden then pushes us out of the way and becomes the voyeur himself: he sees Stradlater as "a Year Book kind of handsome guy," all framed and set for viewing; he follows him to the can to watch this knockout shave; "I just watched him" (ch. 6), he says, as Stradlater undresses. His worries about Stradlater's sexual activities with Jane, his obsession with the idea, suggest also his own voyeuristic delights, his use of Stradlater. So Stradlater is no better for us than Ackley; he too becomes an object, switches places. Where is the voyeur-reader to go?

It's not that Holden never again sets himself up as an object; it's just that he won't stand still and, most of all, won't keep that hunting cap down over his eyes. We may enjoy the Sunny and Maurice interlude, which, though vulgar, does punish Holden and reduces him to powerlessness. But the hotel in which all this takes place, "full of perverts" (ch. 9), seems to bring out the old voyeur in Holden. He peeks regularly out of his own windows and into the windows of others to spot the crummy stuff going on: "Anyway, first he'd take a swallow and squirt it all over *her*, then she'd do it to *him*—they took *turns*, for God's sake. You should've seen them" (ch. 9). *I*? *I* should've seen them? Whatever for? Holden admits, "This kind of junk is sort of fascinating to watch, even if you don't want it to be," an uncomfortable sort of reflection, unless we're fully into the play—which we are.

Even his warmest thoughts of Jane shove us out of the position and role we thought we were in, comforting her as he does and using the opportunity for caresses, "the closest we ever got to necking" (ch. 11). He twice expresses an indifference to how he *looks*, and says he won't commit suicide only because he can't abide the idea of being looked at. What has happened to our cute exhibitionist? Even the later episode with Mr. Antolini, set up to give us, at last, an ideal surrogate in the witty, handsome, and caring older man, turns sour. Antolini has everything the way he (or at least we) want it: a lonely, beautiful boy going to bed right there (minus pajamas). But Holden's panic reduces Antolini and us to fear and pleading.

Worse, Holden begins noticing more and more pedophile objects of his own. First, there's the little boy singing, the "swell kid" with the "pretty little voice," and, even better, "parents who paid no attention to him" (ch. 15). The song he sings, a ballad of guiltless seduction—"If a body kiss a body,/ Need a body cry?"—is a nearly flawless rendition of pedophilic fantasy: playful and gratuitous love. It is made absolutely perfect by Holden's turning the light and transitory "meet a body" into "catch a body," into permanent possession. It is the strategy of the photographer, of the practiced voyeur, of the Lewis Carroll who often spoke of owning the heart-love of a child. He *owns* as Holden *catches*, attempting to change the song, arrest the growth, make the whole world into a Wonderland with the unattached, pretty child always there.

Holden's course continues as he stoops to tighten the little girl's skate: "God, I love it when a kid's nice and polite when you tighten their skate for them or something. Most kids are. They really are" (ch. 16). He happily encounters the small boy with his pants open, winding toward two images of stasis and control: the museum and the endless circling of the carousel. These climactic voyeuristic scenes connect, of course, with his over-affectionate little sister, Phoebe, who is his chief focus throughout. The erotic dimensions of that relationship have been ably traced by James Bryan,[14] but it is worth noting here that it is Holden who paces another's bedroom, picking up, examining, *looking at* her "personal things" (ch. 21): her discarded clothes, the material on her desk, the writing inside her notebooks—"I can read that kind of stuff, some kid's notebook, Phoebe's or anybody's, all day and all night long. Kid's notebooks kill me" (ch. 21). We know the feeling, but we thought we were, in fact, reading something like a kid's notebook. We thought we had a corner on that particular market.

At the end, Holden confirms his voyeuristic power, repeating four times, "I'll watch ya" to Phoebe's invitation to join her on the carousel: "Then the carousel started, and I watched her go around and around" (ch. 25). And around and around and around. Holden has "matured," only if one identifies maturity with an arrest, a paralysis of subject and object: "I felt so damn happy all of a sudden, the way old Phoebe kept

320 / *The Pedophile Reader*

going around and around. I was damn near bawling, I felt so damn happy, if you want to know the truth. I don't know why. It was just that she looked so damn *nice*, the way she kept going around and around, in her blue coat and all. I wish you could've been there" (ch. 25).

C. The Reader Left Playing

Thanks just the same, but we don't exactly want to be there now. There's no place for us to stand, nothing for us to see. Holden has mischievously shoved in front, stolen the scene and all the looking, grabbed all the best lines and the bows. Besides, voyeurs only work solo. Holden has earlier expressed the cute desire to telephone authors with whose sensitivities he feels a kinship: "I'd rather call old Thomas Hardy up. I like that Eustacia Vye" (ch. 3). We had, for a moment, a better deal—not a telephone call but a kind of video tape where we could watch old Holden to our heart's content. Rerun it, freeze the frames. We imagined that we had caught the catcher in our lens. But that clumsy sort of possessive desire is turned back on us, our presumed command of the subject position exposed as foolish posturing, like that of old Spencer or Ackley. But, as an alternative, we are offered a much more supple, lilting form of desire, one which allows us to write criticism as a form of sexualized play, feigning control over this material in order to block the deconstruction of our voyeurism, when we are actually ensuring it. Really, all we want is the game itself, the chance to write for control and fail and then write again, play some more, keep the desire alive and the game spinning along.

Tragic Play With Tess

The game is different with Tess, partly because we have to struggle some to keep her a child, to anticipate and parry her attempts to claim something more. She may fight to give herself substance, to be adult; but our reading tries to keep her as empty as the day she was born. The play, of necessity, becomes a little rough, like a game of tag with sledge-hammers. Trying to hold onto the object, then, we may just happen to murder it; respecting Tess's childhood (and our own erotic needs) may, regrettably, demand her smothering. Such play, as Meredith says, "the devils might appal,"[15] and there's certainly the chance that the grisly direction of the game might send some readers heading for home. This is peculiar play, no longer the self-conscious artfulness of Holden's switcheroos, where voyeurism was never serious about its aims and welcomed being foiled. Here the voyeurism threatens actually to claim its prize, to turn into unrestrained collecting, a full-throated sadistic howl. Tess hasn't the chances to escape that Holden has; we will not give them to her. She starts the game with overwhelming handicaps.

But it is, all the same, a very popular game, in and out of novels. Tess is made available to a discourse of torture in large part because that is the language in which we play with women and children, often making no distinction between the two.[16] Here is play in its most irresponsible form, play conducted with hatchets and machine-guns, play that should be saved from itself, play most in need of the decentering into love. There'll be plenty of time later to worry about what will save us from love. For now, we need to see how play can betray us, can lead us into pleasures we wish we did not relish so.

A. You Did Not Come

"Somebody might have come along that way who would have asked him his trouble, and might have cheered him. . . . But nobody did come, because nobody does; and under the crushing recognition of his gigantic error Jude continued to wish himself out of the world."[17] This is Hardy at the bone: the ache, the plain longing for help, for a kinder scheme of things. The *somebody* who might but does not happen by with a coherent explanation of, variously, Greek grammar, women, or the universe is Hardy's central character. Explanations, compassion, contact of some sort, even a hug or a touch of the hand, ought to be forthcoming. But they are not: "nobody did come, because nobody does." Hardy's fiction runs on this motor, on the propulsive hope for that which, very definitely, will not be, an image which cannot be realized. This absent ghost is called into being in the minds of decent, struggling characters who have somehow attracted to themselves the attention of careless, impersonal agencies who strew pain around, particularly upon the good, without reason and without end. These recurrent tragic or absurdist destructions move always on the ergs of absence; without the impalpable image of what cannot be there, nothing would be possible.[18] Without this never-present *somebody*, there would be no desire and no novel.

As it is, *somebody* doesn't show up, right on cue, and all is well. Not being there, *somebody* is much more energizing than any presence could be. *Somebody* becomes an image that can be decked out in any form whatever and, just as important, used for the exercise of nearly any feeling, erotic ones not excluded. Whoever speaks in Hardy typically assumes a passive role, feels cheated, left hanging by the nonappearance of *somebody*. In fact, that broken appointment provides a motive for extraordinary activity, beginning with the effective killing of *somebody* and continuing with a manipulation of the corpse so as to provide an outlet for all manner of stagings and emotional eruptions. Like a skilled murderous mortician with necrophilic tastes, then, the characters, narrators, and readers can cavort themselves in ways a real live presence would certainly resist. This play of turning absence into malleable image is so often eroticized that I'd like to focus on the process, particularly on the sadistic form that such eroticism usually takes in the novel. But first, as a warm-up, a poem, "A Broken Appointment":

> You did not come.
> And marching Time drew on, and wore me numb.—
> Yet less for loss of your dear presence there,
> Than that I found lacking in your make
> That high compassion which can overbear
> Reluctance for pure lovingkindness' sake
> Grieved I, when, as the hope-hour stroked its sum,
> You did not come.
>
> You love not me,
> And love alone can lend you loyalty;
> —I know and knew it. But, unto the store
> Of human deeds divine in all but name,
> Was it not worth a little hour or more
> To add yet this: Once you, a woman, came
> To soothe a time-torn man; even though it be
> You love not me?[19]

Certainly this woman did us a great favor by staying away; we can scarcely imagine Hardy writing an interesting poem on the subject had she come. And that's because she does the speaker of the poem a great favor too. He can, thereby, set the poem nicely in memory, that great theater for endlessly revisable, self-satisfying drama. He can also transform her absence into an uncomplaining cadaver that will oblige him by taking any form, accepting any imposition of motive, welcoming his desire.

The poem draws its self-pitying force from that which wasn't (because it never is) to be: a joyous and fulfilling meeting with his lover—or what he thought was his lover—at the hope-hour—or what he thought was the hope-hour. Through her non-appearance, Hardy can create, first, a blunt image of faithless bitchiness and a shadow image of beautiful constancy. The reiterated "You did not come" of the first stanza carries a shadow, "You might have come," and the "You love me not" of the second stanza suggests "You still might love me." The hectoring, self-satisfied argument of the first stanza runs: what really grieves me is that I found you a brute, incapable even of common sympathy or compassion. This argument contains within its apparent protective name-calling an alternate strain of wooing, talk of "your dear presence" and of the sweet possibility of "loving-kindness." This is an odd form of courtship, perhaps, though probably not so uncommon. It masks with its lip-quivering acceptance of finality and utter desolation—"you did not come"; "you love not me"—undercurrents that run all this negativity toward hope, twisting the finality into a new beginning. The second stanza, after all, turns to a kind of pleading—couldn't you have done at least this?—and projects for its audience an image of a woman coming to soothe a time-torn man, a fulfillment, a possibility that moves the poem out of the past and into the future. The argument thus runs: you have proved yourself beneath contempt; that's closed and settled—on the other hand, I will hold out to you the prospect that it's not all closed and settled, that you still have a chance to reclaim yourself and, incidentally, me as well.

Benumbed or crushed sexual desire is thus belied by rising sexual expectation. But to read the poem in this way, to foreground a psychology of grief and hope, is, perhaps, to miss all the fun. Another way to receive the poem is as an expression of sexual anger, an exercise in sadistic revelry. Why does the poem, first of all, keep going on past its many endings? "You did not come" in the first line seems conclusive enough; it represents, after all, the extent of his knowledge on the subject. The poem threatens to stop after these four words. Further, "I know and knew it" (l. 11) would seem to close off the inquiry into *why* she didn't come: she doesn't love him; that being so, there is no particular reason why she should come. The poem really works, however, on the extending "Yet" (l. 3) and "But" (l. 11), which function not to qualify but to ignore the conclusions, to keep things proceeding illogically to the real business of the poem: the creation of images and the projection of a psychology of resentment. He hopes not that she will come some other time or learn after all to love him; he hopes to give pain. Thus he creates a host of certainties: she will receive and attend to his message, first of all, feel the full force of these manufactured images. Next, he refuses to consider alternate possibilities for her absence: that she may have been thrown by her horse, struck senseless by a falling timber, eaten by wild beasts. Such things would spoil the narrative he and we are having such fun with, complicate the images we are sneering at.

And what images these are! In the first stanza he concocts her as one missing something in her "make" (her essence and that of her parents too; a genteel equivalent of "Yo mama!"), namely that "high compassion" which would humanize her to the extent that she would not be controlled by something so trifling as mere "reluctance." But with her it's not a question of high compassion or high anything; she cannot manage even "lovingkindness," a kind of undemanding cozying-up we would think even dogs could muster—but not her. She is missing from him, you see, because she is missing a good deal inside. He, on the other hand, has oodles of character, unselfishly lamenting not his own loss but the discovery of her (presumably genetic) character defects. Self-pity, that is, barely masks or cooperates with the delight in furious name-calling, a kind of letter-to-the-editor luxury he allows himself more openly in the second stanza, where he changes the image of himself from one of sturdy, if wounded rectitude to one of time-torn pitiableness in order to extend, with variations, the attack on her. She is so self-consumed, he says, she cannot spare even that "little hour or more." Now why this particular hour ("or more," depending on how things might have developed, one supposes) is "little" might seem unclear, but Hardy's "little hour" is certainly kin to popular conceptions of "little Nell" or "little Eva": packed with sobs. This stanza is also packed with fury. Since she chooses not, or is not fitted, to add to divine deeds, she is, one might presume, Satanic. No poem could more plainly manufacture an image, tell it to go to hell, and then send it there.

Such manufactures are not, of course, turned out by the poem but by us. And that such goods are erotically freighted, sadistically charged, we will admit, confessing also that it is the "loss of your dear presence there" that releases the rage, that in turn creates the obsessive images, and that allows us to pour such fantastic energy out over these images. Nowhere are such energies, released by loss, given such room to play as in *Tess*.

A. Vaporizing Tess

What disappears most emphatically in *Tess* is Tess—and long before she is objectified as the black flag that marks her obliteration. Struggling throughout the novel to bring herself into palpable, demonstrable being, Tess's self, most especially her body, keeps being taken up into mere form, into the handy, self-serving formulations of others. These others objectify her by separating her into parts, submitting these parts to a curious blurring process, and then eroticizing this blur as a wonderfully chameleon image. Tess takes on any shape for those she meets, but always a conveniently empty shape, ready to be filled in and then longed for. In a hazy form, she fits perfectly into erotic fantasies, especially fantasies where sexual feeling and sexual pleasure are not only unfocused, spread all over the body, but somehow totally unindividualized, making no distinctions between the participants, flowing from one to the other.

As we have seen (in ch. 7), this absorbing, non-genital sexual drama is enacted most commonly in the discourse of sex and pain, in erotic spanking fantasies, where the sexual sensation is said to be undifferentiated, both (or all) parties sharing the same generalized and intense erotic feeling. In order to fit Tess into this play, she is subject to continual vanishing acts, acts performed by sadistic and voyeuristic magicians so insistent that they kill her, finding, it seems, the ideal object in a corpse they can dress up and manipulate at will. But this *they*, it is time to admit, is *we* or, if you insist, *me*, acting by way of the novel's two somewhat heavy-handed players, Alec and Angel.[20] These two, by different means, show us how to play the game, even authorize our entry into it. Before turning to these pedagogues, though, these lovers we pretend to hate, I'll look briefly at how Tess is already distanced, blurred, emptied out for us by the novel generally and by our cooperating narrator.

This creation of absence in the novel is intimately connected to a need to distance experience by means of generalization, oversized reflections, abstractions—in short, by "the habit of taking long views"[21] the narrator marks sarcastically as characteristic of the age. This habit, he says, flattens "emotions to a monotonous average" (ch. 1); it also makes so remote the physical and particular that it acts to drain them of substance, to obliterate them. The narrator himself habitually takes the long views he mocks: "It is a vale [Blackmoor] whose acquaintance is best made by viewing it from the summits of the hills that surround it," the details of the "recesses" being apt "to engender dissatisfaction" (ch. 2). We are urged to take our satisfactions from the remote, the soft and pleasing vagueness of the faraway. Too close an acquaintance with details will not do; and it is with people just as it is with landscapes. The narrator makes acquaintance—and keeps acquaintance—with characters in the same way, not only distancing them (and us) with equivocations but treating them as "forms," "shapes," "images."

Tess is introduced as something of a blur: "She was a fine and handsome girl—not handsomer than some others, possibly—but her mobile peony mouth and large innocent eyes added eloquence to colour and shape" (ch. 2). Even those features we look at—the peony mouth and those large eyes—are strangely dissociated, unintegrated, and are, further, quickly dissolved into the murk, made contributory to "colour and shape," whatever they are. "Possibly" there is no difference at all between Tess and the smear of white that constitutes the other girls, apart from her accidental red ribbon, a pathetic insistence on textile particularity that prefigures the black flag that finally contains her. Angel looks down on her from the hill and sees her as a "white shape," ominously "so soft in her thin white gown" (ch. 2) he longs for her even then. Her own family sees her as the same blank "white shape" (ch. 7) as she leaves for the d'Urberville farm. Tess cannot escape these hazy forms: even puberty comes on her only as "a luxuriance of aspect" (ch. 5).

Tess tries somehow to form a being for herself but knows deep down that she is simply a part of an unindividualized historical pattern and that if she reads she will discover "in some old book somebody just like me, and . . . [learn] that I shall only act her part" (ch. 19). To others, she is only a generic image, "a fine and picturesque country girl and no more" (ch. 2), "only a passing thought" (ch. 14), "but a transient impression, half forgotten" (ch. 5). No wonder she repeats after all the historical pattern she had feared, the one so common to women: turning to men and sexual relations in an attempt to establish an existence or a self she can find nowhere else. The men, tragically, are the last ones who want a self thrust at them; they are, like the narrator and like us, only too satisfied with a "white shape."

B. Hating Alec

Poor Alec Stoke d'Urberville is made to bear the load of our desperate wish to dissociate ourselves from responsibility for these sadistic-murdering dynamics, while participating in them at the same time. Alec is set up, as all readers have noted with relief, as an unmistakable, moustache-twirling stage villain, presumably without conscience but with a surplus of animal drives. He is, we guess, all genitals and no heart, and can thus focus and drain off resentment and fear, protecting at the same time our involvement in the play. Tess and most readers position him as a contrast, a black foil to Angel's whiteness (and her own), to the narrator's grim compassion, and to the reader's stalwart decency. We code Alec as a monster—or try to. After all, he likes flash clothes, fast horses, money, and pretty child-women. He not only likes pretty girls; he likes to scare them and to sleep with them. Unlike us.

The series of signals we solidify as "Alec" functions as a loaded and deceptive rhetorical ploy, inviting us to imagine a comforting distance where there is none. It is true that we can see Alec as something of an animated sadism machine; but he differs from customary operations only by being somewhat crude, obvious in his devices (and by being better natured, more kindly than most). He functions all on the surface and threatens to give the game away. We are so bombarded in front with his unsubtle mode of operating that we really ought to be expecting some sneak assault from the rear.

Alec is frightening to us partly because he and the force he represents seem so pleasantly impersonal. He puts Tess on his sexual rack simply because she has wandered by; any other "crumby" girl would do as well. He has no other way of proceeding but by the instruction manual of sadism: absence and pain. The narrator suggests that he performs his erotic torturing acts even on his blind old mother, who loves her son "resentfully," is "bitterly fond" (ch. 9). We are unlikely to notice much the narrator's comment that such ghastly perversion is not so perverse after all but really rather common: "Mrs. d'Urberville was not the first mother compelled to love her son resentfully...."

With Tess, his moves are obvious. He announces as much with his first words, "Well, my Beauty, what can I do for you?" (ch. 5). Tess exists for him, from the beginning, as an abstraction, as "Beauty," that is, as no more than a vaguely formed image. She is, further, *his* Beauty, that he can do for, with, or to, as he likes. This image of Beauty becomes specific for him only in reference to her "luxuriance of aspect" (ch. 5) (breasts?) and her social class: "You are mighty sensitive for a cottage girl" (ch. 8). The ugly snobbishness is less offensive to us than the depersonalizing type-casting. But variations on this same term, "cottage girl," are used by Angel and by the narrator. They read the term a little differently: the narrator personalizes it a little; Angel purifies it idyllically; Alec debases it. But it is a *term* they (and we) are reading, not Tess (whatever we take "Tess" to mean), and it is a purely literary term, adaptable to different genres: the narrator reads it in reference to psychological realism, Alec the pastoral idyll, Alec naturalism. But all deal only in images. Tess is expelled so that the image can prevail.

The image Alec produces then can be terrified and hurt, eroticized and controlled. His driving a horse that he says once nearly killed him and that he nearly killed in return is an obvious instance. He can both pain and master Tess in the same way, and he does: "her large eyes star[ed] at him like those of a wild animal" (ch. 8), says the narrator, who seems to be caught up in Alec's procedures, offering to him and to us the perfect simile. For a *wild* animal exists in this form only to be *tamed*, and that is exactly what Alec sets about doing, stamping her with "the kiss of mastery" (ch. 8) and forcing from her the admission, "See how you've mastered me!" (ch. 12). This mastery involves investing her with the proper response, which is not adoration but anger—"I hate and detest you!" (ch. 8)—an anger basic to sadism and precisely, as the narrator says (ch. 11), what Alec wants.

Her "confused surrender awhile" (ch. 12) follows from all this as a matter of course. It is not that she is stunned by the rape so much as that Alec has successfully sent her packing and can do what he will with the image she has left behind. She is simply caught in the relentless working out of the sadistic plotting. The scene of her rape is presented so entirely in the way of absences that a term like "rape" signals only our need to fill up the emptiness somehow, to suppose that maybe there are two *people* involved. There are, in fact, only forms; at least Tess is only a form. Whatever it is we picture as happening, at any rate, is prefigured by a remarkable scene of grotesque blending: wild dancing, whirling and collapsing figures, clouds of dust, an odd and unreal light, the "twitching entanglement of arms and legs": "of the rushing couples there could barely be discerned more than the high lights—the indistinctness shaping them to satyrs clasping nymphs" (ch. 10). It is a marvelous stroke to make the active shaping agency here "indistinctness" itself. Unwillingly, we are free to suppose, Tess adds to the sadistic foreplay, teasingly offering both resistance and compliance, an indecisiveness Alec is free to read as a flirtatious show, the sadist's dream: "She drew a quick pettish breath of objection, writhing uneasily on her seat, looked far ahead, and murmured, 'I don't know—I wish—how can I say yes or no when—' " (ch. 11).

What is raped or seduced, then, is "a pale nebulousness at his feet, which represented the white muslin figure" (ch. 11). Note that the expulsion of Tess is doubled in force here: she is replaced by the familiar white figure, which in turn is vaporized into an even more adaptable "pale nebulousness," a distant representation of a representation. It is, we note, the narrator who is doing this "figuring" and "nebulousing," though perhaps he is representing, though still cooperatively, Alec's perception. When we leave Alec as he stoops over Tess and join the narrator, however, we do not see much change. The narrator describes whatever it is that is going on as enacted "upon this beautiful feminine tissue, sensitive as gossamer, and practically blank as snow." All this about tissue, gossamer, and blankness should be familiar to us by now. It is the voice of the sadist.

Alec's later career invites us further to compartmentalize and channel our protective outrage, to regard these sadistic currents as little ugly rivulets and not the main channel—certainly not what we are swimming in as we read. Alec stirs within Tess only the feeblest of attempts to assert a being, a presence. When she offers the sad but conventional explanation, "I didn't understand your meaning until it was too late," Alec retorts, "That's what every woman says." This awakens what the narrator calls her "latent spirit," but the best that latent spirit can do is, "Did it never strike you that what every woman says some women may feel?" (ch. 13). Tess can manage only to qualify the generalization, not to specify herself. She is still indistinguishable from "some women," scarcely more individualized than "a cottage girl" or "a white shape." Alec thus has an easy time reappropriating her later on in his devices of sexual play, now refined to include pain for both parties. He has discovered the pleasures of "having a good slap at yourself" (ch. 45) and initiates Tess into those delights. When she whales him with her mace-like glove and bloodies him up, she invites him to "punish me! . . . whip me, crush me" (ch. 47). Perhaps things have developed now to a grim reciprocity, where Tess is able to absent Alec the way he does her, reducing him to "a spot," a figure of blood. But the mechanisms involving us are the same, and it's hardly cheering to see them being exposed so openly; since that puts at risk our own involvement in the sadistic play, which has been, all along, wholehearted.

C. Just Your Average Angel

Angel, we hope, is a different matter. Despicable as we may find him, we want to locate or invent a difference. So does Tess, and she has every apparent justification for doing so. She is lured into the valley that contains Crick's dairy and Angel partly on the basis of its difference from Blackmoor: "The secret of Blackmoor was best discovered from the heights around; to read aright the valley before her it was necessary to descend into its midst" (ch. 16). This spot seems to disdain the terrifying abstractions, the murdering distances, and to promise discrimination, particularity, being. Tess tries to assert that difference immediately, reading on her first view of Angel a "something . . . differing" beneath his ordinary dairyman's attire. She sees the attire as mere camouflage for distinctiveness, as she tries to do unto others what has certainly not been done unto her. Through the vale and through Angel, she wants to individualize and thus escape the nothingness forced on her by earlier sadistic patternings. But Angel is not the ticket out of that Inferno. He is, in fact, only a form himself, "not altogether a distinct figure," containing a "something nebulous" in and about him (ch. 18). Tess, ironically, is beginning to fill him up just as Alec filled her, and she soon, accordingly, finds herself creating erotic sensations mixed inextricably with pain.

Angel sits at an open window strumming on his harp, as Tess wanders in a garden outside (ch. 19). Of course it is, as the narrator insists, the commonplace window of an ordinary dairyman's house; Angels' harp and his musical abilities are frankly "poor"; the garden is a most postlapsarian Eden, slushing over with cuckoo-spittle, mashed snails, slug-slime, and ripping thistles. But Tess slogs her way through Nature's vomit, mesmerized by "a stark quality like that of nudity" in the air and the lousy music, which makes her "undulate" and get all aflame in her cheeks. One wonders what she would have done had Angel been talented. She eroticizes a void, what is really only "a typical summer evening" and a mediocre man and performer. She is playing Alec's game, the only one she knows. Angel spots her, finally and fatally, or rather spots "her light summer gown." There's that white form again, and the two are off and running.

Angel, it turns out, is a much more versatile imagizer than is Alec. He too can see her during their courtship as a "milkmaid" or "daughter of the soil," ominously generic categories he will return to later; but he can do better, turning "the merest stray phenomenon" into "a rosy warming apparition" (ch. 20). Tess and Angel together are so formless they are "impregnated by their surroundings" (ch. 24), Tess being reduced over and over to a portrait, a "cameo" (ch. 24), appearing "ghostly," with "a sort of phosphorescence" in the "luminous gloom" (ch. 20). Sounds like Alec in the Chase all over again, doesn't it? This will-o'-the-wisp phosphorescent gloom not only aids in eroticizing them for one another (and for us); it is the substance of the *them*. "It was then," the narrator tells us, at this strange, insubstantial time, "that she impressed him most deeply. She was no longer the milkmaid, but the visionary essence of woman—a whole sex condensed into one typical form. He called her Artemis, Demeter, and other fanciful names" (ch. 20). These fanciful names represent a fanciful being. Tess's physical self is present to him only as a model for mental reproductions: he studies "the curve of those lips" so intently only so that "he could reproduce them mentally with ease" (ch. 24). The imaginative construction of "essence of woman" becomes so fixed that it takes a great jolt to alter it even slightly. When he learns of Tess's presumably distinguished ancestry, he simply does some touching up, expresses pleasure that the new image will be more presentable to his parents, and speaks quite in the old style of "the well-read woman that I mean to make you." Victor Frankenstein had nothing on Angel.

But what do we make of this construction *we* devise and call Angel Clare? Hardy's narrator explains him often, but the terms of those explanations—"I will not say"; "It might have been that"—give and then take away, in fact seem to take away much more than they give. They leave him blanker than ever. The explanations that seem solid lose their grounding through being multiplied and made to fly all over the map, in circles and in opposite directions. Critics often try to invest with peculiar authority the statement that Angel is "more spiritual than animal," "less Byronic than Shelleyan" (ch. 30), as if these comparatives and sliding more-this-than-thats could be pinned down and as if the problem were purely hormonal. And we are tempted to rush in with what is surely the least interesting explanation available: that Angel has too little of what Alec has too much of in the way of . .uh . .er . .sexual needs. What do we make of the scene where Angel lugs the other girls across the water and then returns to nuzzle and fondle Tess, all sighs and hot breath? What about his claim that Tess and her face are something more than simply lovable: "there was nothing ethereal about it; all was real vitality, real warmth, real incarnation" (ch. 24)? It's all, we are told, very *real*. "It was for herself he loved Tess" (ch. 26), the narrator bluntly explains. For *herself*? Against this we have the statements that his love "inclined to the ethereal" (ch. 30), was rooted "ideally and fancifully" (ch. 32). Even Tess suspects he is in love with an image: "she you love is not my real self, but one in my image" (ch. 33).

One might hush this hubbub a little by arguing that Angel is in love, and passionately, with the very real image he has created, an image, the narrator suggests, which constitutes the only reality anyhow. I'm less interested here, though, in making claims about a single coherent decoding than in arguing for a perception of Angel as part of a pattern of sadistic maneuvering. He is not figured as passionless or sexless; he is drawn to his image of Tess "by every heave of his pulses" (ch. 25). It is just that these pulse-heaves lead him to evacuate Tess and to figure a coalescence of eroticism and pain. Into the emptiness he has formed he intrudes himself, like Alec, as a master. Tess "caught his manner and habits, his speech and phrases, his likings and his aversions" (ch. 32) and becomes focused on but one point, a full cooperation in the sadistic program: "Her one desire, so long resisted, to make herself his, to call him her lord, her own—then, if necessary, to die—had at last lifted her up from her plodding reflective pathway" (ch. 33).

The reference to death makes explicit what she will, in fact, find it "necessary" to do. All along at Talbothay's, Angel, no less than would Alec, has swept through the female population as a smiling, ubiquitous sadist. Not only Tess but all the dairy girls find him "ecstasizing them to a killing joy"; they live in his presence with a "torturing ecstasy" (ch. 23). The narrator, seeking to make explicit the sado-masochistic proceedings, even reaches for direct allusions to, of all people, Swinburne: "pleasure girdled about with pain" (ch. 25). Tess herself sees her life at this time as a lariat, "twisted of two strands, positive pleasure and positive pain" (ch. 28).

All this pleasure and all the pain are directed toward an Angel who is inaccessible and can therefore be filled with qualities that will arouse this twining, this mixture of sexuality and pain. In this sense, the sadism is imaginative, imagistic—however effective. But there is nothing imaginary about the pain Tess feels on her honeymoon, where she jolts Angel's image of her roughly, shatters it, and discovers the real pain during the time when he must cast about for a new mental compartment for her. His erotic energies, for once, are directed outward in one of the most ghastly (yet participatory) scenes of sadistic acrobatics I know of. Angel's considerable eroticism is now no longer contained or controlled; if he were somehow biologically deficient, Tess wouldn't have such a terrible time of it. After her confession, Angel exposes his obsession with sex—or with Tess's sexual past as a narrative he can play and replay in his own mind, really a form of pornographic fixation. This fiction compels sexual energy, a compulsion D.H. Lawrence, describing what he took to be a modern malady, described as "sex in the head." Such sadistic mental novel-writing is so focused in the honeymoon sequence, that I'd like to dwell on it.

The episode, beginning with the end of Tess's tearless, unflinching narrative of her time with Alec, features an immediate blurring of perspective, acting, finally, to blend our vision with what turns out to be Angel's: "but the complexion even of external things seemed to suffer transmutation as her announcement progressed" (ch. 35). Who is seeing this apparent change, the impish fire and the grinning fender? Why does it occur? What does it amount to? On the last point the narrator is bluntly clear: "Nothing had changed since the moments when he had been kissing her; or, rather, nothing in the substance of things. But the essences of things had changed." To whom? Why to Angel, of course—and to us. What is this essence? Is it really the same as the "complexion" of "things"? Surely these *things* and Tess too are the same—or so we would like to think. But the complexion of things, the perception of things—of the fender and of Tess—has changed, and the perception of that complexion, that internal imaging, is, sadly, all the essence that she has. These images are made essences, for the reader and for Angel; and we are pounded to participate with him as he proceeds to unleash his anger on images he can shift at will. Apparently freed now from any inhibitions on his sadism, he writes a series of versatile pornographic scenes for his—and our—pleasure.

Angel first does virtually nothing, stirring the fire in what the narrator calls an "irrelevant act." Such irrelevant delay, however, forces Tess to wait in grinding suspense, a painful tension that is only a prelude. Angel turns on her a blankness, "the most inadequate, commonplace" voice she had heard from him, as he tries to hold onto the old image he had posed: "Am I to believe this? . . . *My* wife, *my* Tess—nothing in you warrants such a supposition as that." Nothing, that is, in his old image can immediately find a place for a Tess who has a past, particularly a sexual past, an existence outside of "*my* Tess."

His befuddlement is amazingly short-lived. After entertaining a very brief period of denial—imagining Tess is out of her mind and the like—he finds the formula he needs. Tess, in her agony, makes her most poignant and, one would suppose, most irresistible appeal: " 'In the name of our love, forgive me!' she whispered with a dry mouth. 'I have forgiven you the same.' " Her logic seems unbreakable here; further, it seems unlikely that a man like Angel Clare would deny anyone at least the words of forgiveness. But if he forgives Tess, the game is up; and the last thing he wants is to end things so quickly. So he evades, disallows the point: "O Tess, forgiveness does not apply to the case! You were one person; now you are another." The hitch in the forgive-me plea is not, clearly, "forgive" but "me." Her *me* exists for Angel only as a construction now shattered, so he proceeds to replace his former picture of an innocent maid with a new one, the corrupted woman, the deceiver, and he can write a new script, safe in the narrative formula he has created. It is a narrative Tess cannot penetrate with reason or with love; she can only suffer.

Angel launches immediately into his sadistic operation with "horrible laughter—as unnatural and ghastly as a laugh in hell." He gets just the effect he is after; Tess's response could have been copied verbatim from an erotic child-spanking novel: " 'Don't—don't! It kills me quite, that!' she shrieked. 'O have mercy upon me—have mercy!' " "I thought, Angel," she says, "that you loved me—me, my very self! If it be I you do love, O how can it be that you look and speak so?" Whether

Tess is any less an imagist in her construction of Angel is uncertain, but this plea for a love of her very self is hopeless: "I repeat, the woman I have been loving is not you." She sees that he regards her now merely as a "species of impostor; a guilty woman in the guise of an innocent one." The terms, guilt and innocence, are less horrifying than the abstraction into roles, into a general "species." She responds with "terror . . . upon her white face," her constricted mouth forming itself into "a round little hole." This is the sort of thing he wants, and he works this image transformation until she finally bursts into tears.

As Tess begins to cry, the narrator offers some surprisingly clear commentary: "Clare was relieved at this change, for the effect on her of what had happened was beginning to be a trouble to him." He had, apparently, been approaching a "trouble," a kind of shut-off point in sadism, an end to pleasure when the pain for the object is too static or too overwhelming. Seeing Tess get some relief in "self-sympathetic tears," he is freed from any impulse to sympathize and can press on. His cold neutrality is among his surest weapons for causing pain. When Tess asks, for instance, whether she is too wicked to allow them to live together, Clare answers, "I have not been able to think of what we can do." Such cruelty probably rips more deeply than direct attack, though he can manage that too: Tess offers to lie down and die for him, and he whips out, "You are very good. But it strikes me that there is a want of harmony between your present mood of self-sacrifice and your past mood of self-preservation." Tess may not quite understand the sarcasm, but she recognizes the anger clearly enough, and is driven into a silence that extends the scene. Later, when he switches centers in the drama and forgives Tess or says he does, Tess asks if he can love her, "to which question he did not answer." Such devices prolong the suffering and the pleasure. That pleasure is most titillated, as always, by absence, conducive both to pain and to image-making: "Tess . . I cannot stay—in this room—just now. I will walk out a little way." So we will miss nothing in this sexual drama, the narrator points out that "cruelty was mighty in Clare now," quotes Swinburne on sadism again ("And the veil of thine head shall be grief, and the crown shall be pain"), and marks the relationship of sadism to absence: "What a weak thing her presence must have become to him!" Clare withdraws to pump back up a sexual feeling that finds presence an irritating distraction.

Tess has surprising insight into what is going on in Angel's mind, but when she threatens to make an entry into his narrative, he retreats to his old, maddeningly self-enclosed formula. Tess says, "It is in your own mind what you are angry at, Angel; it is not in me. O, it is not in me, and I am not the deceitful woman you think me!" "Hm—well," Angel says, "Not deceitful, my wife; but not the same." She can only force him to make small adjustments in his mental fiction; she cannot transform it—nor can she find a real role in it. Like absence, Angel's sadistic fiction-making robs her of any essence outside it. One of the reasons these scenes are so nightmarish (if irresistible) is that Tess's repeated insistence that she is what she has always been, more fundamentally that she *is*, that she exists, is an insistence on a different plot, one we perhaps ought to be anxious to complete in our own minds. But we find ourselves, like Tess, stymied by and, to be candid, quite caught up in Angel's more authoritative plot.

He keeps that plot going the next day (ch. 36) by rehearsing the whole thing—"Tess! Say it is not true!"—and demanding details:

> "Is he living?" Angel then asked.
> "The baby died."
> "But the man?"
> "He is alive."
> ....
> "Is he in England?"
> "Yes."

The brutal way in which he ignores the news of the baby's death, rushing onward without a pause to the man, exposes, I think, his obsessive sexual interest and his desire not so much to gain information as to hurt.

He then explains to Tess his "position," which is one he says "any man" would hold: "I thought—any man would have thought—that by giving up all ambition to win a wife with social standing, with fortune, with knowledge of the world, I should secure rustic innocence as surely as I should secure pink cheeks; but—However, I am no man to reproach you, and I will not." He reproaches her bitterly and then deflects criticism for having done so. The horror (and delight) of all this is not merely that the "position" is simply a self-pitying pose designed to lacerate her but that she is sucked into believing it, participating in its pseudo-logic: "Tess felt his position so entirely that the remainder had not been needed." He then, once again, is free to proceed: "O Tess—you are too, too—childish—unformed—crude, I suppose! I don't know what you are." He is right about the last, at least, though he might have been more honest had he admitted that what he takes to be Tess's unformed childishness was just what attracted him and attracts him still. But his attack causes "a quick shame mixed with

336 / *The Pedophile Reader*

misery" to come on her in renewed force, with such force that she openly suggests the only logical fulfillment of this sadistic program:

> "What were you thinking of doing?" he inquired.
> "Of putting an end to myself."
> "When?"
> She writhed under this inquisitorial manner of his.
> "Last night," she answered.
> "Where?"
> "Under your mistletoe."
> "My good—! How?" he asked sternly.

Note Angel's grisly and quick interest in the narrative details—When? Where? How?—and the absence of concern or even caution. When he does get around to noticing the extremity of her suggestion, it is only to deliver another whiplash: "Wicked! The idea was unworthy of you beyond description." The awkwardness in his prose may suggest that the idea has simply not yet entered his image ("description") of her, interesting as the notion is. Perhaps suicide is not quite the fillip he wants in his pornography; murder would be better, a murder he enacts with her and the nearby tombs in dumb show (ch. 37). It is only with a corpse that he can be tender: "My poor, poor Tess—my dearest, darling Tess! So sweet, so good, so true!" Perhaps necrophilia is indeed the inevitable end of sadism, but not, of course, of sadistic reading, since it would put an end to our desire.

And Tess keeps that going. Though she has been reduced to feeling that she is "so utterly worthless," heroically (and erotically) she will not give up. She again returns to an appeal that has considerable logical and emotional strength: " 'I told you I thought I was not respectable enough long ago—and on that account I didn't want to marry you, only—only you urged me!' She broke into sobs, and turned her back to him. It would almost have won round any man but Angel Clare." Angel now has passed into a state where there is no mechanism of control. His sexual fiction is so powerfully fixed that it can carry him through all that time in Brazil.

In a novel filled with and based on absence, Angel's putting an ocean between them is crucial. As he says, "I think of people more kindly when I am away from them" (ch. 36). He also, clearly, thinks of them more tenderly: while in Brazil, "he almost talked to her in his anger, as if she had been in the room. And then her cooing voice, plaintive in expostulation, disturbed the darkness, the velvet touch of her lips passed over his brow, and he could distinguish in the air the warmth of her breath" (ch. 39). Angel can make passionate love to a carcass or a mental image, even feel her warm breath, perhaps the same "warm breath" Alec feels when he seduces Tess. Angel has not been magically sexualized in Brazil; he is sexualized as he always has been, still controlled by "what Tess was not" (ch. 39), by a vacancy he can fill.

We are, I suppose, free to imagine that Angel comes back with a new "make" and new erotic needs, but we have to engage in some pretty energetic inner remodeling of our own to fix up our image in that transformational way. We are told only that he has acquired some rather cynical and disjointed philosophic views and that he was "arrested" now less by "beauty" than by "pathos" (ch. 49). Sounds pretty dangerously like the old Angel, one might think. His memory is most stirred, after all, by Izz Huett's pathetic honesty: "The words of Izz Huett, never quite stilled in his memory, came back to him. . . . Tess would lay down her life for him, and she herself could do no more" (ch. 49). That image of Tess dead as a doornail proves to be irresistible.

Tess, from this view, replays old scenes, reenters after murdering Alec as the old Tess, the same old white shape for Angel, a mere "figure" (ch. 57). Angel leads her to Stonehenge, where, with Tess saying, "I shall not live for you to despise me!" (ch. 58), he can complete his sadistic exercise, reformulating her as a sacrificial victim and a flag—more images. The use of Liza-Lu, an even more perfect blank than Tess, may seem to us less a sign of rejuvenation than of ghastly reiteration.[22] Tess offers her to Angel as a pure implement: "If you would train and teach her, Angel, and bring her up for your own self! . . . She has all the best of me without the bad of me; and if she were to become yours . . ." (ch. 58). Liza-Lu appears in the second half of the novel also as a "figure" (ch. 49) and at the end ascends a hill with Angel to gaze on Tess's execution from the summit. We are all used by now to these distant prospects, these long views, and what happens to "figures" who join them. Angel and Liza-Lu go off hand-in-hand with the world presumably all before them, but we may suspect it is but a narrow, torture-racked world that Angel (and we) can create.

So we come to the end of a novel figuring a world of flitting phenomena, changing forms. The project to fix or imagine solidity depends on distancing or absenting the corporeal so as to make room for images. Eroticizing these images, then, is a free and unrestricted operation; one can easily turn an absence into a corpse, and sexuality might as well become sadism. Images, after all, are one's own possession and can be whipped or rubbed out at will.

By us, of course, as readers. And it's not that our activity as voyeur-pedophile readers is particularly unusual here in this novel. Angel, our guide and model, is never presented as especially perverse: he is just a "well-meaning young man, a sample product of the last five-and-twenty-years" (ch. 39). All this sadistic revelry is pretty much a matter of course. Even the narrator seems always to turn an erotic Tess into a bleeding Tess: "A bit of her naked arm is visible between the bluff leather of the gauntlet and the sleeve of her gown; and as the day wears on its feminine smoothness becomes scarified by the stubble, and bleeds" (ch. 14). One is reminded of Roland Barthes's orgiastic "gaps," worked on some by Sade. This narrator blandly includes us, even explicitly, in the fun: "Clare had been harsh towards her; there is no doubt of it. Men are too often harsh with women they love or have loved; women with men" (ch. 49). Each man and woman too kills the thing he or she loves—and loves to do it. *Tess* becomes, thus, a titillating snuff movie we run in our minds. The novel offers us not just the suggestion but the demonstration that our own lives are nothing more than this movie in the head, made over in the flesh.

It is perhaps too strong to say that our reading here suggests that happy sexuality can exist only in fictions, constructs of what is not there, inner pornographic narratives or fables, whether of children or not. Still, the power of these negations is dreadful, as if absences were writing the novel in defiance of presence. And playful deconstruction is hard to come by. At one point, Tess complains to her mother, "Why didn't you tell me there was danger in men-folks? Why didn't you warn me? Ladies know how to fend hands against because they read novels that tell them of these tricks; but I never had the chance of learning in that way" (ch. 12). One might suppose that this is offered as a kind of justification for the novel in front of us, a hope that the work will be effectively cautionary, providing the chance for learning. But we know from our own pedophile reading that narratives are never constructed in such a straightforward way. There are always counter-narratives, negations that overwhelm opportunity and freedom. Play offers some wedge out, but it is not easy to play with corpses. In Hardy, at least, one never reads to learn—or learns to read so that desire leads somewhere other than the grave.

Notes

1. This section is adapted from a part of an essay, "Tennyson, Hallam's Corpse, Milton's Murder, and Poetic Exhibitionism," *Nineteenth-Century Literature*, 45 (1990):

176–205. That essay was co-authored with Buck McMullen, who has kindly given his permission for the inclusion of the material here. He is not, however, responsible for any distortions or errors; those are all mine.

2. Sigmund Freud, "Instincts and Their Vicissitudes," XIV, 127. Subsequent references to this essay will be cited by page in the text.

3. Robert Con Davis, "Lacan, Poe, and Narrative Repression," in *Lacan and Narration*, ed. Robert Con Davis (Baltimore: The Johns Hopkins Univ. Press, 1983), p. 987.

4. Davis, "Lacan, Poe," p. 992.

5. Dickens, *David Copperfield*, (ch. iii). Subsequent references will be in the text.

6. Interestingly, although Holden himself uses "cute"—"It did look pretty cute, too" (ch. 17)—he generally professes disdain for the term: "She sings it very Dixieland and whorehouse, and it doesn't sound all mushy. If a white girl was singing it, she'd make it sound *cute* as hell, but old Estelle Fletcher knew what the hell she was doing" (ch. 16). Holden's preference for the black and whorehousey, about which he knows nothing, and his pretenses about music generally all act, ironically, to make him all the cuter. J. D. Salinger, *The Catcher in the Rye* (New York: Bantam, 1964).

7. Salinger, *The Catcher in the Rye*, ch. 9. Subsequent references will be cited in the text by chapter.

8. In an important essay, Carol and Richard Ohmann survey the criticism on the novel and note, in the midst of all the raging disagreement, an identifiable consensus that the novel concerns a search for "self," a consensus they see as clearly, though unconsciously, ideological: "Reviewers, Critics, and *The Catcher in the Rye*," *Critical Inquiry* 3 (1976): 15–37.

9. Duane Edwards, "Holden Caulfield: 'Don't Ever Tell Anybody Anything'," *English Literary History* 44 (1977): 556.

10. The Ohmanns argue that "Holden responds not to the timeless terrors of sex but to the exploitation of girls and women by such types as Stradlater": "Universals and the Historically Particular," *Critical Inquiry* 3 (1977): 775. This molding of a left-wing, ideological Holden is no more and certainly no less "valid" than our molding of a sexualized one.

11. Jones calls it "predictable and boring": "It reflects something not at all rich and strange but what every sensitive sixteen-year-old since Rousseau has felt": "Case History of All of Us," *Nation*, 1 Sept. 1951, p. 176.

12. Edwards, " 'Don't Ever Tell,'" p. 556.

13. As I said earlier, this is not so much a fact of chronology, where Holden is *presented* early on as blind and later as a looker, but of erotic construction. I am suggesting that we build up an exhibitionistic Holden, an object, despite contradictory "evidence" that comes at us, even early on in the novel. The deconstruction of our static, voyeuristic longing is not a matter of evidence piling up on us, though; it is implicit in our erotic maneuverings that the seer will be seen, that looking cannot escape being spied upon.

14. James Bryan, "The Psychological Structure of *The Catcher in the Rye*," *PMLA* 89 (1974): 1065–74.

15. George Meredith, *Modern Love*, Sonnet XVII, "The Memorial Edition of the Works of George Meredith" (London: Constable, 1910), vol. 24, p. 197.

16. Northrop Frye's discussion of the first phase of tragedy, corresponding to the birth

340 / *The Pedophile Reader*

of the hero, mentions *Tess* as an example, even though the hero of this tragedy of extreme innocence might more properly be a baby: "owing to the unusual difficulty of making an interesting dramatic character out of an infant, the central and typical figure of this phase is the calumniated woman": *Anatomy of Criticism: Four Essays* (Princeton: Princeton Univ. Press, 1957), p. 219.

17. Thomas Hardy, *Jude the Obscure*, ed. Norman Page (New York: Norton, 1978), Part I—ch. IV.

18. See an earlier discussion of mine, "Hardy's Absences," *Critical Approaches to the Fiction of Thomas Hardy*, ed. Dale Kramer (London: Macmillan, 1979), pp. 202–14. That discussion, concerned with *Jude* and *A Pair of Blue Eyes*, now seems to me, unhappily, divorced from concerns of sexuality and secretly married to some formalist assumptions. See also J. Hillis Miller, *Thomas Hardy: Distance and Desire* (Cambridge, MA: Harvard Univ. Press, 1970), a splendid book which, however, does not, despite its title, connect very closely with the model or argument here.

19. "A Broken Appointment," *The Complete Poems of Thomas Hardy*, ed. James Gibson (New York: Macmillan, 1982), p. 136.

20. I realize that I am humanizing and solidifying these "characters," but that's for convenience only. What we call "Alec," "Tess," or "Angel" should be regarded not as real people but as vehicles for setting up intricate and various structures of sexual expression and responsiveness. But it's certainly less clumsy to speak of "Alec," "Tess," and "Angel" than of coded vehicles.

21. Thomas Hardy, *Tess of the d'Urbervilles: A Pure Woman Faithfully Presented*, 2nd ed., ed. Scott Elledge (New York: Norton, 1979), ch. 1. Subsequent references will be noted in the text by chapter number.

22. Miller (*Distance and Desire*, p. 155) also suggests that this ending may be read as the beginning of a new cycle of the same thing.

10

The Pedophile Reader: Events

The scenes we enact in our heads answer to and promote needs so insistent they are not going to depend on books alone for their exercise. The fictions we engender have a wider scope, and we find ourselves able to construct them not simply or even mainly by way of novels. We plot the life about us in much the same way, find means for dramatizing our desires and their necessary protections through movies, television, the schools, the athletic fields, the playground, the day-care center, and the courtroom.

We keep the story alive and before us, being told over and over. At the same time, we find ways to deny emphatically that we are authoring this story, much less serving as its leading players. By creating gothic melodramas, monster stories of child-molesting and playing them out periodically (often), we provide not just titillation but assurances of righteousness. Demonizing the child-molester much as we demonize Alec d'Urberville, we can connect to a pedophile drama while pretending to shut down the theater. Most pointedly, we use our legal system to provide us with access to these guilt-free forms of scapegoating pornography. The fact that these trials last longer and longer, occur with greater frequency does not suggest that they are not doing their job. It may be true that we need more of them because they are not providing satisfaction; but it's not satisfaction we are after. We do not want it all to be over with, and these trials perpetuate themselves in order to keep our needs and our desires coursing along. For example, let's take the Buckey matter.

Some Background Designed To Look Factual

The Buckey matter is actually Part II of a spectacle more familiarly called "The McMartin Pre-School Case" that ran from 1983 until

342 / *The Pedophile Reader*

1990. The case, involving a nursery school in the Los Angeles suburb of Manhattan Beach, began on August 12, 1983, when one Judy Johnson made a phone call to the Manhattan Beach Police Department, was connected to juvenile officer Jane Hoag, and claimed that her son had been sodomized by "Mr. Ray" (Raymond Buckey). Johnson later went on to claim that Buckey wore masks, capes, and other costumes, stuck the boy's head in a toilet, and forced an air tube in his rectum. Within a few months she had also accused an AWOL marine, three "models" from a local health club, and her ex-husband of sodomizing the boy. Her dog, she reported, "had some hair missing" and thus was also a likely victim of the same act. McMartin teachers, she said, had run scissors into the boy's eyes, staples into his nipples, and forced his fingers into a goat's anus, while Peggy McMartin Buckey, Raymond's mother, was killing a baby and forcing the boy to drink its blood. In 1985 Johnson was diagnosed as suffering from "acute paranoid schizophrenia" and by 1987 she was dead from alcohol-induced liver disease.[1]

Meanwhile, Officer Hoag, unable after four weeks of work to obtain any corroboration from other children she interviewed or any other substantial evidence, was still somehow convinced by Johnson's initial phone call and turned to Chief of Police Henry L. Kuhlmeyer, Jr. and the Captain of the Investigation Division, John Wehner. These officials immediately (September 8, 1983) sent out to all parents of McMartin pre-school children a letter asking for their "assistance in this continuing investigation" "involving child molestation (288 P.C.)": "Our investigation indicates that possible criminal acts include: oral sex, fondling of genitals, buttocks or chest area, and sodomy, possibly committed under the pretense of 'taking the child's temperature.' Also, photos may have been taken of children without their clothing. Any information from your child regarding having ever observed Ray Buckey to leave a classroom alone with a child during any nap period, or if they have ever observed Ray Buckey tie up a child, is important." The letter was clear on how the parents could gather important information: "Please question your child to see if he or she has been a witness to any crime or if he or she has been a victim." An "information form" was enclosed for the parents' convenience and a week allowed for reporting the results of interrogations.

By the next spring (1984), Raymond Buckey, his sister, mother, grandmother, and three teachers had been arrested, charged with over 200 counts of child-molesting involving 42 children. Eventually, after preliminary hearings and a review of budget constraints, the number of defendants was shrunk to two, Raymond Buckey and his mother, facing only 65 charges. The trial finally commenced in April of 1987 and ran until January 1990, thus establishing the record for the longest criminal trial in our nation's history.

Over the months, the cast changed little, apart from some jury replacements necessitated by health problems faced by two, the career difficulties of a third, the financial crises that came upon a fourth, and the slovenly "inattentiveness" of a fifth. Despite some alarmist talk about a mistrial by reason of jury evaporation, on January 18, 1990 the replacement jury did act, acquitting both defendants on 52 counts and remaining deadlocked on the other 13. The district attorney's office indicated it would accept the verdict and stop the play; and the *Los Angeles Times* announced the curtain in its headline: "McMartin Verdict: Not Guilty." But what the same newspaper later called "extraordinary public lobbying" by way of marches, letter-writing campaigns, press conferences, and appearances with Geraldo and Oprah resulted in the caving-in of the D.A. and his announcement on February 1 that he would produce after all the sequel we were demanding, this time with a single defendant, Raymond Buckey, and only the 13 charges left over from the first stage. During this second trial, three of the children were called back for agonizing reprises and Raymond Buckey, who spent five of these seven years in prison, was again made the subject of a whole series of tales. However, a slimming of the narrative cut the charges to 8 and the second trial to a shadow of its former self that occupied us for only 5 months, ending in a stupefied and deadlocked jury, the declaration of a mistrial on July 27, 1990, and the unleashing of those of us who had become experts on the matter.

On-The-Spot Coverage

"In the Buckey matter, the defendant is in the court with his attorneys, the jury is seated, the people are represented." A judge with a voice, face, and manner washed clean of any expression whatever hums this invocation at the beginning of each recommencement of the trial of Raymond Buckey on 8 counts of child-molesting. But why? Why are we employing this judge to say such things? Why is there a Buckey matter? What interests and cravings are being met and served? What are the people after? Who are the people?

Apart from principals and officials, there are surprisingly few people in the courtroom most days, and those of us who do attend are, each of us, there for one reason: we are writing about the case. Why else would we be there? One might say that we must write in order to excuse our attendance at the trial. One might also say that the trial exists so that we can write about it, so that stories are told. Why have a trial about texts that results in more texts and yet more texts? Who asked me to attend and to write? Who put this event there for the watching and writing—and why?

"I refer the court to Document [inaudible], Appendix [inaudible], of the official Transcript, Page 55,000," says Prosecutor Pam Ferrero on June 25, 1990 at about 2:30. Page 55,000. And after page 55,000, we have not "The End" but page 55,001. We will never have "The End." We will never have "The Truth" either. And that's what the trial is for, I have decided, which is why both the judge and I attend. We are both there to take our parts in a process whereby the end and the truth are centered and held in suspension by being textualized in a way so remarkably sophisticated that our interest will never be exhausted. Never fulfilled, either, but that's the point. The judge and I keep the plot alive, keep the story spinning along. We are neither of us hypocrites or cynics. It's not that we do not believe in truth or in conclusions. We believe in them so wholeheartedly that we will do everything we can and more to keep them alive and fresh, always squirming.

The Buckey matter is matter for story-telling, not surprisingly, since the Buckey matter is itself a fiction. The only point in making a comment like that must be to indicate that there are no easy distinctions to be made between the texts that *are* the Buckey matter and the texts *about* the Buckey matter. In the first case we have stories told by parents and police and investigators and sneaks and experts about the stories told at one time or another by the children and by Raymond Buckey. These stories are then told over by the attorneys, by the judge, and, in secret, by the jury. They are all stories about stories, attempts to retell in such a way as to capture for us more persuasive veracity and authority. They are all stories in search of representational status, stories laying claim to transparency.

Such stories strive to be purely mimetic, to forge a direct connection to the truth by reason of their immediacy. That there are hundreds or even thousands of such stories, each making the same claim and each bearing little or no relation to the others, raises the suspicion of those of us at the trial that these immediate stories are maybe too close to the matter, that they are clouded by interest or emotion or by a perspective that is as distorted as one we allow ourselves in viewing a massive canvas from three inches away, watching the World Series while never taking our eyes off second base. Hence we other text-makers back off, take in the whole field, all 55,000-plus pages and more, much more, in the way of interviews, newspaper accounts, television analyses, scholarly reports, and the findings from archaeological digs.[2] Then, we suppose, we can write a stronger story, one less partial and more in contact with what really happened.

What we are likely to do, I suggest, is to join hands with the more immediate stories, the stories that *are* the Buckey matter, not to correct but to extend them. By so resolutely multiplying the stories of what really happened and by lending to a thousand versions so much plausibility and authority, these narratives manage to make "what really happened" both vital and infinitely plastic. There is no end to the very fine stories about what really happened and no limit to the sincerity, veracity, scrupulous employment of evidence, logical rigor, and disinterestedness of each.

There is nothing bogus about such a process, nor (I hope you understand) about my account of it. The trial is established as an official arena for such narrative multiplications, a way, albeit an expensive way, of getting things started and of generating infinite new possibilities for the telling of this cultural saga. After a time, a very long time in this case, the trial gets out of the way and turns the job over to others, like me. The questions I propose to keep the game going are these: what is the referent for all this signifying? why does our game so much resemble hide-and-seek? My thesis (or the rule for my version of the game) is that the Buckey matter is a matter of truth-telling that is so sincere and exhaustive it renders sincerity irrelevant and exhaustion a source of endless renewal. And, as the judge always says, "the people are represented" in all this—not, indeed, by the comically incompetent duo conducting the prosecution but by writers and text-makers. The people are represented, that is to say, by me.

Telling It Like It Was: The Children

"I believe," Buckey's attorney says, "the children believe what they are saying." What the three children in this second trial are saying is that Raymond Buckey molested them—engaged them in games involving nudity and improper contact, fondled them, forced them into genital and oral sex, sodomized them, urinated on them—and then insured with threats their silence. Asked what he thinks of the children's stories, Raymond Buckey says on the stand that he thinks children are more honest than adults. In fact, he says, "all children are honest as to what they believe." Buckey allows that statement to stand for a dramatic moment before quietly adding: "but that doesn't make what they believe right." To a very large extent, what is at stake in the

Buckey matter is just that: whether what the children believe to be "right" is "right." Perhaps what really matters here at the trial is who has the power to determine that. Perhaps what truly matters to us trial-watchers is the perpetuation of the children's narratives, the narratives about the child.

Oddly, absolutely everyone in the courtroom agrees that the children are now and always have been telling a perfectly straight story (the narrators are reliable), but it is possible, perhaps probable or certain, that these narrators are limited, that they (a) are telling a story that never happened, (b) are telling a story that has been fed to them or severely distorted by others, (c) are telling a story that has shifted over time, (d) are telling a story where the events are right but the actors are not, (e) are telling a story where the actors are right but not the events, (f) many of the above. The argument between defense and prosecution comes down to an argument about narrators, genre, and tone, finally about interpretation. It is a literary argument about texts, a quarrel between authors and critics.

The prosecution claims that the children's evidence should be read in a "straightforward" and "common-sense" way. If they say something happened, it happened; their words are to be interpreted by means of the no-nonsense equipment we bring to bear on any text in daily life. The prosecution claims the texts offered by the children are not, as we used to say, "literature" and need no special attention beyond regarding them as "true." The prosecution further claims, in the manner of authoritative medieval exegesis of scripture, that where discrepancies are unavoidable we take whatever furthers the prosecution's case as true and disregard the rest. Though the children have told many different narratives, denied the truth of narratives told previously and recanted them, switched the modes or settings or even actors in the stories, the prosecution still sticks by its rules of interpretation: the child is always telling the truth when it says molestation occurred (and is never telling the truth when it says it didn't); if the latest version of a child's narrative confirms the prosecution's case, then that story is to be believed (if it doesn't, it isn't); the child's language needs no "interpretation" but is transparent and directly mimetic, says the prosecution (allowing for some few exceptional cases which the prosecution will clarify for us). The prosecution does not really disagree with Mr. Buckey, then: "all children are honest as to what they believe, but that doesn't make what they believe right." The prosecution imposes its own view of how to fix on what truly is "right"; it certainly doesn't trust the children to do that for them. That children are honest as to what they believe, then, simply renders the search for truth more open;

it does not give any authority to the child but rather transfers all power to the adult story-tellers. The child becomes an empty signifier, or, rather, an infinitely plural one. The child's testimony becomes a spilling out of game counters and an invitation to all adults not simply to play but to make up the rules of the game. The child can never author its own story. The prosecution seizes hold and tells the story it must have.

The position of the defense as regards the children is very little different. The child's complete and uncomplicated veracity is accorded a respect almost absurd to anyone who has ever spent more than a few seconds with an actual child. But it serves the purposes of the defense as well as the prosecution to erect this myth of a spotlessly honest child, since it also empties out the child and makes it incapable of any independent action or thought. That the child is completely honest means that the child is incapable of not being honest; its veracity is unwilled and hence merely automatic. The child's relation to the matter under consideration is thus innocent and powerless. The child will report with entire sincerity whatever enters its head and takes up lodging there. Under this figuring, the child is judged unable really to interpret, even to interpret its own story; all it can do is lay out the story in some impossibly unmediated language so that the real interpreters can have a go at it. The prosecution's child cannot author; the defense's child cannot interpret. The honest child cannot write, cannot read; the child of molestation is functionally and conveniently illiterate, not because the pedophile wants it that way but because we do.

For the defense, then, these stories told by the children are no less empty, no less subject to the authority of the adult interpreters. Whereas the prosecution demanded the right to say when it was the child was to be believed and on what terms, however, the defense claims that the child's stories, all of them, are pretty much irrelevant, drained of any authority. The prosecution wants to be author, the defense wants to be critic.

The prosecution's insistence that the proper story must be scoured clean of the child's denials of molestation and constructed entirely out of accusations is not, as we might expect, simply turned upside down by the defense. Rather than making stories out of the children's denials, the defense discredits all the stories and turns to other materials entirely for its narratives. The defense is not seeking better stories but better matter for sophisticated analysis. In order to find such matter the defense must establish convincingly a generic pattern for the children's stories wherein reliable narrators tell hopelessly unreliable yarns. Reversing the old nostrum, the defense argues that we must always trust the teller, but never the tales.

The way into this interpretive mode is to argue that the children are every bit as likely to believe and repeat what is not right as what is. When pressed in cross-examination, Raymond Buckey offered as an example children's sincere attachment to Santa Claus stories. These are telling examples, since Santa Claus is not only not "right" but is also a clear instance of implantation, a story smuggled to the children by outside agencies. In the Buckey matter, the defense has argued that the stories of molestation (along with Satanic ritual, torture, animal sacrifice, blood-drinking, and long-distance airplane rides) have been instilled in the children by parents, police, peers, television, and so forth. The children, they argue, have simply recorded the signals being sent their way and have finally, with a lot of coaching of one sort or another, come to believe the tales they were trained for. All tales, therefore, should be invalidated.

According to the defense, a group known as Children's Institute International has served as head coach and athletic director from the beginning. Employees of CII acted as interviewers of the children back in 1983, as interpreters of their stories, and as advisors to their parents on what stories to believe and how to ensure that the children told those stories. On June 13, 1990 an employee of CII, Sandra Gail Krebs was called to the stand by the defense, clearly in the hopes that she would serve to corroborate their interpretive paradigm by illustrating the way in which the children were provided with stories they could tell and believe. The defense, that is, hoped to demolish the prosecution's method of reading and their means for claiming authority and authorship by ridiculing Ms. Krebs's way of finding stories. Exactly like the prosecution, Ms. Krebs assumes that the children cannot themselves tell a coherent story, not without her help. The way she gives help is to tell the story herself until the child is finally bullied into agreeing with her. That's not the way Ms. Krebs would describe her procedures, of course; that's the way the defense describes them. Ms. Krebs would say she was finding ways to allow the child to "disclose" the truth and the details of molestation.

Ms. Krebs says she is merely bringing to light what was previously hidden. Using her puppets, anatomically correct dolls (i.e., featuring prominent and, with males, erect genitals), and the right sort of questions, she will, as she says, facilitate disclosure, allow an opening-up. She becomes indignant at suggestions that she does anything more than raise the windows of the mind. Echoing the theories of the prosecution, she says that a child will not say such things happened if they didn't; "it is not possible," she says, that these particular children are retelling stories fed to them by way of these interviews.

Now the defense can hardly imagine a construction of "disclose" that is so naive, and it sees Ms. Krebs's procedures as a violent invasion of the child's memory. From the defense's point of view, Ms. Krebs, armed with (they sneeringly disclose) her degrees in theater and journalism, has managed to disclose only her own conviction that molestation had occurred and her willingness to badger the children until they confirmed her groundless beliefs. The defense cites those of Ms. Krebs's techniques that seem to be borrowed from Gestapo-torture movies:

> "You have some yucky secrets, don't you? Wouldn't you like to put them in the box and get rid of them?"
> "Are you really sure you don't have yucky secrets?"
> "C'mon! A lot of your friends have told us their yucky secrets."
> "Mommy and daddy would be very happy if you got rid of those yucky secrets."[3]

And so it goes—or so the defense says it goes. Ms. Krebs sticks to her story; that is, she sticks to her right to tell the one story there is to tell. She says directly that no other story is possible than the one she is telling. She also suggests that such a story is self-sufficient, that it needs no interpreting. The defense-as-critic is outraged by such a claim and asserts the contrary position that no language is self-sufficient, i.e., that no language can stand without the critic interpreting it. The defense, finally, does not need to ridicule the story itself, the story of molestation. The defense simply needs to assert a more cogent theory of language and interpretation, one that transfers authority from author to critic, from one text to another, and causes all stories to evaporate. No story, the defense maintains, stands on its own; no story is free from power. Ms. Krebs and the prosecution have foolishly gambled on taking control of the story, says the defense. The defense is letting everything ride with a different bet: relying on the tendency of texts to spin out into other texts and the corresponding authority of he who can describe the spinning, the defense places all its chips on the power of *un*fixing, of deconstruction. Once something is disclosed, there is no getting it back into the box. Ms. Krebs has let loose the story. Whether she made it or the children or Raymond Buckey there's no knowing and never will be. To tell the truth, we have all lost interest in that question anyhow.

As A Matter Of Fact: The Prosecution

The members of the prosecution team, Joe Martinez and Pam Ferrero, stalk rather than walk, aim and waggle fingers for emphasis, glare at the defendant, the jury, and at me; they are both quite dramatic, or at least theatrical. I think they have not mastered the semiotics of indignation. They give the impression of trying hard to manufacture fury against the defendant and come up with nothing better than grumpiness. When outrage is called for, they produce bad manners; instead of wrath, peevishness. We all agree on this, we courtroom observers/writers-in-attendance; we agree that the prosecution is incompetent. We also think, those of us willing to speak in such terms, that sending out a woman and a Hispanic in this case makes little sense. Child-molesting is not a minority or racial crime; it is pure middle-class, white-on-white stuff, our version of the Crips and the Bloods. Women arguably have a particular stake in all this (hence Ferrero), but that point is erased by Martinez's obtrusive floundering and by the fact that most of us simply do not like Ferrero at all: she seems perpetually aggrieved; and that's annoying, if not threatening. Anyhow, our view is that the prosecution could hardly be worse. That's a curious judgment and a spooky one, considering that none of us has any real legal knowledge and more than half the time do not know what is going on. I wonder whether calling the prosecution incompetent is not a way of protecting ourselves from seeing that it's actually their theory, their reliance on stories, which is wobbly. After all, we have come to court ourselves to get a story and may find it hard to watch as the authority of stories takes such a beating.

I wonder if the jury is also saying that the prosecution is incompetent. Since I have come to admire and put my heart with Raymond Buckey—a way of lying about this is to say I believe him innocent, but, while true, that has little to do with it—I hope the jury does not join in with our ridicule of the prosecutors, even if that team does forget things, mispronounce names, and dress funny. Saying that the prosecutors are incompetent keeps open the possibility that they really do have a fine story to tell (a fine theory) but are bungling the performance. It means that the story is maybe still there if *we* can only disclose it. It means that we might treat the prosecution within the same theoretical model the prosecution uses on the discourse of the children. And that would be too bad for Raymond Buckey.

The prosecution's story is simply our culture's familiar story about the pedophile and his victims. The first trial attempted to complicate the story by adding multiple pedophiles and by making some of them female, but these features were disasters, like so many "improvements" to stories we have come to trust and need. Such changes spoiled things completely, so we told the story again in the second trial in order to get it right. Some of the children simply readjusted their recitations to fit the requirements of the new tale, maintaining unchanged the events but switching the actors so as to fit the new cast. Amy Beeles shifted Raymond Buckey into the molesting role played in her original story, told for the first trial, by Peggy McMartin Buckey, now no longer charged with anything and thus unavailable for the part.[4]

Raymond Buckey himself is the most imperturbable figure in the room, apart from the judge and one jury member who closes his eyes for long periods of time concentrating intently. I read Raymond Buckey's quiet as a dignity and grace born of great suffering. Others detect something sinister in it, but, then, others are wrong, aren't they? Constructed as a pedophile by the prosecution, even Raymond's body conforms: he is handsome in a furtive sort of way, quiet, and squinty-eyed. He has noticed all this himself: "Some people don't like the way I look, [but] I can't do anything about it if they think my eyes are too squinty."[5] By the prosecution's reading, Buckey simply carries out the dictates of this pedophile body, manifesting in every action the well-known mannerisms, habits, and practices of the pedophile.

How these come to be so well-known is not a part of the prosecution's concern, which is focused on the legend itself. According to this fiction, the pedophile is he who can be explained by his love for children, a love that expresses itself inevitably in sexually obsessive forms. So strong is this obsession known to be that there is nothing about the pedophile that cannot be explained by his pedophilia. The pedophile is nothing but a pedophile, and he cannot not be a pedophile. The procedures are very much like those adopted with the children's "disclosures," then: the story-telling that swims along coherently with a buoyant deductive logic. Pam Ferrero sneers to Buckey on the stand, "There is nothing I could ask you that would cause you to admit to molesting children, is there?" Buckey, you see, resists what is so obvious to the prosecution: the authority of the story. And the first rule laid down by that authority is that it must not be resisted. Nothing can exist outside the story. Except the liar. Buckey's obstinacy in the face of the tale's power is, thus, a pretty fair indication that he is lying, since the tale provides only one explanation. Buckey does not exist for the prosecution outside of this fable; their cross-examination amounts to an invitation to come back home, to settle down within the story—as a child-molester. That way he can be.

"What is it you like about children?," Ferrero asks. The asking of the question assumes that, whatever else may be in doubt, guilt isn't, since the question is never raised in this form except in a criminal context. If you need to ask, something is badly wrong. And raising the question raises the criminal context into certain prominence and forces

Buckey into explaining what it is that makes the pedophile tick. He tries to ignore the context: "What's not to like?" But it won't do at all to suggest that we *all* like children. Of course we don't. Only pedophiles like children, and we all know it. If that logic collapses, what case do we have against Buckey and what protections do we have from someone asking us what we ourselves like about children? Isn't this trial staged so we can tell the pedophiles from the rest of us—those in the gallery, say? How are we to do that if Buckey's question—what's not to like?—is allowed air time?

Ferrero also brings out (though it was never really hidden, having been located in one of the legal lootings of Buckey's place and broadcast in the newspapers) that Buckey possessed some copies of *Playboy*. Did he buy them "to read the interviews"? No, he did not, he says. He was not a subscriber; but he does admit to purchasing copies from time to time. Every month? No. Most months? Yes, probably most months. More than 6 times a year? Maybe. As many as 10 times a year? It's all quite Dickensian, quite like Bardell v. Pickwick. Having made this point with *Playboy*—there is general agreement among us that the point has been made—Ferrero passes over, surprisingly, Buckey's copy (also found by the sheriffing swine rooting through his apartment) of *Sexual Secrets*. We who are in on these things—I won't tell you how—know all about the existence of this find and are sure it will form a sequel to the *Playboy* questioning. But it does not. We are surprised. None of us has ever seen *Sexual Secrets* (or anything like it) but we are not tadpoles either and can imagine what it might be. Still, instead of this, the prosecution turns to Raymond Buckey's decision not to use underwear.

I figure myself that the prosecution spent 80% of its cross-examining time on this item. Some of the time was spent showing photographs to Buckey, of when he was playing volleyball, for instance, and asking him, "Are you wearing underwear in this picture?" In all of the pictures, Buckey has on trousers or sweat pants or shorts, I think, so there is never any way he can really tell, not being Ray Milland in *X—The Man with the X-Ray Eyes* and able to peek right through layers of clothing. So Buckey says, "I don't know" or "Maybe" or "Probably not" or "Could be"—mixing them up just to vary things. The prosecution, I assume, has no interest in the specific questions, knows they are something out of Wonderland, but asks them anyway so as to be able to control a context established entirely by the question and independent of the answer. These questions do not so much answer themselves as render answers impertinent, interruptions to a narrative mode that can proceed entirely on snide interrogations. It is the narrative that matters. Asking Buckey repeatedly about his underwear or lack of it keeps the story before us, even if you have no interest (as we do not) in Buckey's underwear or anyone else's. The narrative only needs the image of Raymond naked, and the question provides that by jeering: "Raymond's not wearing underwear! Raymond's not wearing underwear!" By the way, I am puzzled that the prosecution uses the broad term "underwear" when Raymond's T-shirts are not an issue. Maybe it's because the word "underpants" is thought to be indecent. I certainly think it is.

Critical Matter: The Defense

The defense's job is to unsettle the smug securities on which the prosecution's insinuations are built, to make the prosecution's stories seem silly. When did you start not wearing underwear? Many, many years ago. How come? It was more comfortable since I spent so much time on the beach playing volleyball and in and out of the water and since underwear gets wet and doesn't dry very fast and. . . . Yes, well, do you think it improper to dress that way at a pre-school? At the time I didn't. Do you now? Yes.

That's pretty close to accurate, and it illustrates what the defense does with the stories of the prosecution. Here, we first move from the prosecution's sensational/criminal melodrama, where the absence of underwear is a signal of a disgusting premeditation, to an everyday Trollopian realism, where dress indicates nothing more than careless habit and the vague hope of finding some kind of compromise between fashion and comfort. But it is not quite accurate, I think, to say that the defense simply wants to inscribe a different genre or formal pattern on these materials. The defense is actively draining the story's signals of all significance (so they become no signals at all), substituting an absurdist semiotics wherein all stories give up telling.

Buckey himself works within the same mode. Was there an unspeakable game called "Tickle," a game that was part of a monster-narrative of seduction? No. But did he tickle children? Yes, occasionally. Why? "Why does anybody tickle anybody?" You see the point: the tickling is done for no special reason and fits into no causal pattern, no plot: it's not part of an "innocent" narrative but a piece of a strategy to deny all narrative.

You may be thinking that this is just a windy and modish way of saying what is obvious to everyone after fifth-grade civics: under our system, the defense is not required to tell a persuasive story of innocence, simply render untelling the stories of guilt that might otherwise get themselves told. The story of the accused's innocence, a very strong story, has, as it were, already been recited: he simply *is* innocent from the opening bell, and the prosecution must confront a tale we all believe. But you are wrong to think that way. For one thing, the presumption of innocence must somehow buck a rigged rhetorical situation in which the prosecution gets not only the first but the last word too. More to the point, are we really prepared, in the instance of accusations of child-molesting, to tell any sort of innocence-story? Who starts out by believing in Raymond Buckey's innocence? According to a poll (accurate) I took among colleagues here and elsewhere, all pretty much equal in their ignorance of the case and their commitment to the American way, I found only a couple whose immediate response was "I don't know." No one said he was innocent. I only asked half a dozen people, it is true, but that's enough to give me what I need.

The defense, then, must certainly not rest on the strength of the already-told, relying on that and the manifest weakness of the narrative patched together by the awful writers manning the prosecution. The defense must substitute the texts of analysis, precisely because all stories fall eventually into the same culturally determined plot, a plot that spells out excruciating torture and final disaster for Raymond Buckey or anyone else accused of this offense. The defense, then, needs a discourse which contains no plots whatever. The defense's first move, already charted, is to deconstruct the center of the prosecution's tale, the truth-center occupied by the children and their inability not to speak of molestation. Such decentering is meant to point us not to a different story, however, but to the decentering itself.

What the defense sets up to do is to broadcast the power of negation, to tell stories that fade to black, stories that become, in true postmodernist fashion, anti-stories. These stories may pretend to make "points," to make the same point, but it's always that there is no point, that the point is *no*, that the point is the very *process* of erasing. The stories dissolve as narratives right before our eyes. The idea is to rain out the acid words of nothingness all over our prosecution's crops (a metaphor I am proud of) and to call attention not to the wreckage so much as the rain coming down. Did you ever have Amy Beeles as a student? I never saw her. Did you ever take a child's temperature? No; I never took anybody's temperature. Did you ever have a beard? No. A moustache? No. A beard and a moustache? No. Did you ever sodomize a child? No, never. Have you ever done anything to harm a child? No. You see what is happening: no, never, nothing, nada.

In a world without stories, we have no story-tellers. We have critics, deconstructive critics who are capable of setting in motion the most wonderful possibilities but who are impatient with linear and predictable narratives. The possibility set free by the defense is that the children were never damaged by the storyless Raymond Buckey: there were no molestings; no penetrations by the underwear-unencumbered penis of the little, defenseless bodies; no pain. There was no story at all. Nothing. Aren't Buckey and his Derridean attorney shifting us to a world where nothing holds, not even damage?

Our Story

But is that what we want, damage-vanish or even damage-control? How do we respond to the story-killers? After all, we are the ones who constructed the stories in the first place. I think that we ignore the deconstructive operations of the defense and turn even these maneuvers into substance, into material for more stories. Like mine. Our culture has produced a story of molestation that is not only widely believed but, more important, widely sanctioned and, more important still, widely circulated. According to this story, the pedophiles who (alone) endanger children are pretty much everywhere, everywhere except within, of course. They flourish in day-care centers, in churches, social service agencies, schools, and locker rooms. They are all male, maladjusted or sick (but criminal certainly), violent and dangerous, strangers, and photographers. They are in league with and support (or operate) circles of abduction, child-prostitution rings, and a child-pornography racket.

Many of us are dimly aware that there is no reason on earth to have such a story around, apart from our need for it. Social scientists and workers in the field, even the police, tell among themselves (or in safely ineffectual academic journals) a story that is entirely different. This shadow/silent story readjusts every part of the public legend: there is no evidence that any child-abduction or prostitution rings exist; no commercial child-erotica is now published, except by the F.B.I. for Sting operations; pedophiles, such as may exist, are gentle and unaggressive, usually but not always male; almost all child-molesting comes not from outside but from within the family circle. It is perhaps obvious why such a story has no currency.

The loud public tale has the status of what we used to call "myth" when we believed some stories were truer than others. I still do, and I believe the story that is now trapping Raymond Buckey is not only false but baleful. This trial of Raymond Buckey provides a way for texts to spin out endlessly, but to spin always the same web, the one we desire so badly we are happy to be caught in it. Even the defense cannot escape the words that will be wrestled away from deconstructive play and put to work on the same tediously repetitive construction job. And so we haul back into court these children, to save them and to make them help us in our task of—keeping the story going. Amy Beeles, Tori Walsh, Suzanne Goss: back once more to tell the stories we need. Suzanne Goss, Buckey says, was an especially winning and happy little girl, "just a very friendly child." I wonder if she is still? I wonder what we have done by making her and the others, year after year, play parts in this wretched cultural narrative? I wonder what we do to ourselves?

The standard narrative manages to package all the horror gothic-style, fashioning an Outsider as monster and thus protecting us from the more knowing shadow-stories of incest and the seduction of children by those who are loved and trusted (by "love" and "trust"). So much is obvious. But those of us doing our duty at the trial have come to see that the shadow-story is really much the same as the official one, offering simply a more cynical, detective-story or soap-opera modeling of the romance/gothic plot. Substituting a father for a stranger, a criminal (or an illness) for a monster leaves the basic dualisms untroubled. As we sit on courtroom seats that are, though mere benches, surprisingly comfortable, it occurs to us that it might be possible to replot the story by relocating the history and presence of our culturally scripted desire for children. Instead of telling the story one more time, we might tell the story of the story. We could, at some risk, center and speak what is marginal and unspeakable. Now we are not, naturally enough, interested in simple reversals or parodies: we do not want to change places with Raymond Buckey or begin producing banal confessions. That would be less interesting even than the gothic we now have with us; worse, it would be utterly predictable. It would be pretty much the same story. Deconstructing the story we love to tell and believe, the story of the monster does give us a glimpse of another tale to tell, but it is not one where the villain roles go to individuals. Not even to me.

Notes

1. See Mary A. Fischer, "McMartin," *Los Angeles Magazine*, October 1989, pp. 128–29.

2. In the spring of 1990, some of the parents employed a former F.B.I. special agent,

what they said were geologists, professional tunnel-diggers, photographers, and an archaeologist to gouge around and under the school to confirm the existence of secret dens and tunnels, the leavings from Satanic sacrificial rites, and anything else that might be suggested by the debris. The D.A.'s office said that these excavations turned up nothing even remotely useful; the parents disagreed; the specialists were professionally circumspect.

3. For a rich and compelling account of this grilling and other matters relating to the trial, see the essay by a fellow gallery-sitter who writes with more information, alertness, and judiciousness than I: Keith Fitzgerald's "Why I Came to Believe Ray Buckey Is Innocent: A Trial Watcher's Notes," *Reader (Los Angeles)* 12 (July 13, 1990): 3–5.

Ms. Krebs's immediate superior, Kee MacFarlane, also took part in these interviews and seems to have employed similar techniques. Here, in a transcript from a taped interview printed in Fischer (*Los Angeles Magazine*, p. 132), MacFarlane goes after "disclosures" from an eight-year-old former McMartin student, the immediate subject being the alleged game of "Naked Movie Star":

> Boy: "Well, I didn't really hear it [Naked Movie Star] a whole lot. I just heard someone yell it from out in the . . . someone yelled it."
>
> MacFarlane: "Maybe, Mr. Alligator, you peeked in the window one day and saw them playing it, and maybe you could remember and help us."
>
> Boy: "Well, no, I haven't seen anyone playing Naked Movie Star. I've only heard the song."
>
> MacFarlane: "What good are you? You must be dumb."
>
> Boy: "Well, I don't really, umm, remember seeing anyone play that 'cause I wasn't there, when I . . . when people are playing it."
>
> MacFarlane: "You weren't? You weren't. That's why we're hoping maybe you saw . . . See, a lot of these puppets weren't there, but they got to see what happened."
>
> Boy: "Well, I saw a lot of fighting. . . ."
>
> *
>
> MacFarlane: "Can I pat you on the head for that. . . look what a big help you can be. You're going to help all these little children because you're so smart . . . . Okay, did they ever pose in funny poses for the pictures?"
>
> Boy: "Well, it wasn't a real camera. We just played. . . ."
>
> MacFarlane: "Mr. Alligator, I'm going to . . . going to ask you something here. Now, we already found out from the other kids that it was a real camera, so you don't have to pretend, okay? Is that a deal?"
>
> Boy: "Well, I haven't seen any real camera."
>
> MacFarlane: "How about something that goes flash, remember that? I bet if you're smart, you better put your thinking—"
>
> Boy: "Yes, it was a play camera that we played with."
>
> MacFarlane: "Oh, and it went flash?"
>
> Boy: "Well, it didn't exactly go flash."
>
> MacFarlane: "It didn't exactly go flash. Went click? Did little pictures go zip, come out of it?"
>
> Boy: "I don't remember that."
>
> MacFarlane: "Oh, you don't remember that. Well, you're doing pretty good, Mr. Alligator. I got to shake your hand. You remembered who took the pictures and all that; now, just think how your [unintelligible]."
>
> Boy: "I'm getting tired here."

4. See Fitzgerald: "Earlier she [Amy Beeles] said that she didn't remember ever seeing Ray without clothes, that he didn't penetrate her with his finger and penis, and that it was Ray's mother, Peggy, who put a finger in her 'virginia' and rectum. Now, with Peggy acquitted on all counts, Amy says that she definitely saw Ray naked and that he violated her" (p. 4).

5. Mary A. Fischer, "Ray Buckey: An Exclusive Interview," *Los Angeles Magazine*, April 1990, p. 100.

11

Our Own Child-Loving

It has not been a question of getting a new view on pedophilia. This book has, rather, recorded an attempt to use the odd way we place pedophilia to get a new view on our view, a different way to hear our talk. My own role has been to hover round, not to help with anything but to butt in on the conversation with that low-level, one-upmanship, do-it-yourself deconstruction that makes us all cringe. "What makes you say that?," has been my main line throughout, except when I have thought to ask why I have been assuming that anyone *makes* anyone say anything, why I too have been honoring power. Then the question could glide over to "Do we really *want* to say that?" or even "What would it be more fun to say?"

Not that the child and the loving of it have been minor players throughout. It's just that up to now they have not been seen in their familiar form, as a weighty problem, as a cause for little more than alarm. We inside the argument of this book have not been in a position where we could very well hear, much less attend to the pressing questions of our day: "What can we *do* about the way children are loved, about *sexual* attraction, about the exploitation of children, the assaults and the abductions; about the child-pornography industry; about child sex-rings; about the number of children who are molested at one time or other while they are growing up. What are you proposing to do about it?"

And we need to do more with these concerns than argue that they proceed from the way the problem is figured and are hence, though inevitable, no more "real" than the problem they very much need in order to sustain the worries that we have come to depend upon. More is needed, I agree. But not more of the same thing, not more plotting of the problems within the same narrative form and with the same images and cast of characters, since this same thing is so patently ineffective, or, rather, effective only in ensuring the continuation of exactly the same string of problems. That children are sometimes murdered, sometimes kidnapped, sometimes raped and forced to submit in various ways to the needs of others without regard to their own is indisputable. Without doubt, we ladle massive doses of pain into our children, partly in obedience to purblind cultural prescriptions and partly for our own pleasures, some of which are more subtle but no less terrible than the sexual. It is not a question of denying those horrors; it is, for me, a question of asking about the questions, wondering whether the pain itself is in any way contained within and perpetuated by the way we understand the problem—asking about that and about the way we shout down or criminalize any voices which stray outside that understanding. Our children are suffering and we care very much about that, but we seem to care about that suffering to pretty much the same degree that we worry about keeping the applecart steady. We do not want to hear that our solutions are not working; we do not want to hear that our solutions hold hands with the problem, that what needs fixing is the metaphor that allows us to see a cure for power only in more power, in a kind of psycho-cultural arms race with the perverts.

This chapter is meant to confront these issues more directly, perhaps more "seriously," but I cannot alter my tone or stance. I do not, that is, see how the problems can be solved or even addressed within power, the very framework that created them. Children, perhaps most especially, lose within power metaphors; they get power thrown at them, switched across their bodies, driven into their flesh. Power divides things so resolutely and with such a show of clarity that it can, paradoxically, create most enticing shadowiness. The child is so wonderfully set off, set away from us, that its natural connections to us—we were once one, we have them out of our bodies, we have them around us everywhere—are made gossamer-like, gracefully floating off into some Never-Never Land, where this misty Child, the Other has its being. I have argued throughout, then, that the child has been conceived of by power in such a way as to make it both centrally and irresistibly Other, and thus erotic. Responding with arousal, then, is to respond "normally," respond as one is told. We protect against eroticizing the child and thereby write a shadow-story of child-eroticism. The genuine pervert in our culture has been, for the last two hundred years at least, the one who has managed to remain indifferent to the child's blooming, glowing power-driven and power-insured sexual appeal. The rest of us have reacted as we must.

Consequently, we have looked to power for a solution to the mess it has gotten us into; and power has provided us with a story, wherein the effects of power's workings on children are presumably undone. It is a story told to exonerate power. It looks like a story told to help children, but it is not. In this story, we are cast as attractive characters entirely free from desire, children are free from sexual attraction or from any desires of their own, and a few—but not *too* few—sociopathic people are possessed of needs that they then enact in terrible ways. Power has told us that if we rely on this story we cannot go wrong, so long as we repeat it often and loudly enough. Whether we now tell this tale because we need it for reassurance, because it provides us with easy access to the unthinkable ourselves, or both, there seems to be no end to our capacity to find in it charm and gladness.

It is just because this song is not heard, much less sung in the disreputable neighborhoods of pedophilia, that we can nose out there some inside dope on the manufacturing of such hits, such cultural necessities for power. From inside power, we spot the threat of pedophilia and rush to offer a defense, seeking to protect those obviously at risk. We are doing no more than guarding our own from the assaults of the alien. Such exciting tales, we know from our own nation's history, have a way of disguising as heroic defense a fierce imperialist move, a take-over of a continent similar to the take-over of the child. If Milton's God created man according to His whim and then damned him for it, we have created children as we wanted and then protected them for it. These protections do not come cheap.

To protect children from the dangers of sick sexual interests, we cultivate in the child a sharp sense of terror that can serve as a defense. Since children, we figure, are likely to be unable to distinguish a pedophilic advance from any other, we take the safe route and tell them to forget about discriminations, to regard any and all adult comments or signals of recognition as advances, and all advances as perilous. In order to impress this line of thinking on the child, we are urged to make their fear of displeasing us equal to the fear of the Other adult. Nearly any means we might use to convince the child of the gravity of the situation are countenanced.

The following "Dear Abby" offers a retelling of this common but quite remarkable fable. In this column "Arizona Mom" writes about her "adorable" 2½-year-old son whom she is "glad" to say is not at all "shy and withdrawn." In fact, "he runs up to people he has never seen before and puts his arms up, asking to be held—and, of course, these strangers pick him up." "I am concerned," the writer continues, "that his friendliness might lead to his being abducted someday." She has tried telling her son not to "act that way," "but he turns right around and does it anyway." What's to be done?, she asks Abby: how can she "discourage this behavior without offending the stranger?"

Anyone now alive in this country will be able to anticipate what Abby thinks about this concern for the stranger's feelings. So, after dismissing this piffle—the stranger very possibly being a child-molester anyway—Abby turns on the heat:

> Do more than just "tell" your son; forbid him to speak to strangers. Explain that there are people who could do him harm—and one cannot tell by looking at a stranger who is harmless and who is not. If your child defies you, punish him by depriving him of something he considers a treat—but make that punishment memorable.
>
> Be firm, mother. Your child needs to be protected, and it's your responsibility to protect him.[1]

One notices how this fable disguises its own needs. It tells the story about child sexuality again, the story about the monsters who believe in it and do such harm. It tells the story of how alert the rest of us are to the child's needs. And what the child has the most need of should be clear: "Your child needs to be protected." Adequate protection can only be provided if the concerned parent matches force with force, by being *firm*. The only way to meet such a powerful threat is to exercise power, to exercise power on the child so that the child will then have some power of its own. Abby says we might try depriving the child of a treat, *but* that we should make the punishment "memorable," whatever we do. I don't think, judging by Abby's tone, that we ought to pin all our hopes on treat-deprivations. That wouldn't be so very "memorable," probably. In order to cure the child of his dangerous friendliness, more may be required, just so he won't be hurt. So says Abby; so says our culture.[2]

Take the following two scenes enacted in a shopping mall, say, or on the street or in the park: in the first an adult is striking a screaming child repeatedly on the buttocks; in the second an adult is sitting with a child on a bench and they are hugging. Which scene is more common? Which makes us uneasy? Which do we judge to be normal? Which is more likely to run afoul of the law? A society, I believe, which honors hitting and suspects hugging is immoral; one which sees hitting as health and hugging as illness is mad; one which is aroused by hitting alone is psychotic and should be locked up.

The real criminal is not the pedophile but the prescribed attitude to pedophilia: that is the stagy form of the claim I have been making throughout and simply want to recast here in this concluding chapter by placing it briefly in a twentieth-century American context. This is not an analysis of our culture but a glance at it, and of course this "culture" is itself a fiction, a multiple fiction at that. Even a weak description of our grouping together in America would acknowledge a huge number of regional, class, occupational, and linguistic divisions. Sexuality itself (as distinct from "sex"), Foucault says, is "originally, historically bourgeois," inducing class effects gradually.[3] It is likely, then, that my own immersion in bourgeois constructions of sexuality will have some resonance in other strata. In any case, I have neither the room nor the resources here for an explicit account of these multiplicities in the argument which follows: that the child is constructed so as to make its eroticism necessary and the image of the erotic child central and not marginal to our culture; that our denial of this positioning is itself a form of erotic doublespeak; that power's specific maneuverings in this area are dangerous and cruel; and that we might, finally, refigure in some way these issues so as to give us and our children a little relief. Right now we are doing nothing but heavy, hot breathing; we are allowed to do nothing but pant. That's getting tiresome, and it hurts.

Selling the Erotic Child

Children have been central to "entertainment" for many centuries, of course; but it is arguable that not even their presence in Medieval choirs or Renaissance theater could rival the way we have in the last two hundred years made childhood into a self-contained leisure-time industry. Particularly in America but also overseas, nineteenth-century schools turned the students' accomplishments, real or imagined, into the public spectacle of recitations, contests, displays of skill or talent in art, music, drama, sports, and handicrafts. In this century, children and their wares and their bodies are put on display so often that parenthood has become largely an extended series of "watchings." Turn a child loose for a lesson or two in tap, ballet, baton-twirling, tennis, accordion, computer programming, speech, swimming, singing, anything at all and you will find yourself, long before the teachings have had any of the promised effects, going to watch the child demonstrate how much skill she or he has yet to acquire. Even if the child is, happily, withdrawn and nervous about the spotlight, given to private

364 / *Our Own Child-Loving*

activities, you will find yourself going to watch and having her or him watched by many others: a reader will be put on display for having read; a knitter for having knitted; a canner for canning; a tender of animals for managing to keep them from dying. The vast array of Little League/Pee Wee/Junior sports events allows even more in the gazing line. One way or another, there is nothing we do so much of with children as watching them.

Beyond this enormous amateur theater, occupying every village and hamlet, city and suburb across the land, we have the pros, where the most talented and charming of our children are paid salaries and good ones to thrill us so deeply that we are willing to lay out enough money so that there will be some left over for others even after the child stars get theirs. The most open market for display is, of course, advertising, where Brooke Shields and imitators model sweaters and jeans with, so they say, nothing on under them and where, for less money, serviceable anonymous cuties model everything from short swishy skirts to skimpy underwear for catalogues and Sunday stuffers.[4] For pure erotic longevity, however, nothing has been able to top the blond child in the Coppertone ad, the one whose pants are being yanked down from behind[5] so as to expose a chubby bottom fully and who reacts to the exposure with a becoming blush and with no attempt whatever to cover herself.

What of the child in the mainline entertainment media, though, in the movies and television and comic books and Sunday funnies, where the attempt to sell something is not so open? That child is, more or less, one erotic image with slight variations. From the beginning of the century, one form seems to have dominated, to have attracted the desire of the nation. That form, I think, is essentially genderless, blond, vacant, wide-eyed (unsuspecting), and secretive (mischievous); it is also attached to the upper middle class, to a vaguely Protestant but non-denominational and actually not-very-earnest set of values, to urban sophistication (though not street-kid sophistication), and to an indoor, pampered, unathletic, moderately hot house environment; parents are of very little or no importance to these children, though the latter are, as we would expect, much more interested in adults than in other children; these children pay little explicit attention to their bodies, are so far from being vain that they are very nearly unaware that we are watching and certainly don't notice if a shirttail is out, some underwear provocatively flashing, skin exposed. When the figure is nominally female, it is made exceptionally active, even aggressive; when male, more passive, even sneaky; the females are given short hair, distinctive features; the males long hair and soft, hazy features—all merging toward (though not duplicating exactly) an androgynous oneness, the perfect erotic child.

A. Sunday Fun

The American Sunday "funnies," newspaper comic strips, were almost at once dominated by the images of children, especially, I think, this one special figure of the erotic child. There were many fumbling and only moderately successful attempts at good children, joke-telling children, dark-haired children, fat or ugly children; but the ideal formula was soon hit upon and became solidified in Richard F. Outcault's amazingly long-running and commercially adaptable Buster Brown. Buster was never drawn very well, or at least consistently, but he was recognizable for the simplicity of his features, the large, perfect-circle eyes and the exaggerated, bee-sting (lipstick-formed) lips; in profile, he looked much like what was to become the image of the flapper. He had very long blond hair, formed as if in a beauty-shop perm (or eighteenth-century wig). He wore an unusual pantalooned, skirted outfit, so that the arrangements necessary to these clothes when Buster was in his most familiar posture made his spankings indistinguishable from those of his female funnies friends (see Figures A and B).[6] Buster, especially his bottom-under-attack, was pure unisex.

And the attacks on this bottom formed both the central image and the central plot of this immensely popular strip. Now and then Buster aroused readers by appearing naked, usually through the gimmick of having the swimming boy's clothes stolen by a dog or other naughty boys and then showing him making a run for it, a run we view, naturally, from the rear (see Figure C; June 11, 1905). In the little moral tags, infuriating to modern readers and probably to readers of the time too but handy as screens for the erotics, Buster often reflects on how unimportant such things as clothes are, compared to "character," "principle," and other irrelevances. In the strip of January 7, 1906, a naked Buster, howling "Not so hard, Pa!" is whipped by an angry father, a scene so pornographic it is given to readers only in shadow (Figure D). But this is actually an uncharacteristic scene, probably a mistake, in that Buster is not generally nude,[7] the punisher is generally the mother with her hand or a hairbrush and not the father with a stick, and the child is not held at arm's length but cuddled over the lap or slung over a chair so as to bring the buttocks into focus. The characteristic scene, in other words, is less harsh, more tactile and cuddly, more repeatable. Instead of the rather pathetic "Not so hard,

366 / *Our Own Child-Loving*

Figure A

Pa!" Buster's line is often something like "Harder Ma!" (September 1, 1904), "*My*, I did get spanked, but it was worth it" (July 20, 1919), "I have shown very poor judgment again, and I have been very well spanked" (September 25, 1904), and even "Bless her Heart. I fairly enjoyed being spanked again" (September 24, 1905). The spankings are not really climactic, that is, sometimes are not shown at all (to pique the imagination, no doubt) and sometimes are only threatened; it's just that they form both the plot and the atmosphere of the weekly story. A good example is the strip of March 17, 1918: see Figure E. The final box of the top column, "Come on, Ma, Here I am" suggests what this particular Sunday's fun is about. It is fun that seems to have lost all restraint in its frenzy of punishments, gender transformations, and erotic undressings, undressings that reveal how, underneath, the child is simply a wonderfully reproducible form, androgynous and endlessly compliant, cheerfully engaging in just the right sort of mischief, the sort of mischief we love.

The association between Buster and his spankings was so strong that

Our Own Child-Loving / 367

!["But Just Couldn't Mamma!" cartoon with mother holding hairbrush and child saying "Make More Noise, Esser!"]

Figure B

other artists sometimes referred to it in their own strips: see, for instance, the September 25, 1904 "Betsy Bouncer and Her Doll," Figure F. These other strips from the first decades of the century often featured spankings of their own, of course. It wasn't just Buster who was upended and made to sparkle from behind; the same activity was on view in "Angelic Angelina," "Ginger Pop," "Wide Awake Willie," "Reg'lar Fellers," "Bobby Make Believe," and, of course, "The Katzenjammer Kids." Occasionally, as in Sidney Smith's "The Gumps" strip from November 21, 1920 (see Figure G), the delights verge closely on undisguised brutality. While most cartoons really featured the misdeeds and contracted the punishment to a single scene or two, here the punishment and its harsh aftermath occupies the entire strip, the chase being followed by a beating with a strap, then by a spanking with the hand and then by what looks like a grisly punch line, the towheaded child's hope for the death or disappearance of the parents. This is eroticism over the edge.

Figure C

Our Own Child-Loving / 369

Figure D

It was an explicit eroticism carried on for a time in the 1920s and 1930s by a Buster Brown copy, Martin M. Branner's Perry Winkle: see Figure H; January 5, 1930. Perry was drawn with another rosebud mouth, immense round eyes, a perky nose, and very long blond hair.[8] Exactly like Buster, his spanking formed the staple of the strip. Every summer he went swimming and thus lost his clothes and thus appeared naked a few times, but generally he was either being whacked or threatened with it: "So that's his idea of fun, is it!! Wait'll he gets home!! I'll take his clothes offen him and tan him good and proper!!!" (July 15, 1928). In the late 1930s and into the 1940s the tradition endured in "Dixie Dugan," "Joe Palooka," "Apple Mary," "Ella Cinders," "Harold Teen," and "Lil' Abner," gradually losing steam after those decades, or taking more disguised forms, though still popping up now and then in "Little Lulu," "Little Iodine," "Blondie," "Dennis the Menace," "Archie," "Richie Rich," and even "Mary Worth."

B. Moving Pictures

This Buster Brown figure keeps coming back to us, ready for more, in television and cinema. The most obvious and prominent big-eyed, kissy-lipped blonde figures have been Shirley Temple, Jackie Coogan, Freddie Bartholomew, Patty McCormack, Jay North (Dennis the Menace), Tatum O'Neal, Ricky Schroeder, Jodie Foster, Drew Barrymore, River Pheonix, and Macaulay Culkin, not all blonde exactly but otherwise indistinguishable. Nearly every television sit-com has the mandatory child in this mold, often, like *Family Ties*, adding one later if s/he

Figure E

Our Own Child-Loving / 371

Figure F

has been by some blunder left out of the original formula. Long-running displays of child erotica like *The Brady Bunch* cease attracting only when the youngest objects, Bobby and Cindy, pass out of pedophile range.

But it is in films that the fullest exposure is possible, the most complete playing out of the Buster Brown fantasy. The image of Shirley Temple is perhaps most suggestive, as she flirted and seduced and sashayed her way through movie after movie, attaching herself always to adults, winning their hearts and minds, and swishing her short little skirt around above a camera positioned at a remarkably low level. Even more blatant is the career of Mark Lester, a beautifully empty child who looked just like Buster Brown (as they all do). Lester began his career as a pretty decoration, advanced to providing an object for abuse, and ended by dropping his pants. That's crude but true. Most prominently in Carol Reed's *Oliver!* (1968), Lester's body is flung about and dangled in tantalizing partial nakedness (his shirt being pulled out of trousers that are drooping down just as fast) in a long finale that seems arranged not to kill Sikes but to display the boy. From there he moved to school-child films like *Melody* (1972), where he is happily spanked on screen, cries a little, and teams up with a young mate wearing a skirt she doesn't mind the camera shooting straight up. From here it was a short step to *Redneck* (1972), a perverse initiation story, featuring Lester, still prepubescent but barely so, undressing slowly before a mirror in order to examine, quite pointedly, his presumably developing genitals, genitals which we are not shown (having no interest in them) so that the camera may linger fondly over the bared buttocks.

Lester's progress almost exactly duplicates that of Jay North, who had, slightly earlier, moved from cute-but-clothed exhibiting toward

Figure G

Our Own Child-Loving / 373

Figure H

twelve-year-old nudity. North had been for years (1959–1963) television's perfect Buster Brown clone, Dennis the Menace, an image slightly more active than Lester's but physically identical. Like Lester, North progressed to spanking (by Lucille Ball in her *The Lucy Show* comedy series) and then, in a film called *Maya* (1965), to full rearwards nudity. In an extended scene, explained (weakly) in the narrative by a dunk in a river, North stands naked before a fire, rubbing his buttocks and talking, while the camera holds still, breathlessly, unable to believe its luck. After a time, a good long time, he wraps some cloth around him but, so the happy joke goes, is so inexperienced at doing so that he leaves a part of himself exposed. Guess which part.

These bottoms, the Buster Brown bottom reproduced over and over, become featured in an astonishing number of movies. Peter Brook's 1963 artsy *Lord of the Flies* (and its 1990 unartsy remake) are notorious, but even guaranteed wholesome movies like *My Side of the Moun-*

tain (1969) stick in quite gratuitous swimming or bathing or undressing-for-bed scenes so as to give us shots of bottoms. The endless succession of "Boy"s in the endless succession of Tarzan movies were wondrously obliging in this regard, as were more recent films like the determinedly serious *Pretty Baby* (1978) or the decidedly silly *The Blue Lagoon* (1980). Films made by guardians of the cultural center are especially likely to wind toward the rear. Both Walt Disney, who had a positive mania for bottoms, and *The Reader's Digest* manage consistently to get clothes off and cameras positioned for back-end shots. In Disney's *One Little Indian* (1973), for instance, James Garner takes the child across his lap, pulls down his pants, and examines, along with the camera, the buttocks to get clues as to the child's parentage, a scene repeated from the opening of the movie. In *The Reader's Digest*'s right-wing version of *Tom Sawyer* (1973), the reward we get for watching the moronic Nixonite inversion of Twain is a shot of Tom and Huck swimming, both actors arching their backs in turn so that their naked posteriors, emerging from the waves, can be fondled by the camera.

Nearly as good as this are shots of underwear, if they are made properly sneaky, provocative—Barthesian glimpses, flashes of forbidden wonder. The little Buster-Brown skirt-wearers in the long-running *Our Gang* films (1922–1944), the adorable Darla (Hood) most commonly, seemed always willing to pose in convenient positions for the display of underpants, and we see the same thing in any number of later "good kid" Buster-figures, from Luke Halpin in the 1960s *Flipper* movies to Bobby Brady and Ricky Schroeder. But as in the comics, the flash of the child's underwear is by no means made less tempting when the child's moral development is shakier or outright endangered. Film adaptations of Stephen King novels, in which the question of child goodness often comes up, seem remarkable for such exhibits, as in *Cujo* (1983), or, so overtly as to arouse some discomfort, in *Stand By Me* (1986), where the film pivots on a scene of pedophile bliss: four morally fragile Buster Browns in their underwear, wet and revealing, with one of them fumbling around inside, in close-up, at his testicles. Similarly, in Stanley Kramer's *Bless the Beasts and Children* (1971), six "problem" children spend a large part of the film so clad, and while Patty McCormack in that classic film about child-evil *The Bad Seed* (1956) does not actually take off her dress, the camera at one point reduces itself to an impossibly low ground-level, worm's-eye view in order to show us her panties.

In these last two films we have further Buster Brown attractions: the *Beasts and Children* boys are all paddled soundly, rub themselves, and cry. *The Bad Seed* goes even further. Finding no place in the story (or in the Maxwell Anderson play which formed the basis for the film) for some "don't 'ee, please don't 'ee," the film added a joking coda, where not the character ("Rhoda") but the actress (Patty McCormack) is introduced, placed on a sofa, and then turned over the knee of the woman who plays her mother (Nancy Kelly) and firmly, loudly spanked. Such woodshed affairs are frequent for popular entertainments such as Hal Roach's *Our Gang* series; but they are also plentiful in films with far loftier credentials, like Charles Laughton's *The Night of the Hunter* (1955), which seems to figure that with children there, even in the part of pitiable victims, there is finally nothing to do with them but bare their bottoms and whip them.

These are examples that will seem extreme, perhaps, and certainly unsubtle. Still, the image of the cute, huggable, beatable child is likely so powerful that we not only cannot do without it but cannot even recognize our own need. It has become second nature, this desire, this figuring of the Buster Brown in our minds and in our art and in our lives. When somebody brings it to our attention, therefore, it seems absurd.

Just Say No: Denial, DoubleSpeak, EroticSpeak

In the very strength of our denial, the need we have to tell the story so strenuously and so often, always in the same terms exactly, lies perhaps a surer clue to our involvement in the sexualizing of the child. Such frenzied denunciations of the villains, such easy expressions of outrage,[9] such simple-minded analyses of the problem of child-molesting as we love to repeat serve not simply to flatter us but to bring before us once again the same story of desire that is itself desirable, allowing us to construct, watch, enjoy the erotic child without taking any responsibility for our actions. This, one might say, is the sort of pornography that really ought to be banned.

In its most obvious form, it seeks to protect the emptiness of the child, its "innocence," for pedophilic figurings, speaking over and over again of the child's sexuality as if it were not there,[10] as if, in other words, it needed to be guarded, hoarded, reserved for the speaker. Ignoring entirely our own most valued empirical science and insisting thunderously on the "purity" of children constitute ways of raising and thus implanting sexuality on them, a way of imaging them wholly through desire. Denying the child access to sexual feeling is also a way of maintaining unchallenged what are clearly traditional views of gender, family, and authority; if only a few freaks conspire to sexualize children, then nothing is the matter that a little censorship or some entrapment or a few electrocutions won't cure.

The hypocrisy of these protective denials is perhaps most evident in the media displays mentioned earlier and, as Paul Gebhard points out, in such public promotions of sexual desirability as Miss America and Miss Universe contests, where the winners are quite commonly minors, thus proclaiming to one and all that the most sexually prized among us are not sexual beings at all, cannot be by law.[11] In similar ways, magazines like *Chic*, *Hustler*, *Playboy*, and in a slightly different key, *The National Enquirer* lose no opportunity to capitalize on and to denounce pedophilic desires. *Hustler* gives as its reason for keeping these issues and images alive by discussing them the quite orthodox view that "contemptible" as such things certainly are, the magazine, aware of its cultural duties, has a "responsibility" to show that "perverts" "exist—and need to be exposed."[12] We can all rest easier knowing *Hustler* is on guard. Actually, such a system of denial is so widespread and the protections against acknowledging our own child-loving so deeply planted that these blatant contradictions can often exist even without *Hustler*'s cynicism. For instance, the almost painfully enlightened *Show Me!*, a sex-education book of photographs with text for children and parents, has become the standard for what some officials think of as "kiddie-porn" and is doubtless employed by some in private erotic duties (the photographs are of naked children and adolescents, the latter sometimes involved in sex play). It is sadly ironic, then, that this text hauls out the same tired line to justify itself: a child informed by this book on sexual matters will not be such easy prey to "sexual perverts," "psychopaths," and "strangers."[13]

Our doublespeak operations act not simply to generate lots of self-flattery and lots of titillating talk but also to protect what seems to be the most popular sexual activity with children allowed, or indeed mandated, by power: spanking. The same journalists and legislators anxious to take a most visible stand against the sexual exploitation of children in any form are often just as eager to affirm the right of certain adults to chastise at will and with almost no intrusive controls. Parents, we know, are not only allowed to whack away but are now and then encouraged to do so[14]; child-abuse legislation, like public opinion (naturally), therefore expressly excludes from censure or penalty "reasonable corporal punishment" administered by parents or anyone *in loco parentis*. What is assault in another context is here simply a traditional practice of good parenting, the exercise of a freedom we are proud to have wrested away from King George. That it is next to impossible to distinguish "reasonable" child-beating from that which is "excessive" seems to bother us little, so determined are we to take the rights power grants us and to practice them on children. But we might be struck by the anomalies we introduce with this harsh sexualizing of power, the problems that arise in our righteous child-flagellating. Eleven-year-old Justin Miller, for instance, recently reported to authorities that while his parents had been members of a Christian commune, "four men had struck him 140 times with a wooden paddle" to make him a better Christian. Subsequent criminal charges, which the commune leader said had been "hatched in hell,"[15] were dropped however, when the deputy D.A. concluded that there simply was no conclusive medical evidence to support the case: "the physician who examined Miller could not pinpoint if the bruising on his buttocks came from a brief recent swatting or from a serious beating months ago."[16] One can see the physician's point, and the deputy D.A.'s too, and the commune leader's for that matter: why should the court's time be wasted with the trifling bruises from a "swatting," a "brief" one too, perhaps no more than seventy or eighty blows? Kids who complain about such trifles are a nuisance and deserve to be taught a lesson.

And the lesson for us is that we cannot get enough of this subject in the flesh or, more commonly and perhaps more urgently, in print. Aside from spankings, not after all easily available to everyone, our main diet comes from talk, from constant talk on child pornography, incest, child sex slaves, prostitution, child abduction, child sex murders. The excitement generated by such talk can be had for free almost anywhere, not just in *Hustler* and *Playboy* but *Ms.* and *The Nation*, *The National Enquirer* and the *New York Times*, on Geraldo and on MacNeil/Lehrer. We note that there are virtually no curbs on what can be said, the subject promoting a smug certainty that can somehow allow salacious talk and images otherwise completely unacceptable for the media. We may also notice that the customary checks provided by demands for evidence, statistics, reasonable empirical grounding, loose and dubious as these things are in the best of circumstances, become so slack here as to snooze. One can make any sort of claim, so long as it is shocking. And, as suggested above, we notice that there is no political variance on this point, no spectrum at all. The standard liberal line on sexuality—Freud's line, say, about the terrible "injustice" of demanding of everyone "the same standard of sexual life"[17]—is silenced as regards children, heard only from pedophile apologists. The religious Right and the radical Left join happily to repeat the same erotic chant; we are all, as it were, compelled to speak it, have it with our corn flakes every morning, start the day off not with a song but a little child sex talk. It's our pledge of allegiance to power.

Power and the Problem

Power has a way of dealing with "problems" it has created, isolated for attention, and injected with alarm: throw a little force into them. The idea is not to make the problems go away, of course, since they would not have been created in the first place if they did not serve power well. The idea is to keep the problems alive, to assure us that they are still with us, doing their job. If the problems are, as in this case, defined as exciting yet somehow officially distasteful, power can protect us by melodramatic narratives of the criminal. In the case of the sexual attraction to children, mandated by power, the procedures we employ to scratch this itch and keep it going are to: (1) root it in indignation and provide plenty of justification for that response; (2) deny or displace problems that do exist or seem threatening; (3) write the child-love story as a legal issue, with lawyers and jailers as the novelists.

A. Defining the Proper Reaction

We are told to be incensed and to keep being incensed. It is not easy to hold that pose for long, of course; so we get periodic and stern lectures on keeping still, threats on how we will be pinched or shook if we relax. Newspapers, magazines, television, schools, police, social scientists, and preachers all contribute generously to pumping up our outrage and keeping it elevated. But the most resolute if not the most articulate of these lecturers are the lawmen, the legislators, especially when they turn to holding hearings.

The late-1984 hearings on "Child Pornography and Pedophilia," chaired by Senator William V. Roth, Jr., provide a good example. Chairman Roth opened the proceedings by declaring that the activity they were to hear about was "up there beside the most pernicious acts ever committed by so-called organized crime"[18] and ended them by saying he had heard nothing that would cause him to change his mind: "To be frank, I can think of no more pernicious crime than this, the exploitation, utilization of innocent children I think is the most unbelievable act to comprehend" (p. 60). One can see why Senator Roth was the man for this job. He saw that what was wanted was the sort of talk that is impatient with talk: the time had come for that glinty-eyed, narrow-lipped discourse that shows how itchy we are to get at our guns, to kick a little butt: "It seems to me," the Chairman said, "all we are talking about is studying, when what we need is action" (p. 28). Still, he kept his talk-show studyings meandering along, stroking his men-of-action guests with fulsome compliments: "You are doing an enormous service in an area that is unbelievable" (p. 53). (None of us are required to "believe" any of this, it appears, so long as we are roused into motion.) One of those actually out in the field was William von Raab, Commissioner of the U.S. Customs Service, and one of Roth's favorite studiers: "As you know," von Raab said in a wholly characteristic comment, "Amsterdam is sort of the 1984 version of Sodom and Gomorrah" (p. 10). The star of Roth's show was doubtless Professor Kenneth J. Herrmann, Jr., who, as professors will, bored through the crust of statistics and facts and material presences to get to the rhetoric below, the attitude that was, when all was said and done (which it never would be), vital: "Whatever action is taken must contain a strong and uncompromising sense of moral outrage." In fact, this action, whatever it might be (and it doesn't much matter what it is), must not simply *contain* such outrage: "This moral outrage must form the foundation for all intervention" (p. 25).

This outrage can sometimes seep its way into non-Congressional arguments, indeed form their substance: Susan Brownmiller's comments on the subject, for instance, and particularly her charge that most studies of child molestation, particularly psychoanalytic ones, "point a wagging finger at the victim."[19] Brownmiller attacks the "all-forgiving liberal's attitude" and applauds the prison hierarchy which places the child molester on the bottom.[20] This is only one small step away from the infamous Lloyd Martin, of the LAPD, who said pedophilia was "worse than homicide," or J. Edgar Hoover's reflections: ". . . depraved human beings, more savage than beasts, are permitted to roam America almost at will."[21] Propelled by such justifications, we are not encouraged to examine "facts," counter-arguments, or much of anything else. We are speeding by so very fast.

B. Directing Our Outrage

Once provoked, our emotions need to exercise themselves on a few carefully mapped-out and positively determined sites of danger. These targets, in turn, must be interesting and also rather remote perils that can substitute satisfactorily for those too large or too imminent to make for easy and uniform anger. Sitting right over a major geological fault in Los Angeles as I write this, for instance, I am very worried about killer bees. In our culture, two such points of distracting focus have proved especially serviceable: child-pornography and child-abductions.

Whatever may have been the situation in the past, for several years now there has been no large-scale kiddie-porn industry at all in this country (or probably anywhere). There has been nothing at all one could call an "industry": no production and no distribution beyond amateur photography and the swapping of such photos or videos among collectors, and probably no more than a handful of them. The one exception to such sweeping claims (made sweeping, of course, to counter the swoops on the other side) has to do with government publications and mailings in Sting operations. The government is now the only one in the business of kiddie porn. At least some members of the police are willing enough to say this, pointing likewise with some pride to success in stopping not only imports and local activities but in promoting successfully legislation that would remove most anything anyone would ever think to call kiddie porn from the bleeding-heart protections of the First Amendment. Our willingness to tamper with the Bill of Rights here and to sanction so much police activity, local and national, that involves entrapment of the unwary by way of false advertisements in magazines and newspapers and various other lures and lies can only, I think, be justified if we are willing to suppose that there is such an industry and that it is both gigantic and out of control. We must believe, as Customs Commissioner von Raab says President Reagan did, that what is at stake in stamping out this industry is, at the very least, "the Nation's moral health" (p. 4), that, despite all evidence, there is kiddie porn everywhere—the Assistant Chief Postal Inspector for criminal investigation told the Senators conducting the hearings that "its pervasiveness is evident in the number of investigations we have undertaken" (p. 5); further, as von Raab put it, there is "a shocking cause and effect relationship between child molesting and child pornography" (p. 5). What would be shocking is the uncovering of any evidence or even a plausible argument in favor of a cause and effect relationship, if von Raab means that looking at the porn makes one go out and molest. If he means that people who are arrested for this offense often possess the porn, that is true enough; but of course that observation does not begin to establish the causality von Raab needs.

But, equally of course, neither von Raab nor we care two pins about the logic of all this: what we need is the talk and the porn. If we manage to dry up the commercial sources, let the government produce it. We can always invent the justifications later. It is not that the agencies of the law, busy cutting and pasting old porn magazines and racking their brains over the writing of provocative ads, are themselves either perverse or paranoid. They simply do what they are told, take their directions on what constitutes "criminal" from the rest of us and proceed in a manner neither insane nor inventive.

Thus with pornography and, even more vigorously, with the story of the abducted child, the child lured into the passing car, stolen from the streets or playgrounds. Here the police and legislators are perhaps less important, though we do have the important "Missing Children Act" of October 12, 1982 and an enormous number of more recent spin-offs, local and national. Behind all this is a story, the story that makes such good tv and cinema precisely because it is so wide of the mark, because it locates as a danger to children something quite horrible but only slightly more threatening than being swallowed by alligators or vaporized by ether waves. Of course it is true that children are now and then kidnapped. (They are also raped and murdered too, like the rest of us, and I am not claiming that such crimes are myths, only that they differ from the falsely pumped-up kidnapping-for-sexual-purposes story.) But how often? The blunt infrequency of such crimes does not seem to justify the creation of a state of emergency or explain such things as the national delight following the 1983 showing of *Adam* (including President Reagan's introducing NBC's "Adam Roll Call") and the recent wild success of the 1989 *I Know My First Name is Steven* (also NBC), which finished first in the ratings for the week by an enormous margin.[22] Both shows featured graphic depictions of abductions, the second detailing rather explicitly what the abductor purportedly did to the child.

Howard Rosenberg, writing in the *Los Angeles Times*, said of *Steven*, "You don't want to watch, but you can't *stop* watching."[23] With this cultural addiction, we no longer even pretend that we can *stop* any time we like. But so feeding our habit may not only mean directing our attention and fantasies to minor difficulties but also ignoring the real pain of children. Our insatiable interest in abduction even allows some enterprising capitalists to cash in: a very-definitely-for-profit company in Ohio supplying pictures of "missing children" for milk-cartons or an outfit called "Advo-System" providing as "a public service" a picture of seventeen-year-old Michael Masaoay on the front of an offer I received in today's mail from "Miller's Carpet Care." John Crewdson says that of the missing children in police files, 95% are teenage runaways or throwaways and that nearly all the rest are involved in custody battles

382 / *Our Own Child-Loving*

and are with one of the parents; further, "the monumental effort to track down missing children has yet to recover a single child abducted by a stranger."[24] But our need for the story has nothing to do with such things as recovering children; that's not what we meant at all.

C. Police Story

Let's put it most offensively: what power gives us is a form of allowable cultural pornography, managed by power's most savage agents: legislators, lawyers, and cops. The importance of the criminalizing of this story is signaled by the relative rarity of women in the tale and by the odd investment of authority, even intellectual authority, not in the laboratory scientist or physician but in Dirty Harry. This is macho lore, where evil is evil and understanding is not so important as a knee in the gut, a .36 slug to the head.

There are, of course, more genteel public disclosures. After all, the public is the one generating all the interest and all the funds. So they get hearings and media hype and films and trials: molesters brought face to face with our contempt. What we make them do is tell all, tell everything they have to tell. We make them do that by first having the children tell everything they know or have experienced or have heard. This takes some time, but it seems to be worth it somehow, even though the actual judicial results are often disappointing. Perhaps it is not the hanging we want so much as the talking itself.

Of course there are victims. Just as we are more than happy to put up the money for legal spectacles like McMartin, we also seem happy to let others suffer. We would not want to be told that it is the suffering that is, in fact, most pleasing to us, but it is we who are causing most of it. We should make no mistake about the nature of our pleasures: this is blood sport. Our deep concern for the children involved allows us to put them through horrors, to subject them to exposure and trial so we can hear the story we must have. Even worse, they have had to withstand from parents, teachers, peers, and the galaxy of social workers, psychologists, and police what has certainly amounted to an invasion, amounted to molestation. And, as if we cared, there is the issue of the civil rights of the accused: with McMartin, not simply of Peggy McMartin Buckey and her son, but of the five defendants who were toyed with publicly for a while and then released, their lives pretty much destroyed. Our narrative requires that the mere mention of the possibility of child-molesting, the slightest brush not necessarily with suspicion itself but with a distant cousin of suspicion, is tantamount to conviction.

And even children who were certainly never touched by Raymond Buckey or his mother, children miles and years away from the McMartin Day Care Center, may have to pay for this trial and its harsh examination of touching, may have to pay for it by not being touched in any way. David Watchfogel, a former teacher in the area, says that the trial made it "very clear that people could not hug and touch kids. A lot of adults are very careful these days and they will be forever."[25] Adults taking this sort of care take away from children forever more than one can say. As another Manhattan Beach resident says, "Every time I hug my nieces and nephews I think twice about it. Isn't that weird?"[26]

It's as if all the parts in this weird drama were assigned, not chosen. There are no auditions for the role; casting is done by the commandant of Kafka's Penal Colony. We can hardly protest if we should somehow find ourselves within the drama, positioned as child-molester and unable ever to escape. Our role in that case requires that we deny the charges, doing so simply confirming our identity as the criminal. Denial is as good as a confession; they are, in fact, the same thing. Our destiny is to undergo behavior modification treatments ("direct behavioral intervention")[27] or, more likely, be thrown into jail and murdered by inmates playing their parts. In a sadistic parody of traditional legal activity, the rights of the accused are discarded, accusation being made equivalent to proof. The Wonderland proposal that the sentence precede the verdict is in accord with a system whereby, according to what has become widely known as the "accommodation syndrome," the child who has been in fact molested will characteristically be reluctant to make any accusations, will tell a variety of harmless stories at first before making the charge of sexual molestation, and will then withdraw that story and substitute one or more others. The child will lie, in other words, but not about this crime; no harmless stories from the child's lips are to be believed, but horror is never to be doubted. Recanting, admitting that one invented or exaggerated or was wrong, is simply part of the role the victim plays and only confirms that the offense has taken place. If the child says it happened, it happened; if the child says it didn't happen, it happened. That children are so smothered with our own sick fears and suspicions that they can hardly help misinterpreting friendliness was noted with some anger decades ago by Kinsey.[28] That children sometimes realize that their position in this play, however undesirable in so many ways, does provide them with some blackmail possibilities is inevitable, but we ignore all that.

Despite what we say, children of course *do* invent stories about molestation, either because the overlay of suggestion applied by our culture is far too strong to resist or because in some cases they may have something to gain, like vengeance.[29]

That this mandatory scenario, played over and over again, forces all the rest of us into certain positions should be obvious. We are given attitudes to wear, conclusions to draw. We are also blinded to other possibilities for conceiving of the situation. There are questions we need not be ordered to silence because we have been so distanced from them they would never occur to us. However, we might wonder if this melodramatic, personalized fable of monsters running amuck among us is not serving somebody's interests that are not ours or the children's, and that are not the interests of justice, kindness, or mutual understanding, much less play or love. If all the problems can be reduced to perversion, personal illness, or evil (it perhaps matters little which), then larger issues can be ignored, issues like the perilous health of the family-as-institution, the pressure of large-scale economic and social realities, the stark failure of so many of us to provide to children and to one another not just love (which is clearly out of our reach) but something more modest, perhaps what Thomas Hardy called "mere lovingkindness."

The Answer

It is customary to say that the answer is what one doesn't have; but actually answers are much easier to come by than questions that place us outside power. Any paradigm is quick to provide answers; it's the bonus one receives for signing up with the metaphor. Columbia Records gives you a dozen records for a dollar; metaphors give you as many answers as you like. Power has plenty of answers to the pedophilia problem, one of which is to exterminate all the brutes, the others being to exterminate all the brutes. Actually, power does provide a liberal position, one that is despised at present but wholly consistent with our usual operations. If it is a question of power, which of course it must be, that power can be refigured or redistributed in any number of ways consistent with our goal of balancing such power or putting it in the hands of the responsible or hogging it all to ourselves or whatever.

Thus it is available to those within power to see that the protection of the powerless by the powerful, however necessary, does have the unfortunate and sometimes unfair consequence of actually robbing those protected of what power they might lay claim to. If I need to be protected, I admit my weakness and thus invariably give up certain rights. With children, our resolute protecting renders them dependent on our sense of justice for whatever powers they have.

This seems reasonable enough, and most would probably be willing to make some adjustments in the protecting apparatus to restore some of the child's power we have inadvertently taken away. The problem comes when this logic hits the field of sex or sexuality. Does it follow that the pedophilia scare robs children of their sexual rights, their rights to exercise certain wholly legitimate sexual powers? We have no right as adults, one might say, to take over the child's body because we presume to know best, issuing all manner of arbitrary bans. Children, we continue, have the right of full access to sexual force, a real and important power in our culture. But "we," of course, say nothing of the sort. Such a line becomes for us simple pedophile scandal, perhaps common in the Gomorrah of Amsterdam, but over here the sole property of various societies, now mostly extinct, formed to promote sex between the adult and the child. When NAMBLA (The North American Man/Boy Love Association) talks about the sexual rights of the child, we more than suspect that for them only the right of the adult to have sex with the child is at stake. Power analyses in this case do not lend themselves to "fair and equitable balancing," which is probably why there simply is no liberal position on the matter.

Within power, we seem able only to move further in the same direction, promoting for our own pleasure that which we most fear and abhor. It seems to me that little can be gained by reallocating power, giving more to the child. The child does not need sexual power, certainly does not need to be taught the filthy lesson that sex and power are one. Besides, we are slipping them plenty of sneaky power right now; and no study of the actual sexual relations between children and adults has suggested that the child is totally powerless. Power is not the problem in such relations; cruelty, loveless cruelty is the problem. The answer is not to empower the pedophile, certainly. But the answer is just as certainly not to empower children. The answer is to remove them and us to a position that might decenter power, show us what has caused all the trouble and all the pain. *And then to keep moving.* I am not proposing a substitute site, just a mode of transportation. I do not believe there is any narrative that can, when naturalized, avoid the horror. But I think the travel between narratives can do wonders for the complexion of things; the breeze we feel as we move is refreshing, and maybe it can puff away old pain. For starters, we should take all power explanations, most centrally those *obvious* power explanations and play with them. We are right now caught in a terrible, playless, power-game no decent person would want to enter. I want to find a way into a game which plays.

The answer is neither to empower children nor to enfeeble them but to see through them into play. Right now, I should say, that is not easy and may even be dangerous. One has to trust that in waiving the protections we are also waiving the risk, that the power guarding the children has also manufactured the enemies that threaten. Moving to where power is not must not open the child up to exploitation, make the child into easy prey for lustful, sick adults. I propose a refiguring of the fields of being and of desire so that bodies and pleasures, released from power, would also be released from abuse and molestation. I do not think that in play there would be open season on children. I do not think there would be any hunting, any cultural will to resent and to deny and to hurt, as there is now. It seems to me cynical to suppose that we are locked into gazing at milk-carton pin-ups and entertaining ourselves with decade-long child-molesting trials. No alternate center we might travel to will do for us much better in the long run. But perhaps we can escape the long run, hope to find as we lope from place to place, some outlook that freshens, that keeps us from hurting so much those we might, in a different land, learn to look upon with fondness.

The Old Questions

Maybe there's a point in again putting questions in the ugliest way possible, the way of the pedophile. These questions are unfair, rhetorically askew, weighted with criminality. They may also show us something about ourselves. Let's put the most obscene question this way: why do our children so often engage in sexual relations with adults? Instead of hastily providing the answer given to us by power, let's outshout it with some other questions. Why do children engaging in such relations indicate such a positive response to them? Why do studies of such children sometimes argue that negative effects are slight or wholly absent? Why do arrested pedophiles commonly rack up such a shocking record before they are turned in? Why are the children silent? Why do they so often term the pedophile their "best friend"? Why do they say they "love" her or him?

As we have seen (Ch. 5), Theo Sandfort's study of twenty-five boys involved in such relationships concluded that "the different indices paint a coherent picture in which the sexual contacts with the adults appeared to have been a predominantly positive experience for virtually all of the boys." Ten of the twenty-five were unable, even with prodding, to formulate *any* negative response, and of the remaining fifteen, most of the fears or difficulties were induced by their awareness of others' potential disapproval and the consequent need for secrecy.[30] Larry L. Constantine's self-consciously "radical perspective" on the subject is still conscientiously precise: "A careful review of the literature on adult-child sexual encounters . . . indicates that immediate negative reactions are minor or completely absent in the majority of cases and significant long-term psychological or social impairment is rare, truly remarkable findings considering that most studies have dealt with criminal or clinical samples."[31] The fullest empirical study of the pedophile conducted recently concludes that this person is typically unagressive, "gentle and rational" and that there is little evidence to show that "lasting psychological harm is done to a child through sexual contact with adults."[32]

What is remarkable is not that such conclusions are uncontested—of course they are contested—but that they have about them a pertinacity that keeps them hanging around. Perhaps they have some sort of deep, weedy root in our common sense or our observation. Even the F.B.I. admits that their job is made very difficult by the fact that the children involved often do not readily accept the part written for them in our script: the part of victim. The child often sees herself or himself as a fully willing, responsible, even initiating partner. An article in the *FBI Law Enforcement Bulletin* says bluntly, "Children are not forced, compelled, or enticed into acts with threats of harm. They are, in many cases, willing, noncomplaining victims. Some children have actually described the people who molest them as their 'best friends.' "[33]

Again, instead of rushing to supply the "explanation" for all this that is so close at hand—that the child is "seduced" into loving the pedophile and just imagines it is not being harmed—let us suggest that doubtless such an explanation is true and that it does not fully explain. Let us ask if there isn't more to it, if there aren't other possible answers, or questions. Why should a child's best friend be one who pulls that child in some way apart from family, from mainstream values, from the cultural center? Why should the child, in some cases, not only not resist such hugger-mugger, such radical marginalizing but seek it out, initiate it? Why should some children run headlong into trouble and then want to stay there? Isn't it possible that there is something in what we are offering to the child that is not so very attractive? Is it possible that sexual relationships with adults are not always entered into blindly or stupidly or even as a consequence of seduction but with a sense

388 / *Our Own Child-Loving*

that, dangerous as they are, they may give something otherwise not available? What is it we are withholding from the child—or not giving to it because we own so little of it, so little we may, in fact, have run out altogether?

The children in Sandfort's study are clear on what they are looking for. These are not demon boys, the Damiens and Jasons of our child-evil-loving media, but rather children with quite ordinary child needs. They do not, even under questioning, talk a lot about sex. The sex they are having with adults perhaps doesn't bother them; it doesn't seem, one way or the other, to be very central, not what they came to the relationship for in the first place. They came for affection, a sense of being looked at, touched, thought about, hectored, hugged-kidded-tickled, loved. Here are a couple of child-voices from the United States:

> Without guys like Mark, I would probably be dead today, because without someone to love me—well, life wouldn't be worth living.

> ... now I have someone to care for me and love just me for what I am. Does this make any sense to you? You can change this around to sound better. O.K.? Use my name, please. Ed, Philadelphia.

> I love him and I know that he loves me.[34]

One thing seems clear. Pedophiles tend to love children in some way and children who become involved with them love them back. Power gives us no weapons for dealing with all this; it unmistakably allows us to see some things wonderfully well, and it is important that we see them. But it does not offer a clear view of this odd quality of "love." Power is shrewd about the way in which "love" can mask as seduction, create victims, become vile; it is blank about the way such love might come to the lonely and the unwanted. Power is admirably suited to deal with monsters; it does less well with undramatic tales of outcasts, misfits, and the loveless and unlovely. And, to tell the truth, play has not a lot more to offer here, which is why pedophilia seems as unplayful as, from another perspective, it seems exploitative. Play is *maybe* better, or at least different. But it doesn't finally answer, as the Victorians knew. Play allows us to see some of these issues, perhaps clearly enough to turn them into frolics and thus escape the worst of power's traps. Play allows us to stop protecting the child to death; but it gives us no way to make connections.

"All you need is love" is a terrifying slogan; it would be more sanely and healthily phrased, "All you need is kneecaps." No *all* can serve us well, as we must soon learn from our devotion to power, learn that or die. Love as a center has a nice ring to it but is no less a dragon than power, should we let it take up permanent residence. We really have no notion of what it would be like to center love, I think, since the forms of love we have now all seem perverse and battering, pedophilia being in this regard very little different from the rest of them. But it is we who have made them so, we who have dictated the way in which the child must be loved and also despised, cuddled and beaten. No wonder that the child may turn to "perverts" and outlawed forms of affection; compared to normality, all that could seem comparatively healthy and free.

* * *

The criminal and the normal, the pedophile and the rest of us, the outlaw and the inlaw: if such distinctions were serving us well, we would not need to assert them so brutally and heedlessly. We so fear defilement from the forms we have invented to cleanse ourselves that we are compelled to have their names always on our tongues, the bodies of these Others (the sick, the monstrous, the perverted) always before us, on trial or on stage. Perhaps there is less to fear than we have supposed, even a profit to be harvested by putting our Yankee ingenuity to work in promoting a collapse of these binaries.

To be more specific about the present, let's return to the past; and to make things more concrete, let's employ a fable, our normal/outlaw construction of *Oliver Twist*. Here's how it goes, this story of O: Oliver is born, like all children we love, without encumbrances: no parents, no name, no being apart from what we put into him. This is not, however, a fable of bliss, for once the empty child is before us it becomes the target not only of desire but of anxiety, of passion entwined cruelly with panic and dread. In this case, we use Oliver to dramatize our concurrent need for and horror of the urban nightmare, the criminal poor, unchartered sexuality, the dissolution of the family, the innocent child. All these activate our most pressing longings and refusals.

The story we tell of Oliver, whether or not it is Dickens's, is, on one level, wildly incoherent, bouncing the boy back and forth among different worlds without letting him come to rest in any. It is as if we always wanted him somewhere other than where he is, wanted him in motion, always glimpsed and never set. Here's one way to schematize this bouncing: the perfectly vacant child is in and out of (a) the institutional world, (b) the criminal-sexual world, (c) the family world.

In the first—the world of the workhouse, courtrooms, masters and other official overseers—Oliver is brutally and lasciviously mistreated, playing at once to our indignation and our delight. It is interesting to note how readily we adopt the position that the institutions we set up to do our dirty work are themselves abnormal, that they do not reflect us, that they are somehow monstrous. Where do we suppose they came from? They keep the child moving, void of substance, howling, and in need of our help: what would we do without them? But we also need to disown them, which is why we are nearly as ready to suspect the social worker and psychologist as the pedophile, wondering if the child welfare agencies aren't working against our own welfare.

So we fling our child out of that anxiety and into another more stark, the criminal world of child-molesting, Fagin's world. Fagin isn't given a world, of course, but a "den," a Satanic/bestial crawling place where kidnapped children are bludgeoned, used, twisted into enemies of people like us. On the other hand, Oliver and the others seem not to be kidnapped but rescued, not used but loved, not twisted but allowed to play lustily. There's food there and plenty of gin, laughter and games, and sex too. This is what we want so badly for the child and for us that we need to make it unthinkable—just so we can never stop thinking about it. We only fake killing off Fagin in this fable, knowing how vital he is within us and how adept at changing costumes, popping up when we need him in churches, day-care-centers, and scout meetings. Never quite at home, though, never present at the dinner table or when tucking in the kids.

That's the world of the Bedwins and Brownlows and Maylies, the family, where we can play out a different form of the same drama that's running in the other two worlds as well: saving and protecting the child. We also exercise and deny our anxieties about this *family*, the sense that it is not only in pieces but that it is the site of danger. We rush to snatch the child from the stranger offering candy, wrap the little thing in blankets, take it home and—what? In our fable, we take it home to stroke and murmur over and then to smother. Oliver is nestled into a family, odd and disjointed but resolutely a family, that really wants him always in bed, barely conscious, declining. This is a world of paranoid protections so complete they consume us. All the innocents are dead or dying fast. We need Oliver here, but we need to send him out periodically to the pedophile, to Fagin, to get a little life in him, just so we can bring him back for some more interesting and erotic dying.

Our fable then is not so much irresolute as open and continuous, a postmodern fable of ambiguous non-completion. Or, maybe, it's a fable of psychotic repetitions, battering and banging the body of the child between different and distant theatres to enact shows of violence, shows of love. There is not one of these theatres but imagines it is giving the love without the violence, imagines it is offering a haven from the horror. Our fable suggests that it is this belief in havens that promotes the molesting, that makes inevitable the damaged and tearful children we really do wish were somehow whole and happy. In the ghastly, spliced-together ending of *Oliver Twist*, Dickens arbitrarily selects one of these worlds, declares it superior, and pretends it is not linked to the others. Mr. Brownlow adopts Oliver, settles in with him and Mrs. Bedwin and creates a "little society, whose condition approached as nearly to one of perfect happiness as can ever be known in this changing world."[35] But this is the happiness of the tomb or of the pornographic fantasy of the child and pedophile locked together forever in a sound-proof room.

Surely we can imagine a happiness more perfect than this, perhaps, says our fable, by giving up thinking we need to choose between these worlds. For one thing, we seem completely unable to choose anyhow, and, for another, we haven't made these worlds so that any of them offer much to us or to the child. Rather than oscillating wildly between sanctuaries, wondering whether we should cast our lot with Mr. Bumble and Mrs. Sowerberry, Rose Maylie and Mr. Grimwig, or the Artful Dodger and Nancy, perhaps we might bring them all together, collapse the boundaries and loosen the protections. They all really want the same thing, after all. We know that because we want it too.

Notes

1. In *Los Angeles Times* (May 12, 1989), Part V, p. 4.

2. In a later column (*Los Angeles Times*, August 20, 1989, Part VI, p. 2), Abby printed a letter critical of her advice, arguing that such training would produce "a paranoid, anti-social misanthrope out of that friendly little boy before he's 5!" Abby stuck to her guns: "I wouldn't have given that kind of advice 10 years ago, but times have changed. Read on." And what one reads on to find was a letter from "Serving Time in Texas" who claimed to be one of "thousands" of child-molesters roaming the streets and anxious to find friendly little children. He backed Abby to the hilt: "Please tell 'Arizona Mom' *never* to let her little boy out of her sight. . . . If she doesn't follow your advice, I promise you her little boy will be sexually molested many times before he reaches the age of 12." That Abby should regard such a thing as evidence says a great deal about the culture she is reflecting.

3. Foucault, *History of Sexuality*, p. 127.

4. I believe that a study of the erotics of children's fashions would tell us much, since

most of us would agree that Roland Barthes's assertion that clothing is "at the center of all today's eroticism" is not hyperbolic (*Sade/Fourier/Loyola*, p. 19).

5. By a dog, to be sure, a cute little puppy. That makes it all very "innocent," conveniently so; we are invited to look our fill, without risking anything messy, like arrest.

6. Figure A is from the March 17, 1918 *Los Angeles Times* (Sunday "comics" supplement) "Buster Brown" strip; Figure B from the same paper's May 18, 1918 "Mama's Angel Child" Sunday strip. All subsequent comic-strip illustrations, from the *Los Angeles Times* Sunday comic supplements, will be cited in the text by date.

7. In the strip for October 24, 1909, Buster, on a world tour, is caught in "Via Garlico" by a group of Italian toughs who take his clothes from him, one article at a time, making for an incomplete (he is rescued after giving up his pants) but still remarkable slow striptease.

8. Interestingly, his hair was originally black but was changed, doubtless because gentlemen and ladies alike prefer blonds.

9. See Crewdson, *By Silence Betrayed*, pp. 248–50, for a shrewd, regrettably brief, comment on this double-message in our culture.

10. Compare J. W. Mohr: "Children are basically still treated as asexual beings with some cognitive interest in sexuality" ("Age Structures," p. 41); and Stevi Jackson: "Most people are still ready to express horror and outrage at any threat to children's innocence, but now concern has shifted from anxieties about their moral and spiritual well-being to the psychological effects of early contact with sex" (*Childhood and Sexuality*, p. 48).

11. Gebhard et al., *Sex Offenders*, p. 83.

12. Anon., *Hustler* (November, 1983), p. 12.

13. Fleischhauer-Hardt, *Show Me!*, p. 158.

14. Compare Edward Zigler and Nancy W. Hall, "Physical Child Abuse in America: Past, Present, and Future," in Dante Cicchetti and Vicki Carlson, eds., *Child Maltreatment: Theory and Research on the Causes and Consequences of Child Abuse and Neglect* (Cambridge: Cambridge Univ. Press, 1989): ". . . American culture not only condones but actively encourages parents to use physical punishment" (p. 57).

15. Subsequent to the *Los Angeles Times* story from which all this is taken (see note 16), I obtained (was handed while strolling at Venice Beach) the following document, "Tony Alamo: My Side of the Story," purporting to be a "press release" issued on August 9, 1989 by the Rev. Alamo, Pastor of the Holy Alamo Christian Church and the man mentioned in the Miller case. In this document, Alamo quite strongly suggests that those investigating him, the Los Angeles District Attorney, several of his assistants, "and the FBI," are "every single one of them criminals and liars," the District Attorney (Ira Reiner) also being, according to an earlier Alamo charge (based on "reliable informants"), "guilty of child molestation." Despite this, Alamo not only does not deny that he instructs his flock to practice the "spanking" of children but says that attempts to limit our rights in this area violate God's word, sentence us to hell, and cause us in the meantime to live in fear of our children or, just as likely, in imminent bodily peril: "Thousands of people are being murdered today by their children, and it is the government's fault," the government which turns children onto drugs and homicide because they keep us from spanking. "This is Catholic communism," says Alamo; "this is the false prophet, the Mother of Harlots, and the Beast (the beastly government)." Alamo's range, you can see, extends from sociology to scripture, from the F.B.I. to the Babylonian

Whore (if there's any difference). He also has at his disposal a more personal, down-to-earth rhetoric. After all, he says with an easy grin, "I and millions like me have gotten spanked when we were young for things we did wrong and we turned out O.K." Anyone who could resist that is in thrall to the Pope, Ira Reiner, and the Beast!

16. *Los Angeles Times*, August 25, 1989, Part II, pp. 1,5. On this subject see also M.D.A. Freeman, *Violence in the Home* (Westmead: Saxon House, 1979), pp. 45–46; and Pleck, *Domestic Tyranny*, passim.

17. Freud, " 'Civilized' Sexual Morality," IX, 192.

18. "Child Pornography and Pedophilia" hearings, United States Senate Subcommittee on Investigations of the Committee on Governmental Affairs, 98th Congress, 2nd sess., p. 2. Further references will be cited in the text.

19. Susan Brownmiller, *Against Our Will: Men, Women, and Rape* (New York: Simon and Schuster, 1975), p. 275.

20. Brownmiller, *Against Our Will*, p. 272.

21. From the *Los Angeles Times*, May 3, 1981, Part V, p. 14 (quoted in Davis, *SMUT*, p. 111); Hoover, "How Safe is Your Daughter?" *American Magazine*, July 1947, p. 32. Lloyd Martin established LAPD's sexually exploited child unit and has been widely cited as something of an expert on the subject; J. Edgar Hoover, of course, was for decades custodian of America's safety and moral fiber.

22. Shown first May 22 and 23, 1989. For the ratings, see the *Los Angeles Times*, June 1, 1989, Part VI, p. 1. "Part 2" of the movie rated 27.3, "Part 1" 21.6. Behind these top two, a distant third, was *Cheers* at 18.9.

23. May 22, 1989, VI, 6. The appeal of this film was compounded, I think, by the addition of lots of talk about spanking the boy, almost all of it coming from the father (though the abductor also threatens a spanking). The opening section of the movie is consumed by the topic, by the father's threatenings and postponings and the mother's shrewish attacks on him for "not taking care of" the problem. The child is promised at various times a "licking," "beating," "whipping," "spanking"—a whole Thesaurus entry—and on the day of his abduction is returning home, we are told, to a certain carrying out of the long-delayed (and all the more tantalizing) execution of the sentence: "I hope he doesn't hit you too hard!" a friend calls to him after school. The father having vowed that "he won't be able to sit down for a week" doesn't swing our sympathies over to the kidnapper, of course. Rather, we hate him the more since he has robbed us of the scene that would have taken place this time for sure had Steven made it home.

24. Crewdson, *By Silence Betrayed*, pp. 112–13.

25. *Los Angeles Times*, November 19, 1989, Part I, p. 35.

26. *Los Angeles Times*, November 19, 1989, Part I, p. 35.

27. One of the more humane versions of these "interventions" is described in D.R. Laws and A.V. Pawlowski, "An Automated Fading Procedure to Alter Sexual Responsiveness in Pedophiles," *Journal of Homosexuality* 1 (2) (1974): 149–63.

28. Kinsey, *Human Female*, pp. 20–21. "The child," Kinsey says, "who has been raised in fear of all strangers and all physical manifestations of affection," "may ruin the lives" of honorable people. Of course, as Kinsey implies, it is not the child who is doing the actual ruining but the network of assumptions and beliefs neither the child nor we seem able to escape.

29. David Allen Ward, a school bus driver in Escondida, California, was accused of

child molesting by children who later said they had made up the charges to get back at him because he yelled at them and "made them behave." Of course it is surprising that the "accommodation syndrome" theory didn't kick in here and cause the recantation to be ignored. Somehow, though, it did not; and the charges against Ward were dropped: *USA Today,* October 3, 1985, p. 3A.

30. Sandfort, *Sexual Aspects of Paedophile Relations,* pp. 61, 64–65.

31. Larry L. Constantine, "The Sexual Rights of Children: Implications of a Radical Perspective," in Constantine and Martinson, eds., *Children and Sex,* p. 259.

32. Glenn D. Wilson and David N. Cox, *The Child-Lovers: A Study of Paedophiles in Society* (London: Peter Owen, 1983), pp. 122, 129.

33. Seth L. Goldstein, "Investigating Child Sexual Exploitation: Law Enforcement's Role," *FBI Law Enforcement Bulletin* 53 (January 1984): 25. On the ages and forms of "the child" in our culture, see Chapter 1, p. 5–13 and Chapter 2, passim.

34. All these quotes are taken from *Boys Speak Out on Man/Boy Love,* 3rd ed. (San Francisco: North American Man/Boy Love Association, 1986), pp. 7, 8, 11. Not all readers will regard the source as reliable. I believe, however, that the sentiments expressed here are echoed all over, even in police reports, and are entirely representative. There would be no necessity for NAMBLA to invent them, even were they prone to dishonesty, which I do not think they are.

35. Charles Dickens, *The Adventures of Oliver Twist* (London: Oxford Univ. Press, 1949), ch. liii.

Index

Abbott, Rev. Jacob, 97n, 100n, 103n, 129n; on corporal punishment, 110
Abraham, 307
Achilles, 219
Ackley, Robert (*The Catcher in the Rye*), 317–18, 320
Acton, William, 50, 53n, 56n, 57n, 58n, 97n, 99n, 130n, 179n, 181n, 272n; and power, 20; and labeling of sexuality, 21, 50; on language and action, 36; on class, 38–39; and women's sexual passion, 40, 180n; empiricism in, 46; and systems, 47; on definitions of "the child," 69; on the neglect and mistreatment of children, 76; on prostitution, 77, 108, 152; and the body, 108–9, 114; as "representative Victorian," 154–60; on masturbation, 155–57; on child sexuality, 159–60; on whipping, 255
Adam (television movie), 381
Adamson, J.H., 271n
Adler, Alfred, 16
Adolescent, the, 69; and Holden Caulfield, 312–13, 315
Adult, the, distinction from child, 6–7, 13, 15, 62–63, 79; and the home, 83–87; and child-management, 87–95; enfeebled by precocity, 120–4; and the gentle child, 217; and Victorian child-beating, 249–55; and modern child-beating, 261–63; child's imitation of, 277–78; hostility toward in *Peter Pan*, 281–82; entry into Wonderland, 288–94; role in relation to Alice, 293–98; and child in the McMartin Pre-School trial, 345–49; child-watching in our culture, 363–65; *see also* Parent
Advice to a Mother (Chavasse), 166
Advice to a Youth (Cobbett), 151
"Advo-System," 381
Affinity, as alternate center to power, 8; and blurring of gender, 13, 15
"Against Idleness and Mischief" (Watts), 93; parody of in Carroll, 288–89, 292
Age of consent, 70
"Aged Fifteen" (Pim), 226
Alamo, Tony, 392–93n
Albutt, Dr. Henry Arthur, 101n, 119, 131n, 177n, 179n
Alcibiade Fanciullo a Sculoa (Pallavicino), 198
Alger, Horatio, 203
Allen, Elizabeth Akers, 97n
Allen, W. David, 227, 244n
Alice (Lewis Carroll's), 209, 218, 276–79, 288–98; and the pedophile image, 196–97; and Peter Pan, 289, 296, 298
Alice's Adventures in Wonderland, 8, 102n, 235–6, 245n, 276–79, 288–98
Anarchy, and pedophilia, 230–1; and schoolmasters, 231–32
Anderson, Maxwell, 375
"Angelic Angelina" (comic strip), 367
Antolini, Mr. (*The Catcher in the Rye*), 315, 319
Antony and Cleopatra, 12
Aphrodisiacs and Anti-Aphrodisiacs (Davenport), 40
"Apple Mary" (comic strip), 369
Arabian Nights, The, 43
"Archie" (comic strip), 369
Ariès, Phillipe, 61–63, 65, 69, 70, 72,

75, 83–84, 86, 95n, 96n, 97n, 98n, 99n, 100n, 101n
Arnold, Matthew, 173, 182n
Arnold, Thomas, 66, 71, 97n, 98n, 103n, 130n, 131n, 181n, 271n; and the ideal Church, 116; on precocity, 120, 122; on "evil," 169; on whipping, 251, 253, 254
Artful Dodger, The (*Oliver Twist*), 391
Artificial Mother, The (Putnam), 248
Asbestos Diary, The (Dukahz), 206
Ashbee, Henry Spenser, *see* Fraxi, Pisanus
Auerbach, Nina, 290, 299n
Austen, Jane, 131n, 259
Autobiography of a Flea (Anon.), 213n

Bad Seed, The (film), 374–75
Baker, Dr. Isaac Brown, 163
Ball, Lucille, 373
Bamford, T.W., 96n
Barchester Towers, 248
Bardell v. Pickwick, 352
"Bare Knees" (Pim), 227
Barker-Benfield, Ben, 129–30n, 163, 180n
Barrie, J.M., 79, 99n, 243n, 298n; and gender, 51n; and pedophilia, 212n; and photography, 227, 303; on parents and children, 243n; and *Peter Pan*, 278–88; and the Davies boys, 278, 280
Barrymore, Drew, 369
Barthes, Roland, 31, 55n, 265, 267, 273n, 274n, 338, 374, 392n
Bartholomew, Freddie, 10, 369
Bates, David, 245n
Bateson, Gregory, 24, 54n, 105, 128n
Bede, the Venerable, 140
Bedwin, Mrs. (*Oliver Twist*), 390–1
Beeles, Amy (McMartin case), 351, 354, 356
Bell, Alan P., 193, 212n, 213n
Bentham, Jeremy, 40, 42
Bernard, Fritz, 209
"Betsy Bouncer and Her Doll" (comic strip), 367, 371
Bibliography of Prohibited Books (Fraxi), 170–71
Bill of Rights, 380

Birkenhead, Lord, 36
Birkin, Andrew, 99n, 299n
Birnbaum, H. Jean, 211n
Blackstone, Sir William, 137
Blackwell, Elizabeth, Dr., 14, 51n, 58n, 97n, 102n, 130n, 131n, 132n, 177n, 178n, 180n; on mind-body connections, 112, 117; and precocity, 120; on sexual development, 123, 126; on sex and power, 135; and sex education, 143; on masturbation, 166, 167
Blake, Kathleen, 299n
Blake, William, 209
Blanch, William Harnbett, 271n
Blanchot, Maurice, 52n
Bless the Beasts and Children (film), 374–75
Bloch, Dr. Iwan, 270n
"Blondie" (comic strip), 369
Bloxam, John Francis, 199
Blue Lagoon, The (film), 224, 374
Boarding-schools, 86; and "immorality," 140, 168–69; and pederasty, 198–99; and nostalgia, 231–32; and Oscar Browning; 232–33; and William Johnson, 233–34; whipping in, 253–54
"Bobby Make Believe" (comic strip), 367
Body, the, and economic models, 41, 42–43; and exercise models, 41–42, 43; invention of modern form of, 104–5; formation of laws governing, 106–15; and puberty, 107, 124–26; body-centers, 109–15; and nerveforce, 109–10; and chemistry, 110–11; and blood, 111; and electro-magnetism, 111–12; and the brain, 112; and sperm, 112–14; and sex, 114, as self-sufficient and harmonious, 115–17; and development, 116–17; as connected to the mind, 114–20; and precocity, 120–24; and latency, 126–28; and figures of naughtiness, 246–47; and textual desire, 303–38; and the pedophile, 351
Bold, Eleanor (*Barchester Towers*), 248
Book of Instructions for Young Mothers (Rhoda White), 120
Bouidillon, Francis William, 199

"Boy" (Tarzan films), 374
Boy David, The (Barrie), 281, 299n
Boy Makes the Man, The (Anon.), 97n
Boys and Their Ways (Anon.), 100n, 102n, 132n, 220, 243n, 244n, 271n; and nostalgia, 231
Boys for Sale (Drew and Drake), 206, 208
Boys Speak Out on Man/Boy Love (NAMBLA), 394n
Bradbury, Dr. Andrew, 211n
Bradford, Rev. Edwin Emmanuel, 208, 219, 243n
Bradlaugh, Annie, 39
Bradlaugh, Charles, 39
Brady, Bobby, 371, 374
Brady, Cindy, 371
Brady Bunch, The (television series), 64, 371
Bragman, Louis J., 211n
Brand, Jeanne L., 128n
Branner, Martin M., 369
Bratton, J.S., 58n, 96n
Bray, Mrs. Caroline, 88, 101n, 103n, 105, 128n, 131n
Brecher, Edward, 178n
Brigham, Amariah, 130n, 131n
Bristow, Edward J., 99n, 180n, 211n; on Ellis, 182n
Brodie, Miss Jean (Muriel Spark's), 233
"Broken Appointment, A" (Hardy), 322–24
Brome, Vincent, 178n
Brontë, Emily, 51n
Brontës, The, 80
Brook, Peter, 373
Brown, Buster, 64, 203, 269, 365–70, 371, 373–75, 392n
Brown, Tom (*Tom Brown's Schooldays*), 255
Browning, Oscar, 199, 232–33, 234
Browning, Robert, 106
Brownlow, Mr. (*Oliver Twist*), 390–1
Brownmiller, Susan, 379, 393n
Brown-Sequard, Dr., 113–14
Bruns, Gerald, 53n
Bryan, James, 319, 339n
Buckey, Peggy McMartin, 342, 351, 358n, 382–83
Buckey, Raymond, and the McMartin Pre-School trial, 341–46, 348–56, 358n, 382–83
Bullough, Vern L., 54n, 129n, 130n, 167, 177n, 178n, 180n, 181n, 198, 213n
Bumble, Mr. (*Oliver Twist*), 80
Bunker, Edith, 285
Burgess, Ann Wolbert, 54n, 210n, 211n, 214n
Burton, Richard, 43–44, 176, 207
Busby, Dr. (Westminster School), 253
Butler, Josephine, 21, 53n
Butler, Samuel, 113, 130n
Butler, Samuel (the elder), 248, 270n
Byron, George Gordon, Lord, 25, 217, 226, 243n, 257, 331

"Calamites, The," 199
Caliban (Browning's "Caliban upon Setebos"), 106
Cameron, Lucy L., 98n
Carlyle, Thomas, 50
Carpenter, Edward, 106, 128n, 169, 176, 181n; and dynamic models for understanding, 189; and "The Uranians," 199; on democracy, 203
Carpenter, Mary, 76
Carroll, Lewis (Charles Lutwidge Dodgson), 67, 76, 93, 243n, 245n, 293, 298n; parody of Watts, 102n; and gender, 51n; and pedophilia, 196–97, 212n; and the true/false child, 196–97; in *Dreamchild*, 205; and his readers, 218; and photography, 227, 290, 303; and "Speak gently," 235–36; and the Alice books, 278–79, 288–98; on owning children, 319
Catcher in the Rye, The, and pedophile reading, 309–20; and formalism, 309–10; and exhibitionism, 311–17; and voyeurism foiled, 317–20
Caucus Race, The (*Alice in Wonderland*), 291
Caulfield, Allie (*The Catcher in the Rye*), 316
Caulfield, D.B. (*The Catcher in the Rye*), 313
Caulfield, Holden (*The Catcher in the Rye*), 309–20, 321, 339n

Caulfield, Phoebe (*The Catcher in the Rye*), 319–20
Chandos, John, 181n, 244n, 271n
Chavasse, Pye Henry, 91, 97n, 102n, 131n, 171n; on exercise, 117; on precocity, 121; ignoring masturbation, 166
Chetham, Celia (*Middlemarch*), 248
Chic, 376
Child, the: constructedness, 4–5, 11, 61–63, 69; connection to cultural models of the desirable, 4–5, 10, 11–13, 26, 67, 151–53; defined, 5, 68–70; distinction from adult, 6–7, 13, 15, 62–63; and emptiness, 11–13, 78–79; in *Wuthering Heights*, 11–13; and gender, 14–16, 64–65, 106–7, 268; and power, 16–17, 24–25, 28–29, 72–73; mortality rates, 38, 75; and class, 38–39, 123–24, 203; systems of rearing, 49, 65; Phillipe Ariès on, 61–63, 65, 72, 83–84; strangeness of, 63–65, 221–22; and models of development, 66–68; and gradualism, 66; and catastrophic models, 66–67; and nostalgia, 67–68, 228–34; existence of sexual feeling in, 70, 118–28, 140–42, 159–60, 172–76; and puberty, 70, 107, 124–26; nature of, 71–79; and evil, 71–72, 74, 95; and innocence, 72–79, 219–21; and feeling, 74; exportation of, 75; in the work force, 76; as prostitutes, 76–77; as image of happiness, 79–80; and corporal punishment, 109–110, 150–51, 249–55, 261–63; as holy (and dead), 80–82, 234–40; as an object for inquiry, 82–83; and the family, 83–87; and boarding schools, 86, 168–69, 231–34; the management of, 87–95; and habits, 92–93; and obedience, 93–95; and inflaming ideas, 118–19, 140–42; precocity in, 120–24; and latency, 126–28; erotic whipping of (Victorian), 150–51, 255–57; and female sexuality, 161–63; as a "problem," 183–84; in pedophile fantasies, 195–97, 209–10, 217–43; and Lewis Carroll, 196–97, 218; and attraction to pedophiles, 185; and gentleness, 217–43; as living in a separate world, 221–22; and nudity, 223–25; and transience, 225–28; offering nostalgia, 228–34; as erotic corpse, 234–40; in Kilvert, 240–43; and naughtiness, 246–70; and resentment, 247–49; and pain/love (Ellis), 257–59; as Peter Pan, 275–88; as Alice, 275–79, 288–98; as text for voyeurs, 303–38; in *David Copperfield*, 306–9; in *The Catcher in the Rye*, 309–20; in *Tess of the d'Urbervilles*, 320–38; in the McMartin Pre-School trial, 345–49; and our culture, 359–91; on exhibit, 363–65; and advertising, 364; in comic strips, 365–69; in cinema, 369–75; at risk, 378–84; outside of power, 384–91
"Child Is Being Beaten, A" (Freud), 259–61
Child, Mrs. Lydia Maria, 36, 56n, 92, 102n, 132n, 272n; on mental exercise, 122; on puberty, 125; on corporal punishment, 254
Child-abuse: and gender, 15–16; and love, 27; and child-labor, 75–77; and Victorian pornography, 169–72; and pedophilia, 185, 188–89; and Victorian child-beating, 249–55; Victorian opposition to, 254–55; and the McMartin Pre-School trial, 341–58; and politics, 350; in our time, 360, 375, 378–84; *see also* Whipping; Masturbation; Desire; Pedophilia
Child-love, *see* Pedophilia
Children and Sex (Constantine and Martinson), 127
Children and What to Do With Them (Anon.), 93, 102n, 103n, 152, 272n
Children: Their Health, Training, and Education (Anon.), 99n, 102n, 131n, 132n, 152, 270n
Children's Institute International (McMartin case), 348
Children's Petition, The (1669), 255, 272n
Children's Rights (Wiggin), 209
Children's Wrong, The (Anon.), 87, 100n, 101n, 130n, 169, 177n, 181n
Chimney sweepers, 76

Christ's Hospital (School), 254
Clamp, Peter G., 99n
Clare, Angel (*Tess of the d'Urbervilles*), 325, 326, 327, 329–38, 340n
Class, and readings of the past, 38–39; and the Victorian child, 82, 203; and sexual precocity, 123–24; and biology, 175–76; and the gentle child, 217; and pederasty, 219, 223, 232; in *Peter Pan*, 283; and Holden Caulfield, 314–15; and sexuality in our culture, 363
Cleopatra, 282
Clitoridectomy, 162–63, 165
Cobbe, Frances Power, 47, 56n, 57n, 81, 97n, 98n, 100n
Cobbett, William, 86, 101n, 151
Coleridge, Samuel Taylor, 63, 254
Collis, John Stewart, 55n
Columbia Records, 384
Comfort, Alex, 180n
Cominos, Peter T., 57n, 154–55, 179n
Comstock, Anthony, 73, 98n
Comstock, Cathy, 55n
Confessions (Rousseau), 120, 256
Confessions of Nemesis Hunt, The (Anon.), 171, 181n
Confessions of a Royal Rake (Anon.), 273n
Constantine, Larry L., 54n, 96n, 127, 132n, 211n, 387, 394n
Coogan, Jackie, 369
Cook, Mark, 214n
Cope, Jackson I., 213n
Copperfield, David, 13, 179n, 306–9
Copperfield, Mrs. Clara, 306, 308–9
Coppertone (advertisements), 10, 364
"Corvo, Baron," *see* Rolfe
Cory, William, *see* Johnson
Cosby, Bill, 309
Coveney, Peter, 61, 63, 95n, 97n, 98n, 100n, 245n, 298n; on Paul Dombey's death, 236
Cox, David N., 394n
Creakle, Mr. (*David Copperfield*), 308
Crewdson, John, 190, 211n, 213n, 381, 392n, 393n
Crick, Dairyman (*Tess of the d'Urbervilles*), 329
Croft-Cooke, Rupert, 23, 54n, 211n, 213n, 244n; on scandals at Eton, 232–34
Crompton, Louis, 54n, 55n, 56n, 177n, 226, 244n
Cujo (film), 374
Culkin, Macaulay, 369
Curative Magnetism (Shettle), 111
Curiositates Eroticae Physiologiae (Davenport), 40
Currier, Richard L., 182n
Curse of Manhood, The (Verley), 113
Custody of Children Act, 84
Cutt, M. Nancy., 80, 98n, 100n, 271n
"Cycle of abuse," 15, 190

Daily News (London), 232
Damien (*The Omen*), 388
Daniel, 307
Dante Alighieri, 267
Darling, Michael (*Peter Pan*), 222, 284
Darling, Mr. George (*Peter Pan*), 276, 284, 285
Darling, Mrs. (*Peter Pan*), 285, 286
Darling, Wendy (*Peter Pan*), 281; and adult sexuality, 282; as intruder, 285–86; and Alice, 288, 296, 298
Darwin, Charles, 40, 42, 66, 137, 147, 276
Davenport, John, 40–42, 56n, 57n, 130n, 131n, 179n, 272n; on sperm, 113–14; on mind-body links, 119; on whipping, 255
David, King, 250
David Copperfield, 13, 179n, 230; erotic reading of, 306–9; and Holden Caulfield, 312
Davidson, Arnold I., 53n, 58n, 137, 177n
Davidson, Lucretia Maria, 121
Davidson, Michael, 206, 210n, 212n, 214n, 244n; on transience of pedophile relations, 226
Davies family (Barrie's friends), 278, 280, 283, 285
Davis, Murray S., 177n, 210n
Davis, Robert Con, 305, 339n
"Death of the Domini, The" (Thomas Hood), 266
de Boissy, Marquis, 44
Deconstruction, and method of this

book, 3–4, 6–7, 10, 359; of pedophilia, 3–4, 204–10; and power, 7–8, 20, 29–30, 385–86; and politics of book, 10; of gender, 14–15, 189–90; and Freud, 20; and Foucault, 35–36; and essentializing, 50; and innocence, 78; and health/disease, 105; and "latency," 126–28; and gentleness, 218; and naughtiness/goodness, 246–47; and voyeurism/exhibitionism, 309–20, 339n; and the cute, 310; and cultural narratives of child-molesting, 341–58; and the McMartin defense, 349, 353–55
"Defects in the Moral Training of Girls" (Anon.), 101n, 132n
"Dennis the Menace" (comic strip and television series), 369, 373
Derrida, Jacques, 54n, 291, 355; on power and centered structures, 30
Desart, Lord, 36
Desire, and the child, 4–5, 7, 10, 26, 67–68, 183–84; and power, 8, 32; and emptiness, 12–13; Roland Barthes on, 31; perpetuation of, 31–32; and Otherness, 32–33; and Victorian women, 40; and loss, 67, 225–28; nostalgia in, 67–68, 228–34; and prostitution, 108; and child-love, 183–214; as play, 196–97; and gentleness, 217–43; and transience, 225–28; and nostalgia, 228–34; and death, 234–40; and naughtiness, 246–47; and child-spanking, 255–57; and child-beating pornography, 263–66; and Peter Pan, 276–88; in Hook's attraction to Peter Pan, 284–85; and Alice, 276–79, 288–98; and voyeuristic reading, 303–38; and *David Copperfield*, 306–9; and *The Catcher in the Rye*, 309–20; and *Tess of the d'Urbervilles*, 320–38; and child-molesting narratives, 341–58; and the modern child, 359–91; *see also* Pedophilia
Deslandes, L., 114, 130n, 132n, 164, 179n, 180n
Dickens, Charles, 51n, 67, 74, 80, 82, 95, 168, 244n, 245n, 252, 267, 339n, 352, 394n; and Urania House, 108; and pedophilia, 212n; and *Dombey and Son*, 236–38; and *The Old Curiosity Shop*, 238–40; child-resenting in, 249; and *David Copperfield*, 306–9; and *Oliver Twist*, 389–91
Dirty Harry, 382
Disney, Walt, 374
Disorderly Family, The (Anon.), 101n
"Dixie Dugan" (comic strip), 369
Do-The-Girls-Hall, Or Conventual Life Unveiled (Anon.), 102n
Dodo, The (*Alice in Wonderland*), 196, 291
Dombey, Florence, 236, 245n
Dombey, Paul, 81, 236–38; and Little Nell, 238–39
Dombey, Mr., 245n
Dombey and Son, 236–38, 249
Dostoevsky, Fyodor, 80
Dothie, Mrs. Hilton, 129n
Dowson, Ernest, 240
Dracula, Count, 111, 235, 245n
Drake, Jonathan, 197, 206, 208, 214n
Drake, Mrs. Emma F. Angell, 101n
Dreamchild (film), 205
Drew, Dennis, 197, 206, 208, 214n
Drinka, George Frederick, 178n
Drysdale, George, 42–43, 57n, 131n; on mind-body links, 118
Dubois, Jean, 179n, 180n
Duchess, The (*Alice in Wonderland*), 235–36, 290–91; and her baby, 293
Dukahz, Casimir (pseud.), 206, 212n, 244n; on nostalgia, 228
Dukes, Clement, 99n, 101n, 130n, 131n, 178n, 180n, 181n, 182n; on exercise, 117; and child sexuality, 176
Dunbar, Mr. (Wixenford School), 253
d'Urberville (Durbeyfield), Liza-Lu, 337
d'Urberville (Durbeyfield), Tess, 320–38, 340n
d'Urberville (Stoke), Alec, 325, 326–29, 330, 331, 337, 340n; and the child-molester, 341
d'Urberville (Stoke), Mrs., 327
Dworin, William, 212n, 214n
Dyer, Willie, 231–32

E.T. (film), 203, 309
Earnshaw, Catherine (*Wuthering Heights*), 11–13, 51n, 235

Earnshaw, Hindley (*Wuthering Heights*), 11
East, Jeff, 269
Ebbard, Richard, 182n
Ede, Lisa, 299n
Edlestone, John, 217, 226
Edis, Arthur W., 75, 89, 98n, 101n
Edwards, Duane, 339n
Eglinton, J.Z. (pseud.), 197, 212n, 213n, 226, 244n
Electro-magnetic systems, 47, 48; and the body, 111–12
Elements of Social Science (Drysdale), 42–43
"Ella Cinders" (comic strip), 369
Ellis, Havelock, 53n, 54n, 57n, 98n, 129n, 144, 177n, 178n, 180n, 181n, 182n, 211n, 213n, 251, 272n, 273n; on sexual essentializing, 21; and the normal/abnormal distinctions, 22–23, 146, 272n; solemn tone of, 29; on repression, 34; and system-thinking, 47; on children's immodesty, 73; and "erotic symbolism," 136; on Krafft-Ebing, 144, 146–47; analysis of, 146–51; on modesty, 147–48; on homosexuality, 149–50, 169; and female masochism, 163; on masturbation, 165; on infant sexuality, 175; on female sexual impulses, 190; on homosexuality, 191; and "law of contrasts," 201; on love and pain, 257–59
Englishwoman's Domestic Magazine, The, 252–53
Erasmus, Desiderius, 84
Eroticism, *see* Desire
Esoteric Anthropology (Nichols), 87
Etienne, Robert, 95n
Eton, and pederasty scandals, 199, 232–34; and flogging, 253, 255, 256; and Hook, 276
"Eton Boating Song" (Johnson), 233, 234
Evard, Rev. George, 131n
Eve (*Paradise Lost*), 213n
Every Mother's Book (Fennings), 89
Exhibitionism, and texts, 303; and Holden Caulfield, 311–17
Experiences of Flagellation (Anon.), 249, 270n, 274n

Fagin (*Oliver Twist*), 114, 209, 390–91
Falwell, Rev. Jerry, 26
Family: pedophilia as protection of, 26, 390; as centered in the child, 83–87; child-management in, 87–95; and development of the body, 115–16; and growth of privacy, 142–43; and Victorian child-beating, 249–55
Family Ties (television series), 369, 371
Farley, John, 178n
Farrar, F.W., 245n
Fat Boy, The (*Pickwick Papers*), 95
Father's Advice to a Son, A (Anon.), 102n
Fawley, Jude (*Jude the Obscure*), 321
Fawn, the (*Through the Looking-Glass*), 297
FBI Law Enforcement Bulletin, 387
Federal Bureau of Investigation, 355, 356–57n, 387, 392n
Fennings, Alfred, 75, 89, 98n, 101n, 131n
Ferrero, Pam (McMartin case), 344, 349–53
Festus, 255
Few Suggestions to Mothers, A ("A Mother"), 57n, 96n, 252, 271n
Few Words of Advice to a Public Schoolboy, A (Poynder), 166
Findlay, J. J., 98n, 132n
Finn, Huckleberry, 209, 224, 374
Fischer, Mary A., 356n, 358n
Fish, Stanley, 148
Fitzgerald, Keith, 357n, 358n
Flagellation, *see* Whipping
Fleischhauer-Hardt, Helga, 55n, 214n, 392n
Flint, Rev. J.F., 54n, 153, 179n
Flogging-Block, The (Swinburne), 272n
Flynt, Larry, 303
Foster, Jodie, 369
Foucault, Michel, 51n, 52n, 53n, 56n, 100n, 128n, 134, 136, 140, 176n, 177n, 182n, 273n, 391n; on power, 17–20, 21–22, 263, on sex and sexuality, 18; and possibilities for liberation, 30, 139; and reading the past, 34–35; critique of repression in, 34–35; and the family, 84; on the body, 104–5; on the "normal," 138; and Victorian "incitement to discourse"

on sex, 139–40, 142, 152; on child sexuality, 172, 174, 183; and bourgeois origins of sexuality, 363
Fowler, O.S., 135, 166, 177n, 180n
Frankenstein, Victor, 331
Fraser, Morris, 100n, 211n, 213n, 243n, 245n, 298n; and explanation of pedophilia, 212n
"Fraxi, Pisanus" (Henry Spenser Ashbee), 170–71, 181n
Freeman, M.D.A., 393n
Freud, Sigmund, 51n, 52n, 53n, 55n, 56n, 57n, 61, 78, 95n, 96n, 98n, 100n, 102n, 128n, 130n, 132n, 177n, 178n, 181n, 182n, 211n, 244n, 272n, 273n, 339n, 377, 393n; on gender and children, 13, 106, 189; and the powers of children, 16–17; on power generally, 19–20; on child sexuality, 26, 124, 172; on secrets, 33–34; on repression, 34, 35; and empiricism, 46; on the unconscious in children, 64; and latency, 70, 126–27; and family romance, 84; on the impressionable child, 92; on "the mental factor," 112; on puberty, 125; and hysteria, 136; on "normality" and perversion, 138; and sex education, 143–44 and masturbation, 168; on parental idiocy, 173, 176; on women and children, 190; on pedophilia, 201–2; on narcissism, 213n; and idealized sex, 222–23; on children's immodesty, 223; on child-beating, 255–56, 259–61; and masochism, 262; and the child's adult imitations, 277–78; and voyeurism/exhibitionism, 304–5, 310; and Holden Caulfield, 315
Froebel, Friedrich, 61, 79, 95n, 97n, 100n, 130n; and natural development, 116
From Here to Eternity (film), 236
Fruits of Philosophy (Knowlton), 39–40
Fry, Roger, 271n
Frye, Northrop, 267, 339n, 340n
Functions and Disorders of the Reproductive Organs, The (Acton), 69; examination of six editions of, 155–60

Galahad, Sir (Tennyson), 113–14
Gallagher, Jane (*The Catcher in the Rye*), 315, 318

Gargery, Joe (*Great Expectations*), 28, 209
Garner, James, 374
Gaskell, Elizabeth, 80
Gathorne-Hardy, Jonathan, 63, 75, 86, 96n, 99n, 100n, 101n, 102n, 271n
Gay, Peter, 58n
Gebhard, Paul H., 180n, 190, 207, 211n, 212n, 213n, 214n, 376, 392n
Gender, and the Victorian child, 13, 15, 64–65, 106–7; and child-loving, 13–16; and pedophilia, 13–16, 51n, 189–90; and sexual passion, 14; deconstruction of, 14–15; and child-abuse, 15–16; and female sexuality, 160–63; and benefits of orgasm, 186; in Kilvert, 241; and child-beating narratives, 268–70; and Peter Pan, 282, 287–88; and irrelevance to modern erotic child image, 364–65, 366–75
Genesis, 43, 154
Gentle Measures (Abbott), 110
Gentleness, and the child, 217–43; and reading, 218
Gerry, Elbridge T., 141
Gibson, Ian, 271n
Gilbert, Arthur N., 180n, 181n
"Ginger Pop" (comic strip), 367
Gladstone, William Ewart, 108, 178n
Glubb (*Dombey and Son*), 237
Gnat, the (*Through the Looking-Glass*), 196, 297
Goldman, Ronald and Juliet, 133n
Goldstein, Seth L., 394n
Gomorrah, 379, 385
Gorham, Deborah, 51n, 56n, 61, 72, 95n, 96n, 98n, 101n, 129n, 179n, 211n, 299n
Goss, Suzanne (McMartin case), 356
Gray, Donald, 299n
Greek Love (Eglinton), 197
Greenblatt, Stephen, 30, 52n
Greg, W. R., 129–130n
Grimwig, Mr. (*Oliver Twist*), 391
Groser, William H., 99n
Groth, A. Nicholas, 207, 210n, 211n, 212n, 213n, 214n
Gryphon, The (*Alice in Wonderland*), 290
Guiliano, Edward, 299n
"Gumps, The" (comic strip), 367, 372

Hagstrum, Jean, 65, 96n, 182n, 213n
Hall, Calvin S., 193, 212n, 213n
Hall, Nancy W., 392n
Hall, W. Clarke, 97n, 100n
Halpin, Luke, 374
Hansel and Gretel, 12
Hardy, Thomas, 80, 281, 384; and Holden Caulfield, 320; and *Tess of the d'Urbervilles*, 320–38; and *Jude the Obscure*, 321, 340n; and "A Broken Appointment" 322–24
"Harold Teen" (comic strip), 369
Harrow (School), 231
Hartshorne, Henry, 129n
Harville, Captain (*Persuasion*), 117
Hatter, The (*Alice in Wonderland*), 290
Hayes, Sally (*The Catcher in the Rye*), 313, 315
Heathcliff (*Wuthering Heights*), 11–13, 51n, 64, 235
"Heraclitus" (William Johnson), 234
Hereford, Bishop of, 132n
Herrmann, Professor Kenneth J., Jr., 379
Hill, General (*When a Child Loves*), 200, 225
Hill, Rev. Alfred Bligh, 89, 101n
Hints on Child-Training (Trumbull), 91
Hints on Early Education (Anon.), 100n, 102n, 272n
Hirschfeld, Magnus, 29
History, and perception, 4, 34–35, 38–39; and power, 19; narrative emplotments of, 29–30; and estranging, 33–51; in Foucault, 34–35; and reading of silence, 35–36; and class, 38–39; and constructing "the child," 61–63; reading the "masturbation panic" in, 163–68; and explanations of pedophilia, 197–202; and flagellation, 249–50, 252; *see also* Victorian culture
History of European Morals (Lecky), 50
Hoag, Officer Jane (McMartin case), 342
Hogan, Hulk, 303
Holmes, James, 178n
Holmstrom, Linda Lytle, 210n, 214n
Holt, Robert, 57n
Homosexuality, 36; and essentializing, 20, 21; and the "normal," 137; Krafft-Ebing on, 146; Ellis on, 149–50, 169; and dissociation from pedophilia, 188, 190–91; and scandals at Eton, 232–34; and child-beating fantasies, 268–69; and J.M. Barrie, 280; and Holden Caulfield, 315–16
Honey, John Raymond de Symons, 86, 100n, 101n, 131n, 181n, 271n, 274n; and schoolboy immorality, 168–69
Hood, Darla (*Our Gang*), 374
Hood, Thomas, 266, 274n
Hook (*Peter Pan*), 281, 284; and nostalgia, 276; and tie to Peter, 284–85; as pedophile, 285, 286; and his defeat, 287
Hoover, J. Edgar, 379, 393n
Hope, A.R., 67–68, 97n, 232, 244n
Hopkins, Ellice, 103n, 128n, 176, 182n, 271n; on "wholesome terror," 250–51
Horner, Dr. (Eton), 232
Howe, Julia Ward, 118, 131n
Howells, Kevin, 212n
Huett, Izz (*Tess of the d'Urbervilles*), 337
Hugo, Victor, 80
Humpty Dumpty (*Through the Looking-Glass*), 297
Hunt, Leigh, 254
Hunt, William Holman, 236
Hustler, 26, 376, 377, 392n

I Know My First Name Is Steven (television film), 381, 393n
Incest, 36–37; Krafft-Ebing on, 145; and pedophilia, 204; and cultural narratives of child-molesting, 356
Indecent Whippings (Anon.), 271n
Innocence, and eroticizing the child, 13, 175–6, 219–25; and sexual knowledge, 36; and the Victorian child, 72–79; and depravity, 78; and pornography, 141; in Peter Pan, 282; and David Copperfield, 306–9; and Tess d'Urberville, 324–38; and the McMartin children, 347–49
In Memoriam, 267
"Instincts and Their Vicissitudes" (Freud), 304–5
Intuitive Morals (Cobbe), 81
Isaac, 307

Isaiah, 250
Iser, Wolfgang, 303
Ives, George Cecil, 49, 58n

Jackson, A. Reeves, 182n
Jackson, Stevi, 96n, 98n, 140, 177n, 209, 214n
Jason (*Friday the 13th*), 388
Jekyll, Dr. Henry, 157
"Jiggs and Maggie," 206
Jim (*Huckleberry Finn*), 209, 224
"Joe Palooka" (comic strip), 369
Johnson, Judy (McMartin case), 342
Johnson, Mark, 19, 53n
Johnson, William (Cory), 199, 233–34, 244n
Jordan, Thomas Edward, 99n
Joseph (*Wuthering Heights*), 11
Jones, Ernest, 315, 339n
Jones, Tom (Fielding), 13
Jordan, Thomas Edward, 56n, 75
Jude the Obscure, 321, 340n
Jung, Carl, 16
Justinian, 193

Kafka, Franz, 383
"Katzenjammer Kids, The" (comic strip), 367
Keate, Dr. (Eton), 253, 255
Kellogg, J.H., 130n
Kellogg, Mrs. J.H., 101n, 130n
Kelly, Nancy, 375
Kempe, C. Henry, 211n
Kerr, Deborah, 236
Keyes, Edward L., 178n, 181n
Kidrodstock, Lord (pseud.), 273n
Kilvert, Rev. Francis, 240–43, 245n, 266, 274n
Kim (Kipling's), 209
King, Stephen, 99n, 374
Kinsey, Alfred, 53n, 54n, 55n, 57n, 58n, 99n, 132n, 177n, 179n, 180n, 210n, 211n, 212n, 272n; and attack on fixed categories, 21, 189; conspiracy to ignore, 21; on normal/abnormal distinctions, 23; and sexual powers of children, 26, 172; satiric tone in, 29, 34–35; empiricism in, 46; on the child and play, 79; and puberty, 125–6; attack on "latency" in, 127; on the "normal," 137–38; on masturbation, 162, 164; and pedophilia, 185–87, 383, 393n
Kitchner, Henry Thomas, 181n
Knoepflmacher, U.C., 299n
Knowlton, Charles, 39–40, 41, 42, 56n, 177n; on sex and power, 135
Kraemer, William, 212n
Krafft-Ebing, Richard von, 50, 51n, 58n, 96n, 130n, 132n, 144, 176n, 177n, 178n, 179n, 180n, 210n, 211n, 212n, 251, 272n, 273n; and the child's gender, 15, 64–65; on the brain and sexual pathology, 112; on puberty, 125, 132n; and latency, 126, 137; and sex as the center, 134; analysis of, 144–46; on female masturbation, 162–63; on child sexuality, 176; and pedophilia, 184, 191, 193; on whipping, 255
Kramer, Stanley, 374
Krebs (Crabs?), Bernice (*The Catcher in the Rye*), 315
Krebs, Sandra Gail (McMartin case), 348–49, 357n
Kucich, John, 52n, 56n
Kuhlmeyer, Chief Henry L., Jr. (McMartin case), 342

Lacan, Jacques, on voyeurism and "seeing," 305–6
Lady Gay Spanker's Tales (Anon.), 273n, 274n
Lakoff, George, 19, 53n
Lamb, Charles, 254
Lambercier, Mlle. (Rousseau's nurse), 256
Lancaster, Burt, 236
Langford, G.W., 245n
Lardner, Ring, 313
Largen, Mary Ann, 54n
Laslett, Peter, 86, 100n
Latency, 70, 137; and the child's body, 126–28
Laughton, Charles, 375
Lawrence, D.H., 281, 332
Laws, D.R., 212n, 393n
Lecky, William E.H., 50, 58n
Lectures on Diet and Regimen (Willich), 48–49

"Legend of the Water Lilies, The" (F.W. Bouidillon), 199
Lester, Mark, 269, 371, 373
Letters from a Father to His Son (Anon.), 131n
Lewinsohn, Richard, 56n, 61, 95n
Liddell, Alice, 205
"Lil' Abner" (comic strip), 369
Little Children (Anon.), 38, 56n
Little Em'ly (*David Copperfield*), 307
Little Eva, 324
"Little Iodine" (comic strip), 369
"Little Lulu" (comic strip), 369
Little Nell, 64, 67, 81, 82, 324; and erotic dying, 238–40
Little Woodman, The (Sherwood), 249
Lockwood (*Wuthering Heights*), 11–12
Logan, William, 99n, 129n
Lord of the Flies, The (novel and films), 203, 373
Los Angeles Times, 343, 381, 391n, 393n
Louis Phillipe, 44
Love in Earnest (Nicholosn), 206, 228–29
"Lucas, Dr." (pseud.), 135–36, 164, 177n, 180n
Luce, Carl (*The Catcher in the Rye*), 315
Lucian, 255
Lucy Show, The (television series), 373
Lustful Adventures (Anon.), 171, 181n, 213n
Lyttleton, Lord Edward, 153, 169, 178n, 181n

Macaulay, Thomas Babington, 50
MacDonald, George, 245n
MacDonald, Robert H., 180n
MacFarlane, Kee (McMartin case), 357n
MacNeil/Lehrer (television news), 377
MacStinger, Alexander (*Dombey and Son*), 249
Magnet, The, 164
"Mama's Angel Child" (comic strip), 392n
Manhood (Deslandes), 164, 180n
Mantegazza, Professor, 44
Marcus, Steven, 40, 55n, 57n, 178n, 179n, 181n, 270n, 273n, 274n; on William Acton, 153–54; and Victorian pornography, 170–71; on child-beating erotica, 264–65, 268–69
Marlowe, Christopher, 213n
Martin, John Rutledge, 57n, 58n, 137, 154–55, 177n, 179n, 180n; on masturbation, 164; on Victorian moderation, 181n
Martin, Lloyd, 379, 393n
Martinez, Joseph (McMartin case), 349–50
Martinson, Floyd M., 54n, 96n, 127, 132n, 182n
"Mary Worth" (comic strip), 369
Masaoay, Michael, 381
Masson, Jeffrey Moussaieff, 214n, 221, 243n
Masters and Johnson, 272n
Masturbation, 41, 42–43, 48, 91, 123, 135, 142; and vital energy, 109–110; and loss of semen, 113–14; and precocity, 118; Krafft-Ebing on, 145; Ellis on, 149; William Acton on, 155–57, 158; and female sexuality, 161–62; and Victorian culture, 152, 163–68; Kinsey on, 186; and whipping, 251
Matthews, Joseph Bridges, 272n
Maugham, Somerset, 313
Maurice (*The Catcher in the Rye*), 316, 318
May, Margaret, 271n
Maya (film), 373
Mayhew, Henry, 39
Maylie, Rose (*Oliver Twist*), 390–91
Maynard, John, 56n, 154, 179n
McBride, Will, 55n
McCormack, Patty, 269, 369, 374–75
McGhee, Richard, 272n
McHugh, Paul, 129n
McMartin Pre-School trial, 341–58, 382–83; background of, 341–45; and the children; the prosecution in, 349–53; the defense in, 353–55; and us, 355–56
McMullen, Buck, 339n
McNichol, Kristy, 270
M'Choakumchild, Mr. (*Hard Times*), 276
Medusa, 285

Melody (film), 371
"Memoranda from Mr. P——" (Anon., *The Pearl*), 224, 244n
Memory, *see* Nostalgia
Menaker, Esther, 273n
Menken, Adah, 188
Meredith, George, 320, 339n
Merrill, Lynn L., 58n, 144, 178n
Meynell, Viola, 299n
Micawber, Mr. Wilkins, 179n
Middlemarch, 248
Miles (*Turn of the Screw*), 81
Millais, John Everett, 236
Milland, Ray, 352
Miller, Gavin, 205
Miller, J. Hillis, 340n
Miller, Justin, 377, 392n
"Miller's Carpet Care," 381
Milne, A.A., 282
Milton, John, 213n, 361
Miss America, 376
Miss Universe, 376
"Missing Children Act" (1982), 381
Mitchell, William, 100n, 102n, 182n
Mock Turtle, the (*Alice in Wonderland*), 290, 293
Mohr, J. W., 133n, 392n
Moll, Albert, 20, 53n, 69, 98n, 176, 212n; on pederasty and the normal, 191
Mona (*When a Child Loves*), 225, 227, 265
Moon, Michael, 203, 214n
Morrison, W. Douglas, 272n
Morrow, Ernest (*The Catcher in the Rye*), 314
Moser, Barry, 299n
Mother's Best Book or Nursery Companion, The (Anon.), 273n
Mother's Book, The (Mrs. Child), 92, 122
Mother's Medical Adviser, The (Anon.), 97n, 131n
Mother's Thorough Resource-Book, The (Anon.), 131n
Ms., 26, 377
Murdstone, Mr. (*David Copperfield*), 306, 308
My Secret Life (Anon.), 154, 171, 181n
My Side of the Mountain (film), 373–74
Mysteries of Venus (Anon.), 171, 181n

NAMBLA (North American Man/Boy Love Association), 385, 394n
Nancy (*Oliver Twist*), 391
Nardinelli, Clark, 99n
Nation, The, 377
National Broadcasting Company, 381
National Enquirer, The, 376, 377
National Organization of Women (NOW), 26
Naughtiness, and pedophilia, 246–70; and goodness, 246–47; and spanking, 247–57
Neale, R.S., 39, 56n
Nelly (*Wuthering Heights*), 12
Neroni, Madeline (*Barchester Towers*), 249
New historicism, and power, 19, 27
Newman, Francis W., 181n, 189, 211n
Neuberg, Victor E., 271n
Neverland (*Peter Pan*), 277, 278, 283–86
New Testament, 267
New York Times, 377
Nichols, T.L., 87, 101n, 129n, 132n, 180n; on child sexuality, 123; on female sexual desire, 163
Nicholson, John Gambril Francis, 199, 206
Nietzsche, Friedrich, 24, 34, 54n, 55n; on the "normal," 138
Night of the Hunter, The (film), 375
Noah, 66
Normal, the, as regulated by power, 22–23
Norroy, Phyllis (pseud.), 213n
North, Jay, 369, 371–72
Nostalgia, and pedophilia, 228–34; for the dead child, 234–40; and Kilvert, 240–43; in Peter Pan and Alice, 275, 277–79
Notes & Queries, 252
Novick, Jack, 100n
Novick, Kerry Kelly, 100n
Nubbles, Kit (*The Old Curiosity Shop*), 239
Nursery, the, as metaphor, 90–91

Oates, Joyce Carol, 33
Obedience, and Victorian children, 93–95; and the naughty child, 246–70
O'Carroll, Tom, 54n, 133n, 208, 214n

"'Of the Land We Love'" (Anon.), 244n
Offer, Daniel, 132n
Ohmann, Carol and Richard, 339n
Old Testament, 43
Oliver! (film), 371
Oliver Twist, as a fable for our time, 389–91
Omer, Mr. (*David Copperfield*), 308
O'Neal, Tatum, 269, 369
One Little Indian (film), 374
Orgel, Stephen, 213n
Orwell, George, 24
Other Victorians, The (Steven Marcus), 153, 170
Otherness, and desire, 32–33, 195–97; and the child, 221–22, 225–28, 360; and nostalgia, 228–34; and death, 234–40; and the naughty child, 246–47; and spanking, 255–57; in Peter Pan, 275–88; in Alice, 275–79, 288–98; and textual erotics, 303–38; and David Copperfield, 306–9; and Holden Caulfield, 309–20; and Tess d'Urberville, 324–38
Our Children (E.C.), 102n, 182n
Our Gang (films), 374, 375
Outcault, Richard F., 365

Paget, Dr. James, 154
Pair of Blue Eyes, A (Hardy), 340n
Pallavicino, Ferrante, 198
Parent, the, the concept constructed, 84–85; and child sexuality, 173; and sex-talk, 142–43; advice manuals for, 151–52; and *Peter Pan*, 222, 283–84; and child-beating, 249–55, 261–63; and critics, 311; child-watching in our culture by, 363–65
Parr, Joy, 99n
Pater, Walter, 233
Patroclus, 219
Pawlowski, A.V., 212n, 393n
Pearl, The, 224
Pechter, Edward, 27, 54n
Pecksniff, Mr., 148
Pederasty, 43–44, 149, 191; and tourism, 197; and Greek and Roman cultures, 197–98, 208, 219, 223; and Eton, 199, 232–34; and *The Pearl*, 224; and Hook in *Peter Pan*, 282–83; and *The Catcher in the Rye*, 315, 316–17, 319
Pedophilia, 183–214; and knowingness, 3–4; cultural constructions of, 3–4, 5, 26–28; our need for, 5, 25, 26–28, 361–63, 375–78; ritualized discourse on, 6, 25–28; and gender, 13, 51n, 189–90; in males, 15, 190; power explanations of, 15, 24–25, 186–89, 378–84; as means to protect the family, 26; and love, 27–28, 205–10, 242–43; and Victorian pornography, 169–72, 200–2; Krafft-Ebing on, 145–46; our present need for, 184–87; and the Victorians, 184, 197–202; and Kinsey, 185–87; and homosexuality, 188, 190–91; psychological explanations of, 192–97; and play, 195–97, 204–10; and Lewis Carroll, 196–97, 205; historical explanations of, 197–202; social explanations of, 202–4; and inside explanations, 204–10; and T.H. White, 205–6; and J.A. Symonds, 192; gentleness and, 217–43; and nudity, 223–25, 240–41; and transience, 225–28; and voyeurism, 227–28; and nostalgia, 228–34; and death, 234–40; in Kilvert, 240–43; and the naughty child, 246–70; and child-whipping, 248, 255–57; in child-beating pornography, 263–66; and Peter Pan, 276–88; and Alice, 276–79, 288–98; in Barrie, 280; and textual voyeurism, 303–38; and *David Copperfield*, 306–9; and *The Catcher in the Rye*, 309–20; and *Tess of the d'Urbervilles*, 320–38; and the McMartin Pre-School trial, 341–58; and our culture, 359–91; and denial, 375–77; refigured, 384–91
"Pedophilia: The Consequences for the Child" (Bernard), 209
Peggotty, Dan (*David Copperfield*), 307, 308
"Perfectly Contented" (Pim), 220
"Penal Colony, In the" (Kafka), 383
Persuasion (Austen), 117
Peter and Wendy, 276–88
Peter Pan, 276–88; and parents, 222, 299n; and death, 299n

Peter Pan (character), 276–88; and Paul Dombey, 236–37; and Alice, 289
Peterson, M. Jeanne, 154, 179n
Phoenix, River, 270, 369
Photography, and children, 93, 195, 199–200, 227–28; and pedophilia, 227–28; and Carroll, 290, 303; and Barrie, 303
Physiology for Common Schools (Bray), 88
Piccaninny tribe (*Peter Pan*), 283
Pigeon, the (*Alice in Wonderland*), 294–95
Pim, Henry Moore ("A. Newman," pseud.), 220, 226, 227, 243n, 244n
Pip (*Great Expectations*), 28, 209, 255
Pipchin, Mrs. (*Dombey and Son*), 237
Play, as alternate center to power, 8, 30, 386; as negated by power, 18; and Victorian system-building, 46–47; and the child, 79–80; in conceptions of the body, 108–9; and Ellis, 149–50; in pornography, 171–72; and Victorian ideas of gender, 161; and pedophilia, 195–97, 204–10; and child-beating, 266–67; in *Peter Pan*, 276–88; resistance to in Alice books, 276–79, 288–98; and pedophile reading, 303–38; in *The Catcher in the Rye*, 310–11; and our culture, 384–91
Playboy, 352, 376, 377
Pleck, Elizabeth, 271n, 393n
Plummer, C., 140
Plummer, Kenneth, 185, 210n
Podsnap, Mr., 43, 70
Politics, of book and deconstruction, 10; and Victorian views of prostitution, 28; of pedophilia, 230–31; and *Peter Pan*, 283; in *The Catcher in the Rye*, 339n; and child-molesting, 350
Pollock, Linda, 96n, 271n
Pomeroy, H.S., 26, 54n
Pomeroy, Wardell, 172, 181n, 210n
Pornography, fight against, 29; and body as toy, 115; and the power of words, 124; and Victorian culture, 169–72; and the innocence of children, 141; and Victorian children, 200–2; and *The Catcher in the Rye*, 310; and *Tess of the d'Urbervilles*, 333–38; and *The Pearl*, 224–25; scarcity of children in, 224–25; and child-beating (Victorian), 263–6; and cultural narratives of child-molesting, 341; and modern children, 376, 380–81

Power, 16–33; and deconstruction, 7–8, 20, 29; idealizations of, 8, 17–20; alternate centers to, 8; and desire, 8, 32; connections to sex, 15, 135–36, 186–87; used to explain pedophilia, 15, 24–25, 187–89, 378–84; allocations to children, 16–17 24–25, 85–86; Foucault on, 17–20, 21–22; and the new historicism, 19, 27; and the "normal," 22–23; attacks on, 24; and stories of denial, 25–26; protections offered by, 25–26, 28–29; and solemn tone, 29–30; as unifying center, 30–31; and explanations, 32–33; and repression, 35; as myth of liberation, 35; and the family, 85–86; and child-management, 87–95; and the body, 104–5; as alien to pedophilia, 196–97; and naughtiness, 246–70; and child-beating, 249–55, 261–63, 267–68; and Alice, 290–91; and pedophile reading, 303–38; and cultural narratives of child-molesting, 341–58, 360–61; decentering of, 384–91
Poynder, Rev. Frederick, 102n, 166
Precocity, 109–10, 120–24; and Paul Dombey, 237; and erotic child-beating, 256–57, 260
Preservation of Health, The (Dukes), 117
Pretty Baby (film), 374
Prevention of Cruelty to Children Act, 84, 255
"Priest and the Acolyte, The," 81, 234–35
Private Letters from Phyllis to Marie (Norroy), 213n
Problem in Modern Ethics, A (Symonds), 219
Prostitution, Victorian discussions of 27–28; and Victorian children, 76–77, 151; and perception of the body, 107–8
Prostitution (Acton), 108

Protections, of children, 10; and gender, 16; promised by power, 25–26, 28–29; of the quality of innocence, 72; of Victorian children, 254–55; of modern children, 361–62, 382–84
Proudie, Mrs., 135
Puberty, and definitions of the child, 70; and the child's body, 107, 124–26
Public schools, *see* Boarding schools
Pullan, Mrs. Matilda Marian, 102n, 103n, 132n
Purity, and the eroticizing of children, 12, 175–76; and bodily growth, 106; and semen-retention, 113; and Christianity, 198; and social class, 203; and the gentle child, 219–221; in *David Copperfield*, 306–9; in *Tess of the d'Urbervilles*, 320–38; and the modern child, 375–76; *see also* Innocence
"Purity—How Preserved Among the Young" (Seward), 140
Putnam, G.H., 270n
Putnam-Jacobi, Mary, 129n, 132n

Queen of Hearts, The (*Alice in Wonderland*), 290
Quilp, Daniel (*The Old Curiosity Shop*), 239
Quint, Peter (*Turn of the Screw*), 81

Radbill, Samuel X., 55n
Rackin, Donald, 299n
Radley School, 267
Raffalovich, Marc-Andre, 220, 222, 243n
Reade, Brian, 57n, 213n, 214n, 243n
Reader's Digest, The, 26, 374
Reading, and pedophilia, 303–38; and the McMartin case, 341–58
Reagan, Nancy and Ronald, 153, 380, 381
Red King, The (*Through the Looking-Glass*), 297
Redneck (film), 371
Reed, Carol, 371
"Reg'lar Fellers" (comic strip), 367
Reich, Annie, 180n
Reiner, Ira, 392–93n
Reiner, Rob, 99n

Repression, critique of hypothesis, 34–35, 152
Resentment, and the child, 247–49; of Peter Pan, 286–87; of Alice, 294–95, 296–98
Resolutions Respecting the Treatment of My Children (Anon.), 100n, 103n
Rhoda (*The Bad Seed*), 375
Richelot, G., 99n
"Richie Rich" (comic strip), 369
Rivera, Geraldo, 343, 377
Roach, Hal, 375
Robinson, Henry, 76, 99n
"Rod, The" ("Houston's Juvenile Tract"), 250
Rolfe, Frederick ("Corvo"), 199, 213n
Romance of Natural History, The (Merrill), 144
Rosenberg, Howard, 381
Rossman, Parker, 188, 211n, 212n, 213n, 214n
Roth, Senator William V., Jr., 378–79
Rousseau, Jean Jacques, 64, 72, 74, 120, 131n, 174, 272n; and whipping, 256
Ryan, Michael, 51n, 102n, 131n, 132n

Sacher-Masoch, Leopold von, 262
Sade, Marquis de, 150, 256, 265, 338
Salinger, J.D., and *The Catcher in the Rye*, 309–20, 339n
Salway, Lance, 97n
Sandford and Merton (Day), 251
Sandfort, Theo, 24, 54n, 210n, 212n, 214n, 394n; and myths of pedophilia, 184–85; and research on pedophilia, 209, 386–87, 388
Satyricon, 255
Sawicki, Jana, 30, 54n
Sawyer, Sid, 225
Sawyer, Tom, 255, 374
Schroeder, Ricky, 10, 269, 369, 374
Scott, George Ripley, 271n, 272n
Secrets of Life, The ("Dr. Lucas"), 135, 164
Sedgwick, Eve Kosofsky, 51n, 54n, 246, 270n
Setebos (Browning's "Caliban upon Setebos"), 106
Seward, S.S., Rev., 72–73, 98n, 140–41, 177n, 182n

Sewell, Dr. (Radley School), 267
Sex, connections to power, 15, 18, 134–35; and sexuality, 18, 139–51; and violence, 28–29; and repression hypothesis, 34–35, 140; and the Victorians, 34–51, 134–82; and Victorian women, 41, 160–63; and sperm pools, 42–43; and body-laws, 106; and the brain, 112; as center of the body, 114; and puberty, 124–26; and latency, 126–28, 137; invention of, 136–38; and idealism, 222–25; and child-spanking, 255–57; and Peter Pan, 282–83; and Alice, 297–98; and Holden Caulfield, 314–16
Sexology (William Walling), 166
Sexuality, and sex, 18, 139–51; and power, 20; and essences, 20–21; related to normal/abnormal distinctions, 22–23; role of repression hypothesis in, 35; and multiplication of discourses, 35; and silence, 35–37, 139, 151–53; essences and, 49–51; and the child, 70, 118–28, 140–42, 159–60, 172–76; and precocity, 123–24, 140–41; and puberty, 124–26; and latency, 126–28; and the move from "nature" to "norm," 137–38; and explosion of discourse, 139–40; the expert in, 142–44; and Krafft-Ebing, 144–46, 147; and Ellis, 146–51; and William Acton, 154–60; and whipping (Ellis), 257–61; and pedophile reading, 303–38; and *David Copperfield*, 306–9; and *The Catcher in the Rye*, 309–20; and *Tess of the d'Urbervilles*, 320–38; and the McMartin Pre-School trial, 341–58; and the child in our culture, 362–91; *see also* Pedophilia
Sexual Secrets (McMartin case), 352
Sgroi, Suzanne M., 210n, 214n
Shaftesbury, Lord, 89
Sharp, Becky, 249
Shaw, George Bernard, 261, 263
Sheep, the (*Through the Looking-Glass*), 297
Shelley, P.B., 29, 331
Sherwood, Mrs. Mary M., 71, 98, 249
Shettle, Richard C., 57n, 111–12, 129n, 130n

Shields, Brooke, 10, 224, 364
Shipley, Rev. Orby, 101n
Show Me! (Fleischhauer-Hardt), 202, 376
Sikes, Bill (*Oliver!*), 371
Silas Marner, 67, 114
Silence, reading of, 35–37; and sexuality, 35–37, 139, 151–53; and action, 37
Simon, William, 132n
Smike (*Nicholas Nickleby*), 81
Smiles, Samuel, 47–48, 57n, 82, 88, 97n, 100n, 101n, 102n, 129n, 131n; on children and parents, 90; on "energy of will," 109; and precocity, 119
Smirnoff, Victor N., 267, 273n, 274n
Smith, F. Barry, 154, 179n, 180n
Smith, Sarah ("Hesba Stretton"), 65
Smith, Timothy d'Arch, 203, 206, 213n, 214n
Snoopy, 309
Sodom, 379
Sodomy, 43–44
Solomon, 250
Sotadic Zone, 43–44
Sowerberry, Mrs. (*Oliver Twist*), 391
Spanking, *see* Whipping
Spark, Muriel, 233
"Speak gently to the little child" (*Alice in Wonderland*), 235, 293
Spencer, Herbert, 71, 98n, 101n, 128n, 130n, 131n; on the body's accounting, 116
Spencer, Mr. (*The Catcher in the Rye*), 316–17, 320
Spenlow (Copperfield), Dora (*David Copperfield*), 309
Sperm, and economic models, 42–43; and vital energy, 112–14; and retention, 158; and orgasm, 185
Spilka, Mark, 96n
Spock, Jonathan, Dr., 157
Stable, Justice, 183
Stall, Sylvanus, 131n
Stand By Me (film), 374
Stead, William Thomas, 77
Stearns, Carol Z., 55n, 178n
Stearns, Peter N., 55n, 178n
Steele, Brandt, 192, 193–94, 211n, 212n
Stendahl (Marie Henri Beyle), 262, 273n

Stevenson, John, 51n
Stewart, Susan, 228, 244n
Stoker, Bram, 111, 245n
Stone, Lawrence, 61, 95n, 96n
Stone, Lore E., 17, 51n
Stowe, Harriet Beecher, 80
Stradlater, Ward (*The Catcher in the Rye*), 315, 317–18, 339n
Strasser, August Adrian, 271n
Studies in the Psychology of Sex (Ellis), 257
Suburban Souls (Anon.), 171, 181n
Sunday-School Times, 61
Sunday School Union, The, 80
Sunny (*The Catcher in the Rye*), 313, 316, 318
Suransky, Valerie P., 96, 101n, 177n
Swinburne, A.C., 188, 194, 255, 270n; and erotic whipping, 256–57, 308; and *The Whippingham Papers*, 273n; and *Tess of the d'Urbervilles*, 332, 334
Symonds, J.A., 140, 176, 177n, 199, 212n, 240, 243n, 244n; and pedophilia, 192; and fantasy life, 194; and *A Problem in Modern Ethics*, 219; on Willie Dyer, 231–32

Tait, William, 129n
Talbot, James Beard, 129n
Tarzan, 374
Taunton Commission, The, 254
Taylor, Charles Bell, 50, 58n
Taylor, Isaac, 102n
Temple, Shirley, 10, 269, 369, 371
Tennyson, Alfred, Lord, 75, 113–14, 267
Tennyson, Hallam, Lord, 99n
Tess of the d'Urbervilles, and pedophile reading, 320–28; and Alec, 326–29; and Angel, 329–38; and tragedy, 340n
Thomas, Keith, 96n
Through the Looking-Glass, 295–98
Thurmer, Selma (*The Catcher in the Rye*), 314
Tiger Lily (*Peter Pan*), 283
Times (London), 232, 252
Tinker Bell (*Peter Pan*), 281, 286, 287

"'Tis the voice of the sluggard" (*Alice in Wonderland*), 292
Tissot, S.A.D., 164, 167
"To a Sicilian Boy" (Wraitslaw), 221–22
Tom Brown's Universe (Honey), 168
Tom Sawyer (film), 374
Trollope, Anthony, 80, 99n, 212n, 287, 353
Trotwood, Betsey (*David Copperfield*), 309
Trudgill, Eric, 97n, 178n, 298n
Trumbull, H. Clay, 61, 91, 95n, 96n, 102n
Tulliver, Maggie (*Mill on the Floss*), 209
Turn of the Screw, The, 81
Turner, E. S., 274n
Twain, Mark, 374
Tweedle Brothers, the (*Through the Looking-Glass*), 297
Twist, Oliver, 64, 74, 80, 209; and blankness, 223; as a fable for our time, 389–91
Tyler, R.P. "Toby," 17, 51n

Udall, Nicholas, 253; charged with "unnatural crime," 255
Ulrichs, Carl Heinrich, 29
Underwear, and pedophilia, 200; in the McMartin case, 352–53
"Uranians, The," 199
Urwick, Edward Jones, 97n, 132n

Van Buren, Abigail ("Dear Abby"), 361–62, 391n
vand den Berg, J. H., 96n
Venus School-Mistress (Anon.), 274n
Verley, Henry, 113, 130n
Vicinus, Martha, 181n
Victorian Childhood (Jordan), 75
Victorian culture, and Otherness, 4, 32–33, 33–51; and child sexuality, 26; prostitution in, 27–28; repression in, 34–35; and sex-talk, 35–51; and silence, 35–37; the "eccentric" in, 39–51; and the taking of clear positions, 44–45; enthusiasm for inquiry in, 45–46; and empiricism, 46; system-building in, 46–48; and the expert, 48–49; and faith in essences, 49–51;

and view of change, 50–51; and constructions of children, 61–63; the body in, 104–28; and constructions of sex and sexuality, 134–82; Marcus on, 153–55; William Acton as representative of, 154–60; and masturbation, 163–68; and boarding school immorality, 168–69, 231–34; pornography in, 169–72, 200–2; and pedophilia, 185, 197–202; and constructions of gentleness, 217–43; and child-resentment, 248–49; child-beating in, 249–57; reflected in Alice books, 288–94

Vintras, A., 99n

Violence, and sex, 28–29; as a rarity in pedophilia, 207; and Tess, 321, 329, 337–38; and a fable for our time, 390–91

von Raab, William, 379, 380

Voyeurism, and children, 67–68; parental, 91; and photography, 199–200, 303; and transience, 226–27; in Kilvert, 241–43; and spanking, 255–57; and child-beating (Freud), 259–61; in child-beating pornography, 263–66; and Peter Pan, 276; and Alice, 276; in erotic reading, 303–38; and the Freud/Lacan model, 304–6; and *David Copperfield*, 306–9; and *The Catcher in the Rye*, 309–20; and *Tess of the d'Urbervilles*, 320–38; in the McMartin Pre-School trial, 341–58; and the child in our culture, 363–75

Vye, Eustacia (*The Return of the Native*), 320

Wagner, Gillian, 99n
Walker, Alexander, 51n
Walkowitz, Judith R., 129n
Walling, William H., 128n, 131n, 166, 180n
Walsh, Tori (McMartin case), 356
"Walter" (*My Secret Life*), 171
Ward, David Allen, 393–94n
Ward, J.P., 98n
Wardlaw, Ralph, 129n
Warner, Sylvia Townsend, 214n
Warren, Mrs. Eliza, 100n, 102n

Wasp, the (*Through the Looking-Glass*), 298
Watchfogel, David, 383
Watts, Isaac, 93, 102n, 289
"We," and justifications for, 9–10
Weatherly, Lionel, 98n, 131n
Weeks, Jeffrey, 52n, 53n, 54n, 55n, 56n, 58n, 96n, 128n, 179n; on "the body," 104; on William Acton, 154; on S/M, 273n
Wehner, Captain John (McMartin case), 342
Welty, Rev. J.B., 140, 177n
Westminster School, 253
What a Young Boy Ought to Know (Anon.), 118
When a Child Loves (Anon.), 132n, 200, 213n, 244n, 273n, 274n; sadism in, 225; and voyeurism, 227
Whipping, of criminals, 68; of children, 79, 110, 225; and eroticism, 150–51, 255–57; and pornography, 200, 263–66; in Kilvert's *Diaries*, 240; of the naughty child, 246–70; and resentment, 247–49; and love, 248; and Godliness, 249–50; in boarding-schools, 253–54; Ellis on, 257–59; Freud on, 259–61; and gender, 268–70; in J.M. Barrie, 281; and erotic reading of *David Copperfield*, 308–9; and Holden Caulfield, 317; and Tess, 325, 333; of children in our culture, 362, 376–78, 393n; and comic strips, 365–69
White, Hayden, 29, 54n, 55n, 58n, 177n, 244n; on anarchy, 230–31
White, Henry Kirke, 121
White, Rhoda E., 102n, 120, 131n
White, T.H., 205–6, 214n
White Knight, the (*Through the Looking-Glass*), 196, 298
White Queen, the (*Through the Looking-Glass*), 297
Whitman, Walt, 199, 219
Wickham, Mrs. (*Dombey and Son*), 236
"Wide Awake Willie" (comic strip), 367
Wife of Bath, 206
Wiggin, Kate Douglas, 96n, 209
Wilberforce, Bishop, 249
Wilde, Oscar, 25, 44, 81, 100n, 243n,

314; on parents and children, 84; the trials of, 150, 235; as threat to young manhood, 190; and "useless" art, 221; on feasting with panthers, 222; and worship of atmosphere, 233
Willich, A.F.M., 48–49, 58n, 89, 97n, 101n, 104, 105, 128n, 130n
Wilson, Glenn D., 214n, 394n
Winchester School, 253
Winfrey, Oprah, 343
Winkle, Perry, 269, 369, 373
Wixenford School, 253
Wolin, Sheldon S., 52n
Wood-Allen, Mary, 36, 56n, 66, 96n, 130n, 132n, 176n, 179n; on continence, 113; and latency, 126; on sex and power, 134; on masturbation, 161
Wordsworth, William, 63, 67, 72, 74, 87, 248, 281

Wraitslaw, Theodore, 221
Wright, Henry Clarke, 110, 129n
Wuthering Heights, and romantic tragedy, 11–13

X—The Man with the X-Ray Eyes (film), 352

"You are old, Father William" (*Alice in Wonderland*), 292
"Young Beginners" (*The Pearl*), 224, 244n
Young, G.M., 57n
Young, Wayland, 213n
Young Wife's Own Book, The (Anon.), 120
Youth and True Manhood (Anon.), 118, 131n, 169, 181n

Zigler, Edward, 392n

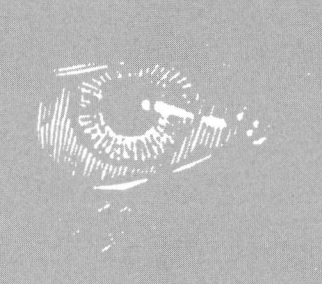

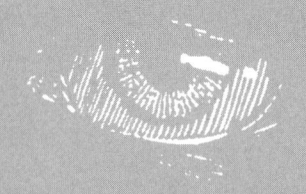